Contemporary Authors®

ISSN 0010-7468

Contemporary Authors®

A Bio-Bibliographical Guide to
Current Writers in Fiction, General Nonfiction,
Poetry, Journalism, Drama, Motion Pictures,
Television, and Other Fields

volume 291

GALE
CENGAGE Learning™

Detroit • New York • San Francisco • New Haven, Conn • Waterville, Maine • London

Contemporary Authors, Vol. 291

Project Editor: Amy Elisabeth Fuller

Editorial: Mary Ruby

Permissions: Margaret Gaston-Chamberlain, Lisa Kinkade, Tracie Richardson

Imaging and Multimedia: John Watkins

Composition and Electronic Capture: Gary Oudersluys

Manufacturing: Drew Kalasky

Gale
27500 Drake Rd.
Farmington Hills, MI, 48331-3535

LIBRARY OF CONGRESS CATALOG CARD NUMBER 81-640179

ISBN-13: 978-1-4144-3956-3
ISBN-10: 1-4144-3956-3

ISSN 0010-7468

This title is also available as an e-book.
ISBN-13: 978-1-4144-5650-8
ISBN-10: 1-4144-5650-6
Contact your Gale sales representative for ordering information.

Printed in the United States of America
2 3 4 5 6 7 14 13 12 11 10

Contents

Preface

Contemporary Authors (*CA*) provides information on approximately 130,000 writers in a wide range of media, including:

- Current writers of fiction, nonfiction, poetry, and drama whose works have been issued by commercial publishers, risk publishers, or university presses (authors whose books have been published only by known vanity or author-subsidized firms are ordinarily not included)

- Prominent print and broadcast journalists, editors, syndicated cartoonists, graphic novelists, screenwriters, television scriptwriters, and other media people

- Notable international authors

- Literary greats of the early twentieth century whose works are popular in today's high school and college curriculums and continue to elicit critical attention

A *CA* listing entails no charge or obligation. Authors are included on the basis of the above criteria and their interest to *CA* users. Sources of potential listees include trade periodicals, publishers' catalogs, librarians, and other users of the series.

How to Get the Most out of *CA*: Use the Index

The key to locating an author's most recent entry is the *CA* cumulative index, which is published separately and distributed twice a year. It provides access to *all* entries in *CA* and *Contemporary Authors New Revision Series* (*CANR*). Always consult the latest index to find an author's most recent entry.

For the convenience of users, the *CA* cumulative index also includes references to all entries in these Gale Cengage Learning literary series: *Authors and Artists for Young Adults, Authors in the News, Bestsellers, Black Literature Criticism, Black Literature Criticism Supplement, Black Writers, Children's Literature Review, Concise Dictionary of American Literary Biography, Concise Dictionary of British Literary Biography, Contemporary Authors Autobiography Series, Contemporary Authors Bibliographical Series, Contemporary Dramatists, Contemporary Literary Criticism, Contemporary Novelists, Contemporary Poets, Contemporary Popular Writers, Contemporary Southern Writers, Contemporary Women Poets, Dictionary of Literary Biography, Dictionary of Literary Biography Documentary Series, Dictionary of Literary Biography Yearbook, DISCovering Authors, DISCovering Authors: British, DISCovering Authors: Canadian, DISCovering Authors: Modules* (including modules for Dramatists, Most-Studied Authors, Multicultural Authors, Novelists, Poets, and Popular/Genre Authors), *DISCovering Authors 3.0, Drama Criticism, Drama for Students, Feminist Writers, Hispanic Literature Criticism, Hispanic Writers, Junior DISCovering Authors, Major Authors and Illustrators for Children and Young Adults, Major 20th-Century Writers, Native North American Literature, Novels for Students, Poetry Criticism, Poetry for Students, Short Stories for Students, Short Story Criticism, Something about the Author, Something about the Author Autobiography Series, St. James Guide to Children's Writers, St. James Guide to Crime & Mystery Writers, St. James Guide to Fantasy Writers, St. James Guide to Horror, Ghost & Gothic Writers, St. James Guide to Science Fiction Writers, St. James Guide to Young Adult Writers, Twentieth-Century Literary Criticism, 20th Century Romance and Historical Writers, World Literature Criticism,* and *Yesterday's Authors of Books for Children.*

A Sample Index Entry:

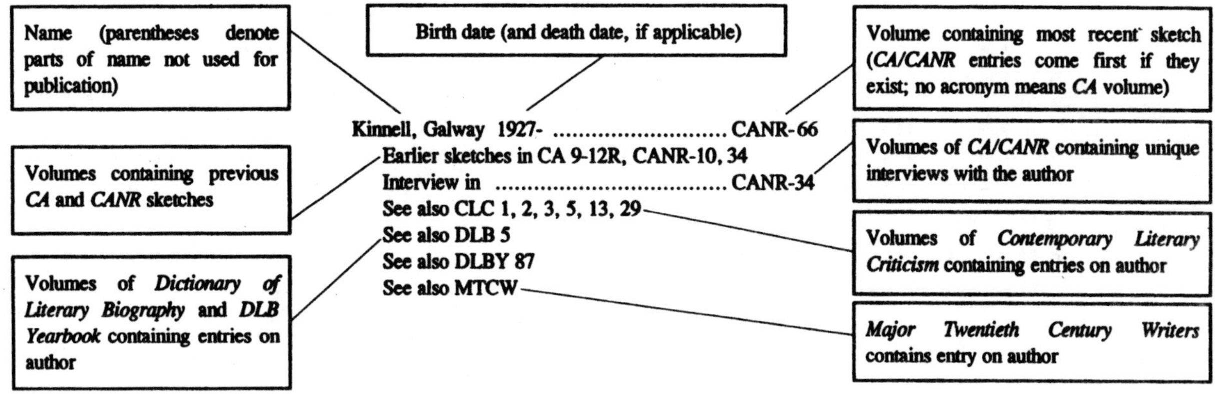

How Are Entries Compiled?

The editors make every effort to secure new information directly from the authors; listees' responses to our questionnaires and query letters provide most of the information featured in *CA*. For deceased writers, or those who fail to reply to requests for data, we consult other reliable biographical sources, such as those indexed in Gale's *Biography and Genealogy Master Index,* and bibliographical sources, including *National Union Catalog, LC MARC,* and *British National Bibliography.* Further details come from published interviews, feature stories, and book reviews, as well as information supplied by the authors' publishers and agents.

An asterisk (*) at the end of a sketch indicates that the listing has been compiled from secondary sources believed to be reliable but has not been personally verified for this edition by the author sketched.

What Kinds of Information Does An Entry Provide?

Sketches in *CA* contain the following biographical and bibliographical information:

- **Entry heading:** the most complete form of author's name, plus any pseudonyms or name variations used for writing

- **Personal information:** author's date and place of birth, family data, ethnicity, educational background, political and religious affiliations, and hobbies and leisure interests

- **Addresses:** author's home, office, or agent's addresses, plus e-mail and fax numbers, as available

- **Career summary:** name of employer, position, and dates held for each career post; resume of other vocational achievements; military service

- **Membership information:** professional, civic, and other association memberships and any official posts held

- **Awards and honors:** military and civic citations, major prizes and nominations, fellowships, grants, and honorary degrees

- **Writings:** a comprehensive, chronological list of titles, publishers, dates of original publication and revised editions, and production information for plays, television scripts, and screenplays

- **Adaptations:** a list of films, plays, and other media which have been adapted from the author's work

- **Sidelights:** a biographical portrait of the author's development; information about the critical reception of the author's works; revealing comments, often by the author, on personal interests, aspirations, motivations, and thoughts on writing

- **Interview:** a one-on-one discussion with authors conducted especially for *CA*, offering insight into authors' thoughts about their craft

- **Autobiographical essay:** an original essay written by noted authors for *CA*, a forum in which writers may present themselves, on their own terms, to their audience

- **Photographs:** portraits and personal photographs of notable authors

- **Biographical and critical sources:** a list of books and periodicals in which additional information on an author's life and/or writings appears

- **Obituary Notices** in *CA* provide date and place of birth as well as death information about authors whose full-length sketches appeared in the series before their deaths. The entries also summarize the authors' careers and writings and list other sources of biographical and death information.

Related Titles in the *CA* Series

Contemporary Authors Autobiography Series complements *CA* original and revised volumes with specially commissioned autobiographical essays by important current authors, illustrated with personal photographs they provide. Common topics include their motivations for writing, the people and experiences that shaped their careers, the rewards they derive from their work, and their impressions of the current literary scene.

Contemporary Authors Bibliographical Series surveys writings by and about important American authors since World War II. Each volume concentrates on a specific genre and features approximately ten writers; entries list works written by and about the author and contain a bibliographical essay discussing the merits and deficiencies of major critical and scholarly studies in detail.

Available in Electronic Formats

GaleNet. *CA* is available on a subscription basis through GaleNet, an online information resource that features an easy-to-use end-user interface, powerful search capabilities, and ease of access through the World-Wide Web. For more information, call 1-800-877-GALE.

Licensing. *CA* is available for licensing. The complete database is provided in a fielded format and is deliverable on such media as disk, CD-ROM, or tape. For more information, contact Gale's Business Development Group at 1-800-877-GALE.

Suggestions Are Welcome

The editors welcome comments and suggestions from users on any aspect of the *CA* series. If readers would like to recommend authors for inclusion in future volumes of the series, they are cordially invited to write the Editors at *Contemporary Authors*, Gale Cengage Learning, 27500 Drake Rd., Farmington Hills, MI 48331-3535; or call at 1-248-699-4253; or fax at 1-248-699-8054.

Indexing note: All *Contemporary Authors* entries are indexed in the *Contemporary Authors* cumulative index, which is published separately and distributed twice a year.

As always, the most recent Contemporary Authors cumulative index continues to be the user's guide to the location of an individual author's listing.

CA Numbering System and Volume Update Chart

Occasionally questions arise about the *CA* numbering system and which volumes, if any, can be discarded. Despite numbers like "29-32R," "97-100" and "291," the entire *CA* print series consists of only 417 physical volumes with the publication of *CA* Volume 291. The following charts note changes in the numbering system and cover design, and indicate which volumes are essential for the most complete, up-to-date coverage.

***CA* First Revision**

- 1-4R through 41-44R (11 books)
  Cover: Brown with black and gold trim.
  There will be no further First Revision volumes because revised entries are now being handled exclusively through the more efficient *New Revision Series* mentioned below.

***CA* Original Volumes**

- 45-48 through 97-100 (14 books)
  Cover: Brown with black and gold trim.
  101 through 291 (191 books)
  Cover: Blue and black with orange bands.
  The same as previous *CA* original volumes but with a new, simplified numbering system and new cover design.

***CA* Permanent Series**

- *CAP*-1 and *CAP*-2 (2 books)
  Cover: Brown with red and gold trim.
  There will be no further Permanent Series volumes because revised entries are now being handled exclusively through the more efficient *New Revision Series* mentioned below.

***CA* New Revision Series**

- CANR-1 through CANR-199 (199 books)
  Cover: Blue and black with green bands.
  Includes only sketches requiring significant changes; **sketches are taken from any previously published CA, CAP, or CANR volume.**

If You Have:	You May Discard:
CA First Revision Volumes 1-4R through 41-44R and *CA Permanent Series* Volumes 1 and 2	*CA* Original Volumes 1, 2, 3, 4 Volumes 5-6 through 41-44
CA Original Volumes 45-48 through 97-100 and 101 through 291	**NONE:** These volumes will not be superseded by corresponding revised volumes. Individual entries from these and all other volumes appearing in the left column of this chart may be revised and included in the various volumes of the *New Revision Series.*
CA New Revision Series Volumes *CANR*-1 through *CANR*-199	**NONE:** The *New Revision Series* does not replace any single volume of *CA*. Instead, volumes of *CANR* include entries from many previous *CA* series volumes. All *New Revision Series* volumes must be retained for full coverage.

A Sampling of Authors and Media People Featured in This Volume

Diane Ackerman
Ackerman has been hailed by several critics not only for her poetry but for her prose explorations into the world of science and natural history. Her voracious appetite for knowledge and her eager appreciation of the natural world are evident in *Jaguar of Sweet Laughter: New and Selected Poems.* Ackerman has also been praised for her skill at observing and then eloquently describing the details of the natural world, and nowhere is that more evident than in *The Moon by Whale Light, and Other Adventures among Bats, Penguins, Crocodilians, and Whales,* a collection of four essays expanded from articles previously published in the *New Yorker.* Allying herself with experts on each species, Ackerman went into the field to gain firsthand experience with these animals. She is from Illinois and has won numerous awards for her writing.

Hélène Berr
Berr was a French woman of Jewish descent who kept a diary about the Nazi occupation of France. She was born March 27, 1921, in Paris, France, to a wealthy Jewish family that had lived in France for several generations. She attended the Sorbonne, studying Russian and English literature. She was not able to take her final examination for a degree, however, because of anti-Semitic laws instituted by the Vichy regime following the Nazi occupation of her country. Faced with increasing restrictions on Jewish life, Berr joined an underground group transferring Jewish children to families in the unoccupied portions of France. Berr was eventually arrested and taken to a concentration camp. Though she survived one of the terrible death marches from Auschwitz to Bergen-Belsen, she was beaten to death in Bergen-Belsen on April 10, 1945, just five days before the Allies freed the prisoners there.

Georgina Spencer Cavendish
Lady Spencer, later Georgiana Spencer Cavendish, the Duchess of Devonshire, was born July 6, 1757, and died March 30, 1806. Hailing from a long line of aristocracy, Cavendish's direct descendents include Diana Spencer, the late Princess of Wales, and Sara Ferguson, Duchess of York. Cavendish, the daughter of John Spencer, the 1st Earl of Spencer, was an avid socialite and celebrated style icon. Cavendish's reaction to her regular exposure to high society is evinced in her book *The Sylph,* which was released in 1779. In her book, *Emma,* a young woman is forced into an arranged marriage with a man she does not love which leads to many problems for the wedded duo.

Christos Gage
American screenwriter and comic book author Gage was born July 17, in New York, but grew up primarily in Athens, Greece, and North Grafton, Massachusetts. Gage was fascinated with storytelling from a young age, learning to read when he was just three. He soon discovered comic books and collected them religiously, keeping them in his closet. Unlike many young boys, he never grew out of his love for comics. When writing for film and television he often collaborates with his wife, writer Ruth Fletcher Gage. Then at the end of 2004, Gage's love for comics came to the foreground and he began to write in that medium as well. Since that time, Gage has written for numerous comics, including popular series for both Marvel and Wildfire/DC.

Jean-Pierre Houdin
Writer and architect Jean-Pierre Houdin was born in 1951 in Paris, France, but grew up primarily in Abidjan, Africa, where his engineer father was working for a construction company. As a child, he became fascinated by both building and design due to his exposure to his father's work, and so eventually ended up studying architecture at École des Beaux-Arts in Paris, graduating in 1976. For the next two decades, Houdin worked as an independent architect and owner of his own firm. He also indulged his interest in art, opening an avant-garde gallery called Les Enfants Gâtés in Paris with his wife, Michelle, and a friend.

Jackie Kessler
Kessler is an American writer of dark fantasy and paranormal fiction. Her "Hell on Earth" series features Jezebel, a four-thousand-year-old succubus who doubles as an exotic dancer and is one step away from being captured by demons from hell. Her human disguise may save her from being captured, but it does not prevent Jezebel from experiencing numerous adventures in this world. Kessler did not always intend to be a writer. By the age of fifteen, she discovered that she enjoyed writing the text for her comics as much as (or perhaps more than) drawing them. She began to write scenarios for her favorite comic books, such as *X-Men* and *Alpha Flight.*

Adam Nimoy
Nimoy is the son of actor and director Leonard Nimoy, most famous for his role as Mr. Spock on the *Star Trek* television series and several features films based on the series. A successful television director, Nimoy is also the author of *My Incredibly Wonderful, Miserable Life: An Anti-Memoir.* The memoir examines Nimoy's life from his time as a child, as he had to deal with a famous

father who was often away working, to the author's own adulthood trials and tribulations, including a failed marriage and a long addiction to alcohol and marijuana.

Sichan Siv

Sichan Siv was a young relief agency worker in Cambodia when Pol Pot's Khmer Rouge army overtook the country and set about eradicating any vestige of western influence. Millions of people, particularly those with formal education, were sentenced to reeducation programs, slave labor, or summary execution. Some two million Cambodians were either killed outright or died of exhaustion or starvation. Siv was one of the few to escape, eventually immigrating to the United States as a refugee. His memoir, *Golden Bones: An Extraordinary Journey from Hell in Cambodia to a New Life in America,* chronicles his ordeal and expresses his gratitude for his new life as an American citizen.

Acknowledgments

Grateful acknowledgment is made to those publishers, photographers, and artists whose work appear with these authors's essays. Following is a list of the copyright holders who have granted us permission to reproduce material in this volume of *CA*. Every effort has been made to trace copyright, but if omissions have been made, please let us know.

Photographs/Art

Ackerman, Diane: All photographs reproduced by permission.

A

** Indicates that a listing has been compiled from secondary sources believed to be reliable, but has not been personally verified for this edition by the author sketched.*

ABEYSEKARA, Tissa 1939-2009

PERSONAL: Born 1939; died April 18, 2009, at Colombo National Hospital, Sri Lanka; wife's name Asanka; children: daughters Aparna, Noriko, Charulatha, and Svetlana, son Dimithra. *Ethnicity:* Sinhalese.

CAREER: Screenwriter, film director, actor, novelist.

MEMBER: Foundation of SAARC Writers and Literature; Sri Lanka Rupavahini Corporation, board member; Aesthetic Institute of Sri Lanka, board member; University of Visual and Performing Arts, council member; National Heritage Trust of Sri Lanka, trustee; Sri Lanka Television Training Institute, director; National Film Corporation, chair, 1999–2001.

AWARDS, HONORS: Gratiaen Prize, Best Piece of Creative Writing in English by a Resident Sri Lankan, for *Bringing Tony Home,* 1996.

WRITINGS:

BOOKS

Ayale Giya Sithaka Satahan, Samajaya ha Samayika Kendraya (Colombo, Sri Lanka), 1991.

Rupavahiniya vivrta Arthikaya/Citrapata Samsthava, Ha Sinamave Arbudaya, Samajaya ha Samayika Kendraya (Colombo, Sri Lanka), 1991.

Pitagamkarayo: Prabandha Kathavaki, Mudra Prakasanayaki (Colombo, Sri Lanka), 1997.

Rupa Sva Rupa, Sarasavi Prakasakayo (Nugegoda, Sri Lanka), 2004.

FILM DIRECTOR

Viragaya Tira Racanaya, Mudra (Battaramulla, Sri Lanka), 1992.

Film director of *Karumakkarayo* and *Mahagedara.*

FILM SCRIPTWRITER

Roots of Paradise: A Film on the Cultural Triangle of Sri Lanka, Central Cultural Fund (Colombo, Sri Lanka), 2006.

Uppalavanna = Uppalawanna/Sumati Citrapata Sinama; Adyaksanaya, Sunil Ariyaratna, Torana Music Box (Colombo, Sri Lanka), 2007.

Film script writer of *Nidhanaya, Ganga Addara, Podi Malli, Delowak Atara, Welikatara, Sakman Maluwa,* and *Uthpalawanna.*

BOOKS IN ENGLISH

Bringing Tony Home: A Story in Three Movements, T. Abeysekara (Rajagiriya, Sri Lanka), 1998.

In My Kingdom of the Sun and the Holy Peak: Being Three Stories of the Betrayal, the Redemption and the Last Phase of a Land and Its People, Vijitha Yapa Publications (Colombo, Sri Lanka), 2004.

Roots, Reflections and Reminiscences, Sarasavi Publishers (Nugegoda, Sri Lanka), 2007.

Bringing Tony Home: Stories, North Atlantic Books (Berkeley, CA), 2008.

SIDELIGHTS: Tissa Abeysekara was a master of nearly all aspects of cinema: directing, acting, and scriptwriting. Abeysekara was born in 1939 in Sri Lanka. He attended Dharmapala Vidyalaya secondary school in Pannipitiya in the early 1950s. While still a teenager he began writing short stories. He later wrote the novel *Pitagamkarayo: Prabandha Kathavaki* and the essays "Ayale Giya Sithaka Satahan" and "Rupa-Svarupa."

In the early 1960s, he had a chance meeting with pioneer director Dr. Lester James Peries who lured him to the varied and artistic world of filmmaking. In the cinema, Abeysekara blossomed as a screenwriter, writing the scripts for *Nidhanaya, Ganga Addara, Podi Malli, Delowak Atara, Welikatara, Sakman Maluwa,* and *Uthpalawanna.*

Abeysekara joined the Government Film Unit and made more than forty documentary films for theaters and television. He took pride in making films that built public awareness. His first feature film was *Karumakkarayo,* based on Dr. Gunadasa Amarasekara's controversial novel about a power-hungry village politician.

Abeysekara later directed *Mahagedara* and the highly acclaimed *Viragaya Tira Racanaya* based on Martin Wickramasinghe's novel about a youth with a traditional Buddhist upbringing clashing with the modern world.

Abeysekara's acclaimed book *Bringing Tony Home: A Story in Three Movements* is a collection of four autobiographical and contemplative stories of childhood memories of a lost dog, rediscovered love, parents and their secrets, and Sri Lankan culture. The book was published in the United States in 1998. A reviewer said in *Publishers Weekly,* "These multilayered stories, worth repeat reading, make a welcome introduction to Abeysekara and his homeland." Another writer commented in *Kirkus Reviews* that *Bringing Tony Home* was "a sophisticated jigsaw of a book, sensitively—sometimes stiflingly—mixing memory and history with regret and rites of passage."

He received many national awards for his films, scriptwriting, directing, and work in television. In 1996 he won the Gratiaen Prize for the best piece of creative writing in English by a Sri Lankan resident for *Bringing Tony Home.* He was honored by then president Chandrika Bandaranaike Kumaratunga in 2005 with the title of Deshabandu, or friend of the country.

From 1999 to 2001 Abeysekara served as chair of the National Film Corporation, where he worked to raise the stature of the cinema industry in Sri Lanka. He was also a member of the Foundation of SAARC Writers and Literature, council member of the University of Visual and Performing Arts in Colombo, and trustee of the National Heritage Trust of Sri Lanka.

In 2004 he wrote *In My Kingdom of the Sun and the Holy Peak: Being Three Stories of the Betrayal, the Redemption and the Last Phase of a Land and Its People.* He followed that up in 2007 with the book *Roots, Reflections and Reminiscences,* a tribute to his parents and cultural legacy and a search for his roots and identity.

Abeysekara died on April 18, 2009, at the age of sixty-nine after a brief illness. Quoted by the BBC, literary critic Saman Wickremarachchi said, Abeysekara had a proven talent of writing on any subject ranging from films, drama, books, philosophy, culture or any social subjects."

BIOGRAPHICAL AND CRITICAL SOURCES:

PERIODICALS

Internet Bookwatch, April, 2009, review of *Bringing Tony Home: A Story in Three Movements.*

Kirkus Reviews, October 1, 2008, review of *Bringing Tony Home.*

Publishers Weekly, September 29, 2008, review of *Bringing Tony Home,* p. 61.

ONLINE

Daily News, http://www.dailynews.lk/ (May 20, 2006), Sandasen Marasinghe, "Cinema Still Holds Appeal: Tissa Abeysekara," interview.

Karen Vanuska Live Journal, http://karenvanuska.livejournal.com/ (February 26, 2009), Karen Vanuska, review of *Bringing Tony Home.*

Random House Online, http://randomhouse.com/ (July 1, 2009), review of *Bringing Tony Home.*

OBITUARIES:

ONLINE

BBC Online, http://bbc.co.uk/ (April 18, 2009), "Tissa Abeysekara Passes Away."

Lankapuvath, http://www.lankapuvath/ (April 19, 2009), "Sri Lankan Film Industry Loses Tissa Abeysekara."

oneSriLanka Online, http://www.spot.lk/ (April 22, 2009), "Tribute to Dr. Tissa Abeysekara, Nation Has Lost a Man of Unparalleled Talent."

Sinhale Hot News, http://sinhale.wordpress.com/ (April 18, 2009), "Veteran Filmmaker Tissa Abeysekara Passed Away."*

* * *

ACKERMAN, Diane 1948-

PERSONAL: Born October 7, 1948, in Waukegan, IL; daughter of Sam (a restaurant owner) and Marcia (Tischler) Fink. *Education:* Attended Boston University, 1966-67; Pennsylvania State University, B.A., 1970; Cornell University, M.F.A., 1973, M.A., 1976, Ph.D., 1978. *Hobbies and other interests:* Gardening, bicycling.

ADDRESSES: *Home*—Ithaca, NY. *E-mail*—inkdream@hotmail.com.

CAREER: Writer. Social worker in New York, NY, 1967; Pennsylvania State University, University Park, government researcher, 1968; *Library Journal,* New York, NY, editorial assistant, 1970; *Epoch,* Ithaca, NY, associate editor, 1971-77; Cornell University, Ithaca, teaching assistant, 1971-78, lecturer, 1978-79; University of Pittsburgh, Pittsburgh, PA, assistant professor of English, 1980-83; Washington University, St. Louis, MO, director of writers program and writer-in-residence, 1984-86; *New Yorker,* New York, NY, staff writer, 1988-94. Host, *Mystery of the Senses,* Public Broadcasting System (PBS), 1995. Writer-in-residence, William and Mary College, Williamsburg, VA, 1983, Ohio University, Athens, 1983; visiting writer, Columbia University, New York, NY, 1986, New York University, New York, NY, 1986; Cornell University, visiting writer, 1987, visiting professor at Society for the Humanities, 1998-99; Atlantic Center for the Arts, New Smyrna Beach, FL, master artist-in-residence, 1988; University of Richmond, Richmond, VA, National Endowment for the Humanities Distinguished Professor. Member of literature panels, including New York State Council on the Arts, 1980-83; member of advisory board, Planetary Society, Pasadena, CA, 1980—. Has participated in readings, residencies, and workshops. Produced the recordings *The Naturalists,* Gang of Seven, Inc., 1992, and *A Natural History of Love,* 1994.

AWARDS, HONORS: Poetry Prize, Academy of American Poets, Cornell University, 1972; Corson Bishop French Prize, Cornell University, 1972, 1977; Abbie Copps Prize, Olivet College, 1974; Rockefeller graduate fellowship, 1974-76; Heermans-McCalmon Playwriting Prize, Cornell University, 1976; National Endowment for the Arts, creative writing fellowships, 1976 and 1986; Creative Artists Public Service fellowship, 1980; Poetry Prize, *Black Warrior Review,* 1981; Associated Writing Programs, member of board of directors, 1982-85; Pushcart Prize VIII, 1984; Peter I.B. Lavan Younger Poet Award, Academy of American Poets, 1985; Lowell Thomas Award, Society of American Travel Writers, 1990; National Endowment for the Arts, member of Poetry Panel, 1991; National Book Critics Circle Award nomination, 1991; Wordsmith Award, 1992; "New and Noteworthy Book of the Year," *New York Times Book Review,* for *The Moon by Whale Light,* 1992, and for *Jaguar of Sweet Laughter,* 1993; Golden Nose Award, Olfactory Research Fund, 1994; named a "Literary Lion" by the New York Public Library, 1994; Journalist-in-Space Project semifinalist; John Burroughs Nature Award, 1998; Guggenheim fellowship, Guggenheim Memorial Foundation, 2003, 2005; D. Litt., Kenyon College, 2006; *The Zookeeper's Wife* was selected as a *Booklist* Editor's Choice Top of the List Winner, 2007; Orion Book Award, 2008.

WRITINGS:

POETRY

(With Jody Bolz and Nancy Steele) *Poems: Ackerman, Bolz, and Steele* (chapbook), Stone Marrow Press (Cincinnati, OH), 1973.

The Planets: A Cosmic Pastoral, Morrow (New York, NY), 1976.

Wife of Light, Morrow (New York, NY), 1978.

Lady Faustus, Morrow (New York, NY), 1983.

Jaguar of Sweet Laughter: New and Selected Poems, Random House (New York, NY), 1991.

(Editor, with Jeanne Mackin) *The Book of Love,* Norton (New York, NY), 1998.

I Praise My Destroyer, Random House (New York, NY), 1998.

Origami Bridges: Poems of Psychoanalysis and Fire, HarperCollins (New York, NY), 2002.

Animal Sense (juvenile), illustrated by Peter Sís, Knopf (New York, NY), 2003.

NONFICTION

Twilight of the Tenderfoot: A Western Memoir, Morrow (New York, NY), 1980, reprinted, Fulcrum (Golden, CO), 2002.

On Extended Wings (memoir), Atheneum (New York, NY), 1985, published as *On Extended Wings: An Adventure in Flight,* Scribner (New York, NY), 1987.

A Natural History of the Senses, Random House (New York, NY), 1990.

The Moon by Whale Light, and Other Adventures among Bats, Penguins, Crocodilians, and Whales, Random House (New York, NY), 1991.

A Natural History of Love, Random House (New York, NY), 1994.

The Rarest of the Rare: Vanishing Animals, Timeless Worlds, Random House (New York, NY), 1995.

Monk Seal Hideaway (juvenile), Crown (New York, NY), 1995.

Bats: Shadows in the Night (juvenile), photographs by Merlin Tuttle, Crown (New York, NY), 1997.

A Slender Thread: Crisis, Healing, and Nature, Random House (New York, NY), 1997.

Deep Play, illustrated by Peter Sís, Random House (New York, NY), 1999.

Cultivating Delight: A Natural History of My Garden, HarperCollins (New York, NY), 2001.

An Alchemy of Mind: The Marvel and Mystery of the Brain, Scribner (New York, NY), 2004.

The Zookeeper's Wife: A War Story, W.W. Norton (New York, NY), 2007.

Dawn Light: Dancing with Cranes and Other Ways to Start the Day, W.W. Norton (New York, NY), 2009.

OTHER

Reverse Thunder: A Dramatic Poem (play; produced in New Brunswick, NJ, 1982), Lumen (Cambridge, MA), 1988.

Ideas (television documentary), 1990.

Mystery of the Senses (television documentary), Public Broadcasting System, 1995.

Also author of the play *All Seasons Are Weather,* in *Texas Arts Journal* (Dallas, TX), fall, 1979. Contributor to books and anthologies, including *The Morrow Anthology of Younger Poets,* edited by Dave Smith and David Bottoms, Morrow, 1985; *Norton Introduction to Literature,* edited by Jerome Beaty and J. Paul Hunter, 4th edition, Norton, 1986; *Norton Introduction to Poetry,* edited by J. Paul Hunter, 3rd edition, Norton, 1986; *The Paris Review Anthology,* edited by George Plimpton, Norton, 1989; *Beyond the Map,* ELM Press, 1995; *Going on Faith: Writing as a Spiritual Quest,* edited by William Zinsser, Marlowe, 1999; (with others) *Food and Faith: Justice, Joy, and Daily Bread,* edited by Michael Schut, 2002; *Within the Stone,* 2004; *Blue Planet Run: The Race to Provide Safe Drinking Water to the World,* 2007; and numerous other poetry and prose anthologies.

Contributor of poems and nonfiction to literary journals, periodicals, and newspapers, including *New Yorker, Poetry, Life, Omni, Kenyon Review, American Poetry Review, Parnassus, Michigan Quarterly Review, Paris Review, Parnassus: Poetry in Review, Discover, World Magazine,* and *New York Times.* Contributor of reviews to *New York Times Book Review.*

ADAPTATIONS: On Extended Wings: An Adventure in Flight was adapted for the stage in 1987 by Norma Jean Griffin.

SIDELIGHTS: Diane Ackerman has been hailed by several critics not only for her poetry but for her prose explorations into the world of science and natural history. Her voracious appetite for knowledge and her eager appreciation of the natural world are evident in *Jaguar of Sweet Laughter: New and Selected Poems,* according to *New York Times Book Review* contributor David Kirby. He asserted, "Diane Ackerman's poems not only operate in the present but press toward the future. . . . Just about everything Ms. Ackerman writes, prose or poetry, is exploratory. . . . [Her] speakers push ahead; they probe, open, take off lids, peel back covers, inspect, taste, sniff." Her constant sense of wonder is the key to the appeal of her work, concluded Kirby: "Ms. Ackerman trains her telescope on the bend in the river, all but pitching over the rail as she strains toward the next surprise."

In his essay in *Parnassus,* Mark Doty compared Ackerman's work to that of another, more "metaphysical" nature poet, Mary Oliver, whose poetic quest remains a search for meaning in what she finds in the natural world. In contrast, Doty maintained, Ackerman "does not look for an overarching metaphysic, a coherence, because she fundamentally doesn't believe there is such a thing. . . . Where Darwin amassed a lifetime's worth of observed detail in order to generalize and arrive at evolutionary patterns, Ackerman prefers the sensuous, puzzling, intractable particular."

Ackerman has also been praised for her skill at observing and then eloquently describing the details of the natural world, and nowhere is that more evident than in *The Moon by Whale Light, and Other Adventures among Bats, Penguins, Crocodilians, and Whales,* a collection of four essays expanded from articles previously published in the *New Yorker.* Allying herself with experts on each species, Ackerman went into the field to gain firsthand experience with these animals. She recorded her observations in detail, along with her thoughts on the folklore of each animal. Fraser Harrison noted in *New Statesman and Society* that Ackerman's depiction of habitats is poetic, "and it is this quality that makes her a considerable nature writer as well as an intrepid, sharp-eyed journalist, for she has the imaginative gift to identify with the character of her animals and the intelligence to keep them in their ecological place."

Michiko Kakutani, writing in the *New York Times,* offered similar praise, writing that Ackerman "has a gift for sparkling, resonant language, and her descriptions of various animals and their habitats are alive with verbal energy and delight. She describes bats as delicately assembled packages of 'fur and appetite' and characterizes their high-pitched cries as 'vocal Braille.'" Kakutani further praised the author for providing a great deal of "fascinating" information about the lives of each species. In addition, Franklin Burroughs, writing in the *Southern Review,* enthusiastically endorsed Ackerman's "fine eye for detail, her adventurousness, and her humor" and noted: "When these essays first appeared in the familiar milieu of the *New Yorker,* they seemed to fall within its civilized, flexible conception of an American middle voice: informative, engaging, modest, witty, and thoroughly *professional,* not subject to the enthusiasms, large claims, and idiosyncrasies of the writer for whom writing itself remains the central, animating adventure."

Ackerman shifted her focus from the animal world to the human province of romantic love with her 1994 collection of essays *A Natural History of Love. Washington Post Book World* contributor Barbara Raskin characterized this volume as "an audaciously brilliant romp. . . . Using an evolutionary history as her launchpad, Ackerman takes off on a space flight in which she describes, defines, theorizes, analyzes, analogizes, apologizes, generalizes, explains, philosophizes, embellishes, codifies, classifies, confesses, compares, contrasts, speculates, hypothesizes and generally carries on like a hooligan about amatory love. It's a blast." Ackerman follows a quick survey of two thousand years of love with an analysis of famous literary passages on romance, the chemistry of love, the effects of lovelessness on children and cultures, and many more subjects. Some critics believed that she included too many topics in the collection and used too many different writing styles. Chris Goodrich, writing in the *Los Angeles Times,* felt that Ackerman "has found a particularly good lens through which to view her subject." He considered the book "a pleasure" and described Ackerman as "a beguiling, even seductive writer." Raskin also emphasized the author's power with words, stating: "Of all the loves Ackerman describes, none is greater than her own love of language. . . . She produces hard-hitting metaphors and sweet constellations of similes that are like confectionery recipes for fresh insights."

In the mid-1990s Ackerman wrote up her observations from two research expeditions to produce her first books for children: *Monk Seal Hideaway,* about monk seals at the Hawaiian Island National Wildlife Refuge, and *Bats: Shadows in the Night,* an account of her trip to Big Bend National Park in Texas accompanied by Merlin Tuttle, a bat expert and photographer. *Bulletin of the Center for Children's Books* contributor Roger Sutton found the tone of *Monk Seal Hideaway* to be "amiable and engaging" and noted that "budding naturalists will appreciate the eyewitness report." *Bats* also won praise as "natural history writing at its best," in the words of Sally Estes in *Booklist.*

Even as Ackerman branched out into writing children's books, she continued to write poetry. Without the guidance and comfort of religious dogma, Ackerman asks in *I Praise My Destroyer,* how does an agnostic face up to the "horror lesson" of death? As John Taylor pointed out in his *Poetry* review, the agnostic's "only certitude is eschatological uncertainty." He praised Ackerman for the "precision and enthusiasm" with which she confronts this dilemma by "exalting the organic processes whereby entities such as ourselves come into existence, exist, then perish." Moreover, the "gently erotic love poems" included in this collection, Taylor observed, "show that we must come to terms not only with our demise, but also sometimes—and no less intensely—with the lover who fled 'the love-brightened room.' . . . We also die . . . several times in the midst of life through amorous leave-takings and unrequited attractions."

Death plays an altogether different role in *A Slender Thread: Crisis, Healing, and Nature,* Ackerman's account of working the night shift of a suicide prevention hotline for one year. Antoinette Brinkman described the book in the *Library Journal* as "intensely interdisciplinary," noting that Ackerman "deftly interweaves moving stories of battered women, the lonely middle-aged, and suicidal teens with observations of nature by day and human nature in the later hours." *New York Times Book Review* critic Kate Jennings noted that the author comes across "as a thoroughly nice person," but pointed out that sentimentality can be "an occupational hazard" among those who write in the first person. In this regard, Jennings cited May Sarton, M.F.K. Fisher, and Annie Dillard, all critically acclaimed authors whose first-person writings nonetheless, like Ackerman's, "walk a fine line, risking self-regard and preciousness as well as sentimentality."

Ackerman's 1999 title *Deep Play* deals with transcendence of the daily norm through forms of "play" such as art, religion, and other human practices that lead to a heightened state of being. Winifred Gallagher observed in the *New York Times Book Review* that Ackerman "writes best when she balances her impressions with objective knowledge, like research on the functions of play in various species or the utility of color in nature." A *Publishers Weekly* reviewer noted that Ackerman's best writing emerges when her subject is "something observable" and she "beguiles readers with fine turns of phrase." The *Publishers Weekly* reviewer was less impressed when Ackerman "indulges her weakness for abstraction," but *Booklist* contributor Donna Seaman found that "the very act of reading this original, exultant, sage, poetic, and generous meditation on the importance of enchantment is deep play."

In *Cultivating Delight: A Natural History of My Garden,* Ackerman takes the reader on a philosophical jaunt through the four seasons as observed in her own backyard landscape. This book is not a gardening manual; Ackerman's interest is not so much in how things grow as in what the natural world does for the human soul and spirit. From this perspective, "Ackerman buzzes productively from idea to revelation to insight," a *Publishers Weekly* reviewer noted, as she "reprises her role as an enchanting intellectual sensualist."

Ackerman's *Origami Bridges: Poems of Psychoanalysis and Fire* documents a year and a half of psychoanalysis with an analyst the poems refer to as "Dr. B." Written in free verse and loose rhyme, the poems are divided into four sections. In a review for the *Library Journal,* Barbara Hoffert commented on the book's "down to the essence" diction, writing, "Ackerman is far too witty and honest a writer to sink us with pretense." Donna Seaman of *Booklist,* who called Ackerman "extraordinarily attuned" and considered her nature writing "beguiling . . . superlatively descriptive and wonderfully present," felt that Ackerman's writing in *Origami Bridges* "is positively incandescent."

One year after *Origami Bridges* was released, Ackerman published *Animal Sense,* a collection of poetry for children. *Animal Sense* contains fifteen poems in five sections, each section focusing on a certain sense, each poem focusing on a different animal. In this collection, Ackerman intertwines her poetry with scientific facts about animals. A *Publishers Weekly* critic noted the beauty of the artwork, but had some reservations regarding the poetry, calling the book "a beautifully designed but unfortunately flawed collection." However, Lauralyn Persson, writing in the *School Library Journal,* noted that "readers who want to go beyond the obvious will savor it."

Published in 2004, *An Alchemy of Mind: The Marvel and Mystery of the Brain* employs Ackerman's flair for metaphor to explain the complex workings of the brain. A *Publishers Weekly* contributor described Ackerman's "sensuous" prose, noting that her metaphors "cascade down every page like waterfalls." The contributor also felt that even the most science-minded readers "should be won over by her uniquely personal perspective." Combining experience, history, literature, and science, Ackerman produces a new sort of study on how and why we think by infusing her trademark poetic language into scientific writing. Booklist critic Donna Seaman called the writing "agile, involving and uniquely far-ranging and insightful." Floyd Skloot, writing in *Newsday,* called Ackerman "a grand, erudite synthesizer, positioning herself at the place where knowledge ends and reporting back to us in the language of lyric."

According to Ackerman, *An Alchemy of Mind* is the natural next step following her previous work. In an interview with Ron Hogan of *Publishers Weekly,* she explained: "All of my books are an effort to discover a little better what it once was like to be alive on the planet: what the passions felt like, what it tasted like, what it smelt like, the whole experience of being alive." Ackerman's wonder at every aspect of life makes up the thread that runs through all of her work. In an interview with Barbara Adams of *Writer's Digest,* Ackerman reflected, "Sometimes people think that I write different kinds of books—some about animals and some about people. But to my mind, it's all part of the same quest, to understand the human condition and what life on Earth feels like."

Ackerman followed *An Alchemy of Mind* with the story of a couple who smuggled more than 300 Jews out of the Warsaw Ghetto during World War II. Based on the diaries of Antonina Zabinski, *The Zookeeper's Wife* recounts how the Warsaw Zoo was mostly destroyed by bombing and shares how the Zabinskis used the empty zoo to hide and shelter Jews to save them from the Nazis' attempted extermination. "Though it reads more extravagantly than most fictions, and features a cast worthy of a novel, the book is meticulously researched and documented," wrote Charles Foran of the Toronto *Globe and Mail.* Wilda Williams, writing in *Library Journal,* stated, "Ackerman has done an invaluable service in bringing a little-known story of heroism and compassion to light." A *Publishers Weekly* critic noted, "Ackerman's writing is viscerally evocative."

The Zookeeper's Wife was selected by *Booklist* as a Top of the List Winner for the Editors' Choice books of 2007. Donna Seaman, reviewing the book for that magazine, felt that "Ackerman has written many stellar works . . . but this is the book she was born to write." Carol Memmott, writing for *USA Today,* noted the role of the animals that remained at the zoo and were allowed to run free, under Antonina's care. She concluded, "Ackerman's story is a treatise on nobility—a word that applies to some humans and all of the animals in *The Zookeeper's Wife.*"

In Ackerman's next book, *Dawn Light: Dancing with Cranes and Other Ways to Start the Day,* the author muses about the earliest hours of the day. The pieces discuss animal and plant life, particularly focusing on birds, as well as rituals and spiritual philosophies about dawn, and the use of dawn lighting in art work. "Ackerman creates a luxuriant word garden brimming with spirited observations, stories, and musings," wrote Donna Seaman in *Booklist.* Sue O'Brien, writing for *School Library Journal,* concluded, "These pieces are accessible and lyrically written." Noting that *Dawn Light* encourages readers to stop and appreciate what goes on around them, Wendy Smith wrote in *Washington Post Book World,* "It's easy to live in the moment when you're immersed in Ackerman's glorious prose, studded with arresting phrases and breathtakingly beautiful images."

AUTOBIOGRAPHICAL ESSAY:

In the small Chicago suburb of Waukegan, Illinois, which for some reason has driven over eighty of its onetime residents to become writers of one sort or another, my family lived in a bay-windowed house on the outskirts of town, where paved streets gave way to vast, flat housing tracts, and the tallest objects for miles were orange bulldozers standing like mastodons in the dirt. Right across the street from us there was a small field and then a plum orchard I sometimes walked through on the way to Greenwood Elementary

Poet and nature writer Diane Ackerman in her garden, 2000s

School. This was not the route preferred by my parents. The woods were overgrown, and, as Frost wrote, dark and deep, and I was just a six-year-old with a Roy Rogers writing tablet and a mop of unruly hair my mother had temporarily tamed in a ponytail.

The route I was supposed to take went around the block, on sidewalk all the way, past the vacant lot on the corner, past the little, blue frame house of Mrs. Griffith, who once phoned my mother to report: "Your daughter is talking to herself again! Lord knows what she talks about. I just thought I'd better tell you, Marcia." Then on past the Book Mobile stop across from the drugstore where I sometimes bought plastic horses and riders. I loved playing with the horses, whether they were ridden by cavalrymen or cowboys, and most of all I liked it when they came with small, red rubber saddles, and reins that slid into the groove in the horse's mouth, and even stirrups you could slide the foot of the rider into. But they were always frozen into a state of alarm or rest: the horses were always galloping, trotting, or standing still at some invisible hitching post. And the riders were always waving their arms or hunkering low in the saddle or sitting up stiffly on parade march. Though I tried to make them move, by bending or heating or twisting, I soon learned, as I would later about real soldiers and cowboys, that they could break beyond repair and disappear from my life. I never thought of them as being frozen in an abstract position. I thought of them being always frightened, always angry, always sad, always silently yelling.

Around the corner from the drugstore stood Victor's house. I called my cousin Tic-Toc, and he was my best friend, until his mother came between us. Once she shrieked to find me talking her son into tying a towel around his shoulders and leaping from the back roof onto the brick barbecue to see if people really could fly. On another occasion, we concocted a gruesome brew of unmentionable fluids to give to Normy Wolf, a nerd who lived across the street. I wanted to see if it would kill him, and we would have found out if Victor's mother hadn't caught us crossing the street with a disgustingly full mayonnaise jar. On another day, I drafted Victor into a bolder experiment. I wondered if it were possible to navigate an entire house without touching the ground. His mother walked in from shopping just as I was jumping from a bannister onto a doorknob, swinging into the living room, and then leaping across the top of the couch and chairs as if they were ice floes. I was not a hyperkinetic child, just curious. I wanted to see if it were possible, and would have, if she hadn't banished me at once. Victor was told to play with boys from then on. It was clear girls were too dangerous.

But I didn't know I was different, truly, irrevocably different, different in what I saw when looking out of the window each day, until one morning when going through the orchard with three schoolmates. We were late for first grade, and there were silhouette drawings none of us wanted to miss, so we cut through the orchard. I can still remember the sheen of the green and red plaid dress that Susan Green wore. She had a matching ribbon in her hair, and a petticoat that made her skirt rustle as she moved. Above us, the trees were thick with dark plums huddled like bats. Susan dragged at my arm and pulled me along because I was dawdling, staring up at the fruit—or bats—and when she demanded to know what I was looking at I told her. She let go of my arm and all three girls recoiled. The possibility of bats didn't frighten them. I frightened them. There were the elaborate fantasies I wove when we played "store," "operator," or "house." My

Diane Ackerman (left), holding the Roy Rogers writing tablet, with brother Howard on the first day of kindergarten, 1953

perverse insistence on giving trees colors other than green in drawings. My doing *boy* things like raising turtles and wearing six-shooters to tapdance lessons. My thinking the toy cowboys we played with had emotions. And now this: plums that looked like bats. All these years later, the look on their faces is indelible. But most of all I remember flushing with wonder at the sight of my first metaphor—the living plums: the bats.

*

When I was eight, we moved to Allentown, Pennsylvania. At first, we lived in a row house on South St. Cloud Street, in a neighborhood swarming with children my age. From my bedroom window, I would lovingly watch Chuckie Steckler walk home from school each day. He wore his dark hair brushed up stiff in the front, Elvis Presley style, and he was shy and athletic. His eyes magnetized me. I thought he was the handsomest creature I had ever seen, and sometimes I dashed downstairs and raced him to the end of the block, which seemed an appropriate way to show affection to a boy.

Alas, Chuckie just passed through my neighborhood on his way home. The kids on the block formed a tight play group. At the south end of the street, we played "high waters," a favorite jumping game in which we ran full-speed, one after another at a rope wall, while two children kept raising the rope higher and higher. At the other end of the street, in a cool dark basement full of mildew and lime stains, we put on television musicals and skits, which I wrote. In the back alley we played "kick the tin can," and once we played "French tag" there, too. I remember how yukky I found the sloppy wet kiss a boy slobbered onto my cheek as I wrestled to get free. He was freckled, had chipmunk cheeks and a crew cut, and I liked him a lot; and, since I was a blaze no one could catch, I *let* him tackle me, though I didn't know why.

I loved to run and climb trees and wrestle and explore things and create fantasy worlds and ride horses. At eleven, I was totally horse-obsessed, an equinemania I've written about at length in *A Natural History of Love.* I even "published" one issue of a horse newspaper, writing out each copy in pencil on notebook paper, but soon scrapped the idea as far too taxing. At twelve, I wrote a short sappy novel about a horse named Stormy and the girl who loved him.

At thirteen, when I went to summer camp in the Poconos, I took with me the beginning of an adventure novel I was trying to write about spies, love, and foreign intrigue. Unfortunately, I didn't know anything (not even the basic mechanics) of sex, and had no experience of gun-shooting, knife-wielding violence. Not to mention espionage. Appreciating that these were vital elements in any spy saga, I had to abandon the novel. I wish to goodness now that I had saved it.

Camp Pinemere sat on a lake deep in the state forest, and there were canoe trips, all the usual crafts and sports, the usual meals at long tables in a dining hall, and the usual nerve-wracking dances. Once, before a dance, an older camper told the more naive of us that a girl could get pregnant if her ears touched a boy's, so we were panicky about slow dances. One girl actually wore Dixie cups on her ears for most of the evening.

The camp staged an amateur musical every summer (it was *Bye Bye Birdie* when I was thirteen), and that taught us about creative teamwork. But what was really unusual about Camp Pinemere was its enthusiasm for folksinging. It was the sixties, many counselors played guitar, and the whole camp gathered in the evenings and on Sunday afternoons to sing wonderful, classic folk songs; ethnic songs being popularized by Theodore Bikel; and new songs sung by Peter, Paul, and Mary, Pete Seeger, Joan Baez, and many others. The music was buoyantly melodic, and often haunting and soulful, or tear-jerkingly mournful, and the words were always charged with meaning.

It was there at summer camp that my intellectual mind first stirred and I began reading serious books and thinking about profound things. All the other girls I knew were giggling about boys and breasts and periods and clothes and rock and roll, and they went blank and bored if I brought up ideas. So I began leading a double life. Most of the time, I hung out with the girls and did normal boy-crazy girl things. We spent a lot of time setting our hair on big plastic pink rollers, reading fan magazines, and talking about "making out," how to use Tampax, and what strategies to use to get a boy you like to notice you. But, without telling the girls (for fear of their ostracizing me), I hung around older people who seemed to talk on another plane. I made friends first with the tennis instructor, Gary Abrams, a college student majoring in philosophy. He gave me Herman Hesse's *Siddhartha* to read, along with other books he thought I could manage and would find stimulating. I read them under covers at night, and we'd sometimes talk about the truths I found in them. I was eager, but shy and awkward with my ideas; and he listened and took them seriously. I never felt tutored, challenged, or judged. We talked ideas, and it was thrilling. Right in the midst of all the mysterious, intense, adolescent, coming-of-age mayhem, he midwifed my awakening mind. In later years, I tried to locate him, but I heard that he had gone to Israel to work on a kibbutz; and so I never had a chance to thank him. That was before the Six Day War. I'd love to know what became of him, but I don't even know if he is alive. I have a photograph of him taken at camp, and I cherish it.

Gary Abrams at Camp Pinemere, 1961

*

When I was a senior in high school, I worked on the school newspaper and bought the first Bob Dylan and Beatles albums. I learned about sex in a high school psychology class when I was seventeen, and though I had a boyfriend with whom I very much wanted to make love, when push came to shove neither of us knew how, so we settled for endless kisses and soulful glances deep and dangerous as the well of our affection. My parents didn't approve of my writing poems and stories, and so I had to do it on the sly. Most girls lied about seeing boys. I lied about writing and often stayed after school to write, or made up excuses to stay home when the rest of my family went out shopping. I hid my writings in my room. I loved taking the bus to Lehigh University's library and would check out many books, some in languages I couldn't read, just to make contact with the friendly mind they contained. One day my mother, searching through my room, found a story I had written about a white woman who married a black man (integration was still quite new and my generation was morally outraged by racial prejudice). My mother was convinced I was having an affair with a black man—there was nothing I could say to persuade her otherwise—and so she put an end to my library trips. That was a blow, but I continued to write in secret, and to read whatever and whenever I could. At last, I went off to college (Boston University) in 1967, the year of the first love-ins, and quickly became a flower child. What good luck to have been an undergraduate in that tumultuous era.

Thinking about the late sixties, I remember the anxious thrill of trying to reinvent society. A generation defined by love-ins, hallucinogenic drugs, and the Vietnam War, we lived in a state of daily commotion. Cynicism and idealism often went hand in hand. Inherited truths no longer fit; we felt it was both our privilege and our duty to reshape them. The roller coaster we rode sometimes took wild curves or went off the track. Fun meant outlandish public pranks. Rock and roll besotted us with high-decibel slogans. We championed integration. The Vietnam War loomed over everything and everyone. We protested. We were arrested. We enlisted. We were drafted. We avoided the draft. We staged sit-ins. We practiced free love. We sampled drugs and learned about extremes of consciousness. Like every generation, we lived with moral dilemmas. On campus, we discussed politics before, after, and during classes, whose curricula we rewrote. That atmosphere of upheaval, social change, and hope had a powerful impact on me, as it did on so many others.

Of course, some people grew older and betrayed their dreams. But I've been heartened to see how many children of the sixties have come of age, gotten into positions of influence, and kept their vision. They don't always agree on issues; but what they share is a belief in the sanctity of life and the perfectibility of people, and a determination to make a difference. At the end of Italo Calvino's *Invisible Cities,* Marco Polo says of his life that his toughest task was to try to figure out who and what in the midst of inferno are not inferno, and make sure they prevail. Although I didn't know it when I was eighteen, that was also my quest. It continues to be. Only the forum has changed, not the underlying idealism. Word processing, the revelations of science, feminism, and other twentieth-century phenomena all have affected my work, but none so profoundly as growing up in the sixties.

For various reasons, in my sophomore year I transferred to Penn State. At Boston University I intended to major in what was then called Physiological Psychology, because I was fascinated by human behavior and the emerging field of brain science; but Penn State's computer mistakenly placed me in English, and, since I had been writing shyly but enthusiastically all my life, I considered it fate. Between developing a social conscience and getting my hormones together, I learned little as an undergraduate at Penn State, except where things were located. Certainly I didn't learn to love knowledge or feel called by literature. A student there was obliged to take *either* Shakespeare or Milton. The only inspiring classes I found were a phenomenology class (Heidegger, Merleau-Ponty, *et al*) taught by a wonderfully eccentric philosopher, Alfonso Lingis, who had an eloquent, poetic mind; and a contemporary literature class taught by novelist Paul West [who contributed to *Contemporary Authors Autobiography Series,* Volume 7, pp. 265-86], which was dazzlingly full of ideas. I began dating West, and his demanding criticism of my poetry helped to discipline it. But no other faculty member advised or counselled me. And the writing courses I took were disappointing. I remember how one writing professor, on the first day of class, gave us a long list of what he would not allow us to write. I often got good marks in my writing classes, but I received helpful criticism from only one poet, Jack McManis, dead now, bless his soul, who believed in my talent and encouraged me. The science classes I sometimes took were dull as ditch water. Graduate school was by no means the obvious choice for me.

*

I had wanted to write books while I did anthropological work somewhere in a jungle or on a veldt, but I ended up making a very difficult choice among three possible paths: going to Tanzania to help with chimpanzee research at Jane Goodall's site; digging up earthquake victims in Peru; graduate work in an MFA program. Cornell offered me a teaching assistantship, financial support, and two years in which to write. Even though I desperately wanted to see the world and be out in nature, I wanted even more to perfect myself as a writer. So, after agonizing and soul-searching, I decided on graduate school, and, looking back, it was as if someone then threw a switch in my life, which suddenly began going in a different direction.

When I arrived at Cornell, I was badly educated, couldn't write prose, and didn't have a trained mind. But I did have a lot of curiosity, a somewhat eccentric and swervy imagination, and what seemed to me then almost limitless mental energy. One day I was listening to Gustav Holst's *The Planets,* and I thought how sad it was that people needed to turn the planet Mars

In high school, 1966

into a war god or the planet Venus into a *femme fatale* in order to appreciate them. I was reading general science books and magazines for fun; and the real planets, with their bizarre atmospheres and mysterious terrains, fascinated me. So, as I began planning a book-length suite of poems based on the science of the planets. I applied to the Department of Science, Technology, and Society for support and was thrilled to receive it. I joined a strange interdisciplinary seminar, which met to discuss awkward problems in biomedical ethics and other topics related mainly to science, ethics, and society. It was a seminar by invitation only, and each year it included faculty from different departments and a couple of graduate students like myself who received fellowships.

While I was there, the other seminar members were always from philosophy or the sciences, and I often felt that I was the token creative person in their midst. My natural urge was to solve the problems we were discussing. I wanted to come up with a list of workable solutions, choose the best one and act on it. This amused them no end. Rather than calling me a writer, they referred to me as a "primary agent," by which they meant that, like a painter or composer, I *did* things, while they, on the other hand, discussed things. I often arrived, fresh from the stable, carrying purple riding chaps and smelling of things earthier, to discuss such thorny subjects as euthanasia, which we were on no account to make up our minds about or to try to resolve in any practical way. But I learned a lot about how other sensibilities worked. I enjoyed thinking about difficult moral issues. I was a twenty-two-year-old poet then; prose was an unknown and frightening terrain, and I hadn't yet learned how to think comfortably in it. Nor to think comfortably at all. I wasn't trained in the dressage of syllogistic argument, and ideas that I offered simply, thoughtfully, and from personal experience, without benefit of philosophical rhetoric, were often dismissed as amusing and well-meant, but amateurish. We each had a brief, lunchtime seminar topic, and the one they assigned me was: "Is There Truth in Poetry?" I think it may shed some light on how my creative mind was evolving, so here is part of the talk I gave:

Poetry is not philosophy, not sociology, not psychology, not politics. One ought not to ask of it what's found to better advantage elsewhere. One should only ask poetry to do what it excels at: (1) reflect the working sensibility of its creator, ideally someone with a unique vision and a unique way of expressing it, (2) remind us of the truths about life and human nature that we knew all along, but forgot somehow because they weren't yet in memorable language, and (3) reveal to us many incidental things that a poem knows so well.

What does a poem know? For openers, it knows the vagaries of linguistic fashion, the arduous, ricochet, and sometimes fanciful evolution of society as reflected in its language. It knows quite a lot about social convention, mob psychology, and mores, as they surface in the euphemisms of twenty ages—words like "lynch," "bloomers," or "fornicate"—and then submerge into normal discourse. A poem knows about Creation, any creation, our creation. It takes a blank and makes something, adds *some thing* to the sum of existence. If a poet describes a panther's cage in a certain vivid way, that cage will be as real a fact as the sun. A poem knows more about human nature than its writer does, because a poem is often a camera, a logbook, an annal, not an interpreter. A poem says: These are the facts. And sometimes it goes on to say: And this is what I make of them. But the facts may be right, and the *what I make of them* hopelessly wrong, in what is nonetheless a meaningful and moving poem. A poem may know the subtlest elisions of feeling, the earliest signs of some pattern or discord. It's only when we encounter Keats's odes as a set that we see budding in the first ones what will openly haunt the last. A book of poems chronicles the poet's many selves, and as such knows more about the poet than the poet does at any given time, including the time when the book is finished and yet another self holds her book of previous selves in her hands. A poem knows a great deal about our mental habits, and about upheaval and discovery, loneliness and despair. And it knows the handrails a mind clings to in times of stress (for Shelley, "veils"; for Rilke, "angels"; for Thomas, "wax"). A poem tells us about the subtleties of mood for which we have no labels. The voluptuousness of waiting, for instance: how one's whole body can rock from the heavy pounding of the heart. It knows extremes of consciousness, knows what the landscape of imagination looks like when the mind is at full-throttle, or beclouded, or cyclone-torn. Especially it tells us about our human need to make treaties. Often a poem is where an emotional or metaphysical truce takes place. Time slow-gaits enough in the hewing of the poem to make a treaty that will endure, in print, until the poet disowns it, perhaps in a second treaty called a "palinode." A poem knows about illusion and magic, how to glorify what is not glorious, how to bankrupt what is. It displays, in its alchemy of mind, the transmuting of the commonplace into golden saliences. It takes two pedestrian items, claps them together, and comes out with something finer than either one, makes them unite in a metaphor's common cause. A good example is Shelley's "the intense inane," where each humdrum word is elevated by the other. A poem records emotions and moods that lie beyond normal language, that can only be patched together and hinted at metaphorically. It knows about spunk, zealousness, obstinacy, and deliverance. It *accretes* life, which is why different people can read different things in the same poem. It freezes life, too, yanks a bit out of life's turbulent stream, and holds it up squirming for view, framed by the white margins of the page. Poetry is an act of distillation. It takes contingency samples, is selective. It telescopes time. It focuses what most often floods past us in a polite blur.

We expect the poet to be a monger of intensity, to pain for us, to reach into the campfire so that, like cautious Girl Scouts, we can linger in the woods and watch without burning ourselves or grubbying up our uniforms. Then, even if we don't feel the fire, we can see the poet's face illuminated by the light, hear her flushed chatter, the blazing wood crackle, and imagine well enough what the fire feels like from our safe remove. Though one can't live at red alert from day to day, we expect the poet to, on our behalf, and to share that intensity with us when we're in the right mood. And if we become frightened or bored, we can simply put the poem back on the shelf. Really, we are asking the poet to live an extravagantly emotional life for us, so we can add her experiences to our own.

Diane at Penn State, nineteen years old

We read poems in part, I think, because they are an elegant, persuasive form of lying that can glorify a human condition feared to be meaningless, a universe feared to be "an unloving crock of shit," as philosopher Henry Finch once said offhandedly. To make physical the mystery is in some sense to domesticate it. We ask the poet to take what surpasses our understanding and force it into the straitjacket of language, to rinse the incomprehensible as free of telltale ambiguity and absurdity as possible. That's not to say that we don't find nature ambiguous or life absurd, only that the temptation to play and land the mystery like a slippery salmon, to freeze it in vocabularic aspic, is irresistible. Surely this is not far afield from the hunting magic of the cave drawings at Lascaux.

We ask the poet to reassure us by giving us a geometry of living, in which all things add up and cohere, to tell us how things buttress one another, circle round and intermelt. Once the poet has broken life into shards, we ask her to spin around and piece it back together again, making life seem even more fluid than before. Now it is a fluency of particulars instead of a nebulous surging. We ask the poet to compress and abbreviate the chaos, so we don't overload from its waterfall of sensations, all of which we nonetheless wish to somehow take in. There's more protein in a tiny piece of steak than in a whole loaf of bread, more food for thought in a line of Donne's than in a sermon (unless it's a sermon of Donne's). Because a poem tells us about the peculiar sensibility of the poet, it has a truth of structure, even when not of content. The poet records the fact of her mortality, though not always as straightforwardly or elegantly as Dylan Thomas does in the "Prologue" to his *Collected Poems:*

> I hack
> This rumpus of shapes
> For you to know
> How I, a spinning man,
> Glory also this star. . . .

The best poems are rich with observational truths. Above all, we ask the poet to teach us a way of seeing, lest one spend a lifetime on this planet without noticing how green light flares up as the setting sun rolls under, or the gauzy spread of the Milky Way on a star-loaded summer night, or what Beckett in *How It Is* calls "the fragility of euphoria among the sponges." The poet refuses to let things merge, lie low, succumb to visual habit. Instead, she hoists things out of their routine, and lays them out on a white papery beach to be fumbled and explored. I don't mean to suggest that the subject of a poem is an end in itself. What it usually is is an occasion, catalyst, or tripwire that permits the poet to reach into herself and haul up whatever nugget of the human condition distracts her at the moment, something that can't be reached in any other way. It's a kind of catapult into another metaphysical country where one has longer conceptual arms. The poet reminds us that life's seductive habits of thought and sight can be broken at will. We ask the poet to shepherd us telescopically and microscopically through many perspectives, to lead us like a mountain goat through the hidden, multidimensionality of almost everything.

We expect the poet to know about a lot of strange things, to baby-sit for us, to help us relocate emotionally, to act as a messenger in affairs of the heart, to provide us with an intellectual calling card, to give us death's dumb show and escape's nimbus. Poetry is a kind of knowing, a way of looking at the ordinary until it becomes special and the exceptional until it becomes commonplace. It both amplifies and reduces experience, paradoxical though that be, shrinks an event teeming with disorder to the rigorous pungency of an epigram, or elasticizes one's perspective until, to use an image of Donne's, a drop of blood sucked by a single flea can accommodate an entire world order. Was abstraction ever so particular, so localized as it is in Donne? Or so orchestral a single glint as it is, say, in Milton's cosmological eye? "Milton's delight," notes Dr. Johnson, "was to sport in the wide regions of possibility; reality was a scene too narrow for his mind." Milton could say "All Hell broke loose" because he knew where (and what) Hell was; he had sent his wife and daughters there often enough, and his vision encompassed it, just as it did the constellations (many of which he introduces into *Paradise Lost*). He could say "Orion rose arm'd" because he'd observed Orion often enough when the arms weren't visible.

Poetry is a kind of attentiveness that permits one both the organized adventure of the nomad and the armchair security of the bank teller, a way of dabbling without being a dilettante. But poems ought not to be looked to as harbors of Truth, or poets as wardens of what is right.

*

Poetry was all I knew at twenty-one. So, it was also the only way I could know the All. Since then, I've struggled to learn to write prose, which doesn't come naturally to me and was a nightmare chore for years. Paul West tutored me and guided my progress. What also helped enormously was writing thirteen very short, densely poetic articles (about American heroes and landmarks that had grown stale in the imagination) for *Parade,* because it taught me how to balance a vast amount of research, observation, and response in a tiny space. I will always be grateful to its editor in chief, Walter Anderson, a tall man who casts a long shadow, for believing in me and setting me a challenge that would teach me priceless skills. How vividly I remember that first assignment from *Parade*—a thousand-word portrait of everything and everyone that happened at Ellis Island. It was dead summer and brutally hot. I'd tried for days to write it, and sobbing, sat down beside the pool where Paul was swimming. I showed him the jumbled manuscript and bawled about how I would never be able to fix it, that I was in over my head, that I had no job, no bank account, no future, and no hope. Holding onto the pool coping, he read the essay lying on the ground in front of him, praised its descriptive passages and intuitions, damned its organization, and reassembled it. "Put this here, and that there, and this bit at the end, and that bit at the beginning, and write a paragraph about those things here, and then it'll be fine!" he said. That's just what I did, and it worked. Structuring prose—whose rhythms, patterns and architecture were so different from poetry's—was the hardest thing for me to learn.

As a Ph.D. student at Cornell, with Paul West, 1979

But at some point, after grueling years of struggle, for reasons I can't explain, something clicked and prose became a familiar country. Now I find it comfortable, fascinating, sometimes even thrilling to write. My muse has become highly miscellaneous. And I feel lucky indeed to have been able to use prose as a passport to some of the most astonishing landscapes on earth.

For example, for a month in 1989, I sailed around Antarctica, a landscape as sensuous as it is remote, whose crystal desert I had wanted to see for a long time. Some months before, I helped to raise baby penguins in quarantine at Sea World in San Diego. One fluffy, brown, yeti-shaped chick, which I became particularly fond of, I named "Apsley," after Apsley Cherry-Gerrard who, in 1911, trekked across Antarctica, and wrote a vivid and poignant book about it, *The Worst Journey in the World.* For two years, I had been writing natural history essays for Robert Gottlieb at the *New Yorker,* the editor who sent me to see and write about penguins in the wild. To be haunted by the ghostly beauty of pastel icebergs and astonished by the Antarctic's vast herds of animals are things few people have ever known, or will ever know, and I felt privileged—and still do. Not so long ago—in the days of Sir Richard Burton, T.E. Lawrence, D.H. Lawrence, Lady Hester Stanhope, Beryl Markham, Herman Melville, Washington Irving, and others—there was a crossroads where physical adventure and literary writing converged. There is also a long history of poets called "nature poets," and we all know that brimming category includes writers as different as Lucretius and Marvell. But my prose now seems to locate me among a small tribe often referred to as "nature writers." How curious that label is, suggesting as it does that nature is somehow separate from our doings, that nature does not contain us, that it's possible to step outside of nature—not merely as one of its more promising denizens, but objectively, as a sort of extraterrestrial voyeur. Still, the label is a dignified one and includes a pastoral ethics that we share, a devotion to the keenly observed detail, and a sense of sacredness. There is a way of beholding nature, which is itself a form of prayer.

In my journal, I wrote: "Tonight the moon is invisible, darkness itself has nearly vanished, and the known world, which we map with families, routines, and newspapers, floats somewhere beyond the horizon. Travelling to a strange, new landscape is a kind of romance. You become intensely aware of the world where you are, but also oblivious to the rest of the world at the same time. Like love, travel makes you innocent again. The only news I've heard for days has been the news of nature. Tomorrow, when we drift through the iceberg gardens of Gerlache Strait, I will be working—that is, writing prose. My mind will become a cyclone of intense alertness, in which details present themselves slowly, thoroughly, one at a time. I don't know how to describe what happens to me when I'm out in 'nature' and 'working'—it's a kind of rapture—but it's happened often enough that I know to expect it."

I had been wondering then about the little penguin, Apsley. Shortly, he would have fledged, replacing his thick brown down with black-and-white feathers, and would look very different. My plan was to gather pebbles from the rookery at Salisbury Plain, on South Georgia (where the egg he hatched from was collected), and take them back to him as a souvenir. Apsley was not the sort of penguin that builds nests from stones, but he might recognize the rich amalgam of smells.

Because I write at length about little-known animals in curious landscapes, people often ask, for example, Do you prefer whales to bats? I prefer life. Each of the animals I write about I find beguiling in and of itself; but in all honesty there is no animal that isn't fascinating if viewed up close and in detail. I chose to write about bats, crocodilians, penguins, whales, and such because each would teach something special about nature and about the human condition. About our terror of things that live by night, or the advantages of cold-bloodedness; about intelligence and music, or our need to withstand most any ordeal to behold a nearly extinct life-form before it vanishes. Before beginning each expedition, I knew some of my motives, but always returned nourished by unexpected experiences. What is necessarily missing from the essays is all the fun, turmoil, stress, and welcome obsessiveness that went into setting them up. The emotional marginalia sometimes included acts of great generosity of spirit, and at others revealed less-becoming sides of human nature, and even periods of pain and personal tragedy.

Much of a nature writer's life is spent living by seasonal time, not mere chronicity, as one waits for nature to go about its normal ways. There are long pastures of quiet, broken suddenly by the indelible thrill of seeing a whale or alligator, and then the long hours afterward, as the excitement mellows. Of course, we also live by chronicity. Shifting one's allegiance between those two perceptions of time is one of the most curious and uncanny things that naturalists do. On the way out into the field, and on the return, there comes a point when the two notions of time meet, as if they were nothing more than high mountain roads converging in the wilderness, and you must leap from one to the other and quickly get your footing. I found this especially true when I was writing "Whales," which required trips to both Hawaii and Argentina. Half the time I fretted about airplane schedules, boat rentals, getting permits and permissions, or fixing my tape recorder in the middle of lengthy interviews. But the other half I spent on the desolate, fossil-strewn beaches of Patagonia, watching the hypnotic movements of mother and baby whales. Falling asleep to their snoring and snuffling sounds, attuned only to their lives, I lived on whale time.

Entering an alternate reality, which has its own social customs, time zones, routines, hierarchies and values, is not easy. You leave all the guideposts, the friends and relatives you rely on, and become part of a social group whose laws are rarely explained, but include you, rule you. You have no bank account of esteem. You are judged by everyone. You are admired for your affiliations rather than your character or qualities. You meet people who wish in one way or another to exploit you. You can become distracted from yourself, and enter a cone of ambiguity where you move like an interloper or an outlaw. It is like waking up in a sci-fi story where people move along a different time line and you slide among them. In one sense, that freedom feels exhilarating, but in another it fills you with unsurpassable loneliness. It is difficult to explain the exact appeal of this paradox. Most field naturalists I know relish being new, anonymous, at their own disposal, untrackable, freed from their past, able (even required) to reinvent themselves; and yet they also tend to phone and write home often when they're in port, many times a day blazing a link to their loved ones.

*

People think I court danger. After all, I straddle alligators and swim up to a whale's mouth and climb down

With Paul West, 1980s

cliffs and stand in the midst of millions of bats and risk frostbite at the ends of the Earth. Although I must confess there have been many times when I was truly frightened, and a sentence such as *Why the hell do you get into situations like this?* ran through my mind, such moments pass quickly. I don't take unreasonable chances. I'm always accompanied by experts who have spent many years working with the animal that we are studying and who have been close to that animal countless times, often enough to know what may be dangerous.

"How could you walk across a lagoon where there were alligators somewhere under the water and not know where the alligators were?" one woman asked, clearly horrified. Simple: I followed the invisible footsteps of Kent Vliet, who was a yard in front of me. Kent and his colleagues had been working with alligators in St. Augustine for some time, and he knew where it was probably safe to walk, and also what to do if attacked. But frightened? My heart was pounding.

"How could you let a big bat tangle in your hair?" That was a different situation—bats aren't dangerous, just misunderstood. So I felt no fear at all or, rather, was fearful for the bat which I didn't wish to hurt in any way.

I often find things renewing about *ordeal.* When I went out into the Texas desert with Merlin Tuttle and his friends, to net wild bats and photograph them, we didn't have two hours of sleep. By day we looked for likely batting spots and set up our nets. By night we patrolled the nets or photographed bats. One night, I spent hours aiming photographic lights for Merlin in an abandoned barn while startled bats peed on me nonstop. On the wall in my study, I have one of the photographs of pallid bats that Merlin took that night, and it makes me smile, because I remember just what the event looked, smelled, and felt like.

There were times handling alligators that I got banged up pretty hard. Climbing off an alligator, I didn't jump back fast enough and it swung its head around and clobbered me on the shin. Alligators have exceedingly powerful heads and this was like being slammed with a baseball bat made of pure bone. My shin bruised savagely, but the bone didn't break. And, frankly, that was a trivial price to pay for the privilege of being able to study an alligator intimately, to touch its mouth and eyes, and the folds of its neck skin, and the claws on its back feet, and really get to know the look and feel of it up close.

At a later time, on an expedition to Japan to see rare albatrosses, I managed to break three ribs. When I was sure I would live through that injury, it then became strictly a matter of pain. The pain was torrential. The top half of my body was paralyzed by pain. Every movement sent lightning forks through my chest and back. Standing absolutely still hurt badly, sitting hurt badly, lying down hurt badly, and trying to keep my balance on a rolling ship was agony. Once I lay down, I could not get up. The muscles were too inflamed to work. On shipboard, leaving the island, I will never forget the crew settling me into one of the tiny capsule bunks, which are small open cubicles recessed into the wall. Some hours later, waking in pain, I discovered that I was trapped in my low-ceilinged, coffin-like bunk. For two hours, I tried everything I could think of to get out. I have never known such helplessness. Because I couldn't expand my chest, I was unable to call for help, hard as I tried. Finally, a Japanese passenger across the room woke up and crawled sleepily from his bunk. I pantomimed that I needed help, that my ribs were broken, and would he drag me carefully out of my narrow bunk. Sliding his arms under my shoulders, he pulled me out like a war casualty, as pain twisted its ragged knives. Then, holding onto the ceiling, I crawled onto the middle deck, and sat against a wall. But this was just pain. I know now that I can withstand great pain. I was much more concerned by how *inconvenient* the injury was for everyone else—they had to leave the island early. That's what I regretted, not that I was in pain. I also learned about the generosity and concern of strangers—my journey out of Japan was strewn with a trail of kindness. However, most of my expeditions cost me no pain as savage as broken ribs (now my benchmark for a tough trip), just the occasional allergy, bruise, protozoan, or heartache.

On the outside of the train station in Washington, DC, these words are inscribed: "He that would bring home the wealth of the Indies must carry the wealth of the Indies with him. So it is with travelling. A man must carry knowledge with him if he would bring home knowledge." That maxim is particularly true for a nature writer. I never mind abandoning habits, preferences, tastes, plans. I prefer to become part of the new landscape, fully available to the moment, able to revise or ad-lib a perspective without warning, open to the revelations of nature. But you also need to know what you're looking at. So I read everything I can—science, folklore, novels, whatever—and then I plague my scientist companions with questions. This all adds to the creative feeding-frenzy that each article sets in motion.

In writing about rock climber Mo Anthoine, A. (Alfred) Alvarez cites a phrase from an unlikely source—Jeremy Bentham. The father of utilitarianism dismisses as *deep play* any activity in which "the stakes are so high," as Alvarez puts it, "that it is irrational for anyone to engage in it at all, since the marginal utility of what you stand to win is grossly outweighed by the disutility of what you stand to lose." Alvarez is wise to see that Bentham despises *deep play* for some of the precise reasons Mo Anthoine cherishes it. Anthoine confesses that a couple of times a year he has to *feed his rat,* as he puts it, by which he means that wonderful mad rodent inside of him that demands a challenge or a trip that will combine adventure, fun, wonder, risk, and ordeal. Although I'm not a rock climber, I know how the rat gnaws, and I must admit there is nothing like *deep play.* In *On Extended Wings,* a memoir about learning to fly, I wrote:

> It isn't that I find danger ennobling, or that I require cheap excitation to cure the dullness of routine; but I do like the moment central to danger and to some sports, when you become so thoroughly concerned with acting deftly, in order to be safe, that only reaction is possible, not analysis. You shed the centuries and feel creatural. Of course, you do have to scan, assess, and make constant minute decisions. But there is nothing like *thinking* in the usual, methodical way. What takes its place is more akin to an informed instinct. For a pensive person, to be fully alert but free of thought is a form of ecstasy.
>
> Being ecstatic means being flung out of your usual self. When you're enraptured, your senses are upright and saluting. But there is also a state when perception doesn't work,

Williamsburg, Virginia, "where I got my pilot's license," 1983

> consciousness vanishes like the gorgeous fever it is, and you feel free of all mind-body constraints, suddenly so free of them you don't perceive yourself as being free, but vigilant, a seeing eye without judgment, history, or emotion. It's that shudder out of time, the central moment in so many sports, that one often feels, and perhaps becomes addicted to, while doing something dangerous.

Although I never take unnecessary chances, a tidy amount of risk, discomfort, pain, or physical challenge does not deter me. At some point, in the writing of each of my nature essays, my rat found sustenance, and there were, above all, wonderful moments of *deep play.*

Why this form of play should include wild animals is no mystery. In many ways, we're totemic creatures, who wear the hides of animals on our bodies and, in affectionate cuteness, at times even address one another by animal names—"pussycat," "honeybunny," "my little minx," etc. Animals share our world, accompany us through life, and frequently figure as symbols of one sort or another. Everyone has a bat story fluttering around in the half-lit mansion of memory. In my case, as I mentioned at the outset of this essay, bats were inextricably linked to the plum orchard across from my house in Illinois, and the first hint that I might be an artist.

People sometimes ask me about all of the science in my work, thinking it odd that I should wish to combine Science and Art, and assuming that I must have some inner pledge or outer maxim I follow. But the hardest job for me is trying to keep Science out of my writing. We live in a world where amino acids, viruses, airfoils, and such are common ingredients in our daily sense of Nature. Not to write about Nature in its widest sense, because quasars or corpuscles are not "the proper realm of poetry," as a critic once said to me, is not only irresponsible and philistine, it bankrupts the experience of living, it ignores much of life's fascination and variety. I'm a great fan of the Universe, which I take literally: as one. All of it interests me, and it interests me in detail.

*

Writing is my form of celebration and prayer, but it is also the way in which I enquire about the world. I seem to be driven by an intense, nomadic curiosity; my feeling of ignorance is often overwhelming. As a result, prompted by unconscious obbligatos, I frequently find myself in a state of complete rapture about a discipline or field, and rapidly coming down with a poem or a book. For as little as six months, perhaps, or as long as three years, I will be obsessed with flying, or whales, love, the senses, or the oceans, and eagerly learn everything I can about the field. Any raw facts I might acquire about the workings of Nature fuel my creative work and are secondary to my rage to learn about the human condition, which I don't think we can see whole from any one vantage point. If I hadn't spent a year as a soccer journalist many years ago, to get atmosphere for a novel set in the soccer world, I would never have learned as much as I did about the history of play, and certainly never written the four soccer poems at the end of *Lady Faustus,* which have nothing at all to do with soccer, but are really about the rhythm of the mind and what it means to *know* something.

I try to give myself passionately, totally, to whatever I'm observing, with as much affectionate curiosity as I can muster, as a means to understanding a little better what being human is, and what it was like to have once been alive on the planet, how it felt in one's senses, passions, and contemplations. I appear to have a lot of Science in my work, I suppose, but I think of myself as a nature writer, if what we mean by Nature is, as I've said, the full sum of Creation.

Poets tend to be bothered by disturbing questions. Only two questions bother me, but they bother me a lot: (1) How do you start with hydrogen and end up with us?

Or, if you like, How did we get from the Big Bang to the whole shebang? and (2) What was it like once to have been alive on the planet? Everything I've written thus far, in poetry or prose, has been an attempt to elaborate or find answers to those two questions. Deep down, I know they should take from birth to death to answer and include all of consciousness. And I suppose some would find that rather overwhelming and fraught with built-in failure. I don't think of it in that way—in terms of goal, success, or self-esteem—but, rather, as a simple mystery trip. The world revealing itself, human nature revealing itself, is seductive and startling, and that's fascinating enough to send words down my spine.

For ten years, I taught writing at many universities around the country, as writers do, but it became increasingly more attractive to support myself through the sweat of my pen, if I could. When I began writing natural history articles for *Life,* the *New Yorker, National Geographic,* and other magazines, that became almost possible. The commercial success of *A Natural History of the Senses*—a book that was great fun to write and a long-term labor of love—clinched it. Though I work like the dickens now, I only write essays for magazines that overlap with whatever book I'm working on, but I'm always working on a couple of projects at once. My real joy is being able to create my own astonishment, to study the intimate life of the loon, if I wish to, or the mysteries of how and why we love, or the sensuality of looking, or patterns in nature, or work on a new poem. I can follow my curiosity wherever it leads, and that makes me lucky indeed. At the moment, I'm getting ready to embark on another great adventure. This time it will be a book in which I hope to combine my favorite fascinations—nature and human nature. But before that I have to clear my desk, which means writing this autobiographical essay, tagging the eleven gray squirrels in my backyard and writing about them for *National Geographic,* polishing up the introduction to *The Rarest of the Rare* (a new book about some endangered animals I travelled the world to find), finishing the narration for the PBS series based on my senses book, and going on a three-week book tour for *A Natural History of Love.* Then it will be August, hot, sultry, death-defying August, when dawn saws through the forest, the leaves are painfully green, the hummingbirds assault the bell-shaped flowers, and the human carnival is at full tilt.

Ackerman contributed the following update to her autobiographical essay, 2009:

With scrub jays in Florida, 1992

I just read the preceding essay with the wistful smile one reserves for her younger self. Were they really more innocent days? Probably not. Each year warps the lens of memory a little more. But I could not have imagined what lay in store for me: *millefiore* events that have run the gamut from unlucky and harrowing to lucky and heartening. And lots of mental mischief.

For five years I volunteered anonymously at a local telephone crisis center. There, almost everything dangerous or poignant that can happen to human beings prompted a call—from depression, suicide, and murder to all the trials, uncertainties, and conflicts of love. Yet it wasn't at all depressing work, but intensely draining and uplifting. It taught me a lot about altruism, resiliency, salvation, how to survive crises, and our ability to heal. It was only after I retired from service that I wrote *A Slender Thread,* in which I set some of my experiences against the backdrop of the natural world I love.

Soon afterward I began a new collection of poetry and one of the strangest writing experiences I've ever known. *Origami Bridges: Poems of Psychoanalysis and Fire* wasn't a planned book, but one that geysered up naturally over a year and a half, during which I was in psychotherapy and wrote a poem almost daily. An unusual aspect of my therapy was that my therapist and I lived in different towns. Once a month or so I

Posing with one of her subjects, 1991

would visit him in his office. Most weeks we spoke by telephone, however, which in some ways allowed greater intimacy and risk, although it deprived us of the lavish visual cues that can be so telling. The voice is lavish, too. After my experience as a telephone crisis-line counselor, I felt comfortable dealing with steep emotions by phone, a drama that has its own fascinating dynamics. Although I didn't know much of my analyst's background, he was a profoundly nuanced listener. Somehow this combination of methods worked remarkably well. A telephone receiver is perforated like a confessional screen, you miss the shame of eye contact, the other's voice seems to originate inside your head, mental portraits of the other form while you're talking, and so on. As in traditional psychoanalysis, you don't see the analyst. But in this case the analyst doesn't see you, either.

A therapist usually provides a safe place in which to meet, his space, full of his belongings, with furniture arranged for his physical and aesthetic comfort. He's in charge of air flow and cushions, and he's used to the ambient noises: from heating pipes that sound like a giraffe choking on an abacus, to a window ledge where doves seem to be warming up for light opera. No, via telephone, you have to find your own private space, free from interruption, and that's not always easy. For example, in one poem, the roofers begin hammering mid-session.

I sent him all the poems that emerged, hot off the heart, and they became an important part of the therapy, another place where we could meet. There's a tradition of using artworks in this way, children's drawings especially, and it opened up some unexpected avenues. So much of life falls between the seams of the sayable. Metaphor thrives in the spaces between words. Of course, psychotherapy and lyrical poetry address many of the same issues, and they both create a space where one can explore one's relationship with oneself and others. Both require rules, tremendous focus, entrancement and exaltation, the tension of spontaneity caged by restraint, the risk of failure and shame, the drumbeat of ritual, the willingness to be shaken to the core. So, though refreshingly different from each other, the two overlap in companionable places.

As I revised each poem, I necessarily restructured some of the feelings the poem captured. That process was also illuminating. My chief goal with this book, however, was to write the best poetry I could; its usefulness in therapy was felicitous but secondary. They remain, after all, simply deeply felt poems about an important relationship in one's life.

It didn't occur to me at the time, but one association I have with origami comes from a trip to Honduras with the doctors of Interplast. In fascination and awe, I watched dozens of operations on severely afflicted children, mainly with cleft mouth and palate. Working with a child's unique deformity and available flesh, the surgeons deftly reassembled faces like the folding of origami. Their own faces read: *If I fold this piece here, and slide that piece there, and angle this other piece between them, and snip a little behind here, and then fold this other edge down . . .* and so on, resolving the geometrical puzzle of a cleft face. One doctor would start a child on the long road to healing, part of whose ultimate goal was being able to smile—coin of the realm for all children—and another doctor would continue the work when Interplast returned the following year with a new crew of volunteers. On my trip, I helped out as a circulating nurse, someone who bridges the sterile and unsterile fields in the operating room, and I became acutely aware of the surgeons' origami, their creative joining of papery flesh.

Curiously enough, at a certain point, I stopped needing to write psychotherapy poems. No doubt much could be said about their order and evolution, the complex role they played and why at a certain stage I no longer required their intermediacy. There may have been a gradual change in how I processed pain, a psychic change that short-circuited my being inspired to write them. Maybe I wasn't feeling the same miasma I had to name if I hoped to manage and explore it.

When I read the book straight through now, I'm surprised by the evolving tones of the relationship, something only visible in hindsight. While writing *Origami Bridges,* I was finishing a prose book, as well, *Cultivating Delight: A Natural History of My Garden,* and some of the poems' moods and themes appear in it. The poems influenced the prose. The reverse was not true, however; the creative flow traveled only in one direction.

I wrote the last of *Cultivating Delight* while wearing a stiff, painful neck collar, because I'd injured my neck in a bicycling accident. It was a time haunted by the fear of paralysis, full of uncertainty and immobility. An aide helped me into the garden each day and ran errands, did the household chores. Yet it was also one of the happiest periods of my life, because I woke up each morning, rubbed my hands together, and said, *Oh, boy. What can I learn about today?* I thought about the psychology and ways of gardeners like me, eternal optimists who need to create worlds of color, scent and beauty. I thought about how a garden quickly becomes an extension of oneself that one can prune and perfect, and about all the surprising things we have in common with plants. When I dip into the book now, I don't remember the neck fright. Instead, *Cultivating Delight* remains one of my favorite books because it conjures up those garden days of curiosity and wonder.

Next came *An Alchemy of Mind,* a sort of secular hymn to the brain, or if you like, a poetics of the brain based on scientific research. In its pages I tried to capture the mystery, experience, and feel of having a brain/mind. I love to focus on a facet of nature we view too narrowly, and try to demystify it, clarify it, give it a human face, celebrate its richness and variety. After all, one can get to the end of life and discover one lived only the length of it, not the width. So, just as one could learn to garden better from reading *Cultivating Delight,* though it's also a book about growth and our relationship with nature (among other things), one could learn the latest neuroscience from reading *An Alchemy of Mind,* though it's also a book about how the brain becomes the mind and the mental fantasia in which we spend our days.

While I was on a book tour for *An Alchemy of Mind,* Paul fell ill with a kidney infection that became systemic, one of those staphylococcus bugs older than sharks or gingko trees, and I hurried home to camp out with him in the hospital. Struggling from bed one evening, he made his way to the bathroom, elated that we would be heading home the following morning. A few moments later he walked back out and stood at the foot of the bed, eyes glazed, his face like fallen ice. Paul had a massive stroke, one tailored to his own private hell. The author of over fifty stylishly written books, a master of English prose with one of the largest working vocabularies, a man whose life revolved around words, he had suffered brain damage to the key language areas of his brain, and could no longer process language in any form. Global aphasia, it's called—the curse of a perpetual tip-of-the-tongue memory hunt. He understood little of what people said, and all he could utter was the syllable "mem." Nothing more.

But Paul could be diabolically determined, and so could I. Over the next four years, he re-loomed vibrant carpets of vocabulary, and his life grew richer in a score of ways. This was Paul's second stroke. He had a TIA (a small stroke from which one can mainly recover) fifteen years earlier, quickly followed by a pacemaker, diabetes, an increasingly irregular heart, several pneumonias, and many other health scares. So for the past twenty years or so, I've been a caregiver. Life can survive in the constant shadow of illness, and even rise to moments of rampant joy, but the shadow remains, and one has to make space for it. As Amelia Earhart once said to reporters after she emerged from a plane crash: "It's all part of the adventure."

*

In 2005, I stumbled upon a little-known true story of World War II, one so admirable, emotionally charged, and full of animals that I felt irresistibly drawn to it. *The Zookeeper's Wife* is about the extraordinary efforts of Jan and Antonina Zabinski, Christian zookeepers horrified by Nazi racism, who capitalized on the Nazi's obsession with pureblood animals in order to save over 300 doomed people. After their zoo was bombed, killing most of the animals, the Zabinskis began smuggling Jews out of the ghetto, sneaking them into the zoo, and hiding them in the empty animal cages. Twenty at a time also hid inside the zookeepers' house, living underground and between walls, but coming out after dark for piano concerts, sculpting, and dinner parties, since the Zabinskis specialized in hiding artists and intellectuals.

They also adopted many orphaned animals and raised them indoors. Because of this bizarre but life-saving mix, the Underground gave the zoo the codename of "The House under a Crazy Star," and it became one of the most successful hideouts during World War II.

I felt very close to Antonina, who differed from me in telling ways: she was Catholic, a Pole born in Russia, orphaned as a child, tall, blond, a gifted pianist who grew up in the early 1900s—just to name a few! But, in important other ways—her mindful senses, how snug nature felt to her, a vertiginous empathy (both for people and for the other animals we call animals)—we were surprisingly kindred spirits. I also shared her optimistic marrow and belief in the basic goodness of people, despite evidence to the contrary. In her case that was a huge *despite,* because she survived wars in both Russia and Poland, and had suffered many calibers of loss.

Studying Poland's natural world provided a steady stream of small astonishments. The sights, sounds, and smells of a zoo depend on the animals it keeps, and I had great fun learning the ways of gibbons, badgers, arctic hares, lynxes, and the other animals that either lived indoors with the Zabinskis or on the grounds. I relished the excuse to learn about Hassidism, Kaballah, and pagan mysticism of the early twentieth century, Nazism's roots in the occult, and other arcana, as well as such practical matters as Polish history and Baltic lampshades of the era.

Then, one autumn weekend in Washington, DC, I attended a dialogue hosted by the Mind & Life Institute, which brought together the fourteenth Dalai Lama and other Buddhists with contemplatives and neuroscientists, to discuss suffering, compassion, meditation, consciousness, and other topics of mutual interest. Blessed with boyish curiosity and a puckish sense of humor, the Dalai Lama sat on stage in the Daughters of the American Revolution Constitution Hall, wearing chrysanthemum-red robes. "My religion is kindness," he explained simply at one point. "My religion is compassion." At the close of this deeply emotional weekend, in which such words as "peace, compassion, loving kindness" flowed freely among talk of "neurons" and "theta waves," I went to the Holocaust Museum. In just a couple of hours, my mental calipers widened to embrace two extremes of human behavior. That evening, I looked back on the day and felt a profound sense of marvel about our species. On the one hand, some people will go to diabolical lengths when they get bored with the mayhem they've invented, and on the other hand, some will perform high-wire feats of compassion, altruism and empathy. For a moment, I paused at a mental overlook, one of those vistas that I cherish, when the human pageant seems to spread out below and my perspective deepens. The whole enterprise of writing *The Zookeeper's Wife,* which took years, was a small price to pay for the gift of that moment.

In my books, as nature and human nature waltz together and each shines light upon the other, most of what I do is just pay attention. For the moment, we can only know the shape and complexion life has found in us here on Earth. It's ironic that we designate certain landforms as natural wonders, when none is as unlikely as we, the tiny bipeds with the giant dreams. I mean our being here at all, given all the twists, turns, sidesteps, leaps, and genetic bottlenecks of evolution. We are natural wonders, creatures easy to know, but hard to know well. *The Zookeeper's Wife* is one more piece of a mosaic that I can never finish, but which, if I could, would help to tell the whole story of human experience.

Today, I'm decompressing from yet another near-death experience of Paul's, which, thank heavens, ended happily. I'm also waiting for the bound galleys of *Dawn Light* to arrive. I began this celebration of nature at dawn in the aftermath of Paul's stroke four years ago, in part because I found solace in the healing power of nature. The short chapters were written in gusts of reverie at dawn, and belong to that quirky genre, *a natural history,* in which I relish something from different perspectives. In this case, the everyday mystery I'm exploring is part of the great parentheses of our lives, a symbol of birth and insight, to many cultures a goddess, a time alive and death-defying, when the deepest arcades of life and matter become visible.

Endlessly fascinated by both mind and matter, I feel grateful to have a calling that allows me to create my own astonishment. Writing continues to be my form of inquiry, celebration, and prayer.

With Paul West, 2000s

BIOGRAPHICAL AND CRITICAL SOURCES:

BOOKS

Ackerman, Diane, *Twilight of the Tenderfoot: A Western Memoir,* Morrow (New York, NY), 1980.

Ackerman, Diane, *On Extended Wings,* Atheneum (New York, NY), 1985.

Contemporary Poets, 6th edition, St. James Press (Detroit, MI), 1996.

Contemporary Women Poets, St. James Press (Detroit, MI), 1998.

Dictionary of Literary Biography, Volume 120: *American Poets since World War II, Third Series,* Gale (Detroit, MI), 1992.

PERIODICALS

Affilia Journal of Women and Social Work, summer, 1998, Catherine Hiersteiner, review of *A Slender Thread: Crisis, Healing, and Nature,* pp. 255-256.

American Biology Teacher, May, 1992, Rita Hoots, *The Moon by Whale Light, and Other Adventures among Bats, Penguins, Crocodilians, and Whales,* pp. 314-315.

Appraisal: Science Books for Young People, fall, 1998, review of *Bats: Shadows in the Night,* p. 5.

Art in America, January, 2006, "Artist Andrea Blu, Parker's Box Gallery Owner Alun Williams, and Art Collector and Benefactor Diane Ackerman Have Been Awarded the Order of Arts and Letters," p. 150.

Biography, fall, 2007, review of *The Zookeeper's Wife,* p. 716; winter, 2008, review of *The Zookeeper's Wife,* p. 212.

Book, May, 1999, review of *Deep Play,* p. 82; November-December, 2002, Stephen Whited, review of *Origami Bridges: Poems of Psychoanalysis and Fire,* p. 89.

Booklist, October 1, 1997, Sally Estes, review of *Bats,* p. 320; March 15, 1998, Donna Seaman, review of *I Praise My Destroyer,* p. 1197; March 1, 1999, Donna Seaman, review of *Deep Play,* p. 1099; September 1, 2001, Donna Seaman, review of *Cultivating Delight: A Natural History of My Garden,* p. 26; September 1, 2002, Donna Seaman, review of *Origami Bridges,* p. 48; February 15, 2003, Gillian Engberg, review of *Animal Sense,* p. 1068; April 1, 2003, review of *Animal Sense,* p. 1407; May 1, 2004, Donna Seaman, review of *An Alchemy of Mind: The Marvel and Mystery of the Brain,* p. 1533; January 1, 2005, review of *An Alchemy of Mind,* p. 768; August, 2007, Donna Seaman, review of *The Zookeeper's Wife,* p. 5; January 1, 2008, "Adult Books, Editors' Choice, 2007," p. 6; June 1, 2009, Donna Seaman, review of *Dawn Light: Dancing with Cranes and Other Ways to Start the Day,* p. 4.

BookPage, October, 2001, review of *Cultivating Delight,* p. 4; April, 2003, review of *Animal Sense,* p. 28.

Bookseller, November 30, 2007, review of *The Zookeeper's Wife,* p. 12.

Bookworld, July, 18, 1999, review of *Deep Play,* p. 7; October 7, 2001, review of *Cultivating Delight,* p. 13; April 27, 2003, review of *Animal Sense,* p. 12; June 13, 2004, Carl Zimmer, review of *An Alchemy of Mind,* p. 13.

Bulletin of the Center for Children's Books, June, 1995, Roger Sutton, review of *Monk Seal Hideaway,* p. 337; September, 1997, review of *Bats,* p. 4.

California Bookwatch, November, 2007, review of *The Zookeeper's Wife.*

Catholic Library World, February 23, 1998, review of *I Praise My Destroyer,* p. 70.

Choice, October, 1997, review of *A Slender Thread,* p. 327.

Christian Science Monitor, October 24, 2001, review of *Cultivating Delight,* p. 19.

Discover, May, 2002, review of *Cultivating Delight,* p. 76; March, 2003, review of *Animal Sense,* p. 73.

Entertainment Weekly, January 17, 1997, Vanessa V. Friedman, review of *A Slender Thread,* p. 58; June 11, 2004, Tina Jordan, review of *An Alchemy of Mind,* p. 128.

Globe and Mail (Toronto, Ontario, Canada), June 12, 1999, review of *Deep Play,* p. D11; December 1, 2001, review of *Cultivating Delight,* p. 1; December 15, 2007, Charles Foran, review of *The Zookeeper's Wife.*

Good Housekeeping, December, 1999, Kathleen Powers, "Lovers: Great Romances of Our Time through the Eyes of Legendary Writers," p. BIH8; September, 2007, "No Matter What Mood You're In, We Have a Great Book for You," p. 203.

Horn Book, January, 2003, review of *Animal Sense,* p. 88.

Kirkus Reviews, April 1, 1998, review of *I Praise My Destroyer,* p. 441; April 1, 1999, review of *Deep Play,* p. 497; August 1, 2001, review of *Cultivating Delight,* p. 1077; December 15, 2002, review of *Animal Sense,* p. 1844; February 15, 2004, review of *An Alchemy of Mind,* p. 161.

Kliatt, March, 2008, Sue Rosenzweig, review of *The Zookeeper's Wife,* p. 54.

Library Bookwatch, November, 2004, review of *An Alchemy of Mind.*

Library Journal, January, 1997, Antoinette Brinkman, review of *A Slender Thread,* p. 125; February 1, 1998, Richard K. Burns, review of *The Book of Love,* p. 84; March 15, 1998, Ann Van Buren review of *I Praise My Destroyer,* p. 67; June 1, 1998, review of *A Slender Thread,* p. 75; September 1, 2001, Daniel Starr, review of *Cultivating Delight,* p. 215; October 15, 2002, Barbara Hoffert, review of *Origami Bridges,* p. 77; April 15, 2003, Barbara Hoffert, review of *Origami Bridges,* p. 90; March 15, 2004, Laurie Bartolini, review of *An Alchemy of Mind,* p. 103; September 1, 2007, Wilda Williams, review of *The Zookeeper's Wife,* p. 147; July 1, 2009, Sue O'Brien, review of *Dawn Light,* p. 118.

Library Media Connection, October, 2003, Judith Beavers, review of *Animal Sense,* p. 63.

Los Angeles Times, July 8, 1994, Chris Goodrich, review of *A Natural History of Love,* p. E8; October 30, 2001, Michael Harris; review of *Cultivating Delight,* p. E3.

Michigan Quarterly Review, winter, 2000, Carolyn Kizer, "Four Smart Poets," pp. 167-172; winter,

2004, "The Personal Lyric and the Physical World," review of *Origami Bridges,* pp. 117-132.
New Leader, September, 2002, review of *Origami Bridges,* p. 33.
Newsday, June 27, 2004, Floyd Skloot, review of *An Alchemy of Mind.*
New Statesman and Society, May 21, 1993, Fraser Harrison, review of *The Moon by Whale Light, and Other Adventures among Bats, Penguins, Crocodilians, and Whales,* p. 35.
Newsweek, February 10, 1997, Jeff Giles, review of *A Slender Thread,* p. 66; March 3, 2008, "Diane Ackerman: A Life in Books," p. 14.
New Yorker, March 24, 1997, review of *A Slender Thread,* p. 83.
New York Times Book Review, November 3, 1991, David Kirby, review of *Jaguar of Sweet Laughter: New and Selected Poems,* p. 14; December 29, 1991, Michiko Kakutani, review of *The Moon by Whale Light, and Other Adventures among Bats, Penguins, Crocodilians, and Whales,* p. 7; February 16, 1997, review of *The Rarest of the Rare: Vanishing Animals, Timeless Worlds,* p. 32; March 2, 1997, Kate Jennings, "Calling Out for Help," p. 11; December 7, 1997, review of *A Slender Thread,* p. 76; April 19, 1998, review of *A Slender Thread,* p. 40; June 20, 1999, Winifred Gallagher, "May the Force Be with You," p. 10; October 21, 2001, Miranda Seymour, "A Poet's Green Plot," review of *Cultivating Delight,* p. 17; October 28, 2001, review of *Cultivating Delight,* p. 30; November 4, 2001, review of *Cultivating Delight,* p. 34; December 2, 2001, review of *Cultivating Delight,* p. 68; October 13, 2002, Scott Veale, review of *Cultivating Delight,* p. 32; December 8, 2002, review of *Cultivating Delight,* p. 32; June 1, 2003, review of *Animal Sense,* p. 24; August 29, 2004, Marina Warner, "Circuits," p. 15; September 9, 2007, review of *The Zookeeper's Wife,* p. 716.
North American Review, November-December, 2003, Vincent F. Gotera, review of *Animal Sense,* p. 58.
Parnassus, fall, 1995, Mark Doty, "Horsehair Sofas of the Antarctic: Diane Ackerman's Natural Histories."
People, March 10, 1997, Thomas Curwin, review of *A Slender Thread,* p. 31; October 29, 2001, review of *Cultivating Delight,* p. 56; July 12, 2004, Moira Bailey, review of *An Alchemy of Mind,* p. 46.
Poetry, December, 1998, John Taylor, review of *I Praise My Destroyer,* p. 182; August, 2003, Christina Pugh, review of *Origami Bridges,* p. 291.
Psychology Today, May-June, 2004, review of *An Alchemy of Mind,* p. 82.
Publishers Weekly, December 15, 1997, review of *The Book of Love,* p. 51; March 1, 1999, review of *Deep Play,* p. 47; July 23, 2001, review of *Cultivating Delight,* p. 58; September 23, 2002, review of *Origami Bridges,* p. 68; December 16, 2002, review of *Animal Sense,* p. 67; May 31, 2004, review of *An Alchemy of Mind,* p. 68; July 23, 2007, review of *The Zookeeper's Wife,* p. 58.
Reference and Research Book News, November, 2004, review of *Within the Stone,* p. 249.
Roundup Magazine, April, 2003, review of *Twilight of the Tenderfoot,* p. 23.
School Library Journal, October, 1997, Patricia Manning, review of *Bats,* p. 141; February, 2003, Lauralyn Persson, review of *Animal Sense,* p. 126.
Science Books and Films, January, 1998, review of *Bats,* p. 20; May-June, 2004, Nancy A. Ridenour, review of *An Alchemy of Mind,* p. 117; May-June, 2005, review of *An Alchemy of Mind,* p. 95.
Science News, March 16, 2002, review of *Cultivating Delight,* p. 175.
Smithsonian, October, 2001, Kathryn Brown, review of *Cultivating Delight,* p. 138.
Southern Review, October, 1992, Franklin Burroughs, review of *The Moon by Whale Light, and Other Adventures among Bats, Penguins, Crocodilians, and Whales,* p. 928.
Tribune Books, December 1, 2002, review of *Cultivating Delight,* p. 6.
Underwater Naturalist, 2002, review of *The Moon by Whale Light and Other Adventures among Bats, Penguins, Crocodilians, and Whales,* p. 47.
USA Today, October 2, 2007, Carol Memmott, "In *Zookeeper's Wife,* Hope Runs Free," p. 06D.
Washington Post Book World, Barbara Raskin, review of *A Natural History of Love,* June 19, 1994, p. 2; October 7, 2001, "As Someone Who Has Yet to Be . . . ," p. T13; October 1-7, 2007, Susie Linfield, review of *The Zookeeper's Wife,* p. 39; September 20-26, 2009, Wendy Smith, "Seize the Day," p. 3.
Women's Review of Books, December, 2004, Peg Aloi, review of *An Alchemy of Mind,* pp. 11-12.
Writer's Digest, September, 1997, Barbara Adams, "Diane Ackerman: Tight Focus in Small Spaces," author interview, p. 29.

ONLINE

Diane Ackerman Home Page, http://www.dianeackerman.com (September 7, 2009).

HarperCollins Web site, http://www.harpercollins.com/authors/20266/Diane_Ackerman/index.aspx (September 7, 2009).

W.W. Norton Web site, http://books.wwnorton.com/books/author.aspx?ID=5220 (September 28, 2009).

* * *

ADAMCHAK, Raoul W. 1953-
(R.W. Adamchak)

PERSONAL: Born November 11, 1953; married Pamela C. Ronald (a professor of plant pathology). *Education:* Clark University, Worcester, MA, B.A.

ADDRESSES: *E-mail*—rwadamchak@ucdavis.edu.

CAREER: Writer, instructor, and organic farmer. *IPM Practitioners,* coeditor; University of California, IPM Manual Group, senior writer; Full Belly Farm, Guinda, CA, partner; California Certified Organic Farmers, inspector; University of California-Davis, Student Farm, Market Garden Coordinator.

MEMBER: California Certified Organic Farmers, former board member and president.

WRITINGS:

(With wife, Pamela C. Ronald) *Tomorrow's Table: Organic Farming, Genetics, and the Future of Food,* Oxford University Press (New York, NY), 2008.

SIDELIGHTS: Raoul W. Adamchak is a writer, instructor, and organic gardener. He was born November 11, 1953, and earned a master's degree in international agricultural development. Adamchak has grown organic crops for more than two decades and was a partner in Full Belly Farm, a private 150-acre organic vegetable farm in California. He also served as board president and member of the California Certified Organic Farmers. Through the organization he inspected more than one hundred organic farms. Adamchak teaches organic production methods and is the Market Garden director and CSA coordinator of the Student Farm at the University of California-Davis.

In 2008 he and his wife, Pamela C. Ronald, a plant geneticist at UC Davis and chair of the school's plant genomics program, published *Tomorrow's Table: Organic Farming, Genetics, and the Future of Food.* The book makes the controversial contention that organic farming methods and crop genetic engineering (GE) can and should coexist in order to meet the planet's increasing need for healthy food. The world's population is expected to reach more than nine billion by 2050, and the authors believe that GE crops that can resist pests, freezing, and flooding raised using environmentally conscious organic farming techniques are what will be needed to feed the world's hungry.

In *Tomorrow's Table* the authors explain what geneticists and organic farmers do, separate the truth from fiction on the debate over the safety of GE food, present a typical Ronald-Adamchak family meal, and offer a timeline of biological technology from 4000 BCE to the twenty-first-century.

Kate Washington said in *Conversations about Plant Biotechnology,* "The book's unusual format—the two authors switch off chapters and range stylistically from personal anecdote to hard science—makes for a lively read, even through some fairly dry and technical material." But she admitted that "with its fresh and intriguing premise, its unconventional style and its passion for improving farming and food production, is worth reading with an open mind." Still skeptical on the merits of genetic engineering after reading the book, organic farmer Jim Profit commented in *Catholic Register,* "The book lacks any real critique of our present food system. The value at the system's core is making profit for the shareholder, not food for the hungry. . . . Whether one agrees with the authors or not, this book makes a great contribution to the debate about genetic engineering."

Writing in *Library Journal,* Joshua Lambert noted that although the book is not a comprehensive review of genetic engineering, it "offers a compelling portrait of how GE and organic farming can coexist for the future betterment." A contributor to *Western Farm Press* said the book "was written for consumers, farmers and policymakers who want to make food choices and policy that will support ecologically responsible farming practices. It is also for consumers who want accurate information about genetically engineered crops and their potential impacts on human health and the environment."

Adamchak told *CA:* "I've been interested in writing for a long time, but I finally had something interesting to write about. I worked for Bill and Helga Olkowski for many years. They broke trail on the idea of integrating the least toxic pest control materials with ecologically based pest control strategies. Their work led me to the view that both organic farming and genetically engineered crops both have something to contribute to sustainable agriculture. I had to write during any free moment I could find. I have a job, kids, a house, cars, and outdoor adventure to take. Often I wrote after the kids went to sleep. My coauthor and I were also part of a writing group. We would write a chapter and read it to the group, get feedback, and rewrite again and again. We also attended a writer's workshop with Kim Barnes, which was very helpful. I hope our book will help people think about organic farming, genetically engineered crops, and sustainable agriculture in a rational way, using evidence-based information. I hope it helps the organic community and the agriculture scientist community to talk civilly with each other. Ultimately, I hope we can all get together to solve the world's agricultural problems using an ecologically based sustainable agriculture that uses the best and most appropriate technology available."

BIOGRAPHICAL AND CRITICAL SOURCES:

PERIODICALS

Booklist, April 1, 2008, Mark Knoblauch, review of *Tomorrow's Table: Organic Farming, Genetics, and the Future of Food,* p. 14.

Choice: Current Reviews for Academic Libraries, December, 2008, M.J. Stone, review of *Tomorrow's Table,* p. 717.

Futurist, May-June, 2008, review of *Tomorrow's Table,* p. 59.

Library Journal, April 15, 2008, Joshua Lambert, review of *Tomorrow's Table,* p. 102.

U.S. News & World Report Online, June 5, 2008, Adam Voiland, "Solving the Food Crisis with an Unlikely Alliance; A New Book Argues for a Marriage of Organic Farming and Genetic Engineering," interview.

ONLINE

Catholic Register, http://www.catholicregister.org/ (March 9, 2009), Jim Profit, "Tempting Morsels Can't Convince This Skeptic," review of *Tomorrow's Table.*

Conversations about Plant Biotechnology, http://www.monsanto.com/ (May 8, 2008), Kate Washington, "Opposites Attract," review of *Tomorrow's Table.*

Oxford University Press Canada, http://www.oupcanada.com/ (July 1, 2009), brief author profile.

Western Farm Press, http://westernfarmpress.com/ (May 28, 2008), "New Book Promotes GMOS and Organic Farming," review of *Tomorrow's Table.*

* * *

ADAMCHAK, R.W.
See ADAMCHAK, Raoul W.

* * *

ANDEREGG, David 1953-

PERSONAL: Born November 11, 1953, in Milwaukee, WI; married Kelley DeLorenzo; children: Francesca and Peter Lorenzo. *Education:* University of Wisconsin, Madison, bachelor's degree; Tufts University, Boston, MA, master's degree, 1981; Clark University, Worcester, MA, Ph.D., 1985.

ADDRESSES: Office—Bennington College, 1 College Dr., Bennington, VT 05201. *E-mail*—Danderegg@bennington.edu.

CAREER: Psychologist, writer, instructor, and pianist. Cambridge School of Ballet, Cambridge, MA, Walnut Hill School, Natick, MA, Concert Dance Company, Boston, MA, and Boston Conservatory, Boston, MA, rehearsal and performance pianist; Harvard Graduate School of Education, Cambridge, and Research Institute for Educational Problems, Cambridge, research assistant; Harvard Medical School, instructor; psychologist in private practice, 1987; Smith College School for Social Work, Northampton, MA, instructor; Bennington College, Bennington, VT, instructor, 1999—. Staff psychologist at a community mental health center.

MEMBER: American Psychological Association.

AWARDS, HONORS: Austen Riggs Center, Stockbridge, MA, postdoctoral fellowship.

WRITINGS:

Worried All the Time: Overparenting in an Age of Anxiety and How to Stop It, Free Press (New York, NY), 2003.

Nerds: Who They Are and Why We Need More of Them, Jeremy P. Tarcher/Penguin (New York, NY), 2007.

Contributor of a chapter to the book *The Psychotherapy of Schizophrenia,* edited by G. Benedetti and P.M. Furlan, Hogrefe & Huber, 1993. Contributor of articles to periodicals and professional journals, including *Psychoanalytic Psychology, American Journal of Psychoanalysis, Psychologist Psychoanalyst, Psychoanalysis and Contemporary Thought, Los Angeles Times, Miami Herald* and *Newsday.* Member of the editorial board of *Psychoanalytic Psychology.*

SIDELIGHTS: David Anderegg is a writer and a psychologist specializing in child psychology. He was born November 11, 1953, in Milwaukee, Wisconsin, but moved to Fond du Lac in Wisconsin where he grew up. He began his education as an applied piano major at University of Wisconsin in Madison but changed to American history. He went to work as a rehearsal and performance pianist for various art schools in the Boston area, including Cambridge School of Ballet, Boston Conservatory, and Walnut Hill School.

While working as a piano tuner and in after-school programs, he became interested in children and how they think and feel, so he decided to study the psychology of children. He earned a master's degree in psychology from the Eliot-Pearson Department of Child Study at Tufts University in 1981 and a Ph.D. in psychology from Clark University in Worcester, Massachusetts, in 1985.

Anderegg worked as a research assistant at the Harvard Graduate School of Education and for the Research Institute for Educational Problems in Cambridge, Massachusetts. He served his predoctoral internship at Beth Israel Hospital in Boston under which he was an instructor in psychology at the Harvard Medical School.

He held several medical and teaching jobs, working at the Austen Riggs Center long-term psychiatric hospital, in his own private practice in 1987, and as a staff psychologist at a community mental health center. He taught at Smith College School for Social Work in Northampton, Massachusetts, in the late 1980s, and in 1999 he went to Bennington College in Bennington, Vermont, where he is still teaching abnormal and clinical psychology and the psychology of creativity.

In 2003 Anderegg published *Worried All the Time: Overparenting in an Age of Anxiety and How to Stop It,* in which he describes the new phenomenon of overly obsessive parents, ones who worry too much despite the fact that children are healthier and safer than in any other time in history. Parents overthink everything, try to make perfect decisions, are too anxious, and overreact when something happens to their children.

Anderegg says that parents have displaced anxiety and are projecting their own fears about the world onto their children. With twenty-four-hour news channels reporting abductions of children and school shootings, parents believe the world to be a more dangerous place than it used to be. Despite the number of school shootings, suicides, and homicides that are reported on school grounds, data shows that school is actually the safest place for children.

For the book, Anderegg drew on extensive social science research and cases from his twenty years of clinical experience. He analyzed attitudes of parents and caregivers, the use of day-care centers and au pairs, the influence of the media, parents' overscheduling of activities for their children, and the potential for drug and alcohol abuse among children.

"Parents will appreciate this accessible and helpful resource," commented Vanessa Bush in *Booklist,* while a writer in *Publishers Weekly* said that although Anderegg provides sensible advice, the book "will be of the most use to parents who have some familiarity with educational and psychological terminology."

"Anderegg is a soothing voice of reason," according to Joe Hartlaub on *Bookreporter.com.* Hartlaub added, "Anderegg isn't totally convincing, but he does an excellent job of discerning issues of concern and discussing them." Maryse Breton wrote in *Library Journal,* "Although the facts are less convincing than the author's interpretations . . . parents will recognize themselves in the numerous examples and take heart."

In 2007 Anderegg published *Nerds: Who They Are and Why We Need More of Them,* an exploration of the history of the nerd and the negative stereotype. Anderegg explores the stereotype of the socially awkward but scholarly person and shows that adolescents and society at large believe that brains and beauty are mutually exclusive. No teenager wants to risk being dateless if he is seen being interested in science and math. Anderegg asserts that denigration of nerds undermines children and the country as a whole.

Not only does the stereotype create unhappiness and loss of self-esteem and achievement in the children who are the target, says Anderegg, it creates a negative impact on America's competitiveness with other countries, such as China and India, in the education of future scientists. He offers the revealing statistic that in 2004 American colleges graduated more sports-exercise majors than electrical engineers.

"One may quibble with his narrow definition of the subspecies, as someone who is interested just in science and math," noted Rachel Hartigan Shea in the *Houston Chronicle,* "but Anderegg's clear-eyed look at a damaging cultural truism does nerds and jocks—all Americans, really—a service."

Benjamin A. Plotinsky wrote in *Commentary* that Anderegg "regards nerds as victims, reiterating constantly that the unattractive stereotype drives promising teenagers away from technical professions. . . . The prototypical nerd is a wholesome, appealingly goofy kid who embraces nerdiness almost unthinkingly; Anderegg wants to make the world safe for such types, to protect them from the social disapprobation that will keep them from flowering."

BIOGRAPHICAL AND CRITICAL SOURCES:

PERIODICALS

Booklist, May 1, 2003, Vanessa Bush, review of *Worried All the Time: Overparenting in an Age of Anxiety and How to Stop It,* p. 1562; December 1, 2007, Vanessa Bush, review of *Nerds: Who They Are and Why We Need More of Them,* p. 10.

Commentary, May 1, 2008, Benjamin A. Plotinsky, "The Rule Followers," p. 63.

Economist, January 12, 2008, "In Praise of Nerds; American Kids," p. 77.

Houston Chronicle, January 20, 2008, Rachel Hartigan Shea, "Nerds? Who Needs 'em? America Does, Psychotherapist Says, and We Should Stop Making Them Objects of Derision," p. 14.

Library Journal, April 15, 2003, Maryse Breton, review of *Worried All the Time,* p. 115.

Los Angeles Times, June 15, 2003, review of *Worried All the Time,* p. 15.

Publishers Weekly, April 7, 2003, review of *Worried All the Time,* p. 58.

ONLINE

Bennington College Web site, http://www.bennington.edu/ (April 1, 2009), author profile.

Bookreporter.com, http://www.bookreporter.com/ (July 1, 2009), Joe Hartlaub, review of *Worried All the Time.*

David Anderegg Home Page, http://www.drdavidanderegg.com (July 1, 2009), author profile.

Geek Studies, http://www.geekstudies.org/ (May 7, 2008), "Notes on David Anderegg's 'Nerds,'" review of *Nerds.*

Psychology Today Web site, http://www.psychologytoday/ (July 1, 2009), author profile.

OTHER

NRO Radio (audio file), February 7, 2008, John J. Miller, "David Anderegg on Nerds: Who They Are and Why We Need More of Them."*

* * *

ANDERSON, Taylor

PERSONAL: Married; wife's name Christine; children: Rebecca. *Education:* Earned master's degree. *Hobbies and other interests:* Gun maker, forensic ballistic archaeologist, and eighteenth- and nineteenth-century artillery collector.

CAREER: Instructor, writer, and technical consultant for movies. Tarleton State University, Stephenville, TX, instructor.

MEMBER: National Historical Honor Society, U.S. Field Artillery Association.

AWARDS, HONORS: Intercollegiate Press Association Awards; Honorable Order of St. Barbara, U.S. Field Artillery Association.

WRITINGS:

One Little Miracle (sound recording), Old Church Records (Centerville, UT), 2002.

"DESTROYERMEN" SERIES

Into the Storm: Destroyermen, Book 1, Roc (New York, NY), 2008.

Crusade: Destroyermen, Book 2, Roc (New York, NY), 2008.

Maelstrom: Destroyermen, Book 3, Roc (New York, NY), 2009.

SIDELIGHTS: Taylor Anderson is a historian and writer of speculative historical fiction. Anderson holds a master's degree in history and taught history at Tarleton State University in Stephenville, Texas. He has written historical articles and short fiction. A gun maker, forensic ballistic archaeologist, and expert in eighteenth-, nineteenth-, and twentieth-century artillery and combat, Anderson has become a historical consultant. He has collaborated with museums, the National Parks Service, and the U.S. Army, and has been a technical and dialogue consultant for films and documentaries, advising sound engineers, shooting off artillery from his own collection, and acting in a few roles.

In 2008 Anderson published *Into the Storm: Destroyermen, Book 1,* the first book in the "Destroyermen" series that blends historical fiction, World War II battleships, science fiction, and time travel. In the story, the USS *Walker,* an old four-stacker destroyer, is engaging Japanese battle cruisers in the Pacific Ocean. During a squall the warship is hurled into a parallel world devoid of humans but populated by an intelligent species of lemurs, called Lemurians, who are in a battle for dominance with evolved raptor reptiles, called Griks.

The first book details the Lemurian society and their fight against the bloodthirsty Griks who exiled them to islands in the Pacific. While Anderson put the action in a fantastical setting, the ships and combat are as accurate as his thousands of hours of research could make it. A writer in *Publishers Weekly* noted that Anderson expanded on "familiar concepts with high-tension nautical battles and skillful descriptions of period attitudes and dialogue." Roland Green wrote in *Booklist,* "That action works out in the context of extremely high-level achievement at both world building and characterization."

The same year, Anderson published the next book in the "Destroyermen" series, *Crusade: Destroyermen, Book 2,* which involves another U.S. destroyer, the *Mahan,* that also enters the parallel world. The *Mahan* and USS *Walker* side with a Lemurian queen in a battle with the Griks, who just acquired the Japanese battle cruiser *Amagi,* which also crossed over into this world. Reviewers praised the book's action sequences. A writer in *Publishers Weekly* said that Anderson's sequel includes, "land battles against overwhelming odds, a massive typhoon and a phenomenal aerial duel." Jackie Cassada noted in *Library Journal,* "[Commander] Reddy is a likable protagonist, epitomizing the best of the wartime American military."

Writing in *Booklist,* Roland Green expected that Anderson's next book will have more of what *Crusade* had, "more intelligent action, more skillful handling of a very large cast, and an obstinately maintained refusal to slow the pace." *Maelstrom: Destroyermen, Book 3,* published in 2009, features a lengthy climactic battle between the Lemurians with the USS *Walker* and the Griks with the *Amagi. Maelstrom* pleased many reviewers. Roland Green said in *Booklist,* "Fans of action—alt-historical, naval, or just plain nonstop—take heart." "Experienced military SF readers will enjoy the attention to technical and historical detail," commented a writer in *Publishers Weekly.*

BIOGRAPHICAL AND CRITICAL SOURCES:

PERIODICALS

Booklist, May 15, 2008, Roland Green, review of *Into the Storm: Destroyermen, Book 1,* p. 30; September 1, 2008, Roland Green, review of *Crusade: Destroyermen, Book 2,* p. 59; February 15, 2009, Roland Green, review of *Maelstrom: Destroyermen, Book 3,* p. 44.

Library Journal, May 15, 2008, Jackie Cassada, review of *Into the Storm,* p. 94.

Publishers Weekly, April 28, 2008, review of *Into the Storm,* p. 116; August 11, 2008, review of *Crusade,* p. 33; December 15, 2008, review of *Maelstrom,* p. 38.

ONLINE

Shrapnel Games.com, http://forum.shrapnelgames.com/ (June 29, 2009), S.R. Krol, review of *Into the Storm.*

Taylor Anderson Home Page, http://www.taylorandersonauthor.com (August 1, 2009).*

* * *

ARMBRECHT, Ann 1962-
(Ann Armbrecht Forbes)

PERSONAL: Born 1962; married; children: two. *Education:* Dartmouth College, B.A., 1984; Columbia University, M.A., 1987; Harvard University, Ph.D., 1995.

ADDRESSES: Home—Montpelier, VT.

CAREER: Anthropologist and writer. University of Vermont, Montpelier, lecturer, 2004; Goddard College, Plainfield, VT, instructor.

WRITINGS:

Settlements of Hope: An Account of Tibetan Refugees in Nepal, Cultural Survival (Cambridge, MA), 1989.

Developing Tibet? A Survey of International Development Projects, Cultural Survival (Cambridge, MA), 1992.

Thin Places: A Pilgrimage Home, Columbia University Press (New York, NY), 2009.

SIDELIGHTS: Ann Armbrecht is an anthropologist who has lived in Nepal to study the Yamphu Rai people. She was born in 1962 and raised in West Virginia. After earning a bachelor's degree from Dartmouth College in Hanover, New Hampshire, in 1984 she applied to the Peace Corps and in 1985 was sent to a remote village in Nepal to teach Tibetan refugees. In 1987 she earned a master's degree from Columbia University but continued to visit Nepal. Her 1989 book *Settlements of Hope: An Account of Tibetan Refugees in Nepal* chronicles her experiences in the region.

Throughout the 1990s, Armbrecht returned to Nepal and Tibet several times to focus on the Yamphu Rai people in northeastern Nepal. She learned how they farmed and related to the land at a time when their land had been designated a national park and conservation area. Her second book, *Developing Tibet? A Survey of International Development Projects,* was published in 1992.

Armbrecht's anthropological studies in both Nepal and Tibet and her research for her two books helped her complete her Ph.D. dissertation at Harvard University in 1995. Armbrecht now lectures in the anthropology department of the University of Vermont in Montpelier and teaches at Goddard College, Plainfield, Vermont.

In 2009 she published *Thin Places: A Pilgrimage Home,* which chronicles her years in Nepal with the Yamphu Rai and their cultural and economic transformation. It is also a memoir that explores her spiritual and intellectual journey in places considered fragile and sacred. Armbrecht wrote, "I was also there because I wanted to discover how to live more simply and more lightly on the earth."

Besides charting her travels in Nepal, the book also reveals her own cultural struggles as a scholar, a Westerner, and a wife in an unhappy marriage. By weaving together stories of the Nepalese and her own life, she describes how one can move between cultures and make a spiritual pilgrimage that ultimately brings you back home.

"This book is stirring on many levels . . . presenting lyrical descriptions of seasons, the enervating weather, the fog-bound and light-scattered terrain," said David

G. Campbell in *Orion* magazine. "There is sanctity in these pages, too. Armbrecht's is a lovely and humble journey: into the Himalayas, into her homeland, and into her heart."

A writer in *Kirkus Reviews* noted, "A difficult, intensely interior journey, both anthropological and emotional," while Rob Williams commented in *Vermont Commons,* "Armbrecht's vulnerability, wisdom and unflinching honesty at a time of great crisis for the West make this story one of the most important books of the last year."

BIOGRAPHICAL AND CRITICAL SOURCES:

PERIODICALS

American Anthropologist, June 1, 1993, James F. Fisher, review of *Developing Tibet? A Survey of International Development Projects,* p. 449.

American Ethnologist, May 1, 1993, Margaret Nowak, review of *Settlements of Hope: An Account of Tibetan Refugees in Nepal,* p. 419.

International Migration Review, March 22, 1992, Gary Fuller, review of *Settlements of Hope,* p. 184.

Kirkus Reviews, October 1, 2008, review of *Thin Places: A Pilgrimage Home.*

Man, September 1, 1991, Cathy Cantwell, review of *Settlements of Hope,* p. 566.

Orion, May 1, 2009, David G. Campbell, review of *Thin Places.*

ONLINE

Arcadia Cafe, http://arcadiacoffee.com/ (December 1, 2008), author profile.

Bearpond Books, http://www.bearpondbooks.com/ (June 1, 2009), short author profile.

University of Vermont Web site, http://www.uvm.edu/ (July 1, 2009), short author profile.

Vermont Commons, http://www.vtcommons.org/ (February 24, 2009), Rob Williams, "Thin Places—Finding the Sacred in the In-Between," review of *Thin Places.**

* * *

ARNOLD, Craig 1967-2009

PERSONAL: Born November 16, 1967; married; presumed dead after a fall off a cliff while hiking, April 27, 2009, in Kuchinoerabu Island, Kagoshima, Japan. *Education:* Yale University, B.A., 1990; University of Utah, Ph.D., 2001.

CAREER: Poet and educator. University of Wyoming, Laramie, assistant professor, 2004-09.

AWARDS, HONORS: Original Writing Award, Utah Arts Council, 1998; New Writers Award, Great Lakes Colleges Association, 1999; Yale Younger Poets Prize, 1999, for *Shells;* Bess Hokin Prize, 2005, for poem "Incubus"; Anthony Hecht Poetry Prize, Waywiser Press, 2006. Recipient of fellowships, including Amy Lowell Poetry Traveling Scholarship, 1996; Creative Writing Fellowship, National Endowment for the Arts, 1998; John Atherton Fellowship in Poetry, Bread Loaf Writers Conference, 1999; Dobie Paisano Fellow, University of Texas, Austin, 2001; Alfred Hodder Fellowship in the Humanities, Princeton University, 2001; Rome Prize in Literature, American Academy of Arts and Letters, 2005; Fulbright Fellowship, 2008; U.S.-Japan Creative Artists Exchange Fellowship, 2009.

WRITINGS:

Shells, Yale University Press (New Haven, CT), 1999.

Made Flesh, Ausable Press (Keene, NY), 2008.

Contributor of poems to literary journals including *Poetry, Paris Review, Denver Quarterly, Barrow Street, New Republic,* and *Yale Review.*

Contributor of poems to anthologies including *Best American Poetry,* 1998, and *Bread Loaf Anthology of New American Poets.*

SIDELIGHTS: Craig Arnold was an American poet and professor who vanished while hiking on a volcanic island in Japan. Born into a U.S. Air Force family on November 16, 1967, Arnold lived in the United States and Europe, and spent four years on the Japanese island of Okinawa as a youngster. As an adult, he lived in Salt Lake City, Utah, intermittently for ten years in the 1990s and early 2000s. Arnold received a bachelor of arts degree in English from Yale University in 1990 and earned his Ph.D. in creative writing from the University of Utah in 2001. He became an assistant professor of poetry in the University of Wyoming in Laramie's MFA program in 2004. In addition to his poetry and teaching, he loved to cook, which is apparent in some of his poems, and he was a musician with the alternative rock band, Iris.

In 1999 Arnold published his first book of poems, *Shells.* Its poems, with such titles as "Hermit Crab," "Oysters," "The Power Grip," "For a Cook," "Artichoke," "Hot," and "Shore," evoke the protective shells, or emotional armor, people express themselves with when experiencing appetites, loss, and secrets. The structure of the poems is long and rambling, some written in two- or three-line stanzas. The themes run from flirtatious and obsessive to erotic and sexually explicit. There is the woman secretly attracted to her roommate, a trip to the aquarium with children, and friends spending time with each other. The poems cause the reader to reflect on personal friendships and longings.

Rachel Barenblat wrote in *PIF Magazine* that "the book plays with the idea of shell as house, shell as casing, shell as self, shell as form. The book's strength is the way its subjects become metonymy [when one word is substituted for another] for each other: sex, food, humanity, the creatures of the sea." Rochelle Ratner said in *Library Journal,* "This extremely accomplished first volume presents difficult poems, both in form and subject matter." *Shells* received the Yale Younger Poets Prize bestowed by renowned poet and literary judge W.S. Merwin.

In 2008 Arnold published his second collection of poetry, *Made Flesh,* which offers poems exploring love, failed romance in Spain, and erotic devotion. He achieves these punches of emotional power through some over-the-top scenes, metaphors of bodily harm, and imagery from nature. His poem "Couple from Hell" uses the example of Persephone and Hades in the underworld to explore images of childhood and the disintegration of a relationship. In the gothic "Incubus," a woman experiences sensation desired by a demon within her body. A contributor to *Publishers Weekly* wrote that Arnold "construct[ed] what might be the strangest and most instinctively powerful poetry book of the season" and that he presented vividly earthy language with disguised philosophical sophistication. Commenting on why Arnold would write so many poems about why things go wrong when his own life was seemingly going along so well, Ben Fulton wrote in the July 1, 2009, edition of *America's Intelligence Wire,* "Call it a deep-seated need to coin a poetic idiom where life's hard truths are mourned and celebrated—perhaps even liberated in language hung on a sound philosophical spine yet, as Arnold described it, not so stiff that the words aren't free to dance."

Arnold's poems have appeared in anthologies and in literary journals, and he became a world traveler due to numerous awards and fellowships. He received the Amy Lowell Poetry Traveling Scholarship, which brought him to Spain and other European countries in 1996. He went to Rome when he received the Rome Prize in Literature in 2005, and attended the Hay Festival of Literature and Arts in Cartagena, Colombia. During 2009 he flew back and forth between the United States and Japan for the Creative Artists Exchange Fellowship.

On April 27, 2009, Arnold failed to return to the inn he was staying in after hiking alone on the small volcanic island of Kuchinoerabu in southern Japan. He was declared missing, and the Japanese government searched for him and even extended their search after the maximum three days. His brother, Chris Arnold, flew to Japan to join the search. His hiking trail was eventually discovered ascending a high cliff, but no trail was found descending. It was presumed that he suffered a fatal fall off the cliff. His family and the poetry community mourned his loss with tributes.

BIOGRAPHICAL AND CRITICAL SOURCES:

PERIODICALS

America's Intelligence Wire, May 2, 2009, Ben Fulton, "Writing It Like It Is: Poetry. U. Alum Craig Arnold Explores Failing Relationships—With an Ear to Their Disconsolate Splendor"; May 6, 2009, "Search for US Poet in Japan to Be Scaled Down"; May 6, 2009, Mari Yamaguchi, "Trackers Find Trail of Missing U.S. Poet in Japan"; May 7, 2009, Mead Gruver, "Team to Look 1 More Day for Missing Poet in Japan"; May 7, 2009, Ben Fulton, "New Search Team Finds Poet's Trail: Missing. Japanese End Search as New Team Finds Evidence"; May 8, 2009, Mead Gruver, "Search for Missing Poet in Japan Down to Final Day"; May 8, 2009, Mead Gruver, "US Team Concludes Island Search for Missing Poet"; May 8, 2009, Ben Neary, "School: Family of Missing Poet Believes He Died"; May 9, 2009, Ben Fulton, "Poet Fell to Death from Cliff: Lost Searchers Say Arnold Did Not Survive Fall from Cliff"; May 13, 2009, Mead Gruver, "Climbing Team to Search for Missing Wyoming Poet"; May 15, 2009, Mead

Gruver, "Climbers Search without Success for Missing Poet"; June 25, 2009, "Friends and Fellow Writers Salute Poet Who Vanished on Trek."

Booklist, March 15, 1999, Ray Olson, review of *Shells,* p. 1271.

Chicago Tribune, May 13, 2009, Mary Schmich, "Search for Poet Grips Like His Words"; May 13, 2009, Mary Schmich, "A Poet Vanishes, His Words Remain."

Japan Times, May 1, 2009, Alex Martin, "American Hiker Believed Missing on Volcanic Isle off Yakushima"; May 2, 2009, Alex Martin, "American Missing on Volcanic Island Is Award-Winning Poet, Assistant Professor."

Library Journal, May 1, 1999, Rochelle Ratner, review of *Shells,* p. 83.

Los Angeles Times, May 9, 2009, Carolyn Kellogg, "Missing Poet Craig Arnold Presumed Dead."

New York Times, May 6, 2009, "No Sign of Poet Lost in Japan," p. C3(L).

Poetry, April, 2000, David Yezzi, review of *Shells,* p. 48; November, 2005, "Announcement of Prizes," p. 165.

Publishers Weekly, March 29, 1999, review of *Shells,* p. 99; June 16, 2008, review of *Made Flesh,* p. 2.

St. Petersburg Times, May 9, 2009, "U.S. Poet Still Missing in Japan," p. 5A.

UPI NewsTrack, May 7, 2009, "Search Goes On for Poet Missing in Japan."

Virginia Quarterly Review, autumn, 1999, review of *Shells,* p. 136.

ONLINE

Digital Emunction, http://www.digitalemunction.com/ (May 8, 2009), Michael Hansen, "Craig Arnold, 1968-2009."

Examiner.com, http://www.examiner.com/ (May 12, 2009), Tad Richards, "Death of a Poet."

Los Angeles Times, http://latimesblogs.latimes.com/ (May 9, 2009), Carolyn Kellogg, "Missing Poet Craig Arnold Presumed Dead."

New York Times, Paper Cuts Blog, http://papercuts.blogs.nytimes.com/ (May 20, 2009), David Orr, "There Will Be No More Poems from Him."

PIF Magazine, http://www.pifmagazine.com/ (July 1, 2009), Rachel Barenblat, review of *Shells.*

Poetry Foundation, http://www.poetryfoundation.org/ (July 1, 2009), author profile.

OTHER

ABC News, http://abcnews.go.com/, (May 2, 2009), Susan Donaldson James, "Poet Craig Arnold Disappears at Volcano"; (May 8, 2009), Susan Donaldson James, "Japanese End Search for Craig Arnold."

All Things Considered (radio transcript), April 30, 2009, "University of Wyoming Professor Missing in Japan."*

* * *

ASHLAND, Monk 1972-
[A pseudonym]
(Chris Rettstatt)

PERSONAL: Born 1972, in AR; married; children: Zoe, Echo (twin daughters). *Education:* University of Illinois, Chicago, B.A. *Hobbies and other interests:* Travel, languages, playing with his daughters.

ADDRESSES: *Home*—Chicago, IL; and Chongquing, China. *E-mail*—rettstatt@gmail.com.

CAREER: Author, transmedia storyteller, and youth media consultant. Star Farm Productions (entertainment company), Chicago, IL, former director of story development; Story Monk Studios (IP development studio), Chongquing, China, director.

AWARDS, HONORS: CYBILS Award, nomination, 2008, for *The Sky Village.*

WRITINGS:

"KAIMIRA" FANTASY SERIES

(With brother, under pseudonym Nigel Ashland) *The Sky Village,* illustrated by Jeff Nentrup, Candlewick Press (Cambridge, MA), 2008.

The Terrible Everything, illustrated by Jeff Nentrup, Candlewick Press (Cambridge, MA), 2010.

Contributor to books, including *Settlers of the New Virtual Worlds.*

SIDELIGHTS: Monk Ashland is the pen name of Chris Rettstatt, the coauthor of the dystopian fantasy *The Sky Village.* The first in the proposed five-book

"Kaimira" series, *The Sky Village* takes place in the future, following the Trinary Wars and the devastation they wrought. Now men must battle wild creatures and intelligent robots called meks in order to survive. Twelve-year-old Mei Long has been sent from China to live in the floating network of hot-air balloons known as Sky Village since her mother was captured by meks. Through the pages of the Tree Book, Mei is able to communicate with a slightly older boy named Rom. Rom lives in the wilds of Las Vegas, and his younger sister is in the clutches of mek-beast hybrid creatures. As Mei and Rom both learn, they each have the Kaimira gene, which endows them with powers they hope to use to rescue their family members.

The Sky Village combines the text of the pseudonymous Ashland brothers ("Nigel Ashland" is also a pen name) with links to online activities referencing the "Kaimira" world. Although Michael Cart wrote in *Booklist* that *The Sky Village* is "short on characterization," young readers will nonetheless "be tantalized." In *Voice of Youth Advocates,* Lynne Farrell Stover found more to like in the novel, cited the story's "strong characters . . . , terrifyingly unpredictable villains, frightening futuristic settings, and wonderfully written action sequences." Stover predicted that the "Kaimira" books will find ready fans among readers who enjoy "adventure, science fiction, and fantasy."

Discussing the growing interest in postapocalyptic fiction with a *YPulse.com* interviewer, Rettstatt noted: "Post-apocalyptic fiction has been going strong for as long as I can remember. Just look at how many times Tokyo has been obliterated on TV and film. And in this Golden Age of YA literature, it makes sense that a few of us are going to . . . create a fresh start and a new sandbox for our imaginary characters.

"That said, when a community experiences a traumatic reminder of its mortality and its vulnerability to destruction, I do think the resulting surge of anxiety tends to erupt in a renewed interest in post-apocalyptic stories. And if there is something in the YA lit Zeitgeist giving a leg up to that sort of fiction, it would be convenient to connect it to modern fears of terrorist attack.

"But my gut feeling is that many of today's post-apocalyptic stories have roots that are older than that. I think these more modern fears will be played out in the stories our children write. It scares me to imagine what forms their fictional disasters will take, oozing from primal fears caused by our generation's mistakes."

BIOGRAPHICAL AND CRITICAL SOURCES:

PERIODICALS

Booklist, July 1, 2008, Michael Cart, review of *The Sky Village,* p. 68.

Kirkus Reviews, June 15, 2008, review of *The Sky Village.*

Tribune Books (Chicago, IL), July 5, 2008, Mary Harris Russell, review of *The Sky Village,* p. 7.

Voice of Youth Advocates, October 14, 2008, Lynne Farrell Stover, review of *The Sky Village.*

ONLINE

Chris Rettstatt Home Page, http://rettstatt.com (November 3, 2009).

Chris Rettstatt Professional Page, http://storymonk.com (December 1, 2009).

Kaimira Web site, http://www.kaimiracode.com (November 3, 2009).

YPulse.com, http://www.ypulse.com/ (August 27, 2008), interview with Rettstatt.

B

BAKER, Tiffany

PERSONAL: Married Edward Baker; children: three. *Education:* Denison University, Granville, OH, bachelor's degree; University of California, Irvine, M.A., Ph.D.

ADDRESSES: *Agent*—Dan Lazar, Writer's House, 21 W. 26th St., New York, NY 10010.

CAREER: University of California, Irvine, CA, instructor; Cooper Union College, New York, NY, instructor.

WRITINGS:

The Little Giant of Aberdeen County: A Novel, Grand Central Publishing (New York, NY), 2009.

Also author of essay, "When Size Is in Your Imagination."

SIDELIGHTS: Tiffany Baker is an instructor and writer living in California. She earned an English degree from Denison University in Ohio, and a graduate degree in creative writing and a Ph.D. in Victorian literature from the University of California at Irvine.

On a hiking trip with her mother in Corsica she met Edward Baker whom she married and moved with to England. A few years later, they moved to New York where she taught humanities at Cooper Union College. She also taught at the University of California, Irvine and lives in Tiburon, California. Wanting to be a writer, Baker wrote on and off over the years while having three children in between.

In 2009 Baker published *The Little Giant of Aberdeen County: A Novel,* about a woman named Truly born with gigantism in a small town in upstate New York. After her mother dies in childbirth because of Truly's size, she lives at first with a sister and drunken father. After her father dies, she lives with caregivers on a horse farm.

With the book, Baker wanted to explore prejudice and society's preoccupation with physicality. She said in an interview for the *Marin Independent Journal,* "I was interested in the habits of little towns—who plays what role and why, what makes the people good or bad or heroes." She added, "I like to think [the book] will give them a chance to connect with people who are not like them, to get a sense of compassion, a celebration of differences."

In addition to Truly, the book is populated by other misfits, such as a wizardly gardener, a beautiful sister, a silent girl, a heartless doctor, and a cruel schoolmistress. Commenting that the colorful people resemble fairy tale characters, Carole Goldberg said in the *Sun Sentinel,* "Baker enters Alice Hoffman territory in this parable about beauty and ugliness, meanness and mercy and magic, and does it with dark humor."

Baker exposes the irony that Truly is so big that she is invisible. The townspeople cannot possibly miss her walking down the street yet they refuse to see her.

Literally no one can embrace her, so figuratively they ignore her presence, her voice, and her contributions to the town. The book is an allegory about the prejudice people have concerning physical appearance. Baker said in an interview in *Publishers Weekly,* "I want people to realize that the world is a strange and wonderful place, and that when you look at another human being, what you see on the outside isn't what might be inside the person."

Reviewers praised *The Little Giant of Aberdeen County* for its quirky characters, warmth, commentary on today's preoccupation with size and looks, and fast-paced story filled with tragedy and joy. "Debut author Tiffany Baker crafts a love letter to the world's outcasts with *The Little Giant of Aberdeen County,* a subtle little pearl of a book that's all the more remarkable for its utter lack of flash," said Joy Tipping in the *Dallas Morning News.*

Although "readers with a soft spot for lovable, saintly freaks may overlook the simplistic characterizations and manufactured plot," according to a writer in *Kirkus Reviews,* Nancy H. Fontaine noted in *Library Journal,* "Baker's brilliant debut is infused with vibrant language and quirky, original characters."

Patty Rhule said in *USA Today,* "[Baker] writes the kind of book you find yourself stealing time from workday chores to read."

BIOGRAPHICAL AND CRITICAL SOURCES:

PERIODICALS

Booklist, December 1, 2008, Marta Segal Block, review of *The Little Giant of Aberdeen County: A Novel,* p. 24.

Book World, January 4, 2009, Ron Charles, "A Small-Town Figure," p. 7.

Dallas Morning News, January 11, 2009, Joy Tipping, "'The Little Giant of Aberdeen County' by Tiffany Baker: Outcast's Story Touches on Universal Themes."

Kirkus Reviews, October 15, 2008, review of *The Little Giant of Aberdeen County.*

Library Journal, October 15, 2008, Nancy H. Fontaine, review of *The Little Giant of Aberdeen County,* p. 52; May 1, 2009, Carol Stern, review of *The Little Giant of Aberdeen County,* p. 48.

Marie Claire, January 1, 2009, Eileen Conlan, review of *The Little Giant of Aberdeen County,* p. 43.

Marin Independent Journal, February 16, 2009, Beth Ashley, "Tiburon Author's First Novel Hits a Nerve," review of *The Little Giant of Aberdeen County.*

Publishers Weekly, September 8, 2008, review of *The Little Giant of Aberdeen County,* p. 33; November 3, 2008, Hilary S. Kayle, "PW Talks with Tiffany Baker: A Behemoth at Center Stage," p. 38; March 30, 2009, review of *The Little Giant of Aberdeen County,* p. 46.

Sun Sentinel, January 25, 2009, Carole Goldberg, review of *The Little Giant of Aberdeen County.*

USA Today, February 12, 2009, Patty Rhule, "A Giant Spirit Rises above a Harsh Life," review of *The Little Giant of Aberdeen County,* p. 05.

ONLINE

Book Lady's Blog, http://thebookladysblog.com/ (January 5, 2009), review of *The Little Giant of Aberdeen County.*

BookPage, http://bookpage.com/ (July 1, 2009), Katherine Wyrick, "A Big-Hearted Heroine," review of *The Little Giant of Aberdeen County.*

Bookworm's World, http://luanne-abookwormsworld.blogspot.com/ (January 1, 2009), review of *The Little Giant of Aberdeen County.*

Curled Up with a Good Book, http://www.curledup.com/ (July 1, 2009), Steven Rosen, author interview.

Divine Caroline, http://www.divinecaroline.com/ (February 1, 2009), author interview.

Everyday Goddess, http://everydaygoddess.typepad.com/ (March 31, 2009), review of *The Little Giant of Aberdeen County.*

MostlyFiction, http://www.mostlyfiction.com/ (March 8, 2009), Jana Perskie, review of *The Little Giant of Aberdeen County.*

Speaking Volumes, http://chplnjbooks.wordpress.com/ (June 17, 2009), review of *The Little Giant of Aberdeen County.*

Tiffany Baker Home Page, http://www.tiffanybaker.com (July 1, 2009), author profile.*

* * *

BARKAN, Josh 1969-
(Joshua Barkan)

PERSONAL: Born 1969, in CA; married. *Education:* Attended Yale University; University of Iowa, M.F.A.

ADDRESSES: Home—New York, NY. *E-mail*—josh@joshbarkan.com.

CAREER: Writer and educator. Harvard University, Cambridge, MA, writing instructor; New York University, New York, NY, writing instructor; Boston University, Boston, MA, writing instructor.

AWARDS, HONORS: Literature fellowship, National Endowment for the Arts, 2006.

WRITINGS:

Before Hiroshima: The Confession of Murayama Kazuo, and Other Stories, Toby Press (London, England), 2000.
Blind Speed: A Novel, Triquarterly Books (Evanston, IL), 2008.

SIDELIGHTS: Josh Barkan is a fiction writer and teacher. He was born in 1969, in California, and spent his childhood in a number of locations, including Kenya, Tanzania, France, and India. He attended Yale University, where he received writing fellowships, and then obtained his M.F.A. from the Iowa Writer's Workshop at the University of Iowa. He has taught writing at Harvard University in Cambridge, Massachusetts; Boston University in Boston, Massachusetts; and New York University in New York, New York. In 2006 he was awarded a literature fellowship by the National Endowment for the Arts.

Barkan's first book is a collection of short stories published in 2000 and titled *Before Hiroshima: The Confession of Murayama Kazuo, and Other Stories.* The title novella is told from the point of view of an elderly Japanese man who confesses that he may have had a chance to prevent the deaths of those killed when bombs were dropped on Hiroshima and Nagasaki.

Barkan's next book, *Blind Speed: A Novel,* was published in 2008. The narrative focuses on Paul Berger a perpetual failure who may lose his job teaching at a community college because he cannot finish his book. Paul's inadequacies are accentuated by the fact that his successful lawyer brother is currently running for Congress, and by an ominous palm-reading session. Over the course of the novel, most of Paul's worst fears come true, as his wedding turns into an unhinged disaster and he becomes embroiled in a series of farcical adventures involving, among other things, eco-terrorists.

A reviewer for the *Porter Square Books* Web log praised the book as being one of the few novels willing to explore failure, explaining, "For some reason, some people don't have what it takes to succeed and exploring this idea makes *Blind Speed* a challenging, often uncomfortable read. Barkan mitigates this challenge by making the book very funny, by making Paul charming (if a little pathetic), and by engaging intelligently with contemporary politics. However, he doesn't let readers get away from the fact that one can do everything right and still end up baffled by life and its consequences." Jonathan Messinger, in a review for *Time Out Chicago,* quoted Barkan, stating, "I wanted to write about failure, . . . actual failure. A lot of stories focus on success, but that's not what a lot of us experience in this country; there's a lot of us still trying to make it somehow."

Luan Gaines, writing for *Curled Up with a Good Book,* also enjoyed *Blind Speed,* noting, "Somehow Barkan fashions a fascinating if fractious novel out of Paul's attempt to make sense of a life in thrall to the interference of fate." Gaines added, "Following the logic of Paul's erratic thoughts is . . . an esoteric Disney ride without a seatbelt." Donna Seaman, writing in *Booklist,* had some reservations, noting that the novel's plot is "raggedy" and that the environmental issues are "muddled." However, Seaman concluded by calling the book "a smart, comedic, and heartfelt attack on hypocrisy and greed."

BIOGRAPHICAL AND CRITICAL SOURCES:

PERIODICALS

Booklist, May 15, 2008, Donna Seaman, review of *Blind Speed: A Novel,* p. 20.
Library Journal, July 1, 2003, review of *Before Hiroshima: The Confession of Murayama Kazuo, and Other Stories,* p. 30.

ONLINE

Curled Up with a Good Book, http://www.curledup.com/ (August 4, 2009), Luan Gaines, review of *Blind Speed.*

Josh Barkan Home Page, http://www.joshbarkan.blogspot.com (August 4, 2009), author profile.

Porter Square Books Blog, http://www.portersquarebooksblog.blogspot.com/ (July 9, 2008), "Joe Barkan and the Literature of Failure," review of *Blind Speed.*

Time Out Chicago, http://www.chicago.timeout.com/ (August 4, 2009), Jonathan Messinger, "Fail Better," review of *Blind Speed.*

Toby Press Web site, http://www.tobypress.com/ (August 4, 2009), author profile.*

* * *

BARKAN, Joshua
See BARKAN, Josh

* * *

BARKER, Stuart 1970-

PERSONAL: Born February 18, 1970, in Galloway, Scotland. *Education:* Received degree from University of Strathclyde, Glasgow, Scotland, 1996.

ADDRESSES: Home—Scotland.

CAREER: Biographer and writer. *Motor Cycle News,* reporter, feature writer.

WRITINGS:

(With Niall Mackenzie) *Niall Mackenzie: The Autobiography,* CollinsWillow (London, England), 2003.

Barry Sheene, 1950-2003: The Biography, HarperCollins (London, England), 2003.

(With Steve Hislop) *Hizzy: The Autobiography of Steve Hislop, 1962-2003,* CollinsWillow (London, England), 2004.

Life of Evel: Evel Knievel, CollinsWillow (London, England), 2004, St. Martin's Press (New York, NY), 2008.

TT Century: One Hundred Years of the Tourist Trophy, Century (London, England), 2007.

David Jefferies: The Official Biography, J.H. Haynes (Somerset, England), 2009.

Contributor of articles to magazines, including *FHM, Superbike, Two Wheels Only,* and *Biker.*

SIDELIGHTS: Stuart Barker writes biographies of motorcycle racers and about motorcycle-related subjects. He was born February 18, 1970, in Galloway, Scotland; he still lives in Scotland. He earned a degree from the University of Strathclyde in 1996. A fan of motorcycle racing, Barker became a news reporter for *Motor Cycle News,* later working for the publication as a feature writer and road tester. As a freelance writer, he has written articles for numerous motorcycle magazines, such as *FHM, Superbike, Two Wheels Only,* and *Biker.*

Barker applied his journalism skills to write a series of biographies of motorcycle racing legends and stuntmen, including Barry Sheene, Evel Knievel, and David Jefferies. He cowrote the autobiographies of Niall Mackenzie and Steve Hislop. Barker also wrote *TT Century: One Hundred Years of the Tourist Trophy* in 2007 about the prestigious series of motorcycle races on the Isle of Man. In 2003 Barker published *Barry Sheene, 1950-2003: The Biography* about the world 500cc Grand Prix motorcycle racing champion who garnered international fame between 1975 and 1982. Sheene won more international 500cc and 750cc Grand Prix titles than any other racer, and won two consecutive world 500cc titles in 1976 and 1977. He was also famous for his near-fatal crashes and his playboy lifestyle. After retiring from racing, he turned motor sport commentator and businessman. He died in 2003 after a battle with cancer. As the only journalist to ride with Sheene as he toured, Barker got a firsthand look at the man some called the most famous bike racer in the world. Barker offers a complete look at the racer by including interviews with friends, teammates, and former rivals.

Barker's *Life of Evel: Evel Knievel* was published in 2004. The author provides an unflinching account of motorcycle daredevil Robert "Evel" Knievel, known for his never-quit attitude, his crashes that left him broken, as well as his successes. His famous stunts included his jump over the fountains at Caesars Palace in Las Vegas in 1967 and his failed attempt to jump Idaho's Snake River Canyon in 1974. Knievel's life was not all glamour and adventure; he admitted to being a womanizer, petty thief, alcoholic, and gambler. In the lively biography, Barker recounts how Knievel was imprisoned for assault, pursued by the IRS for tax evasion, cheated on his wife of thirty-eight years with hundreds (or perhaps thousands) of women, needed a hip replacement and liver transplant, and spent a month in a coma.

Referring to *Life of Evel* as keen and compassionate, a writer in *Kirkus Reviews* commented that "Barker earnestly provides a sympathetic spin by noting that Knievel's greatest stunts occurred during a time in American history when people 'badly needed a hero and an escape from the depressing events.'"

BIOGRAPHICAL AND CRITICAL SOURCES:

PERIODICALS

Kirkus Reviews, October 1, 2008, review of *Life of Evel: Evel Knievel.*

ONLINE

HarperCollins Canada Web site, http://www.harpercollins.ca/ (July 1, 2009), brief author profile and review of *Barry Sheene, 1950-2003: The Biography.*

Independent, http://www.independent.co.uk/ (February 24, 2008), Simon Redfern, review of *Life of Evel.*

Macmillan Web site, http://us.macmillan.com/ (July 1, 2009), brief author profile.

Speed TV Books, http://speedtvbooks.com/ (July 1, 2009), overview of *David Jefferies: The Official Biography.**

*   *   *

BARNES, Peter 1942-

PERSONAL: Born April 16, 1942; partner of Cornelia Durrant; children: Zachary, Eli. *Education:* Harvard University, B.A., 1962; Georgetown University, M.A., 1966.

ADDRESSES: Home—Point Reyes Station, CA. *E-mail*—PeterBarn@aol.com; peter@capanddividend.org; Peter@tomales.org.

CAREER: Entrepreneur, journalist, and writer. *Lowell Sun,* Lowell, MA, reporter; *Newsweek,* New York, NY, Washington correspondent; *New Republic,* Washington, DC, West Coast correspondent; The Solar Center, San Francisco, CA, cofounder and president, 1976—; Working Assets Money Fund, cofounder and vice president, 1983—; Working Assets Long Distance, San Francisco, CA, cofounder and president, 1985—; National Cooperative Bank (now NCB), Washington, DC, director; California State Assistance Fund for Energy, Santa Rosa, director; California Solar Energy Industry Association, Rio Vista, director; TechMar, Inc., Long Beach, CA, director; Tomales Bay Institute, Point Reyes Station, CA, senior fellow.

Member of nonprofit boards including Greenpeace International, Redefining Progress, TV Turnoff Network, Noise Pollution Clearinghouse, Tomales Bay Institute, Family Violence Prevention Fund, and California Tax Reform Association.

AWARDS, HONORS: Socially Responsible Entrepreneur of the Year for Northern California, 1995.

WRITINGS:

Pawns: The Plight of the Citizen-Soldier, Knopf (New York, NY), 1972.

(Editor) *The People's Land: A Reader on Land Reform in the United States,* Rodale (Chicago, IL), 1975.

Who Owns the Sky? Our Common Assets and the Future of Capitalism, Island Press (Washington, DC), 2001.

Capitalism 3.0: A Guide to Reclaiming the Commons, Berrett-Koehler (San Francisco, CA), 2006.

Climate Solutions: A Citizen's Guide, foreword by Bill McKibben, Chelsea Green Publishing (White River Junction, VT), 2008.

Contributor of articles to publications, including the *Economist, New York Times, Newsweek, New Republic, Washington Post, San Francisco Chronicle, Christian Science Monitor, American Prospect, Utne Reader, Yes!, Lowell Sun,* and *Resurgence.*

SIDELIGHTS: Paul Barnes is an entrepreneur and writer who has founded and led several companies. Born April 16, 1942, and raised in New York City, he received a B.A. in history from Harvard University in 1962 and an M.A. in government from Georgetown University in 1966. He started his career as a journalist, working as a reporter at the *Lowell Sun* in Massachusetts. He went on to serve as Washington correspondent for *Newsweek* and as West Coast correspondent for the *New Republic.* In 1976 he cofounded and became president of The Solar Center, a worker-owned solar energy company in San Francisco. In 1983 he was one of the founders of the Working Assets Money Fund, a socially conscious investment fund, and later became president of Working Assets Long Distance, a socially conscious telephone company that contributes a portion of each customer's bill to environmental and social causes. Barnes has also worked as a director in numerous companies, including National Cooperative Bank (now NCB), the California State Assistance Fund for Energy, California Energy Industry Association, and TechMar. He is a senior fellow at the Tomales Bay Institute.

Barnes's first book, published in 1972, was *Pawns: The Plight of the Citizen-Soldier.* Commissioned but ultimately scrapped by the Nixon administration, *Pawns* recommends overhauling the military by moving towards a citizen-soldier militia closer to the original concept of the Founding Fathers. This monograph was followed by *The People's Land: A Reader on Land Reform in the United States,* a collection of writings edited by Barnes and published in 1975.

In 2001 Barnes published *Who Owns the Sky? Our Common Assets and the Future of Capitalism.* The book argues that pollution is hard to regulate because natural resources are not owned by any individual, and therefore their degradation is not valued properly. Barnes argues that this problem can be addressed if natural resources such as the sky are treated as commons, in the way woods or pastures were historically treated as common property. Barnes further suggests that air pollution should be regulated through a market-based, cap-and-trade system. He proposes setting up a "Sky Trust," a nongovernmental organization that would charge companies based on how much they polluted. The money from these companies would then be paid to citizens, used in part to offset the higher fuel prices that are expected to result from more closely regulating pollution.

In 2006 Barnes published *Capitalism 3.0: A Guide to Reclaiming the Commons.* The book argues that capitalism is a positive force, and that it has been instrumental in moving the world from an economy of scarcity to one of surplus. However, Barnes argues that certain aspects of capitalism need to be rethought or upgraded to address several major problems. These challenges include the following: the destruction of the environment, the growing gap between rich and poor, and the fact that despite increases in gross domestic product (GDP), many people report they are not experiencing any increase in happiness. As in *Who Owns the Sky?* Barnes argues that these problems can be addressed by changing the way capitalism deals with the commons—that is, with assets that are held by everyone. Among these commons, Barnes includes natural resources such as the sky, the land, and water, as well as language, music, the Internet, libraries, and other cultural and social goods.

Barnes argues that the value of these commons is often ignored because no one person owns them. To rectify this problem, Barnes suggests establishing nongovernmental trusts that would be charged with safeguarding the commons for future generations. Thus, future generations, or all citizens, would be treated as the trusts' beneficiaries. Users of the commons would then have to pay a fee to the trust. Thus, polluters would have to pay to pollute, which would encourage them to pollute less. Trusts could also place limits on the amount of allowable pollution. The fees raised by the trust could be distributed to citizens or used to fund public good. By ensuring that all citizens were recompensed for their share in the commons, Barnes believes that the problems of income inequality and poor quality of life could be rectified.

Mark Braund, writing in the *Guardian* newspaper, said of *Capitalism 3.0,* "Current economic arrangements constantly encourage politicians into bed with big business. Persuading those with disproportionate economic power that new property rights should be established and placed in trust in perpetuity will not be easy. But by building democracy into the structures of the economy through the creation of publicly-owned trusts, we could start to address the widening wealth gap, preserve the life-sustaining capacity of the planet, and extend the benefits of a dynamic market-driven economy to everyone. We don't need to replace the current operating system, just apply an upgrade. In *Capitalism 3.0* Peter Barnes has provided the code." A reviewer in *California Bookwatch* agreed, noting that Barnes provides "a fine roadmap for preserving capitalism's best features."

In 2008 Barnes published *Climate Solutions: A Citizen's Guide.* The book focuses on the problem of climate change and distinguishes between helpful policy proposals and those that are unlikely to work. Written in a question-and-answer format, the book includes many illustrations, graphs, and maps. Colleen Mondor, writing in *Booklist,* called the work "concisely written" and noted that while it would not provide enough information for advanced investigators, it was "a no-brainer for any teen doing a report on national climate policy." A reviewer in *Internet Bookwatch* described the book as "highly recommended to general interest readers." *Bookwatch* described the book as "highly recommended to general interest readers."

BIOGRAPHICAL AND CRITICAL SOURCES:

PERIODICALS

Booklist, June 1, 2001, David Rouse, review of *Who Owns the Sky? Our Common Assets and the Future of Capitalism,* p. 1804; April 1, 2008, Colleen Mondor, review of *Climate Solutions: A Citizen's Guide,* p. 8.

California Bookwatch, December, 2006, review of *Capitalism 3.0: A Guide to Reclaiming the Commons.*

E, January, 2007, "Pay to Prey."

Ecologist, November, 2001, James Terrell, review of *Who Owns the Sky?,* p. 58.

Internet Bookwatch, June, 2008, review of *Climate Solutions.*

Multinational Monitor, November-December, 2006, Robert Weissman, review of *Capitalism 3.0,* p. 47.

New York Review of Books, April 26, 2001, review of *Who Owns the Sky?,* p. 36.

Personnel Psychology, winter, 2008, review of *Capitalism 3.0,* p. 946.

Publishers Weekly, June 11, 2001, review of *Who Owns the Sky?,* p. 74.

Reference & Research Book News, February, 2007, review of *Capitalism 3.0.*

ONLINE

Capitalism 3.0 Web site, http://capitalism3.com (July 26, 2009), author profile.

Encyclopedia of Earth, http://www.eoearth.org/ (July 26, 2009), author profile.

Field Guide to the U.S. Economy, http://www.fguide.org/ (June 20, 2007), Jonathan Teller-Elsberg, "Econ-Utopia: The Bloodless Revolution, part 1 of 2: A Review of Peter Barnes' Capitalism 3.0."

Guardian Online, http://www.guardian.co.uk/ (October 9, 2007), Mark Braund, "Common Wealth."

Sky Book Web site, http://www.skybook.org/ (July 26, 2009), author profile.

TreeHugger, http://www.treehugger.com/ (July 13, 2008), Jermy Elton Jacquot, "The TH Interview: Peter Barnes, Senior Fellow at the Tomales Bay Institute."

OTHER

Morning Edition, January 27, 1999, "Analysis: Author Peter Barnes with a Mouse-Eye View of the Goings On in Washington," broadcast transcript.

Weekend All Things Considered, September 9, 2001, "Interview: Peter Barnes Discusses His Idea for a Sky Trust as Described in His Book 'Who Owns the Sky?,'" broadcast transcript.

* * *

BAUERMEISTER, Erica 1959-

PERSONAL: Born 1959, in Pasadena, CA. *Education:* Occidental College, Los Angeles, CA, bachelor's degree; University of Washington, Seattle, Ph.D.

ADDRESSES: Home—Seattle, WA. *E-mail*—ericabauermeister@gmail.com.

CAREER: Writer and instructor. University of Washington, Seattle, instructor; Antioch University, Los Angeles, CA, instructor.

WRITINGS:

(With Jesse Larsen and Holly Smith) *500 Great Books by Women: A Reader's Guide,* Penguin Books (New York, NY), 1994.

(With Holly Smith) *Let's Hear It for the Girls: 375 Great Books for Readers 2-14,* Penguin Books (New York, NY), 1997.

The School of Essential Ingredients, Putnam (New York, NY), 2009.

SIDELIGHTS: Erica Bauermeister was born in 1959 in Pasadena, California. During her childhood she moved to the East Coast then again back to California to the northern part of the state. After Bauermeister graduated from Occidental College in Los Angeles, she moved to Seattle, got married, and earned her Ph.D. in literature from the University of Washington. She has taught creative writing and literature at University of Washington and Antioch University in Los Angeles.

When Bauermeister was getting her Ph.D. in literature, she was frustrated by the lack of women authors in the curriculum. This gave her the idea to compile a list of great literature by women. In 1994 she published *500 Great Books by Women: A Reader's Guide,* edited with Holly Smith and Jesse Larsen.

The book's criteria for listing works by women were that they had to be prose pieces, available in English, and still in print, and according to the editors, "found to be thought-provoking, beautiful and satisfying." The books chosen range from the thirteenth century to the present day, represent seventy countries, and include such writers as Jane Austen, Marguerite Duras, Gail Godwin, and Amy Tan. The book includes bibliographic information, annotations by the editors, and several indexes to find listings by author, title, genre, date, and geographic region.

A writer in *Booklist* commented that, "although this work is a welcome addition to the numerous bibliographies pertaining to women, it is not without flaws. First, the compilers' decision to include only in-print works results in a distorted picture of good books by women." Another fault, according to the reviewer, was that, in the nonfiction section, the editors chose to select primarily works about women or women's issues instead of a more general range of subject matter.

Bauermeister followed *500 Great Books by Women* with *Let's Hear It for the Girls: 375 Great Books for Readers 2-14* in 1997, edited with Holly Smith.

The book includes a bibliography of books that feature strong female protagonists who can raise girls' self-esteem. Books appropriate for four age ranges are listed in indexes that are arranged by title, author, time period of the book, subject, and country.

Bauermeister and her family lived in Italy for two years where she learned to like the slower pace of life and gain an appreciation of food. Upon her return to Seattle in 1999 she missed being part of a community of food lovers. To relieve this feeling, she took a cooking class and got the idea to write a novel about a group of people who meet in a cooking class and what the preparation of food meant to them.

In 2007 she published her first book of fiction, *The School of Essential Ingredients,* which follows eight cooking students and their teacher. A series of vignettes follows the characters as they work through their difficult choices and personal demons and build a comforting relationship with the food they cook. Lilian is their teacher who holds the classes in a restaurant's kitchen and watches over her students, sometimes playing matchmaker.

Response to *The School of Essential Ingredients* was mixed. A writer in *Kirkus Reviews* commented, "The book feels less empathetic and more hokey and melodramatic. The stifling humidity of the prose will push a lot of readers out of this kitchen." On the other hand, a writer in *Publishers Weekly* noted, "Bauermeister's tale of food and hope is certain to satisfy." Tom Valeo said in the *St. Petersburg Times,* "Bauermeister deftly combines romance, lyrical language and a dash of sentimentality with themes of love, hope and grief, producing a story that reveals the dark hungers her students harbor."

BIOGRAPHICAL AND CRITICAL SOURCES:

PERIODICALS

Booklist, April 15, 1995, review of *500 Great Books by Women: A Reader's Guide,* p. 1523; March 1, 1997, Ilene Cooper, review of *Let's Hear It for the Girls: 375 Great Books for Readers 2-14,* p. 1176; November 15, 2008, Mark Knoblauch, review of *The School of Essential Ingredients,* p. 27.

Kirkus Reviews, October 1, 2008, review of *The School of Essential Ingredients.*

Library Journal, January 1, 1995, Denise Johnson, review of *500 Great Books by Women,* p. 101; May 1, 2009, Donna Bachowski, review of *The School of Essential Ingredients,* p. 48.

Los Angeles Times, April 13, 1995, Brian Alcorn, "Female Writers Get Their Due: An Exhaustive Guide Lists 500 Titles, All by Women," p. 8.

Ms. Magazine, January 1, 1995, review of *500 Great Books by Women,* p. 71.

Publishers Weekly, November 14, 1994, review of *500 Great Books by Women,* p. 64; December 16, 1996, review of *Let's Hear It for the Girls,* p. 61; October 13, 2008, review of *The School of Essential Ingredients,* p. 36.

St. Petersburg Times, April 15, 2009, Tom Valeo, "Cooking Tips and Dark Secrets," review of *The School of Essential Ingredients,* p. 2.

School Library Journal, May 1, 1997, Kevin Wayne Booe, review of *Let's Hear It for the Girls,* p. 59.

Voice of Youth Advocates, June 1, 1999, review of *Let's Hear It for the Girls,* p. 96.

ONLINE

Australian Women Online, http://www.australianwomenonline.com/ (June 2, 2009), Tania McCartney, "Essentially Erica Bauermeister: Master of Edible Fiction," author interview.

Book Addiction, http://heatherlo.wordpress.com/ (June 14, 2009), Hildra Tague, review of *The School of Essential Ingredients.*

BookBrowse, http://www.bookbrowse.com/ (July 1, 2009), author interview.

Diary of an Eccentric, http://diaryofaneccentric.blogspot.com/ (February 12, 2009), author interview.

Erica Bauermeister Home Page, http://www.ericabauermeister.com (July 1, 2009), author profile.

HarperCollins Web site, http://www.harpercollins.com/ (July 1, 2009), author interview.

Raging Bibliomania, http://zibilee.figearo.net/ (March 4, 2009), review of *The School of Essential Ingredients.*

Setting the Bar, http://legalmama.today.com/ (April 1, 2009), review of *The School of Essential Ingredients.*

S. Krishna's Books, http://www.skrishnasbooks.com/ (February 1, 2009), Hildra Tague, review of *The School of Essential Ingredients.*

Suite101.com, http://self-awareness.suite101.com/ (March 17, 2009), Hildra Tague, review of *The School of Essential Ingredients.**

BEHAN, Eileen

PERSONAL: Education: Brigham and Women's Hospital, Boston, MA, trained for dietitian.

ADDRESSES: E-mail—info@eileenbehan.com.

CAREER: Dietitian and writer. Veteran's Administration Outpatient Clinic, Boston, MA, dietitian; Harvard School of Public Health, dietitian, Boston, MA; Core Physicians, Exeter, NH, dietitian. For the Love of Food Project, founder, 2007.

MEMBER: American Dietetic Association.

WRITINGS:

Microwave Cooking for Your Baby & Child: The ABCs of Creating Quick, Nutritious Meals for Your Little Ones, Villard Books (New York, NY), 1991.

Eat Well, Lose Weight While Breastfeeding: The Complete Nutrition Book for Nursing Mothers, including a Healthy Guide to the Weight Loss Your Doctor Promised, Villard Books (New York, NY), 1992, revised edition published as *Eat Well, Lose Weight, While Breastfeeding: The Complete Nutrition Book for Nursing Mothers,* Ballantine Books (New York, NY), 2006.

Cooking Well for the Unwell: More Than One Hundred Nutritious Recipes, Hearst Books (New York, NY), 1996.

Meals That Heal for Babies, Toddlers, and Children, Pocket Books (New York, NY), 1996.

The Pregnancy Diet: A Healthy Weight Control Program for Pregnant Women, Pocket Books (New York, NY), 1999.

Fit Kids: Raising Physically and Emotionally Strong Kids with Real Food, Pocket Books (New York, NY), 2001.

Therapeutic Nutrition: A Guide to Patient Education, Lippincott Williams & Wilkins (Philadelphia, PA), 2006.

The Baby Food Bible: A Complete Guide to Feeding Your Child, from Infancy On, Ballantine Books (New York, NY), 2008.

Contributor of articles to periodicals, including *Tufts University Diet and Nutrition Newsletter, Washington Post, Parents Magazine, Parenting,* and *Newsweek.*

Writer and producer of *Food for Talk* for Boston public radio.

SIDELIGHTS: Eileen Behan is a registered dietitian who has written numerous books on healthy eating for adults, pregnant women, and children. She trained as a dietitian at Brigham and Women's Hospital in Boston and worked for more than twenty-five years with individuals and families, counseling them on diet and nutrition. She works at Core Physicians in Exeter, New Hampshire.

Behan founded the nonprofit For the Love of Food Project, which informs people about healthy eating and meal plans, based in New Hampshire. She has written on nutrition for publications such as *Newsweek* and the *Tufts University Diet and Nutrition Newsletter,* and appeared on the *Today Show,* CNN, and New Hampshire Public Television.

In 1991 Behan published her first book, *Microwave Cooking for Your Baby & Child: The ABCs of Creating Quick, Nutritious Meals for Your Little Ones,* in which she offers convenient and nutritious meals for young children. She allays parents' fear of "nuking" their children's food and explains proper procedures for microwaving food. She also includes information on organic food; foods that can cause a choking hazard; child versions of adult dishes, such as paella; and tips on graduating baby to solid food. Molly McQuade wrote in *Publishers Weekly,* "In this comprehensive volume, nutritionist Behan simplifies the task of feeding babies and children quickly and healthfully."

Behan wrote *Cooking Well for the Unwell: More Than One Hundred Nutritious Recipes* in 1996. The book provides tips, nutritional information, calorie counts, and encouragement for people who prepare meals for those who are ill or convalescing. She explains the special dietary needs for people with AIDS, cancer, and those on restrictive diets. A writer in *Publishers Weekly* said, "Recipes are quite easy and all have nutritional analyses."

In 2006 Behan published *Therapeutic Nutrition: A Guide to Patient Education.* Written for health-care professionals without a background in nutrition, the book provides discussions on integrating nutrition into medical practice. She offers 135 patient handouts on diet and dietary supplements for children, teens, lactating women, vegetarians, and the obese.

In 2008, Behan wrote *The Baby Food Bible: A Complete Guide to Feeding Your Child, from Infancy On.* In the book she advocates introducing children to a variety of nutritious food early, turning off the television at mealtimes, and watering down sugary drinks. The book includes a chart on portion sizes, tips on healthy eating, and instructions on making homemade baby food. A writer in *Publishers Weekly* commented, "This is an excellent, comprehensive guide worthy of all parents' collections."

BIOGRAPHICAL AND CRITICAL SOURCES:

PERIODICALS

Library Journal, May 1, 1996, Janet M. Schneider, review of *Cooking Well for the Unwell: More Than One Hundred Nutritious Recipes,* p. 120; August 1, 1996, Loraine F. Sweetland, review of *Meals That Heal for Babies, Toddlers, and Children,* p. 100.

Publishers Weekly, December 21, 1990, Molly McQuade, review of *Microwave Cooking for Your Baby & Child: The ABCs of Creating Quick, Nutritious Meals for Your Little Ones,* p. 52; June 17, 1996, review of *Cooking Well for the Unwell,* p. 58; September 2, 1996, review of *Meals That Heal for Babies, Toddlers, and Children,* p. 125; May 19, 2008, review of *The Baby Food Bible: A Complete Guide to Feeding Your Child, from Infancy On,* p. 50.

SciTech Book News, December 1, 2006, review of *Therapeutic Nutrition: A Guide to Patient Education.*

ONLINE

Eileen Behan Home Page, http://www.eileenbehan.com (July 1, 2009), author profile.

Stonewall Kitchen Cooking School, http://www.stonewallkitchen.com/ (July 1, 2009), short author profile.

WebMD, http://www.webmd.com/ (July 1, 2009), author profile.*

* * *

BELBEN, Rosalind 1941-
(Rosalind Loveday Belben)

PERSONAL: Born February 1, 1941, in Dorset, England; daughter of G.D. and Joyce Belben.

ADDRESSES: *Home*—Dorset, England.

CAREER: Author.

AWARDS, HONORS: DAAD Berliner Künstlerprogramm Fellowship, 1987; Fellow of the Royal Society of Literature, 1999; James Tait Black Memorial Prize, 2007, for *Our Horses in Egypt.*

WRITINGS:

Bogies: Two Stories, New Authors (London, England), 1972.

Reuben, Little Hero, Hutchinson (London, England), 1973.

The Limit, Hutchinson (London, England), 1974.

Dreaming of Dead People, Harvester Press (Brighton, England), 1979, Serpent's Tail (London, England), 1991.

Is Beauty Good, Serpent's Tail (London, England), 1989.

Choosing Spectacles, Serpent's Tail (London, England), 1994.

Hound Music, Chatto & Windus (London, England), 2001.

Our Horses in Egypt, Chatto & Windus (London, England), 2007.

SIDELIGHTS: Rosalind Belben is a British novelist. She was born February 1, 1941, in Dorset, England. Her father was a naval officer who died during World War II.

Belben's first work of fiction was *Bogies: Two Stories,* published in 1972. Since then she has published numerous books, some centering on nature and animals, others focusing on history.

In 1989 she published *Is Beauty Good,* the first of her books published in the United States. For the book she took inspiration from her love of German literature and her Berlin Artists-in-Residence fellowship in West Berlin in 1987. Each chapter presents a variety of voices discussing aesthetics, nature, gardening, and animals.

In trying to capture the physical look of "conversation books," scribbled by Beethoven when he was deaf and Kafka when he could not speak due to tuberculosis, she experiments with abbreviations, ellipses, errant use of capital letters, and omission of vowels. She also uses an impersonal third person to create distance and a detached narrative. Penny Kaganoff noted in *Publishers Weekly* that "little is straightforward in this fictional work," and commented that "some anthropomorphic descriptions of plants border on sentimental."

In 2001 Belben published *Hound Music,* a novel set in the world of turn-of-the-century English fox hunting. George Lupis is master of his domain as well as master of the Quarr Fox Hounds. He is gruff and connects better with his beloved hounds than he does with his wife, Dorothy. After his death, she sells off the hounds and the horses and travels to North Africa to get away from the house and the children. Meanwhile, the children revive the fox-hunting tradition by collecting and training a few stray dogs.

Jane Ridley wrote in the *Spectator,* "Rosalind Belben writes beautifully about nature. . . . Her ear for speech is astonishing." Ridley added, "No one has ever written better than she does here about the English upper-class cult of fox-hunting pre-1914. . . . *Hound Music* is a minor classic, perhaps a major one; an enthralling and nonjudgmental evocation of a vanished world." Writing in the *Review of Contemporary Fiction,* Elisabeth Sheffield said that the book "is not an easy treat, as the eccentric point of view and idiomatic diction don't cut the reader much slack." Nevertheless, Sheffield said the book was authentic and worthwhile.

Belben published *Our Horses in Egypt* in 2007. The book delves into the fate of 22,000 horses left in Egypt at the end of World War I to be sold off, worked to death, or die of disease or starvation. The story follows the point of view of Philomena, a British mare that was sent to Egypt to help in the war, her harrowing ship voyage, violent service during the war, and abandonment after it. At the end of the war, her owner, a young war widow, travels to Egypt to retrieve her horse.

Stevie Davies wrote in the *Independent,* "Like most epics, this one closes in a species of failure. But *Our Horses in Egypt,* a radical experiment in narrative, has a sympathetic splendour, leading the blinkered humanist imagination into the realm of creaturely experience." Concerning the parts of the book told from the point of view of the horse, Jane Shilling commented in the *Telegraph,* "Philomena's story is a marvel. I don't think I've encountered a narrative told in the third person but essentially from the point of view of an animal before; indeed it's done so lightly and skillfully that I didn't realise that was what was happening at first."

Our Horses in Egypt received the James Tait Black Memorial Prize for fiction in 2007. The prize is Britain's oldest literary award having begun in 1919. Colin Nicholson, the award's manager, commented, "Rosalind Belben's novel was innovatively plotted and convincingly executed."

BIOGRAPHICAL AND CRITICAL SOURCES:

PERIODICALS

Bookseller, August 29, 2008, "Belben and Hill Win James Tait Black Prizes," p. 7.

Canadian Broadcasting Corporation, August 22, 2008, "Horse Tale Wins Britain's Oldest Literary Award."

Independent, February 23, 2007, Stevie Davies, "Welcome to a Wild, Whickering World," review of *Our Horses in Egypt.*

Publishers Weekly, January 18, 1991, Penny Kaganoff, review of *Is Beauty Good,* p. 54.

Review of Contemporary Fiction, September 22, 2002, Elisabeth Sheffield, review of *Hound Music,* p. 156.

Spectator, September 8, 2001, Jane Ridley, review of *Hound Music,* p. 39; November 24, 2001, review of *Hound Music,* p. 43.

Telegraph, February 25, 2007, Jane Shilling, review of *Our Horses in Egypt.*

TLS. Times Literary Supplement, February 3, 1995, review of *Choosing Spectacles,* p. 22; August 31, 2001, Emma Tristram, review of *Hound Music,* p. 21; February 23, 2007, Mark Thwaite, "Philomena's War," p. 23.

ONLINE

Book World, http://bookworld.typepad.com/ (February 4, 2008), review of *Our Horses in Egypt.*

Insider, http://www.theinsider.com/ (July 1, 2009), "Rosalind Belben, Rosemary Hill Win Literary Award."

Ready Steady Books, http://www.readysteadybook.com/ (May 23, 2007), Mark Thwaite, "Rosalind Belben," author interview.

* * *

BELBEN, Rosalind Loveday
See BELBEN, Rosalind

* * *

BENEDICT, Jeff 1966-

PERSONAL: Born March 14, 1966. *Education:* Eastern Connecticut State University, B.A.; Northeastern University, M.A.; New England College of Law, J.D.

ADDRESSES: Office—Division of Humanities, Southern Virginia University, 1 University Hill Dr., Buena Vista, VA 24416. *E-mail*—jeff@jeffbenedict.com.

CAREER: Writer and educator. Northeastern University's Center for the Study of Society, Boston, MA, director; Southern Virginia University, Buena Vista, professor of advanced writing.

WRITINGS:

NONFICTION

Public Heroes, Private Felons: Athletes and Crimes against Women, Northeastern University Press (Boston, MA), 1997.

Athletes and Acquaintance Rape, Sage Publications (Thousand Oaks, CA), 1998.

(With Don Yaeger) *Pros and Cons: The Criminals Who Play in the NFL,* Warner Books (New York, NY), 1998.

Without Reservation: The Making of America's Most Powerful Indian Tribe and the World's Largest Casino, HarperCollins (New York, NY), 2000.

No Bone Unturned: The Adventures of a Top Smithsonian Forensic Scientist and the Legal Battle for America's Oldest Skeletons, HarperCollins (New York, NY), 2003.

Out of Bounds: Inside the NBA's Culture of Rape, Violence, and Crime, HarperCollins (New York, NY), 2004.

The Mormon Way of Doing Business: Leadership and Success through Faith and Family, Warner Business Books (New York, NY), 2007.

Little Pink House: A True Story of Defiance and Courage, Grand Central Publishing (New York, NY), 2009.

How to Build a Business Warren Buffett Would Buy: The R.C. Willey Story, Shadow Mountain (Salt Lake City, UT), 2009.

SIDELIGHTS: Jeff Benedict, a graduate of Northwestern University and the New England College of Law, is a professor of advanced writing at the Southern Virginia University in Buena Vista, and the author of nonfiction works detailing women's, social justice, and legal history issues. Benedict's publications include: *Without Reservation: The Making of America's Most Powerful Indian Tribe and the World's Largest Casino; No Bone Unturned: The Adventures of a Top Smithsonian Forensic Scientist and the Legal Battle for America's Oldest Skeletons;* and *How to Build a Business Warren Buffett Would Buy: The R.C. Willey Story.*

Benedict's debut publication, *Public Heroes, Private Felons: Athletes and Crimes against Women,* was released in 1997. The text questions the legitimacy of public sports figures who have been given paragon status in American society. The text details instances of physical and sexual assault upon women by several high-profile sports figures and addresses issues of credibility, morality, and legality among those involved in confrontations with celebrity athletes. Moreover, as Sue-Ellen Beauregard observed in an article for *Booklist,* Benedict "examines external factors that may contribute to the crimes" as well as methods intended for the prevention of violent celebrity behavior. The text asserts that crimes perpetuated against the public by celebrities are widely resolved without punishment and that, as a result, these instances are recurring more frequently. Without consequences, Benedict notes, these prominent and popular sports personalities are not bound by the same societal laws as the public majority. Benedict correlates case study data, compiled while he served as director at Northeastern University's Center for the Study of Society, with qualitative assumptions regarding the causes and effects of violence against women by sports celebrities. The result, according to *Library Journal* contributor Valerie Diamond, is data that suggests "that male athletes actually are more likely to commit" violent crimes against women than men without celebrity status. Additionally, Benedict's subsequent publications, *Athletes and Acquaintance Rape* and *Pros and Cons: The Criminals Who Play in the NFL,* also detail specific criminal behaviors whose frequent occurrence can be attributed to those persons listed on sports rosters.

In *Pros and Cons,* a 1998 release, Benedict makes clear that celebrity violence is not merely a women's safety issue. The text provides evidence which suggests a range of criminal behavior, including rape, aggravated assault, and drug possession. These crimes, Benedict reaffirms, go largely unpunished by the perpetrators' employers and professional organizations. Among the information presented in the text regarding celebrity crime is statistical data which explains "that 21 percent" of professional National Football League (NFL) athletes "had been arrested or indicted for serious crimes ranging from fraud to homicide," according to Terry Madden's review for *Library Journal.* Among the more serious incidents catalogued, the text tells of Bryan Boyd and of how he was assaulted outside a Texas bar by four Texas Christian University (TCU) football players. The severe beating Boyd sustained left him brain damaged and paralyzed. The text explains that the assailants were criminally charged but not suspended from the college football team. Furthermore, at least one of Boyd's attackers was drafted by an NFL team. These cases present actualized threats to public safety and place them within the context of a society which does not seek an appropriate retributory amount of justice. In *Out of Bounds: Inside the NBA's Culture of Rape, Violence, and Crime,* Benedict not only chronicles instances of violence and criminality but also the culture that allows and condones such acts. Specifically, a *Publishers Weekly* contributor remarked, "Benedict exposes how life as a touring player in the NBA offers vast . . . free time and sex, encouraging criminal behavior and leading to a warped perception of women." The implications of a culture that is not in accord with its representative society is evinced through the text's discussions of the National Basketball Association (NBA) reactions regarding instances of player misconduct. Like his study of NFL activities, Benedict's representation of the NBA shows the association to have a history of blind acceptance.

In addition to charting criminality among professional athletes, Benedict has written on the subject of how private business affects civil liberties, specifically those pertaining to property ownership. Benedict's *Little Pink House: A True Story of Defiance and Courage,* published in 2009, addresses the government's constitutional right to eminent domain and how this practice has been both beneficial and detrimental to personal property ownership. While the law permits the government to acquire private land for the purpose of public use, the text reveals that the most common dispute regarding the government's acquisition of land stems from value perceptions and relative compensation. Meaning the government's assignment of value and an individual property owner's decided value do not accord in many cases; therefore, the government's afforded compensation is not sufficient for the individual. The text uses the case of *Kelo v. City of New London* to address the concept of eminent domain. Robert S. Poliner, in an article for the *Connecticut Law Tribune,* wrote, "Benedict's book is an account of the day-to-day lives and activities of a number of key players in the case, including Kelo, the other owners of real estate and businesses in the Fort Trumbull section of New London, city officials, officers of the New London Development Corp., Pfizer Inc. (whose plans for a New London research center were at the genesis of the land dispute), and the Institute for Justice." The case illustrates the government's questionable use of eminent domain to condemn personal property and use the land for economic gains. In a review for the *Volokh Conspiracy* Web site, Ilya Somin found, "Benedict also does an excellent job of portraying the human cost of going through an eminent domain case. Kelo and the other targeted property owners had their lives severely disrupted for several years, as they waited to see whether they would lose their homes." Moreover, the public reaction to this case damaged the reputations of the corporate entities that sought to do business with the government. Somin concluded, "*Little Pink House* is an impressive account of the events leading up to the most controversial property rights decision in Supreme Court history."

BIOGRAPHICAL AND CRITICAL SOURCES:

PERIODICALS

American Prospect, May 21, 2001, Michael Nelson, review of *Without Reservation: The Making of America's Most Powerful Indian Tribe and the World's Largest Casino,* p. 43.

Archaeology in New Zealand, March 1, 2004, Jacqueline Craig, review of *No Bone Unturned: The Adventures of a Top Smithsonian Forensic Scientist and the Legal Battle for America's Oldest Skeletons,* p. 69.

Booklist, September 1, 1997, Sue-Ellen Beauregard, review of *Public Heroes, Private Felons: Athletes and Crimes against Women,* p. 37; February 15, 2003, Gilbert Taylor, review of *No Bone Unturned,* p. 1024; February 1, 2007, David Siegfried, review of *The Mormon Way of Doing Business: Leadership and Success through Faith and Family,* p. 11.

California Lawyer, March 1, 2009, Richard M. Frank, review of *Little Pink House: A True Story of Defiance and Courage,* p. 41.

Choice: Current Reviews for Academic Libraries, January 1, 1998, review of *Public Heroes, Private Felons,* p. 909; February 1, 2001, F. Nicklason, review of *Without Reservation,* p. 1136.

Commentary, May 1, 2009, "The Skin Left on the Sidewalk," p. 75.

Connecticut Law Tribune, March 9, 2009, "Time to Change Eminent Domain Law."

Furniture-Today, April 6, 2009, "Book Tells 'R.C. Willey Story,'" p. 1.

Journal of Legal Studies Education, January 1, 2005, S. Catherine Anderson, review of *No Bone Unturned*; January 1, 2005, S. Catherine Anderson, review of *No Bone Unturned.*

Kirkus Reviews, January 1, 2003, review of *No Bone Unturned,* p. 120; January 15, 2003, review of *No Bone Unturned,* p. 120; November 15, 2008, review of *Little Pink House.*

Library Journal, October 15, 1997, Valerie Diamond, review of *Public Heroes, Private Felons,* p. 76; December 1, 1998, Terry Madden, review of *Pros and Cons: The Criminals Who Play in the NFL,* p. 115; February 15, 2003, John Burch, review of *No Bone Unturned,* p. 148.

Marquette Sports Law Journal, September 22, 1999, Daniele J. St. Marie, review of *Public Heroes, Private Felons,* p. 169.

News & Advance (Lynchburg, VA), March 2, 2009, Darrell Laurant, "A True Story of Defiance and Courage."

New York Times Book Review, March 15, 2009, "Driven Out," p. 17.

Northern Ireland Legal Quarterly, June 22, 1999, J. Paul McCutcheon, review of *Public Heroes, Private Felons,* p. 276.

NRO Radio, January 29, 2009, "Jeff Benedict on Little Pink House."

Publishers Weekly, September 8, 1997, review of *Public Heroes, Private Felons,* p. 71; May 1, 2000, review of *Without Reservation,* p. 64; February 3, 2003, review of *No Bone Unturned,* p. 63; June 14, 2004, review of *Out of Bounds: Inside the NBA's Culture of Rape, Violence, and Crime,* p. 56; August 6, 2007, "Eminent Domain," p. 18; October 13, 2008, review of *Little Pink House,* p. 43.

Reference & Research Book News, August 1, 2008, review of *The Mormon Way of Doing Business.*

Social Science Journal, July 1, 2001, Thomas J. Hoffman, review of *Without Reservation,* p. 495.

Sociology of Sport Journal, September 1, 2000, review of *Pros and Cons,* p. 297; March 1, 2002, M.F. Stuck, review of *Public Heroes, Private Felons,* p. 101.

Tribune Books, July 15, 2001, review of *Without Reservation,* p. 6; May 4, 2003, review of *No Bone Unturned,* p. 3.

Wall Street Journal, January 26, 2009, "Evicted, but Not without a Fight: Little Pink House, by Jeff Benedict," p. 13.

Wicazo Sa Review, September 22, 2002, Jace Weaver, review of *Without Reservation,* p. 210.

ONLINE

January Online, http://www.januarymagazine.com/ (January 1, 2009), Stephen Miller, "Viagra v. the Little People."

Jeff Benedict Home Page, http://www.jeffbenedict.com (August 2, 2009).

Southern Virginia University Web site, http://svu.edu/ (August 2, 2009), faculty profile.

Volokh Conspiracy Web site, http://www.volokh.com/ (February 21, 2009), Ilya Somin, review of *Little Pink House.**

* * *

BENJAMIN, Zelda

PERSONAL: Married; children: two.

ADDRESSES: *Home*—South Florida. *E-mail*—alex.martinelli@mac.com.

CAREER: Registered nurse and writer.

WRITINGS:

Brooklyn Ballerina, Avalon Books (New York, NY), 2001.

Chocolate Secrets, Avalon Books (New York, NY), 2008.

Contributor of articles to professional journals, including *Journal of Emergency Nursing* and *Society of Pediatric Nurses Newsletter.*

SIDELIGHTS: Zelda Benjamin is a writer living in South Florida who grew up in Brooklyn, New York, where she sets most of her stories. She is a registered nurse in a pediatric emergency room and finds time to write contemporary romance fiction and professional articles for journals and newsletters.

Benjamin wrote about a pediatric emergency department's successful approach to family-centered care for the *Journal of Emergency Nursing* and wrote "Maintaining a Caring Environment within an Organizational Framework" for *Society of Pediatric Nurses Newsletter.*

Benjamin published her first book, *Brooklyn Ballerina,* in 2001. The book follows prima ballerina Rebecca Carr as she decides to rescue her old dance instructor from financial difficulties and raise funds to save her old school. She meets Jake Fleichman, a financial wiz with street smarts who also happens to be a famous New York chef. Rebecca and Jake soon plan a fund-raising banquet.

In 2008 Benjamin published *Chocolate Secrets,* about feuding families: the Martinellis and Simones. Sal Simone stole a secret chocolate recipe from Max Martinelli years ago, and the two old curmudgeons have forbidden their descendants from interacting. That doesn't stop granddaughter Alex Martinelli from falling for firefighter Mike Simone.

While the families discourage the match-up, Mike's firefighter buddies teach him wooing techniques, dating lessons, and even horoscope consulting to win over Alex. Mike is also on a quest to retrieve the chocolate recipe and win the city's bake-off.

"Endearing characters . . . provide a nice balance to the grumpy gramps," noted Shelley Mosley in *Booklist. Chocolate Secrets* is the first book in a planned "Love by Chocolate" series.

BIOGRAPHICAL AND CRITICAL SOURCES:

PERIODICALS

Booklist, April 1, 2008, Shelley Mosley, review of *Chocolate Secrets,* p. 34.

ONLINE

Avalon Books, http://avalonbooks.com/ (July 1, 2009), author profile.

Zelda Benjamin Home Page, http://www.zeldabenjamin.com (July 1, 2009), author profile.*

* * *

BENTLEY, Barbara 1945-

PERSONAL: Born September 2, 1945. *Education:* Golden Gate University, San Francisco, CA, B.S. (summa cum laude), 1986.

CAREER: Writer, businesswoman, winemaker, and victim's advocate.

WRITINGS:

A Dance with the Devil: A True Story of Marriage to a Psychopath, Berkley Books (New York, NY), 2008.

Contributor to the blog *Barbara Writes,* http://barbarawrites.livejournal.com.

SIDELIGHTS: Barbara Bentley was born September 2, 1945, and grew up in the San Francisco Bay Area in a middle-class town. In 1986, she earned a B.S. degree in marketing from the business school at Golden Gate University, graduating summa cum laude. She was also named Outstanding Undergraduate. Bentley worked in the business sector in quality assurance and retired after a thirty-nine-year career. After a harrowing marriage to a con man who tried to murder her, Bentley settled in Northern California with her new husband. She is now an award-winning wine and label maker who enjoys traveling around the world.

In 1981 when Bentley was thirty-five years old and divorced, some friends matched her up on a blind date with the charismatic Admiral John Perry, a man twenty years her senior. He had many fascinating stories from his career as a Navy SEAL and Congressional Medal of Honor winner. He said he was involved with the CIA and was even Frank Sinatra's best man at the singer's wedding.

Lonely and vulnerable, Bentley believed him and dismissed the red flags that were becoming apparent. As time went on, he misused her credit cards, took out a second mortgage on her house, and cleaned her out financially. After she survived several murder attempts, she finally realized he was a compulsive liar, con artist, and psychopath.

Divorcing him was another hurdle. Even though he was in jail for her attempted murder, according to California's no-fault divorce law, he was entitled to half of her assets. With patience and persistence she successfully changed California divorce law.

In 2008 Bentley published a memoir of her harrowing relationship called *A Dance with the Devil: A True Story of Marriage to a Psychopath.* The book describes the details her fourteen-year marriage to John Perry, who was in fact not an admiral but a skillful predator. Believing she could make a difference, Bentley wrote the book to expose the psychopath's strategy and technique so that other women could protect themselves. To learn the skills to write the book she read other memoirs, joined writing groups, and attended writing workshops.

Commenting about *A Dance with the Devil,* a writer in *Kirkus Reviews* said, "The first-time memoirist narrates this improbable nightmare in an easy-to-read conversational style that makes it all the more unsettling." Writing in *Library Journal,* Daisy Porter noted, "Her memoir of marriage to a charismatic liar . . . succeeds. She holds nothing back." A writer on the blog *Lovefraud,* said, "This book is also the story of escape and recovery. And, it's the story of a woman who turned near-tragedy into something positive."

Bentley is a motivational speaker who visits women's organizations, such as the American Association of University Women, the International Women's Writing Guild, and Children's Advocacy Program giving lectures and presenting workshops. Her story appeared on the Lifetime Television channel's *Final Justice* program and *Dateline NBC.*

BIOGRAPHICAL AND CRITICAL SOURCES:

BOOKS

Bentley, Barbara, *A Dance with the Devil: A True Story of Marriage to a Psychopath,* Berkley Books (New York, NY), 2008.

PERIODICALS

Kirkus Reviews, October 1, 2008, review of *A Dance with the Devil.*

Library Journal, January 1, 2009, Daisy Porter, review of *A Dance with the Devil,* p. 108.

ONLINE

A Dance with the Devil Web site, http://www.adancewiththedevil.com/ (July 1, 2009), author profile.

Lovefraud.com, http://www.lovefraud.com/ (July 1, 2009), "Barbara Bentley Story in the Media," short author profile, and review of *A Dance with the Devil.**

* * *

BERKMAN, Steve 1933-

PERSONAL: Born December 8, 1933.

ADDRESSES: *Home*—Leesburg, VA.

CAREER: Lending operations advisor and investigator. World Bank, Washington, DC, Africa Region Group member, 1983-95, corruption investigator, 1998-2002.

Worked variously in industry and technical education before joining the World Bank. Provided assistance to the U.S. Senate Committee on Foreign Relations in relation to development banks and corruption.

WRITINGS:

The World Bank and the Gods of Lending, Kumarian Press (Sterling, VA), 2008.

Contributor to *The World Bank and the $100 Billion Question.* Also contributor to periodicals, including *Journal of Financial Crime, Monday Developments,* and *International Journal of Technical Cooperation.*

SIDELIGHTS: Steve Berkman is a former advisor and investigator for the World Bank. Born December 8, 1933, he worked variously in industry and technical education before joining the World Bank's Africa Region Group in 1983. He worked in twenty-one countries, providing advice on World Bank-funded projects. He retired in 1995 but returned three years later to help establish the bank's Anti-Corruption and Fraud Investigation Unit. He also served as lead investigator on a number of corruption cases in Africa and Latin America. He retired again in 2002. Berkman has also provided assistance to the U.S. Senate Committee on Foreign Relations in their work on legislation to reform development banks and to pass the United Nations Convention Against Corruption. He has also lectured at several universities in the U.S. and Europe, and given presentations to government agencies on the issue of foreign aid and corruption.

Berkman's first book is *The World Bank and the Gods of Lending,* published in 2008. In the book Berkman argues that the World Bank is crippled by corruption and mismanagement. Instead of fighting poverty, Berkman says, the bank mostly serves to enrich corrupt government officials and to advance the careers of its own executives. Berkman believes that the bank needs to "lend less and supervise more." In support of his allegations, Berkman provides copies of internal bank documents, as well as numerous concrete examples, some drawn from his own experience. In one instance in Nigeria, for example, officials charged a World Bank project budget 2,200 dollars for eighteen cups of tea and some snacks. Nor was this unusual. On the contrary, Berkman says that all of his more than one hundred projects at the bank were mired in corruption.

A reviewer writing in *Publishers Weekly* called *The World Bank and the Gods of Lending* "a blistering exposé." The reviewer found the book's tone occasionally too acerbic but concluded that it was nonetheless "a fascinating firsthand account of the bank's failures." Peter Bossard, writing online at *Pambazuka News,* also praised the book, noting that it "combines number crunching with vivid detail and moral outrage." Bossard was also impressed that "even with such stunning conclusions, Berkman does not give up all hope. . . . He calls for smaller, simpler projects, which do not create a 'feeding frenzy for corrupt government officials.' He says that the bank needs to insist that borrowing governments prosecute, punish and recover the assets of guilty individuals in the same way they would treat other criminals. And he proposes that the bank fully disclose all anti-corruption investigations, government agencies involved and funds stolen in its annual report." A reviewer writing in *Internet Bookwatch* concluded that *The World Bank and the Gods of Lending* "is a look [at] how bad mismanagement can be."

BIOGRAPHICAL AND CRITICAL SOURCES:

BOOKS

Berkman, Steve, *The World Bank and the Gods of Lending,* Kumarian Press (Sterling, VA), 2008.

PERIODICALS

Choice: Current Reviews for Academic Libraries, November, 2008, C. Kilby, review of *The World Bank and the Gods of Lending,* p. 567.

Internet Bookwatch, November, 2008, review of *The World Bank and the Gods of Lending.*

Publishers Weekly, April 28, 2008, review of *The World Bank and the Gods of Lending,* p. 126.

ONLINE

Game as Old as Empire, http://gameasoldasempire.com/ (July 26, 2009), author profile.

Kumarian Press Web site, http://kpbooks.com/ (July 26, 2009), author profile.

Pambazuka News, http://kpbooks.com/ (June 11, 2009), Peter Bossard, "Corruption and the World Bank."

* * *

BERR, Hélène 1921-1945

PERSONAL: Born March 27, 1921, in Paris, France; died April 10, 1945, in Bergen-Belsen Concentration Camp, Germany, by beating; daughter of Raymond (an industrialist) and Antoinette Berr. *Education:* Attended Sorbonne.

MEMBER: General Organization of Israelites in France.

WRITINGS:

Journal: 1942-1944, Tallandier (Paris, France), 2008, translation by David Bellos published as *The Journal of Hélène Berr,* Weinstein Books (New York, NY), 2008.

SIDELIGHTS: Hélène Berr was a French woman of Jewish descent who kept a diary about the Nazi occupation of France. She was born March 27, 1921, in Paris, France, to a wealthy Jewish family that had lived in France for several generations. She attended the Sorbonne, studying Russian and English literature. She was not able to take her final examination for a degree, however, because of anti-Semitic laws instituted by the Vichy regime following the Nazi occupation of her country. Faced with increasing restrictions on Jewish life, Berr joined an underground group transferring Jewish children to families in the unoccupied portions of France. Berr was eventually arrested and taken to a concentration camp. Though she survived one of the terrible death marches from Auschwitz to Bergen-Belsen, she was beaten to death in Bergen-Belsen on April 10, 1945, just five days before the Allies freed the prisoners there.

Beginning on August 2, 1942, Berr kept a diary. At first, the journal concerned the everyday concerns of a normal twenty-one-year-old woman. Berr talked about reading Shakespeare, Hemingway, and Keats, about her love of chamber music, and about her growing love affair with her fellow student, Jean Morawiecki. Slowly, the diary takes on a more somber tone, as Berr grapples with the growing Nazi influence over occupied France. She discusses her guilt at her occasional pleasure in reading even in such horrible times and at her flashes of hatred of the Germans. She also expresses anger at her Paris neighbors, who do nothing about the plight of the Jews, and talks about her fear and sadness. The journal ends on February 15, 1944, with the final entry reading "Horror! Horror! Horror!"

The journal was smuggled a few pages at a time to Berr's fiancé Morawiecki, and it was preserved mostly unseen for more than fifty years. It was finally published in 2008 in France as *Journal: 1942-1944,* where it sold more than 100,000 copies. The same year an English version, translated by David Bellos, was published under the title *The Journal of Hélène Berr.*

A reviewer writing in the *Daily Mail* said that Berr's journal "is a valuable record of what it was like to sit in Paris watching the horror approaching—the arrest of Hélène's father, the polite German officer who calls to look over the family apartment, the lengthening roll call of those taken away; and always the inability to realise what lay in store. Why deport a woman with terminal TB? she asked. 'Are they going to put these invalids to work? They will die on the journey.' The truth was literally unimaginable." Marjorie Kehe, writing in the *Christian Science Monitor,* said that "in intelligent, heart-wrenchingly lucid prose, Berr chronicles the escalating horror of the last couple years" of her family's lives. Kehe added that over the course of the diary, "Berr herself is transformed from a privileged, promising youth into an adult who must grapple firsthand with horrifying questions about the existence of evil in the human experience. What elevates her account to the heroic are the clarity, calm, and compassion which she maintains throughout."

Carmen Callil, writing in the *Guardian,* noted that "because of the heartbreaking story she tells, Berr's *Journal* could be difficult to read. But it is not. Like the diary of Anne Frank, *Journal* is ultimately an uplifting book, because in its pages we meet not so much a great writer—though her prose is fine and elegant—as a human being whose heart is great. Overwhelmed, she feels no 'hatred,' just 'protest, revulsion and scorn.' . . . She longs to live but faces squarely how she might die. Nevertheless, an extraordinary thread of hope—in goodness, in humanity—runs through her *Journal.*"

Michael Dirda, writing in the *Washington Post,* praised particularly the English translation, stating that "David Bellos, the translator and biographer of Georges Perec, as well as a professor of French and comparative literature at Princeton, has created an exemplary American edition of Berr's journal. . . . *The Journal of Hélène Berr* has been an immense best seller in Europe and deserves comparable success in this country. This, alas, is how it truly was when good people were heartlessly abused and their lives were ruthlessly taken from them."

BIOGRAPHICAL AND CRITICAL SOURCES:

BOOKS

Berr, Hélène, *Journal: 1942-1944,* Tallandier (Paris, France), 2008, translation by David Bellos published as *The Journal of Hélène Berr,* Weinstein Books (New York, NY), 2008.

PERIODICALS

Biography, spring, 2008, review of *The Journal of Hélène Berr,* p. 315.

Kirkus Reviews, October 1, 2008, review of *The Journal of Hélène Berr.*

Library Journal, November 1, 2008, Marie Marmo Mullaney, review of *The Journal of Hélène Berr,* p. 74.

Publishers Weekly, October 6, 2008, review of *The Journal of Hélène Berr,* p. 44.

ONLINE

Bookreporter, http://bookreporter.com/ (July 27, 2009), Sarah Hannah Gómez, review of *The Journal of Hélène Berr.*

Christian Science Monitor, http://bookreporter.com/ (November 11, 2008), Marjorie Kehe, review of *The Journal of Hélène Berr.*

Daily Mail, http://www.dailymail.co.uk/ (December 4, 2008), "The Extraordinary Courage of the Women Who Resisted."

Ground Report, http://www.spiegel.de/ (January 12, 2008), "Diary of Helene Berr, France's Anne Frank, Published."

Guardian, http://www.guardian.co.uk/ (November 8, 2008), Carmen Callil, "We Must Not Forget."

Jew Wishes, http://www.jewwishes.wordpress.com/ (June 19, 2009),"Jew Wishes On: The Journal of Helene Berr."

Observer, http://www.guardian.co.uk/ (January 6, 2008), Jason Burke, "France Finds Its Own Anne Frank as Young Jewish Woman's Diary Hits Shelves"; (October 22, 2008), Caroline Moorehead, "The Yellow Star of Courage."

Spiegel Online, http://www.spiegel.de/ (January 6, 2008), Siobhán Dowling, "Hélène Berr's Holocaust Diary Flies off the Shelves."

Telegraph, http://www.telegraph.co.uk/ (October 30, 2008), Elizabeth Grice, "How the Diaries of Hélène Berr, the 'Anne Frank of France', Came to Be Published."

Washington Post, http://www.washingtonpost.com/ (November 23, 2008), Michael Dirda, review of *The Journal of Hélène Berr.*

Written World, http://myreadingbooks.blogspot.com/ (November 14, 2008), review of *The Journal of Hélène Berr.*

* * *

BHABHA, Homi K. 1949-

PERSONAL: Born June 5, 1949, in Mumbai (formerly Bombay), Maharashtra, India. *Education:* University of Bombay, B.A., 1970; Oxford University, M.Phil., 1974, M.A., 1977, D.Phil., 1990.

ADDRESSES: Office—Harvard University, Humanities Center, Barker Center 134, 12 Quincy St., Cambridge, MA, 02138. *E-mail*—hbhabha@fas.harvard.edu.

CAREER: Writer and educator. Harvard University, Cambridge, MA, Anne F. Rothenberg Professor of English and American Literature and Language, 2001-06, Anne F. Rothenberg Professor of the Humanities, Department of English, 2006— director, Humanities Center at Harvard, 2005—; distinguished visiting professor, University College, London, England, 2004—.

WRITINGS:

NONFICTION

(Editor) *Nation and Narration,* Routledge (New York, NY), 1990.

The Location of Culture, Routledge (New York, NY), 1994, reprinted, 2004.

(Contributor) Richard Francis, editor, *Negotiating Rapture: The Power of Art to Transform Lives,* Museum of Contemporary Art (Chicago, IL), 1996.

(With Pier Luigi Tazzi) *Anish Kapoor,* University of California Press (Berkeley, CA), 1998.

(With Carol A. Breckenridge, Sheldon Pollock, and Dipesh Chakrabarty) *Cosmopolitanism,* Duke University Press (Durham, NC), 2002.

(With W.J.T. Mitchell) *Edward Said: Continuing the Conversation,* University of Chicago Press (Chicago, IL), 2005.

(Contributor) Fereshteh Daftari, *Without Boundary: Seventeen Ways of Looking,* Museum of Modern Art (New York, NY), 2006.

(Contributor) Dolores Romero López, editor, *Naciones Literarias,* Servicio de Publicaciones (Madrid, Spain), 2006.

Georges Adéagbo: Grand Tour di un Africano, Frittelli Arte Contemporanea (Florence, Italy), 2008.

SIDELIGHTS: Homi K. Bhabha was born June 5, 1949, in Mumbai, India. Bhabha is a professor of English at Harvard University, a lecturer in postcolonial theory at international venues, and a museum consultant. According to the Harvard Alumni Association, Bhabha "has also served as a Faculty Adviser to the DAVOS World Economic Forum and holds honorary visiting professorships at the University of Michigan and Tsinghua University." In addition to his professional engagements, Bhabha is a published author, having released six nonfiction titles, including *Nation and Narration; The Location of Culture; Anish Kapoor; Cosmopolitanism;* and *Edward Said: Continuing the Conversation.* In an article for the *Harvard Gazette,* Ken Gewertz explained that "the perspective that Bhabha brings . . . represents a departure from the traditional study of literature—one in which literary canons are defined by nationality with only an occasional acknowledgement that artistic influences may seep beyond borders. Bhabha's view of the literary universe is one in which borders are extremely porous and national identities may be exceedingly ambiguous. This view reflects a world in which air travel, the media, the Internet, and globalization have created a greater degree of cultural contact than ever before." This concept of globalization and a developing global culture, which Bhabha refers to as the "third space," is a theme echoed through much of Bhabha's work. In an interview with Christian Hoeller for *Translocation,* Bhabha explained his theories, stating that the idea of third space "came from my interest in the way in which power and authority functioned in the symbolic and subjectifying discourses of the colonial moment. My interest was . . . focused on the domain of cultural relations where the structure of signification or the regime of representation becomes at once the medium of social discourse as well as the operative . . . objective of a political strategy. For instance, the transmission of Christian ethics as part of the civilizing mission required both the institution of the English language as a communicative and pedagogical medium as well as the partial interpellation of an individualistic subject." In other words, postcolonial products are much more complicated than the mere opposition between elements; the intersection of culture is the space within which Bhabha finds a discourse of translation. Emily Eakin, in an article for the *New York Times,* pointed out, "Mr. Bhabha set to work on a new theory. And though it can be hard to make out beneath the aspic of theoretical jargon, its broad outlines are clear enough. Instead of victors and victims, Mr. Bhabha stresses ambivalence and negotiation."

Bhabha's *The Location of Culture,* released initially in 1994 with a reprinted edition published in 2004, is a collection of essays addressing various topics within the postcolonial canon. The text discusses the concept of the formation of national identity, racial hybridity, areas of societal cooperation and conflict, and emergent modernity brought about by the colonizers. Stephen Howe, in a review for the *New Statesman & Society,* found, "There is a seriousness, a care, a real weight of scholarship behind Bhabha's thinking," and continued, "He writes a prose of formidable complexity, allusiveness and abstraction, relying heavily on psychoanalytical theory and especially Lacan." The text employs classic psychoanalytic and deconstructive theory in an attempt to categorize and analyze the key concepts of the postcolonial society. Tim Woods, in an article for the *British Journal of Aesthetics,* concluded, "Bhabha's book divulges incisive thought, provocative ideas and exciting illumination on every page. It establishes him as one of the preeminent postcolonial theorists; and it takes cultural criticism into crucially new and important areas of exploration and debate."

Likewise, Bhabha's *Cosmopolitanism,* released in 2002 via the Duke University Press, discusses the concept of globalized society in the context of postcolonialist literary studies. Moreover, *Cosmopolitanism* also offers a compilation of scholarly essays that address different topics within the context of literary, aesthetic, political, and anthropological studies. Also, the implications of cosmopolitan effects on society are discussed within the sphere of multiculturalism, history, and translocation. The essays question Western influences, oppressive politics, and the potential for a classless society. K. Sivaramakrishnan, in an article for the *Journal of the Royal Anthropological Institute,* explained, "The justification for the project is offered in terms of the proliferation of globalization literatures since the late twentieth century, and the challenges posed to world peace by homogenizing nationalisms and coerced multiculturalisms. The authors also wish to highlight the non-Western origins of cosmopolitanism outside the sphere of Roman and Latin influences. Their ambition, in part, is to trace the relationship of these other cosmopolitan cultures to specific processes of vernacular and regional identity formation." The text contains essays by contributors such as Sheldon Pollock, Arjun Apparurai, Dipesh Chakrabarty, Walter D. Mignolo, and Wu Hung.

BIOGRAPHICAL AND CRITICAL SOURCES:

PERIODICALS

American Literature, March, 1991, review of *Nation and Narration,* p. 181.

Artforum International, April, 2003, "Making Difference: Homi K. Bhabha on the Legacy of the Culture Wars," p. 73; February, 2004, "Untimely Ends: Homi K. Bhabha on Edward Said," p. 19; summer, 2007, "Domesticity at War: Beatriz Colomina and Homi K. Bhabha in Conversation," p. 442.

British Journal of Aesthetics, July, 1995, Tim Woods, review of *The Location of Culture,* p. 292.
Choice: Current Reviews for Academic Libraries, February 1, 1995, review of *Nation and Narration,* p. 901; March, 1995, review of *Nation and Narration,* p. 1059.
Chronicle of Higher Education, July 1, 2005, "Journalism Professor Leaves Florida International U. in Dispute with Dean; Harvard Hires a Leading Voice in Postcolonial Studies; U. of Florida Names a Provost."
Comparative Literature, winter, 1991, review of *Nation and Narration,* p. 112.
Journal of Asian Studies, February, 2003, Bruce Robbins, review of *Cosmopolitanism,* p. 192.
Journal of the Royal Anthropological Institute, September, 2005, K. Sivaramakrishnan, review of *Cosmopolitanism,* p. 606.
Modern Language Review, October, 1992, Peter Mudford, review of *Nation and Narration,* p. 915.
New Statesman & Society, February 25, 1994, Stephen Howe, review of *The Location of Culture,* p. 40.
New York Times, November 17, 2001, Emily Eakin, "Harvard's Prize Catch, a Delphic Postcolonialist," p. 15.
Quadrant, March, 1999, "Bad Writing Contest Winners," p. 32.
Quarterly Review of Film and Video, January, 1993, review of *Nation and Narration,* p. 109.
Times Higher Education Supplement, April 8, 1994, Keith Ansell-Pearson, review of *The Location of Culture,* p. 26.
Times Literary Supplement, September 14, 1990, Bryan Cheyette, review of *Nation and Narration,* p. 979; May 27, 1994, Kwame Anthony Appiah, review of *The Location of Culture,* p. 5.

ONLINE

Harvard Alumni Association Web site, http://staging.barrettcommunications.com/ (July 27, 2009), author biography.
Harvard Gazette Online, http://www.news.harvard.edu/gazette/ (January 31, 2002), Ken Gewertz, "Telling Tales Out of, and in, Class: Bhabha Studies Culture and Genre with a Moral Squint."
Harvard University, Dept. of African and African American Studies Web site, http://aaas.fas.harvard.edu/ (July 27, 2009), faculty profile.
Post Colonial Web site, http://www.postcolonialweb.org/ (July 27, 2009), Benjamin Graves, "Homi K. Bhabha: An Overview."
Translocation Web site, http://www.translocation.at/ (January 26, 1999), Christian Hoeller, "Don't Mess with Mister In-Between."*

* * *

BI, Feiyu 1964-

PERSONAL: Born January, 1964, in Xinghua, Jiangsu, China; married; children: one son.

ADDRESSES: *Home*—Nanjing, China. *Agent*—Susijn Agency, Ltd., 3rd Fl., 64 Great Titchfield St., London W1W 7QH, England.

CAREER: Novelist, screenwriter, and poet. Worked for six years as a journalist for the *Nanjing Daily.*

AWARDS, HONORS: Xu Lun prize, 1995, 1996.

WRITINGS:

IN CHINESE

(Cowriter) *Shanghai Triad,* Sony Pictures Classics, 1996.
Nan Ren Hai Sheng Xia Shen Mo, Shi dai wen yi chu ban she (Changchun, China), 2001.
Di Qiu Shang De Wang JiaZhuang, Xin shi jie chu ban she (Beijing, China), 2002.
Bi Feiyu Xiao Shuo (short stories), Zhongguo she hui chu ban she (Beijing, China), 2006.

IN ENGLISH TRANSLATION

The Moon Opera, translated by Howard Goldblatt and Sylvia Li-chun Li, Telegram (London, England), 2007, Houghton Mifflin Harcourt (Boston, MA), 2009.
Three Sisters, translated by Howard Goldblatt and Sylvia Li-chun Li, Telegram Books (London, England), 2009.

Editor of the literary magazine *Yu Hua.*

SIDELIGHTS: Feiyu Bi is a Chinese novelist and writer. He was born in January, 1964, in Xinhua in the province of Jiangsu, China. He worked as a journalist for the *Nanjing Daily* for six years before becoming a full-time poet and novelist.

Bi has had over twenty books of novels and short stories published. His work has been translated into French and German as well as English. One of his novels served as the basis for the 1996 film *Shanghai Triad.* Bi cowrote the script, and the movie was directed by Zhang Yimou (*Raise the Red Lantern*). The movie features the well-known actress Gong Li, who plays the cabaret singer Xiao Jinbao. Derek Elley, writing in *Variety,* called the film "a stylized but gripping portrait of mob power play and lifestyles in 1930 Shanghai."

Bi's first novel to be translated into English was *The Moon Opera* released in 2007 in Britain with a translation by Howard Goldblatt and Sylvia Li-chun Li. The story focuses on Xiao Yanqiu, a Chinese opera singer who had a promising career before she attacked her understudy's teacher in a fit of jealousy. After the scandal, Yanqiu became a singing teacher for two decades. She suddenly emerges from obscurity, however, when a wealthy industrialist offers to put on a production of "The Moon Opera" on the condition that Yanqiu take the lead role. The novel follows Yanqiu's tragic efforts to regain her triumph, linking her struggle to the decline of the opera form in China, and to the struggle between art and money.

Tatyana Gershkovich, writing in the *San Francisco Chronicle,* felt that *The Moon Opera,* is "occasionally heavy-handed", but she also praised it, noting that "Bi Feiyu's eye for the cinematic is evident on the page. In one beautifully unnerving scene, an intoxicated Yanqiu, desperate to be back onstage, dances alone in her kitchen, breaking bottles of oil and soy sauce." A reviewer writing in *World Literature Forum* added, "For a small novel, *The Moon Opera* packs a surprising amount of content, and digging beyond the superficial there are wonderful layers of depth to pick away at. It's a novel that takes on the subjects of identity, gender roles, and cultural decline, amidst the wider themes of jealousy and regret, and, when the curtain drops, is worthy of a standing ovation. Although there are moments when the writing dips, *The Moon Opera* is quick to recover and rarely hits a wrong note." A reviewer in *Kirkus Reviews* noted that some of the technical details of the opera are difficult to follow and that the glossary is not as helpful as it might be. Nonetheless, the same reviewer concluded that the book was "flawed, but elegantly theatrical and emotionally resonant—just like a good opera." Brad Hooper, writing in *Booklist,* said, "This slender novel . . . resonates with a clear crystalline bell tone. . . . At once a sad and lovely story." A reviewer in *Publishers Weekly* added, "The novel's slimness, simple storytelling and overarching morality lend it a fable-like air."

In 2009 another of Bi's books appeared in English: *Three Sisters,* again translated by Goldblatt and Li-Chun Li. The three sisters of the title are the dignified Yumi, the attractive Yuxiu, and the ambitious Yuyang. The story follows them as they attempt to control their own fates in both the rural and urban China of the 1980s.

Bi lives in Nanjing with his wife and son. He edits the literary magazine *Yu Hua.* Among his other novels in Chinese are *Nan Ren Hai Sheng Xia Shen Mo,* published in 2001; *Di Qiu Shang De Wang JiaZhuang,* published in 2002; and *Bi Feiyu Xiao Shuo,* published in 2006.

BIOGRAPHICAL AND CRITICAL SOURCES:

PERIODICALS

Booklist, November 15, 2008, Brad Hooper, review of *The Moon Opera,* p. 31.

Kirkus Reviews, November 15, 2008, review of *The Moon Opera.*

Publishers Weekly, October 27, 2008, review of *The Moon Opera,* p. 33.

ONLINE

APOOO Bookclub, http://www.apooobooks.com/ (March 10, 2009), review of *The Moon Opera.*

Complete Review, http://www.complete-review.com/ (July 27, 2009), review of *The Moon Opera.*

Paper-republic.org, http://www.paper-republic.org/ (July 27, 2009), author profile.

San Francisco Chronicle, http://www.sfgate.com/ (February 10, 2009), Tatyana Gershkovich, review of *The Moon Opera.*

Susijn Agency Web site, http://www.thesusijnagency.com/ (July 27, 2009), author profile.

Telegram Books Web site, http://www.telegrambooks.com/ (July 27, 2009), author profile.

University of Iowa Web site, http://at-lamp.its.uiowa.edu/ (July 27, 2009), author profile.

Variety, http://www.variety.com/ (May 25, 1995), review of *Shanghai Triad.*

World Literature Forum, http://www.worldliteratureforum.com/ (April 3, 2008), review of *The Moon Opera.*

* * *

BINGHAM, Kelly

PERSONAL: Married; children: five. *Education:* Vermont College, M.F.A.

ADDRESSES: *Home*—Ellijay, GA.

CAREER: Author and illustrator. Worked as a story artist and director for Walt Disney Feature Animation, Burbank, CA, for twelve years.

MEMBER: Society of Children's Book Writers and Illustrators.

AWARDS, HONORS: Best Books for Young Adults citation, American Library Association, for *Shark Girl.*

WRITINGS:

Shark Girl, Candlewick Press (Cambridge, MA), 2007.

SIDELIGHTS: Kelly Bingham is the author of *Shark Girl,* a critically acclaimed young-adult novel about a teenage artist recovering from a horrifying shark attack. The work "is for anyone who likes stories about uncontrollable, life-changing events, and how a person deals with that," Bingham stated in an interview on the *Class of 2K7* Web site. "It's about losing something you think you can't live without, then discovering . . . maybe you can. It's also about fitting in and not fitting in, the importance (and non-importance) of looking 'normal,' the way kids treat each other in high school, the fallout of a disabling injury in a teen's life as well as that of her family, and the capacity we all have to love and to overcome and move on."

An avid reader, Bingham notes that literature has had a tremendous impact on her life. "The act of reading was something that fed my soul, and I read quite a bit growing up," she remarked in her *Class of 2K7* interview. "I loved the 'Little House' books by Laura Ingalls Wilder, and must have reread each one a hundred times. In short, I was always reading, and good or bad, I would lose myself in the story entirely." A former story artist at Walt Disney Feature Animation, she worked on such popular films as *Hercules* and *The Hunchback of Notre Dame* while pursuing a literary career. "I spent over ten years trying to 'learn' how to write for children," she related to Cynthia Leitich Smith on the *Cynsations* Web site. "I took classes and workshops, had a critique group, and wrote a lot. After a long time, I realized my level of writing had plateaued . . . and it wasn't that good." Bingham later attended Vermont College, earning a master's degree in writing for children and young adults. "I learned more there in the first semester than I had in the previous ten years of self-teaching," she recalled to Smith. "And I began working in earnest on the story I had brought with me to my first workshop . . . the manuscript that would become *Shark Girl.*

In *Shark Girl* Bingham introduces fifteen-year-old Californian Jane Arrowood, a promising artist who loses her right arm in a near-fatal shark attack. As she recovers, Jane struggles to remaster simple tasks such as opening cans and buttoning her pants. she also mourns the loss of her ability to draw. Bingham tells her protagonist's story through a series of prose poems, newspaper clippings, and letters; according to *School Library Journal* critic Janet S. Thompson, Jane's "voice is authentic and believable as both a teenager and victim."

Shark Girl received strong reviews. "Powerful without being maudlin or preachy, the book explores hurdles that are bound to follow a physical disfigurement," observed a contributor to *Publishers Weekly,* and Frances Bradburn, writing in *Booklist,* stated that Bingham's novel "offers a strong view of a teenager struggling to survive and learn to live again."

Bingham has a number of writing projects planned for the future. As she told Smith, "I love it when a character begins to take shape in my writing and in my mind, and even begins to 'speak' to me and tell me her own story; what has happened, how she feels, where she's going, what she wants to do. That's very exciting."

BIOGRAPHICAL AND CRITICAL SOURCES:

PERIODICALS

Booklist, May 1, 2007, Frances Bradburn, review of *Shark Girl,* p. 81.
Horn Book, May-June, 2007, Lauren Adams, review of *Shark Girl,* p. 278.
Kirkus Reviews, April 1, 2007, review of *Shark Girl.*
Kliatt, May, 2007, Claire Rosser, review of *Shark Girl,* p. 6.
Publishers Weekly, April 16, 2007, review of *Shark Girl,* p. 52.
School Library Journal, June, 2007, Janet S. Thompson, review of *Shark Girl,* p. 140.

ONLINE

Class of 2K7, http://classof2k7.com/ (March 1, 2008), "Kelly Bingham."
Cynsations, http://cynthialeitichsmith.blogspot.com/ (April 25, 2007), Cynthia Leitich Smith, interview with Bingham.
Kelly Bingham Home Page, http://www.kellybingham.net (March 1, 2008).*

* * *

BLAU, Jessica Anya

PERSONAL: Education: University of California, Berkeley, B.A.; Johns Hopkins University, M.A., 1995.

ADDRESSES: Home—MD.

CAREER: Writer.

WRITINGS:

The Summer of Naked Swim Parties (novel), Harper Perennial (New York, NY), 2008.

Also author of the blog *Jessica Anya Blau.*

SIDELIGHTS: Jessica Anya Blau is a graduate of the University of California, at Berkeley, and Johns Hopkins University. In 2008, Blau released her debut fiction novel titled *The Summer of Naked Swim Parties.* Set in the mid-1970s in Santa Barbara, California, the narrative follows a young girl named Jamie as she perseveres through an adolescence wherein her parents are shamelessly and publically sexually active as well as unabashed drug users. Despite their seeming flaws, Allen and Betty are happily married and provide Jamie with a loving home. In the midst of her unconventional family life, Jamie attempts to assert her individuality and come to terms with her sexuality. While Jamie has misgivings regarding her family's domestic dynamics and enters into a relationship with a boy named Trip, her younger sister Renee actively pursues a more normal environment in the form of a neighboring family. Moreover, to compound the awkward domestic environment and familial relationships, Allen and Betty begin to host summer swim parties that encourage nudity, to the mortification of their children. Although Jamie's boyfriend Tripp does not seem offended by these events, Jamie is ever more unsettled by her parents' public displays. However, her relationship with Tripp provides a temporary distraction from the discomforts of her home life, and she ventures further into romantic territory with her increasing sexual daring. However, the tension between family members eventually becomes disruptive, and the family experiences conflicts with each other and their neighbors. A *Publishers Weekly* contributor mentioned that "Allen and Betty's casual ways result in a disaster that turn the family into pariahs in their middle-class" community, which has a negative impact on their children.

Despite the more serious commentaries regarding domestic conflict, sexual maturity, and public propriety, the text combines humor and nostalgic colloquialisms with scenic descriptions of Santa Barbara that make the text evocative of the 1960s and 1970s beachside subculture. Michael Cart, in an article for *Booklist,* pointed out that Blau "skewers what needs skewering and celebrates the rest with humor, style, and an appropriate degree of affection." The text does not seek to glorify acts of promiscuity, general irresponsibility, or drug use. Instead, Blau employs these elements in an attempt to recreate the freedom of expression, naiveté, and carefree exuberance of the era. Through the perspective of an adolescent girl, the reader gains insight into the joys and challenges of maturing through experience.

BIOGRAPHICAL AND CRITICAL SOURCES:

PERIODICALS

Booklist, April 15, 2008, Michael Cart, review of *The Summer of Naked Swim Parties,* p. 26.

Publishers Weekly, February 25, 2008, review of *The Summer of Naked Swim Parties,* p. 46.

Voice of Youth Advocates, August 1, 2008, Angelica Delgado, review of *The Summer of Naked Swim Parties,* p. 236.

ONLINE

Jessica Anya Blau Home Page, http://www.jessicaanyablau.com (August 5, 2009).

Red Room, http://www.redroom.com/ (August 5, 2009), author profile.*

* * *

BLEVINS, Christine

PERSONAL: Married; husband's name Brian; children: Jason, Natalie, Bob, and Grace. *Education:* Attended design school. *Hobbies and other interests:* Writing.

ADDRESSES: Home—Elmhurst, IL. *Agent*—Nancy Coffey, Nancy Coffey Literary & Media Representation, 240 W. 35th St., Ste. 500, New York, NY 10001. *E-mail*—chris@christineblevins.com.

CAREER: Interior designer; graphics designer.

WRITINGS:

Midwife of the Blue Ridge, Berkley Publishing Group (New York, NY), 2008.

The Tory Widow, Berkley Books (New York, NY), 2009.

SIDELIGHTS: The fourth and youngest child of Ukrainian immigrants, Christine Blevins grew up on Chicago's south side. Books were her refuge from the unpleasantness of her neighborhood, sparking and exciting her imagination and creativity, and she often made up stories in her head, although she never wrote them down. After graduating from design school she worked for a while as an interior designer before marrying her husband, Brian. With him as partner, Blevins started a graphics design business in Chicago and raised four children. The family lives in Elmhurst, Illinois.

During a family vacation in Scotland Blevins was making up another story in her head when she decided to write it down. During the two years it took her to write her first book, Blevins discovered that she enjoyed both the writing and the research needed to create an historical novel.

Midwife of the Blue Ridge begins in 1746 during the battle of Culloden in the Scottish Highlands, where seven-year-old Maggie Duncan is the sole survivor of her village. After helping a wounded soldier get home, she is taken in by his wife who raises her and trains her as a healer. When her mentor dies, Maggie decides to try her luck in America and becomes an indentured servant. Her bond is sold to a frontiersman who takes her home to the Blue Ridge Mountains to help his ill and pregnant wife. Just as she learned to survive in war-torn Scotland, Maggie now learns to survive in her new home.

Reviewers praised *Midwife of the Blue Ridge* for its realistic depiction of the time period and for Blevins's deftness with characterizations. As the reviewer for *Publishers Weekly* put it, she "doesn't soft-peddle the brutal realities" of the time period. "Blevins manages to create an amazing atmosphere in the newly settled America," declared the reviewer for *The Bluestocking Society,* and Lynne Welch, reviewing the book for *Booklist,* commented that Blevins "provides an in-depth and up-close look at what life was really like." The reviewer for *BCF Book Reviews* called the book a "terrific, enthralling story of frontier life in colonial Virginia," adding, "The characters were compelling . . . and the settings were wonderfully described." The reviewer was also pleased by "the balanced depiction of the Native Americans . . . showing them from their own point of view as well as an outsider's."

The Tory Widow takes place in New York City in 1775. Anne, married at a young age to a much older man, is now a widow with a young son. She continues to run her husband's printing business, not caring what her customers' politics are. This policy lands her afoul of the Sons of Liberty, who destroy her press because of the Tory materials she prints. She reopens her business as a coffee house but is kept under surveillance by one of her enemies, Jack Hampton. As war begins to break out, Anne discovers that her sympathies lie with the patriots and that Jack has won her love. She is now in a perfect situation to spy on the Tories who were her husband's friends.

Again, reviewers approved Blevins's realistic depiction of the time period and characters while also enjoying the story. The reviewer for *Devourer of Books* declared, "I liked Anne as a character, she was strong and courageous, but didn't seem out of place in her time period." The reviewer for *Tome Traveler's Weblog* had a similar comment: "The author has painted what feels like a realistic portrait of New York City and its divided residents during the beginnings of the American Revolution. I loved the characters, they are all depicted with positive attributes as well as flaws whether they are American or English. . . . She brings colonial New York to life." Praising the book in her review for *Romance Reader,* Cathy Sova wrote, "Readers who enjoy a strong historical thread in their books will find *The Tory Widow* to be quite engrossing," a feeling echoed by the reviewer for *Medieval Bookworm* who said, "I found this book to be very solid. It's a good, enjoyable read." Confirming this opinion was the reviewer for *Tanzanite's Shelf and Stuff,* who stated, "Overall I thought this was an entertaining read."

BIOGRAPHICAL AND CRITICAL SOURCES:

PERIODICALS

Booklist, July 1, 2008, Lynne Welch, review of *Midwife of the Blue Ridge,* p. 36.

Publishers Weekly, May 12, 2008, review of *Midwife of the Blue Ridge,* p. 33.

ONLINE

BCF Book Reviews, http://bcfreviews.wordpress.com/ (September 4, 2008), review of *Midwife of the Blue Ridge.*

Bluestocking Society, http://thebluestockings.com/ (July 28, 2009), review of *Midwife of the Blue Ridge.*

Christine Blevins Home Page http://www.christineblevins.com (July 28, 2009), profile of author.

Devourer of Books, http://www.devourerofbooks.com/ (March 25, 2009), review of *The Tory Widow.*

Fantastic Fiction, http://www.fantasticfiction.co.uk/ (July 28, 2009), short author profile.

Medieval Bookworm, http://chikune.com/ (July 28, 2009) review of *The Tory Widow.*

Red Room, http://www.redroom.com/ (July 28, 2009), author profile.

Romance Reader, http://www.theromancereader.com/ (July 28, 2009), Cathy Sova, review of *The Tory Widow.*

Tanzanite's Shelf and Stuff, http://shelfandstuff.blogspot.com/ (May 16, 2009), review of *The Tory Widow.*

Tome Traveller's Weblog, http://thetometraveller.blogspot.com/ (June 10, 2009), review of *The Tory Widow.**

* * *

BLOXAM, M.F. 1958-

PERSONAL: Born June 2, 1958. *Education:* Studied theater, anthropology, and museum studies.

ADDRESSES: *Home*—Portsmouth, NH.

CAREER: Writer. Worked in museums.

WRITINGS:

The Night Battles, Permanent Press (Sag Harbor, NY), 2008.

SIDELIGHTS: M.F. Bloxam was born on June 2, 1958. She studied anthropology and worked in museums. She lives in Portsmouth, New Hampshire.

In Bloxam's first book, *The Night Battles,* the protagonist is anthropology professor Joan Severance, who is taking a sabbatical from teaching to work as an historical archivist in Valparuta, Sicily. She is lucky to be examining some newly discovered ancient texts that were brought to light when an earthquake revealed an old stone tower. Shifting through the crumbling manuscripts with the help of Valparuta's official archivist, she learns about the Benandanti, forces of good, who fight against the Malandanti, forces of evil, in ferocious battles that occur out-of-body in the dark of night. Although this was officially a medieval and pagan belief stamped out long ago by the authorities and the Catholic Church, Severance discovers both belief and practice are alive and well in Valparuta, and that all of the inhabitants of the village take part in the struggle. While researching the historical archives, Joan also discovers the secrets of her own family's history. She was born in Valparuta, and her father took her away when her mother was murdered while trying to expose the Mafiosi. Soon Severance begins to show some of the psychic and mystical characteristics of the natives, and finds herself drawn to become one of the Benandanti, fighting against evil both for herself and her mother.

Reviews were enthusiastic, if slightly mixed. Although the reviewer for *Kirkus Reviews* thought the book was "contrived," the reviewer for *Publishers Weekly* called *The Night Battles* an "eerie and satisfying debut novel." Bloxam was praised for her style by Rebecca Rule in her review for the *Nashua Telegraph,* noting the "rich and textured language . . . [and] complex and compelling characters. . . . She squeezes meaning from every scene as the mystery deepens and the suspense mounts." Similarly, Joanne Wilkinson, in her review for *Booklist,* approved Bloxam's "careful and elegant prose." Although Terry Weyna, in a review for *Reading the Leaves,* declared, "I kept wanting more from this book than it was giving me," others were deeply drawn in. Wisteria Leigh, in her review for *Blogcritics,* stated, "This book will stimulate your neurons to that time long ago when we believed. . . . *The Night Battles* commands your attention with mesmerizing intrigue and alluring appeal," and the reviewer for *Booksie's Blog* wrote, "*The Night Battles* is well written, and the tension mounts from the first page. . . . It is a major coup to make such beliefs in modern times appear believable and the mainspring of action."

The Night Battles was nominated for the 2008 Pulitzer, PEN/Hemingway, PEN/Faulkner, and National Book Critics Circle Awards.

BIOGRAPHICAL AND CRITICAL SOURCES:

PERIODICALS

Booklist, December 15, 2008, Joanne Wilkinson, review of *The Night Battles,* p. 24.

Kirkus Reviews, October 1, 2008, review of *The Night Battles.*

Publishers Weekly, September 15, 2008, review of *The Night Battles,* p. 41.

ONLINE

Blogcritics.org, http://blogcritics.org/ (March 2, 2009), Wisteria Leigh, review of *The Night Battles.*

Booksie's Blog, http://booksiesblog.blogspot.com/ (March 22, 2009), review of *The Night Battles.*

Greater Phoenix Digital Library, http://phoenix.lib.overdrive.com/ (August 1, 2009), short author profile.

Nashua Telegraph, http://www.nashuatelegraph.com/ (March 1, 2009), Rebecca Rule, "The Battle Is to Put This Book Down."

Permanent Press, http://www.thepermanentpress.com/ (August 1, 2009), short author profile and review of *The Night Battles.*

Reading the Leaves, http://www.readingtheleaves.com/ (March 2, 2009), Terry Weyna, review of *The Night Battles.*

* * *

BONCOMPAGNI, Tatiana 1977(?)-

PERSONAL: Born about 1977; married Maximilian Hoover (an energy consultant), 2003; children: two. *Education:* Graduate of Georgetown University, School of Foreign Service. *Hobbies and other interests:* Cooking, reading, running, swimming, and yoga.

ADDRESSES: Home—New York, NY. *E-mail*—tatiana@boncompagni.net.

CAREER: Journalist, writer. Has written for *American Lawyer,* New York; *Legal Times,* Washington DC; *Wall Street Journal Europe,* Brussels, Belgium; freelance writer, 2003—.

WRITINGS:

Gilding Lily, Avon (New York, NY), 2008.
Hedge Fund Wives, Avon (New York, NY), 2009.

SIDELIGHTS: Born around 1977, Tatiana Boncompagni grew up in South Dakota and Nashville, Tennessee, and went to high school in Edina, Minnesota, where she was the editor of the high school literary magazine, *Images.* Her father was Jewish and from the Midwest, but her mother claims to be a member of the Italian nobility, who left her heritage behind to marry Boncompagni's father. According to Boncompagni, her mother gave her and her sister her own last name in the hope that they would be able to get Italian passports easily. Boncompagni attended Georgetown University in Washington, DC, graduating magna cum laude from the School of Foreign Service with a degree in international law, organization, and politics. She interned at the Federal Reserve Bank of Minneapolis, the office of U.S. Congressman Jim Ramstad, and CNN, before becoming a reporter for *American Lawyer* in New York, the *Legal Times* in Washington, DC, and the *Wall Street Journal Europe* in Brussels after graduation. In 2003 Boncompagni became a freelance journalist specializing in style and fashion, writing articles for the *New York Times* Sunday Styles section, the *Financial Times* Style and Shopping pages, *Vogue, Cookie,* and *InStyle.* That same year she married Maximilian Hoover, heir to the vacuum cleaner fortune, and entered the world of New York high society, which she used as the subject of her first two novels. She lives in Manhattan, New York, with her husband and their two children.

Gilding Lily draws its inspiration from Boncompagni's own life. Lily is a middle-class girl from the Midwest who marries a man from a wealthy family and becomes the newest star of high society. She loves her husband dearly, but after they are married, real life intervenes. Lily becomes pregnant and her husband quits his job; in the face of these life changes, she begins to find the social scene unfulfilling and empty. Writing about it for the newspaper helps, but Lily faces many challenges to save her marriage.

Reviewers liked *Gilding Lily.* In her review for *Curled Up with a Good Book,* Swapna Krishna praised Boncompagni, saying, "She really knows her stuff, and it shows in her debut novel," and a reviewer for *Publishers Weekly* wrote, "Her protagonist is likable even at her most dastardly."

There was some controversy surrounding Boncompagni's second novel, *Hedge Fund Wives.* According to Boncompagni, her sister, Natasha, with whom she had consulted on the book, secretly copied a portion of the manuscript and attempted to claim coauthorship by copyrighting it. Boncompagni sued her, and Natasha eventually dropped her coauthorship claim, but the lawsuit had become a hot topic in the gossip columns and socialites took sides, especially those with aspirations to publish similar novels. The incident left the sisters estranged and soured Boncompagni on New York high society.

Hedge Fund Wives exposes the scandals, petty jealousies, infidelities, and general unhappiness behind the lush and luxurious lives of the very wealthiest women in New York society. It centers on Marcy Emerson, who moves to New York with her husband, a hedge-fund manager, and finds it difficult to fit into the snobbish society of the other wives in her social sphere. As the financial crisis develops, she discovers that her husband is having an affair, but she is far from alone in facing heartbreak. Everywhere she turns, disaster is unfolding despite the cushion of riches far beyond need.

Reviewers were delighted with *Hedge Fund Wives.* The reviewer for *S. Krishna's Books* said it was "a witty and insightful treatment of today's woman, as she explores the sacrifices they make, the bargains they strike, the rules they follow, and what happens when it all starts to fall apart." In her review for *Booklist,* Hilary Hatton called the book "glitzy and gossipy," and the reviewer for *Publishers Weekly* wrote that it was a "salacious, delightful tale of New York movers and shakers" and that Boncompagni wrote "with a keen eye and irresistible energy." Catherine Tuckwell declared in her review for *Blogcritics,* "*Hedge Fund Wives* is the perfect companion to a lazy Sunday afternoon."

BIOGRAPHICAL AND CRITICAL SOURCES:

PERIODICALS

Booklist, April 1, 2009, Hilary Hatton, review of *Hedge Fund Wives,* p. 18.

Financial Times, May 2, 2009, "Chic, Sleek and Discreet; What, Asks Tatiana Boncompagni, Does a Hedge Fund Wife Look Like These Days?," p. 7.

MPLS-St. Paul Magazine, June, 2009, Steve Marsh, "Just Asking," p. 42.

Private Asset Management, November 3, 2008, "Heidi Throws Spears at Hedgie Wives Book Battle."

Publishers Weekly, May 12, 2008, review of *Gilding Lily,* p. 31; March 23, 2009, review of *Hedge Fund Wives,* p. 48.

Star Tribune, October 9, 2008, "Lily's Author Dishes High Society Style; Watch Out Gossip Girl, There's Another Source about the Scandalous Lives of Manhattan's Elite—and Tatiana Boncompagni Has Minnesota Roots," p. 1.

ONLINE

Blogcritics.org, http://blogcritics.org/ (May 20, 2009), Catherine Tuckwell, review of *Hedge Fund Wives.*

Curled Up with a Good Book, http://www.curledup.com/ (August 1, 2009), Swapna Krishna, review of *Gilding Lily.*

Fantastic Fiction, http://www.fantasticfiction.co.uk/ (August 1, 2009), author profile.

HarperCollins, http://www.harpercollins.com/ (August 1, 2009), author profile.

New York Magazine—Daily Intel, http://nymag.com/ (September 16, 2008), Jessica Pressler, "Social-Lit Author Tatiana Boncompagni Thinks $1,000 Is a Little Much to Spend on a Haircut."

New York Observer, http://www.observer.com/ (September 2, 2008), Irina Aleksander, "Did Tatiana Boncompagni's Fancy Friends Bother to Read Her New Book before Throwing Her a Party? We Say: Probably Not!"

New York Post—Page Six, http://www.nypost.com/ (May 18, 2009), Richard Johnson, "Socialites Ditch Tatiana Boncompagni's Party."

S. Krishna's Books, http://www.skrishnasbooks.com/ (May 29, 2009), review of *Hedge Fund Wives.*

Tatiana Boncompagni Home Page, http://www.boncompagni.net (August 1, 2009), author profile.

W, http://www.wmagazine.com/ (May, 2009), Danielle Stein, "Tatiana's Page Turner."*

* * *

BOURGEAULT, Cynthia 1947-

PERSONAL: Born March 13, 1947. *Education:* Holds a Ph.D.

ADDRESSES: Office—Contemplative Society, P.O. Box 205, Cobble Hill, British Columbia V0R 1L0, Canada.

CAREER: Episcopal priest and writer. Contemplative Society, Victoria, British Columbia, Canada, principal teacher; Vancouver School of Theology, Vancouver, adjunct faculty member. Retreat and conference leader, teacher of prayer, writer. Member of Oblate of New Camaldoli Monastery, Big Sur, CA.

AWARDS, HONORS: Institute for Ecumenical and Cultural Research, St. John's Abbey, Collegeville, MN, fellow.

WRITINGS:

(Translator and adapter) *The Wakefield Resurrection Play: A Fourteenth-Century Play,* Seabury Press (New York, NY), 1974.

(Editor) *The Music of the Medieval Church Dramas,* by William L. Smoldon, Oxford University Press (New York, NY), 1980.

Love Is Stronger Than Death: The Mystical Union of Two Souls, Bell Tower (New York, NY), 1999.

Mystical Hope: Trusting in the Mercy of God, Cowley Publications (Cambridge, MA), 2001.

The Wisdom Way of Knowing: Reclaiming an Ancient Tradition to Awaken the Heart, foreword by Thomas Moore, Jossey-Bass (San Francisco, CA), 2003.

Centering Prayer and Inner Awakening, foreword by Thomas Keating, Cowley Publications (Cambridge, MA), 2004.

Chanting the Psalms: A Practical Guide with Instructional CD, New Seeds (Boston, MA), 2006.

The Wisdom Jesus: Transforming Heart and Mind—A New Perspective on Christ and His Message, New Seeds (Boston, MA), 2008.

SIDELIGHTS: Cynthia Bourgeault was born on March 13, 1947. She is a hermit priest, a writer, and a retreat leader with a doctorate in medieval studies and musicology. Her solitary retreat is on Eagle Island in Maine, and she teaches in Vancouver, British Columbia, at the Contemplative Society, an association that encourages contemplative prayer and meditation, located in Cobble Hill, British Columbia, as well as at Benedictine monasteries throughout Canada and the United States. She is also an adjunct faculty member at the Vancouver School of Theology. An Episcopal priest, she is an oblate of the New Camaldoli Monastery in Big Sur, California. She has studied "centering prayer," a method of silent prayer, with movement founder Father Thomas Keating and Christian Wisdom Tradition, a conceptual framework for the development of the spiritual life, with Father Bruno Barnhart of the Camaldoli Monastery.

Love Is Stronger Than Death: The Mystical Union of Two Souls is Bourgeault's account of the relationship she had with a seventy-year-old hermit monk. Seeking answers to the troubles in her life, Bourgeault was a resident in a retreat house in Colorado in 1990, attending a training workshop in centering prayer, when she met Brother Raphael Robin, with whom she engaged in a three-year conversation about spirituality and the nature of love. The bond between the two became so strong, that even when Raphael died, the conversation continued. Their philosophical discussions on the nature of love and death are at the heart of the book, as is the unfolding of the spiritual union the two of them felt.

Reviewers approved *Love Is Stronger Than Death.* Leroy Hommerding, in his review for *Library Journal,* called it a "well-written telling of an unconventional intimacy," and in her review for *Booklist,* Danise Hoover stated that "for those interested in the issues presented here it is an important find."

In *Mystical Hope: Trusting in the Mercy of God,* Bourgeault examines the subject of mercy. She looks at how it is explained in various linguistic versions of the Bible, recounts illustrative stories such as the voyage of St. Brendan and the trials of Job, and uses examples and quotes from theologians such as Thomas Merton, Meister Eckhart, Thomas Keating, and Sufi master Kabir Helminski, as well as making references to writers such as Leo Tolstoy and personal experiences that were revelatory. Her themes include the search for God's presence and the nature of hope.

In a review for *Christ Bhakta Darshan,* H. Talat Halman wrote, "Bourgeault's book can be a sweet, warm and fast read; at a deeper level, the 'ground of hope' and its evocation of the 'protecting nearness', it calls one repeatedly back to reflect on its meditations more deeply and contemplatively."

Chanting the Psalms: A Practical Guide with Instructional CD is just what the name implies. With a companion compact disc to illustrate techniques, the book is a guide to why and how to engage in chanting the Psalms, suggesting that the practice can help to integrate the spiritual and personal unconscious and awaken intuition.

Reviewers found *Chanting the Psalms* a useful publication. The reviewer for *Publishers Weekly* commented that is was "a helpful guide to those who seek to find a viable daily Christian practice," and the reviewer for *Sojurners* called it "interesting and practical." The reviewer for *Christian Century* declared, "With this book . . . Cynthia Bourgeault attempts to make this tradition more accessible."

The Wisdom Jesus: Transforming Heart and Mind—A New Perspective on Christ and His Message is Bourgeault's lesson on expanding the meaning of Jesus from the savior of mankind to a broader view of Jesus as the teacher who shows us how to encompass divine love. She encourages the reader to delve deeply into the Gospels of Matthew and Luke and provides guides to meditation and chanting to allow for this deeper understanding. The core of her thesis is the importance of turning from self-based analysis to becoming the receiver of divine abundance, giving new meaning to Jesus' death and resurrection. The reviewer for *Publishers Weekly* called *The Wisdom Jesus* "intriguing and engaging."

BIOGRAPHICAL AND CRITICAL SOURCES:

PERIODICALS

Booklist, August, 1999, Danise Hoover, review of *Love Is Stronger Than Death: The Mystical Union of Two Souls,* p. 1994.

Christian Century, August 7, 2007, review of *Chanting the Psalms: A Practical Guide with Instructional CD,* p. 41.
Library Journal, July, 1999, Leroy Hommerding, review of *Love Is Stronger Than Death,* p. 97.
Musical Quarterly, winter, 1983, Alejandro Enrique Planchart, review of *The Music of the Medieval Church Dramas,* p. 120.
National Post, June 3, 2000, review of *Love Is Stronger Than Death,* p. 5.
Parabola, May, 2000, review of *Love Is Stronger Than Death,* p. 134; summer, 2000, Richard Smoley, review of *Love Is Stronger Than Death,* p. 134; February, 2003, review of *Mystical Hope: Trusting in the Mercy of God,* p. 90; spring, 2003, Christopher Bamford, review of *Mystical Hope,* p. 90.
Publishers Weekly, September 13, 1999, review of *Love Is Stronger Than Death,* p. 79; September 25, 2006, review of *Chanting the Psalms,* p. 64; May 26, 2008, review of *The Wisdom Jesus: Transforming Heart and Mind—A New Perspective on Christ and His Message,* p. 57.
Sojourners Magazine, February, 2007, "Spiritual Circuitry," p. 38.

ONLINE

Beliefnet.com, http://www.beliefnet.com/ (August 1, 2009), author profile.
Christ Bhakta Darshan, http://www.christbhakta.com/ (May 13, 2008), H. Talat Halman, review of *Mystical Hope.*
Contemplative Society, http://www.contemplative.org/ (August 1, 2009), author profile.
EnlightenNext, http://www.enlightennext.org/ (August 1, 2009), author profile.*

* * *

BRONLEEWE, Matt 1973-
(Matthew Ryan Bronleewe)

PERSONAL: Born 1973, in Dallas, TX; married, 1994; wife's name Karin; children: George, Cole, and Grace. *Education:* Attended Greenville College. *Religion:* Christian. *Hobbies and other interests:* Reading, taste-testing good food, watching sports, art, architectural design, and science.

ADDRESSES: Home—Nashville, TN. *Agent*—Lydia Wills, Paradigm Literary Talent Agency, 360 Park Ave. S., 16th Fl., New York, NY, 10010. *E-mail*—matt@mattbronleewe.com.

CAREER: Novelist, musician. Jars of Clay, cofounder; independent producer and song writer; Infuze, blogger, 2005-07.

AWARDS, HONORS: Multiple Dove awards for music production.

WRITINGS:

Illuminated, Thomas Nelson (Nashville, TN), 2007.
House of Wolves, Thomas Nelson (Nashville, TN), 2008.

MUSIC

(With Michael W. Smith and Martin Smith) *Healing Rain: Piano, Vocal, Guitar* (score), Windswept, (Milwaukee, WI), 2004.
(With Chris Well and Jeremy Bose) *Mammoth City Messengers: Volume 1* (sound recording), ForeFront Records (Franklin, TN), 2004.

SIDELIGHTS: Matt Bronleewe, one of the founders of the Christian rock band Jars of Clay, was born in Dallas, Texas, in 1973 and raised on a wheat farm in Kansas. It was while he was studying music at Greenville College in Greenville, Illinois, that he, along with his friends Dan Haseltine, Charlie Lowell, and Stephen Mason, started Jars of Clay, named after a Biblical verse that acknowledges the power of God through Jesus Christ. Bronleewe participated in the group's demo album, *Frail,* which quickly gained the attention of the Christian label Essential Records, but although the other members accepted the company's recording offer, Bronleewe left the group to finish his music studies. Since then he has become successful as a song writer and music producer, working for many well-known Christian and country music singers and winning several Dove awards, given in recognition of achievements in Christian and gospel music. In 2007 Bronleewe began a new venture when he published his first suspense novel. He lives in Brentwood, Tennessee, with his wife, Karin, and their three children.

Illuminated introduces August Adams, a Biblical scholar and rare book dealer with a photographic memory. In this first of a series, Adams is attempting to find and decode hidden messages in the illuminations of the original Gutenberg Bible, messages that reveal the answers to certain mysteries. Two secret societies, the Orphans and the Order of the Dragon, have been fighting over possession of this rare book, which Adams has in his possession, since the 1400s. The feud has continued for hundreds of years and now puts Adams and his family in grave danger.

Reviewers thought *Illuminated* showed promise, although they were not in agreement about the quality of the writing. The reviewer for *Publishers Weekly* commented, "Readers may struggle to empathize with the cartoonish characters," but Catherine Newhouse, reviewing the book for *Campus Life's Ignite Your Faith* called it "a brilliant, entertaining story with compelling characters." In his review for *Blogcritics,* Warren Kelly wrote, "This debut novel shows a lot of promise, and I look forward to future books."

In *House of Wolves,* the rare book at the heart of the plot is the illuminated manuscript *The Gospels of Henry the Lion,* the key to the whereabouts of a twelfth-century collection of rare Christian relics. Stolen by the Nazis during World War II, it appears and disappears on the market, but no one knows where it really is. Where it really is, it turns out, is in Adams's briefcase. He thinks it is a fake but soon finds out differently when he and his family come under threat of death from the members of a brutal group known as the Black Vehm, who seek the book for themselves.

In her review of *House of Wolves* for the *Christian Suspense Zone,* Susan Sleeman said, "The writing is crisp with unique descriptions. The many action scenes are tight and fast moving, keeping the story racing forward."

When asked about his interest in writing, Bronleewe told *CA:* "I'd been writing songs for about a decade when I found myself yearning for another creative outlet. Music is storytelling in miniature, you have three minutes to provide a setting, characters, and a full story. In contrast, the idea of having 300 pages to tell a tale seemed like a dream. I've been having fun ever since. I grew up reading a lot of C.S. Lewis and J.R.R. Tolkien. I really enjoy modern writers like Michael Chabon and Jonathan Lethem. There are too many authors to list! I'm driven by a strong interest in history and its relation to the shaping of our future. And I love exploration of the problems and decisions that constantly reshape our lives."

In describing his writing process, Bronleewe said, "It starts with a small idea that eventually grows into a big idea. For instance, with my first book, *Illuminated,* it started with: What if I wrote a book about a book? The 'book' turned into the Gutenberg Bible, the rarest book on earth, and the story went on from there. Quirky, interesting characters are what drive me, though . . . getting in the head of someone completely different than me and throwing them into incredibly difficult situations! The most surprising thing I've learned about writing is that people would react so strongly to my books. I've been so humbled and touched by the kind messages I've received from people all over the world. To be able to bring joy to other people is an amazing feeling!"

Speaking of the effect he hopes his books will have, Bronleewe explained: "Life is messy. Life is hard. Life doesn't usually go the way we would like. My books give a taste of a world where the good guys win and evil is triumphed. And sometimes that's all we need . . . an escape from the ordinary into a place that blows our minds!"

BIOGRAPHICAL AND CRITICAL SOURCES:

PERIODICALS

Campus Life's Ignite Your Faith, June-July, 2008, Catherine Newhouse, review of *Illuminated,* p. 28; spring, 2009, review of *House of Wolves,* p. 23.

Publishers Weekly, June 30, 2008, review of *House of Wolves,* p. 163.

ONLINE

Blogcritics.org, http://blogcritics.org/ (September 7, 2007), Warren Kelly, review of *Illuminated.*

Christian Music Central, http://www.cmcentral.com/ (October 19, 2007), Kevan Breitinger, "Matt Bronleewe: Illuminated."

Christian Suspense Zone, http://www.thesuspensezone.com/ (August 1, 2009) Susan Sleeman, review of *House of Wolves.*

Fantastic Fiction, http://www.fantasticfiction.co.uk/ (August 1, 2009), author profile.

Illuminating Fiction, http://illuminatingfiction.blogspot.com/ (August 21, 2008), review of *House of Wolves.*

International Thriller Writers, http://www.thrillerwriters.org/ (August 1, 2009), Megan Kelley Hall, "Matt Bronleewe Makes the Leap from Music to Thrillers."

Matt Bronleewe Home Page, http://www.mattbronleewe.com (August 1, 2009).

MySpace.com, http://www.myspace.com/mattbronleewe (August 1, 2009), author's MySpace page.

Nelson Ministry Services, http://www.nelsonministryservices.com/ (August 1, 2009), short author profile.

Oasis Audio, http://oasisaudio.com/ (August 1, 2009), author profile.

Red Room, http://www.redroom.com/ (August 1, 2009), author profile.

TitleTrakk, http://www.titletrakk.com/ (August 1, 2009), C.J. Darlington, "Matt Bronleewe Interview."

* * *

BRONLEEWE, Matthew Ryan
See BRONLEEWE, Matt

* * *

BROWNING, Marie 1958-

PERSONAL: Born September 8, 1958. *Education:* Attended Camosun College and the University of Victoria.

CAREER: Writer and designer.

WRITINGS:

NONFICTION

Decoupage Projects II, Plaid Enterprises (Norcross, GA), 1995.

Beautiful Handmade Natural Soaps: Practical Ways to Make Hand-Milled Soap and Bath Essentials: Including Charming Ways to Wrap, Label & Present Your Creations as Gifts, Sterling Press (New York, NY), 1998.

Memory Gifts: Preserving Your Treasured Past in Special Ways, Sterling Press (New York, NY), 1999.

Handcrafted Journals, Albums, Scrapbooks & More, Sterling Press (New York, NY), 1999.

Making Glorious Gifts from Your Garden, Sterling Press (New York, NY), 1999.

Hand Decorating Paper, Sterling Press (New York, NY), 2000.

Melt & Pour Soapmaking, Sterling Press (New York, NY), 2000.

Crafting with Vellum & Parchment: New & Exciting Paper Projects, Sterling Press (New York, NY), 2001.

300 Handcrafted Soaps: Great Melt & Pour Projects, Sterling Press (New York, NY), 2002.

Jazzy Jars, Sterling Press (New York, NY), 2002.

Designer Soapmaking, Sterling Press (New York, NY), 2003.

Wonderful Wraps: Make Your Gifts Mean Even More, Sterling Press (New York, NY), 2003.

Inspired by the Garden, North Light Books (Cincinnati, OH), 2004.

Totally Cool Soapmaking for Kids, Sterling Press (New York, NY), 2004.

Totally Cool Polymer Clay Projects, Sterling Press (New York, NY), 2004.

Purse Pizzazz, Sterling Press (New York, NY), 2005.

Creative Craft Lettering Made Easy, North Light Books (Cincinnati, OH), 2005.

Really Jazzy Jars: Glorious Gift Ideas, Sterling Press (New York, NY), 2005.

Jazzy Gift Baskets: Making & Decorating Glorious Presents, Sterling Press (New York, NY), 2006.

Traditional Card Techniques, Sterling Press (New York, NY), 2006.

Casting for Crafters, Sterling Press (New York, NY), 2006.

Paper Mosaics in an Afternoon, Sterling Press (New York, NY), 2006.

Snazzy Jars: Glorious Gift Ideas, Sterling Press (New York, NY), 2006.

Metal Crafting Workshop, Sterling Press (New York, NY), 2006.

Paper Crafts Workshop: A Beginner's Guide to Techniques & Projects, Sterling Press (New York, NY), 2007.

New Concepts in Paper Quilling: Techniques for Cards and Gifts, Sterling Press (New York, NY), 2008.

Creative Collage: Making Memories in Mixed Media, Sterling Press (New York, NY), 2008.

Creative Photo Collage, Sterling Press (New York, NY), 2008.

SIDELIGHTS: Marie Browning is an accomplished designer and crafts author. In an article detailing Browning's creative involvement with the Purple Tree company, a *CNW Group* contributor observed, "Browning is the best-selling author of numerous craft books, with over a half a million books in print, as well as a creative designer for magazines and manufacturers. Her professional expertise and craft industry experience, coupled with her encouraging way of making anyone feel like they can be creative, makes Marie . . . a true asset." Additionally, in the preface to an interview with Browning, a *Vintage Image Craft* Web site contributor wrote, "Browning stands out among craft authors internationally. Her authoring output is one clear distinction—thirty-two books and counting. Her books are produced by the aptly named "Prolific Impressions" team. Also impressive is her creative merging of computer technology, in the form of digital imagery, with traditional craft techniques." Browning has covered such topics as soap making, scrapbooking, photography, decoupage, gift making, gift wrapping, garden art, children's projects, decorative accessories, gift baskets, casting, card making, mosaics, quilting, metalworking, collages, and mixed media projects. In her interview for the *Vintage Image Craft* Web site, Browning discussed her creative process and stated, "When working on a book I look at everything around me to help motivate and inspire the designs. It helps being on the CHA Designers Trend Team, and reporting on lifestyle trends and their effects on the creative industry. I look at everything differently in terms of the focus of the book, and that generates multiple options. To find a few ideas that work, I need to try a lot that don't. It's a pure numbers game. I keep a simple notebook for each book and write down ideas, paste in clippings, doodle and sketch out ideas and add anything else that inspires me. Upon rereading my notes I discover 90% of the ideas are daft, but what's important are the ten percent that are brilliant!"

In *Memory Gifts: Preserving Your Treasured Past in Special Ways,* Browning's creative diversity is evident in her selection of various projects intended to preserve sentimental or significant moments in one's life. In a mixed-media technique called memory crafting, Browning reveals the objects which lend themselves to artistic representations of life moments when used creatively, such as clothing, office supplies, naturally occurring materials, and calendars. Browning provides illustrations, a materials list, and incrementally explained instructions which render the projects in detailed sections. Moreover, the text contains over fifty individual projects one can choose from in order to create a personal piece of memorabilia.

Browning told the *Vintage Image Craft* Web site contributor, "I love making coasters, trays, and place mats with vintage photographs and images. I coat them with Envirotex Lite to finish them so they are practical and easy to clean. I use them everyday!" In her book, *Creative Collage: Making Memories in Mixed Media,* Browning explores the adaptation of photographs and other paper products in order to create collages. A collage, essentially an incorporation of various individual pieces in order to form a whole work with a discernable motif or theme, can include a range of textures, colors, and different-sized materials. Therefore, the technique used is important to the quality of the piece and the success of the aesthetic appeal. Constance Ashmore Fairchild, in a review for *Library Journal,* noted that *Creative Collage* emphasizes "three-dimensional projects in addition to flat items." The text covers such necessary knowledge as materials choices as well as the history of the craft and major design elements that accord with the practice. Tina Coleman, in an article for *Booklist,* commented on the topical breadth and claimed the text "is sure to inspire and encourage crafters of every stripe and experience level."

Likewise, Browning's subsequent publication, *Creative Photo Collage,* details the materials, methods, and preservation available in order to transform captured moments into an artistic form. Using photographs as her primary media, Browning illustrates how one can simultaneously preserve and display recorded memories. Alternatively, as *Library Journal* contributor Constance Ashmore Fairchild noted, Browning reveals the ease with which one can obtain photographs with the use of digital tools, so the project need not risk valuable materials in the process of experimentation. The text discusses image transfer, decoupage, and gifting in addition to the construction of collages. Similarly, *New Concepts in Paper Quilling: Techniques for Cards and Gifts* discusses the use of paper in order to create sentimental or personal objects. Paper quilling is a centuries old technique wherein one uses lengths of shaped paper in order to create images of objects. Browning makes clear the steps necessary for the successful implementation of the technique in card making and other creative projects. Quilling offers the ability to add a three-dimensional aspect to an otherwise two- dimensional flat object. In this text, Browning showcases the variety of quilling patterns, from beginning to experienced levels of design, and their application in greeting cards, gift wrapping, and merely decorative art. Browning's *Inspired by the Garden* also seeks to present projects in which objects are constructed with both detail and creativity. Using aesthetics gathered from the natural world, Browning shows how one can echo nature in manufactured items. *Booklist* contributor Whitney Scott acknowledged Browning's "well-illustrated approach" to explaining paint techniques such as washes and glazing. Scott also stated, "The projects include clocks, trays, and even a spice bin," and the text comes "complete with a summary on needed supplies."

Browning's skill with crafting materials also extends into the realm of metal working. In *Metal Crafting Workshop,* Browning exposes the opportunities available when one employs metal as an artistic medium. Browning introduces the necessary equipment, specific materials, and introductory techniques of metal crafting, including the use of steel, tin, aluminum, and brass. Jennifer Palmer, in a review for *Booklist,* reported that Browning's "encouraging introduction to metal crafting" displays the material's enhancement potential and "quickly dispels any fear the inexperienced metal crafter may have." Browning also makes clear the almost limitless possibilities that metal affords the hobbyist. *Metal Crafting Workshop* offers information regarding making candle holders, accessories, sculpture, and exterior design pieces.

BIOGRAPHICAL AND CRITICAL SOURCES:

PERIODICALS

Booklist, December 1, 1998, Barbara Jacobs, review of *Beautiful Handmade Natural Soaps: Practical Ways to Make Hand-Milled Soap and Bath Essentials: Including Charming Ways to Wrap, Label & Present Your Creations as Gifts,* p. 644; April 1, 2000, Barbara Jacobs, review of *Making Glorious Gifts from Your Garden,* p. 1424; February 15, 2003, Barbara Jacobs, review of *Jazzy Jars,* p. 1030; February 1, 2004, Whitney Scott, review of *Inspired by the Garden,* p. 941; August 1, 2004, Carolyn Phelan, review of *Totally Cool Soapmaking for Kids,* p. 1921; November 1, 2006, Jennifer Palmer, review of *Metal Crafting Workshop,* p. 15; April 15, 2008, Tina Coleman, review of *Creative Collage: Making Memories in Mixed Media,* p. 18.

CNW Group, October 19, 2005, "Canada's Top Creative Experts, Marie Browning and Sue Warden, Launch Purple Tree in Canada; Canadian Women Reconnect with Each Other and Their Creativity at Purple Tree Events."

Crafts 'n Things, February 1, 2002, review of *Crafting with Vellum & Parchment: New & Exciting Paper Projects,* p. 37; February 1, 2003, review of *Really Jazzy Jars: Glorious Gift Ideas,* p. 73; April 1, 2009, review of *Creative Collage,* p. 93.

Library Journal, June 15, 2000, Constance Ashmore Fairchild, review of *Making Glorious Gifts from Your Garden,* p. 78; October 15, 2000, Constance Fairchild, review of *Handcrafted Journals, Albums, Scrapbooks & More,* p. 66; October 15, 2000, review of *Handcrafted Journals, Albums, Scrapbooks & More,* p. 66; June 15, 2001, Constance Ashmore Fairchild, review of *Hand Decorating Paper,* p. 70; February 15, 2002, Constance Ashmore Fairchild, review of *Melt & Pour Soapmaking,* p. 141; October 15, 2002, Constance Fairchild, review of *300 Handcrafted Soaps: Great Melt & Pour Projects,* p. 70; June 15, 2004, Connie Ashmore Fairchild, review of *Really Jazzy Jars,* p. 68; October 15, 2005, Constance Ashmore Fairchild, review of *Purse Pizzazz,* p. 54; October 15, 2006, Constance Ashmore Fairchild, review of *Casting for Crafters,* p. 60; February 15, 2007, Constance Ashmore Fairchild, review of *Metal Crafting Workshop,* p. 120; February 15, 2008, Constance Ashmore, review of *Paper Crafts Workshop: A Beginner's Guide to Techniques & Projects,* p. 102; June 15, 2008, Constance Ashmore Fairchild, review of *Creative Collage,* p. 66; February 15, 2009, Constance Ashmore Fairchild, review of *Creative Photo Collage,* p. 102.

ONLINE

About.com Web site, http://candleandsoap.about.com/ (August 3, 2009), review of *300 Handcrafted Soaps.*

Marie Browning Creates Web site, http://www.mariebrowning.com (August 3, 2009).

Vintage Image Craft Web site, http://www.vintageimagecraft.com/ (August 3, 2009), "Interview with Marie Browning: 'It's Definitely Genetic . . . '."*

* * *

BRUCE, Alison 1966-

PERSONAL: Born 1966, in Surrey, England; married (a musician); children: Lana and Dean. *Education:* College graduate.

ADDRESSES: Home—Cambridge, England.

CAREER: Writer.

WRITINGS:

Cambridgeshire Murders, History Press (Stroud, Gloucestershire, England), 2005.

Cambridge Blue, SohoConstable (New York, NY), 2009.

Billington: Victorian Executioner, History Press (Stroud, Gloucestershire, England), 2009.

SIDELIGHTS: Alison Bruce was born in Surrey, England, in 1966. She lives in Cambridge, England, with her husband, a musician, and her two children.

Bruce's mystery *Cambridge Blue* has as its protagonist twenty-five-year-old Gary Goodhew, the youngest person to be promoted to Detective Constable in the history of Cambridge's Parkside Station. This is his first murder investigation, and it involves an eccentric local family. He begins his investigation according to the book, but he soon learns that everyone, including his own sister, is lying to him. He decides he must put the rules aside and rely on his own intuition to solve a puzzle that gets trickier as the body count increases. As he comes closer to solving the murders, he is surprised, and not entirely pleased, by his conclusions.

Reviews were hesitantly positive. The reviewer for *Publishers Weekly* called *Cambridge Blue* an "assured debut," and the reviewer for *Kirkus Reviews* said it was "a pleasingly different police procedural." In the review for *Mysterious Reviews* the commentator called the novel "a promising start to this series. The plot, basically a police procedural, has the requisite twists and turns, false leads and blind alleys, but is able to maintain a steady, purposeful pace throughout."

BIOGRAPHICAL AND CRITICAL SOURCES:

PERIODICALS

Kirkus Reviews, October 15, 2008, review of *Cambridge Blue.*

Publishers Weekly, November 17, 2008, review of *Cambridge Blue,* p. 46.

ONLINE

Crimespace, http://crimespace.ning.com/ (August 1, 2009), author profile.

Fantastic Fiction, http://www.fantasticfiction.co.uk/ (August 1, 2009), short author profile.

MySpace, http://www.myspace.com/cambridgedetective (August 1, 2009), author's MySpace page.

Mysterious Reviews, http://www.mysteriousreviews.com/ (August 1, 2009), review of *Cambridge Blue.**

* * *

BUDMAN, Mark 1950(?)-

PERSONAL: Born c. 1950, in the Soviet Union; immigrated to United States, 1980; married; children: two. *Ethnicity:* Russian. *Hobbies and other interests:* Traveling.

ADDRESSES: Home—New York. *Agent*—Waxman Literary Agency, 80 5th Ave., Ste. 1101, New York, NY 10011.

CAREER: Writer and editor. *Vestal Review,* Vestal, NY, publisher and editor, 2000—; *Web Del Sol* online literary journal, interview editor.

AWARDS, HONORS: Grant, Broome County Art Council, 2005.

WRITINGS:

(Editor, with Tom Hazuka) *You Have Time for This: Contemporary American Short-Short Stories,* Ooligan Press (Portland, OR), 2006.

My Life at First Try: A Novel, Counterpoint (Berkeley, CA), 2008.

Contributor to *Flash Fiction Forward: 80 Very Short Stories,* edited by Robert Shapard and James Thomas, W.W. Norton, 2006. Fiction and poetry published in *Mississippi Review, Virginia Quarterly, Exquisite Corpse, Iowa Review, McSweeney's, Cafe Irreal, Another Chicago, Bloomsbury Review, Connecticut Review* and *Stone Canoe.*

SIDELIGHTS: Mark Budman defines flash fiction as both an editor and a writer. Budman is the creator and editor of *Vestal Review,* a magazine that publishes stories under five hundred words. In an interview with Wayne Yang for the blog *Eight Diagrams,* Budman said flash fiction "brings to mind an image of a bolt of lightning, the sound of thunder." Budman told Yang that he sees flash fiction as an extension of today's "instant gratification" culture.

His book *My Life at First Try: A Novel* employs flash fiction to great results; it was called "blazingly fast and funny" by a reviewer for *Publishers Weekly.* It is a semiautobiographical story of immigration and sexual adolescence. Budman grew up in the post-Stalin Soviet Union—he was a toddler when Joseph Stalin died. He immigrated to the United States with his wife in 1980; today they live with their two daughters in upstate New York. His novel's main character is a man named Alex whose childhood infatuation with his American cousin feeds an urge to immigrate. When he finally moves with his wife he finds America is less the country he dreamed of and more the country he makes do with. Identity is never far from the center of the story. "I am a hereditary immigrant. My grandparents immigrated twice without moving out of their house," the narrator quips over the ever-changing borders in Central and Eastern Europe.

That style of writing is what reviewer Marshall Jon Fisher of the San Francisco Chronicle found compelling, but he was also troubled over the pacing. He wrote that multiple themes in the book went unexplored even after their import had been established, "but perhaps that's the point of the flash novel. Life zips by, a cascade of events that we can barely assimilate." Most reviewers had a similarly mixed reaction to the content and the writing. Ron Charles of the *Washington Post* reflected that "Mark Budman has a good ear for sexual frustration and bittersweet comedy, too. The early stories about Alex's buoyant adolescence are delightful, but later chapters about working for a chemical plant or raising his family are sometimes prosaic, more like anecdotes, what might pass for a pleasant newspaper column." Charles also found Alex to be an endearing narrator and said, "This is a novel you don't want to stop reading." Overall, reviewers found the book to be sharp, buoyant, and funny. In an interview for the blog *TaniaWrites,* Tania Hershman called *My Life at First Try* "hilarious" and "eye-opening," adding that "it's tough not to have Alex's buoyant energy rub off on the reader."

BIOGRAPHICAL AND CRITICAL SOURCES:

PERIODICALS

Booklist, November 1, 2008, Leah Strauss, review of *My Life at First Try: A Novel,* p. 24.

Kirkus Reviews, October 15, 2008, review of *My Life at First Try.*

Library Journal, September 15, 2008, David A. Berona, review of *My Life at First Try,* p. 43.

Publishers Weekly, September 1, 2008, review of *My Life at First Try,* p. 33.

ONLINE

Christiancrumlish.com, http://christiancrumlish.com/ezone/ (July 16, 2009), author biography.

Eight Diagrams Web log, http://wayneyang.wordpress.com/ (February 22, 2006), Wayne Yang, "Interview with Mark Budman of Vestal Review."

Official Mark Budman Web site, http://markbudman.net (June 2, 2009).

Red Room, http://www.redroom.com/ (February, 2009), author biography.

San Francisco Chronicle Online, http://www.sfgate.com/ (December 14, 2008), Jon Marshall Fisher, review of *My Life at First Try.*

TaniaWrites Web log, http://titaniawrites.blogspot.com/ (December 8, 2008), Tania Hershman, "Author Interview: Mark Budman."

Time Out Chicago, http://chicago.timeout.com/ (January 15, 2009), Jonathan Messinger, review of *My Life at First Try.*

Virginia Quarterly Review Online, http://www.vqronline.org/ (July 16, 2009), author biography.

Washington Post Online, http://www.washingtonpost.com/ (December 12, 2008), Ron Charles, "Young and Restless: Young Guys Worry about Sex in These Two Coming-of-Age Novels from India and Russia," review of *My Life at First Try.**

* * *

BURTON, Fred

PERSONAL: Male.

CAREER: Writer and former Diplomatic Security Service agent. Texas Border Security Council member, 2007.

WRITINGS:

Ghost: Confessions of a Counterterrorism Agent, Random House (New York, NY), 2008.

SIDELIGHTS: Fred Burton, a former U.S. Diplomatic Security Service (DSS) agent, released his debut autobiographical text, *Ghost: Confessions of a Counterterrorism Agent,* in 2008. The text chronicles Burton's experiences working on a diplomatic security detail in foreign, sometimes hostile, territories. An *On What Grounds?* Web site contributor wrote, "A pseudo spy thriller, the book provides a bit of insight into the DSS, or the Defense Security Service, that Burton had worked for, as well as the inter working of many of the governments bureaucratic processes surrounding the handling of terrorism within the U.S. government." Beginning with his education at the DSS training academy in 1985 when counterterrorism was a burgeoning field in the security landscape. Burton, a former Maryland police officer, tells of how he, along with one other classmate, was recruited into the counterterrorism division of the DSS at the conclusion of their training. Maintaining "a seemingly constant high stress level throughout the book, Burton is always hunting down known terrorists, trying to prevent future terror attacks," claimed the *On What Grounds?* contributor. With a high-level security clearance and an understanding of not only the current threats to the United States but also past events in which surveillance and reconnoitering were employed in an attempt to thwart U.S. interests, Burton describes significant moments in the history of counterterrorism. Within the first twenty pages, the reader gains an understanding of the security climate in which Burton operated. Moreover, Burton reveals details regarding DSS policy, such as dress code and communications techniques.

Laura Axelrod, in a review for the *Gasp!* Web site, found, "Burton makes certain that readers identify with the victims of terrorist attacks. It will be difficult to forget the sad details of the attacks, along with the sociopathic mentality of the terrorists." Throughout the text, Burton discusses the effects of terrorist activities and how these senseless acts of violence linger in the American psyche. A *Kirkus Reviews* contributor remarked that "Burton is critical of officials in both political parties for not being sufficiently proactive, though he does not spend enough time explaining the constraints he ran up against." Burton relies upon general descriptions in order to convey his sentiments, and he does not provide the complete identities of several names mentioned, thus maintaining a degree of confidentiality. *Booklist* contributor David Pitt noted Burton's objectivity and stated that *Ghost* is "a fascinating look at what counterterrorism really means on a day-to-day level."

BIOGRAPHICAL AND CRITICAL SOURCES:

PERIODICALS

Booklist, May 15, 2008, David Pitt, review of *Ghost: Confessions of a Counterterrorism Agent,* p. 9.

Kirkus Reviews, May 1, 2008, review of *Ghost.*

Risk Management, July 1, 2008, Pearl Gabel, review of *Ghost,* p. 23.

Security Management, February 1, 2009, Britt Mallow, review of *Ghost,* p. 73.

ONLINE

Gasp!, http://www.gaspjournal.com/ (June 8, 2009), Laura Axelrod, review of *Ghost.*

On What Grounds?, http://onwhatgrounds.org/ (June 25, 2009), review of *Ghost.*

PoliceOne.com, http://www.policeone.com/ (August 6, 2009), author profile.

Random House Web site, http://www.randomhouse.com/ (August 6, 2009), author profile.*

* * *

BUSCH, Peter 1968-

PERSONAL: Born March 22, 1968. *Education:* Universitat Bochum, B.A., 1994; London School of Economics, M.A., 1994, Ph.D., 2000; University of Dortmund, M.A., 1996.

CAREER: Zweites Deutsches Fernsehen (ZDF), Germany, senior broadcast journalist; King's College London, London, England, department of war studies, senior lecturer, 2004—. Guest lecturer in history and journalism at the Free University of Berlin, University of Erfurt, London School of Economics, and University of Hanover.

WRITINGS:

All the Way with JFK: Britain, the U.S., and the Vietnam War, Oxford University Press (New York, NY), 2003.

Also contributor to books, including *Cold War Britain, 1945-1964,* edited by Michael Hopkins, Michael Kandiah and Gillian Staerck, Palgrave, 2002. Contributed to periodicals including the *Journal of Strategic Studies* and *Cold War History.*

SIDELIGHTS: Peter Busch is a German television journalist and a senior lecturer in the department of war studies at King's College in London, England. In Busch's first major academic text, *All the Way with JFK: Britain, the U.S., and the Vietnam War,* he turns attention away from the United States and instead considers Great Britain's role in the duration and violence of the Vietnam War. He also considers the country's relationship with the United States during that time. Reviewer Michael Hopkins in *Contemporary Review* called Busch's book "impressive and largely convincing reappraisal that compels us to adopt a more nuanced understanding of British attitudes to Vietnam in the early 1960s."

In *All the Way with JFK,* Busch uses historical documents to support his thesis that Britain was interested in maintaining colonial influence in Southeast Asia. According to Busch, that interest influenced the British government's decision not to pursue peace negotiations with the National Liberation Front in Vietnam. Busch examines Britain's role in the South East Asia Treaty Organization and the 1954 Geneva Conference on Indochina. He pays particular attention to the British Advisory Mission to Vietnam (BRIAM), which pushed British military leader Sir Robert Thompson to the forefront of the U.S. counterinsurgency. In the *Journal of Southeast Asian Studies,* reviewer Nicholas B. Cullather said Busch "has given us a close look at Thompson and the work of his British Advisory Mission to Vietnam (BRIAM), dispatched to advise Saigon on anti-guerrilla techniques used in the Malayan insurgency." In *All the Way with JFK,* Busch offers a glimpse of Thompson's approach to leadership and the insurgency with this passage: "SUCCESS leads to KILLS, . . . KILLS to CONFIDENCE, CONFIDENCE to better INTELLIGENCE and INTELLIGENCE to greater SUCCESSES." Peter J. Ling wrote in a review in *American Studies Online* that "the British not only opposed negotiations but strengthened the view that military force was the only way to stop the dominos toppling in Indo-China."

While reviewers agreed overall that Busch's book is insightful, *Contemporary Review* contributor Michael Hopkins wrote that Busch "exaggerates the possibilities for British influence and does not explore the activities of the one figure, the British Ambassador in Washington, 1961-65, David Ormsby Gore, who might have been able to pursue a policy of persuasion." Nonetheless, the book is generally considered a success and a useful tool for college students. Reviewer Judith R. Johnson wrote in *History: Review of New Books,* that *All the Way with JFK* is an "extremely well-written and extensively researched study."

BIOGRAPHICAL AND CRITICAL SOURCES:

BOOKS

Busch, Peter, *All the Way with JFK: Britain, the U.S., and the Vietnam War,* Oxford University Press (New York, NY), 2003.

PERIODICALS

American Historical Review, February 1, 2004, Howard Jones, review of *All the Way with JFK,* p. 160.

Contemporary Review, September 1, 2003, Michael F. Hopkins, "Britain, America and Vietnam," review of *All the Way with JFK,* p. 177.

Diplomatic History, January 1, 2005, Kevin Boyle, "With Friends Like These," p. 215.

English Historical Review, November 1, 2004, Kevin Ruane, review of *All the Way with JFK,* p. 1475.

History: Review of New Books, September 22, 2003, Judith R. Johnson, review of *All the Way with JFK,* p. 14.

International Affairs, July 1, 2003, Matthew Jones, review of *All the Way with JFK,* p. 907.

International History Review, September 1, 2004, Andrew Preston, review of *All the Way with JFK,* p. 687.

Journal of American History, June 1, 2004, Mitchell B. Lerner, review of *All the Way with JFK,* p. 324.

Journal of Military History, October 1, 2003, Lawrence Freedman, review of *All the Way with JFK,* p. 1340.

Journal of Modern History, September 1, 2006, "Anglo-American Relations and Cold War Oil: Crisis in Iran," p. 714.

Journal of Southeast Asian Studies, October 1, 2003, Nicholas B. Cullather, review of *All the Way with JFK,* p. 582.

Political Quarterly, October 1, 2003, review of *All the Way with JFK.*

ONLINE

American Studies Online, http://www.americansc.org.uk/ (November 14, 2005), Peter J. Ling, review of *All the Way with JFK.*

King's College London Web site, https://www.kcl.ac.uk/ (April 2, 2009), author biography.

Times Higher Education Online, http://www.timeshighereducation.co.uk/ (June 13, 2003), Rhodri Jeffreys-Jones, "Old Imperialists Egged on the New," review of *All the Way with JFK.**

* * *

BYRNE, Frank J. 1968-

PERSONAL: Born October 2, 1968. *Education:* Kent State University, B.A.; University of Georgia, M.A., 1994; Ohio State University, Ph.D., 2000.

ADDRESSES: Office—History Department, State University of New York, Oswego, NY 13126-3599. *E-mail*—fbyrne@oswego.edu.

CAREER: Writer and educator. State University of New York, Oswego, associate professor of history, 2001—.

WRITINGS:

Becoming Bourgeois: Merchant Culture in the South, 1820-1865, University Press of Kentucky (Lexington, KY), 2006.

SIDELIGHTS: Frank J. Byrne, a graduate of the University of Georgia and Ohio State University, has served as an associate professor of history at the State University of New York in Oswego since 2001. In 2006, Byrne released *Becoming Bourgeois: Merchant Culture in the South, 1820-1865.* The text chronicles the rising merchant class within the South during the nineteenth century. The merchants responded to consumerist demands, thus settling into a niche economic market. This middle class was perpetuated by the constant demand for goods and services in the South prior to the Civil War. Byrne also calls attention to the function of the merchants in their respective community. Whether a shopkeeper or a grocer, these middle-class small business owners provided a space for social interaction and public patronage. In an article for the *Civil War Book Review,* Aaron W. Marrs wrote, "Byrne illustrates the complex interactions that took place in stores, as well as the repercussions that these events had on merchants as members of a community. In so doing, Byrne effectively creates a three-dimensional image of these merchants; they are not simply economic actors." The text informs that although these merchants brought economy to townships, they were viewed with suspicion and sometimes scorn as they did not fit into the conventional social hierarchy. Merchants as well as genteel land owners relied on slaves for labor services, so the upper class viewed the merchants with distrust because they were redefining the balance of power. Moreover, the merchants often provided the slaves with goods, which undermined genteel traditions of nonaffiliation.

Marrs also noted, "Byrne's fascinating chapter on the antebellum merchant family benefits from his mining a large number of personal papers to uncover material on diverse topics such as courtship, gender relations within marriage, and child-rearing." This insight into family life illustrates how the merchant class maintained their status, established a certain set of values, and facilitated social stability. Scott P. Marler, in a review for the *Journal of Southern History,* pointed out that Byrne "convincingly describes the profound ambivalences that conditioned how rural and small-town shopkeepers were regarded by their neighbors, and by devoting half of the book's six chapters to the Civil War years, Byrne proves especially skillful at detailing the many unique problems that store-owning families faced under the pressures of secession, war, and a new government."

BIOGRAPHICAL AND CRITICAL SOURCES:

PERIODICALS

American Historical Review, October 1, 2007, Beth English, review of *Becoming Bourgeois: Merchant Culture in the South, 1820-1865,* p. 1166.

American Studies, March 22, 2007, Paul D. Escott, review of *Becoming Bourgeois,* p. 148.

Choice: Current Reviews for Academic Libraries, April 1, 2007, P.D. Travis, review of *Becoming Bourgeois,* p. 1397.

Journal of Southern History, May 1, 2008, Scott P. Marler, review of *Becoming Bourgeois,* p. 449.

Journal of the Early Republic, September 22, 2007, Brian P. Luskey, review of *Becoming Bourgeois,* p. 526.

Virginia Magazine of History and Biography, September 22, 2008, L. Diane Barnes, review of *Becoming Bourgeois,* p. 420.

ONLINE

Civil War Book Review Online, http://www.lib.lsu.edu/ (August 5, 2009), Aaron W. Marrs, review of *Becoming Bourgeois.*

SUNY Oswego History Department Web site, http://www.oswego.edu/ (August 5, 2009), faculty profile.

University Press of Kentucky Web site, http://www.kentuckypress.com/ (August 5, 2009), author profile.*

C

CAINE, Alex

PERSONAL: Male.

CAREER: Writer, speaker and consultant. Formerly worked as a contract agent hired by the Canadian government and others to infiltrate criminal and terrorist organizations. *Military service:* Served in the Vietnam War.

WRITINGS:

Befriend and Betray: Infiltrating the Hells Angels, Bandidos and Other Criminal Brotherhoods, Random House Canada (Toronto, Ontario, Canada), 2008, Thomas Dunne Books/St. Martin's Press (New York, NY), 2009.

The Fat Mexican: The Bloody Rise of the Bandidos Motorcycle Club, Random House Canada (Toronto, Ontario, Canada), 2009.

SIDELIGHTS: Alex Caine formerly worked as a contractor who hired himself out to Canadian police and other police forces around the world to infiltrate criminal and terrorist groups. His first book, *Befriend and Betray: Infiltrating the Hells Angels, Bandidos and Other Criminal Brotherhoods,* received favorable reviews. For example, *Examiner* Web site contributor Carly Milne observed: "Caine takes dancing with the devil to a whole other realm," adding later in the same review: "Simply put, it's compelling stuff."

Caine recounts his many exploits as a for-hire undercover agent. The author notes that he began his career as the result of his own troubles with the law. Growing up in a working-class family, Caine did a tour of duty in the Vietnam War and then, after returning to the United States, was arrested for possessing marijuana. After being convicted and spending time in prison, the author found himself becoming a contract agent, referred to as a "kite." He performed this job for nearly the next twenty-five years as he infiltrated various groups, from motorcycle gains and the Klu Klux Klan to Asian Triads and Russian mobsters.

The author recounts many of the operations he was involved with as he assumes numerous identities and personas that he would inhabit for several months to several years at a time. Often he would pretend to be one of the criminal underworld's standard inhabitants, such as a drug dealer, gunrunner, and even a hit man. Other times he would create a more complex identity such as an insurance underwriter who wanted to launder money or an importer of goods that also included sex slaves and drugs. In the process of recounting the cases he was involved with, the author wonders whether or not justice was always served. Caine also examines the toll that such an undercover life takes on someone. He writes in the book's preface: "It had been lucrative. It had been exciting. It had been a job. I may have been doing the work of good, but what had it left me with? Or more exactly, what had it left of me?" For example, the author writes of his two broken marriages and estrangement from his sisters after an investigation he was involved in implicated a family member.

Matthew L. Moffett, writing for *School Library Journal,* called *Befriend and Betray* "immediately enticing and gripping all the way through." Noting that the author "remains resolutely unromantic about his targets and has no problem doing exactly what the book's title directs," a *Kirkus Reviews* contributor added that the book is "a refreshingly open and clearheaded account of the dirty side of law enforcement."

BIOGRAPHICAL AND CRITICAL SOURCES:

BOOKS

Caine, Alex, *Befriend and Betray: Infiltrating the Hells Angels, Bandidos and Other Criminal Brotherhoods,* Thomas Dunne Books/St. Martin's Press (New York, NY), 2009.

PERIODICALS

Kirkus Reviews, December 1, 2008, review of *Befriend and Betray.*

Publishers Weekly, November 10, 2008, review of *Befriend and Betray,* p. 42.

School Library Journal, July, 2009, Matthew L. Moffett, review of *Befriend and Betray,* p. 110.

ONLINE

Examiner, http://www.examiner.com/ (March 8, 2009), Carly Milne, "Entertain Me: *Befriend and Betray* by Alex Caine."

MysteryBooks.ca, http://www.mysterybooks.ca/ (August 9, 2009), brief profile of author.

Random House Web site, Random House, http://www.randomhouse.ca/ (August 9, 2009), brief profile of author.*

* * *

CAMPBELL, Glynnis Talken
See McKERRIGAN, Sarah

* * *

CANEDY, Dana

PERSONAL: Ethnicity: African American. *Education:* University of Kentucky, B.A., 1960.

ADDRESSES: Home—New York, NY. *Office*—New York Times, 620 8th Ave., New York, NY 10018. *E-mail*—ajournalforjordan@gmail.com.

CAREER: Writer and journalist. *Plain Dealer,* Cleveland, OH, reporter, 1988-96; *New York Times,* New York, NY, reporter and Miami, FL, bureau chief, 1996-2003, day editor for the national desk, 2003—.

AWARDS, HONORS: Pulitzer Prize, 2000.

WRITINGS:

A Journal for Jordan: A Story of Love and Honor, Crown Press (New York, NY), 2008.

SIDELIGHTS: Dana Canedy is a Pulitzer-Prize-winning author and a graduate of the University of Kentucky. Canedy is a frequent contributor to the *New York Times* and has also worked for the Cleveland, Ohio, *Plain Dealer.* In 2008 Canedy released *A Journal for Jordan: A Story of Love and Honor* via Crown Press. The text tells the story of Canedy's fiancé, First Sergeant Charles Monroe King, who died as the result of the detonation of an improvised explosive device (I.E.D.). King's message to his family and the circumstances of his death become the focal point of the biographical narrative.

A *Kirkus Reviews* contributor claimed, "In spare, poignant prose, *New York Times* assistant national news editor Canedy bares the human cost of the Iraq war." The story is both personal and familiar, as many survivors experience emotions similar to those that Canedy describes. In a reader-response, question-and-answer session for the *New York Times,* Canedy explained why she felt comfortable sharing her story with the public and stated, "I can tell our story because it honors Charles to do so. He was a remarkable man, and I am proud to let the world know about him. I am a grieving partner and mother first, but I am also a journalist. That is the other reason I am able to tell our story. So many people think of American military men and women in the collective, but I wanted to put a face and a life to the story of at least one brave soldier serving in Iraq."

In the narrative Canedy relates passages of King's journal, which he kept throughout his military duty. King "addressed all the entries to their son, Jordan, born in New York City in March 2006 while his father helped lead the 105 men of Charlie Company in an area called the Triangle of Death, thirty miles south of Baghdad," wrote *Plain Dealer* contributor Kristin Ohlson. King recorded his history with Canedy as well as his ruminations regarding his military duties. Thus, the story fluctuates between Canedy's telling of events and passages from King's journal. Ohlson wrote that "Canedy used her skills as a reporter to dig beneath the official story of King's death." What Canedy discovered through her investigative research is as emotional as the passages from King's journal. For example, King relates how he was pressured into accepting the patrol duty in which he was killed and that he was already aware of the deadly I.E.D. activity in the region of his patrol. Christina Eng, in a review for the *San Francisco Chronicle,* felt, "By writing about King, the author gives her son a lasting, positive impression of his father. She affords a decorated career soldier the dignity and respect he deserves and honors the remarkable commitments he made to his country and colleagues." Canedy reveals the self-sacrifice and bravery that King exhibited as a U.S. Army soldier. Eng also observed, "Most of all perhaps, Canedy's memoir speaks to military families everywhere, to boyfriends and girlfriends, husbands and wives," as well as other family members of slain veterans.

Canedy's story is universal in its telling of loss and the intense pain that a survivor encounters. Moreover, several themes appear in the story, specifically those of enduring love, dedication, honor, and human resilience. In an interview for *News & Notes,* Canedy told Farai Chideya that she embedded several personal lessons into the story, including "the importance of communicating with your family, of speaking to your family, writing about how much you love them before time runs out," and, Canedy stated, "We're an example of that."

BIOGRAPHICAL AND CRITICAL SOURCES:

PERIODICALS

Entertainment Weekly, January 9, 2009, Leah Greenblatt, review of *A Journal for Jordan: A Story of Love and Honor,* p. 67.

Essence, December, 2008, Karen Holt, review of *A Journal for Jordan,* p. 48.

Hollywood Reporter, March 28, 2007, Tatiana Siegel and Borys Kit, "'Journal' from Iraq at Escape (Escape Artists Acquires Rights to 'Journal for Jordan')," p. 1.

Kirkus Reviews, November 1, 2008, review of *A Journal for Jordan.*

Lexington Herald-Leader (Lexington, KY), January 14, 2009, Amy Wilson, "Best-Selling Kentucky Author Shares Her Dead Soldier's Journal for Their Son."

News & Notes, January 5, 2009, Farai Chideya, "Personal War Journal Becomes Gripping Memoir."

News & Observer (Raleigh, NC), January 27, 2009, Adrienne Johnson Martin, "Soldier Leaves Legacy for His Son in 'Journal' from Iraq."

News Tribune (Tacoma, WA), January 21, 2009, Scott Fontaine, "'Journal for Jordan' Author Signs Books Tonight."

New York Times, December 23, 2008, Melissa Fay Greene, "Reminder of War's Cost: A Legacy for a Fatherless Son," review of *A Journal for Jordan,* p. 7.

New York Times Book Review, December 28, 2008, Danielle Trussoni, "A Father's Death," review of *A Journal for Jordan,* p. 10.

Publishers Weekly, October 13, 2008, review of *A Journal for Jordan,* p. 48.

USA Today, January 13, 2009, Craig Wilson, "Fatherly Advice from a Book," p. 5.

ONLINE

Charlie Rose Web site, http://www.charlierose.com/ (August 1, 2009), author profile.

New York Times Online, http://www.nytimes.com/ (July 15, 2009), "Dana Canedy Responds to Reader Questions."

Plain Dealer Online, http://www.cleveland.com/ (December 30, 2008), Kristin Ohlson, "Dana Canedy's *Journal for Jordan* Embraces a Son While Mourning the Loss of Her Career Soldier Husband in Iraq."

Random House Web site, http://www.randomhouse.com/ (August 1, 2009), author profile.

San Francisco Chronicle Online, http://www.sfgate.com/ (December 31, 2008), Christina Eng, review of *A Journal for Jordan.**

CARBIN, Debbie 1968-

PERSONAL: Born March, 1968, in Kent, England; married; children: two. *Education:* Attended Folkestone School for Girls.

ADDRESSES: *Home*—South East Kent, England. *E-mail*—debbiecarbin@yahoo.com.

CAREER: Writer; civil service worker; worked in telesales.

WRITINGS:

Thanks for Nothing, Nick Maxwell, St. Martin's Griffin (New York, NY), 2008.

Three Men and a Maybe, Black Swan (London, England), 2009.

SIDELIGHTS: Debbie Carbin, a lifelong resident of South East Kent, England, wrote her first book when she was only six years old. Titled *The Sweet Shop That Wouldn't Open,* it was about a candy shop with a stuck door that eventually opened, and everyone could go in and eat what they wanted. Carbin admitted that the premise was based on a six-year-old's fantasy of eating all the candy she wanted, but it taught her that with writing, "anything I wanted to happen could happen."

Carbin's first novel, *Thanks for Nothing, Nick Maxwell,* is a romance told from the point of view of Rachel Covington, a young, single, attractive woman. At her telesales job, Rachel meets a handsome new coworker, Nick Maxwell, and they have a brief affair. Rachel, used to being the one to end a relationship, is surprised when Nick shows no interest in continuing theirs. As she ponders Nick's disinterest in her, she begins to experience nausea, moodiness, and other symptoms. It is no great surprise that she is, in fact, pregnant; what she decides to do about it is the crux of the plot. In her desperate and lonely state, Rachel finds a lost cell phone at the supermarket and begins a friendship with its owner, a kind man named Hector, who listens to all of Rachel's confessions. An additional plot complication develops when Rachel sees her friend Sarah's husband, Glenn, kissing another woman. Throughout the novel, Rachel makes frequent asides to the reader as if she is talking to her best friend. Reviewers stated that she also grows and changes enough to become a more likeable character and a helpful friend to Sarah. Critics have described *Thanks for Nothing, Nick Maxwell* as an entertaining piece of literature and a strong debut effort, one that *Booklist* reviewer Hilary Hatton called "a surprisingly sweet novel about the complete turnaround effect a baby can have."

Carbin's second novel, *Three Men and a Maybe,* features Beth Sheridan, a woman in love with her boss, Richard. As her love is unrequited, Beth turns to alternative means of meeting men, such as a speed-dating event and flirtatious e-mails, and she suddenly finds herself dealing with three men. While she is in the process of trying to determine which man is Mr. Right, Richard suddenly comes back into Beth's life. Though many reviewers find the book entertaining, *Thanks for Nothing, Nick Maxwell,* remains the favorite Carbin novel.

BIOGRAPHICAL AND CRITICAL SOURCES:

PERIODICALS

Booklist, July 1, 2008, Hilary Hatton, review of *Thanks for Nothing, Nick Maxwell,* p. 38.

Library Journal, July 1, 2008, Lisa Davis-Craig, review of *Thanks for Nothing, Nick Maxwell,* p. 60.

Publishers Weekly, June 2, 2008, review of *Thanks for Nothing, Nick Maxwell,* p. 29.

ONLINE

Bookbag, http://www.thebookbag.co.uk/ (July 14, 2009), Zoë Page, review of *Thanks for Nothing, Nick Maxwell.*

Chick Lit Reviews & News, http://chicklitreviews.wordpress.com/ (July 14, 2009), review of *Thanks for Nothing, Nick Maxwell.*

Debbie Carbin Home Page, http://www.debbiecarbin.com (July 12, 2009).

Macmillan Web site, http://us.macmillan.com/ (July 12, 2009), author information.

Trashionista, http://www.trashionista.com/ (July 14, 2009), review of *Thanks for Nothing, Nick Maxwell.**

* * *

CARLSEN, Spike 1952-

PERSONAL: Born June 11, 1952; married; wife's name Kat; children: five.

ADDRESSES: *Home*—Stillwater, MN. *E-mail*—carlsen@usinternet.com.

CAREER: Writer; *Family Handyman* magazine, executive editor; owner of a construction and remodeling company; carpenter. Has been a guest on the *CBS Early Show; Good Morning, Texas;* Home and Garden Television Network's *25 Biggest Remodeling Mistakes; USA Radio;* and other media programs.

WRITINGS:

A Splintered History of Wood: Belt Sander Races, Blind Woodworkers, and Baseball Bats, Collins (New York, NY), 2008.

Contributor to periodicals, including *Backyard Living, Fine Homebuilding, Old House Journal,* the Minneapolis *Star Tribune, Reader's Digest,* and *Workbench.*

SIDELIGHTS: Speaking as a man who built his own cabin on Lake Superior and owned a construction and remodeling company for fifteen years, Spike Carlsen has a lot to teach readers about wood. In addition to construction and carpentry, Carlsen was the executive editor of *Family Handyman* magazine, for which he wrote numerous articles, and helped revise and edit a do-it-yourself manual for *Reader's Digest.* He has also written a bimonthly column for *Backyard Living* called "Ask Spike" and many articles for publications such as *Fine Homebuilding, Old House Journal,* the Minneapolis *Star Tribune,* and *Workbench.* He has been a guest on the *CBS Early Show; Good Morning, Texas;* the Home and Garden Television network's *25 Biggest Remodeling Mistakes; USA Radio;* and other media programs. After working in central Tanzania to help provide the Bomalan'ombe Secondary School with electricity and a wood-burning cookstove, Carlsen decided to donate money from his book sales to help the school's tree farm.

Carlsen's *A Splintered History of Wood: Belt Sander Races, Blind Woodworkers, and Baseball Bats* is a 411-page close examination of wood, its history, and its many uses. From toothpicks and matches to Steinway pianos and Stradivarius violins, Carlsen explains the finer points of wood that will be, to many readers, surprising. For example, an English warship of the 1700s required seven hundred large oak trees, which England had aplenty; however, the masts were made of 120-foot trees that often came from the new colonies in America, at least until the colonists cut off England's supply to protest taxation without representation. Interviews include a blind cabinetmaker who uses the sense of touch to create his work, and a chainsaw artist called the "Wild Mountain Man," as a *Publishers Weekly* contributor noted. In the category of offbeat stories falls Barry Bonds's baseball bat, made of maple, which has a greater density than ash; and how wood played a great part in helping investigators solve the Lindbergh kidnapping case of 1932.

Part science and technology, history, and tribute, *A Splintered History of Wood* traces humans' dependence on wood in housing, weapons, transportation, and other areas—ending with the devastating effects this dependence has had on the earth's forests and environment. *School Library Journal* reviewer Robert Saunderson noted that Carlsen's writing, while informative, does not "burden lay readers," but entertains with stories and interviews. With photos and research, the book, critics stated, is a testament to this everyday, wonderful natural resource. A *Publishers Weekly* reviewer called the book an "engaging and exhaustively researched work." On a similar note, Saunderson concluded that *A Splintered History of Wood* is "thoroughly researched, thoughtful, and entertaining."

BIOGRAPHICAL AND CRITICAL SOURCES:

PERIODICALS

Booklist, September 1, 2008, David Pitt, review of *A Splintered History of Wood: Belt Sander Races, Blind Woodworkers, and Baseball Bats,* p. 21.

Publishers Weekly, January 22, 2007, Matthew Thornton, "The Forest and the Trees," p. 16; June 2, 2008, review of *A Splintered History of Wood,* p. 36.

School Library Journal, December 1, 2008, Robert Saunderson, review of *A Splintered History of Wood.*

Star Tribune (Minneapolis, MN), September 28, 2008, Dennis Anderson, "Interesting History Is Made of Wood; A Close Examination of One of Our Most Valuable Commodities," review of *A Splintered History of Wood,* p. 13.

ONLINE

A Splintered History of Wood Web site, http://www.asplinteredhistoryofwood.com (July 14, 2009).

HarperCollins Online, http://www.harpercollins.com/ (July 14, 2009), author information.*

* * *

CARLSON, Paul H. 1940-
(Paul Howard Carlson)

PERSONAL: Born August 3, 1940.

ADDRESSES: Office—Texas Tech University, History Department, 2500 Broadway, Lubbock, TX 79409. *E-mail*—paul.carlson@ttu.edu.

CAREER: Historian, educator, writer, and editor. Texas Tech University, Lubbock, professor of history and director of the Center for the Southwest; formerly professor of history at Texas Lutheran College, Seguin. Also served on advisory committees for the *Handbook of Texas,* the Texas Department of Parks and Wildlife, the Charles Goodnight papers, and several historical associations.

MEMBER: Texas State Historical Association (fellow).

AWARDS, HONORS: President's Excellence in Teaching Award, Texas Tech University, 1993; *The Plains Indians* was named one of the 100 most outstanding books on the American West published in the twentieth century, 2005.

WRITINGS:

(Compiler, with Kenneth D. Yeilding) *Ah That Voice: The Fireside Chats of Franklin Delano Roosevelt,* John Ben Shepperd (Odessa, TX), 1974.

Texas Woollybacks: The Range Sheep and Goat Industry, Texas A&M University Press (College Station, TX), 1982.

(With Donald Abbe and David J. Murrah) *Lubbock and the South Plains: An Illustrated History,* Windsor Publications (Chatsworth, CA), 1989.

"Pecos Bill": A Military Biography of William R. Shafter, Texas A&M University Press (College Station, TX), 1989.

Empire Builder in the Texas Panhandle: William Henry Bush, Texas A&M University Press (College Station, TX), 1996.

The Plains Indians, Texas A&M University Press (College Station, TX), 1998.

(Editor) *The Cowboy Way: An Exploration of History and Culture,* Texas Tech University Press (Lubbock, TX), 2000.

The Buffalo Soldier Tragedy of 1877, Texas A&M University Press (College Station, TX), 2003.

Deep Time and the Texas High Plains: History and Geology, Texas Tech University Press (Lubbock, TX), 2005.

Amarillo: The Story of a Western Town, Texas Tech University Press (Lubbock, TX), 2006.

(Editor, with Bruce A. Glasrud and Tai D. Kreidler) *Slavery to Integration: Black Americans in West Texas,* State House Press/McMurry University (Abilene, TX), 2007.

(With Donald R. Abbe) *Historic Lubbock County: An Illustrated History,* Historical Publishing Network (San Antonio, TX), 2008.

The Centennial History of Lubbock: Hub City of the Plains, chronological histories, bibliography, and photo selection by Donald R. Abbe, introduction by Monte L. Monroe, Donning Publishers (Virginia Beach, VA), 2008.

Also author of articles, essays, and book reviews.

The Plains Indians was published in French.

SIDELIGHTS: Paul H. Carlson is a historian who specializes in the history of America's West with a specific focus on Texas, about which he has written and edited several books. Carlson's *Empire Builder in the Texas Panhandle: William Henry Bush* is a biography of Bush, a businessperson from the North who specialized in everything from wholesale clothing to real estate and who eventually came to Texas and entered the cattle ranching business. Despite the book's focus on Bush, the author notes in the book's preface that he is also interested in imparting other information. Carlson writes: "The purpose of this work is to provide more than a biography of William H. Bush. Its broader purpose is to examine the economic growth of the Texas Panhandle, with emphasis on Amarillo, through tracing the life and work of a Chicago-based entrepreneur who played a little-known but important role in the area's history over a fifty-year period at the turn of the century. I have tried to show how a relatively unknown but large-scale Texas landowner, by adjusting to the shifting economic currents of his day, helped influence the development of Amarillo and the greater Panhandle region."

In 1881, Bush, who was born in upstate New York, purchased the sprawling 250,000-acre Frying Pan Ranch, part of which bordered what would later become Amarillo, Texas. While Bush's ranching enterprise over the next two decades would sucuumb to bad weather and low prices for cattle, Bush eventually turned to leasing parts of the land to farmers and ranchers while, at the same time, buying up Amarillo real estate. The author notes that Bush lived mostly in Chicago but, near the end of his life, began to stay more in Texas, where he became a renowned civic leader and philanthropist. "The author has done a lot of research for this book, delving into newspapers and family archives and conducting interviews," wrote *Business History Review* contributor Wyatt Wells.

The Plains Indians, published in 1998, looks at the history of the Indians so often portrayed by Hollywood. Although he goes back to the time the first Indians to come to America's Great Plains, Carlson primarily explores the period of 1750 to 1890, when the Plains Indian culture was considered to be at its peak. He discusses how their culture encompassed thirty tribes ranging from Saskatchewan, Canada, to the Rio Grande, Texas. He distinguishes two groups among the tribes: those who focused on agricultural and those who were semi-nomadic. According to the author, around 1400 AD marks the beginning of the modern Plain tribes. He explains how these Indians were ultimately transformed from farmers and nomads into warriors with the arrival of Europeans and whites, who brought with them horses and firearms. He traces the Indians' acquisition of horses back to the late 1600s and describes how this event was the most important factor in changing their lives and culture.

Calling the book "a fine account," Jerry Keenan also wrote in his review for *HistoryNet.com:* "In *The Plains Indians,* Paul Carlson provides us with a wonderfully complete and insightful look at these tribes." Fred Egloff, writing for *Booklist,* called the book a "superb and objective overview of the society and culture of the Plains Indians."

The Buffalo Soldier Tragedy of 1877 examines an incident in West Texas in which a troop of buffalo soldiers, that is, African American cavalry soldiers led by white officers, pursued a band of Comanches in an area south of modern Lubbock. Along with forty soldiers and their commanding officer were twenty-two buffalo hunters who served as guides. Several days after they left Fort Concho, a few black soldiers returned and reported that they feared the rest of the troop had died of thirst as the Comanches had led them away from water holes as the Indians escaped into the plains. Although considered a routine scouting mission, the affair had turned into a disaster, even though most of the men eventually returned. However, four men did die. Those who survived did so by drinking their own urine and the blood of their horses. Previous reports on this mission, which resulted in several men facing court martial, rely primarily on the accounts of white officers and buffalo hunters. *Journal of Southern History* contributor Shirley A. Leckie remarked that the author has broadened his scope "through the use of new primary sources and the integration of scholarly insights about the Comanches into his narrative," adding later in the same review: "Readers in southern history, western history, and Texas history will find value in Carlson's study of one event."

Deep Time and the Texas High Plains: History and Geology was published in 2005 and focuses on the natural history and archeology of the Lubbock Lake Landmark. The author discusses the geological forces that formed the Texas High Plains and also explores the 12,000-year history of various human activities in the region, from the ancient Paleoindian and Archaic periods on through to modern times. He concludes with the rise of the city of Lubbock. "Well written, brief, and eminently accessible, *Deep Time and the Texas High Plains* achieves its stated purpose: to provide a clear and concise account for the general reading public," remarked Joseph Locke in his review for the *Journal of Southern History.*

In his 2006 book *Amarillo: The Story of a Western Town,* Carlson provides an in-depth history of the city. He writes of Amarillo's earliest explorers on through to the city's rise as a major city in Texas. In the process, he discusses the city's cultural, social, economic, and political development. The author points out that the area's development stemmed from its potential economic value and the railroad industry. He describes how ranching was replaced by farming and how Amarillo boomed in the 1920s due to oil and gas discovered in the area. Carlson goes on to reflect on how Amarillo suffered during the Great Depression and then enjoyed a resurgence in the 1950s. "Combining an easy-to-read narrative with a generous helping of local color, *Amarillo* is a classic popular history," noted Char Miller in a review for the *Journal of Southern History.*

BIOGRAPHICAL AND CRITICAL SOURCES:

BOOKS

Carlson, Paul H., *Empire Builder in the Texas Panhandle: William Henry Bush,* Texas A&M University Press (College Station, TX), 1996.

PERIODICALS

Agricultural History, January, 1998, Cary DeCordova Wintz, review of *Empire Builder in the Texas Panhandle,* p. 108.

American Historical Review, February, 2000, Craig Miner, review of *The Plains Indians,* p. 221; October, 2004, Michele Butts, review of *The Buffalo Soldier Tragedy of 1877,* p. 1239.

Booklist, September 1, 1998, Fred Egloff, review of *The Plains Indians,* p. 59.

Business History Review, autumn, 1983, William Savage, review of *Texas Woollybacks: The Range Sheep and Goat Industry,* p. 430; winter, 1996, Wyatt Wells, review of *Empire Builder in the Texas Panhandle,* p. 598.

Choice, February, 1997, review of *Empire Builder in the Texas Panhandle,* p. 1023; April, 1999, M.C. Mangusso, review of *The Plains Indians,* p. 1515; July-August, 2000, L.B. Gimelli, review of *The Cowboy Way: An Exploration of History and Culture,* p. 2037; winter, 2004, C.D. Wintz, review of *The Buffalo Soldier Tragedy of 1877,* p. 971.

Civil War History, September, 1990, Marvin Fletcher, review of *"Pecos Bill": A Military Biography of William R. Shafter,* p. 289.

Internet Bookwatch, March, 2007, review of *Amarillo: The Story of a Western Town.*

Journal of American History, September, 1983, review of *Texas Woollybacks,* p. 392; December, 1990, Gregory J.W. Urwin, review of *"Pecos Bill,"* p. 1041; December, 1997, David G. McComb, review of *Empire Builder in the Texas Panhandle,* p. 1100; December, 1999, Loretta Fowler, review of *The Plains Indians,* p. 1315.

Journal of Economic Literature, March, 1997, review of *Empire Builder in the Texas Panhandle,* p. 266.

Journal of Military History, July, 1990, Anne Cipriano Venzon, review of *"Pecos Bill,"* p. 363; October, 2003, Michael L. Tate, review of *The Buffalo Soldier Tragedy of 1877,* p. 1300.

Journal of Southern History, August, 2004, Shirley A. Leckie, review of *The Buffalo Soldier Tragedy of 1877,* p. 700; May, 2008, Char Miller, review of *Amarillo,* p. 480; November, 2008, Joseph Locke, review of *Deep Time and the Texas High Plains: History and Geology,* p. 1038.

Journal of the West, winter, 2005, Michael Pierce, review of *The Buffalo Soldier Tragedy of 1877,* p. 100; winter, 2006, Jean A. Stuntz, review of *Deep Time and the Texas High Plains,* p. 88; spring, 2007, James T. Bratcher, review of *Amarillo,* p. 101.

Library Journal, August 1, 1998, review of *The Plains Indians,* p. 108.

Pacific Historical Review, November, 1991, Paul Andrew Hutton, review of *"Pecos Bill,"* p. 546; November, 1997, Ben Procter, review of *Empire Builder in the Texas Panhandle,* p. 609.

Reference & Research Book News, February 11990, review of *"Pecos Bill,"* p. 40; February, 2006, review of *Deep Time and the Texas High Plains*; August, 2007, review of *Amarillo.*

Roundup Magazine, February, 1997, review of *Empire Builder in the Texas Panhandle,* p. 23; August, 2000, review of *The Cowboy Way,* p. 17; June 1, 2008, D.R. Meredith, review of *Amarillo,* p. 32.

Science Books & Films, March, 1999, review of *The Plains Indians,* p. 69.

Southwestern Historical Quarterly, July, 1991, Graham A. Cosmas, review of *"Pecos Bill,"* p. 106; July, 1999, Donald E. Green, review of *Empire Builder in the Texas Panhandle,* p. 119; July, 2002, William D. Carrigan, review of *The Cowboy Way,* p. 142; October, 2003, Robert Wooster, review of *The Buffalo Soldier Tragedy of 1877,* p. 337; January, 2007, Brian Frehner, review of *Deep Time and the Texas High Plains,* p. 417.

Western Historical Quarterly, August, 1990, Marilynn M. Larew, review of *"Pecos Bill,"* p. 379; autumn, 1997, William W. Savage, review of *Empire Builder in the Texas Panhandle,* p. 426; winter, 1999, Pekka Hamalainen, review of *The Plains Indians,* p. 512; autumn, 2001, John H. Lenihan, review of *The Cowboy Way,* p. 388; summer, 2004, Theodore Harris, review of *The Buffalo Soldier Tragedy of 1877,* p. 238; winter, 2007, David G. McComb, review of *Amarillo,* p. 537.

Wild West, June, 1999, Jerry Keenan, review of *The Plains Indians,* p. 72.

ONLINE

HistoryNet.com, http://www.historynet.com/ (August 10, 2009), Jerry Keenan, review of *The Plains Indians.*

Texas Tech University History Department Web site, http://www.depts.ttu.edu/historydepartment/ (August 10, 2009), faculty profile of author.

Texas Tech University Web site, http://www.texastech.edu/ (August 10, 2009), faculty profile of author.*

* * *

CARLSON, Paul Howard
See CARLSON, Paul H.

* * *

CAVENDISH, Georgiana Spencer, Duchess of Devonshire 1757-1806

PERSONAL: Born July 6, 1757; died March 30, 1806.

CAREER: Writer and socialite.

WRITINGS:

CORRESPONDENCE

William Combe, *A Letter to Her Grace the Duchess of Devonshire,* Fielding & Walker (London, England), 1777.

William Combe, *A Second Letter to Her Grace the Duchess of Devonshire,* Fielding & Walker (London, England), 1777.

Georgiana: Extracts from the Correspondence of Georgiana, Duchess of Devonshire, edited by the Earl of Bessborough, Murray (London, England), 1955.

POETRY

The Duchess of Devonshire's Cow: A Poem, J. Bew (London, England), 1777.

Passage du Mont Saint-Gothard, Lasteyrie (Paris, France), 1802.

The Passage of the Mountain of Saint Gothard: A Poem, Prosper (London, England), 1802.

MUSIC

The Favorite Song, musical score, Longman & Broderip (London, England), 1798.

I Have a Silent Sorrow Here, musical score, Longman & Broderip (London, England), 1798.

Dithyrambe sur L'immortalité de L'âme, Chez Giguet & Michaud (Paris, France), 1802.

Sweet Is the Vale: A Favorite Duet, composition for the piano, G.E. Blake, (Philadelphia, PA), c. 1807, reprinted, G. Graupner (Boston, MA), c. 1818.

PROSE

The Sylph (novel), S. Price & J. Williams (Dublin, Ireland), 1779, reprinted, edited by Jonathan David Gross, Northwestern University Press (Evanston, IL), 2007.

Sheridan: From New and Original Material, including a Manuscript Diary by Georgiana Duchess of Devonshire, Constable (London, England), 1909, reprinted, Folcroft Library Editions (Folcroft, PA), 1980.

Emma, or, The Unfortunate Attachment: A Sentimental Novel, edited by Jonathan David Gross, State University of New York Press (Albany, NY), 2004.

ADAPTATIONS: The Favorite Song and *I Have a Silent Sorrow Here* were adapted for the musical *The Strangers.*

SIDELIGHTS: Lady Georgiana Spencer, later Georgiana Spencer Cavendish, the Duchess of Devonshire, was born July 6, 1757, and died March 30, 1806. Hailing from a long line of aristocracy, Cavendish's direct descendents include Diana Spencer, the late Princess of Wales, and Sara Ferguson, Duchess of York. Cavendish, the daughter of John Spencer the 1st Earl of Spencer, was an avid socialite and celebrated style icon. According to Adrienne Warber, in an article for the *Suite 101* Web site, Cavendish "was a popular hostess. She hosted salons that included the most influential Whig politicians, poets, writers and artists of the day. The playwright Richard Sheridan, the politician Charles James Fox and the artist Thomas Gainsborough were frequent visitors to her salons." Her political activism is also noted in historical records as well as her contributions of musical compositions, poetry, and fiction. Amanda Forman, in an article for the London *Times,* wrote, "When Georgiana married the Duke of Devonshire at the age of sixteen, her sole desire was to please him and not to be an embarrassment in front of his friends. As the eldest daughter of the 1st Earl Spencer, she had been brought up to make a good match. But nothing in her education prepared Georgiana for her sudden fame. The duke's vast wealth and political power as the financial patron of the Whig party placed Georgiana on a tall, lonely pedestal. . . . However, by the end of Georgiana's first year of married life, she had become the darling of 18th-century society."

Cavendish's reaction to her regular exposure to high society is evinced in her book *The Sylph,* which was released in 1779. The text, as Sarah Johnson noted in an article for *Booklist,* was released anonymously and "reflects the author's own unhappy marriage and conflicted view of the late-eighteenth-century aristocracy." In what *Library Journal* contributor Michael Rogers called an "epistolary novel," Cavendish tells the story of Julia Stanley, a young woman who finds her marriage lacking substance and is guided by a mysterious entity known as the Sylph. Likewise, Cavendish's *Emma, or, The Unfortunate Attachment: A Sentimental Novel* exhibits many of the same themes as *The Sylph.* In *Emma,* a young woman is forced into an arranged marriage with a man she does not love which leads to many problems for the wedded duo.

BIOGRAPHICAL AND CRITICAL SOURCES:

PERIODICALS

Booklist, October 1, 2007, Sarah Johnson, review of *The Sylph,* p. 32.

Bookseller, August 27, 2004, "Georgiana's Return," p. 25.

Eighteenth-Century Fiction, January 1, 2003, Li-Ping Geng, review of *The Sylph,* p. 331.

Library Journal, December 1, 2007, Michael Rogers, review of *The Sylph,* p. 171.

ONLINE

Suite 101, http://historicalbiographies.suite101.com/ (April 13, 2009), Adrienne Warber, "Georgiana Cavendish, Duchess of Devonshire: Celebrated 18th Century Socialite and Political Activist."

Times Online, http://entertainment.timesonline.co.uk/ (August 24, 2008), Amanda Foreman, "How Do You Solve a Problem Like Georgiana?"*

* * *

CEPERO, Helen 1951-

PERSONAL: Born 1951. *Education:* North Park University, M.Div.

ADDRESSES: Office—North Park Theological Seminary, 3225 W. Foster Ave., Box 14, Chicago, IL 60625.

CAREER: Writer. North Park Theological Seminary, Chicago, IL, professor and director of spiritual formation.

WRITINGS:

Journaling as a Spiritual Practice: Encountering God through Attentive Writing, IVP Books (Downers Grove, IL), 2008.

SIDELIGHTS: Helen Cepero is the director of spiritual formation and an acting professor at North Park University in Chicago, Illinois. In 2008, Cepero released her debut nonfiction publication titled *Journaling as a Spiritual Practice: Encountering God through Attentive Writing.* The text details the potential for spirituality to manifest in one's writing, and specifically in writings which are routinely personal and targeted at one's self revelation. Cepero argues that this method of spiritual formation has ancient origins and that many of Christianity's leading theologians employed journaling as a means by which they could channel spiritual revelation. However, "What should be observed from the outset is that Cepero does not draw her understanding on journaling from the Scriptures, for nowhere in the Bible is such a practice taught. Whatever she has to offer comes from post-biblical tradition and/or the imagination of more recent times," according to a *Christian Book Previews* Web site article by Gary Gilley. In other words, Cepero finds that, although the historic practice of journaling is not a message specifically presented in the Scriptures, Christians throughout history have found journaling to be a helpful practice in channeling their spirituality in an attempt to become closer to God. Through the routine practice of formalizing thought and recounting events, one can more objectively analyze the places in which spirituality manifests in their life. Gilley wrote, "The Lord allows latitude within biblical parameters to find and use methods to help us worship Him and understand His ways. Writing down our thoughts, insights, struggles, and understanding and application of Scripture can have great benefits."

Cepero reveals in various chapters of how one can initiate a spiritual journal, focus on important themes, decipher the spiritual amidst the mundane, anticipate important subjects, place oneself in a present context, begin a dialogue, and deal with conflict. Cepero also asserts that God can be found within the everyday happenings in one's life and that the practice of journaling can help uncover this aspect of belief. A *Publishers Weekly* contributor pointed out that Cepero offers "suggested exercises to help writers find focus, particularly beginners or those who feel stuck with their writing." Moreover, the text reveals that, though the act of writing may seem fluid, it requires a trained eye to piece together the themes and motifs of one's underlying spirituality. A *Christian Century* contributor found that the text has the ability to "jump-start neophytes who don't know how to journal."

BIOGRAPHICAL AND CRITICAL SOURCES:

PERIODICALS

Christian Century, October 7, 2008, review of *Journaling as a Spiritual Practice: Encountering God through Attentive Writing,* p. 48.

Publishers Weekly, April 28, 2008, review of *Journaling as a Spiritual Practice,* p. 131.

ONLINE

Christian Book Previews Web site, http://www.christianbookpreviews.com/ (July 16, 2009), author profile; (July 16, 2009), Gary Gilley, review of *Journaling as a Spiritual Practice.**

* * *

CHANG, Leslie T.

PERSONAL: Married Peter Hessler (a writer). *Ethnicity:* Chinese. *Education:* Graduated from Harvard University.

ADDRESSES: *Home*—CO.

CAREER: Journalist, writer. Worked variously as an intern for the *Miami Herald,* Miami, FL, and in Prague for an expatriate newspaper; *Wall Street Journal,* correspondent in Hong Kong, Taiwan, and China.

WRITINGS:

Factory Girls: From Village to City in a Changing China, Spiegel & Grau (New York, NY), 2008.

Contributor to periodicals including *National Geographic* and the *Wall Street Journal.*

SIDELIGHTS: Chinese American writer and journalist Leslie T. Chang is the daughter of immigrant parents, raised just outside of New York City and forced through childhood to go to Chinese school on Saturday mornings, a discipline for which she was thankful later in life. Chang graduated from Harvard University and went on to serve as an intern for the *Miami Herald.* She then secured a position writing for an expatriate newspaper in Prague, and eventually landed a job as a correspondent for the *Wall Street Journal,* writing first from Hong Kong, then Taiwan, and ultimately China, a beat for which her heritage and knowledge of the language was a definite asset. It was while writing from China that Chang first became interested in the plight of the young female factory workers so prevalent in that country. She had heard stories and read about these girls in several area newspapers, but the more she learned the more curious she became about this way of life and the need to expose its hardships. What began as research for some short articles for the *Wall Street Journal,* eventually expanded into the makings of a book, and Chang ultimately left her job in order to concentrate on writing it full time. The result is *Factory Girls: From Village to City in a Changing China,* which was published in 2008.

Factory Girls focuses primarily on a factory in the city of Dongguan, which is located in the south of China. The city is heavily populated with factories of the sort that have young girls manning the assembly lines. Most provide the girls with living quarters in the form of dorm-like rooms that house approximately a dozen girls. The girls themselves rarely make friends with each other and in some instances work under false names so that gossip about them—either real or imaginary—has less chance of reaching their families, as the talk often centers around what each girl earns, how long she has worked at the factory, whether or not she is spending her little free time with a boy, and how much money she manages to save. Chang explains that across China there are approximately 130 million migrant workers, people traveling from their homes in hopes of finding work that pays sufficiently to allow them to send money back to their loved ones. This is a sharp contrast to the life of the typical Chinese American, even a new immigrant, and Chang includes comparisons between the way these young girls struggle and her own far more privileged childhood and adolescence.

Over the course of the book, Chang focuses in on Lu Qingmin, a newly arrived migrant worker who has arrived in Dongguan in search of a job. She follows the sixteen-year-old as she learns to navigate the city, finds employment, and follows her as she settles into her new life. Chang also looks at the ways in which young Chinese women are changed by this process, often becoming addicted to the relative freedom of working in the city and earning their own money, and as a result, fewer of them return to the villages where they started to marry and start a family, though that was often their original intention. In a review for *Booklist,* Carol Haggas declared Chang's book to be an "eye-opening and sobering insight into the lives of Chinese teens." A reviewer for *Business Week* remarked that "Chang creates compelling portraits of her female subjects. At times, the material is bleak—factory labor in southern China can be grueling, and the lives of those who do it can be difficult. But a spirit of optimism shines through in most of the women."

BIOGRAPHICAL AND CRITICAL SOURCES:

PERIODICALS

America, February 2, 2009, Peter Heinegg, "Women on the Move," review of *Factory Girls: From Village to City in a Changing China,* p. 38.

Booklist, October 1, 2008, Carol Haggas, review of *Factory Girls,* p. 8.

Business Week, October 20, 2008, "Sweat and Striving on China's Factory Floor," p. 94.

Christian Science Monitor, October 7, 2008, Dan Southerland, review of *Factory Girls,* p. 25.

Kirkus Reviews, September 1, 2008, review of *Factory Girls.*

New Yorker, October 27, 2008, review of *Factory Girls,* p. 87.

New York Times, October 22, 2008, Howard W. French, "Dynamic Young Engines Driving China's Epic Boom," p. C6.

New York Times Book Review, November 9, 2008, Patrick Radden Keefe, "Holding Up the Sky," p. 47.

Publishers Weekly, August 25, 2008, review of *Factory Girls,* p. 11.

ONLINE

China Beat Blog, http://thechinabeat.blogspot.com/ (August 12, 2009), Leslie T. Chang, "Writing Factory Girls"; Susan Jakes and Leslie T. Chang, "China Annals: Factory Girls."

Independent Online, http://www.independent.co.uk/ (August 12, 2009), Justin Hill, review of *Factory Girls.*

Leslie T. Chang Home Page, http://www.leslietchang.com (August 12, 2009).

Random House Web site, http://www.randomhouse.com/ (August 12, 2009), author profile.*

* * *

CHATER, Veronica

PERSONAL: Female.

ADDRESSES: Home—Berkeley, CA.

CAREER: Writer.

WRITINGS:

Waiting for the Apocalypse: A Memoir of Faith and Family, W.W. Norton (New York, NY), 2009.

Contributor of essays and articles to periodicals, including the *Los Angeles Times, San Francisco Examiner, Guardian,* and the *Berkeley Monthly.*

SIDELIGHTS: Veronica Chater, a resident of Berkeley, California, is the author of *Waiting for the Apocalypse: A Memoir of Faith and Family,* released in 2009. "This memoir follows the tradition of the coming-of-age story, told in prose that duplicates the narrator's growing awareness of the need to create her own Weltenschauung, or world-view," according to a *Blogtrotter* Web site contributor. The narrative chronicles Chater's Catholic upbringing, the effects on her family of Vatican II, and her efforts to formulate her own beliefs. Chater relates her family's descent into poverty and their struggle to maintain their rigid adherence to faith in spite of a Church in flux and their relocation to Portugal. The *Blogtrotter* Web site contributor noted, "Chater later takes stock of her dad and the predicament they are in as they seek solace in a community as underground as the first catechumens in imperial Rome. They hold the Latin Mass with renegade priests in a Penney's truck garage, a bankrupt department store, their own two-car garages, and their living rooms. The last mass that the family attends in their Portuguese flight shows the author's skill at pacing a story well." Chater provides a detailed depiction of her parents, Lyle and Marty Chater. As Laura Hughes-Collins, in a review for the *Los Angeles Times* Web site, wrote, Chater's "father may be a ranting domestic tyrant, but he's also intellectually curious, a reader and a writer; he sings silly songs, does the chicken dance when he's feeling jubilant and means no harm to any of them. Her mother, in Chater's depiction, is no pushover, her deference to Lyle notwithstanding. Other children might condemn a mother for failing to protect them from the damage a father inflicts, but Chater never does. Marty is old-school Catholic, and submitting to her husband's will is part of the deal." The story illustrates Chater's evolving opinions regarding the extremity of religious devotion, yet her description of her family is nonjudgmental. In an article for the *San Francisco Chronicle* Web site, Don Lattin remarked, "The most enjoyable parts of Chater's story are her tales from the early years, before her father falls in with Catholic cult leaders and attempts to reconcile his traditionalist views with his neighborhood parish." Moreover, a *Publishers Weekly* contributor found that Chater's story reveals the ease with which one can "get caught up in religious fervor, with emotionally devastating consequences that linger long after faith has been abandoned."

BIOGRAPHICAL AND CRITICAL SOURCES:

PERIODICALS

Book World, March 1, 2009, Juliet Wittman, review of *Waiting for the Apocalypse: A Memoir of Faith and Family,* p. 6.

Entertainment Weekly, February 13, 2009, Tina Jordan, review of *Waiting for the Apocalypse,* p. 61.

Kirkus Reviews, November 1, 2008, review of *Waiting for the Apocalypse.*

Library Journal, November 1, 2008, Erica L. Foley, review of *Waiting for the Apocalypse,* p. 72.

Publishers Weekly, November 17, 2008, review of *Waiting for the Apocalypse,* p. 51.

ONLINE

Blogtrotter, http://fionnchu.blogspot.com/ (May 11, 2009), review of *Waiting for the Apocalypse.*

Los Angeles Times Online, http://www.latimes.com/ (February 22, 2009), Laura Collins-Hughes, review of *Waiting for the Apocalypse.*

Red Room, http://www.redroom.com/ (July 19, 2009), author profile.

San Francisco Chronicle Online, http://www.sfgate.com/ (March 1, 2009), Don Lattin, review of *Waiting for the Apocalypse.*

Veronica Chater Home Page, http://www.veronicachater.com (July 19, 2009).*

* * *

CHEN, Joanne

PERSONAL: Female.

ADDRESSES: Home—New York, NY.

CAREER: Writer.

WRITINGS:

The Taste of Sweet: Our Complicated Love Affair with Our Favorite Treats, Crown Press (New York, NY), 2008.

SIDELIGHTS: Joanne Chen is the author of *The Taste of Sweet: Our Complicated Love Affair with Our Favorite Treats. The Taste of Sweet* "explores the science and culture behind why some of us have insatiable sweet tooths while others do not. The book also pays particularly interest to Americans' love-hate-guilt relationship to sweets and desserts," according to an article by Anna Papoutsakis for the *Food Section* Web site. Papoutsakis interviewed Chen for her article and questioned the variance in tasting ability among members of the general population, and Chen stated, "Super-tasters have a higher density of taste buds than tasters and non-tasters. Our taste preferences are mainly determined by culture and experience, but our density of taste buds influence how intense certain foods might taste." This concept of socially constructed tasting and interpretation of flavor is central to the book's thesis regarding the role of sweets in American culture. Chen also addresses the controversy concerning high fructose corn syrup and why many members of the public consider the substance to be a health risk. Chen backs her claims with information garnered from interviews with scientists and food professionals, and the book relies upon this evidence to discern the critical dialogue regarding sweets. Chen asserts that food cravings should not be wholly ignored and that individuals who substitute a food alternative for their craving of something sweet are merely delaying the inevitable. Chen told Papoutsakis, "I stopped obsessing over them and I gained better control over my eating habits" when she finally stopped suppressing the fulfillment of her cravings for sweet foods. A central question in *The Taste of Sweet* is "why we love—and love to hate—dessert," according to a *Shape* contributor, and the text attempts to address the many stereotypes, assumptions, and myths regarding the consumption of sweets. Francisca Goldsmith, in a review for *School Library Journal,* remarked, "Referencing agricultural history, gastronomic invention, medical research, and social changes, Chen weaves readily between science and art." Chen actively attempts to disentangle the act of eating sweet foods with feelings of guilt, remorse, and pleasure, and she questions why people have such strong emotional associations with sweet foods. *Booklist* contributor Mark Knoblauch noted, "Chen spends days in laboratories, ferreting out the physiological bases for our appetite for sweets." Moreover, a *Publishers Weekly* contributor concluded that the text puts forth "a variety of historical and cultural reasons we Americans are uniquely vulnerable to sweetness because of external factors."

BIOGRAPHICAL AND CRITICAL SOURCES:

PERIODICALS

Booklist, April 1, 2008, Mark Knoblauch, review of *The Taste of Sweet: Our Complicated Love Affair with Our Favorite Treats,* p. 15.

Library Journal, March 1, 2008, Rosemarie Lewis, review of *The Taste of Sweet,* p. 103.

Publishers Weekly, January 28, 2008, review of *The Taste of Sweet,* p. 55.
School Library Journal, June 1, 2008, Francisca Goldsmith, review of *The Taste of Sweet,* p. 172.
SciTech Book News, June 1, 2008, review of *The Taste of Sweet.*
Shape, May 1, 2008, "Change Your Attitude, Drop Pounds," p. 38.

ONLINE

Food Section, http://www.thefoodsection.com/ (May 8, 2008), author interview with Anna Papoutsakis.
Random House Web site, http://www.randomhouse.com/ (July 16, 2009), author profile.*

* * *

CHERRY, Bob

PERSONAL: Male.

ADDRESSES: *Home*—WY.

CAREER: Writer.

WRITINGS:

NOVELS

Spirit of the Raven: An Alaskan Novel, Picaro Press (Seattle, WA), 1999.
West of Empty, One Eyed Press (Cody, WY), 2002.
Inua, One Eyed Press (Cody, WY), 2002.
Little Rains, One Eyed Press (Cody, WY), 2003.
Moving Serafina, TCU Press (Fort Worth, TX), 2007.

SIDELIGHTS: Bob Cherry is the author of several fiction releases, including *Spirit of the Raven: An Alaskan Novel,* a 1999 Picaro Press publication. *Spirit of the Raven* takes place in the small town of Snag Point, Alaska, during the early twentieth century. The story begins with the discovery of the dead body of a local trapper. From this point onward, Cherry continually introduces characters with ties either to the trapper or to the surrounding community, and the suspect pool continually widens. A *Library Journal* contributor noted that although the novel essentially chronicles "the aftermath of a murder," the story "also examines the interactions of a culturally diverse group" in a remote wilderness region of the United States. The suspicions triggered by the murder reveal the prejudice and conflict that breeds in an area that is home to newcomers, natives, and speculators. Likewise, *Inua* also takes place in turn of the century Alaska. In *Inua,* Cherry establishes a set of characters who exemplify the diversity of the region, from returning natives who have become disillusioned by modernity to traditionalists who harbor long-held secrets. In the story, a native Alaskan couple attempts to preserve their natural heritage and the land it was founded on by engaging in politics, but the effort is undermined by personal conflicts.

Cherry's *West of Empty* takes up a new landscape and is set in the vast expanse of late-nineteenth-century West Texas. The story follows the protagonist, Phineas Farrow, as he schemes to take advantage of a train collision in order to make a fortune. Cherry includes sideshow elements into this story about an ambitious opportunist whose scheme to sensationalize an accident transforms a small town. Also set in the American West is Cherry's 2003 release, *Little Rains.* The story centers on the ambitions of two men, Truman Pierce and his nephew, J.D. Mitchell. Mitchell joins Pierce on his ranch and begins to learn that errors are not soon corrected and have a haunting quality. The story also reveals the hard life of the cattleman and how the independent rancher was inundated with outside problems. *Moving Serafina,* published in 2007, further explores the issues of western landownership through a story which centers on the theme of familial loss. The novel also addresses water rights and vigilante justice. In a review for *Booklist,* Ian Chipman claimed "the characters and concerns are pure West."

BIOGRAPHICAL AND CRITICAL SOURCES:

PERIODICALS

Booklist, October 1, 2007, Ian Chipman, review of *Moving Serafina,* p. 43.
Library Journal, February 15, 1999, Charlotte L. Glover, review of *Spirit of the Raven: An Alaskan Novel,* p. 182.

Publishers Weekly, January 18, 1999, review of *Spirit of the Raven,* p. 330.

Roundup Magazine, December 1, 2002, review of *West of Empty,* p. 26; October 1, 2003, review of *Little Rains,* p. 28.

ONLINE

Bob Cherry Home Page, http://www.bobcherry.com (July 19, 2009).

TCU Press Web site, http://www.tamu.edu/upress/ (July 19, 2009), author profile.*

* * *

CHRISTY, Bryan

PERSONAL: Education: Graduate of Pennsylvania State University, Cornell University, and the University of Michigan Law School.

ADDRESSES: Home—Philadelphia, PA. *E-mail*—bryan@bryanchristy.com.

CAREER: Writer.

WRITINGS:

The Lizard King: The True Crimes and Passions of the World's Greatest Reptile Smugglers, Twelve (New York, NY), 2008.

SIDELIGHTS: Bryan Christy is a graduate of Pennsylvania State University, Cornell University, and the University of Michigan Law School; he is also the author of *The Lizard King: The True Crimes and Passions of the World's Greatest Reptile Smugglers,* released in 2008. *The Lizard King* is a "well-researched, globe-trotting, decade-spanning adventure tale which is, at heart, the story of two men," Chris Beplar and Mike Van Nostrand, according to a review for the *Writers and Readers* Web site by Cathy Pickens. Beplar and Van Nostrand both work with reptiles, but their objectives could not be more different. Working for the U.S. Fish and Wildlife Services department, Beplar discovers the extent of the reptile smuggling operation and sets about to curb the illegal enterprise. Van Nostrand, however, is simultaneously perpetuating the smuggling operation through his retail business. Pickens observed, "Over the years, the two men learned what they had in common, as well as the frustrating limits that commercialism and regulation brought to the wildlife world." The story incorporates elements of a crime drama as well as a nonfiction approach to chronicling the organization and perpetuation of illegal smuggling of live animals for distribution and profit. The lucrative nature of the smuggling business, the text illustrates, makes apprehending and prosecuting these criminals a difficult task. *Suite 101* Web site contributor Philip McIntosh reported, "Although most reptiles available in U.S. pet shops are now of legal origin, it wasn't always that way. The Van Nostrands worked their way up until they founded Strictly Reptiles to provide just about anything a collector wanted. Endangered or not, it didn't matter." With a no-questions-asked business model, and a slow legal process, the Van Nostrand family successfully facilitates the sale of hundreds of animals illegally obtained from international locations. Moreover, the text explains how the laws preventing illegal animal collection and smuggling are thwarted by creative criminal elements. In an article for the *Sun Sentinel,* David Fleshler remarked, "Christy immerses himself in the wildlife trade, but never lets the material overwhelm him, writing a tight, focused, gripping story. He writes with a laconic humor that recalls Elmore Leonard." Fleshler also commented, "There is a bureaucratic heroism here, of wildlife agents and prosecutors who refuse to accept the judgment of colleagues that pursuing despoilers of the environment is less important than pursuing John Gotti." Moreover, *Booklist* contributor David Pitt concluded the narrative is "an exciting story of smugglers, lawmen, corrupt government officials, organized crime, and slithery beasts."

BIOGRAPHICAL AND CRITICAL SOURCES:

PERIODICALS

Audubon, November 1, 2008, Jessica Leber, review of *The Lizard King: The True Crimes and Passions of the World's Greatest Reptile Smugglers.*

Booklist, July 1, 2008, David Pitt, review of *The Lizard King,* p. 20.

Kirkus Reviews, May 15, 2008, review of *The Lizard King.*

National Post, August 16, 2008, review of *The Lizard King,* p. 12.

New Straits Times, September 21, 2008, "Obsessed with Meaner, Hotter Creatures."

New York Times, August 7, 2008, "Coldblooded Commerce in Coldblooded Contraband," p. 9.

New York Times Book Review, August 17, 2008, "Cold-Blooded," p. 23.

Publishers Weekly, June 9, 2008, review of *The Lizard King,* p. 41.

Sun Sentinel, September 24, 2008, David Fleshler, "'The Lizard King': A Snake Story with Bite."

Wildlife Conservation, November 1, 2008, Elizabeth L. Bennett, review of *The Lizard King.*

ONLINE

Lizard King Book Web site, http://thelizardkingbook.com (July 19, 2009).

Suite 101, http://sciencetechbooks.suite101.com/ (June 16, 2009), Philip McIntosh, review of *The Lizard King.*

Twelve, http://www.twelvebooks.com/ (July 19, 2009), author profile.

Writers Are Readers, http://www.writersarereaders.com/ (July 19, 2009), Cathy Pickens, review of *The Lizard King.**

* * *

CLARK, Cassandra

PERSONAL: Female.

ADDRESSES: *Home*—London, England.

CAREER: Writer.

WRITINGS:

FICTION

Hangman Blind, Minotaur Books (New York, NY), 2009.

The Red Velvet Turnshoe, John Murray (London, England), 2009.

SIDELIGHTS: Cassandra Clark released her debut novel, *Hangman Blind,* in 2009. The narrative is a historically situated mystery which begins in the year 1382 in England. During this time, King Richard, still a boy, has a tremulous hold on his regency, and England is in a state of political unrest which is fueled by an overly taxed peasant population and a weak leadership community. The protagonist, Hildegard, a recently widowed young nun, is sent to secure the permission of the Church for the establishment of a priory funded with the proceeds of Hildegard's marriage union. In addition to the political unrest, the Church has issues as well, with the contention between Pope Clement VII and Pope Urban V, as the result of the Avignon Papacy. While Hildegard travels to the Abbey of Meaux, in York, she witnesses the results of an atmosphere born of fear and hostility when she discovers the lynched bodies of several peasants. After her arrival at the Hutton estate, where she stops to obtain advice from a friend regarding land available for ownership, Hildegard becomes embroiled in an investigation into the wrongdoings against the lord of Hutton manor. Hildegard thus begins the search for the forces behind the attempted murder of Roger de Hutton assisted by Hutton's steward, a man named Ulf. "As the protagonist of the first of a series of medieval mysteries, Hildegard navigates below the radar, moving quietly from abbey to castle, with a network of friends and potential foes, an uncertain political climate, and a fascination with the man who might well be on the wrong side of the nun's best interests," Hubert de Courcy, wrote Luan Gaines in an article for the *Curled Up with a Good Book* Web site.

Clark's subsequent release, *The Red Velvet Turnshoe,* is the next book in her series. Hildegard resumes her role as the gumshoe protagonist when she is tasked by the Church in the return of a holy artifact, the cross of Constantine. During her quest for the relic, Hildegard becomes involved with a man named Pierrekyn, a musician and the main suspect in a murder, "and, after questioning him she feels that he is innocent and she decides to help him avoid arrest and possible lynching," according to *Euro Crime* Web site contributor Terry Halligan. Thus, Hildegard begins another perilous adventure. A *Europe Intelligence Wire* contributor concluded that the historical mystery series "is well plotted and meticulously researched."

BIOGRAPHICAL AND CRITICAL SOURCES:

PERIODICALS

Europe Intelligence Wire, September 1, 2008, "Novel Came to Author in Her Dreams"; April 8, 2009, "New Books."

Financial Times, March 29, 2008, "Page-Turners: Hangman Blind," p. 41.

Kirkus Reviews, October 1, 2008, review of *Hangman Blind.*

Publishers Weekly, October 20, 2008, review of *Hangman Blind,* p. 38.

ONLINE

Bookworm's Dinner, http://bookwormsdinner.blogspot.com/ (April 2, 2009), Wisteria Leigh, review of *Hangman Blind.*

Curled Up with a Good Book, http://www.curledup.com/ (July 19, 2009), Luan Gaines, review of *Hangman Blind.*

Euro Crime, http://www.eurocrime.co.uk/ (November 1, 2008), Amanda Brown, review of *Hangman Blind;* (March 1, 2009), Terry Halligan, review of *The Red Velvet Turnshoe.*

Guardian Online, http://www.guardian.co.uk/ (October 11, 2008), Joanna Hines, review of *Hangman Blind.*

Macmillan Web site, http://us.macmillan.com/ (July 19, 2009), author profile.

Monsters and Critics, http://www.monstersandcritics.com/ (June 14, 2009), Angela Youngman, review of *The Red Velvet Turnshoe.**

* * *

CLARKE, Suzanna 1961-

PERSONAL: Born 1961, in New Zealand. *Education:* Attended the Queensland University of Technology.

ADDRESSES: Home—Brisbane, Australia.

CAREER: Writer and photographer.

WRITINGS:

A House in Fez, Pocket Books (New York, NY), 2008.

Contributor to the *Courier-Mail, Australian,* and *Bulletin.*

SIDELIGHTS: Suzanna Clarke, a New Zealand native, is a contributor to the *Courier-Mail* and an avid photographer. Clarke, who attended the Queensland University of Technology, has over twenty years of photography experience and frequently travels to areas of historical interest, including France, Morocco, and Vietnam. According to a contributor's biographical article for the *Courier-Mail,* Clarke "worked as a freelance photographer for editorial, commercial and government clients, such as the *Australian* and the *Age* newspapers and the *Bulletin* magazine" throughout the 1980s and 1990s.

In 2008, Clarke released *A House in Fez.* The text chronicles Clarke's experiences while she and her husband, Sandy, set about to restore a two thousand-year-old house in the city of Fez, an ancient community in the northernmost region of Morocco. A *Kirkus Reviews* contributor noted, "Everything in Morocco, the couple discovered, proceeded at a tortoise-like pace, as though everyone was waiting for the hand of God to intervene in even the smallest transaction." Founded circa 789, the city is home to one of the oldest institutions of higher learning in the world and serves as a testament to the history of Islamic culture; however, the city is far from being fully modernized. As Lesley Mason reported in an article for the *Bookbag* Web site, the narrative centers on the ex-patriots' "attempts to come to terms with local customs, archaic laws, unyielding bureaucracy (which occasionally yields in the most inexplicable but helpful fashion), builders with notions of their own, plumbers who fail to arrive, and the slow, painful, process of restoring an ancient property to its former glory—whilst insisting upon modernity in the kitchen and the bathroom (albeit sympathetically rendered, obviously)." With an extremely skewed learning curve which included language, laws, and customs, Clarke sets about to purchase and renovate an ancient and structurally degraded property. Mason claimed, "The contradictions of modern Fez are well-captured in discussions of the incomers risking the destruction [of] that which they've come to enjoy, the slow movement of the Moroccans themselves into a modern world." Clarke provides examples of an evolving nation, such as the conflict between fulfilling modern ambitions while simultaneously maintaining mystical traditions and the juxtaposition of modern technologies with ancient transport vessels. Thus, Clarke exposes Moroccan culture as a blend of the past and the present, and the text exposes the problems which develop when a foreign entity unwittingly assigns their own expectations to the services provided by another culture.

BIOGRAPHICAL AND CRITICAL SOURCES:

PERIODICALS

Kirkus Reviews, October 1, 2008, review of *A House in Fez.*

ONLINE

Australian Online, http://www.theaustralian.news.com.au/ (March 1, 2008), Sharon Fowler, "Suzanne Clarke."

Bookbag, http://www.thebookbag.co.uk/ (July 18, 2009), Lesley Mason, review of *A House in Fez.*

Courier-Mail Online, http://www.news.com.au/ (July 18, 2009), author profile.

Penguin Books Australia Web site, http://www.penguin.com.au/ (January 1, 2009), author profile.*

* * *

COLE, Meredith

PERSONAL: Married; children: one son. *Education:* Smith College, graduated 1992; attended New York University's Tisch School of the Art; American University, master's degree, 1996.

ADDRESSES: *Home*—Brooklyn, NY.

CAREER: Writer, novelist, screenwriter, and movie director. School of Visual Arts, New York, NY, teaches directing. Director of the film *Achilles' Love,* Castle Hill, 2000.

MEMBER: Mystery Writers of America (board member of New York chapter), Sisters in Crime.

AWARDS, HONORS: Kodak film grant; Playwriting/Screenwriting fellow, New York Foundation for the Arts, 2004; winner of St. Martin's Press/Malice Domestic Best Traditional First Mystery Contest for *Posed for Murder.*

WRITINGS:

Posed for Murder (novel), Minotaur Books (New York, NY), 2009.

Contributor to the periodicals *Ellery Queen Mystery* magazine and *EQMM* and the anthology *Murder New York Style,* L&L Dreamspell, 2007. Also screenwriter and director of the film *Floating.*

SIDELIGHTS: Meredith Cole worked primarily as a film director and screenwriter before turning to writing mysteries. In addition to contributions to *Ellery Queen Mystery* magazine, Cole is the author of *Posed for Murder,* her debut mystery novel. In an interview with Sandra Parshall for the *Poe's Deadly Daughters* Web site, Cole commented on her new career focus: "I wanted to be a writer since before I could even read. I would dictate stories to my mother." The author went on to note her efforts in film but added: "Film is an expensive medium, and it's difficult to get films made (even if you win Academy Awards) without big names attached and lots of cash. I realized that I'd always read more books than watched films, and storytelling was storytelling. So I set out to write a book."

Posed for Murder focuses on a photographer Lydia McKenzie. Fascinated with famous murder scenes, Lydia recreates and photographs them using various friends as models. Lydia eventually begins to achieve success with photos shot in the black-and-white mode of old film noir movies. However, during a display of some of her photographs at a gallery exhibition in Williamsburg, Brooklyn, two police detectives, the handsome Romero and his female partner Wong, show up to bring Lydia in for questioning. It turns out that Marie, one of Lydia's friends who posed for her photographs, has been murdered and set in the identical pose that she recreated for Lydia.

Cole told Parshall that the inspiration for the novel's plot comes from the author's love of photography. The author went on to tell Parshall: "I wanted to see a story though the eye of a photographer, and use her special skills to solve it."

In *Posed for Murder,* Wong strongly suspects that Lydia is the murderer but Romero seems more sympathetic. Lydia and her friend Georgia, both of whom also posed for photos, decide to do some investigating on their own as another friend turns up dead and posed in a position reflecting one of Lydia's photographs. When another model disappears, it become apparent that Lydia and her friends are in terrible danger. Lydia suspects that perhaps a member of a critique group for artists may be the murderer, leading to an arrest of a suspect. However, Lydia, who learns defense skills at the insistence of friend, soon discovers that the real murderer may still be out there.

"The ending was definitely a surprise, and a well-written one at that," noted S. Krishna in a review for the *S. Krishna's Books* Web site, adding: "Cole's storytelling ability and imagination should be commended; the entire book is a delight to read!" A *Kirkus Reviews* contributor called *Posed for Murder* "amiable" and "well-plotted."

BIOGRAPHICAL AND CRITICAL SOURCES:

PERIODICALS

Booklist, February 1, 2009, Michele Leber, review of *Posed for Murder,* p. 32.
Kirkus Reviews, December 1, 2008, review of *Posed for Murder.*
Publishers Weekly, December 15, 2008, review of *Posed for Murder,* p. 38.
Video Business, April 15, 2002, Ed Hulse, "Achilles' Love," p. 14.

ONLINE

Crime Space, http://crimespace.ning.com/ (August 11, 2009), profile of author.
Fantastic Fiction, http://www.fantasticfiction.co.uk/ (August 11, 2009), brief profile of author.
L&L Dreamspell Web site, http://lldreamspell.com/ (August 11, 2009), profile of author.
Macmillan Web site, http://us.macmillan.com/ (August 11, 2009), brief profile of author.
Meredith Cole Home Page, http://www.culturecurrent.com/cole/index.html (August 11, 2009).
Meredith Cole MySpace Profile, http://www.myspace.com/meredithscole (August 11, 2009).
Poe's Deadly Daughters, http://poesdeadlydaughters.blogspot.com/ (August 11, 2009), Sandra Parshall, "A New Voice: Meredith Cole," interview with author.
Romantic Times, http://www.romantictimes.com/ (August 11, 2009), Sandra Garcia-Myers, review of *Posed for Murder.*
S. Krishna's Books, http://www.skrishnasbooks.com/ (February 17, 2009), S. Krishna, review of *Posed for Murder.*
Writer House Web site, http://www.writerhouse.org/ (August 11, 2009), "Meet the Instructor: Meredith Cole."*

* * *

CONESCU, William

PERSONAL: Born in New York, NY. *Education:* University of North Carolina, B.A.; North Carolina State University, M.F.A.

ADDRESSES: *Home*—Chapel Hill, NC. *E-mail*—william@williamconescu.com.

CAREER: Writer.

WRITINGS:

Being Written (novel), Harper Perennial (New York, NY), 2008.

Contributor to periodicals, including *Gettysburg Review,New Letters,* and *Green Mountains Review.*

SIDELIGHTS: William Conescu, a graduate of the University of North Carolina and North Carolina State University, is the author of *Being Written.* This debut fiction release details and parodies the act of writing as told from the perspective of the protagonist, Daniel Fisher. However, Fisher is not the protagonist of the story he knows is being written by an unnamed author, whom Fisher can also hear composing through the audible scratching noises made by the author's pencil, which denote creative activity. Incredibly, while Fisher is aware of his character status, he is also aware of his function within the author's story. Conescu told Linda L. Richards, in an interview for *January* magazine, "Daniel is a very minor character—the literary equivalent of a movie extra. When Daniel discovers that the author has taken interest in an unhappy young singer, Daniel inserts himself into her social circle and attempts to reinvent himself to win the author's favor. *Being Written* is about the lengths to which Daniel will go to win a bigger part." While in a bar, Fisher meets the author's protagonist, Delia, and a group of her friends, and Fisher decides to try and facilitate a larger role for himself. This meeting eventually attracts the attention of the author to Fisher's character and his potential role in the story.

As a *Popin's Lair* Web site contributor explained, the construction of the narrative allows one to "wonder if Daniel really is a character in a story, or if he's just crazy." Moreover, Susan Larson, in a review for the *Times-Picayune,* wrote, "Conescu's novel is an adroit riff on literary conventions, turning various genres on their heads." Conescu's character, Fisher, has ambition, and this ambition is the literary element that moves the plot forward. While Fisher attempts to gain more exposure in his own story, events occur in reaction to Fisher's actions. Conescu told an *Olive Reader* Web site contributor that he experienced challenges after college and that he echoes his experiences in the text. Conescu stated, "I was interested in writing about artistically-minded people in their twenties and thirties struggling to figure out how best to live their lives, and then I had this playful idea about a minor character who can hear the author's pencil scratching when other characters are "being written" nearby. There are parallels in these struggles."

BIOGRAPHICAL AND CRITICAL SOURCES:

PERIODICALS

Herald-Sun, September 28, 2008, "Books Roundup: Chapel Hill Writer Examines His Craft."

Publishers Weekly, May 12, 2008, review of *Being Written,* p. 31.

ONLINE

Booking Mama, http://bookingmama.blogspot.com/ (November 27, 2008), author interview.

HarperCollins Web site, http://www.harpercollins.com/ (July 17, 2009), author profile.

January Online, http://januarymagazine.com/ (November 1, 2008), author interview with Linda L. Richards.

Metro Online, http://www.metronc.com/ (September 1, 2008), Art Taylor, "Being You; Tar Heel Voices; Fall Signings Kick Off Book Season."

Olive Reader, http://www.olivereader.com/ (October 1, 2008), author interview.

Popin's Lair, http://proudbookworm.blogspot.com/ (April 12, 2009), review of *Being Written.*

Story's Story, http://jseliger.com/ (June 26, 2009), review of *Being Written.*

Times-Picayune Online, http://blog.nola.com/ (October 1, 2008), Susan Larson, "'Being Written' Is a Clever Riff on Literary Conventions."

William Conescu Home Page, http://www.williamconescu.com (July 17, 2009).

* * *

CONYERS, A.J. 1944-2004

PERSONAL: Born May 29, 1944, in San Bernardino, CA; died July 18, 2004, of cancer. *Education:* University of Georgia, B.A., 1966; Southern Baptist Theological Seminary, M.Div., 1971; Southeastern Baptist Theological Seminary, M.Div., 1979.

CAREER: Writer and educator. Central Missouri State University, Warrensburg, professor, 1979-87; College of Charleston, Charleston, SC, chair, 1987-94; G.W. Truett Theological Seminary, Baylor University, Waco, TX, professor of theology, 1994-2004.

WRITINGS:

NONFICTION

How to Read the Bible, InterVarsity Press (Downers Grove, IL), 1986.

God, Hope, and History: Jürgen Moltmann and the Christian Concept of History, Mercer (Macon, GA), 1988.

Discovering Proverbs, Ecclesiastes, Song of Songs, Guideposts (Carmel, NY), 1989.

The Eclipse of Heaven: Rediscovering the Hope of a World Beyond, InterVarsity Press (Downers Grove, IL), 1992, published as *The Eclipse of Heaven: The Loss of Transcendence and Its Effect on Modern Life,* St. Augustine's Press (South Bend, IN), 1999.

The End: What Jesus Really Said about the Last Things, InterVarsity Press (Downers Grove, IL), 1995.

A Basic Christian Theology, Broadman & Holman Publishers (Nashville, TN), 1995.

The Long Truce: How Toleration Made the World Safe for Power and Profit, Spence Press (Dallas, TX), 2001.

The Listening Heart: Vocation and the Crisis of Modern Culture, Spence Press (Dallas, TX), 2006.

Last Things: The Heart of New Testament Eschatology, St. Augustine's Press (South Bend, IN), 2009.

SIDELIGHTS: A.J. Conyers, a graduate of the University of Georgia and the Southern Baptist Theological Seminary, was born May 29, 1944, and died of cancer on July 18, 2004. Conyers served as a professor of theology for Central Missouri State University, in Warrensburg, and the G.W. Truett Theological Seminary at Baylor University in Texas. During his long scholarly career, Conyers published several texts, including: *How to Read the Bible; God, Hope, and History: Jürgen Moltmann and the Christian Concept of History; Discovering Proverbs, Ecclesiastes, Song of Songs; The Eclipse of Heaven: Rediscovering the Hope of a World Beyond; The End: What Jesus Really Said about the Last Things; A Basic Christian Theology; The Eclipse of Heaven: The Loss of Transcendence and Its Effect on Modern Life; The Long Truce: How Toleration Made the World Safe for Power and Profit; The Listening Heart: Vocation and the Crisis of Modern Culture;* and *Last Things: The Heart of New Testament Eschatology.*

In 2007, the American Library Association awarded *The Listening Heart* with a place on their top ten list of religious books, according to a G.W. Truett Theological Seminary Web site contributor's article. The contributor also wrote, "In a provocative new book . . . Conyers shows that Western culture was once informed by a sense of vocation, that men understood life as a response to a call from outside and above themselves." The text explains how the ideal of vocational responsibility began to decline in the sixteenth century alongside the decline of the concept of a contributory society, and the text discusses how the concept of a profession has developed in non-Christian areas of the world. *The Listening Heart* details the ways in which modernity corrupts the idea of community and explains the consequences of achieving a total autonomy. The Enlightenment is credited with the perpetuation of the modern concept of free will and self realization; however, the text asserts that these features are not markers of progress but rather indications of the unmaking of communal responsibility. Slavery, the text claims, is the end result of a fully autonomous individual; for when one is without a bond to society they are also without their own purpose. This in turn enables an outside entity, like another individual or political enterprise, to exert influence over the seemingly independent person.

Ray Olson, in a review for *Booklist,* found that "Conyers sees in vocation a solution to personal alienation, social fragmentation, and even to overweening political power," and Conyers offers examples of vocation from early Christian communities which demonstrate a spiritual purposefulness. In an article for *Books & Culture,* Ralph C. Wood wrote of Conyers's spiritual legacy and stated, "There are so many good things to say about this man's life and work that one quails at saying anything at all, lest it be pathetically too small. Yet when I think of Chip's unique contribution to Baptist life in particular and to the ecumenical church in general, I think of his steadfast avoidance of cliché. He refused the deadly error of making the obvious still more obvious—as one wag has added—in perfectly obvious terms. . . . With devastating clarity, Chip Conyers came to see that this modern way of living no longer valued human beings as particular persons offering their unique and irreplaceable gifts to a communal enterprise." *The Listening Heart* details Conyers's precise views regarding modernity and the dangers that a life led in pursuit of solely individual objectives poses to humanity. Dave DeChristopher, in an essay for the *National Catholic Reporter,* stated as an example, "The spectacular gains of the First World, Dr. Conyers goes on, reflect the sufferings of the developing world."

BIOGRAPHICAL AND CRITICAL SOURCES:

PERIODICALS

Booklist, May 15, 2001, David Rouse, review of *The Long Truce: How Toleration Made the World Safe for Power and Profit,* p. 1710; November 15, 2006, Ray Olson, review of *The Listening Heart: Vocation and the Crisis of Modern Culture,* p. 9.

Books & Culture, November 1, 2004, "A Man Alive in the Midst of Death."
First Things: A Monthly Journal of Religion and Public Life, March 1, 2007, Gilbert Meilaender, review of *The Listening Heart,* p. 52.
Library Journal, June 15, 2001, George Westerlund, review of *The Long Truce,* p. 78.
Modern Age, June 22, 2001, George A. Panichas, review of *The Long Truce,* p. 275.
National Catholic Reporter, February 8, 2008, "When a Calling Became a Choice: How the Loss of a Sense of Vocation Affects Society," p. 12.
Reference & Research Book News, November 1, 2001, review of *The Long Truce,* p. 124.
Theology Today, July 1, 1990, Barry A. Harvey, review of *God, Hope, and History: Jürgen Moltmann and the Christian Concept of History,* p. 230.

ONLINE

George W. Truett Theological Seminary Web site, http://www.baylor.edu/ (October 15, 2007), "Truett Professor Has Book Named to Top 10."

OBITUARIES AND OTHER SOURCES:

ONLINE

Baylor University Press Web site, http://www.baylor.edu/ (July 16, 2009).
Spence Publishing Web site, http://www.spencepublishing.com/ (July 16, 2009).*

* * *

CORSETTI, Emilio, III 1957-

PERSONAL: Born January 18, 1957, in Rochester, PA. *Education:* St. Louis University, B.S., 1978.

ADDRESSES: Home—Lake St. Louis, MO. *E-mail*—emilio@emiliocorsetti.com.

CAREER: Writer and pilot. Apollo Software, Maryland Heights, MO, president, 1983-91; Odyssey Interactive, Ofallon, MO, creative director and vice president, 1994.

WRITINGS:

35 Miles from Shore: The Ditching and Rescue of ALM Flight 980, Odyssey Press (Lake St. Louis, MO), 2008.

Contributor of essays and articles to periodicals, including *Flying, Professional Pilot,* and the *Chicago Tribune.*

SIDELIGHTS: Emilio Corsetti III, a graduate of St. Louis University, has contributed articles and essays to periodicals such as *Flying, Professional Pilot,* and the *Chicago Tribune.* Additionally, Corsetti is the author of *35 Miles from Shore: The Ditching and Rescue of ALM Flight 980* released in 2008. The text chronicles the flight of ALM 980, the circumstances of its water landing, and the resulting fatalities. Corsetti, in a question-and-answer session on the book's Web site, acknowledged, "This book would not have been possible before the advent of the internet. Even in the days and weeks immediately after the accident it would have been nearly impossible to track down all of the participants." The flight, which departed from John F. Kennedy International Airport in New York, New York, was scheduled to arrive safely on the island of St. Maarten, an incorporated territory of the Netherlands Antilles, on May 2, 1970. However, as the text relates, the flight experienced landing difficulties and was forced to land in water due to low fuel reserves resulting from an initial diversion to San Juan and several missed landing attempts. The crash resulted in thirty-seven injuries and twenty-three fatalities among the crew and passengers. As reported on the book's Web site, Corsetti explained why the crash of flight 980 is significant and stated, "The survivors were in the water for an hour and a half before the first rescue helicopter arrived on the scene. The rescue itself took nearly three hours. Additionally, there were survivors. Unfortunately, most airline accidents of any magnitude have few survivors." These circumstances set flight 980 apart from other large-scale aeronautical accidents. In an interview with Ambrose Musiyiwa for the *Conversations with Writers* Web site, Corsetti talked about the difficulties in writing a story with so many possible perspectives and stated, "Without question the most difficult aspect of writing this book was finding the right balance of background information in the story. If I had too much background information, I would lose the reader in a sea of detail. If I had too little, then I risked confusing the reader. I think I found the right balance, but only after reading a lot of other nonfiction books to see how other authors handled it. . . . I learned that the most important thing in providing background information is that you should only include things that help describe a character or event."

BIOGRAPHICAL AND CRITICAL SOURCES:

PERIODICALS

Booklist, April 1, 2008, Roland Green, review of *35 Miles from Shore: The Ditching and Rescue of ALM Flight 980,* p. 6.

Library Journal, March 1, 2008, John Carver Edwards, review of *35 Miles from Shore,* p. 90.

ONLINE

Blogcritics, http://blogcritics.org/ (May 16, 2008), author interview with Mayra Calvani.

Conversations with Writers, http://conversationswithwriters.blogspot.com/ (May 20, 2008), author interview with Ambrose Musiyiwa.

Emilio Corsetti Home Page, http://www.emiliocorsetti.com (July 17, 2009).

35 Miles from Shore Web site, http://www.35milesfromshore.com (July 17, 2009).

* * *

CORWIN, Tom 1955-

PERSONAL: Born December 11, 1955.

ADDRESSES: *Home*—CA.

CAREER: Writer and musician.

WRITINGS:

Mostly Bob, New World Library (Novato, CA), 2006.

Mr. Fooster Traveling on a Whim, illustrated by Craig Frazier, Doubleday (New York, NY), 2008.

SIDELIGHTS: Tom Corwin, a music producer and fiction writer, was born December 11, 1955. Corwin is the author of *Mostly Bob* and *Mr. Fooster Traveling on a Whim. Mostly Bob,* released in 2006 via New World Library, tells the story of Corwin's relationship with his golden retriever, Bob, who died prior to the book's publication. The narrative, according to the *Mostly Bob* Web site, is dedicated in Bob's memory and originated from a written tribute which Corwin e-mailed to his friends and family after Bob's death. Soon thereafter, the message was shared with many readers and a friend recommended that Corwin compose a full-length narrative detailing Bob's life. The story provides an anecdotal chronology of Bob's life and his impact on those who were fortunate enough to have met him. Corwin ultimately relates the personal fulfillment available through the perpetuation of a relationship between an animal and a human. Additionally, the book cover succinctly features a red background with an imposed solid black dog in the lower right hand corner which has the semblance of a golden retriever.

In Corwin's subsequent release, *Mr. Fooster Traveling on a Whim,* the narrative is told as a graphic novel. The text, illustrated by Craig Frazier, details the abstract musings of the main character, Mr. Fooster. Fooster, having decided upon a walk, encounters strange and extraordinary circumstances as he considers his surroundings and engages with the products of his imagination. A reviewer for *Publishers Weekly* described Fooster as "a tall, rangy, hale fellow in a rumpled suit and hat," a perception that is echoed on the text's front cover which features a thin nondescript man wearing a hat and an overcoat who is in the process of blowing a soap bubble. However, this unlikely character evinces a heroic nonchalance and eventually meanders his way into an imaginative world where his mind is the catalyst for strange and exciting events. The book depicts Fooster's acceptance of an unanticipated transport, his transformation into a living tree, and his discovery of the power of belief. Within 112 pages, Corwin provides a variety of journeys which depict Fooster in several remarkable situations, from being encased in a bubble to having discussions with a butterfly, all of which are rendered in a monochromatic color palette. "Though this looks like a children's book, adults capable of childlike wonder will find it quietly delightful," according to a *Publishers Weekly* contributor.

BIOGRAPHICAL AND CRITICAL SOURCES:

PERIODICALS

Publishers Weekly, April 28, 2008, review of *Mr. Fooster Traveling on a Whim,* p. 114; July 7, 2008, review of *Mr. Fooster Traveling on a Whim,* p. 44.

Sing Out!, June 22, 2005, "Tom Corwin and Tim Hockenberry, Mostly Dylan," p. 158.

ONLINE

Mostly Bob Web site, http://www.mostlybob.com (July 15, 2009).

Random House Web site, http://www.randomhouse.com/ (July 15, 2009), author profile.

Red Room, http://www.redroom.com/ (July 15, 2009), author profile.*

*   *   *

COX, Meg

PERSONAL: Education: Graduate of Northwestern University, 1975.

ADDRESSES: Home—Princeton, NJ. *E-mail*—meg@megcox.com.

CAREER: Writer and journalist.

WRITINGS:

The Heart of a Family: Searching America for New Traditions That Fulfill Us, Random House (New York, NY), 1998.

The Book of New Family Traditions: How to Create Great Rituals for Holidays and Everyday, illustrated by Sarah McMenem, Running Press (Philadelphia, PA), 2003.

The Mini Book of New Family Traditions, Running Press (Philadelphia, PA), 2006.

The Quilter's Catalog: A Comprehensive Resource Guide, Workman Press (New York, NY), 2007.

Contributor of articles to the *Wall Street Journal.*

SIDELIGHTS: Meg Cox, a graduate of Northwestern University, is a writer and frequent contributor to the *Wall Street Journal.* Cox's debut book publication, *The Heart of a Family: Searching America for New Traditions That Fulfill Us,* was released in 1998. The text chronicles the variety of American domestic ritual in an attempt to reveal their function and impact on the family. Cox employs survey material and information gathered from interviews with mental health and educational professionals in order to discern the effect of ritual on the American family. According to a *Publishers Weekly* contributor, Cox "believes that great changes in the traditional American family make it essential to cultivate rituals that bind people together." Due to a shifting paradigm for the family, such as the non-nuclear and nontraditional family dynamic of the twenty-first century, Cox asserts that the function of domestic ritual serves several needs, such as facilitating familial bonding and providing a sense of security through repetitious actions. The text illustrates the diversity of practiced familial rituals, including the celebration of religious holidays, birthday commemoration, and the festivity linked with major life events. Bryce Christensen, in a review for *Booklist,* observed that the text puts forth substantive information regarding the "human need for ritual, especially among children trying to establish a sense of identity and moral orientation." Furthermore, the text includes illustrations and objective commentary regarding specific family practices and a section which offers advice regarding establishing new domestic traditions. Additionally, Cox's *The Book of New Family Traditions: How to Create Great Rituals for Holidays and Everyday,* which was released in 2003, reveals the many ways that a family can create special rites and rituals. The text, much like Cox's initial release, discusses methods for enacting new family customs, and Cox advises that the need for recognition and celebration is essential to healthy child development and maintaining familial relations. The text also includes an analysis of the elements that make up family ritual as well as sections detailing holiday, family, and cursory ritual ideas.

Moreover, in *The Quilter's Catalog: A Comprehensive Resource Guide,* a 2007 Workman Press publication, Cox provides an alternative perspective to traditional domestic practices and details the craft of quilting. As in her previous releases, Cox details the importance of quilting and reports on the groups that perpetuate the craft and their various methods. An *Internet Bookwatch* contributor concluded that the text is "a treat for avid quilters."

BIOGRAPHICAL AND CRITICAL SOURCES:

PERIODICALS

Booklist, September 15, 1998, Bryce Christensen, review of *The Heart of a Family: Searching America for New Traditions That Fulfill Us,* p. 175.

Capper's, April 1, 2008, "Author Says People's Interest in Quilting Has Been Revived," p. 11.

Internet Bookwatch, April 1, 2008, review of *The Quilter's Catalog: A Comprehensive Resource Guide.*

Library Journal, November 1, 1998, Elizabeth Caulfield, review of *The Heart of a Family,* p. 115; May 15, 2003, Douglas C. Lord, review of *The Book of New Family Traditions: How to Create Great Rituals for Holidays and Everyday,* p. 107.

Publishers Weekly, September 21, 1998, review of *The Heart of a Family,* p. 63.

ONLINE

Meg Cox Home Page, http://www.megcox.com (July 15, 2009).

Running Press Web site, http://www.perseusbooksgroup.com/ (July 15, 2009), author profile.

UU World Web site, http://www.uuworld.org (July 15, 2009), author profile.*

* * *

CRABBE, R.
See CRABBE, Richard E.

* * *

CRABBE, Richard
See CRABBE, Richard E.

* * *

CRABBE, Richard E.
(R. Crabbe, Richard Crabbe, Richard Edward Crabbe)

PERSONAL: Born on Staten Island, NY.

ADDRESSES: Home—Staten Island, NY.

CAREER: Writer, advertising sales executive, and novelist. Worked for twenty years in advertising sales for companies such as Advance Publications and Time Warner, and for publications such as the *New York Post* and the *Los Angeles Times.*

WRITINGS:

"BRADDOCK" POLICE DETECTIVE SERIES; NOVELS

Suspension, Thomas Dunne Books (New York, NY), 2000.

The Empire of Shadows, Thomas Dunne Books (New York, NY), 2003.

Hell's Gate, Thomas Dunne Books/St. Martin's Minotaur (New York, NY), 2008.

SIDELIGHTS: Richard E. Crabbe is a writer, advertising sales executive, and novelist. He is the author of the "Braddock" police detective series. The first book, *Suspension,* was inspired by Crabbe's daily commutes on the Staten Island Ferry. During these regular trips across New York Harbor, Crabbe became keenly fascinated by the Brooklyn Bridge. This deep curiosity led him "to do research on the Brooklyn Bridge, its origin, design, and construction, and he then began writing *Suspension*—in longhand—during the course of his daily commutes," noted *Bookreporter.com* reviewer Joe Hartlaub.

Suspension introduces series character Joe Braddock, a detective with the New York City Police Department. Set in the year 1883, the book centers on a world still profoundly affected by the events of the Civil War. Here, a group of former Confederate soldiers plot to destroy the Brooklyn Bridge, still under construction but a glaring symbol of what they lost and what the North represented during the war. The former soldiers and their leader, Captain Thaddeus Sangree, set out to destroy the bridge for ideological reasons. Sangree, however, has a more personal agenda: revenge against Union Colonel Washington Roebling, son of the Brooklyn Bridge designer and chief engineer of the project. Sangree holds Roebling responsible for his brother's death at Gettysburg. With their plan in place, the former Confederates get jobs on the bridge construction crew in order to find its weak spots. When they kill a fellow construction worker who has caught on to their plan, however, the murder is investigated by Detective Braddock. As the investigation unfolds, Braddock learns of the plot against the bridge, and must act with cunning, tenacity, and no small amount of brutality to keep the saboteurs from carrying out their mission.

"Crabbe develops Braddock's character quite nicely, taking great pains not to make him too good," Hartlaub observed. The book stands as "cunningly imagined historical fiction" and a "richly atmospheric thriller," remarked a *Publishers Weekly* contributor. "First novelist Crabbe is a thoughtful writer who provides wonderful detail," commented *Library Journal* writer Karen T. Bilton, who called *Suspension* a "suspenseful, well-researched historical" novel. The *Publishers Weekly* writer concluded that Crabbe "has effectively re-created a time when America was attempting to heal old wounds while steadying itself for a great industrial thrust forward."

Braddock returns in *The Empire of Shadows,* now precinct captain, married to an ex-prostitute and current madam, and father to teenage Mike, a former gang member, and young Rebecca. When Braddock takes his family on a well-deserved vacation to the Adirondacks in the fall of 1889, they cross paths with murderer Jim Tupper, an Indian on the run from a killing in New York. When it appears that Tupper has murdered Mike's new girlfriend, a maid at the hotel where they are staying, Braddock focuses his investigative skills and determines that all is not as it seems. Braddock must track Tupper into the wilderness, an unfamiliar setting where the outdoorsman's nature skills will give him a definite upper hand. The situation is made even worse when it becomes apparent that someone is trailing Tupper and also committing other murders. An "intriguing, multilayered plot, authentically detailed descriptions, and ruthless partnerships" propel this historical novel, commented Rex E. Klett in *Library Journal.*

In *Hell's Gate,* Braddock and son Mike are both police detectives in a New York ravaged by gang violence and territorial battles at places like the Hell's Gate Bridge. Mike Braddock works to disrupt the smuggling operations run by the city's gangs. His actions drive him to pursue an extremely tenuous lead given by a dying smuggler—the name "bottler." Soon, Mike is dragged down into the violent world of the gangsters and their customers and victims. Elsewhere, political machinations from the notorious Tammany Hall will have an effect on Mike Braddock and his law-enforcement partners, and the shadow of the fire on the steamship General Slocum, which claimed more than a thousand lives, will affect Mike, the woman he loves, and the entire population of New York.

BIOGRAPHICAL AND CRITICAL SOURCES:

PERIODICALS

Booklist, May 15, 2008, Jen Baker, review of *Hell's Gate,* p. 24.

Drood Review of Mystery, September, 2000, review of *Suspension,* p. 14.

Kirkus Reviews, October 1, 2003, review of *The Empire of Shadows,* p. 1201.

Library Journal, September 1, 2000, Karen T. Bilton, review of *Suspension,* p. 253; November 1, 2003, Rex E. Klett, review of *The Empire of Shadows,* p. 127.

Publishers Weekly, September 25, 2000, review of *Suspension,* p. 83; April 21, 2008, review of *Hell's Gate,* p. 39.

ONLINE

Bookreporter.com, http://www.bookreporter.com/ (August 9, 2009), Joe Hartlaub, review of *Suspension;* Andi Schechter, review of *The Empire of Shadows.*

Genre Go Round Reviews, http://genregoroundreviews.blogspot.com/ (May 1, 2008), Harriet Klausner, review of *Hell's Gate.*

Macmillan Web site, http://us.macmillan.com/ (August 9, 2009), biography of Richard E. Crabbe.*

* * *

CRABBE, Richard Edward
See CRABBE, Richard E.

CROOKS, Christina

PERSONAL: Female.

ADDRESSES: Home—Portland, OR.

CAREER: Writer.

WRITINGS:

Thrill of the Chase, Five Star (Waterville, ME), 2007.

Stories have appeared in anthologies, including *Hot Blood #13: Dark Passions,* Kensington Publishing, 2007, and *Chimeraworld #4,* Chimericana Books, 2006, and in periodicals, including *Space and Time, Nossa Morte, Quantum Kiss,* and *Aoife's Kiss.* Also contributor to *Wrong World,* a QWAND DVD production.

SIDELIGHTS: Christina Crooks is a fiction writer whose short stories have appeared in anthologies and various periodicals. Her first novel is titled *Thrill of the Chase.* Writing for the *Genre Go Round Reviews* Web site, Harriet Klausner called the book "an interesting contemporary romance that uses drag racing to [refresh] the classic triangle story line. "Similarly, *Booklist* contributor Maria Hatton called the novel an "atypical, up-to-the-minute contemporary romance."

Sarah Matell is an automotive technician who, at a young age, was introduced to cars and car racing by her father, who runs a speed shop. Sarah has had a crush on Craig Keller for years. Craig, a professional drag racer, ignores Sarah, preferring his women fast like his cars. Eventually, Sarah's father hires Gordon Devine to use his business skills to oversee the speed shop. Sarah is not happy about Gordon coming in to run the show, figuring that he may know business but that he doesn't know as much about cars as she does. Likewise, Gordon is not initially enamored of Sarah. He perceives her as a spoiled brat who is more interested in pursuing her dream of becoming a top drag racer than committing to her father's business.

Eventually, Gordon proves to Sarah that he knows what goes on under the hood of car via the prototype dragster he has developed. Although he is beginning to have feelings for Sarah, he knows she is lusting after Craig. Eventually, Sarah convinces Gordon to let her drive his own prototype dragster on the racing circuit, where Sarah is willing to do anything to win. Meanwhile, Craig seems to have changed his mind about Sarah. Gordon knows that letting Sarah go on the circuit where she will constantly be in contact with Craig means he may lose her to Craig. Before long, there is a love triangle as Sarah not only proves herself as a racer but also as a woman, leaving behind her tomboy past and buying a new, sexy wardrobe.

"The adventure of racing, along with an engaging romance, provides readers with an entertaining tale," wrote Patti Fischer in a review for the *Romance Reviews Today* Web site, adding later in the same review: "Even if you're not into drag racing, *Thrill of the Chase* is an enjoyable story of a woman coming to know herself." In her review for the *Genre Go Rounds Reviews* Web site, Klausner referred to the novel as "a fine character driven tale."

BIOGRAPHICAL AND CRITICAL SOURCES:

PERIODICALS

Booklist, October 1, 2007, Maria Hatton, review of *Thrill of the Chase,* p. 40.

ONLINE

Christina Crooks Home Page, http://www.christinacrooks.net (July 17, 2009).

Genre Go Round Reviews, http://genregoroundreviews.blogspot.com/ (October 13, 2007), Harriet Klausner, review of *Thrill of the Chase.*

Romance Reviews Today, http://www.romrevtoday.com/ (July 17, 2009), Patti Fischer, review of *Thrill of the Chase.**

* * *

**CROUSE, David 1967-
(David John Crouse)**

PERSONAL: Born June 9, 1967, in Boston, MA; married Melina Draper (a poet); children: Dylan. *Education:* Bradford College, B.A. (summa cum laude), 1990; University of Alaska, M.F.A., 1996.

ADDRESSES: Home—Fairbanks, AK. *Office*—University of Alaska Fairbanks, Department of English, P.O. Box 755720, Fairbanks, AK 99775-5720. *E-mail*—davidcrouse@acsalaska.net.

CAREER: Writer and educator. Bradford College, Bradford, MA, assistant professor of creative writing, 1995-2000; Chester College of New England, Chester, NH, assistant professor, 2001-05, associate professor of creating writing 2005-07, also served as chair of the Writing and Literature Program; University of Alaska, Fairbanks, assistant professor of English, 2007—. Also director of Educational Services, Iprax Corporation, Lexington, MA, 1995.

AWARDS, HONORS: Raymond Carver Short Story Contest finalist, 1994; Yates Short Fiction Award, 2003; Pushcart Prize nominations, 2003, for short story "Still Running," 2004, for short story "Kopy Kats," and 2005; Flannery O'Connor Award for Short Fiction, 2005, for *Copy Cats;* Mary McCarthy Prize in Short Fiction, 2007, for *The Man Back There and Other Stories.*

WRITINGS:

Copy Cats: Stories, University of Georgia Press (Athens, GA), 2005.
The Man Back There and Other Stories, Sarabande Books (Louisville, KY), 2008.

Contributor to literary journals, including *Greensboro Review, Chelsea, Quarterly West, Arts & Letters, Salamander, Flint Hills Review, Northwest Review, Massachusetts Review, Laurel Review, Sonora Review, Pacific Review, Timber Creek Review, Blue Mesa Review, Poet's Edge, Canadian Literature,* and the *Beloit Fiction Journal.* Has also written in the comic book genre, with work appearing in the graphic novel *The Darkhorse Book of the Dead,* Darkhorse Comics, 2005. Also *Permafrost: A Literary Journal,* University of Alaska, editor, 1992-94; *Salamander* magazine, fiction editor, 2001-05, contributing editor, 2005—.

SIDELIGHTS: David Crouse is a fiction writer whose short stories appear in two collections. As noted in the author's faculty profile for the University of Alaska Web site, the author's themes "are issues of identity and alienation." For example, his short story "Kopy Kats," which was nominated for a Pushcart Prize, tells the tale of a man working in a copy shop who finds that life itself is full of imitations and illusions as he helps a patron who collapses in the shop only to find that the customer sees him as a stranger and an irrelevant one at that.

Crouse's first collection of stories, *Copy Cats: Stories,* was published in 2005 and won the Flannery O'Connor Award for Short Fiction. The collection features seven short stories, and a novella. Like the short story "Kopy Kats," which is included in the collection, the stories' characters ponder the mysteriousness of their identities and the identities of those around them. For example, the story "Cry Baby" features a man who writes a memoir about his childhood living in poverty with a father who was abusive. However, the man can neither tell the truth about his past relationship with his best friend, either in the memoir or to his wife. The novella, "Click," focuses on a man engaged to a traditional woman yet finds himself absorbed with the life of a prostitute and drug addict and feels compelled to photograph her. Noting that the stories' characters are "pervaded by a sense of aloneness, of disconnection even from those with whom the central characters are supposedly most intimate," a *Kirkus Reviews* contributor went on to note in the same review that the author's "bleak outlook is richly complex and deeply felt."

Crouse's second collection, *The Man Back There and Other Stories,* won the 2007 Mary McCarthy Prize in Short Fiction. *San Francisco Chronicle* contributor Casey Cep wrote that the stories in this collection "are like tide pools, miniature worlds of wonder that we can study or admire but that are less steady and more fragile than their oceanic equivalents," adding: "The care and attentiveness with which he renders characters and their situations are moving."

The title story begins with a couple, Sharon and Sweets, outside of a bar right after Sweets has had a confrontation with Sharon's ex-husband. A *Publishers Weekly* contributor remarked that, "although Sharon imagines he is defending her honor, Sweets has his own motivation." In other stories, fear and danger are the motivating factor, such as "The Castle on the Hill," in which a dogcatcher sees the victims of a double murder just before their deaths and then sets out to warn his ex-wife about a world full of danger. In "The Observable Universe," a man who is mentally ill and his sister, a multimedia artist, go to a science fiction convention where they ruminate on the idea of escapism into fictional worlds. Meanwhile, at the convention, the man goes to an event and ends up watching a video that his sister made when he was having his breakdown. As he views the video over and over again, he begins to perceive it as a story of his death.

"A remarkable gathering of short fiction, the nine stories of David Crouse's second collection don't just add to his literary resume: They go a long way toward defining it," wrote Jay Robinson for the *Barn Owl Review* Web site. *Bookslut* Web site contributor Benjamin Jacob Hollars remarked that the author's "sharp sense for setting and dialogue only further contribute to the wealth of strengths he draws upon."

BIOGRAPHICAL AND CRITICAL SOURCES:

PERIODICALS

American Book Review, January-February, 2009, Scott Elliott, "Lonely Voices," review of *The Man Back There and Other Stories,* p. 27.

Choice, March, 2006, M.W. Cox, review of *Copy Cats: Stories,* p. 1225.

Kirkus Reviews, August 15, 2005, review of *Copy Cats,* p. 869.

Publishers Weekly, June 9, 2008, review of *The Man Back There and Other Stories,* p. 33.

San Francisco Chronicle, August 15, 2008, Casey Cep, review of *The Man Back There and Other Stories,* p. E3.

Virginia Quarterly Review, spring, 2006, Zak M. Salith, review of *Copy Cats,* p. 313.

ONLINE

Barn Owl Review, http://www.barnowlreview.com/ (July 17, 2009), review of *The Man Back There and Other Stories.*

Bookslut, http://www.barnowlreview.com/ (July 17, 2009), Benjamin Jacob Hollars, review of *The Man Back There and Other Stories.*

David Crouse Home Page, http://www.davidcrouse house.com (July 17, 2009).

University of Alaska Web site, University of Alaska, http://www.alaska.edu/ (July 17, 2009), faculty profile of author.*

CROUSE, David John
See CROUSE, David

* * *

CUMMING, Charles 1971-

PERSONAL: Born April 5, 1971, in Ayr, Scotland; married. *Education:* Graduated from University of Edinburgh with first class honours, 1994.

ADDRESSES: *Home*—London, England. *E-mail*—author@charlescumming.co.uk.

CAREER: Writer and novelist. Briefly worked with the British Secret intelligence Service (SIS), c. 1995.

WRITINGS:

The Hidden Man, Penguin Paperback (New York, NY), 2004.

A Spy by Nature, St. Martin's Press (New York, NY), 2007.

The Spanish Game, St. Martin's Press (New York, NY), 2008.

Typhoon, Michael Joseph (New York, NY), 2008.

Contributing editor to the *Week* magazine; book review contributor to the *Mail on Sunday.*

ADAPTATIONS: Film rights to *A Spy By Nature* have been purchased by Kudos.

SIDELIGHTS: Charles Cumming is a spy novelist whose entry in the genre was precipitated by his recruitment to the British Secret Intelligence Service (SIS) in 1995. A year later, Cumming began work on his first spy novel based on his time with the British intelligence agency, also known as MI6. Since then he has written several successful spy novels earning him recognition as perhaps Great Britain's preeminent spy novelist and also comparisons to both Graham Greene and John Le Carré.

The author's first novel, *A Spy by Nature,* published in the United States in 2007, features Alec Milius, an ambitious young man stuck in a boring job. Wanting to make his mark in the world, he ends up interviewing with MI6. The novel begins by following Alec through the preliminaries of joining the agency via a number of tests. "He calculates his every move, plotting his contributions to a discussion about international relations as if he were playing chess, declining to evaluate himself for the written record, and choosing, in a one-on-one with a shrink, to lie about his current relationship with his former girlfriend, Kate," noted Kirstin Merrihew in a review for the *Mostly Fiction* Web site.

Rejected for the upper level of British spy operations, Alex ends up working in industrial espionage for an oil company as an undercover operative, where he is assigned the mission of befriending an American couple who may be industrial spies. Although supremely self-confident, Alex begins to make mistakes and soon is in danger. Writing for *Publishers Weekly,* a contributor noted that *A Spy by Nature* "provides plenty of elaborate deceits, double crosses and other trappings of a first-class spy thriller." Commenting on the author's real-life recruitment to MI6, Bill Ott wrote in *Booklist* that the author "appears to speak with authority."

Cumming's novel *The Hidden Man* revolves around the Keen family and the Russia mafia. Christopher Keen is a spy who has been estranged from his two sons, Ben and Mark, for more than two decades. It turns out that the people Mark works for are opening a nightclub in Russia and may have ties with the Russian mafia. Christopher also has ties with unsavory people in Russia. Shortly after Mark and Christopher begin to contact each other, Ben meets his father for the first time only to witness his assassination. There may be a connection between Christopher's death and Mark's business associates, and the two brothers set out to find the truth. "This is a worthy second book from an author worth noting," wrote Susan Bell in a review for the *Europe Intelligence Wire.*

Alec Milius returns in *The Spanish Game* and is no longer actually working in espionage but still lives his life cautiously as though someone is coming to eliminate him. Living in Madrid, he uses a false identification, switches hotel rooms regularly when he meets with a married woman, and suspects his newly arrived best friend was sent by British intelligence to inform on him. Eventually, Alex returns to espionage following the disappearance of a local politician and is now really being pursued by a number of factions, including the police and British intelligence.

"The brilliance of this novel is the complexity with which Cumming paints the picture of Alec Milius and his situation: stroke by stroke, with each stroke adding a layer that changes the big picture," remarked J.B. Thompson writing for *ReviewingTheEvidence.com.* In a review for *Booklist,* Thomas Gaughan wrote that "the complex plot effectively uses real events from the history of the Basque-Spanish conflict."

Typhoon begins in Hong Kong in 1997 just prior to the end of British rule. Various countries and their operatives are competing for influence and position in the soon-to-be China-ruled Hong Kong. At the same time, Joe Lennox, a young MI6 agent, loses his girlfriend to CIA agent Miles Coolidge, who seeks to bed as many women as possible. Even worse, Joe also bungles a case involving a defector who vanishes. A decade later, Joe returns to China much more experienced as he encounters old enemies and uncovers a plot to destabilize China prior to the Olympic games. Noting that the novel has a "le Carré-esque touch," Peter Millar, writing for the London *Times Online,* went on to remark in the same review: "The comparison is a heavy one for a young author, but *Typhoon,* with its deep plotting, flawed characters, climactic conclusion and undercurrent of mistrust is another step in the footprints of the master."

BIOGRAPHICAL AND CRITICAL SOURCES:

PERIODICALS

Asia Africa Intelligence Wire, December 24, 2004, "Spies and Lies," review of *The Hidden Man.*

Booklist, August, 2007, Bill Ott, review of *A Spy by Nature,* p. 49; September 15, 2008, Thomas Gaughan, review of *The Spanish Game,* p. 30.

Europe Intelligence Wire, September 11, 2004, Susan Bell, "Engaging Espionage Tale," review of *The Hidden Man.*

Financial Times, April 15, 2006, Zoe Strimpel, "In Brief—*The Spanish Game,*" p. 33.

Kirkus Reviews, October 15, 2008, review of *The Spanish Game.*

Library Journal, September 15, 2008, Barbara Conaty, review of *The Spanish Game,* p. 44.

Publishers Weekly, May 14, 2007, review of *A Spy by Nature,* p. 31; September 22, 2008, review of *The Spanish Game,* p. 38.

Times Literary Supplement, July 4, 2008, Toby Lichtig, review of *Typhoon,* p. 33.

ONLINE

Charles Cumming Home Page, http://www.charlescumming.co.uk (July 18, 2009).

Charles Cumming MySpace.com Page, http://www.myspace.com/charlescumming (July 18, 2009).

Fantastic Fiction, http://www.fantasticfiction.co.uk/ (July 18, 2009), brief profile of author.

Guardian Online, http://www.guardian.co.uk/ (July 18, 2009), brief profile of author.

Lizzy's Literary Life, http://lizzysiddal.wordpress.com/ (November 21, 2007), Lizzy Siddal, "Charles Cumming—Successor of John Le Carré?"

Mostly Fiction, http://www.mostlyfiction.com/ (December 3, 2007), Matthew Merrihew, review of *A Spy by Nature.*

ReviewingTheEvidence.com, http://www.reviewingtheevidence.com/ (July 18, 2009), J.B. Thompson, review of *The Spanish Game.*

Times Online, http://www.timesonline.co.uk/ (June 12, 2008), Peter Millar, review of *Typhoon.**

* * *

CUROE, Carol 1963(?)-

PERSONAL: Born c. 1963; daughter of Robert and Carole Curoe; partner of Susan Langlee, c. 1989—; children: Patrick and Jonathan.

ADDRESSES: *Home*—Minneapolis, MN.

CAREER: Consultant and writer. Business consultant, Minneapolis, MN. Formerly worked in real estate.

WRITINGS:

(With father, Robert Curoe) *Are There Closets in Heaven? A Catholic Father and Lesbian Daughter Share Their Story* (memoir), Syren (Minneapolis, MN), 2007.

SIDELIGHTS: Carol Curoe is author with her father, Robert Curoe, of *Are There Closets in Heaven? A Catholic Father and Lesbian Daughter Share Their Story.* The father-daughter memoir recounts Carol's coming out as a lesbian in 1990 and her parents resulting shock. "They were from a small, conservative, farming community in eastern Iowa, and were totally unprepared to deal with their daughter's 'coming out' as a lesbian," remarked the *Wild Reed* Web site contributor Michael J. Bayly.

As told in the memoir, Robert is sixty-five when his wife, Joyce, presents him with a letter from Carol announcing her sexual orientation. A farmer from Iowa, Robert is also a devout Catholic from an equally devout Catholic family that includes two sisters who were nuns. In Robert's religious belief, homosexuality is a serious sin. "To say that he was shocked . . . would have been a gross understatement," wrote Dan Clendenin in a review for the *Journey with Jesus* Web site. The book follows the relationship between parents and daughter over the next several years as Robert and Joyce deal with a wide range of negative emotions, including confusion and fear that others will find out about their daughter.

Robert, however, is intent on keeping communications open with his daughter while Joyce initially appears to have more difficulty than her husband in dealing with her daughter's announcement. Having written many letters to his six children when they were in college, Robert begins an epistolary communication with Carol that is included in the memoir. Eventually, Carol lets her parents know that she and her partner are going to have a baby by artificial insemination, which leads Robert and Joyce to finally announce their daughter's sexual orientation to the rest of the family.

The story is told by father and daughter in alternating chapters and goes back to the family's early days working their Iowa farm. As noted by Clendenin in his review for the *Journey with Jesus* Web site, the memoir revolves around four primary themes: the "extended family, their culturally conservative farm community, the . . . arena of legal parity . . . and . . . their religious perspectives."

The memoir reveals that the turning point is the letter to the rest of the family letting them know about Carol's homosexuality. Robert and Joyce are relieved to discover that their family is almost universally positive in their responses to the letter, and that some who cannot completely accept Carol's homosexuality are still supportive. This response leads to Robert and Joyce also "coming out" in the sense that they become active in a gay rights organization and begin to openly discuss their daughter's homosexuality and the need for recognizing gay marriage.

"What makes this beautifully written book a page-turner and sets it apart from a standard coming-out story is Robert Curoe's spiritual journey from unquestioning Catholic to outspoken advocate—even in the face of opposition from the Church—for the rights of his daughter, the family she created, and all gay and lesbian people," wrote Michele St. Martin in a review for the *Twin Cities Daily Planet Online* Web site. *Booklist* contributor June Sawyers remarked: "Painfully personal . . . the Curoes' book proves quite inspiring on its timely topic."

BIOGRAPHICAL AND CRITICAL SOURCES:

BOOKS

Curoe, Carole, and Robert Curoe, *Are There Closets in Heaven? A Catholic Father and Lesbian Daughter Share Their Story,* Syren (Minneapolis, MN), 2007.

PERIODICALS

Booklist, October 1, 2007, June Sawyers, review of *Are There Closets in Heaven?,* p. 20.

National Catholic Reporter, November 2, 2007, Kris Berggren, "Parish Cancels Talk by Father and Lesbian Daughter," p. 7.

Star Tribune, October 23, 2007, Joy Powell, "Archdiocese Discourages Church Talks by Lesbian and Her Father; Two Catholic Priests Agreed Not to Have a Minneapolis Woman and Her Father Talk about Their Book. The Event Was Held Elsewhere," p. 03; November 3, 2007, Jeff Strickler, "Faith & Values; 'Closets' Book on Healing Has Opened Some Wounds; Despite Initial Controversy, Authors of a Coming-Out Journal Are Still Hopeful That Their Book Will Bring People Together," p. 01.

ONLINE

Journey with Jesus, http://www.journeywithjesus.net/ (July 18, 2009), Dan Clendenin, review of *Are There Closets in Heaven?*

New Oxford Review Online, http://www.newoxford review.org/ (July 18, 2009), "Not Peace, But a Sword," profile.

St. Joan of Arc, http://www.stjoan.com/ (July 18, 2009), Phil Klees, review of *Are There Closets in Heaven?*

Twin Cities Daily Planet Online, http://www.tcdaily planet.net/ (February 9, 2008), Michele St. Martin, review of *Are There Closets in Heaven?*

Wild Reed, http://thewildreed.blogspot.com/ (October 20, 2007), "Sharing Their Story," interview with author.*

D

DAVIS, Frank 1942-
(Frank Joseph Davis)

PERSONAL: Born June 16, 1942, in New Orleans, LA.

ADDRESSES: Home—New Orleans, LA. *E-mail*—frankd@frankdavis.com.

CAREER: Chef, radio host, television host, public speaker, consultant, and educator. WWL Radio, New Orleans, LA, hosted call-in cooking show; WWL TV, New Orleans, host of *In the Kitchen with Frank Davis.*

MEMBER: American Federation of Television and Radio Artists, American Culinary Federation.

WRITINGS:

The Frank Davis Seafood Notebook, foreword by Paul Prudhomme, Pelican Publishing (Gretna, LA), 1983.

The Frank Davis Fishing Guide to Lake Pontchartrain and Lake Borgne, Pelican Publishing (Gretna, LA), 1988.

Frank Davis Cooks Naturally N'Awlins, illustrations by Shelby Wilson, Pelican Publishing (Gretna, LA), 1990.

Frank Davis Cooks Cajun, Creole, and Crescent City, foreword by Albert Barrocas, illustrations by Shelby Wilson, Pelican Publishing (Gretna, LA), 1994.

The Fisherman's Tackle Box Bible, Pelican Publishing (Gretna, LA), 2003.

Frank Davis Makes Good Groceries! A New Orleans Cookbook, Pelican Publishing (Gretna, LA), 2008.

SIDELIGHTS: A native of New Orleans, cookbook author Frank Davis first started cooking New Orleans food when he was eight years old. Davis, who has hosted both cooking radio and television programs, calls his New Orleans culinary style of cooking "Strictly N'Awlins," a style he developed after working with several noted Cajun and Creole chefs. He is also the developer of his own special brand of preblended gourmet seasonings for cooking. In addition, Davis teaches about cooking, including conducting classes for major corporations and teaching university students various cooking techniques. He holds cooking shows, primarily in the South, and conducts private cooking classes. Although Davis specializes in Louisiana cuisine, *Booklist* contributor Frank Knoblauch commented that Davis's "cooking stretches beyond traditional Cajun and Creole dishes" and includes influences from a variety of sources, including Chinese and Italian styles of food preparation."

Davis's first book, *The Frank Davis Seafood Notebook,* includes a foreword by noted chef Paul Prudhomme, who specializes in Cajun cuisine. The book includes recipes for both familiar seafood, such as oysters, and more esoteric fare, such as alligators. *Frank Davis Cooks Naturally N'Awlins,* which includes illustrations by Shelby Wilson, focuses on traditional Louisiana recipes and provides basic directions to the novice cook on what to do and not what to do when cooking.

Frank Davis Cooks Cajun, Creole, and Crescent City also includes illustrations by Shelby Wilson and features the author's favorite hometown recipes. However, the author also addresses healthy cooking, providing a chapter on how to cook fat free and the use of healthier substitutions. In his 2003 book *Frank Davis Makes Good Groceries! A New Orleans Cookbook,* Davis combines anecdotes from his life to enhance his discussion of how to buy "good groceries" that help in both cooking techniques and food preparation. He includes recipes for side dishes, discusses how to use leftovers, and lists various alternative seasonings for his recipes. Among the recipes, many of which includes the author's own preblended seasonings, are Crawfish Bread and Creole Rice Pudding. Writing for the *Times-Picayune Online,* Judy Walker noted that the cookbook includes "lots of colorful local dialect and spelling."

Davis, an avid fisherman, also writes fishing guides, including *The Frank Davis Fishing Guide to Lake Pontchartrain and Lake Borgne* and *The Fisherman's Tackle Box Bible.* The latter book focuses on the best fishing spots in southern Louisiana and the Gulf of Mexico. The author includes numerous tips he learned from various fishing guides and from his own experiences. For example, Davis writes about the best time to fish in various areas and the best tackle to use. He also discusses natural versus artificial bait.

BIOGRAPHICAL AND CRITICAL SOURCES:

PERIODICALS

Booklist, April 1, 2008, Mark Knoblauch, review of *Frank Davis Makes Good Groceries! A New Orleans Cookbook,* p. 14.

Christian Science Monitor, January 4, 1984, Phyllis Hanes, review of *The Frank Davis Seafood Notebook,* p. 26.

New Orleans, September, 1998, "Frank Davis," interview with author, p. 9.

Publishers Weekly, May 20, 1983, review of *The Frank Davis Seafood Notebook,* p. 228.

Whole Earth, summer, 1998, review of *The Frank Davis Seafood Notebook,* p. 73.

ONLINE

Frank Davis Home Page, http://www.frankdavis.com (July 18, 2009).

Times-Picayune Online, http://blog.nola.com/ (February 21, 2008), Judy Walker, "Cookbook review: That's Naturally Lagniappe," review of *Frank Davis Cooks Naturally N'Awlins.**

* * *

DAVIS, Frank Joseph
See DAVIS, Frank

* * *

DERFNER, Joel

PERSONAL: Education: Harvard University, B.A.; New York University, Tisch School of the Arts, M.F.A.

ADDRESSES: Home—New York, NY. *E-mail*—joel@joelderfner.com.

CAREER: Writer, poet, composer, lyricist, and memoirist. Composer of music and scores for musicals produced in the United States and abroad. Has worked as a dancer, step aerobics instructor, and math teacher.

WRITINGS:

Gay Haiku, Broadway Books (New York, NY), 2005.

Swish: My Quest to Become the Gayest Person Ever (memoir), Broadway Books (New York, NY), 2008.

Composer of music for plays and musicals such as *Postcards from Another Planet* and *Signs of Life.*

SIDELIGHTS: Joel Derfner is a writer, poet, and composer living in New York City. Originally from South Carolina, Derfner concentrated on "fleeing the south as soon as he possibly could," noted a biographer on the *Joel Derfner* Home Page. He studied linguistics at Harvard University, where he earned his B.A. degree. Later, however, he learned that a mistranslation of a word in the Abkhaz language—he'd been translating the word as "who" when it was actually a verb—rendered his thesis invalid, the biographer reported. From there, he pursued an M.F.A. in musical theater from the Tisch School of the Arts at New York University. He has been a successful composer for the musical theater since moving to New York, and has had musical scores produced in New York, London, and Europe. Derfner is also a composer of cabaret songs, with lyrics by him or with a collaborator.

Gay Haiku is a collection of 110 haiku poems following the well-known three-line structure of five, seven, and five syllables. Here, Derfner presents concise, poetic scenes of gay life in an urban setting. An *Advocate* reviewer found the works presented "clever, hilarious, and even poignant snapshots" of the gay lifestyle in the city.

With *Swish: My Quest to Become the Gayest Person Ever*, Derfner "has again managed to elevate the genre of gay literature to an ecstatic level of wit and sophistication," commented a reviewer on the Web site *In the Fray.* Here, Derfner explores his involvement in activities that appear to be consummately gay, but also considers the moments of interpersonal connection and personal insight that signal his comfort with and acceptance of the homosexual lifestyle. He comments on the sensual delights associated with knitting; his experiences with Cheer New York, the city's gay and lesbian cheerleading squad; the search for sex, love, and acceptance; and the sometimes rocky encounters with family and others over his sexual orientation. For example, though his mother was a liberal civil-rights activist, she never came to fully accept that her son was gay. In presenting such personal revelations, this "superficially facile book becomes more than the sum of its parts," commented *Booklist* reviewer Whitney Scott.

"Though sometimes reducing his insights to stereotypes, he can be incredibly funny and wry," commented David Azzolina, writing in *Library Journal.* In a *Gay & Lesbian Review Worldwide* assessment, David Pasteelick found each chapter of the book to be "brilliantly witty," leading to a "reading experience that will make you laugh, choke up, and think about your humanity." Derfner presents a "story that everyone can relate to if they are willing to honestly understand themselves and the points of view of others," the *In the Fray* Web site reviewer concluded.

BIOGRAPHICAL AND CRITICAL SOURCES:

PERIODICALS

Advocate, June 21, 2005, "Haiku Cool," review of *Gay Haiku,* p. 188.

Booklist, May 1, 2008, Whitney Scott, review of *Swish: My Quest to Become the Gayest Person Ever,* p. 60.

Gay & Lesbian Review Worldwide, September-October, 2008, David Pasteelick, review of *Swish,* p. 46.

Library Journal, April 15, 2008, David Azzolina, review of *Swish,* p. 92.

Publishers Weekly, March 24, 2008, review of *Swish,* p. 63.

ONLINE

In The Fray, http://inthefray.org/ (May 3, 2009), "Joel Derfner Takes Gay Literature to a Higher Level," profile of Joel Derfner.

Joel Derfner Home Page, http://www.joelderfner.com (August 10, 2009).

Red Room, http://www.redroom.com/ (August 10, 2009), biography of Joel Derfner.*

* * *

DiFONZO, Nicholas 1959-

PERSONAL: Born December 19, 1959. *Education:* Lafayette College, A.B., 1981; Rider College, M.A. (with distinction), 1990; Temple University, M.A., 1990, Ph.D., 1994.

ADDRESSES: Office—Rochester Institute of Technology, 3176 George Eastman Bldg., 18 Lomb Memorial Dr., Rochester, NY 14623. *E-mail*—nick@profnick.com.

CAREER: Psychologist, educator, consultant, writer, and editor. Rochester Institute of Technology, Rochester, NY, assistant professor of psychology, 1994-99, associate professor of psychology, 2000-06, professor of psychology, 2006—; founder and administrator of Rumor-GossipResearch@listserver.rit.edu, 2003—.

MEMBER: American Psychological Association, American Psychological Society, Society for the Scientific Study of Religion.

AWARDS, HONORS: Marianthi Georgoudi Dissertation Award, Temple University, for philosophical and theoretical contributions to the field of psychology; *ForeWord* Book of the Year Award in psychology, 2007, for *Rumor Psychology;* recipient of research grants, including a grant from the National Science Foundation.

WRITINGS:

(With Prashant Bordia) *Rumor Psychology: Social and Organizational Approaches,* American Psychological Association (Washington, DC), 2007.

The Watercooler Effect: A Psychologist Explores the Extraordinary Power of Rumors, Avery (New York, NY), 2008.

Author of reports, including *How Top PR Professionals Handle Hot Air: Types of Corporate Rumors, Their Effects, and Strategies to Manage Them,* Institute for Public Relations, 1998. Contributor to books, including *Rumor Mills: The Social Impact of Rumor and Legend,* edited by G.A. Fine, V. Campion-Vincent, and C. Heath, Aldine, 2005; *Advances in Psychology: A Tribute to Ralph L. Rosnow,* edited by D.A. Hantula, Lawrence Erlbaum Associates, 2006; *The Science of Social Influence: Advances and Future Progress,* edited by A.R. Pratkanis, Psychology Press, 2007; *Encyclopedia of Social Psychology,* edited by R.F. Baumeister and K.D. Vohs, Sage, 2007; and *International Encyclopedia of the Social Sciences,* editor-in-chief William A. Darity, Jr., Macmillan Reference USA, 2008.

Contributor to journals and periodicals, including the *Sunday Age, Journal of Employee Communication Management, Group & Organization Management, European Journal of Work & Organizational Psychology, Communications Research Reports, Journal of Applied Social Psychology, Small Group Research, Social Psychology Quarterly, Industrial-Organizational Psychologist, Organizational Dynamics, Diogenes, Organizational Behavior and Human Decision Processes, Public Relations Review, Human Resource, Management,* and *Organizational Behavior and Human Decision Processes.* Consulting editor for the *Journal of Social Psychology,* 2000-08, and *Social Influence,* 2008—.

SIDELIGHTS: Nicholas DiFonzo is a psychologist and educator whose broad interests include social psychology and industrial and organizational psychology. One of his primary areas of research is how rumors spread via networks in both social space and across time. He is also interested in how rumors evolve to become accurate or distorted and what the human motivation is in passing on rumors. Among his other interests concerning rumors are how they affect the people who hear them and how rumors can influence both social and economic behavior.

In his first book, *Rumor Psychology: Social and Organizational Approaches,* DiFonzo and coauthor Prashant Bordia present a scholarly overview of rumor research. They also provide an integrated model of rumor phenomena and present an agenda for future research in the area of rumors. DiFonzo and Bordia note that people work hard to tell the difference between rumor and actual fact and discusses the social psychological and organizations phenomena related to rumor, such as prejudice, stereotyping, personal relationships, and group relationships. As they discuss rumor research, they comment on various aspects of rumors, such as why people spread rumors, the specific attitudes and actions they bring about, and how harmful rumors may be prevented.

Whereas *Rumor Psychology* is a book meant primarily for academics, DiFonzo's next book, *The Watercooler Effect: A Psychologist Explores the Extraordinary Power of Rumors,* presents rumor research findings and analysis in a version more accessible to the general public. Focusing on why rumors spread, why people believe them, and how they affect people's behavior, the author discusses how rumors provide a clarifying look at individual and group psychology and why they have always been a pervading aspect of human experience. He goes on to explain why he believes research shows that rumors result from people's need to make sense of the world as they confront threatening or ambiguous situations and talk to each other about these situations, whether with family, on the Web, or standing around the water cooler at work.

Throughout the book, the author draws on real life examples to discuss a wide range of issues concerning rumors. For example, he discusses the infamous rumor about Proctor and Gamble that the company was associated with Satan worship, which was eventually proved untrue. In addition to defining how rumor, urban legends, and gossip differ, he provides examples of how passing a rumor on is often done for personal gain and how rumors can be halted successfully. DiFonzo points out that there are three basic types of rumors: the wish rumor, the dread rumor, and wedge-driving rumors, with the last two categories making up the greatest majority of rumors. For example, in the dread rumor category, workers may readily spread a rumor that layoffs are on the horizon or that the company is failing. Wedge-driving rumors start out as rumors meant to be divisive in a variety of situations and can be designed to undermine a personal relationship or group loyalties. For example, the author writes that rumors are more likely to spread about people that others don't like. However, he also writes that rumors also get passed on quickly because people have a basic tendency to trust one another.

DiFonzo takes a close look at how the spread of damaging rumors can be halted. He suggests that people research a rumor's accuracy before passing it on, especially within the workplace. The author notes that querying both colleagues and superiors about the rumor is appropriate.

"If nothing else, this book will encourage you to stop and question what you hear, rather than jump to conclusions and spread something that may, in fact, change the course of events as some rumors have," wrote Ruth Douillette for the *Internet Review of Books* Web site, adding: "But along with this basic restraint you'll gain a deeper understanding of just how to navigate what DiFonzo calls the 'soupy rumor fog' in which we exist." A *Publishers Weekly* contributor wrote that the author's "clear explanations and entertaining examples make for thoughtful reading."

BIOGRAPHICAL AND CRITICAL SOURCES:

BOOKS

DiFonzo, Nicholas, *The Watercooler Effect: A Psychologist Explores the Extraordinary Power of Rumors,* Avery (New York, NY), 2008.

PERIODICALS

Choice, August, 2007, W.A. Ashton, review of *Rumor Psychology: Social and Organizational Approaches,* p. 2182; February, 2009, H. Karp, review of *The Watercooler Effect,* p. 1190.

Hawaii Business, March, 2009, Terri Schlichenmeyer, review of *The Watercooler Effect.*

Publishers Weekly, June 23, 2008, review of *The Watercooler Effect,* p. 48.

Reference & Research Book News, August, 2007, review of *Rumor Psychology.*

ONLINE

Internet Review of Books, http://internetreviewofbooks.com/ (July 18, 2009), Ruth Douillette, "Did You Hear . . . ?, review of *The Watercooler Effect.*

Medieval Bookworm, http://chikune.com/ (July 18, 2009), review of *The Watercooler Effect.*

Nicholas DiFonzo Home Page, http://www.profnick.com (July 18, 2009).

Pop Culture Junkie, http://aleapopculture.blogspot.com/ (July 20, 2008), review of *The Watercooler Effect.*

Psychology Today Online, http://www.psychologytoday.com/ (July 18, 2009), brief profile of author.

Rochester Institute of Technology Web site, http://www.rit.edu/ (July 18, 2009), biography of author.

Water Cooler Effect Web site, http://www.thewatercoolereffect.com/ (July 18, 2009).

OTHER

Talk of the Nation: Science Friday, (broadcast transcript from National Public Radio), November 2, 2006, "How Do Rumors Get Started?"*

* * *

DIOTALEVI, Dave 1951-
(David A. Diotalevi)

PERSONAL: Born May 2, 1951.

ADDRESSES: Home—MA. *E-mail*—wheresmyx@yahoo.com; miraclemyx@yahoo.com.

CAREER: Writer, novelist, and poet. Created a trademarked temporary tattoo language system that was licensed to a national marketing corporation.

WRITINGS:

God's Questions: Prayerful Answers for Daily Life, Ragged Edge Press (Shippensburg, PA), 1998.
Miracle Myx (novel), Kunati (Largo, FL), 2008.

Contributor of poetry and nonfiction to periodicals. Also author of Web blog *Where's Myx.*

SIDELIGHTS: Dave Diotalevi was trained in engineering and nuclear physics before turning to writing. His first novel, *Miracle Myx,* revolves around Myx Amens, a fourteen-year-old boy who lives in the small town of Miracle, Massachusetts. Myx, however, is not like the other boys in town in that he has died twice, that is, had two near-death encounters. As a result of the first, in which he was struck by lightning, Myx has a photographic memory. The second near-death encounter, caused by a bully, results in Myx not being able to sleep and also developing an acute case of synesthesia. The condition is characterized by one or more sense simultaneously perceiving something, such as both seeing and tasting light. In some cases, sensory perception also combines with things such as letters, shapes, and numbers.

Myx is a foster child whose grandmother died the first time he had a near-death experience. Because Myx doesn't sleep, he wanders the town of Miracle at all hours of the night and seems to be able to discover various things about people, situations, and places. Myx is even contacted by the police from time to time in case he's seen or heard anything about a recent crime. For example, he has the ability to remember all the license plates he has seen in the course of an evening or night. However, Max uses his abilities for more than just recalling license plate numbers. He often comes to the aid of the little guy, such as a girl who is being tormented by the class bully until Myx blackmails him to stop. In another instance, Myx leaves a large sum of money at a diner so the owners' son can attend medical school.

The novel follows Myx for forty-two hours as the police contact Myx when several corpses are discovered with odd parts of their bodies gone. The plot also features an ancient puzzle box that may hold the secret of the town's surprising origin, as well as why someone is committing gruesome murders in which the killer somehow rips the tattoos off of victims.

"The characters that we see in the forty-two hours in which this book takes place are rich and understandable," wrote a contributor to the *Goshendirector's* blog. Mary Frances Wilkens, writing for *Booklist,* commented that she believed that the novel's most interesting aspect is Myx's synesthesia and the author's incorporation of it to experiment with phraseology. Noting that Myx's condition "enables the author to wax poetic one minute . . . and comic the next," Wilkens went on in her review to call *Miracle Myx* "a wickedly funny, surprisingly moving genre-bending tale."

BIOGRAPHICAL AND CRITICAL SOURCES:

PERIODICALS

Booklist, April 1, 2008, Mary Frances Wilkens, review of *Miracle Myx,* p. 33.

ONLINE

Dave Diotalevi Home Page, http://davewritesbooks.com (July 19, 2009).
Goshendirector's Weblog, http://goshendirector.wordpress.com/ (May 30, 2008), review of *Miracle Myx.*
Kunati, http://www.kunati.com/ (July 19, 2009), brief profile of author.
Where's Myx?, http://wheresmyx.blogspot.com, (July 19, 2009), brief biography of author.

* * *

DIOTALEVI, David A.
See DIOTALEVI, Dave

* * *

DOUGLAS, Anne 1930-
[A pseudonym]
(Anna Macklan, A.M. Priestly)

PERSONAL: Born December 3, 1930.

ADDRESSES: Home—Edinburgh, Scotland.

CAREER: Writer.

WRITINGS:

NOVELS

(As Anna Macklan) *Belcarron,* Piatkus (London, England), 1994.
The Fourth Season, Signet (New York, NY), 1995.
(As Anna Macklan) *The House by the Sea,* Piatkus (London, England), 1996.
Catherine's Land, Piatkus (London, England), 1997.
As the Years Go By, Piatkus (London, England), 1999.
Bridge of Hope, Piatkus (London, England), 2000.
The Butterfly Girls, Piatkus (London, England), 2001.
Ginger Street, Piatkus (London, England), 2002.
A Highland Engagement, Piatkus (London, England), 2004.
The Road to the Sands, Piatkus (London, England), 2006.
The Edinburgh Bride, Piatkus (London, England), 2007.
The Girl from Wish Lane, Severn House (Sutton, England), 2008.
A Song in the Air, Severn House (Sutton, England), 2008.
The Kilt Maker, Severn House (Sutton, England), 2009.

SIDELIGHTS: Anne Douglas is a pseudonym of a romance author who has also written under the pseudonym Anna Macklan. Her book *A Song in the Air,* published in 2008, takes place after World War II and finds Shona MacInnes on a farm on a remote island in Scotland. Shona rebels against the island's rigid gender roles by leaving for Edinburgh to become a veterinarian. She eventually takes a position in the veterinarian office of her childhood friend Ross, who, reflecting his background, doesn't believe that a woman can handle being a veterinarian, especially caring for large animals. Although the two clash, Shona and Ross begin to discover that they are much more than just old friends, even as Shona has made up her mind to move back to the island and take care of the region's farm animals. Hilary Hatton, writing for *Booklist,* called *A Song in the Air* "a quaint and rustic story of never knowing what the world has in store."

The author's romance novel titled *The Girl from Wish Lane* was also published in 2008. The novel takes place in the 1920s in Dundee, Scotland, where the line of demarcation between the wealthy and those struggling is clearly marked. Eva Masson is the daughter of jute mill worker who escapes from working in the mill thanks to a scholarship that the mill owner has awarded her. Before long, Eva is in love with the Nicholas, the son of the wealthy mill owner. However, Eva's family does not approve of the relationship, thinking that Eva is being seduced by Nicholas's wealth and position in society. Further problems arise when Eva becomes involved in labor issues and the union, forcing Eva to face conflicting loyalties and perhaps a compromise in her relationship with Nicholas. *Booklist* contributor Hilary Hatton commented that the author's "gentle novel couches the classic 'wrong side of the tracks' story in historical detail and drama."

BIOGRAPHICAL AND CRITICAL SOURCES:

PERIODICALS

Booklist, April 1, 2008, Hilary Hatton, review of *The Girl from Wish Lane,* p. 25; January 1, 2009, Hilary Hatton, review of *A Song in the Air,* p. 56.

ONLINE

Little, Brown Web site, http://www.littlebrown.co.uk/ (July 19, 2009), brief profile of author.
Romantic Times Online, http://romantictimes.com/ (July 19, 2009), Melinda Helfer, review of *Miss Caroline's Deception.*

* * *

DUFFY, Stella 1963-

PERSONAL: Born 1963, in London, England; immigrated to New Zealand in early childhood; married Shelley Silas (a playwright). *Education:* University graduate. *Hobbies and other interests:* Cooking.

ADDRESSES: *Home*—London, England.

CAREER: Writer, actor, comedian, and improviser.

AWARDS, HONORS: Macallan Short Story Dagger, 2002, for "Martha Grace"; Orange Prize long list, and Stonewall Writer of the Year award, both 2008, for *The Room of Lost Things.*

WRITINGS:

NOVELS, UNLESS OTHERWISE NOTED

Singling Out the Couples, Sceptre (London, England), 1998.
Eating Cake, Sceptre (London, England), 1999.
Immaculate Conceit, Sceptre (London, England), 2000.
(Editor, with Lauren Henderson) *Tart Noir* (short stories; includes "Martha Grace"), Berkley Prime Crime (New York, NY), 2002.
State of Happiness, Thomas Dunne Books (New York, NY), 2004.
Parallel Lies, Virago (London, England), 2005.
The Room of Lost Things, Virago (London, England), 2008.

"SAZ MARTIN" SERIES; CRIME NOVELS

Calendar Girl, Serpent's Tail (New York, NY), 1994.
Wavewalker, Serpent's Tail (New York, NY), 1996.
Beneath the Blonde, Serpent's Tail (New York, NY), 1997.
Fresh Flesh, Serpent's Tail (New York, NY), 1999.
Mouths of Babes, Serpent's Tail (New York, NY), 2005.

Also author of numerous short stories; contributor to magazines and newspapers; writer for radio and theater.

ADAPTATIONS: Immaculate Conceit has been adapted for the stage by the National Youth Theatre of Great Britain.

SIDELIGHTS: Stella Duffy, who has been openly lesbian since age eighteen, is an actor and comedian as well as an acclaimed writer of crime fiction and other novels. She also writes for radio and the stage. Though she is best known in the United States for her crime series featuring lesbian private investigator Saz Martin, Duffy considers these novels—like all her writing—to be primarily about relationships rather than murder mysteries. "I don't think there's anything else that matters in the world," she explained in an interview for the *Shots* Web site. "All life is based on relationship. With friends, with lovers, with people we hate. Though, actually I think all I'm really writing about—in all the books is truth and lies. Truth interests me hugely."

Calendar Girl, which Duffy said in the interview that she saw as "a love story gone wrong," introduces Saz Martin, a celibate lesbian trying to her get new private investigating career off the ground in London. In one of the book's two narratives, Saz discusses a perplexing case in which a man asks her to find a missing woman whose name he does not even know. A parallel narrative is that of Maggie, who recounts her torrid relationship with her girlfriend. Solving the case, which illuminates the connection between the disparate stories, brings Saz into the sleazy world of international drug gangs and high-end prostitution.

In *Wavewalker,* Saz is investigating Max North, a pop-psychology guru implicated in a chain of disturbing murders that have been made to look like suicides. A reviewer for *Publishers Weekly* considered the plot and the culprit relatively obvious, but enjoyed Duffy's entertaining and believable descriptions of hippie-era San Francisco and the book's depiction of "1990s cozy lesbian domesticity."

Saz is hired to protect Siobhan Forrester, lead singer of rock band, from a stalker in the third installment of the series, *Beneath the Blonde.* The action moves between London and New Zealand, where Duffy grew up, and confronts Saz with dangers that are complicated by the fact that Siobhan is hiding something important from her.

Four characters from the trendiest of London's elite groups are featured in *Fresh Flesh.* Patrick Freeman is an emotionally volatile celebrity chef with a wild new trophy wife. Chris Marquand, adopted by wealthy parents, is a successful physician awaiting the birth of his first child. Georgina Leyton, gorgeous and icily sexy, is a top-tier attorney. And Luke Godwin, whose bad temper is notorious, owns the hottest new night spot in town. What connects these characters is an ugly secret that Saz—now married to Molly, who is happily pregnant, must unravel.

Mouths of Babes revolves around a tragic incident from Saz's past that now comes back to haunt her. As a schoolgirl, Saz was part of the popular gang that enjoyed playing pranks on other students. One such prank, however, went badly wrong, and the group tried to cover up their responsibility. Indeed, since leaving school, Saz has wanted nothing to do with her former mates. But as the novel opens, the detective, who is now a mother, receives a phone call alerting her to a blackmail attempt regarding the long-ago incident. The group meets to agree on how to respond, but their decision leads only to further complications. Emily Melton, writing in *Booklist,* called the novel a "taut, riveting, finely paced" story. A reviewer for *Publishers Weekly* also praised the book highly, observing that Duffy "pulls no punches" in addressing the teen brutality that had sparked the book's tragic events.

Among Duffy's other novels, *State of Happiness* and *The Room of Lost Things* have received significant acclaim. Like Duffy herself, the protagonist of *State of Happiness,* Cindy, is in the midst of an exciting and satisfying career when she suddenly receives a diagnosis of cancer. Duffy's breast cancer was treated successfully; Cindy's disease, however, is terminal. But Duffy emphasized to *Planet Sappho* Web site interviewer Naomi Young that she is frustrated when readers call the novel her "cancer book." This labeling, she said, is reductive; she prefers to think of the novel as "about what happens to relationships within illness." Cindy, a cartographer and academic, meets Jack, a television news producer, at a Manhattan cocktail party, and the two hit it off instantly. When Jack receives a job offer in California, Cindy follows him, though she does not have time to warm up to Los Angeles before learning that her illness will eventually kill her. She and Jack embark on the necessary path of medical treatments and procedures, medications, and increasingly exhausting bouts of nausea, pain, and depression, all of which Duffy describes with relentless honestly. Indeed, Cindy is no angelic character who finds spiritual meaning through suffering; she rails against the illness that is destroying her, and at a particularly low moment even wishes a similar "shit life" on her friends and family "so they know exactly how I feel." Such details, remarked *Guardian* writer Carrie O'Grady, inform the novel with emotional authenticity. But at the same time, noted the reviewer, "the realities of cancer spill over any map, obscuring the finer lines." In the end, according to O'Grady, *State of Happiness* is "too realistic to be inspirational, too meditative to be cathartic, too sad to be uplifting." Also noting the novel's unsparing details, a writer for *Kirkus Reviews* found Duffy's treatment of cancer "chilly and pretentious." But *Booklist* contributor Aleksandra Kostovski rated the book much more highly, observing that its "elegant and intelligent prose . . . speaks to both . . . minds and hearts." Similarly, a writer for *Bibliofemme Reviews* Web site commended *State of Happiness* as a "simply written but poignant document of a relationship, the bad times as well as good."

The theme of intolerance informs *The Room of Lost Things,* which *Independent* reviewer Danuta Kean considered the author's most personal book to date. In a radical shift away from her feminist perspective, Duffy tells the story through the voices of two central characters who are male. Robert Sutton, age sixty-seven, is selling his small drycleaning business in Brixton to Akeel, an ambitious younger man from east London. As they hammer out terms of the agreement, Robert shows Akeel a room containing lost items left behind from customers' pockets. These provide the framework for a whole web of interrelated stories, resulting in what Kean called "a spellbinding love song to a part of London usually demonized as home to muggings, shootings and feral gangs." Kean also noted Duffy's sensitive treatment of Akeel's Muslim identity, pointing out that the author "challenges stereotypes of Muslim religious devotion, showing it as more complex than it is often portrayed."

BIOGRAPHICAL AND CRITICAL SOURCES:

BOOKS

Duffy, Stella, *State of Happiness,* Thomas Dunne Books (New York, NY), 2004.

PERIODICALS

Asia Africa Intelligence Wire, October 20, 2002, Tom Baker, "This 'Tart' All Dressed Up with Nowhere to Go."

Booklist, November 1, 2004, Aleksandra Kostovski, review of *State of Happiness,* p. 462; May 15, 2008, Emily Melton, review of *Mouths of Babes,* p. 25.

Bookseller, July 15, 2005, review of *Mouths of Babes,* p. 12.

Europe Intelligence Wire, July 28, 2006, "Trials and Tribulations of Being a Crime Writer—by the Authors Themselves."

Guardian (London, England), January 24, 2004, Carrie O'Grady, review of *State of Happiness.*
Independent (London, England), Danuta Kean, interview with Duffy.
Kirkus Reviews, November 1, 2004, review of *State of Happiness,* p. 1022.
Los Angeles Times, December 1, 2002, review of *Tart Noir,* p. 5.
Publishers Weekly, October 7, 1996, review of *Wavewalker,* p. 67; June 11, 2001, review of *Wavewalker,* p. 65; November 22, 2004, review of *State of Happiness,* p. 40; March 31, 2008, review of *Mouths of Babes,* p. 42.
Tribune Books, November 3, 2002, review of *Tart Noir,* p. 2.

ONLINE

Bibliofemme, http://www.bibliofemme.com/ (August 5, 2009), review of *State of Happiness.*
Book Bath, http://bookbath.blogspot.com/ (August 5, 2009), review of *The Room of Lost Things.*
Contemporary Writers, http://www.contemporarywriters.com/ (August 5, 2009), Jules Smith, "Stella Duffy."
Internet Movie Database, http://www.imdb.com/ (August 5, 2009), Duffy profile.
Little, Brown Web site, http://www.littlebrown.co.uk/ (August 5, 2009), Duffy profile.
Planet Sappho, http://www.planetsappho.com/ (August 5, 2009), Naomi Young, interview with Duffy.
Shots, http://www.shotsmag.co.uk/ (August 5, 2009), interview with Duffy.
Stella Duffy Home Page, http://stelladuffy.wordpress.com (August 5, 2009).
Stella Duffy MySpace Profile, http://www.myspace.com/stelladuffy (August 5, 2009).*

* * *

DUGGINS, Pat

PERSONAL: Married; wife's name Lucia. *Hobbies and other interests:* Cooking, traveling, wildlife photography.

ADDRESSES: Home—Orlando, FL. *Office*—WMFE Orlando, 11510 E. Colonial Dr., Orlando, FL 32817.

CAREER: WMFE, Orlando, FL, senior news analyst; University of Central Florida, Orlando, adjunct professor.

AWARDS, HONORS: National Sigma Delta Chi Award, Society of Professional Journalists; National Headliner Award, and Edward R. Murrow Award, Radio-Television News Directors Association, both for documentary of the first anniversary of the Columbia shuttle accident; SunCoast Regional Emmy Award.

WRITINGS:

Final Countdown: NASA and the End of the Space Shuttle Program, University Press of Florida (Gainesville, FL), 2007.

SIDELIGHTS: Pat Duggins, senior news analyst at Orlando, Florida, public radio station WMFE, has for many years specialized in coverage of the National Aeronautics and Space Administration (NASA). His book *Final Countdown: NASA and the End of the Space Shuttle Program* chronicles the development of the human spaceflight program after the Apollo missions, which culminated in a series of moon landings from 1969 to 1972. Following the Apollo program, NASA focused on the space shuttle, which can return to earth with its crew. It is the first spacecraft designed to reenter the earth's atmosphere and be reused for repeated missions. Work on the shuttle program began in the early 1970s, and the first shuttle flight was launched in 1981. The space shuttle has been used in several successful missions, but public perception of the shuttle program has been dominated by two major accidents: the Challenger explosion in 1986, which killed all seven astronauts aboard just over one minute after takeoff; and the Columbia accident in 2003, in which the spacecraft disintegrated on its reentry to earth's atmosphere, also killing all seven crew members. Duggins's book provides extensive detail about each of these disasters, as well as discussion of NASA's decision to retire the space shuttle in 2010 to focus on development of the Orion spacecraft. This new vehicle is part of NASA's Project Constellation, which plans new moon landings as well as explorations of Mars and other parts of the solar system.

The space shuttle program, as Duggins shows, was the result of political compromise after the completion of the Apollo program. NASA had wanted to begin working on a mission to explore Mars in the early 1970s, but failed to get government support. There was considerable interest in the shuttle, however, which was seen as a cost-effective way to deliver satellites into space for both the military and private firms. Though the shuttle only flew about five percent of the missions that supporters had expected, the program continued to receive political support. During the Clinton administration, writes Duggins, the shuttle was used to highlight the potential for international cooperation in space. The author describes the experiences of several shuttle crew members, showing that the experience of being an astronaut is far from the romanticized stereotype; indeed, much of their time is spent in the tedious activity of monitoring experiments or making repairs. He also discusses the high cost of running the shuttle, as well as questions regarding its ultimate purpose. As of 2008 the shuttle program had cost an estimated 170 billion dollars, and many American taxpayers have questioned whether this high price tag is worth the benefit. Though Duggins does not offer a firm answer to this question in the book, he does suggest that NASA could benefit from clearer focus in the future. As he put it in an interview with Scott Simon on *Weekend Edition,* "Ultimately, the message anyone should take home from the book is, okay, we're going to spend billions of dollars and lose fourteen astronauts, shouldn't it be for something?" Indeed, retiring the shuttle, writes Duggins, "may give NASA a chance to forget its troubled past and pursue the genuine mission it has lacked for years."

Reviewing *Final Countdown* in *American Scientist,* Roger A. Pielke enjoyed the book's accessibility and wealth of detail. Though the book is not an academic history, its narrative and analysis are basically consistent with scholarly literature on the subject, said the reviewer, and offer "a first-rate journalistic history of the space shuttle program." *Booklist* contributor Gilbert Taylor also praised the book for its informative and engaging writing, as did a reviewer for *SciTech Book News,* who called *Final Countdown* a "gripping read."

BIOGRAPHICAL AND CRITICAL SOURCES:

BOOKS

Duggins, Pat, *Final Countdown: NASA and the End of the Space Shuttle Program,* University Press of Florida (Gainesville, FL), 2007.

PERIODICALS

American Scientist, September 1, 2008, Roger A. Pielke, "The Rise and Fall of the Space Shuttle."

Booklist, September 1, 2007, Gilbert Taylor, review of *Final Countdown,* p. 33.

Choice: Current Reviews for Academic Libraries, March 1, 2008, A.M. Strauss, review of *Final Countdown,* p. 1180.

Publishers Weekly, August 13, 2007, review of *Final Countdown,* p. 59.

Quill, June 1, 2006, Chris Speckman, "Documentaries."

Science Books & Films, March 1, 2008, Robert N. McCullough, review of *Final Countdown.*

SciTech Book News, March 1, 2008, review of *Final Countdown.*

Weekend Edition Saturday, July 30, 2005, "Interview: Pat Duggins and Scott Parazynski Discuss Space Walks Staged from Space Shuttles"; November 24, 2007, Scott Simon, "Looking Back on Shuttles Facing 'Final Countdown.'"

ONLINE

University Press of Florida Web site, http://www.upf.com/ (August 10, 2009), Duggins profile.

WMFE Web site, http://www.wmfe.org/ (August 10, 2009), Duggins profile.*

* * *

DUMAINE, Brian

PERSONAL: Male.

ADDRESSES: *Office*—Fortune, Time & Life Bldg., Rockefeller Center, New York, NY 10020-1393.

CAREER: Journalist, editor, and writer. *Fortune* magazine, New York, NY, international editor and assistant managing editor, then global editor, also editor of *Fortune Small Business* magazine. Began working for Time, Inc., c. 1981.

WRITINGS:

The Plot to Save the Planet: How Visionary Entrepreneurs and Corporate Titans Are Creating Real Solutions to Global Warming, Crown Business (New York, NY), 2008.

Contributor of business articles to periodicals.

SIDELIGHTS: Brian Dumaine is a journalist who has worked as an editor for *Fortune* magazine, focusing much of attention on environmental issues and the growing green market as it pertains to corporations, markets, and executive thought. In his fist book, *The Plot to Save the Planet: How Visionary Entrepreneurs and Corporate Titans Are Creating Real Solutions to Global Warming,* Dumaine examines a growing effort among American corporations to develop green technology into the new business movement of the twenty-first century.

Writing in the book's introduction, Dumaine notes: "In this book we'll meet the people who are creating the new business models and the cutting-edge technologies that are driving innovations like solar and wind energy, clean cars, practical biofuels, and energy-smart offices and homes. Some of this work, at this point in our history, may appear impractical, or too expensive, or counterproductive. But, though no single program is likely to solve the problem, taken together these emerging technologies are our best chance to reach a carbon-free future."

The author discusses the efforts of both well-known business people, such as Warren Buffet and Richard Branson, and smaller entrepreneurs who are also seeking to develop alternative fuel sources. He notes that their goal is not just to save the planet but reap the huge potential profits that green energy business promises in the future. According to Dumaine, green energy is becoming increasingly popular for venture capitalists, including typical risk-takers and those who are risk-averse. In the process, the author explores various technologies, from more traditional fossil fuels and nuclear power to non-fossil fuels, wind, and solar energy as investors, entrepreneurs, and environmentalists form an improbable collaboration to produce innovate green technology. For example, the author describes how Wal-Mart has formed a relationship with the Environmental Defense Fund and how General Electric is making a concentrated effort to develop and sell green technologies. According to Dumaine, these plans and many others like them, such as the 2.9 billion dollars invested by venture capitalists into solar energy development, are likely to result in the future's most profitable industry.

Noting that the book "is fairly heavy reading, but pleasantly and interestingly so," a contributor to the *Performance Report* Web site went on in the review to call *The Plot to Save the Planet* "well crafted, nicely paced, and loaded with interesting information." A *Publishers Weekly* contributor wrote that the author separates "the hype from the hope" and presents "an informed and optimistic perspective to the revolution underway."

BIOGRAPHICAL AND CRITICAL SOURCES:

BOOKS

Dumaine, Brian, *The Plot to Save the Planet: How Visionary Entrepreneurs and Corporate Titans Are Creating Real Solutions to Global Warming,* Crown Business (New York, NY), 2008.

PERIODICALS

Publishers Weekly, April 28, 2008, review of *The Plot to Save the Planet,* p. 126.

ONLINE

National Summit Web site, http://www.nationalsummit.org/ (July 19, 2009), brief profile of author.

New York University Stern School of Business Social Enterprise Association Web site, https://nyusternsea.campusgroups.com/ (July 19, 2009), brief profile of author.

Performance Report, http://www.theperformancereport.com/ (September 15, 2008), review of *The Plot to Save the Planet.*

Random House Web site, http://www.randomhouse.com/ (July 19, 2009), brief profile of author.*

E

EBISCH, Glen 1946-
(Glen Albert Ebisch)

PERSONAL: Born 1946; married. *Education:* Rutgers University, A.B., Cornell University, M.A., Columbia University, M.A., Ph.D. *Hobbies and other interests:* Yoga and New England folktales of the supernatural.

ADDRESSES: *Office*—Western New England College, 1215 Wilbraham Rd., Springfield, MA 01119.

CAREER: Educator, writer, and novelist. Western New England College, Springfield, MA, professor of philosophy.

WRITINGS:

FICTION

Behind the Mask, Silhouette (Don Mills, Ontario, Canada), 1986.
Shock Effect, Harlequin (Don Mills, Ontario, Canada), 1987.
Angel in the Snow, Crosswinds (New York, NY), 1988.
The Secret of Bluefish Point, Bookmice.com, 2000.
A Special Power, Bookmice.com, 2000.
Woven Hearts, Avalon Books (New York, NY), 2001.
Unwanted Inheritance, Avalon Books (New York, NY), 2001.
To Breathe Again, Avalon Books (New York, NY), 2001.
A Rocky Road, Avalon Books (New York, NY), 2004.
The Crying Girl, Avalon Books (New York, NY), 2007.
Grave Justice, Avalon Books (New York, NY), 2008.
To Grandmother's House, Five Star (Detroit, MI), 2009.
Ghosts from the Past, Avalon Books (New York, NY), 2009.

"LOU DUNLOP" SERIES FOR YOUNG ADULTS

Lou Dunlop: Private Eye, Harlequin (Don Mills, Ontario, Canada), 1987.
Lou Dunlop: Cliffhanger, Harlequin (Don Mills, Ontario, Canada), 1987.

SIDELIGHTS: Glen Ebisch is a philosophy professor who also writes novels. He began writing books for young adults, including the "Lou Dunlop" series, which includes *Lou Dunlop: Private Eye,* and *Lou Dunlop: Cliffhanger.* The author now primarily writes mysteries for adults, setting his novels in the familiar New England where he lives and works and often incorporating his interest in the region's folklore, as well as the supernatural.

In his 2001 book *Woven Hearts,* Ebisch tells the story of Kate Manning, a fabric shop owner in a small town who suddenly faces competition from a huge chain store. Kate is upset because a young man she just met, Roger Garrison, turns out to be the manager of the new store. Although Roger and Kate are competitors, they cannot deny their interest in each other. However, Kate has another competitor in the form of Melissa Hard-grove, the beautiful assistant manager of Roger's store. The plot takes a twist when someone begins sabotaging Kate's store.

In *Unwanted Inheritance,* siblings Caroline and Michael Comptom have inherited an estate that is falling apart. When interior design painter Heather Martinson signs on to help restore the old mansion, she soon finds herself attracted to Michael. Before long, however, she also faces danger as vandalism and strange accidents occur. *To Breathe Again* finds yoga-studio-owner Summyr Fox losing her lease and her part-time job at a food store. She then meets Steven Rafferty, who is using yoga to rehabilitate his shoulder. While Summyr is attracted to Steven, there is something about him that is suspect. Although a practitioner of yoga, Summyr finds that she cannot keep her emotions in check as she must explore her past to move ahead.

In *A Rocky Road,* Ebisch focuses on Susan Cantwell, who quits her job teaching in the suburbs and signs on as a tour bus guide in the Colorado Rocky Mountains. When passengers begin dying mysteriously on her bus, Susan becomes suspicious and joins forces with Detective James Alston to capture the killer. The author reveals his interest in the supernatural with his novel *The Crying Girl. Roaming New England* magazine editor Amanda Vickers gets a call from an old teacher about an interesting story concerning a New Hampshire inn that is supposedly haunted. However, Amanda's teacher soon dies in a mysterious fall while conducting research at the inn. Amanda decides to investigate, leading her and her associate editor, Marcie Ducasse, to a small New England town in the White Mountains where they soon discover that the townspeople are terribly afraid of something.

Grave Justice features the return of Amanda Vickers and Marcie Ducasse, as they once again investigate supposed supernatural occurrences in a small New England town. This time the story takes them to West Windham, Maine, to investigate the Monster of Lake Opal. Soon the two are also involved in the hunt for a killer after they attend a séance trying to contact the victim. Noting the "fan-favorite plot and satisfying comeuppances," *Booklist* contributor Nina C. Davis went on to write in her review that the author "offers up a solid helping of American cozy fare."

A *Publishers Weekly* contributor called *To Grandmother's House* a "nostalgic cozy." The story revolves around Laura Magee, who loses her job at the Boston Museum and gets hired to work for a newspaper in a small New England town. She is to write the "Ask Auntie Mabel" column, taking over for the previous author of the column, Ann Rickdorf, who was murdered. Someone else is soon murdered in Ravensford, and Laura turns to investigative reporting. A *Publishers Weekly* contributor called *To Grandmother's House* an "old-fashioned blend of romance and detection."

BIOGRAPHICAL AND CRITICAL SOURCES:

PERIODICALS

Booklist, April 1, 2008, Nina C. Davis, review of *Grave Justice,* p. 30.

Publishers Weekly, June 12, 1987, Diane Roback, review of *Lou Dunlop: Private Eye,* p. 86; June 22, 2009, review of *To Grandmother's House,* p. 34.

School Library Journal, April, 1987, Kathy Fritts, review of *Behind the Mask,* p. 115; August, 1987, review of *Lou Dunlop: Private Eye,* p. 92; September, 1987, Susan H. Williamson, review of *Lou Dunlop: Cliffhanger,* p. 195; February 1, 1988, Connie Tyrrell Burns, review of *Shock Effect,* p. 72.

Voice of Youth Advocates, August, 1987, review of *Lou Dunlop: Private Eye,* p. 119; October, 1987, review of *Behind the Mask,* p. 210; December, 1987, review of *Lou Dunlop: Cliffhanger,* p. 234; February, 1988, review of *Shock Effect,* p. 279; April, 1988, review of *Shock Effect,* p. 24; June, 1988, review of *Angel in the Snow,* p. 85.

ONLINE

Fantastic Fiction, http://www.fantasticfiction.co.uk/ (July 20, 2009), "About Glen Ebisch."

Mystery Writers of America Web site, http://www.mysterywriters.org/ (July 20, 2009), brief autobiography.

Western New England College, http://www1.wnec.edu/faculty/ (July 20, 2009), faculty profile of author.*

* * *

EBISCH, Glen Albert
See EBISCH, Glen

EDELMAN, Julie

PERSONAL: Married; children: Luke. *Education:* Graduated from Duke University; attended Oxford University.

CAREER: Author and lifestyle reporter. Former senior vice president, Bohbot Entertainment; former senior vice president/creative director, Saatchi Advertising. Appearances on television include *Rachael Ray, Today, The View, Fox 'n Friends,* and *Real Simple TV;* also appears on ABC Radio Networks in "S.O.S. (Save Our Sanity)" vignettes; featured in *Family Circle, Woman's Day, Glamour, Quick 'n Simple,* and *New York Magazine;* lifestyle anchor, http://oomph.net.

WRITINGS:

(With "Goosie") *Once upon a Recipe* (juvenile), Once Upon a Recipe Press (Maplewood, NJ), 2000.

The Accidental Housewife: How to Overcome Housekeeping Hysteria One Task at a Time, Ballantine Books (New York, NY), 2006.

The Ultimate Accidental Housewife: Your Guide to a Clean-Enough House, Hyperion (New York, NY), 2008.

SIDELIGHTS: Author and spokeswoman Julie Edelman is the author of several books designed to make work easier for women who had never planned on a career of domestic bliss. Her books *Once upon a Recipe, The Accidental Housewife: How to Overcome Housekeeping Hysteria One Task at a Time,* and *The Ultimate Accidental Housewife: Your Guide to a Clean-Enough House* are all designed to help the average homemaker confront the issues for which home economics class left them unprepared. "I set out to connect and 'spread the glove' with other housewives who were feeling the same things I was," Edelman explained in a biographical essay published on her Web site, *The Accidental Housewife.* "I wanted to help them embrace their own fears and imperfections and realize that we are a new generation of housewife who doesn't have nor need to do it all. Most importantly I wanted you to believe that it's OK not to be the perfect mom, wife or housekeeper and to feel pride not guilt if you're doing the best you can."

One solution to the problem of overwork, as Edelman presents it in *Once upon a Recipe,* is to enlist help from the children of the house. *Once upon a Recipe* is a cookbook designed specifically for young children—who can learn to use the microwave even if they are too young to be trusted with operating the oven or the stove. Edelman's son, Luke, who shares in her Web site's essay, became so enthusiastic about cooking that he virtually relieved his mother of that particular chore. The book, the author explained in an autobiographical blurb published on the *Fresh Fiction* Web site, "got my son into cooking and I don't have to anymore unless I want to!"

Edelman's breakthrough book was *The Accidental Housewife,* a compendium of tips and tricks designed to reduce the workload for the modern homemaker and relieve her of the burden of high expectations. Edelman realized that having a career, a marriage, and a family were enough for any woman, and the idea of maintaining the perfect home on top of those goals was too much. The publication of the volume brought Edelman a new career as a spokeswoman presenting tips for cutting housework and keeping a neat and tidy home without overwhelming the worker on television and radio, with appearances on *Rachael Ray, Today, The View,* and *Fox 'n Friends.* She capped her first collection with a second one, *The Ultimate Accidental Housewife,* which shows how to keep a house clean with a minimum of effort. "Room by room," declared Barbara Jacobs in *Booklist,* "the litany of clean only what's dirty continues."

BIOGRAPHICAL AND CRITICAL SOURCES:

PERIODICALS

Booklist, April 15, 2008, Barbara Jacobs, review of *The Ultimate Accidental Housewife: Your Guide to a Clean-Enough House,* p. 14.

ONLINE

Accidental Housewife Web site, http://www.theaccidentalhousewife.com (August 12, 2009), author profile.

Fresh Fiction, http://freshfiction.com/ (August 12, 2009), author profile.

PRWatch.org, http://www.prwatch.org/ (August 12, 2009), author profile.*

* * *

EDWARDS, Laurie 1980(?)-
(Laurie Elizabeth Edwards)

PERSONAL: Born c. 1980; married. *Education:* Georgetown University, B.A.; Emerson College, M.F.A.

ADDRESSES: *Home*—Boston, MA. *Agent*—Matthew Carnicelli, Trident Media Group, 41 Madison Ave., Fl. 36, New York, NY 10010. *E-mail*—laurie.edwards@gmail.com.

CAREER: Journalist, writer, editor, consultant, and educator. Northeastern University, Boston, MA, full-time lecturer.

AWARDS, HONORS: Best Consumer Health Book, 2008, for *Life Disrupted.*

WRITINGS:

Life Disrupted: Getting Real about Chronic Illness in Your Twenties and Thirties, Walker (New York, NY), 2008.

Contributor of essays and articles to periodicals, including the *Boston Globe* and *Glamour,* and online outlets, including *ChronicBabe.com.* Author of the blog *A Chronic Dose.*

SIDELIGHTS: A journalist specializing in health issues, Laurie Edwards is also the author of *Life Disrupted: Getting Real about Chronic Illness in Your Twenties and Thirties.* The book is a guide to coping with chronic disease and is specifically directed at younger people who should be in the prime of their lives but who suffer from debilitating health problems. The author reveals that she is one of these people. She suffers from a rare genetic respiratory disease called primary ciliary dyskinesia, or PCD. She is only one of 1,000 medically documented cases of PCD. In addition, she also has celiac disease, bronchiectasis, and thyroid disease.

The author points out that medical advances have led to more chronically ill young children and teenagers surviving into adulthood. Faced with the usual life challenges, such as going to college, embarking on a career, and starting a family, young people with chronic diseases also have to cope with the circumstances of their illness. One of the issues the author deals with in her book is the need to make sure that the illness does not becomes the primary factor in a person's identity. "The whole idea of identity—that is the root of the book," the author told Fran Metch in an interview for *Library Journal.* The author also told Metch later in the same interview: "You have to be willing to adapt goals and plans and aspirations in light of health status, but adaptation is possible and necessary."

Among the many topics discussed by Edwards in her book for living better with a chronic illness is how individuals can manage their own health care and how they can better deal with physicians and frequent hospitalizations. She also provides tips on developing a career that will accommodate specific health needs. Other important issues addressed by the author are finances and the need to develop good relationships. Edwards also discusses others like her who suffer from more than one chronic illness or medical problem. In the process, the author tells her own story of chronic illness and how she dealt with the issues that arose as a result. Edwards includes advice from a variety of professionals, including health professionals and employment specialists.

In a review for *Library Journal,* Fran Metch commented that the author also writes in "an appropriate tone so that her suffering comes across without becoming the focus." A *Publishers Weekly* contributor called Edwards "wise, generous and a terrific storyteller."

BIOGRAPHICAL AND CRITICAL SOURCES:

PERIODICALS

Booklist, July 1, 2008, Whitney Scott, review of *Life Disrupted: Getting Real about Chronic Illness in Your Twenties and Thirties,* p. 24.

Library Journal, May 1, 2008, Fran Metch, review of *Life Disrupted,* p. 89; June 1, 2008, Fran Metch, "Q&A: Laurie Edwards," p. 116.

Publishers Weekly, May 5, 2008, review of *Life Disrupted,* p. 55.

ONLINE

Chronic Dose, http://achronicdose.blogspot.com/ (July 20, 2009), brief autobiography.

ReachMD, http://www.reachmd.com/ (July 20, 2009), brief profile of author.

Walker Web site, http://www.walkerbooks.com/ July 20, 2009), brief profile of author.

* * *

EDWARDS, Laurie Elizabeth
See EDWARDS, Laurie

* * *

EL RASSI, Toufic 1978-

PERSONAL: Born 1978, in Beirut, Lebanon; immigrated to the United States, 1979. *Education:* DePaul University, B.A., 2000, M.A., 2003.

ADDRESSES: Home—Chicago, IL.

CAREER: Writer, educator, lecturer, artist, and graphic novelist. Oakton Community College, Des Plaines, IL, adjunct instructor in history and political science; Harold Washington City College, Chicago, IL, lecturer in social sciences.

WRITINGS:

Arab in America (graphic novel memoir), Last Gasp (San Francisco, CA), 2008.

SIDELIGHTS: Writer, educator, and graphic novelist Toufic El Rassi was born in Beirut, Lebanon, in 1978. He has served as an adjunct instructor in history and political science at Oakton Community College in Des Plaines, Illinois, and as a lecturer in social sciences at Harold Washington City College in Chicago, Illinois.

El Rassi immigrated to the United States with his family in 1979. Though he grew up fully immersed in American society and culture, he was never far removed from his Arab background, and as he entered his teenage years, he became particularly aware of his ethnicity. This feeling of being of two worlds helped make El Rassi especially observant of the way Arabic people were treated in the United States. In *Arab in America,* a memoir in graphic novel form, El Rassi offers a "deeply personal indictment of America's treatment of the Arab world, from Hollywood's racism to the hypocritical War on Terror," commented *New Statesman* reviewer Yo Zushi.

"At best, El Rassi believes Arabs are simply ignored by Americans; at worst, they are the victims of systemic, never-ending historical racism born of ignorance and anger," observed *Comics Bulletin* reviewer Jason Sacks. El Rassi recounts the many difficulties he faced while growing up, from being called names to being physically threatened. He looks at his own life in America, his interactions with classmates and teachers, and the many milestones he encountered, such as becoming an American citizen. Elsewhere in the book, he considers the casual racism sometimes found in American popular culture, noting that even apparently innocent and well-meaning songs, drawings, and movies can present a negative portrayal of Arabs. He considers the American response to Arabs in the aftermath of such national tragedies as the Oklahoma City bombings and the September 11, 2001, attacks on New York. In large measure, he finds that Americans have consistently reacted poorly to Arabs in their midst. Arabs fare even worse when the specter of terrorism inflames hatred, suspicion, and fear that already exists at varying levels.

Throughout book, El Rassi "does a lot of teaching, some of the most devastating of it about the U.S.," remarked Ray Olson in a *Booklist* review. Sacks found it to be a "sincere and heartfelt expression of a creative person's opinions in comics form," a "complex and emotional" work that "serves to illuminate an unfortunate aspect of American society in the Bush era." Craig Taylor, writing in the London *Guardian,* called El Rassi's autobiographical graphic novel "complex and rewarding," and concluded, "At its best, his personal history is enough to illustrate a life lived constantly on the defensive."

BIOGRAPHICAL AND CRITICAL SOURCES:

BOOKS

Arab in America (graphic novel memoir), Last Gasp (San Francisco, CA), 2008.

PERIODICALS

Booklist, April 1, 2008, Ray Olson, review of *Arab in America,* p. 36.

Guardian (London, England), March 22, 2008, Craig Taylor, "On the Defensive," review of *Arab in America.*

New Statesman, May 26, 2008, Yo Zushi, "Growing Up Different," review of *Arab in America.*

Wall Street Journal, March 29, 2008, Jeffrey A. Trachtenberg, "Comics: Pen Power: A Graphic Novelist's Personal Portrait Tackles Fear, Anger, and History," review of *Arab in America.*

ONLINE

Comics Bulletin, http://www.comicsbulletin.com/ (March 12, 2008), Jason Sacks, review of *Arab in America.*

Toufic El Rassi MySpace Page, http://www.myspace.com/toufícelrassi (July 16, 2009).*

*   *   *

EMBRY, Karen
(Karen Howell Embry)

PERSONAL: Born in Tampa, FL.

ADDRESSES: Home—Tampa, FL. *Office*—Karen Embry Designs, LLC, 4504 Hidden Shadow Dr., Tampa, FL 33614-1471. *E-mail*—KHEdesigns@aol.com.

CAREER: Writer, artist, designer, entrepreneur, and educator. Artist and designer in the licensing industry.

MEMBER: Society of Decorative Painters, Society of Creative Designers, Craft and Hobby Association.

WRITINGS:

Decorative Painting for Home & Garden, Sterling Publishing (New York, NY), 2003.

Painted Scrapbook & Album Covers: 11 Albums, Journals, & Memory Books to Paint, Plaid Enterprises (Norcross, GA), 2004.

Painting on Glass & Ceramic, Sterling Publishing (New York, NY), 2008.

SIDELIGHTS: Karen Embry is an artist, graphic designer, writer, and educator. A third-generation artist, she has spent a great deal of her creative career as an artist and designer in the licensing industry. Embry's work has been showcased in national magazines as well as through her own line of licensed decorative gift items for the home. She is a member of several creative-industry organizations such as the Society of Decorative Painters, the Society of Creative Designers, and the Craft and Hobby Association.

As an author, Embry has written a number of works that focus on painting and related decorative arts, such as *Decorative Painting for Home & Garden* and *Painted Scrapbook & Album Covers: 11 Albums, Journals, & Memory Books to Paint.* Several of her books have been published by Plaid Enterprises, and she serves as an ambassador for that publisher.

In *Painting on Glass & Ceramic,* Embry explores the creative possibilities of modern-day painted ceramics. She notes that many of today's specialized enamel paints and glazes do not require kiln firing, making it easier and faster for all ages to create stylish personalized, handcrafted works. She provides details on the characteristics of these paints and glazes, describing which work best on particular types of surfaces. She covers the practicalities of a variety of painting techniques, including sponging, stenciling, reverse painting, stamping, and many others, as well as the brushes and other tools used with them. *Booklist* reviewer Tina Coleman remarked that the "real gems of this book are Embry's project instructions."

In addition to practical instruction on painting techniques, Embry offers a variety of full-size patterns that can be photocopied and used to create a wide range of projects. She explains how to trace and transfer the patterns to a ceramic surface, how to use substances such as underglazes, and how to make the best use of available tools and supplies. Detailed photographs and comprehensive painting guides contain additional suggestions and instructions.

Throughout the book, Embry presents cheerful, contemporary designs suitable for gift-giving and special occasions. Floral designs for plates and teapots accompany designs for wine carafes and soft-drink pitchers. Holidays and commemorative events are covered with projects showcasing Christmas, Mother's Day, and weddings. Embry provides the creative spark for painting and decorating items such as plates, wine glasses, picture frames, pitchers, and pots. Coleman concluded that *Painting on Glass & Ceramic* is a "truly useful crafting resource."

BIOGRAPHICAL AND CRITICAL SOURCES:

PERIODICALS

Booklist, April 1, 2008, Tina Coleman, review of *Painting on Glass & Ceramic,* p. 16.

School Arts, August-September, 2008, Julie B. Wells, review of *Painting on Glass & Ceramic.*

ONLINE

Iyares, http://iyares.com/ (July 16, 2009), review of *Painting on Glass & Ceramic.*

Karen Embry Designs Web site, http://www.karenembrydesigns.com (July 16, 2009).

Karen Embry Home Page, http://www.karenembry.com (July 16, 2009).

Plaid, http://www.plaidonline.com/ (July 16, 2009), biography of Karen Embry.*

* * *

EMBRY, Karen Howell
See EMBRY, Karen

See EMBRY, Karen

* * *

EPPRIDGE, Bill 1938-
(Guillermo Alfredo Eduardo Eppridge)

PERSONAL: Born March 20, 1938, in Buenos Aires, Argentina; son of a chemical engineer (father); married Adrienne Aurichio. *Education:* Attended the University of Toronto; University of Missouri, B.J., 1960. *Hobbies and other interests:* Flyfishing.

ADDRESSES: *Home*—CT. *E-mail*—bill@billeppridge.com.

CAREER: Photojournalist, educator, and writer. Photojournalist and reporter for prominent national magazines such as *National Geographic, Life, Fortune, Time, People,* and *Sports Illustrated. Life,* staff photographer, 1964-72; *Time,* contract photographer, 1973-76; *Sports Illustrated,* contract photographer, 1976-89, staff photographer, 1998-2006. Instructor at photojournalism conferences and workshops, including the University of Missouri Photojournalism Workshop, Eddie Adams Photography Workshop, and Photography at the Summit. *Exhibitions:* "The Beatles! Backstage and behind the Scenes" (photography exhibition), Allen Lambert Galleria, Toronto, Ontario, Canada, 2004; work has also been exhibited at the Smithsonian Museum of American History, the Museum of Television and Radio, the High Museum of Art (Atlanta, GA), the Visa Pour L'Image (Perpignon, France), and in other galleries throughout the United States and Europe.

AWARDS, HONORS: National Press Photographer's Award, First Prize Pictorial, 1959; Joseph Sprague Award, National Press Photographers; MU Photographer of the Year distinction, University of Missouri, three-time recipient; Missouri Honor Medal, University of Missouri Journalism School; College Photographer of the Year award, National Press Photog-raphers Association, two-time recipient; Inducted into the Missouri Press Association's Hall of Fame.

WRITINGS:

PHOTOGRAPHER

Robert F. Jones, *Jake: A Labrador Puppy at Work and Play,* Farrar, Straus & Giroux, (New York, NY), 1992.

(With Robert R. Jones) *Upland Passage,* Farrar, Straus & Giroux, (New York, NY), 1992.

Hays Gorey, *Robert Kennedy: The Last Campaign,* foreword by Bill Clinton, Harcourt Brace (New York, NY), 1993.

The Beatles! Backstage and Behind the Scenes (exhibition catalogue), ArtVision Exhibitions (Boca Raton, FL), 2004.

A Time It Was: Bobby Kennedy in the Sixties, introduction by John E. Frook, essay by Pete Hamill, Abrams (New York, NY), 2008.

Contributor to books, including *Things As They Are: Photojournalism in Context since 1955,* World Press Photo, 2005.

Also author of the blog *Bill Eppridge, Photojournalist.*

SIDELIGHTS: Bill Eppridge is a prominent and prolific photojournalist whose career has spanned more than forty years and some of the world's most prestigious magazines, cultural icons, and political events. He photographed the cusp of the British Invasion of the early 1960s when the Beatles first came to the United States. "He photographed a young Barbra Streisand—living in a tiny railroad apartment in Manhattan—on the verge of super stardom," the biographer stated. "He was the only photographer admitted into Marilyn Lovell's home as her husband, Jim, made his nail-biting re-entry into the atmosphere in the crippled Apollo 13 spacecraft. He captured Clint Eastwood on the set of Dirty Harry. He was at Woodstock. And he was in Vietnam." Eppridge also took one of the twentieth century's most tragic and emotional photographs: the image of Senator Robert Kennedy moments after the popular politician's 1968 assassination in Los Angeles, cradled in the arms of stunned hotel busboy Juan Romero.

Born in 1938 to American parents in Argentina, Eppridge attended the University of Missouri's School of Journalism. He has contributed photographs to prominent magazines such as *Life, Sports Illustrated, National Geographic, Time,* and *People,* either as a freelancer or a staff photographer. He has also regularly worked as an educator and trainer at workshops and seminars throughout the United States. His photographs have been exhibited at museums and galleries such as the Smithsonian Museum of American History, the Museum of Television and Radio, the High Museum of Art, and other American and European galleries.

Eppridge covered large events as well as small. In *Jake: A Labrador Puppy at Work and Play,* Eppridge presents photographs to accompany text by Robert F. Jones. Eppridge and Jones chronicle the charismatic young dog's early years, his integration into the Jones family (and introduction to the established elder canine of the house), his training, and his blossoming into a self-assured animal that represents the human/dog relationship in all its facets. A *Publishers Weekly* reviewer remarked that Eppridge's photographs "cleanly capture Jake's brand of animal magnetism."

The Beatles! Backstage and behind the Scenes is an exhibition catalogue produced in conjunction with an exhibit of Eppridge's photographs of the iconic music group as they made their first visit to the United States in 1964. In these photos, Eppridge documents the group's phenomenal popularity in the America, the profound early influence they had on rock music, and the genesis of the Fab Four's long-standing cultural impact.

A Time It Was: Bobby Kennedy in the Sixties commemorates the fortieth anniversary of Kennedy's assassination. Here, Eppridge assembles a collection of "his most evocative images" of one of the most towering figures in American political history, noted a *Publishers Weekly* reviewer. Eppridge chronicles three years of Kennedy's political activities, from 1966 to 1968. He presents numerous pictures from Kennedy's 1968 presidential campaign, his conflicts with Eugene McCarthy in the presidential primaries, his victory in California, the senator's shocking murder, and the national reaction to the death of a candidate considered nearly guaranteed to claim the presidency of the United States.

In regard to his famous photograph of the dying Kennedy, Eppridge told *Morning Edition* interviewer Renee Montagne, "I was standing there, looking, and suddenly realized that what I was seeing there was an icon, almost. It was almost like a crucifixion." He told Montagne that taking the pictures of Kennedy "was the right thing to do. I think that kind of a situation has got to be documented, it has to be told, and it has to be told to people who do not understand the horrors that we can face." Eppridge told Montagne that his photographs of Kennedy transcended a simple recording of events. When he took those important photographs of Kennedy, he realized "at that point my profession changed. I became a historian."

"*A Time It Was* both fills your heart with pride and honor for what was, and brings tears to your eyes for what could have been," remarked *BuzzFlash* Web site reviewer Thom Hartmann. The *Publishers Weekly* contributor concluded that Eppridge's collection of Kennedy photographs "speaks powerfully and wordlessly of Bobby Kennedy's charismatic presence in the late '60s." Hartmann concluded, "This marvelous book is not only history in your hand, it is inspiration, transformation, and love. It's essential viewing and reading."

"Photographers like Bill Eppridge are a rare breed," remarked a commentator on *PR Newswire* Web site. "For starters, he's a man who has left such an indelible mark on the field of photojournalism that it's hard to remember the 1960s without thinking of his work," the writer stated. More importantly, "Bill Eppridge's body of work has helped shape how we collectively think about the events he has covered."

Eppridge told *CA:* "I hope that my work makes the world a little better."

BIOGRAPHICAL AND CRITICAL SOURCES:

PERIODICALS

Booklist, November 1, 1992, Leone McDermott, review of *Jake: A Labrador Puppy at Work and Play,* p. 508; August, 1993, Jay Freeman, review of *Robert Kennedy: The Last Campaign,* p. 2034.

Bulletin of the Center for Children's Books, January, 1993, review of *Jake,* p. 149.

Daily News (Bowling Green, KY) February 6, 2009, "Brief: Web Photo: *Life* Magazine Photographer Visits WKU."

News Photographer, August 1, 2008, Stephen Wolgast, "When the Past Is Prescient," review of *A Time It Was: Bobby Kennedy in the Sixties,* p. 24.

PR Newswire, February 4, 2004, "NikonNet and 'Legends behind the Lens' Honor the Iconic Works of Photojournalist Bill Eppridge"; February 10, 2004, "New Collectible Photography Book Commemorates 40th Anniversary of the Beatles' First 1964 U.S. Tour."

Publishers Weekly, October 19, 1992, review of *Jake,* p. 81; May 19, 2008, review of *A Time It Was,* p. 49.

School Library Journal, December, 1992, Kay McPherson, review of *Jake,* p. 96.

ONLINE

Bill Eppridge Home Page, http://www.billeppridge.com (July 16, 2009).

BuzzFlash Web log, http://blog.buzzflash.com/ (December 18, 2009), Thom Hartmann, review of *A Time It Was.*

Missouri School of Journalism Web site, http://www.journalism.missouri.edu/ (July 16, 2009), biography of Bill Eppridge.

OTHER

Morning Edition, June 6, 2008, Renee Montagne, "RFK's Shooting Turned Photographer into Historian," transcript of radio interview with Bill Eppridge.

* * *

EPPRIDGE, Guillermo Alfredo Eduardo
See EPPRIDGE, Bill

* * *

EVANS, Stephen 1955-

PERSONAL: Born March 21, 1955; divorced. *Education:* Attended Georgetown University.

ADDRESSES: Home—Silver Springs, MD. *E-mail*—Steve@writerseeksreader.com.

CAREER: Writer, novelist, playwright, and computer analyst.

MEMBER: Dramatists Guild, Society for Technical Communication.

WRITINGS:

The Marriage of True Minds (novel), Unbridled Books (Denver, CO), 2008.

Author of plays and musicals, including *The Talent Machine* (children's musical) and *Spooky Action at a Distance* (comedy). Also author of the blog *Writer Seeks Reader.* Contributor to Web sites, including *Secrets of the City.*

SIDELIGHTS: Stephen Evans is a writer, playwright, and novelist living in Silver Springs, Maryland. Although Evans pursues a professional career as a computer analyst, he is active in writing for the theater and in creating fiction. His first play was produced in 1990. He is the coauthor of a children's musical titled *The Talent Machine,* which was produced and performed for several summers in Annapolis, Maryland, and served as the inspiration for a theater company of the same name. Evans is also the author of the play *Spooky Action at a Distance,* a comedy set in Las Vegas. He attended Georgetown University and is a member of the Dramatists Guild and the Society for Technical Communication.

Evans is also a first-time novelist. His debut work is *The Marriage of True Minds,* a comic novel set in Minneapolis. Protagonists Lena Grant and Nick Ward were once business colleagues, a pair of the best lawyers the city had ever seen. The two were also husband and wife. The duo's high-powered personal and professional lives unraveled, however, and they reluctantly divorced. While Lena remained in control of their law firm, Nick gradually became more involved in political activism. When Nick gets involved in an outrageous public relations stunt that includes filling the mayor's swimming pool with more than a hundred live lobsters, he faces jail time for his role in the fiasco. His actions were designed to call attention to local animal rights issues, but noble intentions do not prevent him from being committed to a local psychiatric hospital while his legal case drags on. In order to keep him from serving a lengthy jail sentence, Lena agrees to serve as sponsor and supervisor of his rehabilitation. Soon, Nick moves back into the house he and Lena once occupied as a married couple, and their unlikely reunion becomes even more complicated by Nick's current troubles, the duo's unresolved personality clashes, and the resurrected memory of the deep and powerful relationship they used to share.

A reviewer on the *Boston Bibliophile* Web site remarked, "*The Marriage of True Minds* is a quick, fun little read. It's author Stephen Evans' first novel but his background in playwriting has given him a great ear for dialogue and a quick wit." Evans's "delectable debut novel thrums with zesty dialogue and a memorably zany cast of irresistible characters," commented *Booklist* reviewer Carol Haggas. A *Publishers Weekly* contributor observed that Evans's book offers "solid proof that he is just as much a talented novelist as he is a playwright."

BIOGRAPHICAL AND CRITICAL SOURCES:

PERIODICALS

Booklist, April 1, 2008, Carol Haggas, review of *The Marriage of True Minds,* p. 26.

Publishers Weekly, March 10, 2008, review of *The Marriage of True Minds,* p. 57.

ONLINE

Boston Bibliophile, http://www.bostonbibliophile.com/ (June 25, 2008), review of *The Marriage of True Minds.*

Stephen Evans Gather Page, http://trueminds.gather.com (July 18, 2009).

Unbridled Books Web site, http://unbrudledbooks.com/ (July 18, 2009), biography of Stephen Evans.*

* * *

EVERETT, Daniel L. 1951-
(Daniel Leonard Everett)

PERSONAL: Born July 26, 1951, in Holtville, CA; son of Leonard and Billie Jean Everett; married Keren M. Graham, January 31, 1970; children: Caleb, Shannon, Kristene. *Education:* University of Campinas, Sc.D., 1983, M.A., 1980. *Hobbies and other interests:* Music, guitar, singing.

ADDRESSES: Office—University of Pittsburgh, 2816 Cathedral of Learning, Pittsburgh, PA 15260.

CAREER: Writer, educator, editor, anthropologist, and linguist. University of Campinas, Sao Paulo, Brazil, assistant professor, 1983-86; University of Pittsburgh,

Pittsburgh, PA, began as assistant professor, 1988, became professor of linguistics and chair of linguistics department, 1992—.

MEMBER: American Council of Learned Societies (fellow), American Academy of the Advancement of Science, Linguistic Society of American, Brazilian Linguistics Society.

AWARDS, HONORS: National Science Foundation grant, 1984, 1989, 1993; Mellon Foundation grant, 1993-95.

WRITINGS:

A lingua piraha e a teoria da sintaxe: descricao, perspectives e teoria, Editora da Unicamp (Campinas, Sao Paulo, Brazil), 1991.

Why There Are No Clitics: An Alternative Perspective on Pronominal Allomorphy, Summer Institute of Linguistics, University of Texas at Arlington (Dallas, TX), 1996.

(With Barbara Kern) *Wari: The Pacaas Novos Language of Western Brazil,* Routledge (New York), 1997.

Don't Sleep, There Are Snakes: Life and Language in the Amazonian Jungle, Pantheon Books (New York, NY), 2008.

Contributor to magazines, including *Current Anthropology. Journal of Amazonian Languages,* editor, 1995.

SIDELIGHTS: Daniel L. Everett is a writer, editor, educator, and linguist. He has served as a professor of linguistics at the University of Campinas in Sao Paulo, Brazil. He started as an assistant professor of linguistics at the University of Pittsburgh in 1988 and became an associate professor by 1992. Since 1992, he has been a professor and chair of the linguistics department at the University of Pittsburgh.

In *Don't Sleep, There Are Snakes: Life and Language in the Amazonian Jungle,* Everett recounts his more than thirty years of linguistic research and experiences among the Piraha (pronounced pee-da-HAN), a tribe of hunter-gatherers living near the Maici and Marmelos Rivers in an isolated area of western Brazil. Everett first encountered the Piraha in 1977 when he and his wife Keren went to Brazil as Christian missionaries. However, "the Piraha were marvelously impervious to his promise of a life with Jesus," remarked Christine Kenneally in a *Publishers Weekly* review. "They pointed out that Everett simply had no proof for the supernatural world he described, and in the end he found himself agreeing with them."

Everett quickly became fascinated by the Piraha's unusual language, and refocused his attention on the tribe from religious conversion to linguistic study. He discovered that the Piraha language has little in common with any other known language. It consists of only three vowels, eight consonants, and a complex system of tonal meaning. The Piraha language also has no numbers or counting system, and no system of mathematic calculation. It does not have specific terms for colors or quantities, does not offer ways to express past or future events, does not use clauses to create complex sentences, and focuses almost entirely on the present and on the speaker's personal experiences. There are no Piraha words for abstract concepts or distant places. The highly tonal language could often result in conversations that were simply hummed, whistled, or sung, Everett found. Culturally, the Piraha had no religious tradition, no creation myth, no rituals, and no native art forms.

The lack of complex expression in the Piraha language was not due to inability on the tribe's part. They were generally jovial and easygoing, with a wealth of knowledge of hunting and survival in the jungle. However, Everett concluded they simply had no interest in certain specific terms, or in the past or future. In contrast to language theories proposed by prominent researchers such as Noam Chomsky and Steven Pinker, Everett "concluded that the Piraha language, including its grammar, had been shaped by a culture that valued only a person's immediate experience, not past or future events," stated *Science News* writer Bruce Bowers. Everett's "examination of the complex relationship between the way we talk and the way we live is easy to follow," commented Kier Graff in a *Booklist* review.

In his book, Everett describes the seven years he spent among the Piraha and the nearly thirty years of linguistic study he has devoted to the deceptively simple language. He details the controversies that have resulted from his studies of the Piraha language. He also reveals how his experiences with the Piraha caused him to question his own religious convictions, and ultimately to abandon the religion that had first prompted him to contact the Piraha.

"With a clear, detail-rich writing style, Everett provides evocative ethnographic descriptions of Piraha life and culture as well as perceptive linguistic analysis," commented a *Library Journal* commentator. "Everett's views on the significant role culture plays in language . . . are nicely explicated here and will introduce non-specialists to the fascinating ongoing debate about the origin of languages," remarked a *Kirkus Reviews* writer.

BIOGRAPHICAL AND CRITICAL SOURCES:

PERIODICALS

Booklist, November 1, 2008, Kier Graff, review of *Don't Sleep, There Are Snakes: Life and Language in the Amazonian Jungle,* p. 6.

California Bookwatch, January, 2009, review of *Don't Sleep, There Are Snakes.*

Geographical, December, 2008, Mick Herron, review of *Don't Sleep, There Are Snakes,* p. 71.

Journal of Linguistics, July, 2000, Hans Bennis, review of *Why There Are No Clitics: An Alternative Perspective on Pronominal Allomorphy,* p. 443.

Kirkus Reviews, October 1, 2008, review of *Don't Sleep, There Are Snakes.*

Language, March, 2001, Joel A. Nevis, review of *Why There Are No Clitics,* p. 162.

Library Journal, November 1, 2008, review of *Don't Sleep, There Are Snakes,* p. 86.

New Scientist, December 6, 2008, Lucy Dodwell, "Strong Words," p. 45.

Publishers Weekly, September 29, 2008, Christine Kenneally, review of *Don't Sleep, There Are Snakes,* p. 70.

Science News, December 10, 2005, Bruce Bower, "The Piraha Challenge: An Amazonian Tribe Takes Grammar to a Strange Place," profile of Daniel L. Everett, p. 376; January 17, 2009, Bruce Bower, review of *Don't Sleep, There Are Snakes,* p. 29.

Studies in Language, Winter, 1998, Ken Johnson, review of *Why There Are No Clitics,* p. 704.

Times Higher Education, November 20, 2008, Andrew Anthony, review of *Don't Sleep, There Are Snakes,* p. 45.*

* * *

EVERETT, Daniel Leonard
See EVERETT, Daniel L.

F

FARR, Michael 1953-

PERSONAL: Born 1953, in Paris, France. *Education:* Trinity College, Cambridge, M.A.

CAREER: Writer, reporter, translator, and biographer. Worked as a reporter for Reuters and the *Daily Telegraph,* London, England.

WRITINGS:

Vanishing Borders: The Rediscovery of Eastern Germany, Poland, and Bohemia, Viking (London, England), 1991.

Berlin! Berlin! Its Culture, Its Times, Kyle Cathie (London, England), 1992.

Tintin: The Complete Companion, John Murray (London, England), 2001.

(Editor and translator) Yves Horeau, *The Adventures of Tintin at Sea,* John Murray (London, England), 2004.

Tintin, Egmont (London, England), 2007.

Thomson and Thomson, Egmont (London, England), 2007.

Snowy, Egmont (London, England), 2007.

Professor Calculus, Egmont (London, England), 2007.

Captain Haddock, Egmont (London, England), 2007.

Tintin & Co., Egmont (London, England), 2007.

Bianca Castafiore, Egmont (London, England), 2007.

The Adventures of Hergé, Creator of Tintin, John Murray (London, England), 2007.

(Translator) Philippe Goddin, *The Art of Hergé: Inventor of Tintin,* Last Gasp (San Francisco, CA), 2008.

Contributor to magazines and periodicals, including *History Today.*

SIDELIGHTS: Michael Farr is a writer, journalist, translator, and biographer. He was born in 1953 in Paris, France. He studied history at Trinity College, Cambridge, where he earned a master's degree in fine art. He began his career as a reporter with Reuters before becoming a journalist with the *Daily Telegraph* in London.

Farr is also a knowledgeable and dedicated Tintinologist. He is an expert on one of the world's most popular comic strips, *The Adventures of Tintin,* and the feature's creator, Georges Remi, known best by the one-word name Hergé. Tintin debuted in 1929, and the many books dedicated to him recount the sometimes exotic, often danger-filled adventures of a resourceful and dedicated boy reporter and his numerous allies and adversaries. By 2007, the many books in the *Adventures of Tintin* series had sold well over 200 million copies and had been translated into nearly seventy languages, noted Sebastain Horsley, writing in the *Spectator.* In his biography of the prolific Belgian cartoonist, *The Adventures of Hergé, Creator of Tintin,* Farr "tries to explain why" Tintin has enjoyed such tremendous international popularity, Horsley remarked.

In his "rich illustrated biography," Farr presents a "stunning collection of artifacts, including pre-Tintin drawings, Tintin sketches, newspaper clippings, magazine and book covers," pictures of puppets originally created for animation purposes, and personal photographs, commented Steven Heller in the *New*

York Times Book Review. He explores the predominantly private Hergé's life and career; the genesis of his most famous creation; and the long-time career of both cartoon and cartoonist. He explores the worldwide phenomenon surrounding Tintin, still active even though no new books have been produced since Hergé's death in 1983. Farr reports that while Hergé is not extensively known in the United States, he enjoys a status on the order of Walt Disney in Europe and other areas of the world.

Horsley called Farr's biography of Hergé a "most marvelous portrait." In assessing Farr's biography, Horsley stated, "Like Tintin, this book is entertainment. It is beautifully illustrated and written with an old-fashioned air of restraint." Hergé, Horsley concluded, "knew that true longing must always be directed to something unattainable. Tintin is achingly so. He teaches us that when there is a conflict between illusion and reality, reality should be persuaded to give in gracefully."

Farr also served as translator of *The Art of Hergé: Inventor of Tintin,* by Philippe Goddin. Here, Farr presents a collection of Hergé's diverse artwork, including juvenilia and early works, sketchbook drawings, portraits, book illustrations, advertising artwork, political posters, and fashion drawings, "most of it totally unrecognizable as coming from the hand that drew Tintin," remarked *Booklist* reviewer Gordon Flagg.

Farr's biography, *The Adventures of Hergé, Creator of Tintin,* "serves as an excellent introduction to and provides fine background material on European—and to a degree, international—popular culture" throughout the twentieth century, commented a *Publishers Weekly* reviewer.

BIOGRAPHICAL AND CRITICAL SOURCES:

PERIODICALS

Bookbird, Annual, 2002, "Tintin, Le Reve Et La Realite," p. 62.

Booklist, September 1, 1992, Gordon Flagg, "Tintin and the World of Hergé," p. 22; April 1, 2008, Gordon Flagg, review of *The Adventures of Hergé, Creator of Tintin,* p. 15; September 15, 2008, Gordon Flagg, review of *The Art of Hergé: Inventor of Tintin,* p. 33.

Contemporary Review, November, 1992, review of *Berlin! Berlin! Its Culture, Its Times,* p. 280.

New York Times Book Review, February 24, 2008, Steven Heller, "Pretty Ugly," review of *The Adventures of Hergé, Creator of Tintin.*

School Librarian, summer, 2002, review of *Tintin: The Complete Companion,* p. 111.

School Library Journal, March, 2008, Francisca Goldsmith, review of *The Adventures of Hergé, Creator of Tintin,* p. 235.

Slavonic and East European Review, April, 1993, Paul W. Knoll, review of *Vanishing Borders: The Rediscovery of Eastern Germany, Poland, and Bohemia,* p. 380.

Spectator, November 17, 2007, Sebastian Horsley, "Why Does Tintin Never Have Sex?," review of *The Adventures of Hergé, Creator of Tintin,* p. 52.

Times Literary Supplement, April 1, 1988, Savkar Altinel, "Hergé and Tintin Reporters: From *Le Petit Vingtieme* to *Tintin Magazine,*" p. 367; May 22, 1992, Steven Lukes, review of *Vanishing Borders,* p. 33; December 7, 2001, review of *Tintin,* p. 8.

ONLINE

Internet Movie Database, http://www.imdb.com/ (July 19, 2009), bibliography of Michael Farr.

OTHER

Canadian Broadcasting Corporation, January 19, 2009, "Comic Hero Tintin Continues to Appeal at 80," broadcast transcript of interview with Michael Farr.*

* * *

FEDERICO, Meg 1956(?)-

PERSONAL: Born c. 1956.

ADDRESSES: *Home*—Halifax, Nova Scotia, Canada. *E-mail*—megfederico@gmail.com.

CAREER: Freelance writer; CBC Radio, Canada, author of commentaries and documentaries; previously author of column, "Transitions: Issues in Caregiving," for *Halifax Daily News,* Halifax, Nova Scotia, Canada.

WRITINGS:

Welcome to the Departure Lounge: Adventures in Mothering Mother, Random House (New York, NY), 2009.

Contributor to periodicals, including the *National Post, Globe and Mail, Shambhala Sun,* and *Agni.*

SIDELIGHTS: Canadian-based freelance writer Meg Federico is the author of a number of documentaries for CBC Radio, as well as a former contributor for the *Halifax Daily News,* where she wrote the "Transitions: Issues in Caregiving" column. She is a frequent contributor to various periodicals, including the *National Post, Globe and Mail, Shambhala Sun,* and *Agni.* Her debut book, a memoir titled *Welcome to the Departure Lounge: Adventures in Mothering Mother,* was published by Random House in 2009.

Known for her humorous outlook on life, Federico brings that same light touch to a serious situation in *Welcome to the Departure Lounge,* where she chronicles her own experiences and hardships dealing with the news that both her mother and her stepfather had been diagnosed with Alzheimer's. Although she lives in Nova Scotia, Canada, Federico undertakes the arduous burden of helping to care for both of them, flying down to their home in New Jersey with great frequency. The situation is exacerbated by Federico's somewhat distant relationship with her mother and complete lack of closeness to her stepfather, as well as the fact that both parents are heavy drinkers and do nothing to cut back on their habits once their illnesses are diagnosed. Federico peppers her story with a combination of grim honesty—explaining her own difficult position as a typical member of the sandwich generation, caught between her own children and her parents—and with ironic and humorous moments that spring up as a result of the situation. The worse her mother becomes, the more Federico finds herself analyzing her as a person and considering the different life experiences that made her the person she was prior to her illness. In addition, Federico offers sound advice regarding things one should keep in mind when caring for an elderly or ailing parent, using her own experiences as an example of what difficulties might arise.

Reviewers praised Federico's approach to her caregiving experiences. A contributor for *Kirkus Reviews* found the book to be "a funny yet touching portrayal of the indignities of aging." *Maclean's* reviewer Brian Bethune commented that "flowing not very far beneath the surface humor, and made palatable by the laughs, are some dead serious issues that, one way or another, most of us will someday face." A writer for *Publishers Weekly* concluded that "Federico gently delineates the humiliating burden caused by the loss of memory, while humanely portraying a brave new sympathy and understanding" in her relationship.

BIOGRAPHICAL AND CRITICAL SOURCES:

BOOKS

Federico, Meg, *Welcome to the Departure Lounge: Adventures in Mothering Mother,* Random House (New York, NY), 2009.

PERIODICALS

Kirkus Reviews, December 1, 2008, review of *Welcome to the Departure Lounge.*

Maclean's, February 23, 2009, Brian Bethune, "Laughing All the Way to the End: Grand Larceny, a Mother's Madcap Final Months and the Bitter Truth about Aging," p. 63.

Publishers Weekly, November 3, 2008, review of *Welcome to the Departure Lounge,* p. 47; December 8, 2008, "PW Talks with Meg Federico: The Dementia Spiral," p. 55.

Wall Street Journal, February 10, 2009, "Caring but Also Careworn: *Welcome to the Departure Lounge,* by Meg Federico," p. 15.

ONLINE

Meg Federico Home Page, http://www.megfederico.com (August 8, 2009).

National Post Web site, http://network.nationalpost.com/ (March 14, 2009), Merilyn Simonds, review of *Welcome to the Departure Lounge.*

Northwest Indiana Times Web site, http://nwitimes.com/ (May 4, 2009), Jane Ammenson, "Get Healthy: Humorist, Author Meg Federico Shares Her Tales of Mothering Her Mother."

Random House Web site, http://www.randomhouse.com/ (August 8, 2009), author profile.*

FEINBERG, Margaret 1976-

PERSONAL: Born 1976; married Leif Oines. *Hobbies and other interests:* Hiking, eating mangos, movies, books, kayaking, traveling, photography, God, authentic faith, urban tribes, glaciers, New Zealand, China, AIDS & Africa, Rwanda.

ADDRESSES: Office—Transparent Faith, P.O. Box 441, Morrison, CO 80465.

CAREER: Author and speaker at colleges and leadership conferences.

AWARDS, HONORS: "30 Emerging Voices" citation, *Charisma* magazine; "40 Under 40" citation, Christian Retailing.

WRITINGS:

God Whispers: Learning to Hear His Voice, Relevant Books (Lake Mary, FL), 2002.

Simple Acts of Faith: Heartwarming Stories of One Life Touching Another, Harvest House (Eugene, OR), 2003.

Simple Acts of Friendship: Heartwarming Stories of One Friend Blessing Another, Harvest House Publishers (Eugene, OR), 2004.

Twentysomething: Surviving and Thriving in the Real World, W Publishing (Nashville, TN), 2004.

(With husband, Leif Oines) *How to Be a Grownup: 247 Lab-Tested Strategies for Conquering the World,* W Publishing (Nashville, TN), 2005.

Just Married, Harvest House Publishers (Eugene, OR), 2005.

Redefining Life: My Career, Think (Colorado Springs, CO), 2005.

Redefining Life: My Relationships: A Navstudy Featuring the Message Remix, Think (Colorado Springs, CO), 2005.

Simple Prayers of Hope, Harvest House Publishers (Eugene, OR), 2005.

What the Heck Am I Going to Do with My Life?, Tyndale House Publishers (Carol Stream, IL), 2005.

(With Natalie Nichols Gillespie) *Five-Star Living on a Two-Star Budget,* Harvest House Publishers (Eugene, OR), 2006.

Redefining Life: For Women: A Navstudy Featuring the Message Remix, Think (Colorado Springs, CO), 2006.

The Organic God, Zondervan (Grand Rapids, MI), 2007.

The Sacred Echo: Hearing God's Voice in Every Area of Your Life, Zondervan (Grand Rapids, MI), 2008.

Scouting the Devine, Zondervan (Grand Rapids, MI), 2009.

Contributor to periodicals, including *Christianity Today, Relevant,* and *HomeLife.* Author of blogs, http://margaretfeinberg.blogspot.com; http://washingtonpost.com.

SIDELIGHTS: Author and public speaker Margaret Feinberg tries to connect the practical with the spiritual in her writings. "My calling," Feinberg explained to an interviewer for the Web site *Faithful Reader,* "is simply to make sure any talents that I've been given, no matter how small, aren't buried."

Feinberg's books include *Simple Acts of Faith: Heartwarming Stories of One Life Touching Another, Simple Prayers of Hope,* and *What the Heck Am I Going to Do with My Life?* The latter book is in many ways an examination of how personal faith can help guide a person out of a midlife crisis. "Faith is a cornerstone of the book in regard to the fact that the one who knows what you're supposed to do with your life is God," Feinberg told the *Faithful Reader* Web site interviewer. "He's the one who created you. He's the one who gifted you. He's the one who equipped you. And he's the one who called you. So, a relationship with him is a huge part of figuring out what the heck."

Both *The Organic God* and *The Sacred Echo: Hearing God's Voice in Every Area of Your Life* focus on changing one's relation with the Divine by changing one's understanding of who God really is. *The Organic God* emphasizes the need to understand the characteristics of God behind the screens we erect. "We, as a society, are very focused on adding things to God—rules, regulations and expectations," explained Jill Hart in a review of the book published on the *Blogcritics* Web site. These things divert us from the nature of God and prevent us from fully realizing our faith. By eliminating them, concluded a reviewer for the *Campus Life's Ignite Your Faith* Web site, we approach a "God who loves us beyond our wildest imaginations."

The Sacred Echo: Hearing God's Voice in Every Area of Your Life approaches the problem of learning to hear and understand the voice of God in our mundane lives. "The sacred echo is the persistent voice of God," Feinberg told Jim and Sheri Mueller in an interview for the Web site *growthtrac.* "It's that moment when we wake in the morning, and maybe we're spending time in Scripture, and a certain passage or a certain verse just pops off the page. . . . Then we have a conversation with a friend later up in the week, and maybe that topic comes up again. Then we flip open the page on our Christian calendar or day planner and—boom—there is the passage again. It's the idea that God is so persistent in the way that he speaks." "In *The Sacred Echo,*" explained Paula Friedrichsen, reviewing the book for the *CBN.com* Web site, "she encourages readers to perk up their ears and begin to listen with increased sensitivity to what God is saying through those sacred echoes." By recounting her own struggles to understand the voice of God, stated a *Today's Christian Woman* contributor, "she trains other eager ears to hear his voice." "Feinberg," a *Publishers Weekly* reviewer concluded, "brings an authentic voice to a perennially difficult subject, and her book" serves as a reminder that learning to listen for the voice of God is a discipline that must be practiced regularly.

BIOGRAPHICAL AND CRITICAL SOURCES:

PERIODICALS

Book World, April 1, 2007, review of *The Organic God,* p. 9.

Campus Life's Ignite Your Faith, November 1, 2007, "Spiritual Growth."

Publishers Weekly, May 26, 2008, review of *The Sacred Echo: Hearing God's Voice in Every Area of Your Life,* p. 58.

Today's Christian, May 1, 2006, Eugene Pratt, review of *Five-Star Living on a Two-Star Budget.*

Today's Christian Woman, July 1, 2004, "Next Generation"; September 1, 2008, review of *The Sacred Echo.*

ONLINE

Blogcritics, http://blogcritics.org/ (July 22, 2009), Jill Hart, review of *The Organic God.*

CBN.com, http://blogs.cbn.com/ (July 22, 2009), Paula Friedrichsen, review of *The Sacred Echo.*

Faithful Reader, http://www.faithfulreader.com/ (July 22, 2009), author profile.

growthtrac, http://www.growthtrac.com/ (July 22, 2009), Jim and Sheri Mueller, "A Conversation with Margaret Feinberg."

Margaret Feinberg Home Page, http://www.margaretfeinberg.com (July 22, 2009), author profile.

Margaret Feinberg MySpace Page, http://www.myspace.com (July 22, 2009), author profile.

Zondervan Web site, http://www.zondervan.com/ (July 22, 2009), author profile.

* * *

FERNANDES, Edna

PERSONAL: Born in Nairobi, Kenya.

ADDRESSES: Agent—Aitken Alexander Associates, 18-21 Cavaye Pl., London SW10 9PT, England. *E-mail*—ednamailbox@gmail.com.

CAREER: Journalist for AP-Dow Jones and Reuters in London, England, and *Financial Times,* New Delhi, India.

AWARDS, HONORS: TR Fyvel Prize shortlist, Index on Censorship (United Kingdom), and Ramnath Goenka Excellence in Journalism Best Book Award, both for *Holy Warriors: A Journey into the Heart of Indian Fundamentalism.*

WRITINGS:

Holy Warriors: A Journey into the Heart of Indian Fundamentalism, Viking (New York, NY), 2006.

The Last Jews of Kerala: The Two Thousand Year History of India's Forgotten Jewish Community, Skyhorse Publishing (New York, NY), 2008.

Contributor to periodicals, including *Wall Street Journal* and *International Herald Tribune.*

SIDELIGHTS: Journalist Edna Fernandes's first book, *Holy Warriors: A Journey into the Heart of Indian Fundamentalism,* is a study of the ways that religious divisions have torn India apart in recent years. It is in part an examination of the phenomenon of *Hindutva:* the idea that the nation of India (historically famous as a cradle of tolerance toward different religions) is in fact only a nation of Hindus; members of other religious groups have no place in that society. Such attitudes go a long way in explaining the political violence that has racked the nation in the decades since the country gained its independence from Britain. "Shiv Sena and the radical groups behind India's former governing party, the BJP, believe in . . . an ideological merger of Holyland with Fatherland," explained Guy Mannes-Abbott in a review of the volume for the *Independent.* "For these admirers of Nazism, the pain is a millennium of external conquest."

At the same time, Fernandes also examines the root of radical Islam by looking at the effects of the British suppression of indigenous dissent in India in the nineteenth century. "In 1866, nine years after the Indian Mutiny in which the British crushed the insurgency of Muslim and Hindu soldiers," Fernandes wrote in a *History Today* article, "a group of Muslim elders established a *madrassa,* or Islamic school, called *Darul Uloom,* the 'House of Knowledge', in northern India. Nurtured by a hatred of foreign rule and cultural 'pollution', Darul Uloom promised to be a haven of Islamic purity and learning, based in the nondescript town of Deoband, in what is today Uttar Pradesh. The *madrassa*'s spiritual ideology was forged in the fires of the Mutiny and would become known as Deobandi Islam." That ideology was the founding of the modern Al Qaida and Taliban movements. The effect of this bifurcation on India, declared Avelino D'Souza, writing on the *Goanet* Web site, is a profoundly conflicted society in which religion can be both central and inconsequential to political discourse. "In one moment India is paranoid about terrorism yet it seems far more restrained in its response than the level of paranoia would suggest," D'Souza stated. "Sometimes Indian society seems to overflow with religious zealotry, at other times we can retreat into the comfortable illusion that religion is an epiphenomenon; it is really all about employment and jobs."

In *The Last Jews of Kerala: The Two Thousand Year History of India's Forgotten Jewish Community,* Fernandes examines the dying Jewish community of the southwestern Indian state of Kerala—remnants of the diaspora caused by the Roman destruction of Jerusalem and expulsion of the Jews from Judea in the second century. She finds that the Keralan community is both small and divided against itself. Less than fifty members of the community remain, and they are separated by racism, fear, mistrust of strangers, and debility from one another and from the rest of the world. Through a combination of "apartheid, centuries of interbreeding, mental illness, and a latter-day exodus from Kerala," stated George Cohen in *Booklist,* the ancient Jews of India have brought their historic culture to the brink of extinction in their homeland. "The small world views of the remaining inhabitants . . . mean that Fernandes has to turn elsewhere for meaningful commentary on their plight," stated Ben Rich in the *New Humanist.* "As a result the story—whilst told at a cracking pace and with the easy accessibility one would expect from an experienced journalist—veers, often uncomfortably, between a series of colourful interviews, a historical pamphlet and a travelogue." "Edna Fernandes's material is fascinating," declared a reviewer for the *Economist,* even though the review went on to criticize the author for her "cliche-ridden and sometimes annoyingly gushy prose." Nonetheless, the *Economist* reviewer continued, "the story of these Jews is so compelling, and the author's reporting of it so assiduous, that she deserves leniency." "Indeed," the contributor concluded, "she has unearthed gems."

BIOGRAPHICAL AND CRITICAL SOURCES:

PERIODICALS

Booklist, June 1, 2008, George Cohen, review of *The Last Jews of Kerala: The Two Thousand Year History of India's Forgotten Jewish Community,* p. 26.

Economist, August 16, 2008, "Living Far Apart; Kerala's Jews."

Far Eastern Economic Review, January 1, 2009, Ben Frumin, review of *The Last Jews of Kerala.*

History Today, February 1, 2009, "School of Shariah: Edna Fernandes Visits a Madrassa in Northern India Founded in the Wake of the Indian Mutiny. One of the First Islamic Fundamentalist Schools, Its Influence Has Spread into Pakistan and Afghanistan, among the Taliban and Followers of Osama Bin Laden," p. 3.

Independent (London, England), August 14, 2007, Guy Abbott-Mannes, review of *Holy Warriors: A Journey into the Heart of Indian Fundamentalism.*
Kirkus Reviews, May 15, 2008, review of *The Last Jews of Kerala.*
New Humanist, July-August, 2008, Ben Rich, review of *The Last Jews of Kerala.*
Publishers Weekly, May 26, 2008, review of *The Last Jews of Kerala,* p. 53.
Reference & Research Book News, February 1, 2009, review of *The Last Jews of Kerala.*

ONLINE

Edna Fernandes Home Page, http://www.ednafernandes.com (July 22, 2009), author profile.
Goanet, http://www.mail-archive.com/ (July 22, 2009), Avelino D'Souza, review of *Holy Warriors.**

* * *

FISCHER, Debbie Reed 1967-

PERSONAL: Born 1967; married; children: two sons. *Education:* University of Miami, B.A., 1991.

ADDRESSES: *Home*—South FL. *Agent*—Steven Chudney, The Chudney Agency, 72 N. State Rd., Ste. 501, Briarcliff Manor, NY 10510. *E-mail*—info@debbiereedfischer.com.

CAREER: Writer; previously worked as a model booker and an English teacher.

WRITINGS:

YOUNG ADULT NOVELS

Braless in Wonderland, Dutton Books (New York, NY), 2008.
Swimming with the Sharks, Flux (Woodbury, MN), 2008.

Maintains a blog at http://debbierfischer.livejournal.com.

SIDELIGHTS: Florida-based writer Debbie Reed Fischer earned her undergraduate degree in screenwriting from the University of Miami in 1991. While still a student, she wrote and directed a number of films and also worked as a host for a local cable news program aimed at a teen audience. However, after graduation she found herself drawn into the business side of the film business in South Beach, and ultimately ended up working for a firm where she booked models for various projects, including film, commercials, music videos, and print. Eventually, Fischer left the film business in favor of education, and spent five years teaching English at the middle grade and high school levels before turning her attentions toward raising a family and reviving her own writing ambitions. Inspired in part by the teens she met working with models, Fischer decided she would focus on writing novels for young adults. She honed her craft while reading published young adult novels and attending various workshops and writers' conferences. Her debut novel, *Braless in Wonderland,* was released in 2008, followed by her sophomore effort, *Swimming with the Sharks.*

Fischer's *Braless in Wonderland* is heavily reliant on her own experiences working as a booker for models. The story revolves around Allee, a girl from a small town who has always considered herself a strong feminist, but whose entire life gets upended when she is spotted by a talent scout in her local mall and sent off to Miami to model, much to the surprise of her family, especially her younger and prettier sister. While Allee has a low opinion of the modeling profession on the whole, considering models to be focused on nothing but their appearance, she has to face the reality that she is in need of money to finance her college education; she is headed to Yale University in the fall. Modeling might be a brainless activity, but it pays well, and so this opportunity might be her one chance to come up with the cash that she needs. In Fischer's humorous take on the classic *Alice in Wonderland,* Allee has her first experience in the real world, and begins to learn that generalizations leave a great deal of room for surprises and new discoveries. She comes to realize that any industry has its smart individuals, and that it pays to watch your back no matter where you are. She also comes to a new understanding of feminism and her own definition of self. Claire Rosser, in a review for *Kliatt,* pointed out that "Allee learns that she may be book smart, but naive when it comes to understanding other people (or herself)," and praised Fischer for her detailed, realistic handling of the modeling industry. Reviewing for *School Library Journal,* Terri Clark opined that the book "a fun, in-depth peek into the modeling world," as well as "a rabbit hole that teens will enjoy exploring." A contributor for *Kirkus Reviews* noted Fischer's deft yet humorous handling of issues that are commonly faced in the modeling industry, such as drug use and profiling based on ethnic background, concluding that *Braless in Wonderland* is "not just a smart read but one that is often very funny as well." Elizabeth Petroelje Stolle, writing for the *Journal of Adolescent and Adult Literacy,* commented of the book that "Fischer has written an engaging story that will keep readers wondering about the next twist. The realities of the modeling world, the conflict between friends, and the complexity of choices all come together in a climax with the expansion of an identity, the rebuilding of relationships, the revelation of secrets, and the pursuit of a dream."

BIOGRAPHICAL AND CRITICAL SOURCES:

PERIODICALS

Journal of Adolescent & Adult Literacy, November 1, 2008, Elizabeth Petroelje Stolle, review of *Braless in Wonderland,* p. 257.

Kirkus Reviews, August 1, 2008, review of *Braless in Wonderland.*

Kliatt, March 1, 2008, Claire Rosser, review of *Braless in Wonderland,* p. 12.

School Library Journal, July 1, 2008, Terri Clark, review of *Braless in Wonderland,* p. 98.

Voice of Youth Advocates, December 1, 2008, Cindy Faughnan, review of *Swimming with the Sharks,* p. 432.

ONLINE

Authors Unleashed Blog, http://authorsunleashed.blogspot.com/ (August 28, 2009), "Interview with Debbie Reed Fischer."

Debbie Reed Fischer Home Page, http://www.debbiereedfischer.com (August 28, 2009), author profile.

Debbie Reed Fischer MySpace Page, http://www.myspace.com/debbiereedfischer (August 28, 2009), author profile.

Romantic Times Online, http://www.romantictimes.com/ (August 28, 2009), Raven Haller, review of *Braless in Wonderland.*

Writer Musings Blog, http://tabwriter.blogspot.com/ (August 28, 2009), "Interview with Debbie Reed Fischer."*

* * *

FISHBURNE, Rodes

PERSONAL: Born in VA. *Education:* Graduated from Emory & Henry College; attended St. Peter's College, Oxford.

ADDRESSES: Home—San Francisco, CA. *Agent*—Fredrica Friedman, Fredrica S. Friedman & Co., 136 E. 57th St., 14th Fl., New York, NY 10022. *E-mail*—rodesmail@gmail.com; rodes@sfgrotto.org.

CAREER: Author and journalist. Former editor, "Big Issue," *Forbes ASAP.* Also worked as a fly-fishing guide in AK. Member, Grotto (writers collective).

AWARDS, HONORS: "Best Novels of 2009" citation, Independent bookstores and *Amazon.com,* for *Going to See the Elephant.*

WRITINGS:

Going to See the Elephant (novel), Bantam Dell (New York, NY), 2009.

Also author of one-act plays *Note to Self,Gaggle,* and *Waiting for Henry to Snow,* produced by Drilling Company at West 78th Street Theatre, New York, NY; author of play *Eternity: A Play in 30 Minutes,* for Alfred P. Sloan Foundation. Editor and author of introduction, *The Best of the Big Issues.* Contributor to periodicals, including *New Yorker, New York Times, San Francisco Chronicle Magazine,* and *Forbes ASAP.*

SIDELIGHTS: Journalist, playwright, and novelist Rodes Fishburne is the author of *Going to See the Elephant,* the story of an aspiring writer who "comes to San Francisco with only a trunk full of first-edition 19th-century novels and an equally heavy load of gumption," wrote Jonathan Kiefer on the Web site *Rumpus.* "Slater Brown wants to be a writer—and not just any writer, but a famous writer; and not just any famous writer, but a justly famous writer. All he lacks is skill and experience and perspective." "I was walking down Polk Street in San Francisco in 2003," Fishburne explained to Kiefer, "and out of the corner of my eye I saw a young man in a coffee shop hunched over a table furiously writing away. He had fourteen empty espresso cups around him, and everything he wrote he either crossed out, or crumpled up." Watching the frenetic writer at work was a revelation to Fishburne, the author continued; it showed him that San Francisco is a place of dreams for people who hope to realize their artistic ambitions. "'Going to see the elephant' was a phrase used for those who traveled West during the gold rush," explained *San Francisco Chronicle* contributor Justin Berton. "Instead of riches, Slater Brown sets out make literary history in the City by the Bay."

Brown's ambitions are quickly frustrated. "He spends his first San Francisco evening writing in an Irish bar," declared Scott Hutchins in a review published on *Rumpus,* "taking breaks to sharpen his cedar pencil with a pocketknife. After washing out as a fiction writer—he spends a tortured twelve days at it—he seeks employment at the offices of a local newspaper, the *Trumpet,* in a three-piece pinstripe suit and a black fedora. Strangely enough, he gets the job." Brown's fortunes only begin to turn around, however, after he receives a unique radio that tunes into private conversations—especially conversations that the city's mayor would prefer remained private. "Brown turns this occult accident into a scoop," wrote a *Kirkus Reviews* contributor, "one that begins a series of successes that help put the *Trumpet* back on firm popular and financial footing." "The book is partly in homage to the possibility of youth," stated a contributor to *America's Intelligence Wire,* "but ultimately it is a serenade to the city that invigorates this author and provides his characters with a fluid and mesmerizing backdrop." Featuring a "shrewdly stylized Jazz Age tone," Donna Seaman wrote in a *Booklist* review, "this old-fashioned yet newfangled tale puts a clever, global-warming-era spin on the superhero story."

BIOGRAPHICAL AND CRITICAL SOURCES:

PERIODICALS

America's Intelligence Wire, March 27, 2009, "Bowdoin College: Book Review: Fishburne Lights Up San Francisco with Colorful Satire in 'Elephant.'"

Booklist, November 15, 2008, Donna Seaman, review of *Going to See the Elephant,* p. 30.

Kirkus Reviews, October 15, 2008, review of *Going to See the Elephant.*

Publishers Weekly, November 10, 2008, review of *Going to See the Elephant,* p. 33.

San Francisco Chronicle, January 15, 2009, Justin Berton, review of *Going to See the Elephant,* p. G-13.

ONLINE

Big Think, http://bigthink.com/ (July 22, 2009), author profile.

Pop Culture Junkie, http://aleapopculture.blogspot.com/ (July 22, 2009), review of *Going to See the Elephant.*

Random House Web site, http://www.randomhouse.com/ (July 22, 2009), author profile.

Red Room, http://www.redroom.com/ (July 22, 2009), author profile.

Rodes Fishburne Home Page, http://rodesfishburne.com (July 22, 2009), author profile.

Rumpus, http://therumpus.net/ (July 22, 2009), Jonathan Kiefer, "The Shorty Q&A with Rodes Fishburne"; Scott Hutchins, review of *Going to See the Elephant.*

Used Books Blog, http://usedbooksblog.com/ (July 22, 2009), review of *Going to See the Elephant.**

* * *

FLEISHMAN, Jeffrey

PERSONAL: Married; wife's name Clare (a journalist).

ADDRESSES: *Home*—Cairo, Egypt. *Office*—Los Angeles Times, 202 W. 1st St., Los Angeles, CA 90012. *E-mail*—jeffrey.fleishman@latimes.com.

CAREER: European correspondent in Rome, Italy for *Philadelphia Inquirer; Los Angeles Times,* bureau chief in Berlin, Germany, 2002-07, bureau chief in Cairo, Egypt, 2007—. Former Neiman Fellow, Harvard University.

AWARDS, HONORS: Pulitzer Prize finalist, 1997, for reporting on Buddhist monks and nuns escaping from Tibet; Goldsmith Prize for Investigative Reporting finalist (with Loretta Tofani), Harvard University, 1998, for "Inside Tibet: A Country Tortured."

WRITINGS:

Promised Virgins: A Novel of Jihad, Arcade Publishing/Hachette Book Group (New York, NY), 2009.

SIDELIGHTS: Los Angeles Times Cairo bureau chief Jeffrey Fleishman is the author of *Promised Virgins: A Novel of Jihad,* the story of a war correspondent named Jay Morgan and his search through the war-torn Balkans for a mysterious armed figure known as "the Dateman," who is rumored to be planning new terrorist attacks against the West in the name of holy war, or *jihad.* The author himself draws on his personal experience in war zones across the world; during the Kosovo conflict he worked as a war correspondent for the *Philadelphia Inquirer* in the Balkans, and in 1997 a story he wrote on the escape of a group of Tibetan monks and nuns across the Himalayas was nominated for the Pulitzer Prize. In addition, he reached the final elimination for Harvard University's Goldsmith Prize for Investigative Reporting in 1998 for another article on the political situation in Tibet.

Despite the fact that it is set in the 1990s, during the civil war that destroyed Yugoslavia, Fleishman's novel evokes the "specter of 9/11," revealed a *Publishers Weekly* reviewer, and that image "hangs over Fleishman's account of war, which is often filled with rich and provocative insights." Joined by his translator Alija (herself the victim of war crimes) and his colleague Brian Conrad, Jay moves through the Bosnian landscape like a man possessed. "Haunted by the death of Linda, his photographer wife, in Beirut, he sometimes doubts whether he has the temperament to survive it," explained Michael Leonard on the *Curled Up with a Good Book* Web site. "Meanwhile, Alija is haunted by the destruction of her family. Gang-raped and beaten, her village destroyed and her parents now in a refugee camp, Alija still holds out hope of finding [her brother] Ardian alive." Together the three search mass graves, brave the daily violence inflicted by the Serbian military police, and move through villages destroyed by the ethnic violence, in search of both Ardian and the Dateman. Finally, "after much searching, and with help from those sympathetic to the rebel cause," declared a *Kirkus Reviews* writer, "Jay succeeds in having a brief and enigmatic interview with the shadowy figure known as Abu Musab." He also finds Ardian, who has been recruited by the terrorists to become one of the suicide bombers that threaten Western targets. "*Promised Virgins,*" wrote Orlando *Sun-Sentinel* reviewer Jean Patteson, "is an adventure story in the manner of Graham Greene or Ernest Hemingway. It's a terrific tale of action and suspense, trust and betrayal, age-old enmity and newly forged comradeship."

BIOGRAPHICAL AND CRITICAL SOURCES:

PERIODICALS

Kirkus Reviews, November 15, 2008, review of *Promised Virgins: A Novel of Jihad.*

Nieman Reports, December 22, 2008, "Jeffrey Fleishman," p. 106.

Publishers Weekly, November 10, 2008, review of *Promised Virgins,* p. 31.

Sun-Sentinel (Orlando, FL), March 22, 2009, Jean Patteson, review of *Promised Virgins.*

ONLINE

Arcade Publishing Web site, http://www.arcadepub.com/ (July 22, 2009), author profile.

Curled Up with a Good Book, http://www.curledup.com/ (July 22, 2009), Michael Leonard, review of *Promised Virgins.*

Los Angeles Times Online, http://www.latimes.com/ (July 22, 2009), author profile.

Ute Körner Literary Agency, http://uklitag.com/ (July 22, 2009), author profile.*

* * *

FLYNN, Daniel J. 1949-

PERSONAL: Born October 24, 1949, in Cambridge, MA; married; children: one son. *Education:* University of Massachusetts—Amherst, B.A. *Religion:* Roman Catholic.

ADDRESSES: Home—MA.

CAREER: Writer and political commentator. Has appeared as a guest on *Fox News, CNN, MSNBC, Showtime, CSPAN,* and *Court TV. Military service:* U.S. Marine Corps Reserve, 1994-2002; honorably discharged with the rank of sergeant.

WRITINGS:

Why the Left Hates America: Exposing the Lies That Have Obscured Our Nation's Greatness, Forum (Roseville, CA), 2002.

Intellectual Morons: How Ideology Makes Smart People Fall for Stupid Ideas, Crown Forum (New York, NY), 2004.

A Conservative History of the American Left, Crown Forum (New York, NY), 2008.

SIDELIGHTS: Daniel J. Flynn is a writer and political commentator who argues against what he sees as the damaging influences to the American social fabric of left-wing attitudes and policies. In his first book, *Why the Left Hates America: Exposing the Lies That Have Obscured Our Nation's Greatness,* he identifies "five big lies" that he says the left perpetuates about the United States: that American women are oppressed by a patriarchal system; that of all nations, the United States poses the greatest threat to the world's environment; that the United States is a fundamentally racist country; that the United States is an imperialist power; and that the American system is set up to increase wealth for the rich and keep the poor from advancing. "I think if we continue to tell the truth about traditional American values we will overwhelm the America-haters on the left as completely as we did the 'evil empire' of the Soviet Union," Flynn told *Insight on the News* interviewer Stephen Goode. "Lies rest upon a false foundation, and when they are exposed they crumble and fall."

To claims that the United States is an empire, for example, Flynn stated in the Goode interview that, unlike Britain, the Soviet Union, and the Ottoman Empire, the United States has not used its military power "to subjugate other peoples, but to encourage their self-determination and to advance the evolution of democratic institutions throughout the world." In *Why the Left Hates America* the author identifies the roots of anti-Americanism as stemming from the legacy of communism and cultural Marxism, as well as from relativism and multiculturalism. Communist activism, he writes, contributed to a milieu in which followers reflexively blame the United States for world crises, without first researching and analyzing relevant facts. Such responses, Flynn says, tolerate every excess of the left but automatically reject every idea from the right. Citing conservative publications such as the *Washington Times* and media outlets such as Fox News, Flynn told Goode that these outlets have helped to balance the media's leftist bias, and added that respectful debate will expose the errors of anti-American ideas. Though some online commentators appreciated Flynn's thesis, Joyce M. Cox, writing in *Library Journal,* criticized *Why the Left Hates America* as a work of "gross generalizations and virulent depictions" of leftist activists.

Flynn expounds on similar themes in *Intellectual Morons: How Ideology Makes Smart People Fall for Stupid Ideas.* His purpose in the book, he explained to *Front Page* Web site writer Jamie Glazov, is "to get more people to think with their brain rather than their ideology." Many prominent intellectuals, he said, have been shown to condone dishonesty when it furthers their beliefs—one example is Rigoberta Menchu, winner of the 1998 Nobel Peace Prize, whose autobiography recounting several acts of political oppression in Guatemala was later found to contain substantial inaccuracies and falsehoods. Similarly, Flynn objects to the left's embrace of Margaret Sanger as an early champion of women's reproductive rights. Citing a speech that Sanger gave to Congress in 1932, Flynn sees Sanger as a champion of eugenics who argued that millions of poor and uneducated Americans, as well as drug users, criminals, and others she deemed unfit to reproduce, should be kept in a system of concentration camps. Famed linguist Noam Chomsky, too, receives scornful attention from Flynn, who discredits several of Chomsky's widely quoted statements on U.S. foreign policy, such as his dismissal of Pol Pot's genocide in Cambodia as a relatively minor event with executions numbering no more than a few thousand.

Such comments, said Flynn in the interview, are accepted because "ideology acts as a mental straitjacket. It blinds adherents to reality, breeds fanaticism, and rationalizes dishonesty. It makes smart people stupid." But *Intellectual Morons* is not simply an attack on individuals; Flynn analyzes the utopian roots of leftist thinking to explain how acceptance of intellectual dishonesty became entrenched. It is easy to cling to a socialist mindset, he told Glazov, because "imperfection and tragedy must be constant realities of human life. For many humans, however, the easiest thing intellectually is to believe that this can be fixed and that heaven can be built on earth—an experiment that always leads to hell on earth. And so the Left will remain powerful and continue to build more human hells in its utopian experiments, which now involves the glorification of the suicide bomber."

Flynn's *A Conservative History of the American Left,* wrote *First Principles Journal* Web Site reviewer Bill Kauffman, is "a well-written, pugnaciously argued, and consistently interesting account of the American Left" that makes controversial arguments but does so from an informed perspective. Observing that the left cannot be trusted to write its own history because it prefers to forget things in its past that are inconsistent with its present existence, Flynn shows that twenty-first century secular liberals are the descendants of religious extremists. Many of these were utopian visionaries who espoused free love, pacifism, and tolerance, and advocated against slavery, but others were openly racist. The ideals of the earliest American socialists were eventually challenged by infighting, Flynn's narrative shows, and from the 1930s the progressive movement was dominated by Soviet ideology. After World War II, the New Left embraced nonviolent social change and participatory democracy, but Flynn argues that its actions have continued to be based on standard Marxist thinking. As *Booklist* reviewer Bryce A. Christensen pointed out, the book presents "a decidedly unflattering investigation into progressive origins," and highlights the many contradictions in the leftist legacy—such as self-described 1960s pacifists building bombs to use against the government.

Writing in the *Weekly Standard,* Ronald Radosh hailed *A Conservative History of the American Left* as "a well-rounded history . . . that should be read by anyone interested in the subject—and that includes those who call themselves left or liberal." *Nation* contributor Michael Kazin, however, felt that Flynn presents his views through "the crude lens of a propagandist." Though the reviewer found the author's "passionate, undeveloped assertions about the past" often puzzling and unconvincing, Kazin nevertheless said that the book is "worth taking seriously." Fred Siegel, writing on the *City Journal* Web site, considered the book "highly readable and informative," concluding that "with messianic hopes now being invested in the candidacy of Democrat Barack Obama, Flynn's history is a timely demonstration of some disturbing continuities in left-wing thought."

BIOGRAPHICAL AND CRITICAL SOURCES:

PERIODICALS

Booklist, April 1, 2008, Bryce Christensen, review of *A Conservative History of the American Left,* p. 8.

Insight on the News, January 7, 2003, Stephen Goode, "Exposing Lies of the American Left: Daniel J. Flynn Fights for the Right at Accuracy in Academia and as Author of a Book That Explores Knee-Jerk Anti-Americanism in Arenas of Radical Influence," p. 42.

Library Journal, October 1, 2002, Joyce M. Cox, review of *Why the Left Hates America: Exposing the Lies That Have Obscured Our Nation's Greatness,* p. 116.

Nation, June 3, 2008, Michael Kazin, review of *A Conservative History of the American Left.*

Publishers Weekly, August 23, 2004, review of *Intellectual Morons: How Ideology Makes Smart People Fall for Stupid Ideas,* p. 49.

Weekly Standard, May 12, 2008, Ronald Radosh, "Radical Revision; Reclaiming the History of the Left from Leftist Historians."

ONLINE

Accuracy in Media, http://www.aim.org/ (July 21, 2009), Kinga Krisko, review of *Intellectual Morons.*

American Spectator Online, http://spectator.org/ (July 21, 2009), Paul J. Cella, review of *Intellectual Morons;* Daniel McCarthy, review of *A Conservative History of the American Left.*

American Thinker, http://www.americanthinker.com/ (July 21, 2009), Judith Reisman, review of *A Conservative History of the American Left.*

Big Hollywood, http://bighollywood.breitbart.com/ (July 21, 2009), "Daniel J. Flynn."

Blog Critics, http://blogcritics.org/ (July 21, 2009), Sean Hackbarth, interview with Flynn.

Campus Report Online, http://www.campusreportonline.net/ (July 21, 2009), Malcolm A. Kline, review of *Intellectual Morons.*

City Journal, http://www.city-journal.org/ (July 21, 2009), Fred Siegel, review of *A Conservative History of the American Left.*

Daniel J. Flynn Home Page, http://www.flynnfiles.com (July 21, 2009).

Enter Stage Right, http://www.enterstageright.com/ (July 21, 2009), W. James Antle III, review of *A Conservative History of the American Left.*

First Principles Journal, http://www.firsprinciplesjournal.com/ (July 21, 2009), Bill Kauffman, review of *A Conservative History of the American Left.*

Front Page, http://www.frontpagemag.com/ (July 21, 2009), Jamie Glazov, interview with Flynn on *Intellectual Morons;* Jamie Glazov, interview with Flynn on *A Conservative History of the American Left.*

Human Events, http://www.humanevents.com/ (July 21, 2009), Timothy P. Carney, review of *Intellectual Morons.*

Lew Rockwell.com, http://www.lewrockwell.com/ (July 21, 2009), Thomas J. DiLorenzo, review of *Intellectual Morons.*

Newsmax.com, http://archive.newsmax.com/ (July 21, 2009), John le Boutiller, review of *Why the Left Hates America;* John le Boutiller, review of *Intellectual Morons.*

Random House Web site, http://www.randomnhouse.com/ (Jul 21, 2009), Flynn profile.

Sobran's, http://www.sobran.com/ (July 21, 2009), "The Myth of the Tolerant Left."

Sullivan County, http://www.sullivan-county.com/ (July 21 2009), Jim Jeffries, review of *Why the Left Hates America.*

World Net Daily, http://www.worldnetdaily.com/ (July 21, 2009), Judith Reisman, review of *Why the Left Hates America.**

* * *

FOLEY, Conor

PERSONAL: Male.

ADDRESSES: *Home*—Brazil.

CAREER: Author and development consultant; humanitarian aid worker in Kosovo, Afghanistan, Colombia, Sri Lanka, Indonesia and Bosnia-Herzegovina. Research fellow, Human Rights Law Centre, University of Nottingham.

WRITINGS:

Ireland: The Case for British Disengagement, National Organisation of Labour Students & Labour Committee on Ireland, 1988.

Slaughter on Britain's Building Sites, Connolly Association (London, England), 1990.

Legion of the Rearguard: The IRA and the Modern Irish State, Pluto Press (London, England), 1992.

(With Sharron Nelles) *Racism: The Destruction of Civil and Political Liberties,* Liberty (London, England), 1993.

(With Charlotte Wright, the Southall Black Sisters, and Change) *Women's Rights, Human Rights: Violations of Women's Civil and Political Liberties,* National Council for Civil Liberties (London, England), 1994.

Sexuality and the State: Human Rights Violations against Lesbians, Gays, Bisexuals, and Transgendered People, National Council for Civil Liberties (London, England), 1994.

Democracy and Human Rights in the UK, Liberty (London, England), 1994.

(With Sue Pratt) *Access Denied: Human Rights and Disabled People,* Liberty (London, England), 1994.

Human Rights, Human Wrongs: The Alternative Report to the United Nations Human Rights Committee, Paul (Concord, MA), 1995.

(With Sue Shutter) *The Last Resort: Violations of the Human Rights of Migrants, Refugees, and Asylum Seekers,* edited by Kate Wilkinson, National Council for Civil Liberties (London, England), 1995.

Northern Ireland: Human Rights and the Peace Dividend, edited by Kate Wilkinson, Liberty (London, England), 1995.

Human Rights and Racial Discrimination: The UK's Compliance with the International Convention on the Elimination of All Forms of Racial Discrimination, Liberty (London, England), 1996.

(With Keir Starmer) *Signing Up for Human Rights: The United Kingdom and International Standards,* Amnesty International United Kingdom (London, England), 1998.

Global Trade, Labour and Human Rights, Amnesty International United Kingdom (London, England), 2000.

Nothing Ever Burns Down by Itself: Political Protest in Britain, 1971-2001, Rivers Oram (London, England), 2002.

Combating Torture: A Manual for Judges and Prosecutors, Human Rights Centre, University of Essex (Colchester, England), 2003.

A Guide to Property Law in Afghanistan, Norwegian Refugee Council/UNHCR, 2005.

The Thin Blue Line: How Humanitarianism Went to War, Verso (New York, NY), 2008.

Columnist, *Guardian.*

SIDELIGHTS: Development consultant, and humanitarian aid work Conor Foley is the author of numerous studies and reports on the state of human rights around the world. His works range from works on the situation in Northern Ireland (*Ireland: The Case for British Disengagement* and *Legion of the Rearguard: The IRA and the Modern Irish State*) to documentation of the state of political and racial politics in the United Kingdom (*Human Rights and Racial Discrimination: The UK's Compliance with the International Convention on the Elimination of All Forms of Racial Discrimination* and *Nothing Ever Burns Down by Itself: Political Protest in Britain, 1971-2001*) to ethical studies of the situations found in Iraq and Afghanistan (*Combating Torture: A Manual for Judges and Prosecutors* and *A Guide to Property Law in Afghanistan*). His most widely reviewed book, however, is *The Thin Blue Line: How Humanitarianism Went to War,* "a first-hand account of the failure of humanitarian intervention," explained a reviewer for the Verso Books Web site, "from Somalia to Iraq."

The Thin Blue Line documents the changes that humanitarianism went through in the 1990s to become an aspect of national politics. "Human rights and humanitarianism became powerful movements in the 1980s and '90s," wrote Scott Malcolmson in the *New York Times Book Review,* "and by now Amnesty International UK 'has over a quarter of a million members, overtaking . . . the British Labor Party.' This shift from class politics to values politics occurred across the Western political spectrum, particularly in the prosperous '90s. Nongovernmental organizations, or NGOs, proliferated; governments integrated human-rights advocacy into their budgets and their diplomacy." "Soon enough," Malcolmson continued, "a transnational 'common culture,' in Foley's phrase, of human rights and humanitarianism had taken hold among a surprisingly large number of people." Humanitarian intervention, Foley suggests, now takes place not because it helps people, but because governments and businesses believe they can make money from it. It has, in the words of a *Kirkus Reviews* contributor, "become a multibillion-dollar industry that significantly influences foreign-policy decisions in Europe and the United States." In addition, many non-Western countries now view humanitarian missions as an extension of the political aims of Western nations and reject human rights aid as an unwarranted interference in their right to self-government. "The war in Iraq has made it all too easy for the absolutists to claim that the United States and other Western countries will cite the moral imperative of R2P [the 'right to protect' one's citizens against atrocities, ratified by the United Nations General Assembly in 2005] to intervene when and where they wish," declared James Traub in *Foreign Policy.* "Perhaps that's a real danger, but what seems far likelier is that Iraq has poisoned the logic of humanitarian intervention for years to come." "This intelligent book," concluded Tristan Quinn in the *New Statesman,* "raises important questions about how far humanitarians should compromise their neutrality."

BIOGRAPHICAL AND CRITICAL SOURCES:

PERIODICALS

Foreign Policy, November 1, 2008, "A Fight to Protect."

Kirkus Reviews, October 1, 2008, review of *The Thin Blue Line: How Humanitarianism Went to War.*

New Statesman, November 10, 2008, "Whose Line Is It Anyway?," p. 57.

New Statesman & Society, July 3, 1992, Jo-Ann Goodwin, review of *Legion of the Rearguard: The IRA and the Modern Irish State,* p. 38; July 21, 1995, review of *Human Rights, Human Wrongs: The Alternative Report to the United Nations Human Rights Committee,* p. 40.

New York Times Book Review, December 14, 2008, Scott Malcolmson, "When to Intervene."

Publishers Weekly, September 15, 2008, review of *The Thin Blue Line,* p. 54.

Survival, February 1, 2009, Gilles Andreani, review of *The Thin Blue Line.*

ONLINE

Foreign Policy Online, http://www.foreignpolicy.com/ (July 22, 2009), "How Humanitarian Intervention Failed the World."

Guardian Online, http://www.guardian.co.uk/ (July 22, 2009), author profile.*

* * *

FOOT, John 1964-

PERSONAL: Born November 8, 1964; son of Paul Foot (a political journalist).

ADDRESSES: Office—University College London, Department of Italian, Gower St., London WC1E 6BT, England. *E-mail*—j.foot@ucl.ac.uk; johnfoot@alice.it.

CAREER: Writer, filmmaker, educator; University College London, London, England, department of Italian, professor of modern Italian history.

WRITINGS:

Milan since the Miracle: City, Culture, and Identity, Berg (Oxford, England), 2001.

(Editor, with John Dickie and Frank M. Snowden) *Disastro! Disasters in Italy since 1860: Culture, Politics, Society,* Palgrave (New York, NY), 2002.

Modern Italy, Palgrave Macmillan (New York, NY), 2003.

(Editor, with Robert Lumley) *Italian Cityscapes: Culture and Urban Change in Contemporary Italy,* University of Exeter Press (Exeter, England), 2004.

Winning at All Costs: A Scandalous History of Italian Soccer, Nation Books (New York, NY), 2007.

Italy's Divided Memory, Palgrave Macmillan (New York, NY), 2009.

FILMS

Ringhiera: Storia di una casa, music by Alberto Morelli, John Foot/Dan Sayer [Italy], 2004.

Story of a House: Piazzale Lugano, 22, music by Alberto Morelli, John Foot/Dan Sayer [Italy], 2004.

Pero: Citta d'immigrazione, John Foot/Dan Sayer (Pero, Italy), 2005.

SIDELIGHTS: British writer, filmmaker, and educator John Foot was born November 8, 1964, the son of Paul Foot, a well-known political journalist. He serves on the faculty of the University College London in London, England, as a reader of modern Italian history in the department of Italian. Foot is the writer and producer of several Italian films *Ringhiera: Storia di una casa, Story of a House: Piazzale Lugano, 22,* and *Pero: Citta d'immigrazione.* In addition, he is the author of a number of books on Italian culture and sports, including *Milan since the Miracle: City, Culture, and Identity; Modern Italy; Calcio: A History of Italian Football; Winning at All Costs: A Scandalous History of Italian Soccer;* and *Italy's Divided Memory.* Foot has also served as editor of *Disastro! Disasters in Italy since 1860: Culture, Politics, Society,* with John Dickie and Frank M. Snowden, and of *Italian Cityscapes: Culture and Urban Change in Contemporary Italy,* with Robert Lumley.

In *Milan since the Miracle,* Foot looks at the cultural history of Milan, Italy, with a particular emphasis on the years following 1950. While the book provides a brief history of the region, it is chiefly concerned with how the city gradually shifted from a primarily industrial region to a major metropolis with heavily consumerist leanings. Anna Centro Bull, writing for the Institute of Historical Research Web site, declared that "this is a hugely enjoyable work, which brought back many memories of a city which seems to attract and repulse in equal measures." Bull concluded, "As well as making fascinating reading, the book stimulates new ideas and offers new incentives for research, and I do not think more could be asked of it."

Calcio offers readers a history of the Italian sport of football—known as calcio—the first book of its kind to be written in the English language. Unlike other sports, this Italian variety of football is considered to be a sport only comprehended by the Italian native, with outsiders struggling forever to get an understanding of the sport and its nuances. Foot attempts to offer a fresh perspective on the game, all the while showing his understanding of its importance in Italian society and identity. He explains the events that surround the matches, which bear a great deal of importance on the overall understanding of the sport and its fans. Where in other nations, the most important moments take place between the players during the game, in Italy the political and social occurrences that surround the play are just as vital. James Richardson, in a review for the London *Guardian Online,* remarked that "all in all, *Calcio* does a stand-up job of taking a complex foreign phenomenon and making it both simple and entertaining. It's an ideal companion for anyone interested in either the Italian game or Italians in general."

BIOGRAPHICAL AND CRITICAL SOURCES:

PERIODICALS

Booklist, October 1, 2007, Keir Graff, review of *Winning at All Costs: A Scandalous History of Italian Soccer,* p. 16.

Choice: Current Reviews for Academic Libraries, September 1, 2002, S.F. White, review of *Milan since the Miracle: City, Culture, and Identity,* p. 174.
European History Quarterly, October 1, 2005, R.J.B. Bosworth, review of *Modern Italy,* p. 590.
Reference & Research Book News, February 1, 2004, review of *Modern Italy,* p. 37; November 1, 2004, review of *Italian Cityscapes: Culture and Urban Change in Contemporary Italy,* p. 40.
Times Literary Supplement (London, England), June 23, 2006, "Inter and Ultras," p. 36.
Urban Geography, November 16, 2002, Brian J.L. Berry, review of *Milan since the Miracle,* p. 795.

ONLINE

Guardian Online, http://www.guardian.co.uk/ (June 3, 2006), James Richardson, review of *Calcio: A History of Italian Football.*
Institute of Historical Research Web site, http://www.history.ac.uk/ (April 1, 2002), Anna Centro Bull, review of *Milan since the Miracle.*
London Review of Books Web site, http://www.lrb.co.uk/ (July 17, 2009), author profile.
Soccerphile Web site, http://www.soccerphile.com/ (July 17, 2009), Sean O'Conor, author interview.
University College London Faculty Web site, http://www.homepages.ucl.ac.uk/ (July 17, 2009), author faculty profile.
University College London Web site, http://www.ucl.ac.uk/ (July 17, 2009), author profile.

* * *

FORBES, Ann Armbrecht
See ARMBRECHT, Ann

* * *

FORD, James Mark
See FORD, Jamie

* * *

FORD, Jamie 1968-
(James Mark Ford)

PERSONAL: Born July 9, 1968; married; children: two sons, two daughters. *Education:* Art Institute of Seattle, A.A., 1988; Attended Orson Scott Card's Literary Boot Camp.

ADDRESSES: Home—Great Falls, MT. *Agent*—Kristin Nelson, Nelson Literary Agency, 1732 Wazee St., Ste. 207, Denver, CO 80202.

CAREER: Writer, advertising art director/copywriter.

MEMBER: Squaw Valley Community of Writers.

AWARDS, HONORS: Winner of Clarity of Night Short Fiction Contest, 2006; winner of numerous advertising awards, including more than four hundred Addys and seven Best-of-Show awards.

WRITINGS:

Hotel on the Corner of Bitter and Sweet: A Novel, Ballantine Books (New York, NY), 2009.

Contributor to industry publications, including *Adweek, Advertising Age, Graphis,* and *Communication Arts.* Contributor to periodicals, including *Picolata Review,* and online journals, including *Flashing in the Gutters* and *Fictional Musings.*

SIDELIGHTS: Writer and art director Jamie Ford was born July 9, 1968, and grew up primarily in Seattle, Washington. He graduated from the Art Institute of Seattle, where he earned an associate's degree in graphic design, and then took a job in advertising, working both on visuals and writing copy. He eventually worked his way up to the position of art director, and over the course of his career has won numerous awards for his advertisements. Always interested in writing fiction, as well, he worked his way through Orson Scott Card's Literary Boot Camp and also spent time as a member of the Squaw Valley Community of Writers. In 2006 he won the Clarity of Night Short Fiction Contest, and he has placed well in a number of other writing competitions. Of Chinese decent on his father's side, Ford is the great-grandson of Min Chung, an immigrant from Kaiping, China, who traveled to San Francisco, California, in 1865, eventually settling in Nevada where he worked as a miner. It was Min Chung who took the American name of Ford. Ford is heavily influenced by his personal family history and by stories he heard growing up near the Chinatown neighborhood of Seattle. His father's childhood, in particular, has served as inspiration for Ford's writing, as the senior Ford grew up during World War II, at a time when many Chinese Americans found themselves the victims of discrimination, lumped together with the Japanese with whom the country was at war. Ford's debut novel, *Hotel on the Corner of Bitter and Sweet: A Novel,* sprang in part from his father's mention of the "I Am Chinese" button that he wore in the aftermath of the attack on Pearl Harbor. Along with other family remembrances and the results of his own copious research into the era and how the times affected the Pacific Northwest, Ford includes a wealth of history and cultural detail in his story.

Hotel on the Corner of Bitter and Sweet takes place in 1940s Seattle, telling the story of Henry Lee, a twelve-year-old Chinese American whose father insists he declares his heritage by wearing a button like the one Ford's father wore. The button does not help Henry, however, who attends an all-white prep school and is bullied mercilessly. His one friend is a new student, a Japanese girl named Keiko, and it is their innocent friendship that forms the backbone of a novel that looks at the meaning of love, race, and prejudice over the course of the next forty years. Interwoven with the past is a more modern tale, as the now-elderly Henry recalls the day the Japanese residents of Seattle were rounded up and put into internment camps, including Keiko and her family. Many of their belongings were stored in the old Panama Hotel, only to be rediscovered decades later. The sight of these items being removed when the hotel is sold—including a very familiar parasol that Henry knows belonged to Keiko—sends his memories reeling. The reader sees the changes between a young boy fascinated by jazz music and willing to risk disinheritance should his parents learn of his friendship with a Japanese girl and the man whose adult relationships—including with his son—are foundering in his old age. A contributor to *Kirkus Reviews* dubbed the book "a timely debut" which "reminds readers of a shameful episode in American history" and "cautions us to examine the present and take heed we don't repeat those injustices." A reviewer for *Publishers Weekly* criticized some of the cultural clichés that Ford included in the book but remarked that "the wartime persecution of Japanese immigrants is presented well." In a review for *School Library Journal,* Angela Carstensen stated that the book's "setting and quietly moving, romantic story are commendable." *Library Journal* reviewer Joanna M. Burkhardt concluded that *Hotel on the Corner of Bitter and Sweet* "is a vivid picture of a confusing and critical time in American history."

BIOGRAPHICAL AND CRITICAL SOURCES:

PERIODICALS

Kirkus Reviews, October 15, 2008, review of *Hotel on the Corner of Bitter and Sweet: A Novel.*

Library Journal, October 1, 2008, Joanna M. Burkhardt, review of *Hotel on the Corner of Bitter and Sweet,* p. 56.

New York Times Book Review, February 18, 2009, Amy Virshup, review of *Hotel on the Corner of Bitter and Sweet.*

Publishers Weekly, September 15, 2008, review of *Hotel on the Corner of Bitter and Sweet,* p. 40.

School Library Journal, May 1, 2009, Angela Carstensen, review of *Hotel on the Corner of Bitter and Sweet,* p. 140.

Star Tribune, January 25, 2009, "Predictable Hotel' Houses Poignant Tale; This Love Story Set in Wartime Seattle Is Likable, but Don't Expect Great Literature," review of *Hotel on the Corner of Bitter and Sweet,* p. 12.

USA Today, February 19, 2009, "New Voices," review of *Hotel on the Corner of Bitter and Sweet,* p. 3.

Weekend Edition Saturday, February 7, 2009, review of *Hotel on the Corner of Bitter and Sweet.*

ONLINE

Book Reporter, http://www.bookreporter.com/ (January 30, 2009), author interview.

Fantastic Fiction, http://www.fantasticfiction.co.uk/ (July 17, 2009), author profile.

Jamie Ford Home Page, http://www.jamieford.com (July 17, 2009).

Jamie Ford MySpace Page, http://www.myspace.com/jamieswords (July 17, 2009).

Random House Web site, http://www.randomhouse.com/ (July 17, 2009), author profile.*

* * *

FRALE, Barbara 1970-

PERSONAL: Born 1970. *Education:* University of Venice, Ph.D.

ADDRESSES: *Home*—Viterbo, Italy.

CAREER: Writer, historian; Vatican Secret Archives, Vatican City, historian.

WRITINGS:

Orte 1303-1367: la città sul fiume, Vecchiarelli Manziana (Rome, Italy), 1995.

L'ultima battaglia dei Templari: dal codice ombra d'obbedienza militare alla costruzione del processo per eresia, Viella (Rome, Italy), 2001.

Il papato e il processo ai Templari: l'inedita assoluzione di Chinon alla luce della diplomatica pontificia, Viella (Rome, Italy), 2003.

I Templari, Mulino (Bologna, Italy), 2004, translation Italian by Gregory Conti published as *The Templars: The Secret History Revealed,* foreword by Umberto Eco, Arcade Publishing (New York, NY), 2009.

Processus Contra Templarios, Archivio Segreto Vaticano (Vatican City, Vatican), 2007.

SIDELIGHTS: Writer and historian Barbara Frale earned her doctorate from the University of Venice, and makes her home in Viterbo, Italy. She serves as a historian for the Vatican Secret Archives, and is also the author of numerous volumes on the history of Italy, focusing in particular on the papacy, the Crusades, and various secrets of the nation, such as the work of the Knights Templar. While the most of Frale's work is available only in Italian, *The Templars: The Secret History Revealed* was published in translation in 2009, with the English text provided by Gregori Conti and a foreword by Umberto Eco.

In *The Templars,* Frale delves into the complicated and mysterious world of the organization founded in the wake of the First Crusade that came to be known as the Knights Templar. This group served both a military and a religious purpose; their goal was to protect and promote the spread of Christianity and to help maintain a Christian foothold in the Holy Land. They answered to no one other than the pope. After the Crusades came to an end, however, the Templars continued on, evolving their purpose to suit the new needs of Europe as well as their own membership. They began to function as a bank, catering only to the most wealthy individuals in Western Europe. Their strict rules regarding to whom they were willing to extend loans put them in a precarious position when France's King Philip IV took umbrage at their selectivity. He ordered the arrest of every Templar, unbeknownst to the current pope, Clement V. However, Clement ultimately capitulated to the king's wishes, and declared a formal disbanding of the Knights Templar. Philip IV ordered the execution of the highest members of the order on accusations of treason. Frale traces the history of the Templars as well as the stories and rumors that have been handed down through the years since they ceased to be an official arm of the Vatican, using documents discovered in the Vatican Archives to provide a framework for her story.

Reviewers had mixed reactions to Frale's account of the history of the Knights of the Templar. A reviewer for *Reference & Research Book News* declared that the volume "gives a generally accurate account of the history of the order, free of conspiracy and secret treasure theories," but noted that not all of the conclusions are accurate. However, Ray Olson, writing for *Booklist,* remarked that readers might "consider this little book the first-choice primer on its legend-laden subject."

BIOGRAPHICAL AND CRITICAL SOURCES:

PERIODICALS

Booklist, December 15, 2008, Ray Olson, review of *The Templars: The Secret History Revealed,* p. 15.

English Historical Review, December 1, 2005, A.J. Forey, review of *I Templari,* p. 1420.

Journal of Ecclesiastical History, April 1, 2006, Jonathan Riley-Smith, review of *I Templari,* p. 334.

Kirkus Reviews, November 15, 2008, review of *The Templars.*

Library Journal, December 1, 2008, Daniel Harms, review of *The Templars,* p. 141.

Reference & Research Book News, May 1, 2009, review of *The Templars.*

Speculum: A Journal of Medieval Studies, January 1, 2006, Elena Bellomo, review of *I Templari,* p. 188.

ONLINE

Arcade Publishers Web site, http://www.arcadepub.com/ (August 28, 2009), author profile.

Chico News and Review Web site, http://www.newsreview.com/ (August 28, 2009), Matthew Craggs, review of *The Templars.**

* * *

FREDERICK, Heather Vogel

PERSONAL: Born in Peterborough, NH; father an elementary teacher and principal; married; children: two sons. *Education:* Principia College, B.A.; attended University of Cologne on a Fulbright grant.

ADDRESSES: *Home*—Portland, OR.

CAREER: Journalist and author. *Christian Science Monitor,* Boston, MA, staff writer and editor, then children's book review editor. Freelance writer; presenter at schools.

AWARDS, HONORS: Books for the Teen age designation, New York Public Library, Amelia Bloomer Project inclusion, American Library Association, and Oregon Book Award for Young Adults, all 2003, Sequoyah Book Award finalist, Oklahoma Library Association, and Lamplighter Award finalist, both 2004, Beacon of Freedom Award finalist, 2005, Connecticut Nutmeg Children's Book Award finalist, 2006, and Arizona Young Readers Award finalist, 2007, all for *The Voyage of Patience Goodspeed;* Amelia Bloomer Project inclusion, 2005, for *The Education of Patience Goodspeed;* 100 Titles for Reading and Sharing listee, New York Public Library, 2005, and Oregon Book Award finalist, 2006, both for *For Your Paws Only;* West Sussex, England, Children's Book Award shortlist, 2007, Garden State Book Award finalist, 2008, and Hawai'i Nene Award nominee, 2010, all for *The Black Paw;* Massachusetts Children's Book Award nomination, 2009, for *Goldwhiskers.*

WRITINGS:

FOR CHILDREN

The Voyage of Patience Goodspeed (novel), Simon & Schuster Books for Young Readers (New York, NY), 2002.

The Education of Patience Goodspeed (novel), Simon & Schuster Books for Young Readers (New York, NY), 2004.

Babyberry Pie (picture book), illustrated by Amy Schwartz, Harcourt (New York, NY), 2010.

Hide-and-Squeak (picture book), illustrated by C.F. Payne, Simon & Schuster Books for Young Readers (New York, NY), 2010.

"SPY MICE" SERIES

The Black Paw, illustrated by Sally Wern Comport, Simon & Schuster Books for Young Readers (New York, NY), 2005.

For Your Paws Only, illustrated by Sally Wern Comport, Simon & Schuster Books for Young Readers (New York, NY), 2005.

Goldwhiskers, illustrated by Sally Wern Comport, Simon & Schuster Books for Young Readers (New York, NY), 2007.

"MOTHER-DAUGHTER BOOK CLUB" NOVEL SERIES

The Mother-Daughter Book Club, Simon & Schuster Books for Young Readers (New York, NY), 2007.

Much Ado about Anne, Simon & Schuster Books for Young Readers (New York, NY), 2008.

Dear Pen Pal, Simon & Schuster Books for Young Readers (New York, NY), 2009.

Contributor to periodicals, including *Child, Family Life,* and *New York Times;* former contributing editor, *Publishers Weekly.*

SIDELIGHTS: Although Heather Vogel Frederick has fulfilled her childhood dream of making writing her life, she worked as a journalist for many years and only turned to children's books while raising her own two children. Beloved by the young fans of her fanciful "Spy Mice" series, Frederick is also the author of the award-winning middle-grade historical novel *The Voyage of Patience Goodspeed.* Her popular "Mother-Daughter Book Club" novels, which include *The Mother-Daughter Book Club, Much Ado about Anne,* and *Dear Pen Pal,* have inspired modern 'tweens with an appreciation for the role good books can play in shaping one's own life.

While growing up in New England, Frederick followed in her family's tradition: she loved books and loved telling stories. "My mother used to say that if Heather had her nose in a book, the house would have to burn down around her before she'd sit up and take notice!" the author recalled on her home page. "Those are the best books, though, aren't they? The ones that take your imagination by storm and spirit you off into a different world?" After attending college and marrying, Frederick became a journalist and worked for several years on the staff of the highly respected *Christian Science Monitor* newspaper.

Frederick published her first book, the historical novel *The Voyage of Patience Goodspeed,* in 2002. Set on Nantucket Island, off the coast of Massachusetts, in 1835, the story follows twelve-year-old Patience Goodspeed as she joins her younger brother Thaddeus and her father, Captain Goodspeed, on a prolonged whaling voyage. Aboard the *Morning Star* Patience misses the studious home life she had enjoyed, and the countless chores allow her few opportunities to channel her intellectual curiosity. However, the girl's math skills soon qualify her to assist the ship's navigator, and when the crew mutinies, stranding the family on a barren island, she uses her newfound skills to aid in their survival. Describing the many dangers faced by New England whalers during the nineteenth century, Frederick effectively captures "the personalities and activities on board," making *The Voyage of Patience Goodspeed* "a voyage readers will be glad to make," according to *Booklist* contributor Diane Foote. Comparing Frederick's novel to Avi's award-winning novel *The Adventures of Charlotte Doyle,* a *Kirkus Reviews* writer praised the story's "feisty heroine" and "rich" details, while a *Publishers Weekly* critic wrote that the well-researched novel is further buoyed by "atmospheric details" and an "eclectic cast and crew."

The adventures of Frederick's young heroine continue in *The Education of Patience Goodspeed,* as Patience and Thaddeus find themselves boarding with a missionary family on the Hawaiian island of Maui while the *Morning Star* takes on provisions in Lahaina. While Patience butts heads with Reverend Wiggins over his constraining views of "a woman's place," a troublesome neighbor from Nantucket arrives and tries to ingratiate herself with the widowed Captain Goodspeed. According to a *Kirkus Reviews* writer, the "tart narration" of the now-thirteen-year-old Patience "is . . . smart and funny," as well as "deftly done." Calling *The Education of Patience Goodspeed* "action-packed," Ginny Gustin added in *School Library Journal* that Frederick "skillfully portrays Patience's emotional development and growing maturity."

In *The Mother-Daughter Book Club,* Frederick introduces four typical middle graders: book-loving Emma, shopaholic Megan, sports-loving Cassidy, and country girl Jess. Together with their moms, the girls join a local book club that meets once a month. With their mothers' encouragement, the girls grudgingly tackle Louisa May Alcott's *Little Women,* and they are surprised to find that the century-old novel with its beloved characters Jo, Beth, Amy, Meg, and Marmee, has much to teach today's tech-savvy sixth grader. Told in alternating chapters by each of the girls, *The Mother-Daughter Book Club* features "plenty of detail," according to *Booklist* critic Heather Booth. Teens "will be easily pulled along" by Frederick's story, predicted Booth, and a *Publishers Weekly* critic suggested that "the club's success . . . may well inspire readers to start one of their own."

The cast of *The Mother-Daughter Book Club* returns in several other novels for preteen readers. In *Much Ado about Anne,* the girls are in seventh grade and *Anne of Green Gables* is on the reading list. The plot of L.M. Montgomery's classic novel seems more than timely to Jess; she has just learned that her family may have to sell off their farm. Although the girls worry when their moms invite stuck-up Becca Chadwick and her mother to join the club, the new member proves her worth in a busy year full of camping trips, school challenges, and helping each other fulfill their dreams. The club membership may change in *Dear Pen Pal* as Jess is offered a full scholarship to a well-known boarding school. Meanwhile, each of the other girls encounters changes in her own life, and reading Jean Webster's novel *Daddy-Long-Legs* speaks to each of the girls while it captures Jess's dilemma. Although Maria B. Salvadore found the grown-up characters "cliched," she described the teen girls as "gutsy problem-solvers" in her *School Library Journal* review of *Much Ado about Anne.* "The pace is fast, the concerns and emotions real," the critic added of Frederick's "satisfying" series installment.

Geared for readers in the upper elementary grades, Frederick's whimsical "Spy Mice" books include *The Black Paw, For Your Paws Only,* and *Goldwhiskers.* The books focus on a boy named Ozymandias "Oz"

Levinson. When his father moves the family from Seattle to Washington, DC, in order to take a job at the International Spy Museum café, Oz meets some tiny mouse spies and quickly becomes involved in a citywide battle between the mice and the rats. In *The Black Paw,* Oz joins a field-mouse secret agent named Morning Glory Goldenleaf in her effort to battle the nefarious work of rat kingpin Roquefort Dupont. Dupont is intent on taking control of the entire rodent world and he sets the stage for this revolution by uniting all the rats of Europe in *For Your Paws Only.* Now it is up to Oz and his bewhiskered secret-agent friends at the Spy Mice Agency to travel to the Big Apple and stop this global rodent threat. Kidnapping (or rather, mousenapping) figures in the plot of *Goldwhiskers,* as Oz and company travel to London on a holiday, only to find themselves in the center of a mystery involving the crown jewels and a group of mouse orphans. In *Publishers Weekly,* a reviewer called *The Black Paw* "a lighthearted, clever combination of fast-moving adventure and talking-animal fantasy," while *School Library Journal* critic Elizabeth Bird praised *For Your Paws Only* as "fast-paced without becoming too predictable." Praising the amusing cartoon art by Sally Wern Comport, another critic for *Publishers Weekly* enjoyed the "engaging banter" in *The Black Paw,* predicting that Frederick's "tale of tails will especially tickle aspiring sleuths."

BIOGRAPHICAL AND CRITICAL SOURCES:

PERIODICALS

Booklist, June 1, 2002, Diane Foote, review of *The Voyage of Patience Goodspeed,* p. 1722; July, 2005, Todd Morning, review of *The Black Paw,* p. 1924; June 1, 2007, Heather Booth, review of *The Mother-Daughter Book Club,* p. 75.

Kirkus Reviews, June 15, 2002, review of *The Voyage of Patience Goodspeed,* p. 880; August 1, 2004, review of *The Education of Patience Goodspeed,* p. 741; September 15, 2005, review of *For Your Paws Only,* p. 1025.

Publishers Weekly, June 17, 2002, review of *The Voyage of Patience Goodspeed,* p. 65; July 18, 2005, review of *The Black Paw,* p. 206; April 2, 2007, review of *The Mother-Daughter Book Club,* p. 57.

School Library Journal, October, 2004, Ginny Gustin, review of *The Education of Patience Goodspeed,* p. 163; October, 2005, Elizabeth Bird, review of *The Black Paw,* p. 160; December, 2005, Elizabeth Bird, review of *For Your Paws Only,* p. 147; August, 2007, Susan Moorhead, review of *The Mother-Daughter Book Club,* p. 116; November, 2008, Maria B. Salvadore, review of *Much Ado about Anne,* p. 120.

ONLINE

Heather Vogel Frederick Home Page, http://www.heathervogelfrederick.com (November 15, 2009).

Heather Vogel Frederick Web log, http://heathervogelfrederick/wordpress.com (November 15, 2009).

* * *

FREEMAN, Bruce

PERSONAL: Married; children: two. *Education:* State University of New York, Binghamton, B.A.; Long Island University, M.A.

ADDRESSES: *Home*—Livingston, NJ. *E-mail*—Bruce@SmallBusinessProf.com.

CAREER: ProLine Communications, Livingston, NJ, president; Scripps Howard News Service, syndicated national columnist of the "Small Business Professor" columns; News12 New Jersey, host of "Be Your Own Boss" segment of *New Jersey Business* program. Serves as adjunct professor of marketing and entrepreneurship at Kean University, Union, NJ, and Ramapo College, Mahwah, NJ.

MEMBER: Society of American Business Editors and Writers.

AWARDS, HONORS: U.S. Small Business Administration Journalist of the Year Award, SBA New Jersey District Director, 2006; Stillman School of Business, Seton Hall University, Excellent Adjunct Professor Award, 2007-08.

WRITINGS:

(With Karin Abarbanel) *Birthing the Elephant: The Woman's Go-for-It! Guide to Overcoming the Big Challenges of Launching a Business,* Ten Speed Press (Berkeley, CA), 2008.

Maintains a blog at http://smallbusinessprof.blogspot.com; syndicated columnist for Scripps Howard News Service.

SIDELIGHTS: Writer and marketing expert Bruce Freeman earned his undergraduate degree from the State University of New York at Binghamton and then continued his education at Long Island University, where he earned his master's degree. He serves as president of ProLine Communications, a marketing and public-relations company in Livingston, New Jersey, and also writes a syndicated column, the "Small Business Professor," for the Scripps Howard News Service. In addition, he hosts the "Be Your Own Boss" segment on a local television station, News12 New Jersey. Over the course of his career, Freeman has been honored with a number of awards, including the U.S. Small Business Administration Journalist of the Year Award from the SBA New Jersey District Director in 2006, and the Excellent Adjunct Professor Award from the Stillman School of Business, Seton Hall University, for 2007-08. Freeman serves as a member of the Society of American Business Editors and Writers, and is a past president of the Technology Leaders' Council and of the Northeast Technical Association. In 2008, Freeman's debut book, *Birthing the Elephant: The Woman's Go-for-It! Guide to Overcoming the Big Challenges of Launching a Business,* written with Karin Abarbanel, was released by Ten Speed Press.

In *Birthing the Elephant,* Freeman and Abarbanel offer readers a humorous yet honest guide to starting a business and making it work. Most small businesses fail, and this book goes over many common mistakes that typically result in failure or at least make success more difficult. The authors offer a step-by-step description of the different stages necessary in planning a new business and putting the plan in motion. As examples, they draw on a number of successful and well-known entrepreneurs, including makeup guru Bobbi Brown; the mother of modern maternity clothing, Liz Lange; and many others working in a wide variety of industries, from technology to baking. In particular, the book focuses on the necessary state of mind that enables an entrepreneur to step out on their own, rather than relying on traditional employment structures to keep one's head above water. A reviewer for *Publishers Weekly* commented that "the authors devote particular attention to commitment, courage, persistence and other traits," while *Booklist* reviewer Barbara Jones opined that beginning "entrepreneurs will find advice that's worth the price of the book alone."

BIOGRAPHICAL AND CRITICAL SOURCES:

PERIODICALS

Booklist, 2008, Barbara Jacobs, review of *Birthing the Elephant: The Woman's Go-for-It! Guide to Overcoming the Big Challenges of Launching a Business.*

Publishers Weekly, January 7, 2008, review of *Birthing the Elephant.*

ONLINE

Small Business Professor Web site, http://www.smallbusinessprof.com (August 10, 2009), author profile.*

* * *

FREEMAN, Charles 1947-

PERSONAL: Born October 11, 1947.

ADDRESSES: *Home*—Suffolk, England.

CAREER: Independent scholar and lawyer.

WRITINGS:

The World of the Romans, advisory editing by J.F. Drinkwater and Andrew Drummond, Oxford University Press (New York, NY), 1993.

The Ancient Greeks, Oxford University Press (New York, NY), 1996.

Egypt, Greece, and Rome: Civilizations of the Ancient Mediterranean, Oxford University Press (New York, NY), 1996, 2nd edition, 2004.

The Legacy of Ancient Egypt, advisory editing by John D. Ray, Facts on File (New York, NY), 1997.

The Rise of the Nazis, Raintree Steck-Vaughn (Austin, TX), 1998, reprinted, Lucent Books (Detroit, MI), 2005.

Crisis in Rwanda, Raintree Steck-Vaughn (Austin, TX), 1999.

The Greek Achievement: The Foundation of the Western World, Viking (New York, NY), 1999.

The Closing of the Western Mind: The Rise of Faith and the Fall of Reason, Heinemann (London, England), 2002, A.A. Knopf (New York, NY), 2003.

The Horses of Saint Mark's: A Story of Triumph in Byzantium, Little, Brown (London, England), 2004.

AD 381: Heretics, Pagans, and the Christian State, Pimlico (London, England), 2008.

A New History of Early Christianity, Yale University Press (New Haven, CT), 2009.

SIDELIGHTS: Charles Freeman is an British independent scholar and lawyer. Born on October 11, 1947, he published his first book, *The World of the Romans,* in 1993. In 1996 Freeman published *Egypt, Greece, and Rome: Civilizations of the Ancient Medi-terranean.* The account incorporates Egypt and the Near East kingdoms as a part, if not a precursor, to the origins of Western civilization, opening new insight into politics, culture, society, and religion.

M. Edmund Hussey, writing in the *Antioch Review,* said that with this groundbreaking book, Freeman "has given us an interesting, readable, and erudite introduction " to these three ancient cultures of the Mediterranean. Hussey remarked that *Egypt, Greece, and Rome* "not only alerts us to the best results of recent pertinent research but also allows us to discover the strong links between these civilizations, which modern scholarship increasingly stresses." Hussey added that "even in asides, Freeman is thought-provoking." *Booklist* contributor Gilbert Taylor observed that "the text is captionlike but knowledgeable and complements this pop-oriented volume." Taylor appended that *Egypt, Greece, and Rome* is "a sumptuous volume that will bring visual splendor to history courses." Robert J. Andrews "highly recommended" the book in a review in *Library Journal,* noting that "this work is a useful introduction to the ancient Mediterranean civilizations."

In 1999 Freeman published *Crisis in Rwanda.* The book is organized and formatted in the form of a magazine article, presenting a survey of who the main factions and their leaders were during the Rwandan genocide in the 1990s. *Booklist* contributor Hazel Rochman observed that "this is a stirring, nonexploitative, accessible account of what happened, written with clarity and fairness and a strong commitment to human rights."

Freeman also published *The Greek Achievement: The Foundation of the Western World* that same year. The account removes the varnish from Greek conquests, showing how members of this greatly admired culture also subjugated women, encouraged slavery, and took pride in the enormous bloodshed wrought during their battles. At the same time, though, he shows how Greek culture established the foundation for Western civilization.

A contributor writing in *Publishers Weekly* remarked that this book is on "par with" the "Hinges of History" series by Thomas Cahill. The same contributor, though, described Freeman as "a more rigorous historian than Cahill, and he never lets enthusiasm obscure the distinction between fact and myth, between events and their interpretation." Writing in *History Today,* Paul Cartledge noted that "Freeman's long but rarely tedious volume is commendably up to the minute," adding that "chapters of narrative are interspersed with ones that systematically survey the religious, political, social, economic and, not least, cultural achievements of the ancient Greeks. He is especially hot, and rightly so, on the need to give due recognition to Greek science and mathematics."

Freeman first published *The Closing of the Western Mind: The Rise of Faith and the Fall of Reason* in 2002; the work was published the following year in the United States. The account argues that fourth-century Christianity, under the patronage of Roman Emperor Constantine, suppressed free thinking and innovation, a mindset that lasted until the Renaissance.

Booklist contributor Brendan Driscoll noticed that Freeman seemed "mournful" over the retreat from logic in Western thinking in the lead-up to its return with Thomas Aquinas. However, Driscoll related that *The Closing of the Western Mind* "is simply too impressively erudite to dismiss as polemic or, indeed, to set down." A contributor writing in *Kirkus Reviews* found it to be "a vigorous study," adding that it is also "a lucid, accessible contribution to intellectual history, and a worthy companion to Elaine Pagels's recent *Beyond Belief.*"

Charles Taliaferro, reviewing the work in *World and I,* commented that "the book is engaging and clearly written." Freeman blames Christianity for "suppressing the virtues of ancient, pagan culture." Taliaferro called the text "polemical and . . . unsympathetic to what the author calls faith," though he conceded that Freeman has good things to say about Christianity, even if "his criterion for Greek success is certainly more generous than his measure for the maturity or intellectual adequacy of Christian culture." Taliaferro complimented Freeman's style, noting its smooth, flowing nature. Taliaferro ultimately summarized Freeman's argument as insistent that "the medieval era was indeed the 'Dark Ages.'" While it was excessively harsh and brutal by modern standards, noted the critic, many good and noble things occurred during this period, including advances in the arts, agriculture, and diplomacy. Taliaferro advised reading *The Spirit of Medieval Philosophy,* by Etienne Gilson, for a "more balanced look" at the many accomplishments and developments that occurred during medieval times.

Reviewing the book in *Library Journal,* James A. Overbeck "highly recommended" *The Closing of the Western Mind,* appending that "this book will appeal to the general educated reader." Richard H. Schlagel, writing in the *Review of Metaphysics,* concluded that "this needed, emended history of early Christianity is clearly written, a pleasure to read, and documented by a vast range and depth of scholarship. It is certainly one of the best accounts available for anyone seeking a factual understanding of the actual origins of Christian doctrine in their historical setting." Mark Edwards, reviewing the account in *History Today,* found the book's title to be "most questionable" for its seeming justification that paganism was rational through its practice of tolerance. But Edwards also commented that "the narrative is clear and fluent, nomenclature is studiously precise, and every judgment is supported by appeal to some authoritative historian or quotation of ancient texts."

Freeman published *AD 381: Heretics, Pagans, and the Christian State* in 2008. The account argues that Roman Emperor Theodosius's decree forcing Christianity onto his people led to the abandonment of open intellectual debate and religious tolerance.

Steven E. Alford, reviewing the book in the *Houston Chronicle,* concluded that "clearly written, well organized, and compellingly argued, *AD 381* provides an absorbing window into 'one of the most important moments in the history of European thought.'" A contributor writing in *Kirkus Reviews* admitted that "questions remain, but Freeman does a good job in forcing a reexamination of this crucial turning point." A contributor writing in *Contemporary Review* pondered whether or not Freeman may be "a prisoner of his own set views." Nevertheless, the same contributor granted that "this is an interesting and sometimes thought-provoking book." David Keymer, reviewing the book in *Library Journal,* said that among "the many excellences" of *AD 381,* "not least are the eloquence, grace, and subtlety of argument with which he presents his case." Keymer labeled the book as an "invaluable" asset to any academic book collection.

BIOGRAPHICAL AND CRITICAL SOURCES:

PERIODICALS

Antioch Review, fall, 1997, M. Edmund Hussey, review of *Egypt, Greece, and Rome: Civilizations of the Ancient Mediterranean,* p. 499.

Booklist, December 15, 1996, Gibert Taylor, review of *Egypt, Greece, and Rome,* p. 706; December 15, 1998, Hazel Rochman, review of *Crisis in Rwanda,* p. 741; December 15, 2001, Hazel Rochman, review of *Crisis in Rwanda,* p. 723; September 15, 2003, Brendan Driscoll, review of *The Closing of the Western Mind: The Rise of Faith and the Fall of Reason,* p. 198.

Book Report, March-April, 1994, Dorothy J. MacRitchie, review of *The World of the Romans,* p. 48; January-February, 1999, Audrey Irene Daigneault, review of *The Rise of the Nazis,* p. 80.

Choice: Current Reviews for Academic Libraries, June, 1997, review of *Egypt, Greece, and Rome,* p. 1717; May, 2004, L.E. Mitchell, review of *The Closing of the Western Mind,* p. 1715.

Contemporary Review, autumn, 2008, review of *AD 381: Heretics, Pagans, and the Christian State,* p. 407.

Curriculum Review, December, 1996, review of *The Ancient Greeks,* p. 12; April, 1998, review of *The Rise of the Nazis,* p. 12.

History Today, November, 1999, review of *The Greek Achievement: The Foundation of the Western World,* p. 56; March, 2000, Paul Cartledge, review of *The Greek Achievement,* p. 58; November, 2002, review of *The Closing of the Western Mind,* p. 64; December, 2002, Mark Edwards, review of *The Closing of the Western Mind,* p. 60.

Houston Chronicle, April 17, 2009, Steven E. Alford, review of *AD 381.*

Kirkus Reviews, July 15, 2003, review of *The Closing of the Western Mind,* p. 947; December 1, 2008, review of *AD 381.*

Library Journal, January, 1997, Robert J. Andrews, review of *Egypt, Greece, and Rome,* p. 119; September 15, 2003, James A. Overbeck, review of *The Closing of the Western Mind,* p. 69; January 1, 2009, David Keymer, review of *AD 381,* p. 97.

Los Angeles Times, November 9, 2003, review of *The Closing of the Western Mind,* p. 13.

Publishers Weekly, June 10, 1996, review of *The Ancient Greeks,* p. 101; July 5, 1999, review of *The Greek Achievement,* p. 49.

Reference & Research Book News, February, 1994, review of *The World of the Romans,* p. 8.

Review of Metaphysics, June, 2005, Richard H. Schlagel, review of *The Closing of the Western Mind,* p. 894.

School Librarian, spring, 1998, review of *The Rise of the Nazis,* p. 51.

School Library Journal, September, 1996, Cynthia Sturgis, review of *The Ancient Greeks,* p. 214; July, 1998, David A. Lindsey, review of *The Rise of the Nazis,* p. 105; February, 1999, Andrew Medlar, review of *Crisis in Rwanda,* p. 116.

Times Educational Supplement, July 3, 1998, review of *Crisis in Rwanda,* p. 25; July 3, 1998, review of *The Rise of the Nazis,* p. 25.

Times Higher Education Supplement, December 13, 2002, Peter Watson, review of *The Closing of the Western Mind,* p. 33.

Times Literary Supplement, February 4, 1994, review of *The World of the Romans,* p. 28; March 14, 1997, Christopher Kelly, review of *Egypt, Greece, and Rome,* p. 24; January 17, 2003, Kate Cooper, review of *The Closing of the Western Mind,* p. 12.

World and I, February, 2004, Charles Taliaferro, review of *The Closing of the Western Mind,* p. 220.*

G

GAGE, Christos
(Christos N. Gage)

PERSONAL: Born July 17, in NY; married Ruth Fletcher (a writer). *Education:* Brown University, B.A.; American Film Institute, M.A.

ADDRESSES: *E-mail*—christosgage@aol.com.

CAREER: Writer, screenwriter, comics author. Writer of screenplays, comic books, and books.

WRITINGS:

COMIC BOOKS AND GRAPHIC NOVELS

Union Jack, four-issue series, illustrated by Mike Perkins, Marvel Comics (New York, NY), 2006.
Iron Man/Captain America: Casualties of War, illustrated by Jeremy Haun, Marvel Comics (New York, NY), 2007.
(With Doug Mahnke) *Post Human Division: Storm Watch 1,* Wildstorm/DC Comics (New York, NY), 2007.
World War Hulk: X-Men (miniseries), illustrated by Andrea DiVito, Marvel Comics (New York, NY), 2007.
Iron Man, issues 19-20, illustrated by Butch Guice, Marvel Comics (New York, NY), 2007.
(With Scott Beatty) *Wildstorm: Revelations,* Wildstorm Productions (La Jolla, CA), 2008.
The Authority: Prime, Wildstorm Productions (La Jolla, CA), 2008.
Wildstorm: Armageddon, Wildstorm Productions (La Jolla, CA), 2008.
Marvel Comics Presents 5-7 ("The Savage Land"), three-part series, illustrated by Joyce Chin, Marvel Comics (New York, NY), 2008.
Thunderbolts: International Incident, illustrated by Ben Oliver, Marvel Comics (New York, NY), 2008.
Annihilation Conquest: Quasar, illustrated by Mike Lilly, Marvel Comics (New York, NY), 2008.
The Lion of Rora, Oni Press (Portland, OR), 2008.
X-Men/Spiderman, four-issue series, Marvel Comics (New York, NY), 2009.
GI Joe: Cobra, four-issue series, IDW Publishing (San Diego, CA), 2009.
Civil War: House of M, five-issue series, illustrated by Andrea DiVito, covers by Mike Perkins, Marvel Comics (New York, NY), 2009.

Author of screenplays of episodes for television series including, *Law & Order: Special Victims Unit,* National Broadcasting Corporation (NBC), 2003, 2004; and *Numb3rs,* Columbia Broadcasting System, 2005. Also author of the screenplays *The Breed,* 2001; *Teenage Caveman* (and associate producer), 2002; and *Paradox,* 2009; author of online Webisode for GameTap, *Laura Croft: Tomb Raider: Revisioned.*

Also author of *Avengers: The Initiative,* Marvel Comics; *Wildcats,* Wildstorm/DC Comics; *The Man with No Name,* Dynamite Entertainment; *Iron Man: Director of Shield,* issues 33-35, Marvel Comics; *Thunderbolts,* issues 122-25, Marvel Comics; *Iron Man Movie* exclusive comic; *The Authority: Prime,* Wildstorm/DC Comics; *House of M: Avengers,* Marvel Comics; *What*

If? Civil War, Marvel Comics; *Iron Man Annual,* issue 1, Marvel Comics; *Armageddon,* Wildstorm/DC Comics; *Stormwatch: PHD,* Wildstorm/DC Comics; *Annihilation: Heralds of Galactus,* issue 1, Marvel Comics; *X-Men: Endangered Species,* Chapters 8-11, Marvel Comics; *Wildstorm: Revelations,* Wildstorm/DC Comics; *Thunderbolts: Reason in Madness,* Marvel Comics; *Red Sonja,* issue 31, Dynamite Entertainment; *Thunderbolts: International Incident,* Marvel Comics; *Thunderbolts: Breaking Point,* Marvel Comics; *New Line Cinema's House of Horror: A Nightmare on Elm Street,* Wildstorm/DC Comics; *Savage Tales: Red Sonja,* issue 3, Dynamite Entertainment; *The Midnighter,* issue 8, Wildstorm/DC Comics; *Worldstorm,* issue 2, Wildstorm/DC Comics; *Batman: Legends of the Dark Knight,* issues 201-203, 214, DC Comics; *Spiderman Unlimited,* issue 12, Marvel Comics (New York, NY); *Deadshot,* DC Comics (New York, NY); *Absolution,* 2009.

SIDELIGHTS: American screenwriter and comic book author Christos Gage was born July 17, in New York, but grew up primarily in Athens, Greece, and North Grafton, Massachusetts. Gage was fascinated with storytelling from a young age, learning to read when he was just three. He soon discovered comic books and collected them religiously, keeping them in his closet. Unlike many young boys, he never grew out of his love for comics. He attended Brown University, majoring in American civilization, a broad subject that was flexible enough to allow Gage to study everything from spy novels to blues music. He then studied screenwriting at the American Film Institute and earned a master of arts degree there. Since 1997 when he sold his first screenplay, Gage has considered himself to be a professional writer, never desiring to do something else in his career. He has written a number of screenplays, selling some while others stayed on the shelf, and also began writing for episodic television, including several episodes of *Law & Order.* When writing for film and television he often collaborates with his wife, writer Ruth Fletcher Gage. Then at the end of 2004, Gage's love for comics came to the foreground and he began to write in that medium as well. Since that time, Gage has written for numerous comics, including popular series for both Marvel and Wildfire/DC. He has also written an online Webisode for GameTap, *Laura Croft: Tomb Raider: Revisioned.*

Wildstorm: Armageddon, which is part of the DC Comics universe, offers readers the darker side of that world they know and love, featuring edgier superheroes as opposed to the cleaner-cut, all-American variety. The stories that come out of this series tend to include more violence and more blood, as well as more sex, creating a truly adult look at crime and heroics. Many of the characters appear to be darker counterparts to similar heroes in the DC universe, such as Midnighter compared to Batman. This particular title serves as a crossover for a number of the series within the "Wildstorm" universe, linking six different groups of characters in one adventure. When a giant spaceship crashes into earth turning the planet upside down in such a way that it is nearly always night and suddenly monsters begin to roam the planet, it takes the combined efforts of these heroes to go up against the evil that remains in the wake of the catastrophe. Neale Monks, reviewing for the *SFCrowsnest* Web site, found the divisions of the story difficult to follow, given that each of six series must be addressed in one book that is scheduled to be the first of a trilogy. However, Monks concluded: "*Wildstorm: Armageddon* is entertaining and an impressive opening to the series."

Absolution is the result of a trip to Los Angeles, California. Gage and his wife, Ruth, were attending a convention there when they met Avatar publisher William Christensen, a fan of Gage's work. They ended up discussing what Gage might be able to do for Christensen, and Ruth ultimately came up with an idea. In an interview with Charles Webb for the *Comics Bulletin* Web site, Gage remarked: "Ruth, in one of her typical moments of genius, suggested a superhero serial killer, and things kind of fell into place from there." John Dusk, the resulting hero, works within the confines of law enforcement officially, so that when he decides to go on a killing spree, he knows precisely which criminals are most deserving of such a fate. Naturally, such an advantage is also a disadvantage, as he feels guilty knowing that he is responsible for the crimes, and in fact, his girlfriend, a homicide detective, is assigned to some of the murder cases for which John is responsible.

BIOGRAPHICAL AND CRITICAL SOURCES:

PERIODICALS

Booklist, October 1, 2007, Tina Coleman, review of *Post Human Division: Storm Watch 1,* p. 43.

Daily Variety, December 22, 2008, "Arcana Picks Up 'Paradox,'" author information, p. 8.

Library Media Connection, November 1, 2008, Kathleen McBroom, review of *Wildstorm: Armageddon.*

ONLINE

Christos Gage Home Page, http://web.mac.com/christosgage (July 20, 2009).

Comic Book Database Web site, http://comicbookdb.com/ (July 20, 2009), author profile.

Comics Bulletin Web site, http://www.comicsbulletin.com/ (July 20, 2009), Charles Webb, "Christos Gage: The Question of Moral Obligation."

Internet Movie Database, http://www.imdb.com/ (July 20, 2009), author profile.

Marvel Web site, http://marvel.com/ (March 5, 2009), "Writer Christos Gage Explains How the Teen Hero from Marvel Super Hero Squad Lands in the *Avengers: The Initiative.*"

SF Crowsnest Web site, http://www.sfcrowsnest.com/ (January 4, 2009), Neale Monks, review of *Wildstorm.**

*   *   *

GAGE, Christos N.
See GAGE, Christos

*   *   *

GAGNON, Michelle 1971-

PERSONAL: Born July 4, 1971. *Education:* Wesleyan University, B.A., 1993.

ADDRESSES: Home—San Francisco, CA. *Agent*—Philip G. Spitzer Literary Agency, Inc., 50 Talmage Farm Ln., East Hampton, NY 11937. *E-mail*—michelle@michellegagnon.com.

CAREER: Writer. Worked previously as a modern dancer, dog walker, bartender, freelance journalist, personal trainer, model, and a Russian supper club performer.

MEMBER: Sisters in Crime, Mystery Writers of America, Romance Writers of America, and International Thriller Writers.

WRITINGS:

"KELLY JONES" MYSTERY NOVELS

The Tunnels, Mira (Don Mills, Ontario, Canada), 2007.

Boneyard, Mira (Don Mills, Ontario, Canada), 2008.

The Gatekeeper, Mira (Don Mills, Ontario, Canada), 2009.

SIDELIGHTS: Michelle Gagnon, born July 4, 1971, has had a diverse career, with a broad range of jobs, including a modern dancer, dog walker, bartender, freelance journalist, personal trainer, model, and a Russian supper club performer, before finally becoming a novelist. A graduate of Wesleyan University, Gagnon specializes in mystery novels and is a member of a number of professional organizations, including Sisters in Crime, Mystery Writers of America, Romance Writers of America, and International Thriller Writers. She is the author of the "Kelly Jones" mystery novel series, which starts with *The Tunnels,* published in 2007, and continues with *Boneyard* and *The Gatekeeper.*

Gagnon introduces Kelly Jones in *The Tunnels,* her first mystery novel. Kelly is a special agent with the U.S. Federal Bureau of Investigation, well known for tracking serial killers over the previous ten years. So she is the one called in when a serial killer begins to murder people on a New England college campus, making use of an intricate system of tunnels beneath the campus grounds that has long been abandoned in order to travel the area unseen and to stash the bodies of his victims. Two young women, both students, are found in the tunnels, their bodies horribly mutilated and laid out in odd positions. The killer has also painted strange symbols on the tunnel walls just near the bodies. Kelly is not just called in because of her expertise with such situations but also because as a former student of the college in question, she has an added advantage. As more bodies are discovered and a pattern begins to emerge, it becomes clear that the serial killer has engaged in a teasing dance with Kelly, luring her into becoming a potential victim herself. A writer for the *Mysterious Reviews* Web site found some weaknesses with the story but remarked that "Gagnon has created an intelligent, confident character in Kelly Jones who grows more complex and, not coincidentally, more interesting as the story progresses."

Kelly Jones returns in Gagnon's next mystery, *Boneyard.* Someone is killing people along the northern stretch of the Appalachian Trail, where it moves into Massachusetts and Vermont, and Kelly is sent to investigate. The first six victims are mere skeletons, left unburied, and are all identified as gay hustlers who, because of their offbeat lifestyles, caused little or no fuss when they first disappeared. As more bones are discovered, Kelly begins to suspect that there are actually two killers at work, with one serving as a copycat of the first. A *Publishers Weekly* reviewer stated that "Gagnon plays the antagonism between the two villains nicely." Carolann Curry, reviewing for *Library Journal,* found this second installment in the series to be "an engaging and quick read."

BIOGRAPHICAL AND CRITICAL SOURCES:

PERIODICALS

Library Journal, June 1, 2008, Carolann Curry, review of *Boneyard,* p. 90.

Publishers Weekly, April 16, 2007, review of *The Tunnels,* p. 38; April 28, 2008, review of *Boneyard,* p. 117.

ONLINE

Hey Lady!, http://heylady.net/ (December 2, 2008), review of *Boneyard.*

International Thriller Writers Web site, http://www.thrillerwriters.org/ (July 18, 2009), author profile.

Michelle Gagnon Home Page, http://www.michellegagnon.com (July 18, 2009).

Michelle Gagnon MySpace Page, http://www.myspace.com/kellyajones (July 18, 2009).

Mysterious Reviews, http://www.mysteriousreviews.com/ (July 18, 2009), review of *The Tunnels.*

Mystery Writers of America Web site, http://www.mysterywriters.org/ (July 18, 2009), author profile.

Reaction to Reading, http://reactiontoreading.wordpress.com/ (March 24, 2009), review of *The Tunnels.*

Red Room, http://www.redroom.com/ (July 18, 2009), author profile.*

* * *

GALLO, Marcia M.

PERSONAL: Born in Wilmington, DE. *Education:* City University of New York, Ph.D., 2004.

ADDRESSES: Office—University of Nevada at Las Vegas, Department of History, 4505 Maryland Pkwy., Box 455020, Las Vegas, NV 89154-5020. *E-mail*—marcia.gallo@unlv.edu.

CAREER: Writer, educator; Lehman College, City University of New York, New York, NY, adjunct assistant professor, 2004-05, visiting assistant professor, 2005-08; University of Nevada at Las Vegas, department of history, assistant professor, 2008—. Previously worked at American Civil Liberties Union, San Francisco, CA, field director; Funding Exchange Foundation, New York, NY, director of development and donor relations.

AWARDS, HONORS: Lambda Literary Award for *Different Daughters: A History of the Daughters of Bilitis and the Rise of the Lesbian Rights Movement,* 2006; Passing the Torch Award, Center for Lesbian and Gay Studies at the City University of New York, 2007.

WRITINGS:

Different Daughters: A History of the Daughters of Bilitis and the Rise of the Lesbian Rights Movement, Carroll & Graf Publishers (New York, NY), 2006.

SIDELIGHTS: Writer and educator Marcia M. Gallo was born in Wilmington, Delaware. She earned her doctorate from the City University of New York (CUNY), where she studied history and specialized in gender and sexuality in particular. Over the course of her career, she has worked in several different capacities, serving as the director of development and donor relations at the Funding Exchange Foundation in New York, New York, then later moving to San Francisco,

California, where she worked for the American Civil Liberties Union. Once she entered academia, Gallo served on the faculty of Lehman College of CUNY until 2008, at which time she moved on to take a position in the department of history at the University of Nevada at Las Vegas. Gallo's book *Different Daughters: A History of the Daughters of Bilitis and the Rise of the Lesbian Rights Movement,* published in 2006, has received a number of accolades including the 2006 Lambda Literary Award. Gallo was also awarded the Passing the Torch Award from the Center for Lesbian and Gay Studies at CUNY in 2007.

Different Daughters was developed from Gallo's doctoral dissertation and looks at the history of the Daughters of Bilitis, the first lesbian organization to be formed in the United States. The group got its start in San Francisco in 1955, at which time the prevailing culture was highly conservative and anything considered outside of the accepted norms of sexual interest or practice was considered deviant behavior. Though the group has previously been mentioned in various books about gay and lesbian life in the United States, Gallo's is the first volume to give detailed attention to the Daughters of Bilitis, focusing entirely on the organization. Over the course of her research, Gallo interviewed thirty-six individuals who are former members of the group in order to offer readers a clear picture of how the group was formed in such a limited climate, the actions its members took in an attempt to shift society in their favor, and the reasons why the organization was eventually disbanded. Lillian Faderman, in a review for *Lambda Book Report,* commented that "Gallo makes the reader understand from the beginning that [Daughters of Bilitis]'s mere existence in the climate of 1950s and [19]60s was a tremendous act of courage." A reviewer for *Publishers Weekly* declared that "this is a respectful, respectable look at an organization overdue for recognition." *Booklist* contributor Whitney Scott found the work to be "an essential addition to the popular literature of sociopolitical issues, women's studies, and gay-lesbian history."

BIOGRAPHICAL AND CRITICAL SOURCES:

PERIODICALS

Booklist, November 1, 2006, Whitney Scott, review of *Different Daughters: A History of the Daughters of Bilitis and the Rise of the Lesbian Rights Movement,* p. 9.

Gay & Lesbian Review Worldwide, September 1, 2007, Vernon Rosario, "Of Living Rooms and Liberation Politics," review of *Different Daughters,* p. 31.

Lambda Book Report, September 22, 2006, Lillian Faderman, review of *Different Daughters,* p. 4.

Publishers Weekly, September 25, 2006, review of *Different Daughters,* p. 57.

ONLINE

Gerberhart Web site, http://www.gerberhart.org/ (July 18, 2009), author profile.

University of Nevada at Las Vegas Department of History Web site, http://history.unlv.edu/ (July 18, 2009), author faculty profile.*

* * *

GANJI, Akbar 1960-

PERSONAL: Born January 31, 1960, in Tehran, Iran.

ADDRESSES: Home—Iran. *E-mail*—contact@akbarganji.org.

CAREER: Journalist, writer, political activist. Has written for numerous dissident newspapers in Iran; previous member of the Revolutionary Guards.

MEMBER: Honorary member of the American, Canadian, and English PEN Centers.

AWARDS, HONORS: International Press Freedom Award, Canadian Journalists for Free Expression, 2000; Golden Pen of Freedom Award, World Association of Newspapers, 2006; Martin Ennals Award for Human Rights Defenders, 2006; John Auchbon Freedom of the Press Award, National Press Club, 2006; John Humphrey Freedom Award, 2007; honorary citizen of Florence, Italy.

WRITINGS:

Tarik'khanah-'i ashba: Asib'shinasi-i guzar bih dawlat-i dimukratik-i tawsi'ah'gara, Tarh-i Naw (Tehran, Iran), 1999.

Talaqqi-i fashisti az din va hkumat, Tarh-i Naw (Tehran, Iran), 2000.

Naqdi bara-yi tamam-i fusul: Guft va gu-yi Akbar Ganji ba 'Abd Allah Nuri: Bih payvast-i matn-i istizah-i Abd Allah Nuri dar Majlis-i panjum, Tarh-i Naw (Tehran, Iran), 2000.

Alijanab-i surkhpush va 'alijanaban-i khakistari: Asib'shinasi-i guzar bih dawlat-i dimukratik-i tawsi'ah'gara, Tarh-i Naw (Tehran, Iran), 2000.

Islahgari-i mi'maranah: Asib'shinasi-i guzar bih dawlat-i dimukratik-i tawsi'ah'gara, Tarh-i Naw (Tehran, Iran), 2000.

The Road to Democracy in Iran, introduction by Joshua Cohen and Abbas Milani, Massachusetts Institute of Technology Press (Cambridge, MA), 2008.

SIDELIGHTS: Akbar Ganji was born January 31, 1960, in Tehran, Iran. Known as a strong-minded and forthright investigative journalist, he is highly vocal in his opposition to the political and social situation in his homeland and has spent a large portion of his career writing for dissident publications and speaking out at various rallies and protests. He spent six years in jail as a result of his beliefs and his willingness to stand up for them and speak against the government. Over the course of his career, Ganji has been honored with numerous awards, both for his writing and for his human rights efforts, including the International Press Freedom Award from the Canadian Journalists for Free Expression, the Golden Pen of Freedom Award from the World Association of Newspapers, the Martin Ennals Award for Human Rights Defenders, the John Auchbon Freedom of the Press Award from the National Press Club, and the John Humphrey Freedom Award. In addition, he has been made an honorary member of the American, Canadian, and English PEN Centers, as well as an honorary citizen of Florence, Italy. His articles have been published both individually and in collections, and his first book to appear in English, *The Road to Democracy in Iran,* was published by the Massachusetts Institute of Technology Press in 2008.

Ganji has always been politically minded. During his youth, he was in favor of the Iranian revolution and participated where it was possible. Then during the 1990s, he began to feel disheartened with the way that the government was run and how the Iranian people were treated. In the wake of the murder of a number of dissident authors, referred to as the "Chain Murders of Iran," Ganji began to write against the government, using these murders as the focal point for a series of news stories. His work resulted in his arrest, and Ganji was sentenced to serve time in the Evin Prison in Tehran. He wrote extensively from his prison cell, and was ultimately released briefly during his sentence due to poor health. He continues to both write about the situation under Fundamental Islam in Iran and to advocate a secular, democratic government for the good of the people.

In *The Road to Democracy in Iran,* which originated as a series of lectures before being combined into a book, Ganji addresses the concept of human rights and various human rights issues around the globe before focusing in on the situation in Iran. Ganji proposes that it is possible for Iran to reform its policies and to conduct itself in accordance with basic human rights, despite the current regime and the strict, fundamentalist outlook. Unlike some political dissidents, Ganji firmly believes that Iran can only change for the better by working on its policies and political system itself, as Western intervention can only lead to more strife due to the differences in religious and social beliefs. Only the Iranians can truly understand the issues at hand in Iran, and therefore they must be responsible for their own positive political transformation. Over the course of the book, he suggests ways in which this change might come about, stressing the importance of fair treatment and equality between the sexes, among other points. John P. Miglietta, in a review for the *Middle East Journal,* commented that "while the author makes a compelling case, he does not deal with the global economic, political, and strategic realities of globalization that are working against this. Nevertheless, this work is valuable, as it illustrates that there are progressive voices around the world, including in Iran, calling for change." Gilbert Taylor, writing for *Booklist,* declared that "Ganji's aspirations—some idealistic, some practical—will resonate with all engaged with the human rights movement."

BIOGRAPHICAL AND CRITICAL SOURCES:

PERIODICALS

Booklist, April 1, 2008, Gilbert Taylor, review of *The Road to Democracy in Iran,* p. 11.

Economist, December 9, 2000, "Iran's Killing Machine; an Iranian Journalist Hits Back," author information, p. 1; December 10, 2005, "A Top Dissident Refuses to Give In; Iran," author information, p. 56.

IPR Strategic Business Information Database, July 31, 2001, "Iran: Press Reflects Poor Human Rights Situation," author information.

Los Angeles Times, August 13, 2006, "Iranian Dissident Urges Caution: A Critic of the Islamic Regime Says U.S. Intervention Would Lead to More Oppression, Some in 'Irangeles' Question His Motives," p. 1.

MEED: Middle East Economic Digest, December 15, 2000, "Iranian Journalist Names Officials Allegedly behind Killings," p. 3; February 9, 2001, "Akbar Ganji," author information, p. 2; March 24, 2006, "Ganji Freed after Five Years: 20 March," p. 5.

Middle East, March 18, 2006, "Iran Frees Prominent Journalist from Jail," author information.

Middle East Journal, September 22, 2008, John P. Miglietta, "The Quest for Democracy in Iran: A Century of Struggle against Authoritarian Rule," p. 712.

Middle East Quarterly, January 1, 2006, "Akbar Ganji: 'Justice in the Face of Tyranny,'" p. 73.

National Review, August 8, 2005, "Iranian Journalist and Political Prisoner Akbar Ganji Was on Hunger Strike for Nearly 40 Days before Being Transferred, Shortly before This Magazine Went to Print, from the Infirmary of Iran's Evin Prison to a Tehran Hospital, Apparently for Emergency Treatment," p. 10.

New Statesman, April 15, 2002, "Writers in Prison," author information, p. 42.

New York Times, November 10, 2000, "Iranian Journalist, in Court, Says Security Forces Tortured Him," p. 7; January 14, 2001, "Iran Hands Stiff Sentences to Reformists," p. 6; March 19, 2006, "Iranian Writer Released after Serving 6-Year Prison Term," p. 3; July 16, 2006, "Iranian Seeks Release of Political Prisoners," p. 14.

Time, March 6, 2000, "'Playing with Death': How Akbar Ganji's Fiery and Courageous Journalism Helped Change Iran's Politics," p. 4.

Time International, March 6, 2000, "Iran's Conscience: Ignoring Death Threats, a Muckraking Journalist Takes on the High and Mighty," p. 20.

ONLINE

Akbar Ganji Home Page, http://www.akbarganji.org (July 19, 2009).

Boston Review Online, http://www.bostonreview.net/ (May 26, 2008), Alan Klehr, author interview.

Free Europe Radio Liberty Web site, http://www.rferl.org/ (July 28, 2006), Fatemah Aman, "Iran: Radio Farda Interview with Dissident Akbar Ganji."

Immanent Frame Blog, http://blog.ssrc.org/ (December 23, 2008), Nader Hashemi and Danny Postel, "A Secular Age: Akbar Ganji in Conversation with Charles Taylor."

PEN American Center Web site, http://www.pen.org/ (July 19, 2009), author profile.

Sourcewatch Web site, http://www.sourcewatch.org/ (July 19, 2009), author profile.*

* * *

GEARY, Theresa Flores

PERSONAL: Education: Holds a Ph.D.

ADDRESSES: Home—Moriarty, NM. *E-mail*—Theresa@beadbible.com.

CAREER: Writer, bead artist; retired clinical psychologist.

WRITINGS:

Native American Beadwork: Projects & Techniques from the Southwest, Sterling Publishing (New York, NY), 2003.

Creative Native American Beading, Sterling Publishing (New York, NY), 2005.

The Illustrated Bead Bible: Terms, Tips & Techniques, photographs by Debra Whalen, Sterling Publishing (New York, NY), 2008.

SIDELIGHTS: Theresa Flores Geary was raised in southern New Mexico, where she developed an appreciation for Native American art, particularly bead work, as a member of the San Carlos Apache tribe. She earned her doctorate and worked as a clinical psychologist in Tucson, Arizona. Once she retired, Geary returned to New Mexico and settled in the town of Moriarty, where she now works as a bead artist and writes about her craft. In recent years, she has also become fascinated with gourds as an artistic medium, adding gourd dolls to her creative repertoire and combining them with beads, which she uses as embellishment. In addition to her art, Geary has begun to grow gourds, both for her own use and to share with other artistic friends and family members, and takes pride in cultivating an intriguing variety of shapes. Geary is the author of several books on beading, including *Native American Beadwork: Projects & Techniques from the Southwest, Creative Native American Beading,* and *The Illustrated Bead Bible: Terms, Tips & Techniques,* which includes photographs by Debra Whalen.

In *Native American Beadwork,* Geary offers readers a how-to guide in Native American beadwork. The book reveals that a majority of modern beadwork is derived from some cultural base, with ethnic customs determining not just the way in which the beads are woven together but the designs that result from that method. The book includes directions for eighteen projects, marked with their degree of difficulty and how new techniques can be applied in each instance. The projects include traditional Southwestern designs, including bear earrings, a kokopelli pin, and an amulet bag, among others. Barbara Jacobs, in a review for *Booklist,* opined that the book helps the reader "to see why the very act of beading can be a perfect relaxation therapy."

Creative Native American Beading serves as a follow-up book to *Native American Beadwork,* building on the foundations of the first volume and providing readers with a new set of projects and designs using their newly acquired beading skills. Constance Ashmore Fairchild, writing for *Library Journal,* recommended the book particularly "for libraries needing more beading material."

The Illustrated Bead Bible is a clear and comprehensive encyclopedia of beading techniques, terms, and concepts. This thorough guidebook answers numerous questions about beading, offers examples of various stitches used in the craft, and gives an overview of the history of beading. Barbara Jacobs, writing for *Booklist,* noted readers should not assume a simple reference book: "Don't overlook its value nor the very practical directions and wealth of information Geary has amassed."

BIOGRAPHICAL AND CRITICAL SOURCES:

PERIODICALS

Booklist, December 15, 2003, Barbara Jacobs, review of *Native American Beadwork: Projects & Techniques from the Southwest,* p. 716; May 15, 2008, Barbara Jacobs, review of *The Illustrated Bead Bible: Terms, Tips & Techniques,* p. 15.

Library Journal, February 15, 2004, Constance Ashmore Fairchild, review of *Native American Beadwork,* p. 124; February 15, 2006, Constance Ashmore Fairchild, review of *Creative Native American Beading,* p. 116; June 15, 2008, Constance Ashmore Fairchild, review of *The Illustrated Bead Bible,* p. 66.

Reference & Research Book News, August 1, 2008, review of *The Illustrated Bead Bible.*

ONLINE

Bead Bible Web site, http://www.beadbible.com (August 10, 2009).

New Mexico Gourd Society Web site, http://www.newmexicogourdsociety.org/ (August 10, 2009), author profile.*

* * *

GEIST, Mary Ellen 1956(?)-

PERSONAL: Born c. 1956; daughter of Woody (former chief executive officer of an auto parts company and a jazz singer) and Rosemary (an artist and educator) Geist. *Education:* Attended Kalamazoo College.

ADDRESSES: Home—Detroit, MI; Walloon Lake, MI.

CAREER: Writer, journalist. WPZ Radio, Petoskey, MI, reporter, anchor; WJML Radio, Petoskey, news anchor; Columbia Broadcasting System/Fox Video, scriptwriter, producer; served as assistant director on an independent horror film; Metro-Goldwyn Mayer/United Artists, Los Angeles, CA, worked for director/writer Andy Tennant; KFWB Radio, Los Angeles, "Morning Streets" reporter; KGO Radio, San Francisco, CA, morning reporter, noon news anchor, and morning news anchor, over twelve-year period; WCBS Radio, New York, NY, morning anchor, 2004-05; previously worked variously as a waitress, jazz singer, actress, and singing telegram deliverer.

AWARDS, HONORS: Associated Press Television and Radio Association Best News Reporting, 1994; Associated Press Best Investigative Reporting, 1999; Associated Press Bill Stout Award, 2000; Associated Press Best Live Coverage of a News Story, 2002; National Edward R. Murrow Award for Best Newscast for the KGO Radio Morning News, 2004; Regional Edward R. Murrow Award for Best Newscast, KGO Radio Morning News, 2004; Associated Press Best Newscast for KGO Radio Morning News, 2004.

WRITINGS:

Measure of the Heart: A Father's Alzheimer's, a Daughter's Return, Springboard Press (New York, NY), 2008.

SIDELIGHTS: Writer and radio reporter Mary Ellen Geist was educated at Kalamazoo College, spending her junior year in Sierra Leone, West Africa, where she first began to consider working in journalism. After graduating, she worked a number of odd jobs but eventually started her journalism career working for WPZ Radio in Petoskey, Michigan, as a reporter and an anchor. From there she moved on to WJML Radio, also in Petoskey, where she served as news anchor. She has worked for Columbia Broadcasting System/Fox Video as a scriptwriter and a producer, and even served as an assistant director for an independent horror film under writer and director Andy Tennant. In Los Angeles, California, Geist spent time working for KFWB Radio, where she was their "Morning Streets" reporter. From there, Geist continued on to KGO Radio in San Francisco, California, holding positions including morning reporter, noon news anchor, and morning news anchor over a twelve-year period. In 2004, she moved to New York, New York, where she spent a year as the morning anchor for WCBS Radio. However, in 2005, Geist quit her job and headed to her parents' home in Michigan, where her father, Woody Geist, a former chief executive office of his own auto parts firm and a jazz singer who spent a number of decades performing with an a capella group, was suffering from Alzheimer's disease. Geist moved in and began helping her mother care for her father, an experience she has chronicled in her book, *Measure of the Heart: A Father's Alzheimer's, a Daughter's Return.*

Measure of the Heart tells a story that is becoming more and more common in the twenty-first century, as people live longer but not always in the best of health. While it has long been considered the role of the unmarried daughter to care for aging or ill parents, modern shifts in attitudes have led to a new type of caregiving. In many instances, single women have highly successful careers, yet some, like Geist, are willing to give them up in order to care for their parents when necessary. In an interview with Jane Gross for the *New York Times,* Geist explained: "I lived a very selfish life. I'd gotten plenty of recognition. But all I did was work, and it was getting old. I knew I could make a difference here. And it's expanded my heart and given me a chance to reclaim something I'd lost." Many women find it necessary to quit their jobs to fulfill the task of caring for a parent, as to maintain both responsibilities at once proves too difficult. In Geist's case, she moved into the attic bedroom suite she once shared with her sisters, and her mother pays her a small salary for her assistance, so that she is not entirely without funds. In return, she ensures that her father gets to adult day care, and that her mother has a measure of time for herself. Geist offers readers advice about dealing with a loved one who has Alzheimer's, all while sharing her own experiences. *Booklist* reviewer Donna Chavez remarked of Geist's effort that "in a very personable style, she shares tips, lessons learned (some the hard way), [and] resources."

BIOGRAPHICAL AND CRITICAL SOURCES:

BOOKS

Geist, Mary Ellen, *Measure of the Heart: A Father's Alzheimer's, a Daughter's Return,* Springboard Press (New York, NY), 2008.

PERIODICALS

Booklist, July 1, 2008, Donna Chavez, review of *Measure of the Heart,* p. 20.

Houston Chronicle, November 27, 2005, "Trading in Careers for Caregiving; Many Successful Women Returning Home to Help Care for Aging Parents," p. 2.

New York Times, November 24, 2005, Jane Gross, "Forget the Career, My Parents Need Me at Home," author interview.

Publishers Weekly, June 2, 2008, review of *Measure of the Heart,* p. 40.

ONLINE

Caring Web site, http://www.caring.com/ (July 18, 2009), Camille Peri, "Talking with Author Mary Ellen Geist: Don't Stop the Music."

Fresh Fiction Web site, http://www.freshfiction.com/ (July 18, 2009), author profile.

Hachette Book Group Web site, http://www.hachettebookgroup.com/ (July 18, 2009), author profile.

Mary Ellen Geist Home Page, http://www.maryellengeist.com (July 18, 2009).*

* * *

GENOVA, Lisa
(Lisa Genova Seufert)

PERSONAL: Children: one son, one daughter. *Education:* Bates College, B.S.; Harvard University, Ph.D.

ADDRESSES: *E-mail*—lisa@stillalice.com.

CAREER: Writer, actor, research scientist. National Alzheimer's Association, online columnist; has performed various scientific research pertaining to molecular etiology of depression, Parkinson's disease, drug addiction, and memory loss following stroke. Also performs on stage and in independent films.

MEMBER: Dementia Advocacy & Support Network International, DementiaUSA.

WRITINGS:

Still Alice, Pocket Books (New York, NY), 2008.

Contributor to the National Alzheimer's Association Web site.

SIDELIGHTS: Lisa Genova studied biopsychology at Bates College, where she earned a bachelor of science degree and graduated as valedictorian. She later attended Harvard University from which she earned a doctorate in neuroscience. Her scientific research interests cover a number of topics, including the molecular etiology of depression, Parkinson's disease, drug addiction, and memory loss in the wake of a stroke. Genova belongs to both the Dementia Advocacy & Support Network International and to DementiaUSA. In addition, she writes a regular column for the National Alzheimer's Association Web site. Outside of her scientific efforts, Genova is also interested in the arts. She performs regularly on stage, primarily in Boston, Massachusetts, and has acted in a number of independent films. Her debut novel, *Still Alice,* was published in 2008.

In *Still Alice,* Genova merges her scientific curiosity regarding Alzheimer's disease with the horror she felt when her beloved grandmother succumbed to the illness in her mid-eighties. When her grandmother was first was diagnosed with the disease, Genova began to research the illness, learning as much as she could about what was taking place inside her grandmother's brain. Much of the scientific material she studied discussed the molecular results of the disease's progress. Beyond that, however, she read more personal nonfiction accounts of living with Alzheimer's, much of which was written either by caregivers or clinicians analyzing the illness. Ultimately, however, her grandmother was too far along in the progression of the disease to tell Genova what she most wanted to know, which was how it actually felt to suffer from Alzheimer's. That burning question and Genova's search for an answer served as the origin for the novel. Genova tells the story of Alice Howland, a professor at Harvard University and a high-achiever, who begins to suffer symptoms of Alzheimer's and gradually, over a two-year period, is ravaged by the illness. Genova depicts Alice as a much younger Alzheimer's patient than is typical, having her first begin her decline at the age of forty-nine. This choice serves to show the extremes of the disease, including how it can rob a person of their livelihood, well-being, and self-respect, all within a short period of time. A reviewer for *Publishers Weekly* declared that "it's impossible not to feel for Alice and her loved ones, but Genova's prose style is clumsy." However, a contributor to *Kirkus Reviews* found the book "worthy, benign, and readable, but not always lifelike." Joanna M. Burkhardt, in a review for *Library Journal,* dubbed Genova's effort "realistic and compelling."

BIOGRAPHICAL AND CRITICAL SOURCES:

PERIODICALS

Kirkus Reviews, November 1, 2008, review of *Still Alice.*

Library Journal, May 1, 2009, Joanna M. Burkhardt, review of *Still Alice,* p. 50.

MBR Bookwatch, May 1, 2008, Mary Cowper, review of *Still Alice.*

Publishers Weekly, October 20, 2008, review of *Still Alice,* p. 31.

ONLINE

Lisa Genova Home Page, http://www.lisagenova.com (July 18, 2009).*

* * *

GERSHOW, Miriam 1970-

PERSONAL: Born November 18, 1970; married. *Education:* Graduated from the University of Michigan, Ann Arbor; University of Oregon, M.F.A., 2002.

ADDRESSES: Home—Eugene, OR. *Agent*—Emily Forland, The Wendy Weil Agency, 232 Madison Ave., Ste. 1300, New York NY 10016.

CAREER: Writer, educator. University of Oregon, Eugene, writing instructor. Previously taught writing at the University of Wisconsin and through the gifted high school student program at Johns Hopkins University.

AWARDS, HONORS: Fiction Fellowship, Wisconsin Institute for Creative Writing; Oregon Literary Fellowship; AWP Intro Journals award.

WRITINGS:

The Local News: A Novel, Spiegel & Grau (New York, NY), 2009.

Contributor to journals including the *Georgia Review, Quarterly West, Black Warrior Review, Nimrod International Journal, Journal,* and *Gulf Coast;* contributor to anthologies including *100 Distinguished Stories of The Best American Short Stories 2007* and *2008 Robert Olen Butler Prize Stories.*

SIDELIGHTS: Eugene, Oregon-based writer and educator Miriam Gershow was born November 18, 1970. Raised in Detroit, she graduated from the University of Michigan in Ann Arbor, then, after moving to Oregon in 1994, went on to earn a master of fine arts degree from the University of Oregon in 2002. Over the course of her career, she has taught writing at the University of Wisconsin and as part of a special program for gifted high school students through Johns Hopkins University, eventually settling at the University of Oregon. In addition to her educational endeavors, she is a regular contributor of fiction to literary journals, including the *Georgia Review, Quarterly West, Black Warrior Review, Nimrod International Journal, Journal,* and *Gulf Coast.* Her work has also appeared in several anthologies, including *100 Distinguished Stories of The Best American Short Stories 2007* and *2008 Robert Olen Butler Prize Stories.* Gershow's debut novel, *The Local News: A Novel,* was published in 2009.

In *The Local News,* Gershow offers readers a story that was inspired by her strong memories of growing up with her sister, a figure she states figured heavily in all of her earliest experiences. In an essay for the Random House Web site, Gershow explained: "When I think of childhood, I think of my older sister. She and I existed in a particular sort of family, the kind where parents were nearby but in their own orbit of adult preoccupations. . . . Rebecca, even though she was three years older, still revolved in the same cartoon-watching, sprinkler-jumping, stuffed-animal-collecting orbit as I did." Gershow took that close-knit relationship and used it as a foundation for her novel, which tells the story of Lydia, a young teenager whose older brother Danny, an eighteen-year-old football hero, disappears one day. The pair were very close as small children, but the age gap and Danny's bullying behavior as they grew older had driven them apart by the time he vanishes. Through Lydia's eyes, Gershow recounts how the tragedy affects the entire family, shifting relationships and altering the way in the remaining members treat each other. Terry Miller Shannon, in a review for the *Book Reporter* Web site, remarked that "readers are transported wholly into Lydia's life, which, although fascinating, is often a truly discomforting experience. Lydia is a refreshingly not-at-all-beautiful, intelligent and witty narrator with a black sense of humor. Her story is unvarnished, lacking in white wash and grittily realistic." Janet Maslin, writing for the *New York Times Book Review,* noted that "this story is full of insightful, implicit hindsight as it illustrates how the trauma involving Danny will shape Lydia's adulthood and forever stunt her ability to get along with others."

BIOGRAPHICAL AND CRITICAL SOURCES:

PERIODICALS

Kirkus Reviews, December 1, 2008, review of *The Local News: A Novel.*

Library Journal, November 15, 2008, Kevin Greczek, review of *The Local News,* p. 60.

Marie Claire, February 1, 2009, Eileen Conlan, review of *The Local News,* p. 55.

New York Times, February 16, 2009, "With a Disappearance, Life Turns Upside Down," p. 7.

Publishers Weekly, October 27, 2008, review of *The Local News,* p. 29.

Register-Guard, March 1, 2009, "First Time's a Charm," p. 29.

School Library Journal, February 1, 2009, Francisca Goldsmith, review of *The Local News,* p. 130.

ONLINE

Book Reporter, http://www.bookreporter.com/ (August 10, 2009), Terry Miller Shannon, review of *The Local News.*

Boston Bibliophile, http://www.bostonbibliophile.com/ (April 16, 2009), review of *The Local News.*

Miriam Gershow Home Page, http://www.miriamgershow.com (August 10, 2009).

Random House Web site, http://www.randomhouse.com/ (February 12, 2009), author interview.*

* * *

GERST, Eric D.

PERSONAL: Male.

ADDRESSES: Home—Newtown, PA.

CAREER: Writer, retired attorney. Previously served as senior partner for a law firm based in Philadelphia, PA, and Washington, DC.

WRITINGS:

Vulture Culture: Dirty Deals, Unpaid Claims, and the Coming Collapse of the Insurance Industry, American Management Association (New York, NY), 2008.

SIDELIGHTS: Eric D. Gerst is a retired attorney who spent more than three decades serving as both a lawyer and a legal consultant. He eventually became a senior partner at a firm based in Philadelphia and Washington, DC, where his focus was the insurance business. Gerst represented a national insurance brokerage company as their general counsel along with various other clients, both corporate and individual. He went before the Senate Banking, Housing, and Urban Affairs Committee to press for a national catastrophe fund designed to help the owners of houses on the coasts that are vulnerable to severe storm damage, and also testified before Congress regarding various ways in which the insurance industry has been abusing their role. In 2008, Gerst's debut book, *Vulture Culture: Dirty Deals, Unpaid Claims, and the Coming Collapse of the Insurance Industry,* was published by the American Management Association.

In *Vulture Culture,* Gerst delves into all of the tricks of the trade and the refusals of service that have made the insurance business an unreliable safety net for so many Americans. When Gerst had an insurance claim of his own turned down, he decided to research the industry in order to see precisely why his claim was denied. As a result, he discovered the myriad of loopholes in the system that allow the insurance companies to refuse payment for claims their customers truly believe are valid. Over the course of the book, Gerst explains how state regulations are inconsistent and points out that there is no system of checks and balances on a federal level to make up for this lack of uniformity. As a result, the entire system in skewed in such a way that the insurance companies are favored in the majority of cases, to the detriment of those individuals who believe themselves to be insured. Gerst also looks at specific instances of insurance companies managing to shirk their responsibilities to their clients, delving into the scandals so prevalent in the industry between 2004 and 2006. He then goes on to outline a number of potential remedies to the situation, advocating a federal oversight system and various ways of regulating business practices so that they are fair to the consumers, and reversing some of the flaws in the existing system. Kathryn Price, in a review for the *Women's Radio Network* Web site, praised Gerst's effort for "pointing out where those flaws lie and how extreme the danger of the imminent collapse of the health insurance industry is."

BIOGRAPHICAL AND CRITICAL SOURCES:

PERIODICALS

Booklist, May 1, 2008, Mary Whaley, review of *Vulture Culture: Dirty Deals, Unpaid Claims, and the Coming Collapse of the Insurance Industry,* p. 61.

ONLINE

Women's Radio Network, http://www.womensradio.com/ (August 10, 2009), Kathryn Price, review of *Vulture Culture.**

* * *

GEUS, Mireille 1964-

PERSONAL: Born 1964, in Amsterdam, Netherlands; married; children: one son, one daughter.

ADDRESSES: Home—Haarlem, Netherlands.

CAREER: Author and writing coach.

AWARDS, HONORS: Vlag en Wimpel award, 2004, for *Virenzo en ik,* and 2008, for *Naar Wolf;* Golden Pen award, 2006, for *Big.*

WRITINGS:

Virenzo en ik, Lemniscat (Rotterdam, Netherlands), 2003.

Big, illustrated by Mies van Hout, Lemniscat (Rotterdam, Netherlands), 2005, translated by Nancy Forest-Flier as *Piggy,* Front Street Books (Asheville, NC), 2008.

Naar Wolf, Lemniscat (Rotterdam, Netherlands), 2007.

SIDELIGHTS: Dutch author Mireille Geus focuses her writing for young teens, mixing spare, compelling prose with stories that reflect the concerns of modern-day middle graders. Her first three books—*Virenzo en ik, Big,* and *Naar Wolf*—were honored with major awards in Geus's native Netherlands, and *Big* was also translated for English-language audiences as *Piggy.*

In *Piggy,* readers meet twelve-year-old "Dizzy" Lizzy Bekell and, through her deliberately paced narration, see the world through her eyes. Lizzy is considered an outsider by the other children in her neighborhood, who call her retarded. Because of her autism, Lizzy goes to a different school and knows few of her neighbors, so when another lonely girl welcomes her efforts at friendship, Lizzy is elated. Unfortunately, Margaret (whose nickname is "Piggy") views the relationship differently. An aggressive girl, she manipulates the emotionally needy Lizzy and ultimately involves the naïve and autistic girl in her plan to exact retribution on some local bullies while risking a tragic outcome. The "slightly confused" narration allows readers to experience Lizzy's mistreatment at the hands of her new "friend," wrote *School Library Journal* critic Wendy Smith-D'Arezzo, the critic praising *Piggy* as "a strong story with believable characters." "Geus creates suspense" by threading Lizzy's narrative with her later interrogation by the police, and introduces "standout" adults that support the girl, wrote a *Kirkus Reviews* writer, and in *Horn Book,* Sarah Ellis praised *Piggy* as a "short, powerful novel" that is "structured like a detective novel, and told with the spare tautness of a mystery."

BIOGRAPHICAL AND CRITICAL SOURCES:

PERIODICALS

Horn Book, January-February, 2009, Sarah Ellis, review of *Piggy,* p. 91.

Kirkus Reviews, September 1, 2008, review of *Piggy.*

School Library Journal, January, 2009, Wendy Smith-D'Arezzo, review of *Piggy,* p. 100.

ONLINE

Lemniscaat Web site, http://lemniscaat.nl/ (November 15, 2009), "Mireille Geus."

Mireille Geus Home Page, http://www.mireillegeus.nl (November 15, 2009).*

* * *

GIBSON, Fiona

PERSONAL: Married; children: twin sons, Dexter and Sam, and one daughter. *Hobbies and other interests:* Drawing, running 10k races, playing her saxophone, and lying in the bath with a big glass of wine.

ADDRESSES: Home—Scotland. *E-mail*—hello@fiona gibson.com.

CAREER: Freelance journalist. *Sunday Herald,* London, England, weekly columnist; previously served as editor for periodicals, including *More, Just Seventeen,* and *Bliss;* contributor to various radio programs for BBC.

WRITINGS:

Babyface, Red Dress Ink (Don Mills, Ontario, Canada), 2004.

Wonderboy, Red Dress Ink (Don Mills, Ontario, Canada), 2005.

The Fish Finger Years, Hodder & Stoughton (London, England), 2006.

Lucky Girl, Hodder & Stoughton (London, England), 2006.

Mummy Said the F-Word, Hodder & Stoughton (London, England), 2008.

Something Good, Red Dress Ink (Don Mills, Ontario, Canada), 2008.

Contributor to periodicals, including the *Observer, Guardian, Marie Claire, Red, New Woman, Top Sante,* and *Elle.*

SIDELIGHTS: Scottish-based freelance writer Fiona Gibson is a weekly columnist for the London *Sunday Herald,* where she writes about her family life. Over the course of her career, she has served as an editor for a number of publications, including *More, Just Seventeen,* and *Bliss.* In addition to her columns, she provides material to the BBC radio for various programs and contributes to periodicals such as the *Observer, Guardian, Marie Claire, Red, New Woman, Top Sante,* and *Elle.* In 2004, she turned her attention to writing fiction, as well, and the result was her first novel, *Babyface.* Subsequent titles include *Wonderboy, The Fish Finger Years, Lucky Girl, Mummy Said the F-Word,* and *Something Good.*

Babyface kicks off when journalist Nina and software programmer Jonathan meet through an off-the-cuff personal ad. Although the pair would not consider each other the perfect match, Nina gets pregnant and they decide to give the relationship a go, and plan to marry once they've settled and had the child. However, when Nina lends baby Ben to a stylist-friend for a spur-of-the-moment shoot, he becomes the next it-baby in the child modeling scene. Knowing that Jonathan would not approve, Nina sneaks off to a number of modeling jobs with the baby. When Jonathan inevitably learns of her deception, sparks fly. A reviewer for *Publishers Weekly* remarked that "while Gibson doesn't quite get at the heart of Nina's relationship with Jonathan, she does charmingly evoke the bittersweet bond of motherhood."

In *Wonderboy,* Gibson looks at a young family in transition. Rowena Skews and her husband, Marcus, have decided to move from their home in London into the countryside, a move they hope will be a good thing for their five-year-old son, Tod, who is somewhat antisocial. Though Ro is not all that thrilled with the prospect of country life, she acknowledges that her child might find a country school less pressurized and easier to make friends. Unfortunately, the house they choose, called Gorby Cottage, requires a great deal of work to make it truly habitable, and Ro finds herself much occupied by that task. At the same time, she feels her marriage is falling apart. Marcus becomes more and more distant, and once he starts calling out the name of another woman in his sleep, Ro is certain he is cheating on her. It does not help that Ro begins to find their new neighbor, Joe, rather sexy herself. Kristine Huntley, reviewing for *Booklist,* opined that the book would particularly appeal to "young mothers facing suburban life for the first time."

Lucky Girl is an offbeat tale of a young woman who finds family in an unlikely place. Stella Moon is a flute player with relationship issues, probably stemming from her feelings of neglect growing up when her father put his job above everything else, including his two daughters, even after their mother died. Stella herself has failed to maintain a long-term relationship and has just been dumped by her latest boyfriend as the book begins. However, when a new family moves in next door, Stella finds herself adopted in a sense by ten-year-old Jojo and her seven-year-old sister Midge. Their mother, Diane, is something of a flake and the girls show up at Stella's house all too often for Stella's initial liking. However, as she gets to know them and even begins teaching one of them the flute, Stella finds herself warming to their antics and grateful for their presence. Kristine Huntley, again writing for *Booklist,* dubbed the book "a touching tale about embracing family, imperfections and all."

Something Good is a mother-daughter story about the way that relationship can change when a teenage girl finds her rebellious streak. Jane Deakins and daughter Hannah have always been close, as mother took child in a divorce when she learned her husband, Max, was being unfaithful. However, when Hannah turns fifteen, the dynamic shifts, as Hannah begins sneaking out to see a boy and becomes friends with the wild-child daughter of her father's current girlfriend. *Booklist* reviewer Kristine Huntley declared that "Gibson's novel is more unpredictable and realistic than most chick-lit fare."

BIOGRAPHICAL AND CRITICAL SOURCES:

PERIODICALS

Booklist, September 15, 2005, Kristine Huntley, review of *Wonderboy,* p. 44; October 15, 2006, Kristine Huntley, review of *Lucky Girl,* p. 28; April 15, 2008, Kristine Huntley, review of *Something Good,* p. 28.

Publishers Weekly, June 14, 2004, review of *Babyface,* p. 42.

ONLINE

Fiona Gibson Home Page, http://www.fionagibson.com (August 11, 2009).

Genre Go Round Reviews Blog, http://genregoroundreviews.blogspot.com/ (March 25, 2008), Harriet Klausner, review of *Something Good.*

Observer Online, http://www.observer.co.uk/ (November 9, 2003), Fiona Gibson, "Exploitation! My Babies Didn't Get Out of Bed for Less Than 250 Pounds."

Trashionista, http://www.trashionista.com/ (May 1, 2009), review of *Mummy Said the F-Word.**

* * *

GILDER, Louisa 1978(?)-

PERSONAL: Born c. 1978. *Education:* Graduated from Dartmouth College, 2000.

CAREER: Writer.

WRITINGS:

The Age of Entanglement: When Quantum Physics Was Reborn, Alfred A. Knopf (New York, NY), 2008.

SIDELIGHTS: Writer Louisa Gilder graduated from Dartmouth College in 2000. She is the author of *The Age of Entanglement: When Quantum Physics Was Reborn.* The book, while a work of nonfiction, is written with the sensibilities of a novel, incorporating imagined dialogues for and between the many intellectual giants responsible for the scientific age and pertaining to the study of quantum physics. The subject matter is difficult, given that the science itself has served as a battleground between experts for decades, but Gilder does her best to deliver both the early history of quantum physics and the more modern approach to this branch of science in an easily understood, engaging manner.

Beginning with the early part of the twentieth century, Gilder addresses the theories of both relativity and quantum physics, their relationship to each other and to the universe, and the brilliant minds that devoted themselves to its study, such as Albert Einstein—whose theory of relativity jump-started these new scientific concepts by serving as a bridge between Newtonian physics and the ideas of the future, and those who worked on quantum physics itself, including Niels Bohr, Werner Heisenberg, Erwin Schrödinger, and Max Born. This shift marks a major change in the way scientific theory was approached, as Einstein was able to work on his own to make his discoveries, while quantum physics proved so complex and difficult to comprehend that a large number of scientists working together took decades in order to come up with a serviceable understanding of the concept. Gilder spends the first half of *The Age of Entanglement* discussing this process.

What makes Gilder's work stand out, however, is the second half of her book, which looks at the progress of quantum physics since 1927. Modern quantum physics is the result of scientists working, not in Germany but rather from around the world, from the University of California, Berkley, to Harvard University, to the large accelerator at CERN outside of Geneva, Switzerland. Gilder analyzes the work and character of individuals ranging from David Bohm, a former student of Robert J. Oppenheimer—whose political leanings resulted in his being brought up before the House Un-American Activities Committee, to Irish theorist John Bell—whose theories pushed the study of quantum physics to a new level in the early 1960s. Jack W. Weigel, in a review for *Library Journal*, stated that Gilder's effort "makes for entertaining light reading but doesn't dig very deeply into the current understanding of entanglement." However, Peter Galison, writing for the *New York Times Book Review*, remarked that "what had been for generations a story of theoretical malcontents now intrigues spooks and start-ups. All this radiates from Louisa Gilder's story. Quantum physics lives."

BIOGRAPHICAL AND CRITICAL SOURCES:

PERIODICALS

Booklist, November 15, 2008, Bryce Christensen, review of *The Age of Entanglement: When Quantum Physics Was Reborn*, p. 8.

Book World, December 7, 2008, "Very Small, Very Weird," review of *The Age of Entanglement*, p. 2.

Choice: Current Reviews for Academic Libraries, May 1, 2009, M.C. Ogilvie, review of *The Age of Entanglement*, p. 1743.

Kirkus Reviews, October 1, 2008, review of *The Age of Entanglement*.

Library Journal, November 1, 2008, Jack W. Weigel, review of *The Age of Entanglement*, p. 98.

Magazine of Fantasy and Science Fiction, March 1, 2009, Charles de Lint, review of *The Age of Entanglement*, p. 32.

New York Times Book Review, March 29, 2009, Peter Galison, review of *The Age of Entanglement*.

Publishers Weekly, September 1, 2008, review of *The Age of Entanglement*, p. 44.

Reference & Research Book News, February 1, 2009, review of *The Age of Entanglement*.

ONLINE

Random House Web site, http://www.randomhouse.com/ (July 18, 2009), author profile.*

* * *

GILLESPIE, Hollis 1962(?)-

PERSONAL: Born c. 1962; children: one daughter.

ADDRESSES: *Home*—Atlanta, GA. *E-mail*—hollisthewriter@gmail.com; hollis.gillespie@creativeloafing.com.

CAREER: Writer, columnist. *Creative Loafing* alternative weekly magazine, Atlanta, GA, author of "Moodswing" column; *Paste* magazine, author of "The Ugly American" travel column; *BeE WOMAN* magazine, author of humorous financial column; regular commentator for National Public Radio and Georgia Public Radio; has appeared on various television and radio programs, including *The Tonight Show with Jay Leno, TBS Storyline, Monica Kaufman's Close-Ups, Good Day Atlanta,* and *TV Land.* Previously worked as a flight attendant for Delta Airlines.

AWARDS, HONORS: *Writer's Digest* Breakout Author of the Year; named best columnist, 2001, 2002, 2005, 2006, 2007, and best local author, 2004, 2005, 2006, in the *Creative Loafing* Best of Atlanta Readers Survey; named best "Tell-All" by *Atlanta* magazine, 2006.

WRITINGS:

Bleachy-Haired Honky Bitch: Tales from a Bad Neighborhood, Regan Books (New York, NY), 2004.

Confessions of a Recovering Slut and Other Love Stories, Regan Books (New York, NY), 2005.

Trailer Trashed: My Dubious Efforts toward Upward Mobility, illustrations by James Polisky, Skirt!/ Globe Pequot Press (Guilford, CT), 2008.

ADAPTATIONS: Film rights under option by Home Box Office for *Bleachy-Haired Honky Bitch: Tales from a Bad Neighborhood,* with Laura Dern to star.

SIDELIGHTS: Writer and columnist Hollis Gillespie started her career working as a flight attendant for Delta Airlines, an odd choice given that she was afraid of flying. The decision, however, proved to her that facing her fears enabled her to tap into her personal creativity, and writing became something she did in her free time between trips, particularly when she found herself on a layover in a foreign country where she did not speak the language, making it more difficult to wile away the hours watching television. Gillespie is the author of the syndicated "Moodswing" column for the Atlanta-based alternative magazine *Creative Loafing,* and also writes a travel column, "The Ugly American," for *Paste* magazine and a financial column for *BeE WOMAN* magazine. She is a regular commentator for National Public Radio and Georgia Public Radio, and has appeared on various television and radio programs, including *The Tonight Show with Jay Leno, TBS Storyline, Monica Kaufman's Close-Ups, Good Day Atlanta,* and *TV Land.* She is the author of the books *Bleachy-Haired Honky Bitch: Tales from a Bad Neighborhood, Confessions of a Recovering Slut and Other Love Stories,* and *Trailer Trashed: My Dubious Efforts toward Upward Mobility.*

Gillespie got her first book deal as the result of an e-mail. She had written to a publisher at HarperCollins, sending along some of her clips from her columns and noting that she would be in New York soon. She received an immediate response that asked her to meet with the publisher in question the same day she was due in the city. Gillespie did not even have to sell her idea; the publisher offered her a contract for a two-book deal immediately upon meeting her, just based on the quality and tone of her writing. The resulting first book, *Bleachy-Haired Honky Bitch,* is a humorous memoir in which Gillespie pokes fun of virtually every aspect of her own life, from her bleached-blonde hair to her oddball relatives, her father's drinking to her own search for a house. Keir Graff, reviewing for *Booklist,* remarked of Gillespie's anecdotes that "some are quite successful, although the book isn't entirely compelling as a front-to-back read." A reviewer for *Publishers Weekly* remarked that "sometimes tender, but mostly just wry and a bit wild, Gillespie's writing is like the best radio commentary, leaving fans hungry, for more." The book has been optioned for a new Home Box Office cable television series, with Laura Dern set to star.

In *Confessions of a Recovering Slut and Other Love Stories,* Gillespie continues her humorous look at the trials and tribulations of her own life, with this installment finding her unmarried and pregnant, and facing the decision of whether to tackle motherhood on her own. The book continues once daughter Milly is born, and Gillespie begins to see the world through different eyes, particularly the hard neighborhood in which she lives and the choices she has made about her day-to-day life. Allison Block, in a review for *Booklist,* commented that "Gillespie's perspective remains deliciously demented and endearingly askew."

Trailer Trashed tracks Gillespie's attempts to become a landlord and the pitfalls of having to oversee various renovations and the process of finding tenants, as well as her ongoing personal life, including her efforts to sell her first book to Hollywood and the ever-difficult search for an acceptable man to date. A reviewer for *Publishers Weekly* noted that Gillespie has a tendency to swear fluently and to include subject matter that might make some readers squirm. While that in itself is not a problem, the same reviewer noted that "Gillespie's potty-mouth style makes most of her stories sound alike." In an interview for *Entertainment Weekly,* Gillespie herself admits: "A lot of people, because my name is androgynous, don't know I'm a girl. I have dude humor."

BIOGRAPHICAL AND CRITICAL SOURCES:

BOOKS

Gillespie, Hollis, *Bleachy-Haired Honky Bitch: Tales from a Bad Neighborhood,* Regan Books (New York, NY), 2004.

Gillespie, Hollis, *Confessions of a Recovering Slut and Other Love Stories,* Regan Books (New York, NY), 2005.
Gillespie, Hollis, *Trailer Trashed: My Dubious Efforts toward Upward Mobility,* illustrations by James Polisky, Skirt!/Globe Pequot Press (Guilford, CT), 2008.

PERIODICALS

Booklist, February 1, 2004, Keir Graff, review of *Bleachy-Haired Honky Bitch,* p. 934; July 1, 2005, Allison Block, review of *Confessions of a Recovering Slut and Other Love Stories,* p. 1880.
Entertainment Weekly, March 5, 2004, "Prepare for Takeoff," p. 72.
Publishers Weekly, January 12, 2004, review of *Bleachy-Haired Honky Bitch,* p. 46; May 23, 2005, review of *Confessions of a Recovering Slut and Other Love Stories,* p. 70; June 16, 2008, review of *Trailer Trashed,* p. 44.

ONLINE

About.com, http://contemporarylit.about.com/ (July 18, 2009), author profile.
Decatur Book Festival Web site, http://www.decaturbookfestival.com/ (July 18, 2009), "AJC Decatur Book Festival Presented by DeKalb Medical."
HarperCollins Web site, http://www.harpercollins.com/ (July 18, 2009), author profile.
Hollis Gillespie Home Page, http://www.hollisgillespie.com (July 18, 2009).
WOW: Women on Writing, http://wow-womenonwriting.com/ (July 18, 2009), Marcia Peterson, "20 Questions Answered by Hollis Gillespie."*

* * *

GOLDMAN, Arthur Steven
See GOLDMAN, Steven

* * *

GOLDMAN, Marlene 1963-
(Marlene B. Goldman)

PERSONAL: Born 1963. *Education:* University of Victoria, M.A., 1989; University of Toronto, Ph.D., 1993.

ADDRESSES: Office—University of Toronto at Scarborough, Division of Humanities, 1265 Military Trail, Scarborough, Ontario M1C 1A4, Canada. *E-mail*—mgoldman@chass.utoronto.ca.

CAREER: University of Toronto, Toronto, Ontario, Canada, Division of Humanities, professor of English.

WRITINGS:

Paths of Desire: Images of Exploration and Mapping in Canadian Women's Writing, University of Toronto Press (Buffalo, NY), 1997.
Rewriting Apocalypse in Canadian Fiction, McGill-Queen's University Press (Ithaca, NY), 2005.

SIDELIGHTS: Writer and educator Marlene Goldman earned her master's degree from the University of Victoria in 1989, then went on to complete her doctorate at the University of Toronto in 1993. She serves on the faculty of the University of Toronto where she is a professor of English. Her academic and research interests include the contemporary literature of Canada, women's writing, and feminist and critical theory. Goldman's books include *Paths of Desire: Images of Exploration and Mapping in Canadian Women's Writing,* which was published in 1997, and *Rewriting Apocalypse in Canadian Fiction,* released in 2005.

Paths of Desire takes a look at the work of five Canadian women writers and analyzes it in terms of how the narrative and the language relates to various images of mapping and exploration within the text. Goldman's examination of this imagery, in part, serves to refute the assessment of some other literary critics that Canadian women are not revolutionary in their writing techniques, instead focusing on the traditional structures of narrative over fresh, innovative styles. She uses the texts mentioned as a way of showing how Canadian women writers do delve into more radical and subversive aspects of the creative process. Ruth Dyckfehderau, in a review for *Resources for Feminist Research,* called Goldman's effort "a beautifully written, carefully structured, and critically thoughtful book that brings to my attention a number of important insights into white Canadian women's writing," and concluded that "this is a critically astute and important piece of writing, one to which I will undoubtedly refer time and again."

In *Rewriting Apocalypse in Canadian Fiction,* Goldman looks at the ways in which Canadian authors write about the images and ideas traditionally associated with an apocalypse as depicted in Revelations, rather than any modern-day issues of financial collapse or global warming. The imagery most commonly addressed in these authors' writings include the concept of division of the population between those destined to be saved and those who will not be, as well as the idea of a new dawn, where clear vision and transformation is the result of an apocalyptic event. Because Goldman focuses on the act of "rewriting," she looks more toward apocalyptic literature that concerns those who have been marginalized by society and its ideas of who is worth saving. The book addresses the works a number of well-known authors, such as Michael Ondaatje and Margaret Atwood, but considers their apocalyptic writings in terms of that subgenre, rather than as part of each author's body of work. In a review for the *Canadian Literature* Web site, Jennifer Bowering Delisle remarked that "the book is strongest when Goldman discusses her texts in terms of biblical allusion and the specific structural features of apocalypse that she identifies, such as intertextuality, allegory, witnessing, and revelation."

BIOGRAPHICAL AND CRITICAL SOURCES:

PERIODICALS

Canadian Book Review Annual, January 1, 1998, review of *Paths of Desire: Images of Exploration and Mapping in Canadian Women's Writing,* p. 268.

Canadian Literature, December 22, 1998, Christl Verduyn, review of *Paths of Desire,* p. 177.

Choice: Current Reviews for Academic Libraries, March 1, 1998, review of *Paths of Desire,* p. 1190.

Reference & Research Book News, February 1, 1998, review of *Paths of Desire,* p. 146.

Resources for Feminist Research, March 22, 2001, Ruth Dyckfehderau, review of *Paths of Desire.*

University of Toronto Quarterly, December 22, 1998, Kathy Mezei, review of *Paths of Desire,* p. 579.

ONLINE

Canadian Literature, http://www.canlit.ca/ (August 11, 2009), Jennifer Bowerling Delisle, "Apocalptic Revisions."

University of Toronto Web site, http://www.utsc.utoronto.ca/ (August 11, 2009), faculty profile.*

*　*　*

GOLDMAN, Marlene B.
See GOLDMAN, Marlene

*　*　*

GOLDMAN, Steven 1964-
(Arthur Steven Goldman)

PERSONAL: Born 1964, in Winston-Salem, NC; married; children: two sons. *Education:* Haverford College, B.A., 1986; Columbia University Teachers College, M.A.; Emerson College, M.F.A. *Religion:* Jewish.

ADDRESSES: Home—Boston, MA. *E-mail*—steven@stevengoldmanbooks.com.

CAREER: Author. Formerly taught middle school.

AWARDS, HONORS: Rainbow Project Outstanding Book selection, American Library Association Gay, Lesbian, Bisexual and Transgendered Round Table/Social Responsibilities Round Table, 2008, for *Two Parties, One Tux, and a Very Short Film about "The Grapes of Wrath."*

WRITINGS:

Two Parties, One Tux, and a Very Short Film about "The Grapes of Wrath," Bloomsbury Children's Books (New York, NY), 2008.

Contributor, under name Arthur Goldman, to journals and magazines, including *Ascent, Educational Digest, Gettysburg Review, In the Family, Nimrod, Phi Delta Kappan,* and *Teachers and Writers.*

SIDELIGHTS: In *Two Parties, One Tux, and a Very Short Film about "The Grapes of Wrath,"* Steven Goldman tells the story of what it is like to be a teen and be different. A former middle-school teacher, the author became interested in writing for young adults while working toward his M.F.A. at Emerson College. As Goldman told *Boston Globe* contributor Ellen Steinbaum, his novel "is about how groups accept and reject people. My interest is in how that happens. I like to inhabit a character and see it from that perspective."

Eleventh-grader Mitchell, the protagonist of *Two Parties, One Tux, and a Very Short Film about "The Grapes of Wrath,"* is a gawky, socially inept teen with little experience of either life or love. Fortunately, Mitchell is saved from social limbo by his best friend, David, but what to do when David confides to him that he is gay? Meanwhile, Mitchell's social life gets a lift when he decides to make a problematic claymation film in lieu of submitting the required book report, and soon he finds himself with two potential dates for the junior prom. In his first novel, Goldman serves up "a side-splitting slice of male adolescence," according to *School Library Journal* contributor Rhona Campbell in a review of *Two Parties, One Tux, and a Very Short Film about "The Grapes of Wrath."* While Campbell maintained that the novel's storyline—flush with talk of parties, beer-drinking, and the potential for sex—"takes a backseat to gems of dialogue," she concluded that the novel is "so funny and yet so realistic." Noting the "dry wit" running through the novel, a *Kirkus Reviews* contributor praised Goldman's ability to capture the "angst and . . . absurdities of high-school politics" in Mitchell's "strangely flat" and humorous narration and concluded that the author "clearly understands how teen boys think and speak." *Two Parties, One Tux, and a Very Short Film about "The Grapes of Wrath"* "speaks to the importance of friendship regardless of one's sexual orientation," asserted Dan Waxman, addressing the story's underlying theme in a review for *Gay and Lesbian Review Worldwide.*

BIOGRAPHICAL AND CRITICAL SOURCES:

PERIODICALS

Boston Globe, March 22, 2009, Ellen Steinbaum, interview with Goldman.

Gay and Lesbian Review Worldwide, March-April, 2009, Dan Waxman, review of *Two Parties, One Tux, and a Very Short Film about "The Grapes of Wrath,"* p. 43.

Kirkus Reviews, August 15, 2008, review of *Two Parties, One Tux, and a Very Short Film about "The Grapes of Wrath."*

School Library Journal, October, 2008, Rhona Campbell, review of *Two Parties, One Tux, and a Very Short Film about "The Grapes of Wrath,"* p. 146.

ONLINE

Steven Goldman Home Page, http://www.stevengoldmanbooks.com (November 5, 2009).*

* * *

GOODHIND, J.G.
See JOHNSON, Jeannie

* * *

GORDON, Grant 1956-

PERSONAL: Born January 2, 1956.

ADDRESSES: Office—Institute for Family Business, 32 Buckingham Palace Rd., London SW1W 0RE, England.

CAREER: Institute for Family Business, London, England, general director; also former senior executive for the family business in the drinks sector.

WRITINGS:

(With Nigel Nicholson) *Family Wars: Classic Conflicts in Family Business and How to Deal with Them,* Kogan Page (Philadelphia, PA), 2008.

SIDELIGHTS: Writer and businessman Grant Gordon was born January 2, 1956. He serves as the general director for the Institute for Family Business in

London, England, and previously was a senior executive at his own family-run business, a United Kingdom-based drinks company of which he is the fifth generation to be a member. These credentials prove an ideal background for the writing of *Family Wars: Classic Conflicts in Family Business and How to Deal with Them,* which Gordon wrote with academic Nigel Nicholson, and which was published in 2008.

Family Wars takes a look at the problems that can arise when disagreements between family members lead to chaos within the parameters of a family-owned and family-run business. While these sorts of issues can affect any size business, including the smallest mom-and-pop organization, they can be far more devastating when the company in question is a major, world-renowned corporation with numerous employees. Particularly vulnerable are companies that have been owned by a family for generations, in which the ideals held by founding family members differ from the younger members of the dynasty. Over the course of the book, Gordon and Nicholson include examples from a variety of famous family-owned businesses, showing how anything from small disagreements to major rivalries can send the company into a tail spin. Families mentioned include the likes of Gucci, Guinness, Gallo, Mondavi, Pritzker, Ford, and Redstone.

The book then goes on to analyze the different problems inherent in running a family business and looks a various strategies to keep the corporate and the family issues separate. It also provides a wealth of advice for how to handle issues if and when they do arise, in a way that will destroy neither the company nor the relationships within the family structure, and even includes tips regarding how to see such issues coming before they become too large and contentious to solve in a reasonable manner. In a review for *Booklist,* Mary Whaley praised the book, but also pointed out its specific target audience, stating that "lessons from this excellent book apply primarily to family companies, although there is thoughtful leadership insight." A reviewer for *Reference & Research Book News* had a similar opinion, noting the book is "for people who are involved in family firms . . . and for general readers with an interest." A contributor for *Internet Bookwatch* commented that the book is best suited for anyone involved in a family business who would hate for "money [to] get in between people and their devotion to family."

BIOGRAPHICAL AND CRITICAL SOURCES:

PERIODICALS

Booklist, April 15, 2008, Mary Whaley, review of *Family Wars: Classic Conflicts in Family Business and How to Deal with Them,* p. 12.

California Bookwatch, November 1, 2008, review of *Family Wars.*

Internet Bookwatch, June 1, 2008, review of *Family Wars.*

Reference & Research Book News, May 1, 2008, review of *Family Wars.*

U.S. News & World Report Online, May 16, 2008, "How to Keep Drama out of a Family Business; Q&A with Nigel Nicholson, Coauthor of *Family Wars.*"

ONLINE

Kogan Page Web site, http://www.koganpage.com/ (August 12, 2009), author profile.*

*　*　*

GORGANI, Fakhraddin (Fakhraddin Asaad Gorgani)

PERSONAL: Male.

CAREER: Eleventh-century Persian poet.

WRITINGS:

Khulasah-i Vis va Ramin, Intisharat-i Tus (Tehran, Iran), 1356, published in English as *Vis and Ramin,* translated from the Persian by George Morrison, Columbia University Press (New York, NY), 1972, translated from the Persian by Dick Davis, Mage Publishers (Washington, DC), 2008.

ADAPTATIONS: Vis and Ramin has been translated into various languages, including French and German.

SIDELIGHTS: Fakhraddin Gorgani was a Persian poet who lived and wrote during the eleventh century. Little is known for certain about this writer, but historians and scholars have researched his background as thoroughly as modern resources allow, and as a result have pieced together a vague amount of information that is thought to pertain to him—though in some instances it might very well refer to another individual from that time period. The name Gorgani suggests that the poet was born in the town of Gorgan, or at the very least that his father was from that area, which lies to the east of the Caspian Sea. He was thought to have been a member of the retinue for the ruler of Isfahan during his lifetime, and is also commonly credited with writing the epic poem *Vis and Ramin,* probably at some point between the years 1050 and 1055. A great love story set in rhyming couplets, the poem is considered the first significant romance to be written in Persia. Historically, the work is of great importance as it served as a foundation for much of the romantic poetry that followed in Persia, and was most likely the inspiration for the story of Tristan and Isolde, which is first recorded in Europe approximately a hundred years later.

The story itself is based in the archaic and complex royal marriage customs that were vital in Persia during that time, in which the married queen of Mah, Shahru, receives another offer of marriage, from King Mobad of Marv, which she in turn rejects. However, to soften the blow, she promises that if she should give birth to a girl, she will give her daughter to him to marry instead. When her daughter Vis is old enough to marry, however, Shahru has forgotten her promise to Mobad and gives the girl in marriage to someone else. The back and forth that results from this broken vow illustrates the complexity of the marriage system during that time, and also portrays characters that come to life for the reader in a way that was unusual for the writing of the period.

Vis and Ramin has appeared in various translations through the centuries, most notably in a modern English version that was translated from the Persian by Dick Davis, a noted poet and scholar who used the heroic couplet form to capture the original flow of the language as closely as possible. Ray Olson, in a review for *Booklist,* dubbed the work "a masterpiece of both its author's and its translator's arts."

BIOGRAPHICAL AND CRITICAL SOURCES:

PERIODICALS

Booklist, April 15, 2008, Ray Olson, review of *Vis and Ramin,* p. 20.

Choice: Current Reviews for Academic Libraries, August 1, 2008, W.L. Hanaway, review of *Vis and Ramin,* p. 2147.

ONLINE

Iranian Web site, http://www.iranian.com/ (February 19, 2008), Balatarin Balatarin, review of *Vis and Ramin.*

W.H. Smith Web site, http://www.whsmith.co.uk/ (August 12, 2009), author profile.*

* * *

GORGANI, Fakhraddin Asaad
See GORGANI, Fakhraddin

* * *

GRANN, David 1967-

PERSONAL: Born March 10, 1967; married; children: two. *Education:* Graduated from Connecticut College, 1989; Tufts University, Fletcher School of Law & Diplomacy, M.A. (international relations); Boston University, M.A. (creative writing).

ADDRESSES: Home—New York, NY. *Office*—New Yorker, 4 Times Sq., New York, NY 10036. *E-mail*—davidgrann@gmail.com.

CAREER: New Republic, Washington, DC, senior editor; *The Hill,* Washington, DC, executive editor, 1995-96; *New Yorker,* New York, NY, staff writer, 2003—.

AWARDS, HONORS: Thomas Watson Fellowship.

WRITINGS:

The Lost City of Z: A Tale of Deadly Obsession in the Amazon, Doubleday (New York, NY), 2009.

Contributor to anthologies, including *What We Saw: The Events of September 11, 2001, The Best American Crime Writing* (2004 and 2005 editions), and *The Best American Sports Writing* (2003 and 2006 editions). Contributor to periodicals, including the *Atlantic, Washington Post, Boston Globe, Wall Street Journal, Weekly Standard,* and *New York Times* magazine.

ADAPTATIONS: The Lost City of Z: A Tale of Deadly Obsession in the Amazon has been optioned for film by Brad Pitt's Plan B production company and Paramount Pictures.

SIDELIGHTS: David Grann graduated from Connecticut College and then attended Tufts University's Fletcher School of Law & Diplomacy, where he earned a master's degree in international relations. Grann also holds a master's degree in creative writing from Boston University. Following his academic career, Grann joined the *New Republic* as senior editor. He then served as an executive editor at *The Hill* newspaper. In 2003, he became a staff writer at *New Yorker.* Grann's book *The Lost City of Z: A Tale of Deadly Obsession in the Amazon* was released in 2009. The volume examines the life and disappearance of Percy H. Fawcett. Indeed, as Grann notes in the book, Fawcett believed that a lost city, "Z," existed in the Amazon jungle. He set out in 1925 to find it, only to disappear.

Discussing the book in an online *World Hum* interview with Frank Bures, Grann remarked: "I had always considered myself a disinterested reporter and at least at the outset I intended to simply write a biography about Fawcett and all the people who disappeared and died looking for this ancient city in the Amazon. But after I uncovered a chest full of Fawcett's diaries and logbooks, which held unprecedented clues to what happened to him and the location of the City of Z, I became much more consumed by the mystery and its romantic nature." In another interview for the *Afterword* Web site, Grann told Mark Medley that "the fascination with lost cities seems eternal. I suspect that part of it, like the earlier searches for mythical kingdoms . . . reflects a longing to find some place that is better or richer or more fabulous than the one we inhabit." Grann continued: "I also think there is a deep curiosity about how real civilizations, such as the Incas or Mayans, once flourished and eventually died out." He also commented that Fawcett is one of the more colorful early twentieth-century explorers. "I am not sure if explorers will ever hold the same place in the popular imagination," he observed, "Fawcett's legend once contributed to radio plays, novels . . . , poems, documentaries, movies, stamps, children's stories, comic books, ballads, stage plays, graphic novels, and museum exhibits. . . . [N]ot only geographical circumstances . . . made these figures legends; there was an array of cultural forces as well." Notably, Grann's book includes a great deal of his own impressions as he researches Fawcett, and he told *Publishers Weekly* interviewer Pete Croatto: "I became much more part of the story in a way I never expected, in that the more research I did the more I found myself becoming consumed by it."

Writing about *The Lost City of Z* for the *Cleveland Plain Dealer,* Michael Kroner, noted that "Grann alternates the story of his own research with Fawcett's adventures, chapter by chapter." Kroner added: "By linking himself to Fawcett, the author puts himself into history, emphasizing that not much more is known about the region now than when Fawcett tromped through a century ago." Michiko Kakutani observed in the *New York Times Book Review* that Grann "ends his narrative with a fascinating visit with the archaeologist Michael Heckenberger, who has been excavating what Mr. Grann describes as 'a vast ancient settlement' in the very region where Fawcett is believed to have vanished." Kakutuni concluded, "As for Mr. Grann's book, it reads with all the pace and excitement of a movie thriller and all the verisimilitude and detail of firsthand reportage."

A *Kirkus Reviews* contributor called the book "a colorful tale of true adventure, marked by satisfyingly unexpected twists, turns and plenty of dark portents." Lev Grossman, writing in *Time,* commended Grann's narrative pacing. The reviewer stated: "What keeps you going is the backstory. The theory that the Amazon basin conceals the capital of an advanced civilization has a long history—it's one of those ideas that's just too romantic to die." Mick Herron, in *Geographical,* described the narrative as "all great fun, enhanced by Grann's . . . tendency to fictionalise—the passages set in Victorian London are full of jolly cliches about brothels, blacking factories and newspaper boys crying 'Orrible murder!'" he commented. "This does rather compromise any claim the book—by virtue of its detailed research—might have to being a work of scholarship, but getting on Fawcett's trail is the main business," Herron added, and concluded, "It's a cracking read."

BIOGRAPHICAL AND CRITICAL SOURCES:

PERIODICALS

Archaeology, May-June, 2009, "Lost in the Land of Z," p. 14.

Booklist, November 1, 2008, Keir Graff, review of *The Lost City of Z: A Tale of Deadly Obsession in the Amazon,* p. 4.

Book World, March 8, 2009, Marie Arana, "Lost in the Jungle," p. B7.

Christian Science Monitor, February 26, 2009, Jeremy Kutner, review of *The Lost City of Z,* p. 25.

Cleveland Plain Dealer, March 5, 2009, Michael Kroner, review of *The Lost City of Z.*

Details, January-February, 2009, Timothy Hodler, "Travel Writers Gone Wild," p. 33.

Entertainment Weekly, February 27, 2009, Thom Geier, review of *The Lost City of Z,* p. 61.

Geographical, March, 2009, Mick Herron, "Missing, Presumed Crazy," p. 61.

Kirkus Reviews, December 1, 2008, review of *The Lost City of Z.*

Library Journal, November 1, 2008, review of *The Lost City of Z,* p. 86; June 1, 2009, Risa Getman, review of *The Lost City of Z,* p. 59.

Nation, April 13, 2009, Greg Grandin, "Green Acres," p. 32.

New York Review of Books, May 14, 2009, Joshua Hammer, "Mad Dreams in the Amazon," p. 14.

New York Times, March 22, 2009, Richard B. Woodward, "Armchair Traveler," p. 6(L).

New York Times Book Review, March 1, 2009, Rich Cohen, "On the Road to El Dorado," p. 16(L); March 17, 2009, Michiko Kakutani, "An Explorer Drawn to, and Eventually Swallowed by, the Amazon."

Publishers Weekly, October 13, 2008, review of *The Lost City of Z,* p. 44; November 3, 2008, Pete Croatto, "PW Talks with David Grann: In Search of a Legendary Explorer," p. 48.

Time, March 2, 2009, Lev Grossman, "Jungle Fever," p. 62.

USA Today, January 15, 2009, Jocelyn McClurg, review of *The Lost City of Z,* p. 6D; February 24, 2009, Don Oldenburg, "*Lost City of Z* Follows the Trail of Lost Explorer," p. 7D.

Washington Post, April 12, 2009, Marie Arana, "Lost in the Jungle: *The Lost City of Z* Is David Grann's Tale of an Explorer's Obsession with the Amazon," p. B7.

ONLINE

Afterword, http://network.nationalpost.com/ (March 26, 2009), Mark Medley, author interview.

David Grann Home Page, http://www.davidgrann.com (August 7, 2009).

World Hum, http://www.worldhum.com/ (March 3, 2009), Frank Bures, author interview.

OTHER

Talk of the Nation (broadcast transcript), February 24, 2009, "Explorer's 'Deadly Obsession' with Lost City."*

* * *

GRAY, Tyler

PERSONAL: Male.

ADDRESSES: Office—New York, NY.

CAREER: Writer, journalist, editor. *Blender* magazine, New York, NY, senior editor; appears periodically as pop culture and news commentator on television networks, including ABC, CNN, MSNBC, FOX, and Comedy Central's *The Daily Show with Jon Stewart.*

WRITINGS:

The Hit Charade: Lou Pearlman, Boy Bands, and the Biggest Ponzi Scheme in U.S. History, Collins (New York, NY), 2008.

Contributor to periodicals such as the *New York Times, Esquire, Radar, Men's Journal, New York Daily News, Orlando Sentinel,* and the *St. Petersburg Times.*

SIDELIGHTS: Writer, editor, and journalist Tyler Gray serves as the senior editor for *Blender* magazine, which is based in New York City. He has contributed to numerous periodicals over the course of his career, including the *New York Times, Esquire, Radar, Men's Journal, New York Daily News, Orlando Sentinel,* and the *St. Petersburg Times.* In addition, he makes frequent guest appearances as a commentator on various television networks, such as ABC, CNN, MSNBC, FOX, and Comedy Central's *The Daily Show with Jon Stewart,* talking primarily about the news and pop culture. Gray's debut book, *The Hit Charade: Lou Pearlman, Boy Bands, and the Biggest Ponzi Scheme in U.S. History,* was published in 2008.

In *The Hit Charade,* Gray offers readers a thorough inside look at the rise and fall of Lou Pearlman. Pearlman became known in the 1990s for his deft touch and sharp eye regarding the potential of young male singers, making a fortune through his management of the mega-star boy bands that dominated the pop charts during that period, The Backstreet Boys and 'N Sync. Although these boy bands were initially known for their clean images and relatively wholesome reputations, Pearlman himself was later revealed to be involved in a number of shady operations on the side, including a number of ongoing scams revolving around fake airline companies and accusations of questionable behavior toward the young singers in his charge, including bilking them for half of their royalty money.

Most serious, however, was a long-term investment scam that revolved around false retirement plans, which resulted in investors, including some of Pearlman's own friends and family members, losing a total of approximately 500 million dollars. Over the course of his book, Gray reveals the details of Pearlman's deceptions and the lengths to which he would go in order to make money. He researched Pearlman's life and dealings primarily through interviews with his associates and people who suffered from his schemes, but also interviewed Pearlman himself once while he was in prison. Bill Baars, writing for *Library Journal,* remarked that "this sordid story receives a tabloid-like treatment." A contributor for *Kirkus Reviews* noted that "despite Pearlman's crimes, he comes off as a surprisingly sympathetic figure," and concluded that Gray's book is "a uniquely American story of ambition, kitsch and monstrous appetites." In a review for *Publishers Weekly,* one writer commented that "Gray has a keen eye for business, and he writes fluently."

BIOGRAPHICAL AND CRITICAL SOURCES:

PERIODICALS

Kirkus Reviews, October 1, 2008, review of *The Hit Charade: Lou Pearlman, Boy Bands, and the Biggest Ponzi Scheme in U.S. History.*

Library Journal, October 15, 2008, review of *The Hit Charade,* p. 71.

Publishers Weekly, September 15, 2008, review of *The Hit Charade,* p. 58.

Reference & Research Book News, February 1, 2009, review of *The Hit Charade.*

ONLINE

HarperCollins Web site, http://www.harpercollins.com/ (July 18, 2009), author profile.*

* * *

GREEN, Matthew 1975-

PERSONAL: Born October 17, 1975, in Kingston-upon-Thames, England. *Education:* Graduated from Balliol College, University of Oxford.

ADDRESSES: *Home*—Lagos, Nigeria.

CAREER: Journalist. *Financial Times,* London, England, West African correspondent based in Nigeria; has also worked as journalist for Reuters, 1998—; regular commentator for BBC World Service.

WRITINGS:

The Wizard of the Nile: The Hunt for Africa's Most Wanted, Olive Branch Press (Northampton, MA), 2009.

Contributor to periodicals, including the *Economist, Times* (London, England), *Arena,* and *Esquire.*

SIDELIGHTS: Matthew Green is a British writer and journalist, who was born October 17, 1975, in Kingston-upon-Thames, England, and graduated from Balliol College at the University of Oxford. Over the course of his journalism career, Green has contributed to a number of prominent periodicals, including the *Economist, Times* (London, England), *Arena,* and *Esquire.* He serves as a West Africa correspondent for the *Financial Times,* based in Lagos, Nigeria, and has worked for Reuters as a regular contributor since 1998. Green is the author of *The Wizard of the Nile: The Hunt for Africa's Most Wanted,* a result of his time spent writing and researching in Africa.

The Wizard of the Nile focuses on the role of Joseph Kony, the warlord in charge of the Lord's Resistance Army, which is a pivotal group in the decades-long civil war decimating Uganda. After twenty years, the war continues to ravage the nation, resulting in numerous deaths and causing strife not only within Uganda's own borders, but in the nations that surround it as well. This terrible situation is only worsened by the fact that many of the "soldiers" fighting the battles are in fact mere children, often kidnapped from their families and put to work fighting on behalf of the warlord who snatched them. Kony's underlings are some of the worst offenders, in many instances raping, torturing, and killing untold numbers of people, and the Lord's Resistance Army is in many respects responsible, maintaining the war for so many years, despite the fact that they operate with so many of the kidnapped children in their ranks. The children, in fact, are relatively easily trained, and, though forced, often take to their roles as cold-blooded soldiers with relative ease. While they might take small items over the course of a raid—things that appear trivial and the choices of schoolboys—they are equally capable of helping to capture numerous women to be used as sex slaves. Green took time off from his work as a correspondent to travel to Uganda in search of Kony, hoping to get the inside story. Over the course of his book, he discusses his search, and what he found. Catherine Bond, writing for *New Statesman,* found fault with the result, declaring that "Green's short history of this strange war is an honest and factual account, devoid of the sort of exaggeration and self-aggrandizement to which journalists are prone. But a book isn't just something that's long—it also has to be finely focused, and in all its extraneous detail, *The Wizard of the Nile* shows the gap between what good journalists and good writers do." However, a contributor for *Kirkus Reviews* found Green's book to be "a searching work of investigative, on-the-ground reporting from the front lines of a long-roiling conflict in the heart of Africa," going on to conclude that the volume is "essential for anyone interested in understanding the politics of modern Africa."

BIOGRAPHICAL AND CRITICAL SOURCES:

PERIODICALS

African Business, March 1, 2008, "Searching for Kony: Uganda's Running Sore," p. 72.

Kirkus Reviews, October 1, 2008, review of *The Wizard of the Nile: The Hunt for Africa's Most Wanted.*

Library Journal, November 15, 2008, Rachel Bridgewater, review of *The Wizard of the Nile,* p. 87.

New Statesman, April 14, 2008, "Horror in Uganda," p. 57.

Reference & Research Book News, February 1, 2009, review of *The Wizard of the Nile.*

ONLINE

Matthew Green Home Page, http://www.matthewgreenreports.com (July 18, 2009).*

* * *

GREENBERG, Murray

PERSONAL: Education: Graduated from Brandeis University.

ADDRESSES: Home—Floral Park, NY.

CAREER: Writer, former attorney.

WRITINGS:

Passing Game: Benny Friedman and the Transformation of Football, PublicAffairs (New York, NY), 2008.

SIDELIGHTS: Former attorney Murray Greenberg is an alumnus of Brandeis University in Waltham, Massachusetts. It was through this academic connection that he first came up with the idea of writing his book, *Passing Game: Benny Friedman and the Transformation of Football,* which focuses on the little-known college football player Benny Friedman who played for the University of Michigan during the 1920s, then went on to coach at Brandeis University, and contributed significantly to bringing the sport around to a more modern system of play. Greenberg attended a tribute dinner for Friedman several years before writing his book, an evening that left a lasting impression upon him. Friedman was the son of Russian Jewish immigrants, growing up in Cleveland, Ohio, and like many of the boys in his neighborhood had become interested in sports. His parents did not approve of his new pastime, considering it too noisy and rowdy, and would have far preferred for him to pursue purely intellectual activities. Greenberg points out in an interview with Ron Kaplan for the *New Jersey Jewish News* Web site, that though Jews were generally considered to be intellectuals over athletes, "a lot of young Jewish boys were looking to break out of that way of thinking and smash that stereotype." This attitude among the younger generation led to an increased interest in sports, and football in particular, as it was by far the most physical of the activities popular during that time. Friedman, small in stature, faced a great deal of adversity and ridicule while trying to improve his football skills, and eventually resorted to lifting weights in order to achieve a more appropriately intimidating frame. By the time he got to the University of Michigan, he was a notable player, and it was there that he became well known for his affinity for what was known as the passing game. He was the first player to make the pass an intrinsic part of his playing style, and his focus resulted in a far more exciting style of play overall. His efforts, both as a player over eight years as a professional and later as a coach, helped the up-and-coming National Football League take root, and contributed to the increased popularity of the sport on a national level. However, Friedman was all but forgotten after he retired, inducted into the Hall of Fame only after his death. Greenberg's book helps shine a light on a significant career. A contributor for *Kirkus Reviews* remarked that "Greenberg sets an unimpeachable case on behalf of this essentially unknowable man," and went on to opine that the book "will surprise even those who think they know the game."

BIOGRAPHICAL AND CRITICAL SOURCES:

PERIODICALS

Houston Chronicle, December 28, 2008, "Why Benny Was Forgotten; Personality, Not Religion or Ethnicity, Likely Cost Football Great Friedman His Place in History," p. 15.

Kirkus Reviews, October 1, 2008, review of *Passing Game: Benny Friedman and the Transformation of Football.*

ONLINE

New Jersey Jewish News Web site, http://www.njjewishnews.com/ (November 13, 2008), Ron Kaplan, "Author Takes a Look Back at a Forgotten Hero."*

* * *

GREENWOOD, T. 1969-
(Tammy Greenwood-Stewart, Tammy Greenwood)

PERSONAL: Born 1969, in VT; married Patrick Stewart; children: two daughters.

ADDRESSES: Home—Takoma Park, MD. *Office*—English Department, George Washington University, Rome Hall, 760801 22nd St. N.W., Washington, DC 20052. *E-mail*—stewbalms.@verizon.net.

CAREER: Writer. George Washington University, Washington, DC, teacher of creative writing.

AWARDS, HONORS: Grants from the Sherwood Anderson Foundation, Christopher Isherwood Foundation, and National Endowment for the Arts.

WRITINGS:

NOVELS

Breathing Water, St. Martin's Press (New York, NY), 1999.
Nearer Than the Sky, St. Martin's Press (New York, NY), 2000.
Undressing the Moon, St. Martin's Press (New York, NY), 2002.
Two Rivers, Kensington Publishing (New York, NY), 2009.

Author of a blog.

SIDELIGHTS: Novelist T. Greenwood writes what a *Kirkus Reviews* contributor described as "Northern Gothic" fiction. Set in small towns in northern New England, Greenwood's books explore complex emotional bonds among characters who often harbor dark secrets. Her debut novel, *Breathing Water,* tells the story of Effie Greer, a young woman who returns to her grandmother's home in Vermont to confront the effects of her breakup with Max, a destructive alcoholic whom she left seven years earlier after he negligently caused the death of an eleven-year-old African American girl who had been visiting the family. The return allows Effie to come to terms with the dynamics of her relationship with Max, and to understand how she allowed herself to assume the role of victim. She also becomes able to open herself to the possibility of a more positive relationship with Devin Jackson, a local handyman and artist. Though a *Publishers Weekly* reviewer found the novel occasionally "maudlin" and "platitudinous," the reviewer nevertheless deemed *Breathing Water* a "poignant debut." Similarly, *Booklist* contributor Danise Hoover deemed the book "an impressive first novel."

In *Nearer Than the Sky,* Indie Brown is summoned from her happy existence in the Maine woods back to Arizona, where her sister needs help caring for their mother, who has been hospitalized after a possible suicide attempt. Reluctantly leaving her lover, Peter, behind, India takes charge in Arizona, bringing her mother home from the hospital and organizing affairs. At the same time, she begins to piece together discomfiting clues about her childhood that suggest the presence of mental illness in the family. Believing that being struck by lightning at age four gave her a special psychic sense, Indie tries to recall why her older brother died, and why her sister was so frequently ill as a little girl. What Indie begins to suspect is that their mother suffers from Munchausen syndrome, an illness that causes a person to create the symptoms of illness in herself or others. Calling the novel a "lyrical investigation into the unreliability and elusiveness of memory," a reviewer for *Publishers Weekly* praised Greenwood's skill in creating a story "rich with evocative details about its heroine's inner life."

Undressing the Moon tells the story of Piper Kincaid, a thirty-year-old woman dying of cancer. When Piper was fourteen, her mother ran off with another man, and now Piper relives those years of abandonment as she prepares for her impending death. She dredges up unhappy memories of her mother's betrayal, but also acknowledges an instance in which she wrongly blamed a high school teacher of assault when she was attacked by a group of boys. Pondering whether to accept her mother's offer of reconciliation, Piper decides against it. A contributor to *Kirkus Reviews* described this story as "victimhood in all its glory," while a writer for *Publishers Weekly* considered the book "lyrical [and] delicately affecting."

Set in rural Vermont in 1980, *Two Rivers* explores the devastating consequences of an earlier crime. Harper Montgomery, the railroad worker who narrates the story, is struggling to raise his daughter after his wife died twelve years earlier in a terrible car crash. That same year, as Greenwood shows through flashbacks, Harper was involved in the murder of a black man, and he is still haunted by guilt over that incident. Things begin to change, however, when he saves a pregnant black teenager from a train wreck. She says she is en route to Canada from New Orleans, escaping the man who raped her, and Harper decides to help her. Thus begins the process that allows Harper, finally, to forgive himself for his part in the earlier killing. The novel, said Greenwood in an interview with *Bookreporter.com* writer Alexis Burling, "is, in many ways, an examination of what happens when someone fails to act and that failure has tragic consequences. . . . It's easy to vilify the perpetrators of . . . horrific violence. What's difficult is allowing them, these criminals, to be human. I needed to understand how a real man, a good man, might find himself involved in something so despicable."

A writer for *Kirkus Reviews* considered *Two Rivers* "overwrought," but others assessed the book more favorably. Hailing the book as an "evocative novel of redemption," a *Publishers Weekly* contributor concluded that Greenwood "is a writer of subtle strength."

BIOGRAPHICAL AND CRITICAL SOURCES:

PERIODICALS

Booklist, May 15, 1999, Danise Hoover, review of *Breathing Water,* p. 1667; July 1, 2000, Danise Hoover, review of *Nearer Than the Sky,* p. 2008.

Kirkus Reviews, October 1, 2001, review of *Undressing the Moon,* p. 1383; November 1, 2008, review of *Two Rivers.*

Library Journal, October 1, 2001, Bette-Lee Fox, review of *Undressing the Moon,* p. 140; December 1, 2008, Leslie Patterson, review of *Two Rivers,* p. 110.

Publishers Weekly, April 5, 1999, review of *Breathing Water,* p. 220; July 10, 2000, review of *Nearer Than the Sky,* p. 44; October 22, 2001, review of *Undressing the Moon,* p. 41; October 13, 2008, review of *Two Rivers,* p. 37.

ONLINE

Bookreporter.com, http://www.bookreporter.com/ (July 22, 2009), Alexis Burling, interview with Greenwood.

Fantastic Fiction Web site, http://www.fantasticfiction.co.uk/ (July 22, 2009), Greenwood profile.

Reading Is My Superpower, http://superfastreader.com/ (July 22, 2009), review of *Two Rivers.*

T. Greenwood Home Page, http://www.tgreenwood.com (July 22, 2009).*

* * *

GREENWOOD, Tammy
See GREENWOOD, T.

GREENWOOD-STEWART, Tammy
See GREENWOOD, T.

* * *

GRIFFIN, Bethany

PERSONAL: Married; has children. *Education:* Holds an M.Ed.

ADDRESSES: *Home*—Louisville, KY.

CAREER: English teacher and writer.

WRITINGS:

Handcuffs (young adult novel), Delacorte Press (New York, NY), 2008.

Author maintains a blog at http://bethanygriffin.livejournal.com.

SIDELIGHTS: Bethany Griffin holds a master's degree in education and has worked for several years as an English teacher. Yet, as she explained on her home page: "I didn't ever really give up on writing, I just went through a long period where all I wanted to do was READ. I'd write a paragraph, read a book or two, write another paragraph. And for a long time, all of my creativity was consumed by this teaching gig I'd taken on." Still, she went on, "at some point the creativity reasserted itself. That point shall be known as The Summer of 2005. I wrote my first YA book between that summer and Christmas Vacation. It's around here in a shoe box. . . . Spring 2006, I wrote *Handcuffs.* Then I revised it. I hooked up with the world's greatest critique partners, got an agent (also world's best, but this is getting a little effusive for me), revised some more, my agent sold the book, revised some more." Griffin's young adult novel *Handcuffs* was published in 2008. The book features sixteen-year-old Parker, who is caught by her parents while fooling around with her ex-boyfriend. What follows is Parker's attempts to deal with her parents' disappointment.

In a review on the *All Things Girl* Web site, Melissa A. Bartel stated that "Griffin's story has a starkly realistic tone," but noted that due to its sexual content it is more suitable for mature readers. Bartel concluded that "it's an interesting, well-written book." A reviewer for *Gracetopia* commented that "while the plot is a good one—fast-paced, twisty—it was really the characters that grabbed hold and wouldn't let me leave." A reviewer wrote on the *YA Reads* Web site: "I was biting my nails all the way till the end." The contributor went on to declare that Griffin "captures the essence of adolescence superbly. Her characters are believable, raw, honest and absolutely engaging. Teenage girls everywhere will be able to relate to Parker's pain and angst, her self-doubt and her hormonal desires."

BIOGRAPHICAL AND CRITICAL SOURCES:

PERIODICALS

Bulletin of the Center for Children's Books, December, 2008, Karen Coats, review of *Handcuffs,* p. 154.

Kirkus Reviews, November 15, 2008, review of *Handcuffs.*

School Library Journal, January, 2009, Johanna Lewis, review of *Handcuffs,* p. 102.

Voice of Youth Advocates, February, 2009, Kimberly Paone, review of *Handcuffs,* p. 528.

ONLINE

All Things Girl, http://allthingsgirl.net/ (January 1, 2009), Melissa A. Bartel, review of *Handcuffs.*

Bethany Griffin Home Page, http://www.bethanygriffin.com (August 7, 2009).

Bethany Griffin MySpace Page, http://www.myspace.com/bethanygriffin (August 7, 2009).

Gracetopia, http://gracetopia.wordpress.com/ (February 23, 2009), review of *Handcuffs.*

YA Reads, http://www.yareads.com/ (January 2, 2009), review of *Handcuffs.**

H

HARDING, Paul 1967-

PERSONAL: Born December 19, 1967. *Education:* University of Iowa, M.F.A.

ADDRESSES: *E-mail*—pharding@fas.harvard.edu.

CAREER: University of Iowa, Iowa City, instructor; Harvard University, Cambridge, MA, instructor. Drummer for the band Cold Water Flat.

WRITINGS:

Tinkers, Bellevue Literary Press (New York, NY), 2008.

SIDELIGHTS: Paul Harding is a novelist and writing instructor. He was born December 19, 1967. He earned an M.F.A. in writing from the Iowa Writers' Workshop and taught writing at the University of Iowa and the Harvard Extension School. He lives in the Boston area with his wife and two sons. Harding was a drummer with the band Cold Water Flats and toured the United States and Europe. The music damaged his hearing, leaving him with tinnitus.

In 2008 Harding published *Tinkers,* a fictionalized memoir of his grandfather and great-grandfather. Set in eastern Maine, the story centers on George Washington Crosby, a clock repairman, who is old and dying. On a rented hospital bed set up in his living room, he waits to die with his family around him. As he dips in and out of consciousness, he imagines that his house is falling down around him. The sky is exposed, and George travels up through the roof and back in time seventy years to be reunited with his father, Howard, who abandoned the family when George was twelve.

Howard was a tinker, traveling salesman, and repairman. With his mule-drawn cart at the turn of the century, he traveled the impoverished villages and back roads of Maine fixing pots, delivering babies, transporting supplies, cutting hair, and performing whatever other tasks needed to be done. Howard's secret was that he suffered from epilepsy, a seizure disorder. When his wife was about to have him committed to an institution in an effort to safeguard their children from his epileptic fits, Howard disappeared.

Harding drew on facts and inspiration from his own family history to write the novel. He apprenticed with his grandfather, who repaired clocks. His great-grandfather had epilepsy and left the family when his grandfather was twelve. Harding noted in interviews that although his elderly family members refused to talk about the impoverished life they led in the woods of Maine, they did tell one- and two-sentence anecdotes about the times, such as, "I made it out of the woods and what happened in the woods, stayed in the woods." Harding used these few sentences as the basis of his story, imagining words and sentences that may have come before and after.

Structuring the book as a metaphor of repairing clocks, Harding includes detailed descriptions of the inner workings of clocks as well as images of nature and carefully drawn peripheral characters to populate the book. George was profoundly affected by his father's abandonment, living a ruined life of poverty and despair. With meticulous examination, filled in with imagination, of the life gone by, at the end of his life George works to repair relations with his father.

Harding correlates the precision of time pieces with the ethereal nature of the forests and the people of Maine. The hermit who lives in the woods and survives the harsh winters alone, the few Native Americans who are left to tend to the natural environment around them, the growing corn that soars green and tall in the summer and yields bountiful harvests, and even the lightning strikes that characterize Howard's seizures all fit together with their own precision and logic.

Reviewers found Harding's study of a father-son relationship heartbreaking and life affirming. Donna Seaman wrote in *Booklist,* "Harding has created a rare and beautiful novel of spiritual inheritance and acute psychological and metaphysical suspense." A writer in *Publishers Weekly* noted, "This is an especially gorgeous example of novelistic craftsmanship."

"In Harding's skillful evocation, Crosby's life . . . becomes a mosaic of memories," said a writer in the *New Yorker,* while a writer in *Kirkus Reviews* commented that Harding filled the book with Whitmanesque descriptions of the world and gave shape to "the extraordinary variety in the thoughts of otherwise ordinary men. An evocative meditation on the nonlinear nature of a life."

BIOGRAPHICAL AND CRITICAL SOURCES:

PERIODICALS

Booklist, December 1, 2008, Donna Seaman, review of *Tinkers,* p. 26.

Kirkus Reviews, October 15, 2008, review of *Tinkers.*

Library Journal, October 15, 2008, Josh Cohen, review of *Tinkers,* p. 55.

New Yorker, January 12, 2009, review of *Tinkers,* p. 69.

Publishers Weekly, September 29, 2008, review of *Tinkers,* p. 58.

ONLINE

BookBrowse, http://www.bookbrowse.com/ (December 30, 2008), short author profile.

Bookslut, http://www.bookslut.com/ (July 1, 2009), Michele Filgate, "An Interview with Paul Harding."

Harvard University Summer School Web site, http://www.summer.harvard.edu/ (April 6, 2009), author profile.

Holt Uncensored, http://www.holtuncensored.com/ (March 12, 2009), Fritz Holt, review of *Tinkers;* (April 7, 2009), Fritz Holt, "A Personal Look at 'Tinkers.'"

Rumpus, http://therumpus.net/ (March 10, 2009), James Scott, review of *Tinkers.*

* * *

HARRIS, Jonathan 1961-

PERSONAL: Born 1961.

ADDRESSES: *Office*—Department of History, Royal Holloway, University of London, Egham, Surrey, TW20 0EX, England. *E-mail*—jonathan.harris@rhul.ac.uk.

CAREER: Historian and writer. Royal Holloway College, University of London, London, England, lecturer.

WRITINGS:

Greek Emigrés in the West, 1400-1520, Porphyrogenitus (Camberley, England), 1995.

Byzantium and the Crusades, Hambledon & London (New York, NY), 2003.

(Editor) *Palgrave Advances in Byzantine History,* Palgrave Macmillan (New York, NY), 2005.

Constantinople: Capital of Byzantium, Hambledon Continuum (New York, NY), 2007.

SIDELIGHTS: Jonathan Harris was born in 1961. A historian, he conducts research focusing on the relationship between Byzantium and Western Europe during the Crusades and the Italian Renaissance. He has published extensively on Byzantine history in the later period of 1100-1453 and lectures on Byzantine studies at Royal Holloway College, part of the University of London.

In 2003 Harris published *Byzantium and the Crusades,* part of a series called "Crusader Worlds" that brings the most current research to a wide-ranging audience. In this work Harris explores the complex and often strained relationship between the Byzantine empire and western Europe during the time of the Crusades.

Western, or Latin, powers mistook the Byzantine foreign policy of eschewing conquest in favor of self-preservation as weakness. Byzantine policy was to persuade neighbors to acknowledge the power of the suzerainty, or ruling authority, through negotiations rather than war. This method succeeded in holding off invaders until 1204, when the capital city of Constantinople was sacked by an army of the Fourth Crusade and held for two generations. Relations between Byzantium and the West grew ever more hostile due to cultural differences and contrary religious, political, and military agendas.

Byzantium and the Crusades was praised for its combination of thorough research and accessibility by readers. James A. Brundage commented in *History: Review of New Books* that the book "is a work of synthesis and interpretation. Harris tells a lively story and gracefully argues his case." Gilbert Taylor remarked in *Booklist,* "Assured and fluid, Harris perceptively narrates events in this tempting presentation for the history buff."

"On the level of narrative, Harris provides a well-written account with considerable detail for a volume of this size. He introduces his work with two chapters that set forth his approach. Readers will find his description of Constantinople rich and fascinating, his view of the imperial office and administration informative," wrote James M. Powell in *Church History.*

Paul Crawford noted in the *Historian* that "Harris's presentation of events is fascinating, compelling, and stimulating, and if one is stimulated to argue with him, then the book is surely still successful. The author, in *Byzantium and the Crusades,* offers both instruction and pleasure. Indeed, he provides a template for how to incorporate both into one work of history."

Harris published *Constantinople: Capital of Byzantium* in 2007. The book provides an overview of the famous Byzantine capital from its foundation by the Roman emperor Constantine in 324 to its conquest and downfall by the Ottoman Turks in 1453. Harris focuses the story of the city on the unsurpassed splendor of its heyday around 1200, providing detailed descriptions of the political intrigues and maneuvers of the elite class, the layout and furnishings of the imperial palace and other adorned buildings, the trade the city amassed due to its strategic location at the crossroads of Europe and Asia, and the pottery and expertly crafted goods it produced.

In 1204 the city was sacked during the Fourth Crusade. Despite the city's loss of population and descent from its former magnificence, Harris argues that Byzantium was not stagnant during its last few hundred years and remained a center of wealth and politics. The book ends with the city's fall to an Ottoman Turkish army in 1453.

Reviewers praised the book's readability. As Jay Freeman noted in *Booklist,* "Harris provides a compact, easily digestible history of the city up to the Ottoman conquest in 1453." Wrote William Caraher in *History: Review of New Books,* "Harris's book tends heavily toward narrative, using short, vivid, descriptive vignettes to present the various aspects of urban society. Only rarely does Harris deal directly with primary sources in an explicit way." Richard Fraser, commenting in *Library Journal,* called the work "a readable, informative, and vivid book, offering an evocative picture of the city."

BIOGRAPHICAL AND CRITICAL SOURCES:

PERIODICALS

American Historical Review, October, 2004, Norman Housley, review of *Byzantium and the Crusades,* p. 1293.

Booklist, May 15, 2003, Gilbert Taylor, review of *Byzantium and the Crusades,* p. 1636; December 1, 2007, Jay Freeman, review of *Constantinople: Capital of Byzantium,* p. 14.

Choice: Current Reviews for Academic Libraries, March, 2004, K.W. Harl, review of *Byzantium and the Crusades,* p. 1353; December, 2008, N. Bihasa, review of *Constantinople,* p. 759.

Church History, June, 2005, James M. Powell, review of *Byzantium and the Crusades,* p. 355.

Historian, fall, 2005, Paul Crawford, review of *Byzantium and the Crusades,* p. 567.

History: Review of New Books, winter, 2004, James A. Brundage, review of *Byzantium and the Crusades,* p. 74; fall, 2007, William Caraher, review of *Constantinople,* p. 30.

Journal of Ecclesiastical History, July, 2004, Jonathan Shepard, review of *Byzantium and the Crusades,* p. 575.

Library Journal, November 15, 2007, Richard Fraser, review of *Constantinople,* p. 69.

ONLINE

Royal Holloway University of London Web site, http://rhul.ac.uk/ (August 8, 2009), author profile.

* * *

HART, Peter 1955-

PERSONAL: Born January 10, 1955; married Polly Napper; children: Lily, Ruby. *Education:* Liverpool University, 1973-76; Crewe & Alsager College, postgraduate teaching course, 1976-77; Liverpool Polytechnic, postgraduate librarianship, 1979-80.

ADDRESSES: E-mail—pmhart@btinternet.com.

CAREER: Imperial War Museum Sound Archive, London, England, oral historian, 1981-2008.

WRITINGS:

(With Nigel Steel) *Defeat at Gallipoli,* Papermac (London, England), 1995.

To the Last Round: The South Notts Hussars, 1939-1942, Leo Cooper/Pen & Sword Books (Barnsley, South Yorkshire, England), 1996.

(With Nigel Steel) *Tumult in the Clouds: The British Experience of the War in the Air, 1914-1918,* Hodder & Stoughton (London, England), 1997.

At the Sharp End: From Le Paradis to Kohima: 2nd Battalion, the Royal Norfolk Regiment, Cooper (Barnsley, South Yorkshire, England), 1998.

The Heat of the Battle: The 16th Battalion Durham Light Infantry, 1943-1945, L. Cooper (London, England), 1999.

(With Nigel Steel) *Passchendaele: The Sacrificial Ground,* Cassell (London, England), 2000.

Somme Success: The Royal Flying Corps and the Battle of the Somme, 1916, L. Cooper (Barnsley, South Yorkshire, England), 2001.

(With Nigel Steel) *Jutland, 1916: Death in the Grey Wastes,* Cassell Military (London, England), 2003.

Bloody April: Slaughter in the Skies over Arras, 1917, Weidenfeld & Nicolson (London, England), 2005.

The Somme, Weidenfeld & Nicolson (London, England), 2005, published as *The Somme: The Darkest Hour on the Western Front,* Pegasus Books (New York, NY), 2009.

Aces Falling: War above the Trenches, Sterling (London, England), 2007.

1918: A Very British Victory, Weidenfeld & Nicolson (London, England), 2008.

SIDELIGHTS: Peter Hart is former oral historian at the Imperial War Museum Sound Archive in London, England. He has written several works on British military history, including such regimental accounts as *To the Last Round: The South Notts Hussars, 1939-1942* and *The Heat of the Battle: The 16th Battalion Durham Light Infantry, 1943-1945.* Much of his work focuses on the British military experience in World War I. These include several books on aerial warfare, which, because of advances in aviation technology, became a major component of military strategy in the early twentieth century. *Tumult in the Clouds: The British Experience of the War in the Air, 1914-1918,* written with Nigel Steel, draws on first-person accounts to present a composite portrait of those who served in the Royal Flying Corps. *Somme Success: The Royal Flying Corps and the Battle of the Somme, 1916* focuses particularly on the Somme offensive, and *Aces Falling: War above the Trenches* examines changes in aerial warfare strategy from the spring of 1918 to the end of the war. Until early 1918, the military used planes in order to take aerial photos for reconnaissance; actual air combat, in the earlier phases of the war, had been conducted much like cavalry battles, with champion flying aces challenging each other in daring dogfights that often won them romanticized acclaim. But in order to support its huge ground offensive in the spring of 1918, Germany ordered its pilots to fly ground attack missions. The resulting rise in fatalities took a significant toll on pilots' morale. Hart also explains that, because pilots often flew at high altitudes in open cockpits without oxygen, they suffered consequent health effects.

Hart's *The Somme,* published in the United States as *The Somme: The Darkest Hour on the Western Front,* received considerable critical attention. *Washington Post Book World* reviewer Robert Bateman described the book as a "memorial" to the men who fought in this 1916 battle, a military campaign of epic carnage. The battle of the Somme, launched in response to the crushing losses suffered by the French army at the ongoing battle of Verdun, began on July 1, 1916. On that first day alone the British army sustained 57,470 casualties; of these, 19,240 soldiers were killed—the worst losses ever suffered by the British army in a single day. Continuing over several more weeks in what could more accurately be described as a series of battles, the Somme offensive finally ended in November, 1916, with British losses numbering 131,000 dead and total casualties at a staggering 419,654. The French army suffered some 204,253 casualties, with German casualties estimated at between 230,000 and 450,000. Though the result of the campaign was not a clear-cut victory, the Allies did gain some ground, and historians have argued that the Somme laid the groundwork for the eventual Allied victory in the war.

The Somme has come to be seen as a carnival of slaughter precipitated by stubborn and incompetent military leaders. Though Hart acknowledges the staggering scope of the battlefield losses, he argues that the campaign was more complex than this stereotype admits. As reviewer Alan Judd observed in the *Spectator,* "No one had fought a war like this before and no British commanders had any experience of fighting a battle on the scale of the Somme." Hart takes a relatively sympathetic view of Somme commander Sir Douglas Haig, who had not been able to choose the time and place for the offensive but was ordered to conduct it under inauspicious conditions. Hart says that Haig and his generals made many mistakes, but that they understood that victory could only come through a war of attrition. Though the commanders "may have been unimaginative," he writes, "they were definitely ruthless when required, but above all they were hard, practical men and they were entirely right."

As Hart makes clear, the military advantage in the campaign lay with the German army in their defensive position. The attacking troops had to try to advance against three lines of solid defensive trenches, constant machine gun and artillery fire, miles of barbed wire, and the threat of nerve gas. British command had hoped that their artillery would be enough to disable the German army, and were unprepared for the relentless fire that the infantry soldiers drew as soon as they charged out of their trenches into no-man's-land. Hart, wrote *Boston Globe* reviewer Chuck Leddy, "does an outstanding job explaining the strategy of the Franco-British alliance, and an even better job detailing the lethal realities of the World War I battlefield."

Quoting extensively from accounts of soldiers in the field, *The Somme* reveals the horrors under which soldiers fought in the campaign. Veterans mention the squalid conditions in the sodden trenches, and describe how they lay facedown in mud with bullets filling the air and their comrades dead or dying all around them. The author's use of these first-person accounts, wrote Judd, is "vivid and varied, never less than compelling, and it amounts to the most comprehensive and insightful account of the vast tragedy of the Somme that I have read." *New York Times Book Review* contributor Max Boot also praised *The Somme* highly, observing that "Hart superbly depicts these months of brutal combat in all their complexity."

One of Hart's major points is that, despite the view of the Somme as an epic blunder, it is "inane to adopt the morbid sentimentality of portraying the men who took part as helpless victims. . . . On the contrary, many were actively looking forward to the moment when they could finally prove themselves as fully-fledged 'warriors.'" Indeed, the author includes accounts from soldiers who were able to consider themselves victors.

While some reviewers expressed disappointment that *The Somme* does not give equal weight to the experiences of German soldiers, they rated the book as an important and superbly written account of the British side of the campaign. The book, wrote Bateman, "brings to life the men who fought at the Somme in an accurate and precisely detailed history of one of the most gut-wrenchingly obscene desecrations of humanity our species ever perpetrated upon itself."

BIOGRAPHICAL AND CRITICAL SOURCES:

BOOKS

Hart, Peter, *The Somme,* Weidenfeld & Nicolson (London, England), 2005.

PERIODICALS

Booklist, October 15, 2007, Gilbert Taylor, review of *Aces Falling: War above the Trenches,* p. 22; December 15, 2008, Roland Green, review of *The Somme,* p. 15.

Boston Globe, February 20, 2009, Chuck Leddy, review of *The Somme.*

Contemporary Review, May 1, 2003, review of *Jutland, 1916: Death in the Grey Wastes,* p. 319; October 1, 2005, review of *Bloody April: Slaughter in the Skies over Arras, 1917,* p. 250; June 22, 2008, review of *Aces Falling,* p. 267.

Esprit De Corps, April 1, 2006, Norm Shannon, review of *Bloody April,* p. 44.

History Today, September 1, 2008, Nigel Jones, "1918: A Very British Victory," p. 64.

Infantry Magazine, January 1, 2000, Harold E. Raugh, review of *The Heat of the Battle: The 16th Battalion Durham Light Infantry, 1943-1945.*

Kirkus Reviews, November 1, 2008, review of *The Somme.*

Library Journal, February 1, 2009, Jim Doyle, review of *The Somme,* p. 80.

New York Times Book Review, January 4, 2009, Max Boot, review of *The Somme,* p. 17.

Publishers Weekly, November 3, 2008, review of *The Somme,* p. 52.

Spectator, July 9, 2005, Alan Judd, review of *The Somme,* p. 37.

Times Literary Supplement, January 12, 2001, Michael Carver, review of *Passchendaele: The Sacrificial Ground,* p. 36.

Washington Post Book World, March 22, 2009, Robert Bateman, review of *The Somme,* p. 7.

ONLINE

Peter Hart Home Page, http://peterhartmilitary.com (July 24, 2009).

* * *

HAWORTH, Danette

PERSONAL: Born in Battle Creek, MI; daughter of an Air Force recruiter; married Steve Haworth; children: three. *Education:* Earned bachelor's degree in English.

ADDRESSES: Home—Orlando, FL. *E-mail*—dhaworthbooks@yahoo.com.

CAREER: Author. Worked as a technical writer, a travel writer for an automobile club, and a freelance writer and editor.

MEMBER: Society of Children's Book Writers and Illustrators.

WRITINGS:

Violet Raines Almost Got Struck by Lightning (novel), Walker (New York, NY), 2008.

The Summer of Moonlight Secrets (novel), Walker (New York, NY), 2010.

Me and Jack (novel), Walker (New York, NY), 2011.

Also contributor of short stories to periodicals and online publications.

SIDELIGHTS: A former technical writer and travel writer, Danette Haworth is the author of *Violet Raines Almost Got Struck by Lightning,* a sensitive coming-of-age tale. "When I got a hold of Violet, she was so complete, so real, I could have dropped her into any situation and I would have known exactly how she would react," Haworth remarked to *Writers Inspired* online interviewer Mary Jo Campbell. "Boy, was she feisty! I wanted to come up with a story that would be a match for her."

Haworth knew from a young age that she wanted to be a writer. "My sister and I used to sit in my grandma's basement and write volumes of poetry," she told Courtney Summers in an online interview, adding, "I created all sorts of comic books featuring Peter Pan; they make me laugh when I look at them now, but they did actually contain conflict and resolution (and a cliff-hanger with Captain Hook raising his sword shouting, 'I'll get you, Pan!')." Haworth attempted her first novel while in seventh grade, took creative writing courses throughout high school, and graduated from college with a degree in English. As she related to Summers, "My first professional job was as a technical writer and though that might sound a bit dry, I found it very interesting. It was also weird that I could edit these huge reports discussing DIS and ET without knowing the engineering behind it." She later found work as a travel writer with an automobile club. "In this new job," she told Summers, "I worked with ten or eleven other editors. Oh! It was wonderful. We could use our big words with each other. Lunchtime conversations were most erudite and quite lofty. I loved it!"

Haworth also began writing short stories and submitting them to periodicals. "When I had a piece published in a national magazine," she recalled to *Writing for Children and Teens* contributor Cynthea Liu, "I finally felt like a 'real writer.' Even that wasn't enough. I wanted to write a book. I started reading books on the craft of writing, researching writing Web sites, and connecting to other writers." The inspiration for Haworth's debut novel came from her mother's childhood experiences. "I thought I was going to write an adult book, a kind of mother/daughter thing with issues," she related to Sandy Nawrot in an online interview. "Then Violet walked in one day and took over! She came to me as a complete character, her attitude, her looks, her accent; she even brought her friends with her!"

Set in the small, backwoods town of Mitchell Hammock, Florida, *Violet Raines Almost Got Struck by Lightning* centers on the title character, a spunky eleven-year-old who still enjoys playing with dolls and exploring the riverbank near her home. When Melissa Gold arrives in town, Violet finds that her best friend, Lottie, has taken an interest in the mature, tough-talking newcomer, which brings dramatic changes to Violet and Lottie's relationship. "Violet passes through the last doors of childhood and into the uncertain entryway of junior high with acute sensitivity," D. Maria LaRocco commented in *School Library Journal,* and a contributor in *Kirkus Reviews* observed that readers will appreciate Haworth's "competent management of such crucial tween issues as best friends, fidelity and impending maturity."

BIOGRAPHICAL AND CRITICAL SOURCES:

PERIODICALS

Bulletin of the Center for Children's Books, October, 2008, Deborah Stevenson, review of *Violet Raines Almost Got Struck by Lightning,* p. 73.

Kirkus Reviews, August 15, 2008, review of *Violet Raines Almost Got Struck by Lightning.*

School Library Journal, October, 2008, D. Maria LaRocco, review of *Violet Raines Almost Got Struck by Lightning,* p. 148.

ONLINE

Courtney Summers Web log, http://courtneysummers.ca/blog/ (October 19, 2007), "Interview with Danette Haworth."

Danette Haworth Home Page, http://www.danettehaworth.com (November 1, 2009).

Danette Haworth Web log, http://summerfriend.blogspot.com/ (November 1, 2009).

Jillian Clemmons Web site, http://jillianclemmons.com/ (May 15, 2009), "Interview with Danette Haworth, Author of *Violet Raines Almost Got Struck by Lightning.*"

Sandy Nawrot Web log, http://sandynawrot.blogspot.com/ (March 18, 2009), "An Interview with Danette Haworth, Author of *Violet Raines Almost Got Struck by Lightning.*"

Writers Inspired Web log, http://writerinspired.wordpress.com/ (May 26, 2009), Mary Jo Campbell, "Book Blog Tour: Danette Haworth, Author of *Violet Raines Almost Got Struck by Lightning.*"

Writing for Children and Teens Web site, http://www.writingforchildrenandteens.com/ (June 19, 2008), Cynthea Liu, "Authors on the Verge: Meet Danette Haworth, Middle-Grade Novelist."

* * *

HAYASHI, Seiichi 1945-

PERSONAL: Born March 7, 1945, in Japan.

ADDRESSES: *Home*—Japan.

CAREER: Illustrator, animator, and mangaka.

WRITINGS:

Hayashi Seiichi Sakuhinshu, Seirindo (Tokyo, Japan), 1972.

Red Colored Elegy, translated by Taro Nettleton, Drawn & Quarterly (Montreal, Quebec, Canada), 2008.

ADAPTATIONS: Red Colored Elegy was adapted as an anime film directed by the author, 2007.

SIDELIGHTS: Seiichi Hayashi, born March 4, 1945, is known as an illustrator, an animator, and the creator of mature and sophisticated avant-garde manga. Manga is a form of illustration that utilizes dynamic black- and-white cartoon panels to tell a story. Extremely popular among Japanese audiences of all ages and interests, manga, since its resurgence after World War II, has been strongly influenced by American comic books, but reflects the cultural and aesthetic traditions of Japan. At the end of the twentieth century, manga morphed into anime, the video form of manga designed for television and movies.

Hayashi originally produced *Red Colored Elegy* around 1970. The 1960s had been an unsettling time for the Japanese people, with political upsets and emerging cultural shifts that seemed to be moving the country to a promising future. The economic downturn that subsequently took over the country led to many expressions of angst among the artists of the time, and a youth culture developed that showed confusion and disillusionment regarding their view of themselves and the world around them. *Red Colored Elegy* reflects this state of mind and is credited with taking manga to a new level of artistic expression.

The story is about a young couple, Ichiro and Sachiko. Both are artists working in unsatisfying jobs, but they have no ambition and live an angst-ridden, depressed life together. Ichiro spends his time sleeping, drinking, smoking, and fighting with Sachiko, while she performs the practical drudgeries of housekeeping. Sachiko's parents want to arrange a marriage for her, but she is uninterested. She is lost in a male-dominated world and can see no way forward and no choices that appeal to her. The two attempt a relationship, but it is half-hearted. Although they want to escape the strictures of their culture and create meaning for themselves, they seem stuck and unable to move beyond a restless and dissatisfied status quo.

What makes *Red Colored Elegy* unique among other manga is Hayashi's style. The story is not so much told as suggested. The faces of the protagonists are always hidden or drawn as incomplete, the backgrounds blank, with the merest indicators of the surrounding space. Hayashi presents an elided and elliptical story line, with little dialogue and simple drawings, as though he has stripped down the characters and their world to the barest essentials. The careful manner in which he places text, characters, lines, contextual objects, and the conjunction of panels serves more to create a mood than to narrate a series of events. This is very different from common forms of manga, which feature detailed drawings of the characters engaged in energetic activities in service to a linear story line. Hayashi's characters, by contrast, live in internal, unexpressed introspection, as he makes clear with the artful manipulation of his pen. An anime version of *Red Colored Elegy* was produced in 2007, directed by the Hayashi.

Although *Red Colored Elegy* was published in the United States many decades after its original publication in Japan, reviewers were quick to see its historical significance as well as to express appreciation for Hayashi's delicate and subtle artwork. The reviewer for *Drawn & Quarterly* wrote, "The quiet melancholy lives of a young couple struggling to make ends meet are beautifully captured in this poetic masterpiece." "What is clear is the power and mastery of Hayashi's art," declared the reviewer for *Completely Futile,* and Eddie Campbell, in his review for *Fate of the Artist,* pronounced it "a good read." In a review for *Anthem,* Nik Mercer commented, "Hayashi's genius is that he was able to essentially pare down his manga story to its bare minimum—if he removed any more, it would truly be a blank slate—without losing the raw emotive power it has."

BIOGRAPHICAL AND CRITICAL SOURCES:

PERIODICALS

Booklist, May 15, 2008, Ray Olson, review of *Red Colored Elegy,* p. 28.

Publishers Weekly, June 2, 2008, review of *Red Colored Elegy,* p. 35.

ONLINE

Anime News Network, http://www.animenewsnetwork.com/ (July 30, 2009), listing of staff for anime version of *Red Colored Elegy.*

Anthem, http://www.anthemmagazine.com/ (August 1, 2008), Nik Mercer, "Seiichi Hayashi's *Red Colored Elegy.*

Completely Futile, http://completelyfutile.blogspot.com/ (May 18, 2004), "The Manga Corner: Seiichi Hayashi."

Drawn & Quarterly, http://www.drawnandquarterly.com/ (July 30, 2009), review of *Red Colored Elegy.*

Fate of the Artist, http://eddiecampbell.blogspot.com/ (August 27, 2008), Eddie Campbell, review of *Red Colored Elegy.*

Kurutta, http://kurutta.blogspot.com/ (May 1, 2009), drawings by author.

Madinkbeard, http://madinkbeard.com/ (November 2, 2008), review of *Red Colored Elegy.*

Village Voice, http://www.villagevoice.com/ (November 30, 2004), Ed Halter, "In the Realm of the Senses: Sampling Japan's Avant-Garde."*

* * *

HIGGINS, Kristan

PERSONAL: Married; children: two. *Education:* College of the Holy Cross, Worcester, MA, B.A. *Hobbies and other interests:* Baseball, bicycling, running, and baking.

ADDRESSES: *E-mail*—k.higgins@snet.net.

CAREER: Copywriter and author.

AWARDS, HONORS: Romance Writers of America, RITA Award for Best Single Title Contemporary Romance, 2008, for *Catch of the Day.*

WRITINGS:

Fools Rush In, Harlequin (Don Mills, Ontario, Canada), 2006.

Catch of the Day, Harlequin (Don Mills, Ontario, Canada), 2007.

Just One of the Guys, Harlequin (Don Mills, Ontario, Canada), 2008.

Too Good to Be True, Harlequin (Don Mills, Ontario, Canada), 2009.

SIDELIGHTS: Kristan Higgins is a copywriter turned author who lives in Connecticut. She earned a B.A. in English from the College of the Holy Cross in Worcester, Massachusetts. She worked as a copywriter until she got married and had children, when she began writing romance novels about women finding love and entangling themselves in opposites-attract situations. Higgins wrote on her home page. "I love to write books about relationships, since the search for love and security is one of the driving forces of life."

Higgins's first romance novel was the 2006 title *Fools Rush In.* In the story physician Millie returns to her home on Cape Cod and pursues her childhood crush, Joe. In her efforts to learn about him, she stalks him and then undergoes a makeover, loses weight, and gets a new wardrobe. When fantasies and wishes about Joe do not turn out the way she had planned, Millie turns to her sister's ex-husband, Sam.

Writing in *Romance Reader,* Shirley Lyons commented, "I disliked this heroine through much of the book. . . . Hopefully [Higgins's] second book will have more likable and sympathetic characters." However, Susan Mobley in *Romantic Times Online* called the book a "pleasant, fairly lighthearted romance."

In 2007 Higgins published her second romantic comedy, *Catch of the Day.* In the book Maggie, owner and operator of a diner in a small, gossipy town in Maine, is the focus of good-hearted joking when her romantic disasters become public knowledge. Maggie's search for a man reaches a desperate level when she starts to eye the local priest. But before things get uncomfortable, the priest turns matchmaker for Maggie. Along comes Malone, a reclusive lobsterman of few words; he and talkative Maggie seem like an odd pair.

Marilyn Weigel wrote in *Romantic Times Online* that "Higgins has crafted a touching story brimming with smart dialogue, sympathetic characters, [and] an engaging narrative." *Catch of the Day* won the 2008 Romance Writers of America RITA Award for Best Single Title Contemporary Romance.

Higgins next published *Just One of the Guys* in 2008. The romance novel tells the story of Chastity, a newspaper editor in upstate New York with four firefighter brothers. In her thirties and tired of feeling like one of the guys, she goes in search of a husband. The man who wants her is a handsome surgeon. The man she wants is firefighter Trevor who thinks of her as just a friend.

The story is infused with slapstick, ribald humor, and oddball subplots, such as Chastity's divorced parents and a receptionist at the newspaper who sabotages her. *Just One of the Guys* received four stars from *Romantic Times Online* magazine. Whitney Kate Sullivan wrote in *Romantic Times Online,* "Higgins's latest [book] is packed full of drama." A writer in *Publishers Weekly* commented, "Higgins provides an amiable romp that ends with a satisfying lump in the throat."

In 2009 Higgins published *Too Good to Be True,* a romance about Grace, whose fiancé left her three weeks before their wedding and is now dating her younger sister, Natalie. When her family hounds her to find another man, she gives them what they want. Her new beau is handsome, charming, a successful surgeon, and almost too good to be true. In fact, he is; she made him up. Meanwhile the charming Callahan moves in next door. She learns that he is an ex-convict, certainly not a boyfriend her family would find acceptable. Annette Elton wrote in *Romantic Times Online,* "Higgins has a unique and fresh writing style that captures your heart and imagination." The book was "cheeky, cute, and satisfying," according to Hilary Hatton in *Booklist.*

BIOGRAPHICAL AND CRITICAL SOURCES:

PERIODICALS

Booklist, February 15, 2009, Hilary Hatton, review of *Too Good to Be True,* p. 42.

Publishers Weekly, July 7, 2008, review of *Just One of the Guys,* p. 43.

ONLINE

About Books, http://www.norarobertsismyqueen.com/ (September 13, 2008), review of *Fools Rush In.*

All about Romance, http://www.likesbooks.com/ (August 9, 2009), Abi Bishop, review of *Fools Rush In.*

Dear Author, http://dearauthor.com/ (September 19, 2008), review of *Catch of the Day.*

Fresh Fiction, http://freshfiction.com/ (August 9, 2009), author profile.

Kristan Higgins Home Page, http://www.kristanhiggins.com (August 9, 2009), author profile.

Love Romance Passion, http://www.loveromancepassion.com/ (July 8, 2009), review of *Too Good to Be True.*

Romance Reader, http://www.theromancereader.com/ (August 9, 2009), Shirley Lyons, review of *Fools Rush In.*

Romantic Times Online, http://www.romantictimes.com/ (August 9, 2009), Annette Elton, review of *Too Good to Be True;* Whitney Kate Sullivan, review of *Just One of the Guys;* Susan Mobley, review of *Fools Rush In;* Marilyn Weigel, review of *Catch of the Day.*

S. Krishna's Books, http://www.skrishnasbooks.com/ (April 20, 2009), review of *Too Good to Be True.*

* * *

HOLLINGTON, Kris

PERSONAL: Male.

ADDRESSES: *Home*—London, England. *Agent*—Andrew Lownie Literary Agency, Ltd., 36 Great Smith St., London SW1P 3BU, England. *E-mail*—info@assassinology.org.

CAREER: Writer and investigative journalist. Has also worked as a sales assistant, a bicycle stunt rider, a fire juggler, a London bike courier, a radio presenter, and a magazine columnist.

WRITINGS:

Diamond Geezers: The Inside Story of the Crime of the Millennium, Michael O'Mara (London, England), 2004.

Wolves, Jackals, and Foxes: The Assassins That Changed History, St. Martin's Press (New York, NY), 2007, published as *How to Kill: The Definitive History of the Assassin,* Century (London, England), 2007.

(With Brian Paddick) *Line of Fire: The Autobiography of Britain's Most Controversial Policeman,* Simon & Schuster (London, England), 2008.

(With Harry Keeble) *Crack House,* Pocket Books (New York, NY), 2009.

(With Harry Keeble) *Baby X: Britain's Child Abusers Brought to Justice,* Pocket Books (London, England), 2010.

(With Cameron Addicott) *Narco Warrior,* Michael Joseph (London, England), 2010.

Contributor to newspapers and periodicals, including the *Sunday Times, Guardian, Mail on Sunday, News of the World, Evening Standard, Arena,* and *Loaded.*

SIDELIGHTS: Kris Hollington is an author and investigative journalist living in London, England, who focuses on international crime and assassination. His books include *Diamond Geezers: The Inside Story of the Crime of the Millennium,* published in 2004, and *Line of Fire: The Autobiography of Britain's Most Controversial Policeman.* With his 2007 work, *Wolves, Jackals, and Foxes: The Assassins That Changed History* (published in England as *How to Kill: The Definitive History of the Assassin*), Hollington presents "a history of the late 20th century punctuated by gunshots," according to Greg Woolf in London's *Sunday Telegraph.* Hollington provides an encyclopedic account of high-profile assassinations or assassination attempts. The book speculates on the death of Joseph Stalin, the failed 1950 attempt on President Harry Truman, the John F. Kennedy assassination, the assassination of Martin Luther King, the attempt on Pope John Paul II, and attempts on presidents Richard Nixon, Jimmy Carter, Ronald Reagan, and George W. Bush. Among celebrity assassinations is that of John Lennon, killed by a stalking fan, Mark Chapman. There are also lesser-known events, such as a failed 1974 skyjacking attempted by the Black Panther Samuel Byck, and the poison-umbrella assassin Francesco Giullino. Hollington goes into exhaustive detail, describing not only motive but also a great variety of means, from exploding telephones to bullets made of teeth to a urine bomb. Hollington also shows how many of these assassinations had a profound effect on contemporary history, for example the killing of Prime Minister Patrice Lumumba of the Congo, who was beaten to death in a plot implicating the CIA and Belgian operatives. There were also the unintended consequences of assassination, especially when state-sponsored. The rise of Saddam Hussein, for example, was bolstered in large part by his early work as an assassin for Egyptian and U.S. intelligence agencies. Hollington further classifies the assassins into three categories: jackals, who are the paid professionals; foxes, the amateurs, whose killing is for some cause they feel passionately about; and the wolves, the loners desperately seeking fame.

In an interview with Neal Conan of National Public Radio, Hollington noted that a full one-third of all assassins manage to escape after their crimes. While some want the fame that comes with committing a spectacular crime, "not all of them want notoriety . . . you know, they do end up in jail. . . . They don't get much chance to bask in glory except perhaps in a very limited circle." Hollington also noted in this interview that "they do tend to be caught and put away, and largely forgotten about, so certainly they don't get a public voice." Asked if he had met an assassin during the course of his research, Hollington replied: "I have met some—I have met—a paid hitman in London and that was a very scary experience I have to say . . . the paid hitmen tend to be very different . . . people who assassinate presidents, they tend to be either critical or, you know, just plain crazy. The hitmen who were paid . . . they're focusing usually on the criminals because they're being paid by criminals, too . . . the professional hitman is a very, very rare, breed in and outside of the world of criminality."

Hollington's book won praise on both sides of the Atlantic. Writing for the *Euro Crime* Web site, Amanda Brown called the work "a gripping walk through the last 60 years of history and how assassinations can and have changed the world." Reviewing the American edition, *Booklist* contributor David Pitt felt that *Wolves, Jackals, and Foxes* would "appeal to a wide spectrum of readers, from political-science students to history buffs to thriller and true-crime fans." For a *Publishers Weekly* reviewer, the same book was "a riveting glimpse of random and sanctioned killing."

When asked about his writing process and interest in writing, Hollington told *CA:* "My agent sends me people with the most amazing stories to tell. I start at 6 a.m. and try to get a thousand words done before breakfast, then whatever happens, happens. Although it is the best job in the world, being an author is not as stress-free as you'd imagine. I love all my books equally. The 'best' one is always the one that is most recently published. The hope I have for my books is that they will thrill, entertain and enlighten."

BIOGRAPHICAL AND CRITICAL SOURCES:

PERIODICALS

Booklist, July 1, 2008, David Pitt, review of *Wolves, Jackals, and Foxes: The Assassins That Changed History,* p. 22.

Bookseller, February 16, 2007, review of *Crack House,* p. 15.

Publishers Weekly, June 23, 2008, review of *Wolves, Jackals, and Foxes,* p. 50.

Sunday Telegraph (London, England), June 28, 2007, Greg Woolf, review of *How to Kill: The Definitive History of the Assassin.*

ONLINE

Andrew Lownie Literary Agency Web site, http://www.andrewlownie.co.uk/ (July 8, 2009), "Kris Hollington."

Assassinology, http://www.assassinology.org/ (July 8, 2009), Kris Hollington, "Near Death of a President."

Euro Crime, http://www.eurocrime.co.uk/ (July 1, 2007), Terry Halligan, review of *How to Kill;* (March 1, 2009), Amanda Brown, review of *How to Kill.*

Macmillan Web site, http://us.macmillan.com/ (July 8, 2009), "Kris Hollington."

Random House Web site, http://www.randomhouse.co.uk/ (July 8, 2009), "Kris Hollington."

Screenjabber, http://screenjabber.com/ (July 8, 2009), "Interview: 'Hitman' Kris Hollington."

Simon & Schuster Web site, http://authors.simonandschuster.co.uk/ (July 8, 2009), "Kris Hollington."

OTHER

National Public Radio, August 11, 2008, Neal Conan, "Interview: The Lives of Assassins," radio broadcast transcript.

* * *

HOLMES, Jon 1973-
(Jonathan Richard Holmes)

PERSONAL: Born April 24, 1973. *Education:* Graduate of University of Kent Canterbury, Christ Church College.

ADDRESSES: Agent—Vivienne Clore, The Richard Stone Partnership, 2 Henrietta St., London W1A 2AS, England. *E-mail*—jon@jonholmes.net.

CAREER: Script writer, broadcaster, and comedian. Writer for radio, television, newspapers, and magazines, 1999—.

AWARDS, HONORS: Sony Gold Award for Best Entertainment Show and Commercial Radio Award for Best New Presenter, 2000, for *Jon Holmes on Music Radio;* Sony Bronze Award for Best Comedy for *The Now Show;* Sony Bronze Award for Best Comedy, 2000, for *The Very World of Milton Jones;* British Comedy Award, Sony Gold Award for Best Comedy, and Broadcasting Press Guild Award, all 2001, all for *Dead Ringers;* Sony Silver Award for *Charm Offensive.*

WRITINGS:

Rock Star Babylon: Outrageous Rumors, Legends, and Raucous True Tales of Rock and Roll Icons, Plume (New York, NY), 2007.

Status Quo and the Kangaroo: And Other Rock Apocryphals, Michael Joseph (London, England), 2007.

SIDELIGHTS: Comedian Jon Holmes was born on April 24, 1973. He attended Christ Church College at the University of Kent in Canterbury, receiving a dual degree in English and radio, film, and television. He immediately began working for BBC Radio 4, for which he wrote a show called *Grievous Bodily Radio,* a project that gained him wide attention, if not always praise. He has worked ever since as writer and broadcaster for British radio and television, winning a host of awards for his work. Among these were the Sony Gold Award for Best Entertainment Show and the Commercial Radio Award for Best New Presenter, both for *Jon Holmes on Music Radio*; the Sony Bronze Award for Best Comedy for the politically based *The Now Show*; the Sony Bronze Award for Best Comedy for *The Very World of Milton Jones;* the British Comedy Award, the Sony Gold Award for Best Comedy, and the Broadcasting Press Guild Award, all for the very popular and much acclaimed *Dead Ringers;* and the Sony Silver Award for *Charm Offensive,* created with Scottish comedian Armando Iannucci. Holmes also has his own radio comedy series, *Listen*

Against and is writer and co-presenter for *The Day the Music Died.* Besides writing for radio and television, Holmes has written many articles for newspapers and magazines, including the *London Times,* the *Guardian,* the *Telegraph,* the *Independent, Time Out,* and *Radio Times,* with a monthly column in the *Sunday Times* entitled "Motormouth."

Rock Star Babylon: Outrageous Rumors, Legends, and Raucous True Tales of Rock and Roll Icons is Holmes's compendium of stories and vignettes from the world of rock and roll. Many of the stories are rumors and Holmes's speculations about them, and many involve sexual and scatological themes. Mike Tribby commented in his review for *Booklist* that *Rock Star Babylon* contained "some pretty foul language, but [is] an enjoyable exposure of rock's underbelly."

Status Quo and the Kangaroo: And Other Rock Apocryphals is Holmes's collection of humorous stories about well-known figures in the music industry. It consists of eighty rock-and-roll legends and myths that he has compiled, followed by his attempts to prove or disprove them, all the while joking and poking fun at his subjects, with occasional wanderings into peripheral areas along the way. In her review of *Status Quo and the Kangaroo* for *WalesOnline,* Hannah Jones declared, "There is plenty about Holmes' tome to enjoy, and there are more than a handful of laugh-out-loud moments," but she also commented that music fans would be familiar with all of the stories.

BIOGRAPHICAL AND CRITICAL SOURCES:

PERIODICALS

Booklist, April 15, 2008, Mike Tribby, review of *Rock Star Babylon: Outrageous Rumors, Legends, and Raucous True Tales of Rock and Roll Icons,* p. 17.

ONLINE

Jon Holmes, http://www.jonholmes.net (July 30, 2009), author's Web site.

TimeOut London, http://www.timeout.com/ (May 29, 2007), John O'Connell, review of *Status Quo and the Kangaroo: And Other Rock Apocryphals.*

WalesOnline, http://www.walesonline.co.uk/ (June 16, 2007), Hannah Jones, review of *Status Quo and the Kangaroo.**

* * *

HOLMES, Jonathan Richard
See HOLMES, Jon

* * *

HOUDIN, Jean-Pierre 1951-

PERSONAL: Born 1951, in Paris, France; son of Henri Houdin (an engineer) and a doctor mother; married: wife's name Michelle. *Education:* Graduated from École des Beaux-Arts, 1976.

CAREER: Writer, architect, entrepreneur. Ran his own architecture firm until 1999; Les Enfants Gâtés gallery, Paris, France, co-owner; joined his father in investigating the structure of the Great Pyramids, 1999—, Association of the Construction of the Great Pyramid, 2003—.

AWARDS, HONORS: Received Montgolfier Prize.

WRITINGS:

(With father, Henri Houdin) *La pyramide de Khéops: sa construction integralement expliquée* (title means "The Pyramid of Kheops: The Integral Construction Explained"), Linteau (Paris, France), 2003.

Kheops: les secrets de la construction de la grande pyramide, Linteau (Paris, France), 2006, translation published as *Khufu: The Secrets behind the Building of the Great Pyramid,* Farid Atiya Press, 2007.

(With Bob Brier) *The Secret of the Great Pyramid: How One Man's Obsession Led to the Solution of Ancient Egypt's Greatest Mystery,* Smithsonian (Washington, DC), 2008.

SIDELIGHTS: Writer and architect Jean-Pierre Houdin was born in 1951 in Paris, France, but grew up primarily in Abidjan, Africa, where his engineer father was working for a construction company. As a child, he became fascinated by both building and design due to his exposure to his father's work, and so eventually ended up studying architecture at École des Beaux-Arts in Paris, graduating in 1976. For the next two decades, Houdin worked as an independent architect and owner of his own firm. He also indulged his interest in art, opening an avant-garde gallery called Les Enfants Gâtés in Paris with his wife, Michelle, and a friend. Then in 1999, Houdin's father, Henri, retired and began to hypothesize regarding his own personal interest in the structure of the pyramids in Egypt. He came up with the idea that these structures had actually been built from within, a concept he suggested to his son, piquing the younger Houdin's interest. Because of Houdin's experience as an architect and with graphics rendered in three dimensions, he agreed to go and assist his father with his research, leaving his architectural business behind in order to do so. The pair joined with a research team that had investigated the pyramid of Khufu during the mid-1980s, and together they analyzed the design of the pyramid, including plans that had been put together for academic purposes. Thanks to the new point of view, they realized that a spiral structure within the pyramid itself was most likely not a structural support, but a ramp that might have been utilized to bring materials up to the higher levels of the pyramid during its initial construction. Houdin continued working on the theory with his father and the other members of the research team, and eventually was awarded the Montgolfier Prize for his research efforts. He has written several books on the secrets of the pyramid and the research behind these newest theories and discoveries, including the English-language texts *Khufu: The Secrets behind the Building of the Great Pyramid* and, with Bob Brier, *The Secret of the Great Pyramid: How One Man's Obsession Led to the Solution of Ancient Egypt's Greatest Mystery.*

The Secret of the Great Pyramid offers readers a teasing story of how Houdin and coauthor Brier, an expert on Egyptian mummies, first became acquainted, before going on to explain Houdin's theories regarding the Great Pyramid and how it was built. The book provides details about Houdin's research with his father, and also discusses the extreme likelihood that the resulting theory will be soon be considered fact. All that is required is for Egyptian authorities to allow thermal photographs to be taken of the interiors of the structure to provide verification. The Great Pyramid, located in Giza, has been considered a mysterious feat of engineering for centuries, so this discovery is of prime importance in the world of historical architecture and Egyptology. The book is filled out with other historical information about the pyramid itself, which was built in honor of Khufu by his brother Hemienu, and supposedly took 25,000 construction workers, all paid Egyptians, approximately twenty years to complete. Modern technology, specifically the ability to use computer graphics to render three-dimensional mappings of the pyramid, were instrumental in proving the feasibility of Houdin's theory regarding the means of construction. A reviewer for *Publishers Weekly* remarked that "the authors' prose is lucid, aided by drawings and photos, and the theories are intriguing." John E. Dockall, writing for *Library Journal,* found the book to be "a welcome addition to Egyptology and monumental architecture scholarship." *Booklist* reviewer Gilbert Taylor opined that the work is "an intriguing resource on a popular subject for personal reading or reports."

BIOGRAPHICAL AND CRITICAL SOURCES:

PERIODICALS

Archeology, May-June, 1999, Bob Brier, "How to Build a Pyramid."

Booklist, October 15, 2008, Gilbert Taylor, review of *The Secret of the Great Pyramid: How One Man's Obsession Led to the Solution of Ancient Egypt's Greatest Mystery,* p. 8.

Internet Bookwatch, May, 2007, review of *Khufu: The Secrets behind the Building of the Great Pyramid.*

Library Journal, November 1, 2008, John E. Dockall, review of *The Secret of the Great Pyramid,* p. 85.

Publishers Weekly, August 25, 2008, review of *The Secret of the Great Pyramid,* p. 62.

ONLINE

HarperCollins Web site, http://www.harpercollins.com/ (August 12, 2009), author profile.*

* * *

HURLEY, Tonya

PERSONAL: Born in Uniontown, PA; married Michael Pagnotta; children: Isabelle Rose. *Education:* University of Pittsburgh, B.A.

ADDRESSES: Home—New York, NY. *E-mail*—info@tonyahurleyproductions.com.

CAREER: Author, screenwriter, and filmmaker. Director of animated and live-action short films, including *Kiss My Brain, The Biblical Real World, Solo-Me-O, Baptism of Solitude: A Tribute to Paul Bowles,* and *best friEND.* Television series work includes: (coproducer and a cowriter) *In Action!,* 2000-01; and (cocreator and coproducer) *So Little Time,* ABC. Director of television commercials; content provider for Web sites; creator of video games, board games, and dolls. Formerly worked as a publicist in New York, NY.

MEMBER: Writers Guild of America.

AWARDS, HONORS: Rockefeller Foundation Award in film nomination, 2001; Canadian International Film Festival second-place award in animated short category for *Kiss My Brain;* Webby Award nominations, 2006, 2007, both for *ghostgirl.com;* numerous official selections for film festivals.

WRITINGS:

Ghostgirl, Little, Brown (Boston, MA), 2008.
Ghostgirl: Homecoming, Little, Brown (New York, NY), 2009.

Author of scripts for short films, including *Kiss My Brain,* 1997, *The Biblical Real World,* 1998, *Solo-Me-O,* 1999, *Baptism of Solitude: A Tribute to Paul Bowles,* 2000, and *best friEND,* 2001. Scriptwriter for television, including *In Action!* (animated series), ABC, 2000-01; and *Big, Big World,* PBS.

ADAPTATIONS: Ghostgirl, narrated by Parker Posey, was adapted as an audiobook, Recorded Books.

SIDELIGHTS: An independent filmmaker and writer, Tonya Hurley took the first step toward her sideline career as a children's writer when she was developing her unique Web site *ghostgirl.com.* Full of strong graphic images, opportunities for creative expression, and a wry take on teen enui, *ghostgirl.com* struck a chord with many teens, and Hurley captures the same theme in her novels *Ghostgirl* and *Ghostgirl: Homecoming.*

When readers first meet her, drab, unstylish, and listless high-school misfit Charlotte Usher is barely a blip on her school's social scene. Her scheme to change her status at Hawthorne High is tragically derailed, however, when the teen chokes on a gummy bear and dies on the first day in physics class. Charlotte's lust for popularity is enough to keep her spirit in limbo, however, and in *Ghostgirl* Hurley follows Charlotte's humorous efforts to win over her still-living high-school crush and get her first kiss as his date at the Fall Ball. Calling *Ghostgirl* "a prime exemplar of . . . a growing subgenre of satire about teens who will not or cannot die," a *Publishers Weekly* critic cited Hurley for her "consistent wit" and "polished dark and deadpan humor." Threading her story with morbid song lyrics and her own stylishly inky Goth art, Hurley creates "pitch-perfect dialogue and clever names . . . [to] keep readers laughing," according to *School Library Journal* critic Shelley Huntington. *Ghostgirl* also boasts what a *Kirkus Reviews* writer described as "a kooky slew of offbeat minor characters," all of whom help energize a story that is "goofy, ghastly, intelligent, [and] electrifying."

As Hurley told Deidre Futon in an online interview posted on the novelist's home page, "Teen years are the most formative in anyone's life, socially. I think we're all stuck there to some extent, insofar as our insecurities are born there, our personalities are cultivated there. It's the best of times and, for a lot of us, the worst. It can be cruel but it's really where you learn to survive. It's the time when you find out who you are, who you want to be, and who you don't. It's the most fertile territory imaginable for a writer. It fascinates me."

BIOGRAPHICAL AND CRITICAL SOURCES:

PERIODICALS

Bulletin of the Center for Children's Books, September, 2008, April Spisak, review of *Ghostgirl,* p. 22.
Kirkus Reviews, July 1, 2008, review of *Ghostgirl.*
Publishers Weekly, July 14, 2008, review of *Ghostgirl* p. 66.
School Library Journal, August, 2008, Shelley Huntington, review of *Ghostgirl,* p. 124; August, 2009, Emily Garrett Cassidy, review of *Ghostgirl: Homecoming,* p. 104.

Voice of Youth Advocates, August, 2008, Lauri Vaughan and Denzil Sikka, review of *Ghostgirl,* p. 261.

ONLINE

Ghostgirl.com, http://www.ghostgirl.com (November 5, 2009).

Tonya Hurley Home Page, http://www.tonyahurley.com (November 5, 2009).*

* * *

HUSTAD, Megan

PERSONAL: Education: Graduate of the University of Minnesota.

ADDRESSES: E-mail—megan.hustad@gmail.com.

CAREER: Editor and writer. Random House, Knopf Group, Basic Books, and Counterpoint Press, editor.

WRITINGS:

How to Be Useful: A Beginner's Guide to Not Hating Work, Houghton Mifflin Harcourt (New York, NY), 2008.

Contributor of articles to periodicals and professional journals, including *New York Times, Salon.com, Slate,* and *Daily Beast.*

SIDELIGHTS: Megan Hustad is a writer and editor originally from Minnesota but now living in New York. She earned a degree in history from the University of Minnesota. After a few stints in retail, she worked for five years as an editor in corporate publishing in New York at such firms as Random House, Knopf Group, Basic Books, and Counterpoint Press. She left the office life to become a freelance writer. Hustad's essays and commentaries have appeared in the *New York Times, Salon.com, Slate, The Daily Beast,* and on American Public Media's *Marketplace* radio program on business and economics.

In 2008 Hustad published *How to Be Useful: A Beginner's Guide to Not Hating Work,* a practical and humorous manual for twenty- and thirty-year-olds to survive the stifling, tedious, solitary, and soul-damaging environment of the modern corporate office. To write the book, Hustad combed nineteenth-, twentieth-, and twenty-first-century books on self-improvement, business, and advice on achieving success. She surveyed dozens of "how to succeed" books, from C.B.C. Amicus's nineteenth-century *Hints on Life* through Andrew Carnegie, Stephen R. Covey, Napoleon Hill, and Donald Trump. Hustad also adds a dash of memoir from her days as a corporate office dweller.

Hustad wants to warn the privileged, middle-class youth entering the workforce that they are in for a shock. Young people who have been coddled and praised all their life and told they can achieve anything they set their mind to have developed a feeling that they are too advanced for their menial, entry-level jobs or internships.

One important message Hustad brings to her readers is that despite being encouraged all their lives to "just be yourself," this advice will not work once they enter office life. She explains that specific personality types get further in corporate settings than others.

In an interview conducted by Christine N. Ziemba in *LAist,* Hustad said, "If you think you have some obligation to represent your true and soulful essence every waking moment of the day, and you're working in an underling or assistant capacity, you will get frustrated and angry with yourself really, really fast." She explained that telling young people that they can say or do anything as long as they are sincere and work hard will not benefit them.

To help navigate office life, Hustad presents ten categories of office commandments in her book. Among her rules is not to say, "Oh, yeah, I smoked pot with him," when asked by a boss if you know someone. She also provides advice on finding something nice to say and how to win friends.

Despite her negative portrayal of the institution, Hustad offers the promise of some benefit from life in an office setting. "There's life around—look at it," she said in an interview on *GalleyCat* Web site. "There are things to be grasped about human nature, human nature in groups, the fragility of egos, the use and abuse of power, the use and abuse of tenderness. . . . The office (esp. an unhappy one) is a good place to study these things. May be my own brand of naiveté, but I'm convinced that people who notice and understand these organizational dynamics will wind up more successful."

Commenting on *How to Be Useful,* Barbara Jacobs wrote in *Booklist,* "The writing is bright, brassy, and only occasionally awkward or annoying." Jacobs noted that Hustad's tips and hints are off the wall or just plain wrong, such as when she advises people not to be nice.

Alexandra Jacobs wrote in the *New York Times Book Review,* "On the one hand, 'How to Be Useful' is a relaxed ramble through the history of the genre, a wry distillation of years of positive thinking. On the other . . . it is itself packaged as a self-help manual, pitched directly to the artfully tousled whippersnappers currently in the market for entry-level positions."

BIOGRAPHICAL AND CRITICAL SOURCES:

BOOKS

Hustad, Megan, *How to Be Useful: A Beginner's Guide to Not Hating Work,* Houghton Mifflin Harcourt (New York, NY), 2008.

PERIODICALS

Booklist, April 1, 2008, Barbara Jacobs, review of *How to Be Useful,* p. 12.

Maclean's, June 16, 2008, "Finally, a Book about . . . 20th-Century Advice," review of *How to Be Useful,* p. 59.

New York Times Book Review, June 8, 2008, Alexandra Jacobs, "Dry Your Hair; Wear Shoes," p. 24.

Publishers Weekly, July 11, 2005, Steven Zeitchik, "Former Counterpoint Editor Megan Hustad Is Poised to Sell a Guide to Being 'Useful' to Amanda Cook at Houghton, via Trident," p. 10.

Seattle Post-Intelligencer, May 22, 2008, Joseph Tartakoff, "A Moment with . . . Megan Hustad, Author."

ONLINE

GalleyCat, http://www.mediabistro.com/ (April 15, 2009), "Just Two Questions: 'How to Be Useful' Author Megan Hustad Explains How to Succeed in Publishing by Actually Trying," author interview.

How to Be UsefulWeb log, http://howtobeuseful.com (August 9, 2009), short author profile.

LAist, http://laist.com/ (May 24, 2008), Christine N. Ziemba, "LAist Interview: Author Megan Hustad on How Not to Hate Your Job," author interview.

Megan Hustad Home Page, http://meganhustad.com (August 9, 2009), author profile.

Save the Assistants, http://savetheassistants.com/ (May 22, 2008), "The STA Interview: Megan Hustad."*

* * *

HUTCHINSON, Carolyn 1945-
(Carolyn Margaret Hutchinson)

PERSONAL: Born October 28, 1945.

CAREER: Gardening writer.

WRITINGS:

(With Richard M. Jackson) *How to Win at Container Gardening,* HarperCollins (London, England), 1996.

(With Richard M. Jackson) *How to Win at Gardening,* HarperCollins (London, England), 1996.

(With Richard M. Jackson) *How to Win at Patios and Small Gardens,* HarperCollins (London, England), 1997.

(With Richard M. Jackson) *Hanging Baskets & Window Boxes,* HarperCollins (London, England), 1998.

(With Richard M. Jackson) *How to Win at Gardening: A Practical A-to-Z Guide to a Better Garden,* Reader's Digest Association (Pleasantville, N.Y.), 1998.

The Once-a-Week Gardener: Time-Saving Tips and Essential Tasks Season-by-Season, Mitchell Beazley (London, England), 1999.

Time-Saving Gardener: Tips and Essential Tasks, Season by Season, Firefly Books (Buffalo, NY), 2008.

SIDELIGHTS: Carolyn Hutchinson, born October 28, 1945, is a gardening writer. She has written and co-written a number of books giving advice on many aspects of gardening, as well as articles for many gardening publications. Her subjects include gardening on and around a patio, container gardening, the use of hanging baskets and window boxes, and seasonal tasks to maintain a year-round garden. Her articles include in-depth profiles of plants and practical advice for gardening and the care and management of property.

In *Time-Saving Gardener: Tips and Essential Tasks, Season by Season,* Hutchinson provides a step-by-step framework for caring for a garden throughout the calendar year. Written for the beginning gardener, the book is categorized by season, explaining each chore that needs attention during each time of the year. Photographs and colored illustrations highlight each activity for added clarification. Subjects covered include fall clean-up, mulching vegetable and flower beds, pruning shrubs, creating and planting container and kitchen gardens, propagating new plants and the best times to plant them, creating and caring for borders and pools, maintaining fences and walls, trimming hedges, dealing with perennial weeds, and preventing and combating pests and plant diseases. Hutchinson uses a system of symbols to indicate the importance of a given chore and gives estimates of how long each tack should take the gardener to perform. She explains the reasons for doing certain activities at particular times of year, such as mowing the lawn for the first time in the spring, cleaning tools and containers, and protecting plants from frost and snow. Sidebars offer extra tips for special circumstances, including protection of pool fish from predators, computerized water systems for conservation of precious resources, and garden design with special plants such as alpines in garden walls. The book includes a list of easy-to-care-for plants and a glossary of gardening and plant terminology.

Reviewers liked the practical suggestions Hutchinson makes in *Time-Saving Gardener.* In her review for *Booklist,* Alice Joyce praised the book, saying Hutchinson's "systematic approach explains what is necessary to undertake each season." Donna L. Davey, reviewing *Time-Saving Gardener* for *Library Journal,* declared it "packed with common sense and great ideas." The reviewer for *Publishers Weekly* commented, "This book gives stressed-out gardeners practical advice on how to keep their backyard jungles tamed."

BIOGRAPHICAL AND CRITICAL SOURCES:

PERIODICALS

Booklist, May 15, 2008, Alice Joyce, review of *Time-Saving Gardener: Tips and Essential Tasks, Season by Season,* p. 14.

Library Journal, August 1, 2008, Donna L. Davey, review of *Time-Saving Gardener,* p. 106.

Publishers Weekly, February 18, 2008, review of *Time-Saving Gardener,* p. 151.

ONLINE

Firefly Books Web site, http://www.fireflybooks.com/ (July 31, 2009), summary of *Time-Saving Gardener* and short author profile.*

* * *

HUTCHINSON, Carolyn Margaret
See HUTCHINSON, Carolyn

* * *

HYLTON, Sara
(Lilian Unsworth)

PERSONAL: Female.

CAREER: Writer.

WRITINGS:

Caprice, St. Martin's Press (New York, NY), 1980.

Carradice Chain, Hutchinson (New York, NY), 1981.

Jacintha, St. Martin's Press (New York, NY), 1981.

The Crimson Falcon, St. Martin's Press (New York, NY), 1983.

The Talisman of Set, St. Martin's Press (New York, NY), 1984.

The Whispering Glade, St. Martin's Press (New York, NY), 1985.

Glamara, Century (London, England), 1986.

The Hills Are Eternal, St. Martin's Press (New York, NY), 1986.

Desert Splendor, St. Martin's Press (New York, NY), 1987.

Tomorrow's Rainbow, St. Martin's Press (New York, NY), 1987.

My Sister Clare, Century (London, England), 1988.

Fragile Heritage, St. Martin's Press (New York, NY), 1990.

Summer of the Flamingoes, St. Martin's Press (New York, NY), 1991.

The Chosen Ones, St. Martin's Press (New York, NY), 1992.

The Last Reunion, St. Martin's Press (New York, NY), 1993.

In the Shadow of the Nile, St. Martin's (New York, NY), 1994.

Reckmire Marsh, St. Martin's Press (New York, NY), 1995.

Melissa, St. Martin's Press (New York, NY), 1996.

The Sunflower Girl, St. Martin's Press (New York, NY), 1997.

Footsteps in the Rain, St. Martin's Press (New York, NY), 1998.

Easter at the Lakes, St. Martin's Press (New York, NY), 1999.

April Wedding, Piatkus Books (London, England), 2000.

Separate Lives, St. Martin's Press (New York, NY), 2000.

Rosie's Journey, Piatkus Books (London, England), 2001.

The Last Waltz, Piatkus Books (London, England), 2003.

An Arranged Marriage, Piatkus Books (London, England), 2004.

The Longest Day, Piatkus Books (London, England), 2005.

The Legacy of Anger, Severn House (London, England), 2008.

Too Many Yesterdays, Severn House (London, England), 2009.

SIDELIGHTS: Sara Hylton is a writer of romantic fiction. She published her first novel, *Caprice,* in 1980. In 1990 Hylton published *Fragile Heritage.* In this novel Ellen Adair is constantly criticized by her father while her poor Irish friend, Kitty McGuire, is the target of a Yorkshire community's bigotry. The two flee to Liverpool and separate, each attempting to make it big at great expense. Sybil Steinberg, writing in *Publishers Weekly,* recalled that "in her laconic, first-person narration . . . there are entertaining moments." However, Steinberg did not find the romances to be very "convincing."

The following year Hylton published *Summer of the Flamingoes.* Lisa Hamilton attends her grandmother's funeral with mixed emotions, having been raised by this grandmother but never earning her approval due to a scandal of her parents' making. Steinberg, again writing in *Publishers Weekly,* observed that the author "unfolds her story smoothly if unsurprisingly."

In 1993 Hylton published *The Last Reunion.* The plot continues the stories of a cast of characters first introduced in her 1992 novel *The Chosen Ones.* Nancy and Noel struggle while living together in the Middle East, Maisie worries about her daughter while tending to her farm, and Amelia avoids her problems by drinking too much. A contributor writing in *Publishers Weekly* found the account "engaging and well-paced, if overburdened by lengthy characterizations."

Hylton published *In the Shadow of the Nile* in 1994. Laura Levison-Gore's mother brings her two daughters to Cairo in hopes that Laura will be able to convince her cousin's wealthy fiancé to marry her instead. The plans go wrong, however, when Laura finds love with an English-raised Egyptian prince. A contributor writing in *Publishers Weekly* remarked that the narrative is "hampered by stereotyped characters." The same contributor criticized that it also "never regains the passion and momentum lost upon the prince's death."

The following year Hylton published *Reckmire Marsh.* Joanna Albemarle inherits her family's Reckmire mansion after her grandparents die and World War II splits up her family. In order to save the family mansion, however, she marries a man who can help accomplish this feat but for whom she has complicated feelings. Kathleen Hughes, reviewing the novel in *Booklist,* said that "the carefully paced narrative, meticulous attention to detail, and elements of surprise" made the novel "hard to put" aside. A contributor writing in *Publishers Weekly* remarked that "there's no depth here, but Hylton . . . has command of her atmospheric setting and maintains a quick pace."

In 1996 Hylton published *Melissa.* Ginny Lawrence's family takes in young Melissa, who is evacuated to their countryside home from London during World War II. While there, Melissa trains to become a singer and succeeds in becoming an opera diva. Ginny marries Alastair and the pair move to Italy, where they meet Melissa. The diva steals Ginny's husband but dumps him not long after Ginny and he divorce. Melissa attempts to befriend Ginny afterwards but again makes inappropriate moves into Ginny's personal life. A contributor writing in *Publishers Weekly* claimed that in this novel, "Hylton, through rich characters, psychological insight, and plot twists aplenty, delivers her tightest, most entertaining romance to date."

The following year Hylton published *The Sunflower Girl.* Marie Claire Moreau and Earl Andrew Martindale have an affair that ends when he returns to England. Marie Claire is kicked out of school and leaves home after having their child, Chantal, out of wedlock. Marie Claire goes on to become the mayor of Dijon and obsesses for the rest of her life about getting revenge on Andrew. *Booklist* contributor Kathleen Hughes admitted that "Hylton manages to hold the reader's interest to the end by avoiding a contrived story line." A contributor writing in *Publishers Weekly* remarked that the novel "manages to be entertaining despite its reliance on stereotypes about gender and class." The same contributor mentioned that "as always, Hylton renders characters and events with sprightly ease."

Hylton published *Footsteps in the Rain* in 1998. Amanda Dexter grew up in British India but is forced to live with her elderly grandparents in England during World War I. Homesick, she is relieved to return to India ten years later, where she briefly finds love and learns of the wrongs of colonialism. Melanie Duncan, writing in *Booklist,* noted that with this novel, "Hylton weaves an enjoyable and richly atmospheric period romance." Duncan suggested that *Footsteps in the Rain* "may appeal to inspirational-fiction fans." A contributor writing in *Publishers Weekly* commented that despite the topic, the novel did not contain any "real threat of weightiness." The same contributor mentioned that "Hylton is always one to make sure love triumphs in the end." Andrea Lee Shuey, writing in *Library Journal,* noted that "the contrasting settings of the Orient and an English mill town are well drawn."

In 1999 Hylton published *Easter at the Lakes.* The account centers on the lives of a number of guests at a castle-hotel in the Lake District of England. Susan Scribner, reviewing the novel in *Romance Reader,* found it "impossible to tell why one character falls in love with the other," adding that "their demonstrations of love are so mundane I almost nodded off." Scribner also complained that "Mary lets her mother and sister walk all over her for so long that I just wanted to shake her." *Booklist* contributor Holly Cooley claimed that "Hylton's immensely readable style makes us care about these characters," suggesting that readers would be "captivated by the various intertwining relationships."

In 2000 Hylton published *Separate Lives.* The account tells of two generations who live on a Greek island and who seem to bring tragedy and death to most of the inhabitants. *Booklist* contributor Diana Tixier Herald remarked that even though the stories are "enigmatic," they are "not exactly romance and not exactly suspense."

Hylton published *The Legacy of Anger* in 2008. Margaret Gates finds romantic opportunity after the wife of her beloved boss dies. The pair enter into an affair that ends when Margaret's boss leaves for a business trip to China and later returns with a new wife. *Booklist* contributor Herald suggested that "readers who enjoy Hylton's new novel will also like works by Linda Sole and Catherine Cookson."

BIOGRAPHICAL AND CRITICAL SOURCES:

PERIODICALS

Booklist, May 15, 1992, Denise Perry Donavin, review of *The Chosen Ones,* p. 1662; September 1, 1993, review of *The Last Reunion,* p. 34; July, 1994, Denise Perry Donavin, review of *In the Shadow of the Nile,* p. 1922; October 15, 1995, Kathleen Hughes, review of *Reckmire Marsh,* p. 385; June

1, 1997, Kathleen Hughes, review of *The Sunflower Girl,* p. 1658; September 15, 1998, Melanie Duncan, review of *Footsteps in the Rain,* p. 212; September 15, 1998, Sally Estes, review of *The Sunflower Girl,* p. 220; July, 1999, Holly Cooley, review of *Easter at the Lakes,* p. 1929; April 15, 2000, Diana Tixier Herald, review of *Separate Lives,* p. 1523; May 15, 2008, Diana Tixier Herald, review of *The Legacy of Anger,* p. 27.

Library Journal, December 1, 1980, Barbara Parker, review of *Caprice,* p. 2515; January 15, 1982, review of *Jacintha,* p. 195; August, 1984, review of *The Talisman of Set,* p. 1467; December 1, 1986, A.M.B. Amantia, review of *The Hills Are Eternal,* p. 136; November 15, 1990, A.M.B. Amantia, review of *Fragile Heritage,* p. 90; May 15, 1992, Sue Mevis, review of *The Chosen Ones,* p. 120; June 1, 1994, Betsy Larson, review of *In the Shadow of the Nile,* p. 160; September 1, 1995, Marion Hanscom, review of *Reckmire Marsh,* p. 208; November 15, 1996, Andrea Lee Shuey, review of *Melissa,* p. 88; October 15, 1998, Andrea Lee Shuey, review of *Footsteps in the Rain,* p. 98.

Publishers Weekly, November 14, 1980, Barbara A. Bannon, review of *Caprice,* p. 45; December 11, 1981, Barbara A. Bannon, review of *Jacintha,* p. 50; April 1, 1983, review of *The Crimson Falcon,* p. 50; June 1, 1984, review of *The Talisman of Set,* p. 56; October 11, 1985, review of *The Whispering Glade,* p. 56; October 11, 1985, review of *The Whispering Glade,* p. 56; October 24, 1986, Sybil Steinberg, review of *The Hills Are Eternal,* p. 59; May 12, 1989, Sybil Steinberg, review of *My Sister Clare,* p. 279; October 5, 1990, Sybil Steinberg, review of *Fragile Heritage,* p. 90; April 12, 1991, Sybil Steinberg, review of *Summer of the Flamingoes,* p. 43; April 27, 1992, review of *The Chosen Ones,* p. 252; August 9, 1993, review of *The Last Reunion,* p. 461; June 6, 1994, review of *In the Shadow of the Nile,* p. 58; September 18, 1995, review of *Reckmire Marsh,* p. 115; October 21, 1996, review of *Melissa,* p. 71; June 23, 1997, review of *The Sunflower Girl,* p. 71; October 5, 1998, review of *Footsteps in the Rain,* p. 81; July 12, 1999, review of *Easter at the Lakes,* p. 79; March 27, 2000, review of *Separate Lives,* p. 55.

School Library Journal, March 1, 1986, review of *The Whispering Glade,* p. 179.

ONLINE

Romance Reader, http://www.theromancereader.com/ (July 31, 2009), Susan Scribner, review of *Easter at the Lakes.**

J

JACKSON, Troy 1968-

PERSONAL: Born 1968; married; children: three. *Education:* Princeton Theological Seminary, M.Div.; University of Kentucky, Ph.D. *Religion:* Christian.

ADDRESSES: *Office*—University Christian Church, 245 W. McMillan, Cincinnati, OH 45219. *E-mail*—ttjackson@yahoo.com.

CAREER: Pastor, historian, instructor, and writer. University Christian Church, Cincinnati, OH, pastor, 1994—.

WRITINGS:

(Editor) *The Papers of Martin Luther King, Jr., Vol. 6: Advocate of the Social Gospel, September 1948–March 1963,* University of California Press (Berkeley, CA), 2007.

Becoming King: Martin Luther King, Jr. and the Making of a National Leader, University Press of Kentucky (Lexington, KY), 2008.

SIDELIGHTS: Troy Jackson is a pastor, historian, college instructor, and writer. He was born in 1968. He earned his master of divinity degree from Princeton Theological Seminary in Princeton, New Jersey, and his Ph.D. in United States history from the University of Kentucky.

Jackson participated in the Sojourners grassroots organizing pilot project, the Vote Out Poverty Campaign, in Ohio. He is also part of the King Papers Project at Stanford University, an endeavor to collect and publish the papers, sermons, and speeches of Reverend Martin Luther King, Jr. Jackson currently serves as senior pastor at University Christian Church in Cincinnati.

In 2008 Jackson published *Becoming King: Martin Luther King, Jr. and the Making of a National Leader,* which concentrates on the relationship between King and the Montgomery, Alabama, bus boycott of 1955-56. King arrived in Montgomery as a twenty-five-year-old doctoral student from Boston University. As the new pastor of Dexter Avenue Baptist Church, King implemented his mission to tackle racial inequality in Montgomery and in the process was transformed into a world leader.

King received support from activists in the black community in Montgomery that included National Association for the Advancement of Colored People (NAACP) leader E.D. Nixon, civil rights lawyers Virginia and Clifford Durr, and Women's Political Council president Jo Ann Robinson, all of whom had been laying the foundation for civil rights since the late 1940s. Jackson explained in the book that it was not so much that King was an instrumental part of the Montgomery civil rights movement as the Montgomery movement was instrumental in creating Martin Luther King, Jr., and propelling him into national prominence.

Steve Goddard commented in *Steve Goddard's History Wire* that so many books have been written about King and his development as a preacher and civil rights leader that "one wonders how much another biography can add. . . . Much of [Jackson's] book is a retelling of oft-told tales."

To the contrary, a writer in *Kirkus Reviews* said the book was "a unique portrait of the civil-rights struggle in Montgomery, Ala. . . . [and] an informed investigation of the struggles that defined a time and place—and the man who gave them a voice." Anthony Edmonds noted in *Library Journal* that Jackson "has written a convincing reinterpretation of the role" King played during the bus boycott of Montgomery.

"Ultimately, *Becoming King* is an interesting read filled with several new layers of information," said William Sturkey in *African American Book Reviews.* He continued, "This book could have benefitted from a further discussion of King's influences prior to Montgomery, but it is an intriguing look into the development of the civil rights movement's most visible figure."

BIOGRAPHICAL AND CRITICAL SOURCES:

PERIODICALS

Kirkus Reviews, October 1, 2008, review of *Becoming King: Martin Luther King, Jr. and the Making of a National Leader.*

Library Journal, September 15, 2008, Anthony Edmonds, review of *Becoming King,* p. 61.

ONLINE

African American Book Reviews—Southwest Journal of Cultures, http://southwestjournalofcultures africanamer.blogspot.com/ (February 11, 2009), William Sturkey, review of *Becoming King.*

Beliefnet.com, http://blog.beliefnet.com/ (March 19, 2008), short author profile.

Steve Goddard's History Wire, http://www.historywire.com/ (December 30, 2008), Steve Goddard, review of *Becoming King.*

University Christian Church, http://www.universitychristianchurch.net/ (August 9, 2009), short author profile.

* * *

JAIN, Anita 1972-

PERSONAL: Born June 24, 1972, in Udaipur, Rajasthan, India; immigrated to United States at six months old; daughter of Shri Ashok Kumar and Kanta Devi Singatwadia; married Anubhav Jain, February 2, 1998; children: Vidit. *Education:* Mohan Lal Sukhadia University, Udaipur, India, B.Sc., 1991, M.Sc., 1993, Ph.D., 2000; graduate of Harvard University, 1994.

ADDRESSES: Office—Lab of Ethnobotany and Agrostology, Mohan Lal Sukhadia University, Udaipur, Rajasthan 313001, India. *Agent*—Esmond Harmsworth, Zachary Shuster Harmsworth, 1776 Broadway, Ste. 1405, New York, NY 10019. *E-mail*—anita@anitajain.net.

CAREER: Botanist, researcher, journalist, and writer. Mohan Lal Sukhadia University, Udaipur, India, research scholar, 1997-98, research associate, 2002, teacher, 2002; Vidhya Bhavan Rural Institute, Udaipur, India, teacher, 2000-02.

MEMBER: Indian Botanical Society.

WRITINGS:

Marrying Anita: A Quest for Love in the New India, Bloomsbury USA (New York, NY), 2008.

SIDELIGHTS: Anita Jain is a journalist and writer. She was born June 24, 1972, in Udaipur, Rajasthan, India, but immigrated to the United States when she was only six months old. During her childhood her family traveled around the country, living in Baltimore, Maryland, and Las Vegas, Nevada, before settling in Sacramento, California. After earning her undergraduate degree in 1994 from Harvard University, she worked as a financial journalist traveling all over the world to places like Mexico City, Singapore, London, and New York.

During her twenties, Jain's search for a husband provided a reflection on Indian and American cultural differences regarding marriage, love, and duty. In 2005 Jain wrote the article "Is Arranged Marriage Really Any Worse Than Craigslist?" for *New York* magazine about her traditional American dating experiences and her father's traditional Indian use of matchmakers and arranged marriages.

Jain spent a decade looking for love in New York City, using the traditional American custom of meeting dot-com millionaires, overachieving financial executives who state up front that they will put their work before their family, closeted gays, and married men looking for affairs. She commented in her article, "I began to feel baffled by Western norms of dating, what one Indian friend calls 'dating for dating's sake.'"

She was ready to consider the matches her father found for her on Indian American Web sites for arranged marriages. In her article she wrote, "My father took to the Websites like a freshly divorced 42-year-old who's just discovered Craigslist." Before long she was receiving contacts. "Strange e-mails from boys' fathers and stranger dates with those boys themselves—has become so much a part of my dating life that I've lost sight of how bizarre it once seemed," she wrote.

Unmarried in America, the thirty-two-year-old Jain moved back to her homeland, to Delhi, for a year to continue her search for a husband. Expanding on her magazine article, she published *Marrying Anita: A Quest for Love in the New India* in 2008, a memoir of her search for a broad-minded groom and her rediscovery of her homeland.

In the new, modern India she finds that the dating scene is not much different from the one in New York; indeed, it is filled with a thriving club scene, one-night stands, rampant egos, friends with benefits, and men who do not return calls. She begins to feel that in both countries being a thirty-something professional woman is a hindrance to finding a mate. In India she even has problems renting an apartment because landlords will not rent to single women, fearing they are prostitutes or will bring men home.

In her memoir Jain explores whether modern views on dating and marriage are really progress and an enemy of intimacy, that women in any culture still feel imprisoned by loneliness, and that perhaps her mother was right when she said, "It's not that there isn't love. It's just that it comes after marriage."

Renuka Rayasam commented in *Wilson Quarterly,* "Unfortunately, Jain seems more interested in stringing together amusing dating anecdotes than in making a sincere attempt at cross-cultural understanding. Many of the people she encounters in America and India read like caricatures." While Rayasam praised Jain's descriptions of modern India, Jain "falters when she focuses inward. Often, she blames her romantic failures on the overused emigrant's complaint of neither fitting in here nor there," said Rayasam.

Other reviewers found the book refreshing. "A sparkling, enjoyable look at how globalization affects love," said a writer in *Kirkus Reviews.* Karen Sobel commented in *Library Journal* that the book was "written in a literary yet compulsively readable voice and with remarkably fresh and merciless analyses of dating trends." A contributor to *Publishers Weekly* said, "With her world-weary yet earnest voice that finds humor in humiliation, Jain is sure to delight readers."

BIOGRAPHICAL AND CRITICAL SOURCES:

BOOKS

Marrying Anita: A Quest for Love in the New India, Bloomsbury USA (New York, NY), 2008.

PERIODICALS

Entertainment Weekly, July 25, 2008, Tina Jordan, review of *Marrying Anita,* p. 75.

Kirkus Reviews, May 15, 2008, review of *Marrying Anita.*

Library Journal, May 1, 2008, Karen Sobel, review of *Marrying Anita,* p. 74.

New York, March 26, 2005, Anita Jain, "Is Arranged Marriage Really Any Worse Than Craigslist?"

New York Times Book Review, August 31, 2008, Lori Gottlieb, "The Arrangement," review of *Marrying Anita.*

Publishers Weekly, May 26, 2008, review of *Marrying Anita,* p. 49.

Wilson Quarterly, autumn, 2008, Renuka Rayasam, "Spouse Hunt," review of *Marrying Anita,* p. 103.

ONLINE

Anita Jain Home Page, http://anitajain.net (August 9, 2009), author profile.

Bloomsbury, http://www.bloomsbury.com/ (July 1, 2009), author profile.

Fatjuicyoyster, http://www.fatjuicyoyster.com/ (April 16, 2009), review of *Marrying Anita.*

Sepia Mutiny, http://www.sepiamutiny.com/ (August 6, 2008), review of *Marrying Anita,* author interview.*

* * *

JAL, Emmanuel 1980(?)-

PERSONAL: Born c. 1980, in Tonj, Warab, Sudan.

CAREER: Musician. Former child soldier. Spokesman for various campaigns, including Make Poverty History, the Coalition to Stop the Use of Child Soldiers, and Control Arms; Gua Africa charity founder.

AWARDS, HONORS: American Gospel Music Award, 2005, for best international artist.

WRITINGS:

(With Megan Lloyd Davies) *War Child: A Child Soldier's Story,* St. Martin's Press (New York, NY), 2009.

SIDELIGHTS: Emmanuel Jal is a Sudanese musician. Described by a contributor to *African Business* as "one of the hottest rappers to explode out of the African music scene," Jal comes from a background of tragedy. Born in war-torn southern Sudan in the early 1980s, he was orphaned and recruited into a militant group in Ethiopia to defend from the Arabs of northern Sudan before he was a teenager. With the assistance of a British aid worker, he was able to escape the region, growing up in Kenya, where he learned to cope with his tragic youth through song.

In an article with Christina McGairk, Jal admitted: "My music comes out of pain and what I see on TV." In an interview with the *New Statesman,* Jal claimed that art and music are capable of making a difference in the world "because it speaks to your mind, your soul and spirit." In reflecting on the current situation in his beloved country, he noted that "it breaks my heart to have to witness what is going on in Sudan."

In an interview on *Day to Day* with Christian Bordal, Jal recalled: "My childhood wasn't fun. I was born in the times when the war that already happened. We were always moving, running, bombs dropping. Funerals after funerals, sad songs every now and then." Upon returning home to make a documentary of his life, Jal shared with Bordal that "what made me sad was to realize the war has reached the core of my family. People have been scarred, scars that will haunt you until the day you die. My little sister was raped several times in that war. And my bigger sister, she was married when she was 13 to one of the war lords and she was like a sex slave to him."

Farai Chideya, interviewing Jal in *News & Notes,* asked him about the role his music has played. To this query, Jal responded: "I'm hopeful because it's helped me as a person, and it's communicating for my country. . . . I meet different people, and they say, I've listened to your music, and you're inspiring. And I thought I had so much problem, but just listening to what you saying. And looking up to you just make me keep on moving." Jal added: "It used to depress me, talking about my story and doing all this, but it energize somebody, and it makes somebody appreciate life. That's what, also, encouraged me to say, OK, nothing just happens. Everything happens for a reason."

With the assistance of Megan Lloyd Davies, Jal published his memoir, *War Child: A Child Soldier's Story,* in 2009. The account touches on his memories and the deaths of his parents, his militant youth, the kindness of strangers, and becoming an international music phenomenon with a valuable message. Edna Gundersen, interviewing Jal in *USA Today,* recorded Jal discussing his personal reflections on his own behavior during his youth. Jal confessed that "the killing and stealing I did in war, I can justify with what happened in my home. I don't feel guilty, but I'm haunted. I used to say, 'Why didn't I die?' Now I know I'm here to tell my story."

Carolyn See, writing in the *Washington Post Book World,* remarked that the account is "very much worth reading." See reported that Jal is "broke a lot of the time—a star in Kenya, maybe, but unknown on the larger stage. He's often tired and sad and lonely, but in *War Child* he succeeds in making this crazy war and all its ramifications utterly grounded, specific and real." See concluded that "you'll come away from this book loving Emmanuel Jal. He might even prod you into a good deed or two." A contributor writing in *Kirkus Reviews* observed that "a touching reunion with his sister, a studio album and a 2008 documentary about his life make for a happy" conclusion to this part of his life. The same contributor labeled the book as a "searing portrait of a war-torn youth turned community advocate and role model."

Booklist contributor Hazel Rochman commented that "teens will be haunted by this incredible memoir of overcoming violence and hatred on the way to rap success." Howard W. French, writing in the *New York Times,* remarked that "the writing is usually sturdy, and in a middle section that relates a long death march through the south it even rises to an urgency that recalls Jerzy Kozinski's novel *The Painted Bird.* Elsewhere, though, it sometimes feels dreamily like Technicolor when color would do, and admits insufficient room for reflection on many themes, notably fear and hatred." French later mentioned that "some of the book's most interesting observations seem almost inadvertent, depriving the reader of context that is important to understanding this conflict, and African conflicts in general."

BIOGRAPHICAL AND CRITICAL SOURCES:

BOOKS

Jal, Emmanuel, and Megan Lloyd Davies, *War Child: A Child Soldier's Story,* St. Martin's Press (New York, NY), 2009.

PERIODICALS

African Business, October, 2005, "Worlds Apart Come Together: A Tribute to Peace," p. 66.

Booklist, December 15, 2008, Hazel Rochman, review of *War Child: A Child Soldier's Story,* p. 15.

Day to Day, May 16, 2008, Christian Bordal, "A Rapper out of Sudan's Civil War."

Jet, August 18, 2008, Christina McGairk, "Sudanese Child Soldier Turns Rapper," p. 36.

Kirkus Reviews, December 1, 2008, review of *War Child.*

Library Journal, November 1, 2008, Ingrid Levin, review of *War Child,* p. 74; February 1, 2009, review of *War Child,* p. 42.

News & Notes, May 6, 2008, Farai Chideya, "A Sudanese 'Warchild' All Grown Up."

New Statesman, April 28, 2008, "The Way I See It: Emmanuel Jal," p. 41.

New York Times, February 17, 2009, Howard W. French, "Surviving a Hitch in an Army of Boys," p. 6.

Rolling Stone, May 15, 2008, Evan Serpick, "Emmanuel Jal: Behind the Warchild."

Time, September 25, 2005, Michael Brunton, "10 Questions: Emmanuel Jal."

USA Today, March 14, 2005, Rob Crilly, "Ex-child Soldier Now Kenya's Hottest Rapper," p. 8A; June 27, 2008, Edna Gundersen, "Rapper Jal, Living to Tell about It," p. 6E.

Variety, June 2, 2008, Ronnie Scheib, "War Child," p. 40.

Washington Post Book World, February 6, 2009, Carolyn See, review of *War Child,* p. C3.

ONLINE

Afrobeat Blog, http://afrobeatblog.blogspot.com/ (February 18, 2009), author interview.

Emmanuel Jal Home Page, http://www.emmanueljal.org (August 22, 2009), author biography.

Emmanuel Jal MySpace Profile, http://www.myspace.com/emmanueljal/ (August 22, 2009), author profile.

Gua Africa, http://www.gua-africa.org/ (August 22, 2009), author profile.

UNICEF Web site, http://www.unicef.org/ (August 25, 2008), Ticiana Maloney and Elizabeth Njinga, "Former Child Soldier Emmanuel Jal Is Now a Hip Hop Star with a Message of Peace."*

* * *

JOHNSON, Gregory C.V.

PERSONAL: Married; wife's name Jill; children: four. *Education:* Denver Theological Seminary, M.Div.

ADDRESSES: Home—UT. *Office*—Standing Together, P.O. Box 685, Lehi, UT 84043. *E-mail*—info@standingtogether.org.

CAREER: Ordained Baptist minister. Standing Together, Lehi, UT, founder and president, 2001—; Washington Heights Baptist Church, Ogden, UT, former minister of outreach and discipleship; Ogden Valley Baptist Church, Huntsville, UT, founding pastor; Orem Evangelical Free Church, Orem, UT, pastor of ministries.

WRITINGS:

(With Robert L. Millet) *Bridging the Divide: The Continuing Conversation between a Mormon and an Evangelical,* Monkfish Book Publishing (Rhinebeck, NY), 2007.

SIDELIGHTS: Gregory C.V. Johnson is the author of *Bridging the Divide: The Continuing Conversation between a Mormon and an Evangelical* with Brigham Young University religious education professor Robert L. Millet. The book is a study of the ways in which the two different faiths reach a dialogue on their common ground. Johnson is uniquely positioned to understand both viewpoints; an ordained Baptist minister and the leader of a significant Evangelical organization, he was raised Mormon and turned to Evangelicalism in high school. In 2001 Johnson and Millet first voiced their differences in public through a series of debates and demonstrated that the items on which they agreed far outweighed the questions on which they diverged. "People like Millet and Johnson cozy up for one reason: They simply can't help themselves," declared Jerry Earl Johnston in the *Deseret News.* Johnston added, "I'm convinced when faith is authentic, it doesn't want to polarize, it wants to make connections. Honest faith, by its nature, wants to reach out."

Over fifty times in the following six years, Johnson and Millet met to discuss the issues that separated them. They "have held 'A Conversation between a Mormon and an Evangelical' in the [United States], Canada and England," explained Lawn Griffiths in the *East Valley Tribune.* Griffiths added, "Between genial ribbing and sharing their own spiritual journeys, they posed questions about problematic parts of each other's religion. . . . At the outset of the dialogue, they promised no winner or loser. 'It is important to get along, but that is not the thrust of our approach,' Johnson said. 'Bob and I are not willing to trade off on our doctrines,' he said. 'I am not conceding the Trinity (God, son and Holy Ghost) if you give up the baptism of the dead.'" Nonetheless, the two individuals—and the two faiths they represent—find common ground in their approaches to their religions. They are convinced that there is a need for the two groups to come together both to resist hostility from the secular world and to celebrate the community of faith to which, despite their differences, both authors belong. In fact, they find that the most important part of their dialogue is not the content of their faiths but rather the ways in which they express it and the concern and care they show for one another. In the relationship between Johnson and Millet, Bryce Christensen wrote in *Booklist,* "readers still see friends who share a sincere commitment to God and his work of salvation."

BIOGRAPHICAL AND CRITICAL SOURCES:

PERIODICALS

Booklist, October 1, 2007, Bryce Christensen, review of *Bridging the Divide: The Continuing Conversation between a Mormon and an Evangelical,* p. 20.

Deseret News, December 23, 2007, Dennis Lythgoe, "Profound 'Divide' Explores 2 Faiths"; January 10, 2008, Jerry Earl Johnston, "Tone Is Key in Talks with Evangelicals."

East Valley Tribune, July 10, 2009, Lawn Griffiths, "Mormon, Baptist Respect Differences in Faith."

ONLINE

Bridging the Divide Web site, http://www.bridgingthedivide.net (July 29, 2009).

Standing Together Web site, http://www.standingtogether.org/ (July 29, 2009), author profile.*

* * *

JOHNSON, Jeannie
(J.G. Goodhind)

PERSONAL: Born in South Bristol, England; children: one daughter. *Ethnicity:* British. *Education:* Bristol Central Secondary Commercial School, Bristol, England. *Hobbies and other interests:* Breeding Irish Setters.

ADDRESSES: Home—Wye Valley, Wales.

CAREER: Worker in probation service, tourism, and hotel management; historical novelist.

AWARDS, HONORS: British Broadcasting Corporation (BBC) New Writers Initiative, Radio Bristol (England), for the script "Second Time Around."

WRITINGS:

The Rest of Our Lives, Orion (London, England), 2002.

A Penny for Tomorrow, Orion (London, England), 2003.

Loving Enemies, Severn House (New York, NY), 2006.

Where the Wild Thyme Blows, Severn House (Sutton, England), 2007.

Secret Sins, Severn House (Sutton, England), 2007.

Bitter Harvest, Severn House (Sutton, England), 2008.

"STRONG" SERIES

Like an Evening Gone, Orion (London, England), 2004.

Just before Dawn, Orion (London, England), 2005.

Forgotten Faces, Orion (London, England), 2005.

"HONEY DRIVER" SERIES; UNDER PSEUDONYM J.G. GOODHIND

Something in the Blood, Severn House (Sutton, England), 2007.

A Taste to Die For, Severn House (Sutton, England), 2007.

Walking with Ghosts, Severn House (Sutton, England), 2008.

Menu for Murder, Severn House (Sutton, England), 2009.

SIDELIGHTS: Jeannie Johnson grew up in South Bristol, England. While attending Victoria Park Junior Girls, Marksbury Road Secondary, and Bristol Central Secondary Commercial School she learned not to stick out. As a way to fit in, she told stories and wrote plays and musicals, despite her schools' lack of encouragement in art and writing.

Johnson worked a variety of jobs in law, probation service, tourism, hotel management, and Irish Setter breeding. She was also a supporting actress in *Casualty* and *Holby City.* As part of a new talent search, she received the BBC New Writers Initiative at Radio Bristol for a script she wrote entitled "Second Time Around."

Publishing *The Rest of Our Lives* in 2002 was the beginning of Johnson's prolific writing career. The book chronicles three women waiting at the train station for their men and how their relationships with their loved ones changed their lives.

Johnson wrote three novels in the "Strong" series, *Like an Evening Gone, Just before Dawn,* and *Forgotten Faces,* about the wealthy Strong family who owns sugar plantations in the West Indies. Despite tragedy, secrets, and loss of their inheritance, Tom Strong and Horatia Strong will do anything to keep the family's status.

Johnson's book *Loving Enemies,* published in 2006, follows Mary Anne Randall, a pregnant laundress and pawnbroker with an abusive drunken husband. Soon Mary Ann falls for a young foreigner. Set during World War II, the challenges of the lives of England's working class "are brought gently to life in Johnson's touching story," said Patty Engelmann in *Booklist.*

Secret Sins follows the story begun in *Loving Enemies.* After Mary Anne's home is bombed, she and her eleven-year-old son live hand-to-mouth and are pursued by her abusive husband, who wants her back. Lynne Welch wrote in *Booklist* that readers who are interested in World War II stories "will appreciate the glimpses into both civilian and military lives."

In 2008 Johnson published *Bitter Harvest.* Set between World Wars I and II, the story follows Catherine, the illegitimate daughter of the head of a winemaking family. Catherine's world falls apart when she is married off to a man for business reasons and when her mother commits suicide. Lynne Welch wrote in *Booklist,* "This powerful novel . . . encompasses both tragedy and triumph."

Beginning in 2007, Johnson published the "Honey Driver" cozy mystery series under the pseudonym J.G. Goodhind. Honey is a hotelier in Bath, England, and an amateur sleuth who assists the local police on behalf of the Bath Hotels Association. Solving crimes and locking up the perpetrators is good for business.

The first book in the series, *Something in the Blood,* involves the mystery of an American tourist who disappears from a local bed-and-breakfast inn. Honey offers her detective skills to the local police and notices the attractive sergeant Steve Doherty. A writer in *Kirkus Reviews* praised "the kickoff to Goodhind's new mystery series—fast-moving, with a likable heroine and an impeccably rendered Bath background."

Another Honey Driver book, *A Taste to Die For,* followed. During a cooking competition, two of the great chefs of Bath, England, are found murdered, and Honey and detective Steve go into action searching for a link between the victims.

Emily Melton wrote in *Booklist,* "The detailed descriptions of one of England's loveliest cities will appeal to ardent Anglophiles." A writer in *Kirkus Reviews* said, "This sequel to Honey's bright debut . . . is another hit."

The third book in the "Honey Driver" series is *Walking with Ghosts.* During a ghost walk with her guests, Honey meets an American calling herself Lady Templeton-Jones. After Jones turns up strangled to death, Honey and Steve weed out the many suspects to find the killer. A writer in *Kirkus Reviews* noted, "Honey's third is just the thing for cozy-loving Anglophiles."

BIOGRAPHICAL AND CRITICAL SOURCES:

PERIODICALS

Booklist, December 15, 2006, Patty Engelmann, review of *Loving Enemies,* p. 29; May 1, 2007, Patty Engelmann, review of *Where the Wild Thyme Blows,* p. 73; October 1, 2007, Lynne Welch, review of *Secret Sins,* p. 32; January 1, 2008, Emily Melton, review of *A Taste to Die For,* p. 50; July 1, 2008, Lynne Welch, review of *Bitter Harvest,* p. 33.

Kirkus Reviews, August 15, 2007, review of *Something in the Blood;* December 15, 2007, review of *A Taste to Die For;* October 15, 2008, review of *Walking with Ghosts.*

ONLINE

Fantastic Fiction, http://www.fantasticfiction.co.uk/ (August 9, 2009), author profile.

Jeannie Johnson Home Page http://www.jeanniejohnson.net (August 9, 2009), author profile.*

* * *

JOHNSON, Kenneth C. 1942-

PERSONAL: Born October 26, 1942, in Pine Bluff, AK. *Education:* Graduate of Carnegie Mellon University.

ADDRESSES: Office—4461 Vista Del Monte Ave., Sherman Oaks CA 91403. *E-mail*—KennyCJohnson@aol.com.

CAREER: Television creator and writer.

Director of television films and of episodes of television shows, including *Alan King Looks Back in Anger: A Review of 1972,* 1973; *Alan King in Las Vegas: Part I,* 1973; *Alan King in Las Vegas, Part II,* 1973; *Adam-12,* National Broadcasting Company (NBC), 1973; *The Secret Empire,* National Broadcasting Company (NBC), 1979; *The Curse of Dracula,* National Broadcasting Company (NBC), 1979 (also producer); *Zenon: Girl of the 21st Century,* Disney Channel, 1999; *Don't Look under the Bed,* Disney Channel, 1999; *Seven Days,* UPN, 1999-2001; *JAG,* Columbia Broadcasting System (CBS), 2002-04; *Easy Money,* CW Television Network, 2008.

Instructor at film schools including University of California at Los Angeles and University of Southern California Film Schools, and English National Film and Television Schools.

AWARDS, HONORS: Viewers for Quality Television Award; Sci-Fi Universe Lifetime Achievement Award; multiple Saturn Awards, Academy of Science Fiction, Fantasy, and Horror Films.

WRITINGS:

NOVELS

V: The Second Generation, Tor (New York, NY), 2007.

V: The Original Miniseries, Tor (New York, NY), 2008.

SIX MILLION DOLLAR MAN/BIONIC WOMAN

(And producer) *The Six Million Dollar Man: The Secret of Bigfoot*, American Broadcasting Company (ABC), 1975.

The Six Million Dollar Man: The Bionic Woman, American Broadcasting Company (ABC), 1975.

(And producer of twenty-one episodes) *The Six Million Dollar Man,* eleven episodes, American Broadcasting Company (ABC), 1975.

(And producer of thirty-three episodes; and director of three episodes) *The Bionic Woman,* fifty-seven episodes, American Broadcasting Company (ABC), 1976.

INCREDIBLE HULK

(And director) *The Incredible Hulk*, Columbia Broadcasting System (CBS), 1977.

The Incredible Hulk: Death in the Family, Columbia Broadcasting System (CBS), 1977.

(And director) *The Incredible Hulk: Married*, Columbia Broadcasting System (CBS), 1978.

(And executive producer of eighty episodes; and director of three episodes) *The Incredible Hulk,* five episodes, Columbia Broadcasting System (CBS), 1978.

V

(And executive producer and director) *V: The Original Mini-Series*, National Broadcasting Company (NBC), 1983.

(And executive producer) *V: The Final Battle*, National Broadcasting Company (NBC), 1984.

V: The Series, nineteen episodes, National Broadcasting Company (NBC), 1984.

ALIEN NATION

Alien Nation, twenty-two episodes, Fox, 1989.

Alien Nation: Body and Soul, Fox, 1995.

Alien Nation: Millenium, Fox, 1996.

Alien Nation: The Enemy Within, Fox, 1996.

Alien Nation: The Udara Legacy, Fox, 1996.

Also developer, executive producer, director of TV movies and one television episode, and composer of theme music.

MISCELLANEOUS TELEVISION

(And producer and director) *An Evening of Edgar Allen Poe,* American-International Television (AIP-TV), 1972.

Adam-12, "Keeping Tabs" and "The Beast," National Broadcasting Company (NBC), 1973.

(And director of one episode.) *Griff*, American Broadcasting Company (ABC), 1973.

(And executive producer and director) *The Girl Who Saved the World*, Universal TV, 1979.

(And executive producer and director) *Senior Trip*, Columbia Broadcasting System (CBS), 1981.

(And executive producer and director) *Hot Pursuit*, 1984.

(And executive producer and director) *Shadow Chasers*, American Broadcasting Company (ABC), 1985.

(And executive producer and director) *The Liberators*, American Broadcasting Company (ABC), 1987.

(And director) *Sherlock Holmes Returns*, Columbia Broadcasting System (CBS), 1993.

(And executive producer) *The Master Race*, Showtime Network, 2001.

(And executive producer and director) *Venus Rising*, Pax Films, 2002.

(And director) *The Valley of Secrets*, TBS Superstation, 2002.

FEATURE FILMS

(And director) *Steel*, Warner Brothers, 1997.

SIDELIGHTS: Kenneth C. Johnson is a television writer, director, and producer He was born in Pine Bluff, Arkansas, on October 26, 1942, and graduated from Carnegie Mellon University's department of drama.

Johnson is best known for his work on science-fiction series. He was the creator of the television series *The Six Million Dollar Man* which ran from 1974 to 1978 following three television movies in 1973, all starring Lee Majors. The series was about the adventures of Steve Austin, a man who received cybernetic attachments after an accident, giving him super-strength and other powers. Johnson also created the spin-off series *The Bionic Woman* starring Lindsay Wagner, which ran from 1976 to 1978. Following the cancellation of those two shows, Johnson created the popular series *The Incredible Hulk* which ran from 1978 to 1982. The Hulk of the title was a super-strong, green-skinned monster, who had first appeared in Marvel Comics.

In 1983 Johnson created, wrote and directed the miniseries *V,* about the infiltration and takeover of earth by seemingly friendly aliens who eventually reveal themselves to be dangerous predatory reptiles. The miniseries was successful enough to spawn a sequel, *V: The Final Battle,* for which Johnson again created the original concept and an early script. However, he left the project after creative differences with the broadcaster, NBC. Johnson was not involved in the following weekly series *V: The Series*, though he does have writing credits on a number of episodes.

Johnson's next high-profile project was the 1989 television series *Alien Nation,* loosely based on the movie of the same name. As in *V,* the story revolves around an alien race arriving on earth. In this case, however, the aliens are friendly, and the story uses the culture differences between humans and "Newcomers" to explore issues of racism, bigotry, and cultural difference. The series was cancelled after one season on Fox. However, Johnson was able to continue the story in a series of five television movies that ran from 1994 to 1997.

In an interview with the Web site *Deadbolt,* Johnson explained his development of the *Alien Nation,* series. "I wasn't that enamored with the movie. I felt it had a great premise that sort of went awry and sort of turned. I always characterize it as sort of Miami Vice with Coneheads and I just felt that they had missed this golden opportunity and I wasn't really that interested. Then I got to this one scene where the alien cop waved goodbye to his family as he went off to work one morning and there was only one shot of his family in the movie, this little alien woman and her two little alien kids. When I saw that it was like a bell went off and I said, 'Wait a minute, I see what this is.' I went back to Fox and said, 'You think you've got Lethal Weapon with aliens.' And they said, 'Yeah, yeah.' I said, 'No. What you've got is In the Heat of the Night. Let me do a piece about what it's like to be the world's newest minority, to be the latest people off of the bus from below the border, the dregs of society, to be the ones everybody looks down on and has a bad word about. That's a show that's not only interesting to me, but it's a show that's got legs. It's a show that's got the ability to just go on and on.'"

There have been various plans to develop either a new *V* miniseries or a feature film. Though none of these has yet come to fruition, Johnson has written a sequel to the original series in novel form titled *V: The Second Generation.* The novel is set twenty years after the original mini-series. The alien Visitors still control earth, but the human resistance fighters gain new allies in another alien race, the insectile Zedti. Carl V. Hayes writing in *Booklist* said "Johnson's energetic, though merely workmanlike, prose should give long-suffering V fans some new thrills."

Johnson also wrote a novelization of *V: The Original Miniseries,* which was published in 2008.

BIOGRAPHICAL AND CRITICAL SOURCES:

PERIODICALS

Booklist, October 1, 2007, Carl Hays, review of *V: The Second Generation,* p. 42.

ONLINE

Deadbolt, http://www.thedeadbolt.com/ (July 17, 2009), Troy Rogers, "Back in Time with Alien Nation Creator Kenneth Johnson."

Kenneth Johnson Home Page, http://www.kennethjohnson.us (July 17, 2009), author profile.

LA Times-Hero Complex Blog, http://www.latimesblogs.latimes.com/ (December 12, 2008), Lee Margulies, "'V' Creator Kenneth Johnson Talks about a Return to Reptiles."

* * *

JOHNSON, Norma Tadlock 1929-
(Kay Kirby, a joint pseudonym)

PERSONAL: Born March 27, 1929; married Elvin R. Johnson (deceased); children: Janice Kay Johnson, Karl. *Education:* Washington State College (now

Washington State University), B.A. (cum laude); Mexico City College (now University of the Americas).

ADDRESSES: Home—Burlington, WA. *E-mail*—norma@normatadlockjohnson.com; cozymystery@yahoo.com.

CAREER: Writer.

MEMBER: American Association of University Women (former president, local chapter), Skagit Vally Writers League, Delta Gamma.

WRITINGS:

Inca Gold, Walker (New York, NY), 1984.
Too Hot to Handle, Walker (New York, NY), 1985.
Bats on the Bedstead, Houghton Mifflin (Boston, MA), 1987.
Witch House, Avon Camelot (New York, NY), 1987.
Donna Rose and the Slug War, Five Star (Waterville, ME), 2004.
Soldiers of the Mountain: The Story of the 10th Mountain Division of World War II, PublishAmerica (Frederick, MD), 2005.
Donna Rose and the Roots of Evil: A Cedar Harbor Mystery, Five Star (Detroit, MI), 2009.

WITH DAUGHTER, JANICE KAY JOHNSON, UNDER JOINT PSEUDONYM KAY KIRBY

Summertime Love, New American Library (New York, NY), 1982.
Autumn Beginning, New American Library (New York, NY), 1982.
Winter Interlude, New American Library (New York, NY), 1982.

SIDELIGHTS: Norma Tadlock Johnson is a writer of novels, nonfiction, and books for younger readers. She was born March 27, 1929, and graduated cum laude from Washington State College. She also pursued graduate studies at Mexico City College. She has lived in Washington, Oregon, California, and Mexico, with summers in Wyoming, and currently resides in Burlington, Washington.

Johnson first published a series of romances written with her daughter, Janice Kay Johnson, under the joint pseudonym Kay Kirby. Among those titles were *Summertime Love, Autumn Beginning,* and *Winter Interlude.* Writing solo, Johnson then produced two romantic suspense novels, *Inca Gold,* published in 1984, and *Too Hot to Handle,* published in 1985.

Johnson subsequently moved into juvenile books. *Bats on the Bedstead,* published in 1987, describes an eleven-year-old boy named Ricky. When his family moves into an old house, Ricky has to fight a flock of evil bats. Though he tries to warn the family of the danger, they do not believe him, and Ricky must try to convince them both of their peril and of his sanity. In 1987 Johnson also published *Witch House,* another juvenile book.

In 2004 Johnson published *Donna Rose and the Slug War,* inspired in part by Johnson's own experiences serving on a local water board and battling slugs in her garden. Donna Galbreath, a retired schoolteacher, discovers the body of the water board chair while she is out digging for clams. Soon the chair's widow is poisoned, and Donna herself becomes the victim of an attack. With the help of her neighbor Cyrus Bates, Donna sets out to find the murderer and solve the mystery. Rex E. Klett, writing in *Library Journal,* praised the book, noting that "outspoken, smart, . . . and caring, Donna makes a perfect sleuth."

Johnson's next project was a foray into wartime history entitled *Soldiers of the Mountain: The Story of the 10th Mountain Division of World War II,* published in 2005. The book describes the experiences of the U.S. Army's 10th Mountain Division, which fought in the mountains of Italy. The men of the 10th were much celebrated in their day, and photographs of their preparations for fighting in the wintery Alps became well known in the United States. The division's most famous battle ended in a defeat of the Germans at Mount Belvedere. Johnson, whose husband, Elvin, won the purple heart and the bronze star while serving as a platoon leader in the 10th, interviewed a number of veterans for this book. She uses their stories and correspondence to flesh out her history of the 10th.

In 2009 Johnson published a sequel to *Donna Rose and the Slug War* entitled *Donna Rose and the Roots of Evil: A Cedar Harbor Mystery.* The story begins with the death of incompetent police Chief Donniker, who collapses while dining at a banquet given in his honor. Further investigation reveals that he has been poisoned with monkshood, a flowing plant used to deadly effect in the first Donna Rose mystery. Donna's friend, officer Jake Santorini, is accused of the crime, so once again it is up to Donna and her neighbor Cyrus to find the real killer.

A reviewer in *Kirkus Reviews* greeted this sequel with enthusiasm, commenting: "The bourgeoning romance between Johnson's . . . older sleuths . . . is likely to make them even more popular with the cozy crowd." Judy Coon, writing in *Booklist,* added that *Donna Rose and the Roots of Evil* would be "pleasant reading for gardeners and for those who enjoy small-town mysteries." Harriet Klausner, writing on the Web site *Mystery Gazette,* added "Although the story line is a bit thin, fans will enjoy Donna Rose's second . . . due to a strong cast who bring alive the Puget Sound area."

Johnson told *CA:* "I got interested in writing from being an avid reader. I'd always intended to write 'someday,' but one day, my daughter and I were discussing romances which were just beginning to be popular. We decided that we could write a better one! She has now written over sixty books for Super Romance plus two historical and a children's picture book, been nominated six times for Romance Writers Rita award, and won it last year for best contemporary romance of the year."

When asked about her influences, Johnson said, "Naturally, my daughter, as well as my local Skagit Writer critique group, which is outstanding. I originally was in a critique group in Snohomish County, headed by Willo Davis Roberts, who also were a positive influence."

She then explained her writing process: "I don't know who said it, but I've heard that we are either 'plungers' or 'plotters.' I definitely am a plunger. I wish I were more methodical. I start with an idea—my characters introduce themselves as well as name themselves, and then I'm off. Fortunately, critique groups are great as brainstormers."

BIOGRAPHICAL AND CRITICAL SOURCES:

PERIODICALS

Booklist, January 1, 2009, Judy Coon, review of *Donna Rose and the Roots of Evil: A Cedar Harbor Mystery,* p. 53.

Drood Review of Mystery, July 1, 2004, Melinda C. Burton, review of *Donna Rose and the Slug War.*

Kirkus Reviews, October 15, 2008, review of *Donna Rose and the Roots of Evil.*

Library Journal, August 1, 2004, Rex E. Klett, review of *Donna Rose and the Slug War,* p. 59.

Publishers Weekly, April 24, 1987, Diane Roback, review of *Bats on the Bedstead,* p. 71.

Reading Teacher, October 1, 1987, Sam Leaton Sebesta, review of *Bats on the Bedstead,* p. 97.

School Library Journal, April 1, 1987, Lisa Smith, review of *Bats on the Bedstead,* p. 96.

ONLINE

Mystery Gazette, http://www.themysterygazette.blogspot.com/ (November 13, 2008), review of *Donna Rose and the Roots of Evil.*

Norma Tadlock Johnson Home Page, http://www.normatadlockjohnson.net (July 17, 2009), author profile.

* * *

JONES, Ricky L. 1967-

PERSONAL: Born July 13, 1967; son of Shelly Stewart (a marketing executive, activist, and author). *Education:* Morehouse College, B.A. (with honors); University of Kentucky, M.A., Ph.D., c. 1996.

ADDRESSES: Office—Department of Pan-African Studies, 445 Strickler Hall, University of Louisville, Louisville, KY 40292. *E-mail*—ricky.jones@louisville.edu.

CAREER: University of Kentucky, Lexington, graduate assistant, 1994-96, instructor, 1995-96; University of Nebraska, Lincoln, visiting scholar, 1995; University of Louisville, Louisville, KY, assistant professor, 1996-2002, associate professor, department of Pan-African Studies, 2002—, vice chair, 2002-03, chair, 2004-08, director, Center for the Study of Crime and Justice in Black Communities, 2007—.

MEMBER: National Council of Black Studies (board of directors), Kentucky American Civil Liberties Union (board of directors).

AWARDS, HONORS: Achievement Award, Lexington (KY) Alumni Chapter of Kappa Alpha Psi, 1994; Polemarch's Award, 1998; Lyman T. Johnson Graduate Fellow, University of Kentucky, 1992-95; Order of Omega Fraternal Honor Society, 1995; National Science Foundation Teaching Fellow, University of Nebraska, 1995; Office of Minority Affairs Faculty Appreciation Award, 1998; Eleanor Young Love Award for Distinguished Scholarship, University of Louisville, 1999; Most Influential Leaders under 40, *Louisville Magazine,* 2002; Guiding Light Award, Association of Black Students, 2004; Most Influential Black Leaders Recognition, *Louisville Courier Journal;* Best Minority/Women's Reporting, Society of Professional Journalists, 2004, 2005, 2006, for "Message to the People" column; YMCA Adult Achiever, 2006.

WRITINGS:

Black Haze: Violence, Sacrifice, and Manhood in Black Greek-Letter Fraternities, State University of New York Press (Albany, NY), 2004.

What's Wrong with Obamamania? Black America, Black Leadership, and the Death of Political Imagination, State University of New York Press (Albany, NY), 2008.

Contributor of chapters to scholarly books and of articles to journals, including *Western Journal of Black Studies, Challenge: A Journal of Research on African American Men, Journal of African American Men, International Journal of African Studies, Negro Educational Review, Griot, Black Scholar, Western Journal of Black Studies, Negro Educational Review, Diverse Issues in Higher Education,* and *International Journal of Africana Studies.* Contributor of a monthly column, "Message to the People," to the *Louisville Eccentric Observer.* Contributor of book reviews to New York University Press and Greenwood Press. Member of the advisory board of *Louisville Cardinal Student Newspaper,* 2004-06. Member of the editorial board of *Journal of African American Studies,* 2006—.

SIDELIGHTS: Ricky L. Jones is a writer, an activist, and an associate professor in the Department of Pan-African Studies at the University of Louisville. Born July 13, 1967, he is the son of Shelly Stewart, a businessman and activist. Jones was raised by his maternal grandmother in the housing projects in Atlanta, Georgia. He was the first member of his family to graduate from high school, and went on to receive a B.A. in political science from Morehouse College and a Ph.D. in political science from the University of Kentucky. He specialized in political philosophy and comparative politics.

Jones's first book is *Black Haze: Violence, Sacrifice, and Manhood in Black Greek-Letter Fraternities,* a study of fraternity hazing. Jones himself was a fraternity chapter president and national committee representative, and the book draws on that experience as well as on research in five different black fraternities. Jones argues that black hazing rituals are more violent than those in other fraternities. He maintains that this is because, as an oppressed group, blacks see the ability to withstand punishment and physical abuse as important aspects of building black male identity. Lamont A. Flowers, writing in *Journal of College Student Development,* praised Jones's work as "an important addition to the scholarship" on Greek organizations.

Jones's second book is *What's Wrong with Obamamania? Black America, Black Leadership, and the Death of Political Imagination,* published in 2008. The book uses the excitement surrounding Barack Obama's run for president as an occasion to examine changes in black leadership. Jones argues in particular that Obama's unwillingness to directly address issues of race means that he may not have the positive impact on race and black America that many hope. Jones discusses the history of black leadership, from W.E.B. DuBois to Martin Luther King, Jr. He also examines modern black institutions, such as megachurches, and hip-hop culture. Jones also notes that the black community has sometimes in the past idealized black leaders, and he argues that such an approach is dangerous, since it can lead to disappointment and unfair expectations. A reviewer writing in *Publishers Weekly* praised the book, saying that it "provides a level of racial analysis and exploration that is almost entirely absent in the mainstream media." Vanessa Bush, writing in *Booklist,* was also impressed with *What's Wrong with Obamamania?* noting that though the book is "a bit academic at times," overall it "is a penetrating look at how race politics has evolved."

In addition to his academic work, Jones is an activist and writes an award-winning column for the alternative weekly *Louisville Eccentric Observer.* The column, "Message to the People," has raised controversy on several occasions. For example, in one column Jones accused two leading Louisville pastors of selling out to Republican members of Congress who had secured federal grants for the city.

In one of his columns, published on June 17, 2009, Jones discussed his next book project: *The End of Race: Moments and Movements in Post-Racial America.* Jones says his book "asks pressing questions. Is it easier and healthier to deny race, ethnicity and religious divisions than deal with them? Is the first question moot because America has already dealt with these problems? Are those of us who remain on the American left simply wrong, and have our views on race, ethnicity and other American cleavages outlived their usefulness? Have we really crossed the post-racial/post-ethnic/post-religious affiliation frontier?"

Jones is a member of the editorial board of *Journal of African American Studies* and was a member of the advisory board of the student newspaper *Louisville Cardinal.* His articles have appeared in numerous academic journals.

BIOGRAPHICAL AND CRITICAL SOURCES:

PERIODICALS

Booklist, May 15, 2008, Vanessa Bush, review of *What's Wrong with Obamamania? Black America, Black Leadership, and the Death of Political Imagination,* p. 19.

Journal of College Student Development, May-June, 2005, Lamont A. Flowers, review of *Black Haze: Violence, Sacrifice, and Manhood in Black Greek-Letter Fraternities,* pp. 328-331.

Publishers Weekly, April 21, 2008, review of *What's Wrong with Obamamania?,* p. 48.

ONLINE

Courier-Journal Online, http://www.rickyljones.com/ (June 8, 2003), Larry Muhammad, "When Conscience Calls."

Ricky L. Jones Home Page, http://www.rickyljones.com (July 20, 2009).

University of Louisville Web site, http://louisville.edu/ (July 20, 2009), faculty profile.*

*   *   *

JONES, Sabrina 1960-

PERSONAL: Born October 6, 1960, in Philadelphia, PA; married Steve Stern (a novelist). *Education:* Attended Pratt Institute; School of Visual Arts, M.F.A.

ADDRESSES: Home—Brooklyn, NY. *E-mail*—sabjonze@yahoo.com.

CAREER: Writer, illustrator, and scenery painter.

MEMBER: United Scenic Artists.

WRITINGS:

Isadora Duncan: A Graphic Biography, Hill & Wang (New York, NY), 2008.

Cofounder and editor of *Girltalk.* Contributor of art and writing to serial comics publications, including *Real Girl, Girltalk,* and *World War 3 Illustrated.* Contributor of historical comics to *Wobblies! A Graphic History of the Industrial Workers of the World.*

SIDELIGHTS: Sabrina Jones is a comic book creator. She was born October 6, 1960, in Philadelphia, Pennsylvania, where she spent her childhood. She studied painting at the Pratt Institute in New York, New York, and received her master of fine arts degree from the School of Visual Arts in the same city. In the mid-1990s, she cofounded and edited the first issues of the comics anthology *Girl Talk.* She has also contributed to the comics *Real Girl* and, more recently, *World War 3 Illustrated.* Her comics were also included in the book *Wobblies! A Graphic History of the Industrial Workers of the World.* She lives in Brooklyn, New York, and paints scenery for film, theater, and television. She is married to novelist Steve Stern.

Jones's first book is *Isadora Duncan: A Graphic Biography,* published in 2008. The book, which Jones both wrote and drew, relates in black-and-white comic-book form the life of Isadora Duncan, the early-twentieth-century American dancer. Duncan was a pioneer of modern dance, who moved away from traditional ballet to a more improvisational and emotional performance. She was known for her sometimes scandalous personal life and for an idiosyncratic style that included flowing gowns and homemade sandals. Duncan was also an advocate for social causes and for women's independence. Jones draws on Duncan's autobiographical writing and on numerous prose biographies for this narrative. For the illustrations, Jones used the many sketches and illustrations of Duncan's performances by painter Abraham Walkowitz and other artists. Jones also used some still photographs, and she looked at modern performances of Duncan's choreography.

In an interview with *Comic Book Resources,* Jones explained what drew her to the biography of Duncan: "Her impact on the field of dance alone is pivotal, the equivalent of Picasso in painting, James Joyce or Whitman in writing. She also looked beyond the stage, advocating for justice and liberation, especially for women and poor children. Throw in an outsized personality and a major appetite for love. . . . At the same time, I realize she might have driven me up a wall if I knew her personally. To paraphrase her student Irma: She had no common sense, but if she did, then she wouldn't have been a genius."

A contributor to *Kirkus Reviews* felt that Jones could have dealt more explicitly with the more scandalous details of Duncan's life, such as her romantic relationships with women, her suicide attempts, and her public drunkenness. However, the same reviewer noted, "With bold strokes and supple lettering, Jones's pen-and-ink drawings attempt to animate Duncan's boundary-smashing style, onstage and off." A reviewer in *School Library Journal* praised *Isadora Duncan,* noting that drawings of Duncan "capture her free spirit." Francisca Goldsmith, writing in *School Library Journal,* called the book "a fine . . . account for dancers, artists, and those interested in American rebels."

BIOGRAPHICAL AND CRITICAL SOURCES:

PERIODICALS

Kirkus Reviews, October 1, 2008, review of *Isadora Duncan: A Graphic Biography.*

School Library Journal, November 1, 2008, Francisca Goldsmith, review of *Isadora Duncan,* p. 156; April 1, 2009, review of *Isadora Duncan,* p. 54.

ONLINE

Comic Book Resources, http://www.comicbookresources.com/ (January 7, 2009), Van Jensen, "Sabrina Jones Dances with Isadora Duncan."

Macmillan Web site, http://us.macmillan.com/ (July 20, 2009), author profile.

Sabrina Jones Home Page, http://www.sabrinaland.com (July 20, 2009).*

* * *

JORDAN, Toni 1966-

PERSONAL: Born 1966, in Brisbane, Queensland, Australia; married. *Education:* University of Queensland, B.S.; RMIT University, Diploma of Arts in Professional Writing.

ADDRESSES: Home—Melbourne, Victoria, Australia.

CAREER: Writer and educator. RMIT University, Melbourne, Victoria, Australia, creative writing instructor.

Worked variously as a research assistant, a molecular biologist, a quality control chemist, a door-to-door saleswoman, a marketing manager, a shop assistant, and a copywriter.

AWARDS, HONORS: Best Fiction, UK Medical Journalists Association, for *Addition.*

WRITINGS:

Addition, William Morrow (New York, NY), 2009.

Contributor of articles to *Sunday Age, Sun-Herald* and *Monthly* (Australia).

SIDELIGHTS: Toni Jordan is an Australian novelist. She was born in 1966 in Brisbane, Queensland, Australia, and majored in science at the University of Queensland. She held a number of jobs, including working as a molecular biologist and a door-to-door saleswoman, before she became an advertising copywriter for a vitamin company. To sharpen her copywriting skills, she enrolled in a course at RMIT University in Melbourne, Victoria, Australia. She took a novel-writing course in order to fulfill a requirement and found that it unexpectedly sparked an interest in fiction. Her first novel, *Addition,* appeared in 2008 and is being published in fifteen countries.

Addition is narrated by Grace Lisa Vandenburg, a woman obsessed with numbers. She counts the number of times she brushes her hair, the number of times she brushes her teeth—the number of times she does everything. Her obsessive compulsive disorder (OCD) is so severe that it keeps her from holding down a job or having a boyfriend. One day, however, she meets a man named Seamus, and inspired by the prospect of romance, she seeks out a cure. The medications she takes to control her disorder, though, make her drab, dull, and slow, and Grace begins to worry that in an effort to conform, she may be losing herself.

Sarah Hague, writing for the Web site *Trashionista,* said, "*Addition* is full of humour and charm. It takes a tender look at the way people suffer from OCDs but does not descend into whimsy." A reviewer writing in *Publishers Weekly* agreed, noting that "the novel does everything a sweet, agreeable romantic comedy should." Allison Block, writing in *Booklist,* added, "Jordan's debut is witty and wise." A contributor to *Kirkus Reviews* called the book "gemlike" and praised it as "a smartly written comedy that cheekily suggests recovery may not be for everyone." Anika Fajardo, writing in *School Library Journal,* noted that fans of Steve Martin's story of obsessive compulsive disorder, *The Pleasure of My Company,* might particularly enjoy Jordan's novel. Fajardo concluded that *Addition,* is "highly recommended for all popular fiction collections."

Laurie Hertzel, writing in the Minneapolis *Star Tribune,* felt that love interest Seamus was perhaps too perfect and that Grace's therapists were perhaps too oblivious. However, Hertzel said these were "just quibbles" and concluded that Grace "herself is a joy—witty, dry, perfectly aware of her situation and how it is affecting her life, occasionally regretful and often the most sensible person around." Charity Vogel, writing in the *Buffalo News,* enjoyed the unusual narration but was even more impressed that "Jordan nails down a deeply seated cause to her heroine's mental gymnastics in an episode from her past that floats to the surface late in the story, to devastating effect." Vogel added, "Don't be fooled by this novel's candy-colored cover. It looks light and fluffy. Wrong, wrong—once you begin the story inside, this love story that's unlike any you've read before, you'll be turning pages long after you should've called lights out."

When interviewed by Fiona Gruber for an article in the *Sydney Morning Herald,* Jordan said of her novel, "At heart, it's a romantic comedy and I wouldn't like the fact that Grace has a few quirks to move it too far from [that] identity. That's what I like about writing and reading but I don't think that means a book can't make you think or a book can't speak to you; it doesn't have to be light and fluffy." Jordan also said that the sex scenes "were the easiest things to write out of the whole novel. I don't care for euphemisms. I think you've got to call it what it is and I think it's a really wonderful tool for a novelist because the way that someone makes love reveals so much about their character. You can really use it to draw a very vivid picture."

Jordan lives in Melbourne with her husband. She teaches creative writing at RMIT University.

BIOGRAPHICAL AND CRITICAL SOURCES:

PERIODICALS

Booklist, January 1, 2009, Allison Block, review of *Addition,* p. 42.

Book World, February 1, 2009, Ron Charles, "Counting on Love," review of *Addition,* p. 6.

Buffalo News, March 9, 2009, Charity Vogel, "*Addition* an Impressive Debut from Australia Native Toni Jordan."

Kirkus Reviews, November 15, 2008, review of *Addition.*

Library Journal, January 1, 2009, Anika Fajardo, review of *Addition,* p. 78.

Pharmacy News, February 14, 2008, "Comic Love Story Adds Up to a Great Read," review of *Addition,* p. 22.

Publishers Weekly, November 10, 2008, review of *Addition,* p. 29.
Star Tribune (Minneapolis, MN), March 25, 2009, "Quirky Main Character Is the Base for *Addition,*" p. 6.

ONLINE

Daisy's Book Journal, http://lazydaisy0413.blogspot.com/ (February 27, 2009), review of *Addition.*
HarperCollins Web site, http://www.harpercollins.com (January 26, 2008), author profile.
PerthNow, http://www.news.com.au/ (April 19, 2008), Brian Crisp, "A Lovely Set of Numbers," review of *Addition.*
Readings, http://www.readings.com.au/ (January 31, 2008), Louise Swinn, "Toni Jordan."
Sydney Morning Herald, http://www.smh.com.au/ (January 26, 2008), Fiona Gruber, "A Romance That Counts."
Toni Jordan Home Page, http://www.tonijordan.com (July 20 2009).
Trashionista, http://www.trashionista.com/ (July 20, 2009), Sarah Hague, review of *Addition.**

* * *

JULIANI, Richard N. 1938-
(Richard Nicholas Juliani)

PERSONAL: Born August 11, 1938. *Education:* University of Pennsylvania, Ph.D.

ADDRESSES: Office—St. Augustine Center for the Liberal Arts, Rm. 277, Sociology, 800 Lancaster Ave., Villanova, PA 19085. *E-mail*—richard.juliani@villanova.edu.

CAREER: Writer, educator, sociologist. Villanova University, Villanova, PA, professor.

AWARDS, HONORS: University Research Award, Villanova University, 1999.

WRITINGS:

The Social Organization of Immigration: The Italians in Philadelphia, Arno Press (New York, NY), 1980.
(Editor, with Sandra P. Juliani) *New Explorations in Italian American Studies: Proceedings of the 25th Annual Conference of the American Italian Historical Association, Washington, DC, November 12-14, 1992,* The Association (Washington, DC), 1994.
Building Little Italy: Philadelphia's Italians before Mass Migration, Pennsylvania State University Press (University Park, PA), 1998.
Priest, Parish, and People: Saving the Faith in Philadelphia's 'Little Italy', University of Notre Dame Press (Notre Dame, IN), 2007.

SIDELIGHTS: A professor of sociology at Villanova University, Richard N. Juliani has written several books dealing with Italian immigration to Philadelphia and the creation of the area known as Little Italy. With his 1998 book *Building Little Italy: Philadelphia's Italians before Mass Migration,* Juliani employs his three decades of research to provide a picture of Italian settlement in Philadelphia. Juliani noted in the introduction to that volume: "A famous scholar once declared that we really do not know America, unless we know the history of its peoples. He might have added that the history of any American city is a story of each of the groups that has made up its population. So the history of Philadelphia is not the saga of a single people, but of many different groups. Although they often met in a shared mainstream, each also had its own experiences. It is only when we see how these different pathways sometimes intersected and fused, but at other moments diverged and remained distinct, that we begin to understand the complicated labyrinth that is the American city."

In *Building Little Italy,* Juliani notes that because earlier works provided little information about Italians in Philadelphia prior to the large wave of immigration that began in the 1880s, his work would purposely concentrate on the earlier era. He shows that Italians first began arriving in Philadelphia in the middle of the eighteenth century, that is, in pre-Revolutionary times. They worked as tradesman, businessmen, scholars, and artists, and from this humble beginning a corner of Philadelphia became a destination for thousands more Italians in later years. The numbers of Italians remained relatively small in Philadelphia, however, until the 1850s. Juliani shows how these early immigrants mostly hailed from the Ligurian coast near Genoa. He uses church records and naturalization records to trace this nascent Italian community, showing how they became sponsors or witnesses for each other in weddings, baptisms, and immigration matters. Juliani also points out that early settlement was centered in the Moyamensing district of Philadelphia, around which grew what became known as Little Italy. This area of South Philadelphia would, by the twentieth century, contain one of the largest Italian American communities in the nation. Some of the early trades these people were involved in included construction, sculpture, and street music. By 1850 there were about 200 Italians in the city, but twenty years later this had grown to 760, a number that included children born in the United States. Ten years later, it was more than double that number. With these numbers, the Philadelphia Italians began to create community foundations and produce civic leaders. The community was granted a Catholic parish, St. Mary Magdalen de Pazzi, as well.

Reviewing Juliani's book for the *H-Net* Web site, Roger D. Simon felt that "the research is extraordinarily meticulous and truly painstaking as [Juliani] traced individuals through various records despite misspellings and Americanization of names." Simon did complain, however, that "Juliani essentially cuts off his narrative story in the mid-1870s, which is just a little too soon," as the community thereafter really became established. Yet overall, Simon praised the work: "Rarely have historians of a major immigrant group invested as much effort in tracing the early pioneers as has Juliani in this work. Juliani has sympathetically reconstructed the initial stages of immigrant community formation and imaginatively drawn from a wide range of sources. He provides new insight into the process of how a discrete group of individuals formed social networks and worked to create the base for Philadelphia's large Italian American community." Similarly, *Canadian Review of Sociology and Anthropology* contributor Sam Migliore concluded, "Juliani has provided us with important insights into the life circumstances early Italian settlers encountered in Philadelphia, their efforts to establish an Italian community for themselves and their children, and the many contributions they made to the development of the city itself." Michael Miller Topp, writing for *International Migration Review,* thought the work was "diligently researched," as well as a "valuable look at a relatively unexplored era of Italian migration." Further positive comments came from *Journal of American Ethnic History* reviewer Diane C. Vecchio, who noted, "One of the many strengths of Juliani's book is his examination of early immigrant communal development within the political, commercial, and intellectual context of the city." Vecchio added, "In addition, Juliani skillfully explains emigration against the backdrop of political developments in Italy." Likewise, *Labor History* contributor Robert M. Zecker observed, "Juliani's important scholarship has filled a gap in the way we conceive of immigrant community building in America."

In his 2007 work *Priest, Parish, and People: Saving the Faith in Philadelphia's 'Little Italy',* Juliani describes a more narrowly focused investigation of Philadelphia's Little Italy. He traces the development of communal relationships in the neighborhood by researching the St. Mary Magdalen de Pazzi parish, which was founded in 1853. He also looks at the work of one of the early rectors of that parish, Antonio Isoleri, who served from 1870 to 1926. Isoleri is a vital part of Juliani's narrative, which demonstrates that this priest was important to the Italian community in several ways. He not only was a bridge for his parishioners between Italy and their new American homes, but he also served as a bridge to different liturgical forms from the Old World to the New World, and as a champion for the new immigrants, attacking the labor agents, or *padrones,* who exploited immigrant laborers they sponsored. And finally, Isoleri also let his parishioners know that there was no conflict between being a good Catholic and being an Italian nationalist. Noting the narrow scope of the work, *Church History* reviewer Joseph P. Chinnici still felt that Juliani "has . . . added considerably to our knowledge of the complexity of the immigrant experience." Joseph Casino, writing for the *Catholic Historical Review,* also was enthusiastic about this work, noting, "Throughout this work, Juliani enriches our understanding of a historical evolution with sociological insights," and further commenting, "If it were not for the erudition and craftsmanship of its author, this work might have choked on its own richness."

BIOGRAPHICAL AND CRITICAL SOURCES:

BOOKS

Juliani, Richard N., *Building Little Italy: Philadelphia's Italians before Mass Migration,* Pennsylvania State University Press (University Park, PA), 1998.

PERIODICALS

American Historical Review, April, 2008, Leslie Woodcock Tentler, review of *Priest, Parish, and People: Saving the Faith in Philadelphia's 'Little Italy',* p. 512.

Canadian Review of Sociology and Anthropology, November, 1999, Sam Migliore, review of *Building Little Italy: Philadelphia's Italians before Mass Migration,* p. 604.

Catholic Historical Review, April, 2008, Joseph J. Casino, review of *Priest, Parish, and People,* p. 404.

Choice, December, 1998, review of *Building Little Italy,* p. 743; October, 2007, P. Kivisto, review of *Priest, Parish, and People,* p. 363.

Church History, March, 2008, Joseph P. Chinnici, review of *Priest, Parish, and People,* p. 205.

Contemporary Sociology, May, 1999, Richard D. Alba, review of *Building Little Italy,* p. 331; November, 2007, Jualynne E. Dodson, review of *Priest, Parish, and People,* p. 568.

Ethnic and Racial Studies, September 1, 2000, Phylis Cancilla Martinelli, review of *Building Little Italy,* p. 935.

International Migration Review, summer, 1999, Michael Miller Topp, review of *Building Little Italy,* p. 500.

Journal of American Ethnic History, January, 1999, Diane C. Vecchio, review of *Building Little Italy,* p. 139; January, 2008, Jordan Stanger-Ross, review of *Priest, Parish, and People,* p. 111.

Journal of American History, June, 1999, Salvatore J. LaGumina, review of *Building Little Italy,* p. 267; December, 2007, Evelyn Savidge Sterne, review of *Priest, Parish, and People,* p. 947.

Journal of Social History, winter, 1999, Donna R. Gabaccia, review of *Building Little Italy,* p. 490.

Labor History, May, 1999, Robert M. Zecker, review of *Building Little Italy,* p. 239.

Reference & Research Book News, November, 1998, review of *Building Little Italy,* p. 54.

ONLINE

H-Net, http://www2.h-net.msu.edu/ (September 1, 1998), Roger D. Simon, review of *Building Little Italy.*

Penn State University Press Web site, http://www.psupress.org/ (July 14, 2009), brief author biography.

Villanova University Web site, http://www.villanova.edu/ (July 14, 2009), "Richard N. Juliani."*

* * *

JULIANI, Richard Nicholas
See JULIANI, Richard N.

K

KAGEN, Lesley

PERSONAL: Born in Milwaukee, WI; married Peter Kagan; children: Casey (son), Riley (daughter). *Education:* Attended Marquette University and University of Wisconsin.

ADDRESSES: *E-mail*—lesleykagen@gmail.com.

CAREER: Actor, restaurant proprietor, and writer. WZMF (radio station), Milwaukee, WI, disc jockey; Licorice Pizza, Los Angeles, CA, producer, writer, and voice actress for commercials, 1976-86; Restaurant Hama, Milwaukee, WI, co-owner, c. 1997—. Worked variously as a voice actress and on-camera actress.

WRITINGS:

Whistling in the Dark, NAL Accent (New York, NY), 2007.

Land of a Hundred Wonders, New American Library (New York, NY), 2008.

SIDELIGHTS: Lesley Kagen is a former actress, a restaurant owner, and a novelist. She was born in Milwaukee, Wisconsin, and majored in radio and television at the University of Wisconsin. She worked as a morning drive disc jockey at one of the first alternative radio stations, WZMF. In 1976, she moved to Los Angeles, California, where for ten years she wrote, produced, and did the voice work for advertisements for Licorice Pizza. She went on to do other voice work and some acting, including commercials and an episode of the television show *Laverne and Shirley.* She met her husband, Peter, in California, though he too was originally from Milwaukee. After the birth of their two children, they moved back to their home town in 1990. A few years later they opened a Japanese restaurant, Restaurant Hama.

In an interview with the Web site *Authors Unleashed,* Kagen explained how she became a writer. "I was that kid that everyone thought would grow up to be a writer because I was such a readaholic. But I fooled everyone and became an actress instead. I spent most of my adult life doing voice-overs for radio and TV. I've done thousands of commercials. It wasn't until much later in life that I decided to write."

Kagen published her first book, *Whistling in the Dark,* in 2007. The novel is set in Milwaukee in the summer of 1959. The narrative focuses on Sally O'Malley, a ten-year-old girl whose father recently died in a car crash. The neighborhood has witnessed a series of murders, and Sally, who swore to her father that she would protect her younger sister, Troo, is determined to fulfill her promise. Sally thinks her neighbor, a policeman, may be responsible for the murders, but she has no one to share her fears with: her mother is in the hospital, her new stepfather is an alcoholic, and her older sister is in love. So, without adult help, it falls to Sally and Troo to investigate the suspect and discover the shocking truth for themselves.

Harriet Klausner, writing on the Web site *Best Reviews,* noted that *Whistling in the Dark* is primarily about the lives of children and only secondarily a mystery.

Klausner added, "Readers will obtain a feel for Milwaukee . . . but it is the cleverly developed warning that children think differently that makes" the book special. A reviewer writing in *Publishers Weekly* also considered the mystery "sketchy" but found Sally "an enchanting protagonist." A reviewer writing on the Web site *Never Not Reading* also felt that "Sally was a wonderful character." The same reviewer noted, "There were . . . many poignant moments in this book that brought the hint of tears to my eyes."

Whistling in the Dark was a *New York Times* best seller. An interviewer with *OnMilwaukee.com* asked Kagen whether she was surprised by the success of the book, to which Kagen responded, "Not surprised, gobsmacked! The chances of having even a moderately successful novel these days is astronomical. To make The New York Times Best Seller List, it, shoot, now you're making me cry. I've considered having that engraved on my tombstone, by the way. Here lies Lesley Kagen. She was a New York Times Bestseller author, you know."

Kagen's second novel, *Land of a Hundred Wonders,* was published in 2008. It is set in Kentucky in the early 1970s and focuses on Gibby McGraw, a twenty-year-old who was mildly brain damaged in the same car accident that killed her parents. "NQR" (for "Not Quite Right") Gibby lives with her grandfather and self-publishes a newspaper, *Gibby's Gazette.* One day she discovers the body of a local politician, and she devotes herself to solving the crime and proving that she can be a real newspaperwoman. A reviewer in *Publishers Weekly* called *Land of a Hundred Wonders* "winsome" and characterized Gibby as a "wonderfully wise Nancy Drew."

BIOGRAPHICAL AND CRITICAL SOURCES:

PERIODICALS

Books, April 29, 2007, review of *Whistling in the Dark,* p. 8.

Publishers Weekly, March 12, 2007, review of *Whistling in the Dark,* p. 40; June 30, 2008, review of *Land of a Hundred Wonders,* p. 162.

Voice of Youth Advocates, February 1, 2008, Pam Carlson, review of *Whistling in the Dark,* p. 525.

ONLINE

Authors Unleashed, http://authorsunleashed.blogspot.com/ (February 19, 2009), "Interview with Lesley Kagen."

Best Reviews, http://thebestreviews.com (May 18, 2007), Harriet Klausner, review of *Whistling in the Dark.*

Lesley Kagen Home Page, http://www.lesleykagen.com (July 20, 2009), author profile.

Never Not Reading, http://nevernotreading.blogspot.com/ (April 29, 2009), review of *Whistling in the Dark.*

OnMilwaukee.com, http://www.onmilwaukee.com/ (August 4, 2008), "Milwaukee Talks: Author Lesley Kagen."

* * *

KALTNER, John 1954-

PERSONAL: Born November 12, 1954. *Education:* State University of New York at Oswego, B.A.; Maryknoll School of Theology, M.A.; Pontifical Biblical Institute, S.S.L.; Drew University, Ph.D.

ADDRESSES: *Office*—Rhodes College, 2000 N. Parkway, Memphis, TN 38112-1690. *E-mail*—kaltner@rhodes.edu.

CAREER: Writer, educator, and theologian. Rhodes College, Memphis, TN, Virginia Ballou McGehee Professor of Muslim-Christian Relations.

AWARDS, HONORS: Jameson M. Jones Award for Outstanding Faculty Service, Rhodes College, 2007.

WRITINGS:

The Use of Arabic in Biblical Hebrew Lexicography, Catholic Biblical Association of America (Washington, DC), 1996.

Ishmael Instructs Isaac: An Introduction to the Qur'an for Bible Readers, Liturgical Press (Collegeville, MN), 1999.

(Editor, with Steven L. McKenzie) *Beyond Babel: A Handbook for Biblical Hebrew and Related Languages,* Brill (Boston, MA), 2002.

Inquiring of Joseph: Getting to Know a Biblical Character through the Qur'an, Liturgical Press (Collegeville, MN), 2003.

Islam: What Non-Muslims Should Know, Fortress (Philadelphia, PA), 2003.

(Editor, with Louis Stulman) *Inspired Speech: Prophecy in the Ancient Near East: Essays in Honor of Herbert B. Huffmon,* T & T Clark International (New York, NY), 2004.

(With Steven L. McKenzie) *The Old Testament: Its Background, Growth and Content,* Abingdon Press (Nashville, TN), 2007.

(With Howard R. Greenstein and Kendra G. Hotz) *What Do Our Neighbors Believe? Questions and Answers about Judaism, Christianity, and Islam,* Westminster John Knox Press (Louisville, KY), 2007.

(With Steven L. McKenzie and Joel Kilpatrick) *The Uncensored Bible: The Bawdy and Naughty Bits of the Good Book,* HarperOne (San Francisco, CA), 2008.

SIDELIGHTS: A professor of religious studies, John Kaltner is a scholar of the Bible, Arabic, and Islam. Many of his books attempt to create an atmosphere of understanding among these major world religions. In *Ishmael Instructs Isaac: An Introduction to the Qur'an for Bible Readers* and *Inquiring of Joseph: Getting to Know a Biblical Character through the Qur'an,* Kaltner shows points of connection between Islam and Christianity. In *Islam: What Non-Muslims Should Know,* Kaltner provides an overview to Islam, with an emphasis, according to *Interpretation* contributor Michael T. Shelley, on the point "that Islam is a complex religion, and while Muslims share certain beliefs and practices, there is a rich diversity among them." Thus, Kaltner argues that it is wrong to look at the Muslim world as monolithic, especially in light of the terrorist activities of some fundamentalists. He covers the biography of Mohammed, the founding and general practices of the religion, Islamic law, the differences between the two main branches of Islam (Sunni and Shi'a), the role of women in Muslim society, and also the concept of the holy war, or jihad. Shelley termed the book "a sympathetic presentation of Islam that is solid and well written." Similarly, *Currents in Theology and Mission* contributor Mark C. Mattes felt that *Islam* "is particularly welcome in an America that increasingly has an Islamic community and is becoming exposed to the wider Islamic world." Mattes further remarked that Kaltner's work "is especially helpful in describing Islam's reaction toward Western modernity," and in general that the author "does an excellent job in giving Americans an objective portrait of Islam."

With Steven L. McKenzie, Kaltner edited the 2002 collection of essays *Beyond Babel: A Handbook for Biblical Hebrew and Related Languages.* The book collects essays from eleven authors that give a general picture of the most important ancient languages used in the study of the Bible, including Egyptian, Hittite, Aramaic, Hebrew, and Akkadian. Not only do the contributors supply an overview of each language, but they also discuss its importance in the study of the Old Testament and list some of the major resources in the language in focus.

Working again with McKenzie, Kaltner wrote the 2007 title *The Old Testament: Its Background, Growth, and Content.* The authors provide an introduction to "the content, historical and literary background, composition and editing, and selected interpretive issues for each book of the [Old Testament]," according to James P. Ashmore writing in *Interpretation.* Ashmore also noted, "Because it avoids scholarly jargon and employs an accessible writing style, this book will also be a useful reference for pastors and educators."

Again teaming with McKenzie, and with the journalist Joel Kilpatrick, Kaltner provides a somewhat lighter exploration of Biblical themes in *The Uncensored Bible: The Bawdy and Naughty Bits of the Good Book,* published in 2008. As a *Publishers Weekly* contributor noted, the authors deal with "juicy tales of sex, dysfunctional families and body parts" from the Hebrew Bible. Some of the stories they investigate include the theory that Eve was actually not formed from Adam's rib, but from his penis; that Joseph may have liked to indulge in wearing female clothing; that Ruth and Boaz may have been doing more than making wheat on the threshing room floor; and that Ehud, the murderer of King Eglon, got away by crawling through a privy. Some of these and other theories they dismiss out of hand, while others receive a serious if somewhat tongue-in-cheek treatment. A *Publishers Weekly* review of *The Uncensored Bible* described it as an "unexpectedly delightful (if juvenile) little book." Similarly, *Booklist* reviewer June Sawyer thought that for those not easily offended, "this is high entertainment that well may lead to many stimulating conversations."

BIOGRAPHICAL AND CRITICAL SOURCES:

PERIODICALS

Booklist, April 1, 2008, June Sawyers, review of *The Uncensored Bible: The Bawdy and Naughty Bits of the Good Book,* p. 6.

Catholic Biblical Quarterly, October, 1997, A.H. Mathias Zahniser, review of *The Use of Arabic in Biblical Hebrew Lexicography,* p. 736; July, 2003, Christopher A. Rollston, review of *Beyond Babel: A Handbook for Biblical Hebrew and Related Languages,* p. 486.

Currents in Theology and Mission, June, 2003, Ralph W. Klein, review of *Beyond Babel,* p. 226; October, 2004, Mark C. Mattes, review of *Islam: What Non-Muslims Should Know,* p. 400; June, 2005, review of *Inspired Speech: Prophecy in the Ancient Near East: Essays in Honor of Herbert B. Huffmon,* p. 221.

Interpretation, April, 2004, Michael T. Shelley, review of *Islam,* p. 222; January, 2009, James P. Ashmore, review of *The Old Testament: Its Background, Growth, and Content,* p. 88.

Journal of Biblical Literature, winter, 1999, Lester L. Grabbe, review of *The Use of Arabic in Biblical Hebrew Lexicography,* p. 711.

Journal of Near Eastern Studies, October, 2006, D.M. Clemens, review of *Beyond Babel,* p. 291.

Journal of Theological Studies, April, 2000, Geoffrey Khan, review of *The Use of Arabic in Biblical Hebrew Lexicography,* p. 173.

Publishers Weekly, April 21, 2008, review of *The Uncensored Bible,* p. 55.

ONLINE

HarperCollins Web site, http://www.harpercollins.com/ (July 14, 2009), "John Kaltner."

Rhodes College Web site, http://www.rhodes.edu/ (August 24, 2007), "Dr. John Kaltner Receives Jameson M. Jones Award for Outstanding Faculty Service"; (July 14, 2009), "John Kaltner."

KEATS, Jonathon 1971-

PERSONAL: Born October 2, 1971, in New York, NY; son of Andrew Terry and Adrienne Keats. *Education:* Amherst College, B.A., 1994.

ADDRESSES: *Home*—San Francisco, CA.

CAREER: Writer, journalist, critic, and conceptual artist. *San Francisco Magazine,* San Francisco, CA, art critic and senior editor, 1997; *Artweek,* San Francisco, culture columnist, 2004; *Wired,* San Francisco, columnist. Writer-in-residence, University of Arizona Poetry Center, Tucson, 2000, Ucross Foundation, Clearmont, WY, 2002; Yaddo, Saratoga Springs, NY, 2003; MacDowell Colony, Petersborough, NH, 2004; McNamara Foundation, Westport, ME, 2006. Artist-in-residence, Montana State University, Bozeman, MT, 2009.

Exhibitions: "Twenty Four Hour Cogito," 2000; "Every Entity Is Identical to Itself," 2002; "1,001 Concertos for Tuning Forks and Audience," 2002; "Brain Trust," 2003; "The God Project," 2004;

MEMBER: Last Supper Society, Philosophical Society of San Francisco (founding member), National Book Critics Circle (board of directors).

WRITINGS:

The Pathology of Lies, Warner Books (New York, NY), 1999.

Control + Alt + Delete: A Dictionary of Cyber Slang, Lyons Press (Guilford, CT), 2007.

The Book of the Unknown: Tales of the Thirty-Six, Random House (New York, NY), 2009.

Also author of novel *Lighter Than Vanity* (in Russian translation), Eksmo Publishers, 2006. Contributor to periodicals, including *Washington Post, Boston Globe, Popular Science, Art in America, Prospect, Forbes Life,* and *Salon.com.*

SIDELIGHTS: Jonathon Keats is a conceptual artist and writer, whose written works include the novel *The Pathology of Lies,* a dictionary entitled *Control + Alt*

+ *Delete: A Dictionary of Cyber Slang,* and the collection of fables *The Book of the Unknown: Tales of the Thirty-Six.* As a conceptual artist, Keats is known for his "thought art." Indeed, his first such "piece" was a marathon of sitting and thinking—for twenty-four hours—at a San Francisco gallery with a nude model in front of him, after which he offered to sell his thoughts to the public. Since that time he has created bee ballets, exhibited plant pornography, attempted to genetically re-create God, and created a ring tone from a silent composition by composer John Cage. Describing Keats's conceptual work for the *Good Magazine* Web site, Theo Schell-Lambert and Jen Dessinger remarked: "Keats's art is essentially that of an earnest philosopher—its driving method an intentional naiveté, a put-on innocence about the way the world works. Playing a bit dumb opens up questions most people assume are already answered, questions that often illuminate something new."

Keats's written works are somewhat more conventional, yet still inspire questioning. His debut novel, *The Pathology of Lies,* provides an "interesting twist on the psycho-killer mystery-thriller," according to *Booklist* contributor Denise Blank. The novel features Gloria Greene, who has just become the new editor of San Francisco's prestigious *Portfolio* magazine. The promotion stirs controversy and interests the FBI, for Greene's predecessor was murdered and his cut up pieces sent to the magazine's subscribers around the nation. Greene, formerly the food editor at the magazine—though she knows little about food—has precious few management skills. When it becomes known that she is a suspect in the murder of the editor, Greene plays it up and turns herself into a celebrity, hoping to win a Pulitzer from all of the coverage. She flaunts her ongoing incestuous affair with her surgeon father and makes light of the fact that she grew up scalpel in hand, dissecting cadavers. She also manages to confound the investigators from the FBI, who become increasingly assured that she is the murderer. A *Publishers Weekly* contributor found this novel a "shrewd satire" and although not living up to its "Dostoyevskian aspirations" still thought "it does succeed at being slick and sassy." Blank had similar praise for the work, noting that Keats is "deft, harsh, and flip, and his novel is a success."

Keats's next novel, *Lighter Than Vanity,* appeared in Russian translation in 2006. It tells the story of a young female college student, Anastasia, who wants to make a career as an American literature scholar. She works at her college library to help pay the bills, and it is there, in a box donated by art dealer Simon Stickley, that she discovers a lost manuscript by the American writer Ernest Hemingway. This is literary gold for Anastasia, but before she announces the discovery, she seeks out Simon, who is apparently ignorant of the manuscript. She and Simon begin dating, and soon Anastasia decides on a bold plan: she will publish the Hemingway manuscript as her own. In the event, it is a huge success, and she and Simon are married. But when it comes time to produce the contractual second novel, things begin to turn awkward.

Keats turned lexicographer for his 2007 title *Control + Alt + Delete,* a reference book introducing the lingo of high-tech. The author provides 272 pages of definitions, from "analog" to "word processor."

In *The Book of the Unknown,* Keats gathers a group of stories around the Jewish concept of Lamedh-Vov. This Talmudic principle maintains that in order for the world to continue, there must be at all times thirty-six righteous souls—people who are in fact saints but have no idea they are saints. Keats presents a dozen stories of such righteous souls, all gathered by the fictional narrator of the book, Jay Katz. The protagonists are not the usual figures of folk tales; they include gamblers, liars, idiots, thieves, and even a golem made of mud, Yod the Inhuman, who, after learning to feel pain and sadness, becomes a whore for the whole village.

In an interview with Kevin Berger of *Salon.com,* Keats explained that his tales in *The Book of the Unknown* present a break with modernism: "There's nothing harmful about modernism per se, but it is rather retrograde. Life is fractured and confused, there's no denying that, yet in their efforts to mimic those qualities, the modernists and their postmodernist imitators abandoned the very reason for telling stories, which is that stories reconceive life. Myths and folk tales and fables are alternate realities, simplified and stripped of current events, microcosms that we can enter into completely while recognizing their artifice. They are akin to the philosophical thought experiments that motivate my conceptual art."

In each story, what might initially appear to be a bad action or impulse develops into a good outcome. For example, in the tale of Gimmel the Gambler, the protagonist loses his fortune to a peasant woman who in turn enjoys enough wealth to become the bride of the king. Heyh the Clown is a circus performer who did not make the grade, but still provides enough humor to charm royalty. Each of the protagonists deals with "moralistic adversity yet continues striving for goodness," noted *Booklist* contributor Blair Parsons. "Although they might stumble, they eventually find redemption and happiness." A reviewer for *Publishers Weekly* felt that "the accomplishment of this book is more about stylistic mimicry than originality." Higher praise came from a *Kirkus Reviews* contributor who concluded, "Unusual and charming stories that successfully revive a nearly forgotten form of storytelling." The same contributor commended this "high-concept collection's engaging stories," comparing them to the work of Sholom Aleichem and Isaac Bashevis Singer.

BIOGRAPHICAL AND CRITICAL SOURCES:

PERIODICALS

Booklist, May 15, 1999, Denise Blank, review of *The Pathology of Lies,* p. 1668; December 1, 2008, Blair Parsons, review of *The Book of the Unknown: Tales of the Thirty-Six,* p. 21.

Kirkus Reviews, November 15, 2008, review of *The Book of the Unknown.*

Publishers Weekly, November 17, 1999, review of *The Pathology of Lies;* September 8, 2008, review of *The Book of the Unknown,* p. 33.

San Francisco Chronicle, February 12, 2009, Justin Berton, review of *The Book of the Unknown,* p. F23.

School Library Journal, January 1, 2009, Connie Williams, review of *The Book of the Unknown,* p. 137.

ONLINE

Good Magazine, http://www.good.is/ (July 1, 2008), Theo Schell-Lambert and Jen Dessinger, "Fun with Art."

Random House Web site, http://www.randomhouse.com/ (July 14, 2009), "Jonathon Keats."

Red Room, http://www.redroom.com/ (July 14, 2009), "Jonathon Keats."

Salon.com, http://www.salon.com/ (March 9, 2009), Kevin Berger, "'If I'm Blaspheming, It Means I'm Doing My Job.'"

SF Weekly, http://www.sfweekly.com/ (August 18, 2004), Lessley Anderson, "God of the Flies."

Wired, http://www.wired.com/ (October 10, 2003), Ryan Singel, "He Thinks, Therefore He Sells."*

* * *

KEEGAN, Claire 1968-

PERSONAL: Born 1968, in County Wicklow, Ireland. *Education:* Attended Loyola University; University of Wales, M.A.; Trinity College, M.Phil.

ADDRESSES: Home—Ireland.

CAREER: Writer and creative writing teacher. Writer-in-residence at University College, Dublin, Ireland, and Dublin City University. Heimbold Professor of Irish Studies, Villanova University, Villanova, PA, 2008.

AWARDS, HONORS: Hugh Leonard Bursary, Macauley fellow, Martin Healy Prize, Kilkenny Prize, Tom Gallon Award, William Trevor Prize, Rooney Prize for Irish Literature, Olive Cook Award, and Davy Byrnes Irish Writing Award, 2009, all for short story "Foster."

WRITINGS:

Antarctica, Faber & Faber (London, England), 1999, Atlantic Monthly Press (New York, NY), 2001.

Walk the Blue Fields, Faber & Faber (London, England), 2007.

SIDELIGHTS: An award-winning author of short stories, Claire Keegan was born in rural County Wicklow, Ireland, where she grew up on a farm as the youngest member of a large family. She studied English and political science at Loyola University in New Orleans, then returned to Ireland. She began writing in 1994 when, during a spell of unemployment, she submitted her first story to a televised writing contest and saw her creation attain the list of top ten out of 10,000 entries. Encouraged, she enrolled at the University of Cardiff, Wales, where she earned a master's degree in creative writing while developing her narrative voice and a talent for storytelling. After another success in 1996, taking fourth place in the Francis McManus Short Story Competition, she encountered literary scout David Marcus, who eventually brought her work to the attention of publisher Faber and Faber. This resulted in the publication of *Antarctica,* her first collection, in 1999. Of her taste for the short story form, Keegan told interviewer Declan Meade on the *Stinging Fly* Web site, "I find the short story form deeply attractive. I think it's just slightly beneath poetry for me. . . . The short story is like a poem in that there is nothing lost. Everything is savoured. There is a strictness about it which I really admire and it takes your breath away if it's good."

The fifteen stories of *Antarctica* are set in Ireland and the southern United States. The collection describes the coming of age of a new generation in Ireland. The often-rebellious female characters are young, eager for experience, and set in family situations that offer very little comfort or encouragement. On its cover, the book offered an enthusiastic recommendation from William Trevor, a legendary Irish storyteller whose endorsement for a debut book by a young and relatively unknown author surprised the literary world. Other reviewers, on both sides of the Atlantic, offered similarly enthusiastic praise. A *Publishers Weekly* contributor offered that "while Keegan's imagery occasionally bears the clear brand of the M.F.A. program, these moments are few and are outweighed by the restraint with which she deploys such imagery, and by her stern refusal to fall back on anything that might resemble a happy ending." Max Brzezinski, writing in the *Antioch Review,* noted that "Keegan writes confidently and with great insight and has produced a livewire collection that is alternatingly terrifying and endearing."

About her writing method, Keegan revealed to interviewer Meade: "It doesn't start with a concept or an idea: I'm going to write about so and so because that's interesting. That never occurs to me. When I begin a story I have no idea how it will end. . . . The guilt is what makes you sit down. You know that you have the capacity to write and you have something in your mind that will not go away. . . . Then you can go back and you can fix it. I love that part too. I love being brutal with the first draft, paring it down and seeing the skeleton of the prose."

The author's second story collection, *Walk the Blue Fields,* was published in 2007. This collection of seven stories is taken from the author's own vivid experiences in rural Ireland, where tragedy is a familiar outcome and human relationships have the quality of timelessness. In her storytelling, the author recalls Irish folktales and myths, while citing the Russian nineteenth-century author Anton Chekhov and setting her characters firmly in the complex, often-harsh circumstances of the twentieth century. Reviewer Anne Enright in the *Guardian* commented: "This is a rural world of silent men and wild women who, for the most part, make bad marriages and vivid, uncomprehending children. It is most clearly seen through the eyes of the young because 'to be an adult was, for the greatest part, to be in darkness'. . . . Keegan makes stories as you might knock a window into the lives of the people she describes; shedding light, conferring power, inviting escape." In a admiring review on the Web site *Bookslut,* Cynthia Reeser concluded, "Keegan is promising as a storyteller, particularly when she leaves herself out of the equation. In her case, emotionally distant and detached narrators work in her favor; sometimes less is more. Her sense of pacing, narrative flow and characterization propel the sharp edges of her Ireland into solid, memorable storytelling." *Publishers Weekly* gave the author further encouragement: "Keegan's poetic prose, spot-on dialogue and well paced plot twists keep the pages turning through sadness, grief, rage and compromise."

BIOGRAPHICAL AND CRITICAL SOURCES:

PERIODICALS

America, January 7, 2002, "Forbidden Fruits," p. 24.

Antioch Review, March 22, 2002, Max Brzezinski, review of *Antarctica,* p. 340.

Booklist, June 1, 2001, Danise Hoover, review of *Antarctica,* p. 1845.

Irish Literary Supplement, September 22, 2002, "A Winning First Effort," p. 26.

Library Journal, June 1, 2001, Heather McCormack, review of *Antarctica,* p. 220.

London Review of Books, January 24, 2008, "Red Flowers at a Wedding?," p. 21.

Los Angeles Times, July 8, 2001, review of *Antarctica,* p. 10; December 2, 2001, review of *Antarctica,* p. 3.

Newsweek, August 27, 2001, review of *Antarctica,* p. 58.

New York Times Book Review, July 29, 2001, "All the Lonely People: A Debut Story Collection Explores the Couplings and Uncouplings of Its Characters," p. 10; September 7, 2008, "Watchers and Tellers," p. 20.

Publishers Weekly, June 18, 2001, review of *Antarctica,* p. 54; May 26, 2008, review of *Walk the Blue Fields,* p. 38.

ONLINE

Bookslut, http://www.bookslut.com/ (May 1, 2008), Cynthia Reeser, review of *Walk the Blue Fields.*

Fantastic Fiction, http://www.fantasticfiction.co.uk/ (August 12, 2009), author biography.

Guardian, http://www.guardian.co.uk/ (August 25, 2007), Anne Enright, "Dancing in the Dark."

Independent, http://www.independent.co.uk/ (May 4, 2008), Brandon Robshaw, review of *Walk the Blue Fields.*

Stinging Fly, http://www.stingingfly.org/ (August 12, 2009), Declan Meade, "Claire Keegan."

Winter with the Writers, http://tars.rollins.edu/winterwiththewriters/ (August 12, 2009), author biography.*

* * *

KESSEL, Brent 1969(?)-

PERSONAL: Born c. 1969; married Britta Bushnell (a yoga instructor). *Education:* University of California, Los Angeles, B.A. Studied yoga with Chuck Miller and Pattabi Jois; studied meditation with teachers including Thich Naht Hanh, the Dalai Lama, Eckhart Tolle, Jon Kabat-Zinn, and Adyashanti.

ADDRESSES: *Office*—Abacus Portfolios, 17383 Sunset Blvd., Ste. A360, Pacific Palisades, CA 90272.

CAREER: Financial planner, business person, educator, and writer. Abacus Wealth Management (now Abacus Wealth Partners), Pacific Palisades, CA, founder and CEO, 1996— Abacus Portfolios, Pacific Palisades, CEO. Since 1998, has taught a workshop on "The Yoga of Money," in venues around the country.

WRITINGS:

It's Not about the Money: Unlock Your Money Type to Achieve Spiritual and Financial Abundance, HarperOne (New York, NY), 2008.

Contributor of a column on money to *Yoga Journal.*

SIDELIGHTS: Brent Kessel is a financial planner, a business person, an educator, and a writer. He received a degree in economics with a minor in psychology from the University of California, Los Angeles. He worked as a financial planner, and in 1996 founded and became chief executive officer (CEO) of his own financial planning company, Abacus Wealth Management, located in Pacific Palisades, California. In 2004, the company merged with Sherman Financial to form Abacus Wealth Partners; Kessel remained on as CEO. Kessel is also the CEO of Abacus Portfolios, a money management firm associated with Abacus Wealth Partners. Abacus Wealth Partners was named one of the 250 top U.S. wealth management firms by *Bloomberg Wealth Manager.*

Kessel has a long-standing interest in yoga and has been involved actively in it since 1989. He has studied with teachers Chuck Miller and Pattabhi Josi and has progressed through the fourth series of Ashtanga. He has also studied meditation with a number of teachers, including Thich Naht Hanh, the Dalai Lama, and Eckhart Tolle. In 1998, Kessel began to integrate yoga and financial planning, eventually creating a workshop on money and personal growth called "The Yoga of Money." Kessel has taught this workshop around the country. He also writes a regular column on money for *Yoga Journal.*

Interviewed by Ellen Uzelac for a feature story that appeared in *Research,* Kessel explained the relationship he sees between yoga and money management. "The thing that's important in yoga is paying attention to what's happening in your body and in your life. We apply that to financial planning with a look at what's really happening: actual spending, assets, returns. . . . Here, you approach limitations with awareness. You get right up against it. That's what I try to do with money. It's just approaching a different area with compassion and sensitivity and awareness."

Kessel published his first book, *It's Not about the Money: Unlock Your Money Type to Achieve Spiritual and Financial Abundance,* in 2008. The book encourages readers to reflect on their relationship to finance. Kessel argues that many people in the United States have a "wanting mind," which continually seeks new objects and experiences and is never content. Kessel encourages self-reflection, asking readers to think about their fears and painful memories associated with money. To help in the process of self-analysis, Kessel categorizes individuals' attitudes toward wealth into eight archetypes, such as the guardian, the pleasure seeker, the caretaker, and the empire builder. He then discusses techniques to break out of each archetypical mode in order to create a happier, healthier relationship with money.

Barbara Jacobs, writing in *Booklist,* noted, "This is a financial-planning guide unlike any other on the market." A reviewer in *Publishers Weekly* commented that those "interested in an Eastern-influenced approach will find useful advice . . . as well as insight into what makes us tick."

In an interview with Kimberly Palmer that appeared in *U.S. News & World Report Online,* Kessel explains why he decided to write his book: "I saw that people were struggling in their relationship with money. No matter if they are rich or poor, everyone struggles with money. I counsel people who have hundreds of millions . . . and others who are 100,000 dollars in debt. The money doesn't seem to make a difference. The patterns that people are stuck in seem to go on and on, year after year. . . . So I decided to look to yoga, meditation, and other wisdom traditions." Kessel continued, "I noticed people approached their financial problems from the outside in. . . . How can I save more, invest better, pay credit cards off? It's never about me. . . . Yoga and meditation approach it completely differently. If you want change, you have to look inside yourself first."

BIOGRAPHICAL AND CRITICAL SOURCES:

PERIODICALS

Booklist, December 1, 2007, Barbara Jacobs, review of *It's Not about the Money: Unlock Your Money Type to Achieve Spiritual and Financial Abundance,* p. 11.

Publishers Weekly, October 15, 2007, review of *It's Not about the Money,* p. 50.

Research, November 1, 2003, Ellen Uzelac, "Financial Soul Searcher: Brent Kessel's Unusual Advisory Practice Explores Clients' Relationship to Money," p. 28.

ONLINE

Brent Kessel Home Page, http://www.brentkessel.com (July 21 2009), author profile.

U.S. News & World Report Online, April 9, 2008, Kimberly Palmer, "Mixing Meditation, Yoga, and Money Management," review of *It's Not about the Money.**

* * *

KESSLER, Jackie 1971(?)-
(Jacqueline H. Kessler)

PERSONAL: Born c. 1971, in Brooklyn, NY; married; children: two.

ADDRESSES: *Agent*—Miriam Kriss, Irene Goodman Literary Agency, 27 W. 24th St., New York, NY 10010. *E-mail*—jax@jackiekessler.com.

CAREER: Writer. Wild Child Publishing, Culver City, CA, fantasy editor; senior editor for a management consulting company.

MEMBER: Science Fiction & Fantasy Writers of America, SF Novelists, Romance Writers of America.

WRITINGS:

"HELL ON EARTH" SERIES

Hell's Belles, Zebra Books/Kensington Publishing (New York, NY), 2007.

The Road to Hell, Zebra Books/Kensington Publishing (New York, NY), 2007.

Hotter Than Hell, Zebra Books/Kensington Publishing (New York, NY), 2008.

"THE ICARUS PROJECT" SERIES

(With Caitlin Kittredge) *Black and White,* Ballantine Books (New York, NY), 2009.

(With Caitlin Kittredge) *Shades of Gray,* Bantam Spectra (New York, NY), 2010.

Contributor of short stories to numerous collections and anthologies. "Hell on Earth" series additions include "A Hell of a Time" (novella), in *Eternal Lover,* Zebra Books/Kensington Publishing (New York, NY), 2008; "When Hell Comes Calling" (short story), in *Lilith Unbound,* Popcorn Press, 2008; and "Hell on Earth" (novella), in *A Red Hot Valentine's Day,* Avon (New York, NY), 2009.

SIDELIGHTS: Jackie Kessler is an American writer of dark fantasy and paranormal fiction. Her "Hell on Earth" series features Jezebel, a four-thousand-year-old succubus who doubles as an exotic dancer and is one step away from being captured by demons from hell. Her human disguise may save her from being captured, but it does not prevent Jezebel from experiencing numerous adventures in this world. Kessler did not always intend to be a writer, as she explains on her Web site. "Me, I wanted to draw comic books. Not Archie comics, either—superhero comic books." By the age of fifteen, she discovered that she enjoyed writing the text for her comics as much as (or perhaps more than) drawing them. She began to write scenarios for her favorite comic books, such as *X-Men* and *Alpha Flight.* Kessler further notes on her Web site: "I wanted to write about power. About magic. About hot guys in spandex. And about beating those guys bloody and senseless." Later, as an editor of fantasy fiction, Kessler interviewed numerous authors and began to see how she might put her own vision into novel form.

Speaking with an *AccessRomance* Web site interviewer, Kessler explained the inspiration for her first published novel and the opening book in the "Hell on Earth" series: "When I started tinkering with the idea for the book, I knew I wanted to write about a demon no longer in Hell. And I wanted the demon to be female. That just automatically meant 'succubus' to me. And so, Jezebel the (former) succubus was born." Kessler also explained in the same interview that she took inspiration from the work of Neil Gaiman, especially his *Sandman* and its articulation of Lucifer and Hell. "That got me thinking about Hell, and the reason for Hell in the first place, and what would happen with a management change," Kessler noted. In an interview with a contributor for the *ParaNormalRomance* Web site, Kessler detailed her plans for the "Hell on Earth" series, projected at nine titles: "The main story arc is the story of Jezebel/Jesse Harris and her various relationships: with her lover Paul, with her buddy Daunuan, with her best friend Megeara . . . and with her own humanity and demonic tendencies. Major changes are happening in Hell, and Jesse isn't done with the Abyss. Or, more accurately, the Abyss isn't done with her."

In the first novel in the series, *Hell's Belles,* readers are introduced to the basic premise of Jezebel on the run from Hell and her growing infatuation with human Paul Hamilton, who has dark secrets in his past. Friends from Hell—the Fury known as Megeara and the incubus Daunuan—soon find her posing as a stripper named Jesse. This former enchantress is also pursued by various enemies from Hell, including Lillith, Queen of Hell, making Jezebel's life on earth uncomfortable, to say the least. The contributor for the *ParaNormalRomance* Web site commented, "Sex, strippers, and demons; what's not to like?" Writing for the *Media Blvd* Web site, Christina Radish commented, "Blending her snarky tone with humor and scorching sex appeal, *Hell's Belles* . . . introduced readers to 4,000-year-old former succubus turned erotic dancer Jezebel, who is on the run from Hell." Further praise for *Hell's Belles* came from *Associated Content* Web site reviewer Julie David, who wrote, "Anyone who loves steamy urban fantasies will gobble this up."

Jezebel's story is continued in *The Road to Hell,* in which Jesse is still seeing her vice-cop boyfriend Paul. However, Hell's tentacles are still trying to draw her back in. Megeara's sister arrives telling Jesse that Meg needs her desperately, and the sexy incubus Daunuan is attempting to take her away from Paul. Lillith also is once again out for revenge, making life difficult if not deathly dangerous for Jesse. Reviewing the first two books in the series for the *Green Man Review* Web site, Michael M. Jones observed, "I found the plots of both books to be rather fast-paced and compelling, with events moving at enough of a pace that it was hard to stop reading." Jones also commented on the heavy dose of sex in these books: "Kessler has a real flair for turning up the heat, taking full advantage of her characters' natures and histories to keep things at a fever pitch. It's hard to open either book and not find a scene where Jezebel isn't taking her clothes off, seducing someone, or being seduced in return, and yet the way it's presented, it's all part of the story." Writing for *Booklist,* Diana Tixier Herald found the second installment "lighthearted and funny" despite some graphic scenes of sex and torture. Similarly, a *Publishers Weekly* reviewer termed *The Road to Hell* a "raunchy blend of heaven, hell and eros."

In *Hotter Than Hell,* the focus turns to Daunuan. A test is set for him before he can become Pan's second-in-command as Hell's lords of lust: he must seduce a woman meant for Heaven. Easy enough, Daunuan figures, but he did not count on falling in love with his intended victim or with having to deal with his feelings for Jesse at the same time. A *Publishers Weekly* reviewer praised this book's "sexy and bold" plot. Kessler has provided further installments of this series in a pair of novellas and a short story, all published in anthologies.

Working with author Caitlin Kittredge, Kessler premiered a new series with the 2008 novel *Black and White.* Here Kessler gives full vent to her love for superhero comics, creating a dueling pair of former friends, Callie Bradford—known as Iridium—and Joannie Greene, also known as Jet, who are now mortal enemies. Their friendship began to dissolve following an incident at a school for young superheroes, and now they are the light and dark side of New Chicago. Jet, with her powerful Shadow, is thought to be the hero of the city, while Iridium is looked upon as a loose canon. An investigative journalist goes missing; while Jet thinks Iridium might be somehow involved, the truth is much more complex. A *Publishers Weekly* reviewer felt that Kessler and Kittredge managed to fabricate a "dark world where the narrow line between hero and vigilante is defined by corporate interests."

In her interview for *ParaNormalRomance,* Kessler remarked on a vital aspect of her fiction: world building. "I think that the challenges of world building are twofold: you have to make it believable, and you have to make it consistent. You set rules when you create worlds, and that means your characters have to obey those rules (or have a damn good reason for breaking them). If you break those rules without a reason, or if your world isn't real, then there's the very big risk of either yanking your readers out of the story or breaking their trust."

BIOGRAPHICAL AND CRITICAL SOURCES:

PERIODICALS

Booklist, September 15, 2007, Diana Tixier Herald, review of *The Road to Hell,* p. 48.

Publishers Weekly, September 17, 2007, review of *The Road to Hell,* p. 35; June 16, 2008, review of *Hotter Than Hell,* p. 33; May 4, 2009, review of *Black and White,* p. 38.

Times Union (Albany, NY), Stephanie Earls, February 3, 2008, "This Is Hell."

ONLINE

AccessRomance, http://www.accessromance.com/ (July 14, 2009), "Interview with Jackie Kessler."

Associated Content, http://www.associatedcontent.com/ (December 1, 2008), Julie David, review of *Hell's Belles.*

Book Smugglers, http://thebooksmugglers.com/ (May 26, 2009), review of *Black and White.*

Eclectic Book Lover, http://www.eclecticbooklover.com/ (June 8, 2009), review of *Black and White.*

Green Man Review, http://www.greenmanreview.com/ (July 14, 2009), Michael M. Jones, review of *Hell's Belles* and *The Road to Hell.*

Jackie Kessler Home Page, http://www.jackiekessler.com (July 22, 2009).

Media Blvd., http://www.mediablvd.com/ (April 14, 2008), Christina Radish, "Jackie Kessler's 'Hell on Earth.'"

ParaNormalRomance, http://paranormalromance.org/ (July 14, 2009), "Jackie Kessler."

Random House Web site, http://www.randomhouse.com/ (July 14, 2009), "Jackie Kessler."

SciFiGuy.ca, http://www.scifiguy.ca/ (June 29, 2009), review of *Black and White.*

Wendy Nelson Tokunaga blog, http://blog.wendytokunaga.com/ (August 4, 2008), Wendy Nelson Tokunaga, review of *Hotter Than Hell.**

* * *

KESSLER, Jacqueline H.
See KESSLER, Jackie

KIM, Mike 1976-

PERSONAL: Born December 11, 1976, in Chicago, IL. *Education:* Graduated from University of Illinois, Urbana-Champaign, 1999; also attended Georgetown University McDonough School of Business.

ADDRESSES: Home—Washington, DC.

CAREER: Financial planner, human rights worker, missionary, and writer. Crossing Borders, Glenview, IL, founder, 2003—.

WRITINGS:

Escaping North Korea: Defiance and Hope in the World's Most Repressive Country, Rowman & Littlefield (Lanham, MD), 2008.

SIDELIGHTS: Mike Kim is a financial advisor and a human rights worker. He was born December 11, 1976, to a Korean American family in Chicago, Illinois, where he also spent his childhood. He graduated from the University of Illinois at Urbana-Champaign and established his own financial advising business in Chicago. In 2001 he went on a two-week vacation in China. While there, he met a number of North Korean refugees. Their stories of the torture, sexual abuse, and desperation they faced in both North Korea and China affected him deeply. He soon gave up his business, and moved to California to learn Chinese and Korean. In 2003 he moved to the China-North Korea border. He became a student of tae kwon do, and used this as cover to help North Koreans defect and to aid them after they did so. In order to get refugees out of North Korea, Kim had to help them travel a 6,000-mile route through China and four other countries until they reached Thailand, which accepts refugees from North Korea. To help in his mission, Kim established Crossing Borders in 2003. Since its founding, the organization has set up five orphanages and twenty-five refugee shelters. The organization also testified before Congress in hearings on the topic of human trafficking in China.

Speaking to a writer for a feature which appeared in *Blue & Gray Online,* Kim explained why he had left his business to do human rights work in North Korea. "I distinctly remember sitting across from clients talking about mutual funds, retirement plans and insurance while feeling completely disengaged by it all. . . . The North Korean refugees I had met on my trip weighed heavily on my heart. At that moment I knew what I had to do—I had to go to China to help."

Huma N. Shah, writing in *Harvard Crimson,* reported on a talk Kim gave at Harvard in which he discussed his experiences and insights into North Korea. During the talk, Kim noted that even feeding North Korean refugees is illegal in China, and characterized the plight of North Korean refugees as "one of the worst human rights crisis in the world." He also discussed the terrible conditions facing North Koreans in their own country, noting that hunger was so great there that one of the teenagers he worked with had "received a bowl of white rice for his birthday gift every year."

In 2008 Kim published a book about his experiences in North Korea and China titled *Escaping North Korea: Defiance and Hope in the World's Most Repressive Country.* A reviewer writing in *Publishers Weekly* said that Kim's experiences gave him a "unique" perspective from which "to synthesize current research . . . on conditions in North Korea with affecting real-life testimonials.

Following his work in North Korea, Kim returned to the United States to pursue an MBA at Georgetown University. He continues to be involved in Crossing Borders and to speak to the media about conditions in North Korea.

BIOGRAPHICAL AND CRITICAL SOURCES:

BOOKS

Kim, Mike, *Escaping North Korea: Defiance and Hope in the World's Most Repressive Country,* Rowman & Littlefield (Lanham, MD), 2008.

PERIODICALS

Japan Times, June 6, 2009, "Refugees Having Big Impact on North Society."

Publishers Weekly, June 23, 2008, review of *Escaping North Korea,* p. 50.

ONLINE

Blue & Gray Online, http://www.thecrimson.com/ (August 7, 2009), "Risking His Life for North Korean Refugees."

Harvard Crimson Online, http://www.thecrimson.com/ (August 7, 2009), Huma N. Shah, "Korean Rights Activist Speaks."*

* * *

KINNAMAN, David 1973-

PERSONAL: Born 1973. *Education:* Attended Biola University.

ADDRESSES: Home—Ventura, CA. *E-mail*—tgorka@barna.org.

CAREER: Writer. Barna Group, Ventura, CA, president, 1995—.

WRITINGS:

(With Gabe Lyons) *Unchristian: What a New Generation Really Thinks about Christianity . . . and Why It Matters,* Baker Books (Grand Rapids, MI), 2007.

SIDELIGHTS: David Kinnaman, a resident of Ventura, California, is the president of the Barna Group, a research development and communications firm with a Christian philosophy. Kinnaman is also the author, with Gabe Lyons, of *Unchristian: What a New Generation Really Thinks about Christianity . . . and Why It Matters,* which was released in 2007. *Unchristian* is the end result of several years of research conducted with the goal of discerning how American culture, particularly youth culture, receives and responds to Christianity. Kinnaman told *Relief* Web site contributor Kimberley Culbertson that the project began as an attempt to "confirm a gut-level suspicion that people's emotional and perceptual barriers to Christ were higher than ever." Kinnaman continued, "And that's exactly what our research ended up bearing out: we have an image problem, but part of the reason for that is because we fail to understand or empathize with the skepticism and disillusionment that people have with us as Christians. It's nothing new that Christianity has an image problem. Jesus himself promised that we would be misunderstood for our faith. But it is worse than ever; it is harder to be a Christian these days—at least it is here in our American context." The text thus chronicles the circumstances which led to the increased barrier between American culture and Christian spirituality.

In a survey of those persons born between 1965 and 1983, labeled the Busters, and those born between 1984 and 2002, labeled the Mosaics, Kinnaman found that most of the participants self identified as being non-Christian. Additionally, of those participants that claimed a Christian affinity, a high percentage of the religiously inclined do not accord, as Culbertson described, "with what Christ really expects from his followers." So, the text sets about to find an answer to why the American culture is highly cynical of Christianity and why the Christian population is experiencing declining numbers. Culbertson observed, "The book focuses on six key areas in which Christians fall short of a Christ-like persona. The research shows that Christians are perceived as hypocritical, conversion-centric, anti-homosexual, sheltered, too political, and judgmental." These six attributes, identified by survey participants, help to contextualize the negative perception of the Christian Church held by many Americans. When asked by Culbertson if any of these attributes came as a surprise to the authors, Kinnaman replied, "One surprise was the intensity of the anti-homosexual perception. Christians are seen to elevate that sin above other sins and to be contemptuous toward gays and lesbians. Certainly this is a complex subject, and the Bible is clear that homosexuality is not consistent with Christian discipleship. Yet, anytime we stray toward treating homosexuals in the "older brother" mindset—feisty, arrogant, nonrelational, and condescending—it contributes little or nothing to restoring people to God's purposes." *Unchristian* addresses the negative perceptions of Christianity as an issue involving the Church's image which is perpetuated by not only non-Christians but also Christians who label and judge those who operate outside of the Church. In an interview with Keith Brenton for the *New Wineskins* Web site, Kinnaman stated, "The young people who are not Christians—they're having a harder time seeing themselves as ever wanting to become Christ-followers because of all the negative baggage that now surrounds what it means to be a Christian."

Marcia Ford, in a review for the *FaithfulReader.com,* acknowledged that, despite the text's large amount of statistical data, "the authors did a masterful job of surrounding those numbers with eye-opening anecdotes and highly accessible analysis. And they included sidebars featuring commentary from other authors who have their ear to the ground on all this, including Rick Warren, Andy Crouch, Brian McLaren and *Faithful Reader.com* Web site reviewer Margaret Feinberg. Their insights help enliven the chapters and put a human face on the stats." Moreover, in an article for the *SOMA* Web site, Robert Cornwall wrote that the text's "conclusion—that "Outsiders" (their term for persons outside the Christian faith) see Christians as hypocritical, concerned only with getting converts, anti-homosexual, sheltered, overly political, and judgmental—is useful information." In nine chapters, the text analyzes the major elements which contribute to a negative perception of the Christian faith. Not only does the text discuss the six aforementioned facets of unchristian behavior, but it also describes how these elements are individually and collectively projected. *Unchristian* asserts that Christian followers need to reexamine the fallibility of their lives and employ a more humble and understanding approach to ministry and missionary activities. Although the text itemizes the major faults facing the Church, the tone is nevertheless sanguine in that the language stresses possibility. A *Christianity Today* contributor noted that the text reminds Christians to treat others "the way a missionary approaches a host society—with eyes and ears open, expecting differences but seeking points of connection." In other words, one needs to employ respect and sympathy in order to make constructive progress.

BIOGRAPHICAL AND CRITICAL SOURCES:

PERIODICALS

Atlanta Journal-Constitution, October 6, 2007, "Faith & Values: Christians' 'Image Problem': Book Details Attitudes about Faithful," p. 6.

Booklist, October 1, 2007, June Sawyers, review of *Unchristian: What a New Generation Really Thinks about Christianity . . . and Why It Matters,* p. 28.

Christianity Today, December 1, 2007, "Who Do People Say We Are? It Doesn't Hurt to Listen to What Non-Christians Think of Us," p. 21.

Herald & Review, June 14, 2008, "Interest in Faith Is Growing among Teens."

Leadership, January 1, 2008, David Swanson, review of *Unchristian,* p. 65.

Library Journal, September 15, 2007, Steve Young, review of *Unchristian,* p. 65.

Publishers Weekly, August 13, 2007, review of *Unchristian,* p. 65.

ONLINE

Calvin College Web site, http://www.calvin.edu/ (July 22, 2009), author profile.

Common Grounds Online, http://commongroundsonline.typepad.com/ (July 22, 2009), Les Newsome, review of *Unchristian.*

Crusader Web site, http://media.www.crusaderonline.com/ (February 26, 2009), Corey Beebe, "Q&A with David Kinnaman."

FaithfulReader.com, http://www.faithfulreader.com/ (July 22, 2009), Marcia Ford, review of *Unchristian.*

Forever Yours Web site, http://brentbailey.blogspot.com/ (April 18, 2009), Brent Bailey, review of *Unchristian.*

New Wineskins, http://www.wineskins.org/ (June 13, 2008), author interview with Keith Brenton.

Relief, http://www.reliefjournal.com/ (May 16, 2008), Kimberley Culbertson, "Changing the UnChristian Perception with David Kinnaman."

SOMA, http://www.somareview.com/ (July 22, 2009), Robert Cornwall, review of *Unchristian.*

Unchristian Web site, http://www.unchristian.com (July 22, 2009).

Xposed2Jesus, http://brianford.wordpress.com/ (December 17, 2007), Brian Ford, review of *Unchristian.**

* * *

KIRBY, Kay
See JOHNSON, Norma Tadlock

KISER, John W., III 1942-

PERSONAL: Born 1942. *Education:* University of North Carolina, B.A.; Columbia University, M.A.; University of Chicago, M.B.A. Also attended Goettingen University.

ADDRESSES: Home—Sperryville, VA. *E-mail*—jwk@copper.net.

CAREER: Consultant and writer of nonfiction. U.S. Department of State, Washington, DC, private consultant, 1975-81; Kiser Research Inc., Washington, DC, president, 1981-94.

MEMBER: William and Mary Greve Foundation (chair), Urals Branch of Russian Academy of Science (honorary member), World Council for Religion and Peace (board of trustees), International Center for Religion and Diplomacy (director), University of Virginia Center for Advanced Studies in Culture (adjunct fellow).

AWARDS, HONORS: Siloe Prize, 2006, for *Monks of Tibhirine: Faith Love and Terror in Algeria.*

WRITINGS:

Report on the Potential for Technology Transfer from the Soviet Union to the United States, Kiser Research (Washington, DC), 1977.

Commercial Technology Transfer from Eastern Europe to the United States and Western Europe, Kiser Research (Washington, DC), 1980.

Communist Entrepreneurs: Unknown Innovators in the Global Economy, F. Watts (New York, NY), 1989.

Stefan Zweig, Death of a Modern Man, University of Toulouse Press (Toulouse, France), 1998.

The Monks of Tibhirine: Faith, Love, and Terror in Algeria, St. Martin's Press (New York, NY), 2002.

Commander of the Faithful: The Life and Times of Emir Abd El-Kader, Monkfish Book Publishing (Rhinebeck, NY), 2008.

Contributor of articles to the *Marine Corps Gazette, Harvard Business Review, Foreign Policy Magazine, Wall Street Journal,* and *Washington Post.*

SIDELIGHTS: John W. Kiser III's first three books, written between 1977 and 1989, were analyses of business and technological opportunities created by the exchange of ideas between the Soviet Union and the United States. Following the collapse of the Soviet Union, Kiser shifted his interests back to history and cultural studies. His next book was *Stefan Zweig, Death of a Modern Man.* Zweig was a highly influential Jewish philosopher and novelist in the 1930s and 1940s. Kiser explains on his Home Page: "I became perplexed by Zweig's suicide in 1942, living safely in Brazil, wealthy, world famous and with young new wife. Still read in Europe, Zweig today is virtually unknown in the United States."

Kiser is most noted for his two books exploring the interactions of Christians and Muslims in Algeria. The first of these is *The Monks of Tibhirine: Faith, Love, and Terror in Algeria,* which explores the lives of a small, long-standing enclave of Christian Trappist monks living in Muslim Algeria. In the 1990s, during one of Algeria's many internecine uprisings, these monks were kidnapped and executed by Islamic extremists. A contributor to *Kirkus Reviews* wrote, "In his debut, technologies broker Kiser builds up the drama leading to the monks' death with the skill of a novelist," resulting in what Kathleen Hipson, writing for *Tampa Tribune,* called "an absorbing account of the monks, their history and their fate, making them more than simply a footnote to history." Writing in *Booklist,* Margaret Flanagan noted that, instead of highlighting the martyrdom of the Christian monks, Kiser offers "a tale of courage, faith, and respect forged by culturally and religiously diverse people." A reviewer with *Publishers Weekly* likewise said that Kiser's complex book was "a must for patient American readers interested in the evolution of independent Islamic politics out of a history of European imperialism."

Several reviewers argued that *The Monks of Tibhirine* neatly captured the complexity of nuanced power struggles within the Muslim world. According to M. Basil Pennington, writing for *America,* "Kiser's book is not heavy; in fact, it is an easy and enjoyable read. Yet anyone looking for a good summation of the history of the Trappists through the centuries and through the vicissitudes of post-Vatican II renewal will not be disappointed. Kiser captures the spirit and the very down-to-earth way this life was lived at Tibhirine. . . . At the same time, he also presents Islam in its richness and depth and the historical vicissitudes it has experienced in Algiers through the centuries and in the evolution of the new Muslim nation." Joseph V. Montville wrote in the *Middle East Journal* that "*The Monks of Tibhirine* is a profoundly instructive study of some of the most important issues facing the world in the twenty-first century, including the sociology of Islamist terrorism, the courage of Muslim clergy to resist terrorist pressure to provide religious justification for the killing of innocents, and above all the capacity for Muslims and Christians to respect, honor and, yes, love each other under the most trying circumstance. These insights come in a compelling and moving narrative that reads at times like a John Le Carre novel, but with much more spiritual and emotional depth."

By far, Kiser's most notable work is *Commander of the Faithful: The Life and Times of Emir Abd El-Kader.* El-Kader, an Islamic scholar, led the first Algerian resistance to French colonial expansion, from 1832-1847. Although his resistance failed, he was celebrated throughout the world for his humane behavior in battle and ethical rigor, earning praise from newspaper columnists, average citizens, French generals he had battled, French soldiers he had held captive, Pope Pius IX, President Abraham Lincoln, and others. According to Tim Gebhart, writing for the *Blogcritics* Web site, "shortly before his death the *New York Times* described him 'among the foremost of the few great men of the century.' . . . Today, it is virtually impossible to imagine major world publications praising an Arab Muslim who led his people in a jihad against an invading superpower. *Commander of the Faithful* helps us understand how that could occur and, more important, sheds light on how our views of Islam and the Middle East continue to be affected by misconceptions or ignorance." According to Roger Kaplan, writing in the *Weekly Standard,* "John Kiser's elegant biography, with just enough contextual history to allow the reader to situate a Sufi mystic tribal leader in his times, ought to be of interest to anyone trying to figure out whether or not we should sigh and embrace another 150 years of Huntingtonian pessimism regarding clashing civilizations."

Although some reviews were uncharitable (according to a contributor to *Kirkus Reviews,* the book is "indifferently written and burdened by invented dialogue, but notable for illustrating that the meeting of civilizations need not always produce a clash"), most raved about its depth, breadth, and drama. John Burgess wrote in *Middle East Policy* that "Kiser gives an excellent overview of the politics of the time, the different actors and their motivations. He also covers the nascent conflict between and among the various religious groups in Lebanon, then still part of the same Ottoman province. . . . The book is most satisfying in its comprehensiveness. . . . As an early exponent of political Islam and pan-Islamism, singular in his lack of extremism and in his sense of a renewed, albeit restricted caliphate, Abd el-Kader makes a fascinating subject." According to Peter Steinfels of the *New York Times:* "Kiser insists on the religious dimension of what might otherwise be read as a story of military and political maneuvering. But *Commander of the Faithful* is hardly a theological study. It is a dramatic story of quarreling tribes, of Sufi sects and brotherhoods, of treacherous Ottoman officials, rival French generals, secret negotiations, broken truces, terrible atrocities and new forms of insurgency and counterinsurgency warfare. . . . It is hard to read *Commander of the Faithful* without thinking of more recent events. . . . [Kiser hopes] the book might help people 'to find in France's adventure and its ultimate failure some lessons about the world we're entering today.'"

BIOGRAPHICAL AND CRITICAL SOURCES:

PERIODICALS

America, April 8, 2002, M. Basil Pennington, "Inshallah!," p. 31.

Booklist, January 1, 2002, Margaret Flanagan, review of *The Monks of Tibhirine: Faith, Love, and Terror in Algeria,* p. 780.

Christian Century, January 16, 2002, review of *The Monks of Tibhirine,* p. 28; December 13, 2003, review of *The Monks of Tibhirine,* p. 22; December 13, 2003, review of *The Monks of Tibhirine,* p. 22.

Commonweal, August 16, 2002, review of *The Monks of Tibhirine,* p. 24.

Kirkus Reviews, December 1, 2001, review of *The Monks of Tibhirine,* p. 1664; September 15, 2008, review of *Commander of the Faithful: The Life and Times of Emir Abd El-Kader.*

Library Journal, January 1, 2002, Steve Young, review of *The Monks of Tibhirine,* p. 111.

Middle East Journal, September 22, 2003, Joseph V. Montville, review of *The Monks of Tibhirine,* p. 665; January 1, 2009, "Who Commands the Faithful?," p. 141.

Middle East Policy, March 22, 2009, John Burgess, review of *Commander of the Faithful,* p. 160.
New York Times, November 22, 2008, "Reviving a Novel-Worthy Tale of War and Religion," p. 19.
Parabola, February 1, 2003, review of *The Monks of Tibhirine,* p. 86; March 22, 2003, "Mutual Charity: A Review of the Monks of Tibhirine," p. 86.
Publishers Weekly, January 14, 2002, review of *The Monks of Tibhirine,* p. 55.
Reference & Research Book News, November 1, 2003, review of *The Monks of Tibhirine,* p. 25.
Tampa Tribune, October 20, 2002, "New in Nonfiction," p. 5.
Tribune Books, February 23, 2003, review of *The Monks of Tibhirine,* p. 6.
Wall Street Journal, February 19, 2002, "Islamic Radicals, Extreme Agenda, Grisly Death," p. 24.
Weekly Standard, January 5, 2009, "Algeria's Patriot; the Meaning for the Present of France's Colonial Past."

ONLINE

Blogcritics, http://www.blogcritics.org/ (January 15, 2009), Tim Gebhart, review of *Commander of the Faithful.*
Explore Elkader Iowa Web site, http://www.elkader-iowa.com/ (July 25, 2009), profile of author.
Macmillan Web site, http://us.macmillan.com/ (July 25, 2009), profile of author.
Read the Spirit, http://www.readthespirit.com/ (May 13, 2009), David Crumm, "Conversation about a Forgotten Muslim Hero—Perfect for Our Times."
True Jihad Web site, http://www.truejihad.com/ (July 25, 2009), profile of author.*

* * *

KLEINFELD, Lenny 1948(?)-

PERSONAL: Born c. 1948; married Ina Jaffe (a radio correspondent). *Education:* Attended University of Wisconsin, Madison.

CAREER: Playwright, journalist, screenwriter, and novelist.

MEMBER: Writers Guild of America, Mystery Writers of America.

WRITINGS:

Shooters and Chasers (novel), Five Star (Detroit, MI), 2009.

Also author of plays and screenplays. Former columnist for *Chicago* magazine. Contributor to publications including *Chicago Reader, Chicago Tribune, Playboy, New York Times,* and *Los Angeles Times.*

SIDELIGHTS: Lenny Kleinfeld is a playwright, journalist, screenwriter, and novelist. His first novel, *Shooters and Chasers,* mixes suspense and comedy elements. It focuses on two Chicago homicide detectives, Mark and Doonie, who are investigating the murder of an architect. A reviewer for the Web site *Mysterious Reviews* said that the multiple points of view in the novel are "done exceptionally well." The same reviewer felt that the ending was not sufficiently "polished" but concluded that the book "is a cleverly developed mystery with compelling characters that is thoroughly entertaining." Harriet Klausner, writing in *Mystery Gazette,* also praised the book, noting that "with several twists and a strong cast on both sides of the law, readers will appreciate this fabulous whodunit." A contributor for *Kirkus Reviews* said that the book had "appealing heroes and villains, a quirky love story, wit, style, suspense, plus . . . the authenticity of an Ed McBain procedural."

BIOGRAPHICAL AND CRITICAL SOURCES:

PERIODICALS

Kirkus Reviews, November 15, 2008, review of *Shooters and Chasers.*
Publishers Weekly, November 17, 2008, review of *Shooters and Chasers,* p. 46.

ONLINE

Chicago Reader Online, http://www.chicagoreader.com/ (August 7, 2009), Michael Miner, "Slow Torture in the Age of Speed."
Lenny Kleinfeld Home Page, http://lennykleinfeld.com (August 7, 2009).

Mysterious Gazette, http://www.mysteriousreviews.com/ (August 7, 2009), Harriet Klausner, review of *Shooters and Chasers.*

Mysterious Reviews, http://www.mysteriousreviews.com/ (August 7, 2009), review of *Shooters and Chasers.*

Wisconsin State Journal Online, http://www.madison.com/ (August 7, 2009), Doug Moe, "Moe: Husband, Wife Unravel a Mystery."*

* * *

KONIGSBERG, Bill 1970-

PERSONAL: Born 1970; partner of Chuck Cahoy. *Education:* Columbia University, B.A., 1994; Arizona State University, M.F.A., 2005.

ADDRESSES: *Home*—Billings, MT. *E-mail*—bkonigsberg@gmail.com.

CAREER: Sports journalist and young-adult author. Worked for newspapers, magazines, online publications, and wire services; *ESPN.com,* assistant editor, c. 2001; Associated Press, writer and editor, 2005-08.

AWARDS, HONORS: GLAAD Media Award, Gay and Lesbian Alliance Against Discrimination, 2002, for article "Sports World Still a Struggle for Gays"; Lambda Literary Award for Children/Young Adults, 2009, for *Out of the Pocket.*

WRITINGS:

Out of the Pocket, Dutton (New York, NY), 2008.

Also author of the *Bill Konigsberg Web Log.* Contributor to periodicals, including *Out, Denver Post, Miami Herald, New York Daily News, New York Times, San Francisco Chronicle,* and *North Jersey Herald and News,* and to Outsports.com and ESPN.com. Author of weekly syndicated column about fantasy baseball.

SIDELIGHTS: Beginning his career in journalism in the mid-1990s, Bill Konigsberg has covered the sporting world for a variety of news outlets, including the Associated Press, the *Denver Post,* the *Arizona Republic,* and ESPN.com. Konigsberg first became known to sports fans when he used a computer program to calculate the theoretical outcome of Major League Baseball's 1994 season after that season was shortened by a player's strike. In 2001 Konigsberg once again earned attention as the result of an article he wrote as assistant editor at ESPN.com. Openly announcing his homosexuality, he also discussed the absence of openly gay figures in professional athletics, a void Konigsberg had begun to notice as a teen. As he shared on his home page, "When I started to realize I was gay I thought it meant that I wasn't supposed to be an athlete, because I didn't know of a single role model who played sports and was gay." After learning of the suicide attempt of a former college football player who had been troubled by his inability to express himself as a homosexual in a rigidly defined heterosexual sports environment, Konigsberg channeled his concern into a young-adult novel.

Published in 2008, *Out of the Pocket* follows the experiences of Bobby Framingham, a senior quarterback who hopes to transition from his California high school football team to a career in college and perhaps even in the National Football League. While an outstanding athlete, the teen soon becomes known not for his success on the gridiron but for his sexual status after a friend reveals to others that Bobby is gay. For his admission, the teen receives overwhelming attention, ranging from gossipy fellow students to national media coverage. Bobby discovers how quickly his world has changed when some fellow teammates stop speaking to him, his coach initially refuses to acknowledge his orientation, and opposing players make him a target for particularly vicious hits. Compounding his troubles at school, he must also witness his father's health slowly decline as the elder Framingham battles cancer.

For his first novel, Konigsberg earned widespread praise from reviewers who cited his ability to bring to life a teen-aged boy facing the challenge of being openly gay in the hyper-masculine world of football. Calling *Out of the Pocket* "a thoughtful, powerful novel," *Booklist* critic Todd Morning added that the author creates a narrator with an "authentic first-person voice." In *School Library Journal* Megan Honig described Bobby as "a likable narrator" and considered the book "a thought-provoking, funny, and ultimately uplifting story of self-actualization." A *Kirkus Reviews* contributor noted that Konigsberg's message of "being who you are" comes through strongly in an "unusual hybrid that juxtaposes hard-hitting, play-by-play football action with scenes of psychological soul-searching." In addition to finding *Out of the Pocket* "an amazing first novel," *Journal of Adolescent and Adult Literacy* writer James Blasingame maintained that Konigsberg does not compromise on either the sports-action elements of the book nor the complex emotions Bobby encounters during his journey as an openly gay athlete. "The author's knowledge of sports is impeccable," Blasingame wrote, "and his understanding of the social interaction of teenagers weaves the story together to make it funny, heartbreaking, and heartwarming." *Out of the Pocket* won a Lambda literary award in 2009.

Konigsberg's second novel, *Openly Straight,* deals with a well-adjusted, openly gay high school senior whose problem is not acceptance, but confining labels. One of the first YA novels to deal with a gay protagonist while not focusing on homophobia, the novel focuses on seventeen-year-old Rafe Goldberg, who trades in his comfortable high school existence in Boulder, Colorado, for a label-free existence at an all-boys' boarding school in Natick, Massachusetts.

BIOGRAPHICAL AND CRITICAL SOURCES:

PERIODICALS

Booklist, September 1, 2008, Todd Morning, review of *Out of the Pocket,* p. 110.

Journal of Adolescent and Adult Literacy, October, 2008, James Blasingame, review of *Out of the Pocket,* p. 170.

Kirkus Reviews, August 15, 2008, review of *Out of the Pocket.*

School Library Journal, September, 2008, Megan Honig, review of *Out of the Pocket,* p. 188.

ONLINE

Bill Konigsberg Home Page, http://www.billkonigsberg.com (November 10, 2009).

* * *

KRITZLER, Ed

See KRITZLER, Edward

KRITZLER, Edward 1941-
(Ed Kritzler)

PERSONAL: Born 1941. *Religion:* Jewish.

ADDRESSES: Home—Kingston, Jamaica. *E-mail*—edkritzler@yahoo.com.

CAREER: Historian and journalist. Jamaican Tourist Board, Kingston, Jamaica, travel writer; Government of Jamaica, film liaison officer; tour guide.

WRITINGS:

Jewish Pirates of the Caribbean: How a Generation of Swashbuckling Jews Carved Out an Empire in the New World in Their Quest for Treasure, Religious Freedom—and Revenge, Doubleday (New York, NY), 2008.

SIDELIGHTS: Edward Kritzler, born in 1941, is a journalist and an authority on the island of Jamaica. He worked for the Jamaica Tourist Board for ten years, arranging and guiding tours for representatives of various media from all over the world. As the film liaison officer for the government of Jamaica, he has worked on a host of feature films and television documentaries. In addition, Kritzler has written extensively about Jamaica, its history, its society, its government, and its people. Because he has contacted so many Jamaican citizens through both his work and his everyday life, he has become a well-known figure all over the island, which he uses to his advantage when acting as a personal tour guide. His vast knowledge of the people and terrain of Jamaica allows him to target his tours to the specific interests of his clients, introducing them to important sports, arts, and cultural personalities and taking them to secluded and unusual locations.

Kritzler's research led him to the discovery that there were many Jewish enclaves and traders active in Jamaica and other areas of the New World from the 1400s, a fact he had not realized before. During the Inquisition, members of the Jewish community were confined to ghettos, threatened into forced conversions, and routinely persecuted, their lands and goods confiscated, their lives forfeit. The resulting diaspora scattered Jews all over the world, including the high seas. In his book *Jewish Pirates of the Caribbean: How a Generation of Swashbuckling Jews Carved Out an Empire in the New World in Their Quest for Treasure, Religious Freedom—and Revenge,* Kritzler tells how some of these disenfranchised Jews, banished from Spain in 1492, had by the seventeenth century become pirates, partly out of a quest for adventure and personal gain, and partly to take revenge on the Spanish government by plundering Spanish fleets and damaging Spain's shipping trade.

He recounts how Jewish merchants set up profitable trade routes in coffee, sugar, and precious metals, at one point cornering the silver trade, but once these businesses were established, European rulers had no more use for the "infidels" who were running them, and they called in the Holy Inquisitors to kill the leaders and confiscate their wealth. The result was that Jewish sailors and merchants went undercover and began to work against Spanish interests. According to Kritzler, undercover Jews, referred to as "Portugals," sailed with explorers Christopher Columbus and Vasco de Gama, assisted Hernán Cortés in looting Mexico and Francisco Pizarro as he plundered the South American coast, and even commanded their own fleets, sailing freely between Holland, which saw the Spanish and Portuguese as enemies, and Jamaica, where descendants of Columbus established sanctuary for Jews, as both traders and buccaneers.

Although reviewers found fault with Kritzler's scholarship and writing style, they nonetheless were enjoyably entertained by *Jewish Pirates of the Caribbean.* In his review for the *Jewish Journal,* Adam Kirsch stated, "Edward Kritzler's new book, despite its serious flaws of scholarship and interpretation, has the merit of reminding us that, in fact, Jews and the descendants of Jews played a significant role in the European colonization of the New World as merchants, diplomats, spies, and yes, even pirates," and the commentator for *Kirkus Reviews* said, "Kritzler supplies squalls of detail, occasionally at the risk of distracting attention from the overarching narrative." In his review for *Booklist,* Jay Freeman commented that the book "captures the spirit of that violent, lawless epoch . . . with an interesting ethnic perspective." Paul Kaplan, in his review for *Library Journal,* praised Kritzler's "journalist's eye for detail" and called *Jewish Pirates of the Caribbean* an "entertaining book." Writing for the *Houston Chronicle,* Steve Weinberg declared, "The narrative comes across as disconnected at times, but the material is so rich that the book is never boring."

BIOGRAPHICAL AND CRITICAL SOURCES:

PERIODICALS

Booklist, October 15, 2008, Jay Freeman, review of *Jewish Pirates of the Caribbean: How a Generation of Swashbuckling Jews Carved Out an Empire in the New World in Their Quest for Treasure, Religious Freedom—and Revenge,* p. 15.

Book World, December 14, 2008, "On the High Seas," p. 4.

Houston Chronicle, November 16, 2008, "Oy, Matey; Jewish Pirates Once Sailed the Caribbean," p. 17.

Kirkus Reviews, October 1, 2008, review of *Jewish Pirates of the Caribbean.*

Library Journal, November 1, 2008, Paul Kaplan, review of *Jewish Pirates of the Caribbean,* p. 88.

Times Literary Supplement, January 30, 2009, Nathan M. Greenfield, review of *Jewish Pirates of the Caribbean,* p. 29.

ONLINE

Jewish Journal, http://www.jewishjournal.com/ (August 12, 2009), Adam Kirsch, "Edward Kritzler's History of Jewish Pirates Is Uneven."

Jewish Pirates of the Caribbean Web site, http://www.jewishpiratesofthecaribbean.com (August 12, 2009), YouTube author interview and personal testimonials.

Random House Web site, http://www.randomhouse.com/ (August 12, 2009), short author profile and summary of *Jewish Pirates of the Caribbean.*

Ynetnews, http://www.ynetnews.com/ (August 12, 2009), Lilith Wagner, "Aaaargh, Jewish Pirates."*

L

LANDMAN, Tanya

PERSONAL: Born in Gravesend, Kent, England; partner of Rod Burnett (a puppeteer); children: Isaac, Jack. *Education:* Holds a university degree.

ADDRESSES: *Home*—Bideford, Devon, England. *E-mail*—tanyalandman@tantraweb.co.uk.

CAREER: Writer and actor. Storybox Theatre, Bristol, Devon, England, administrator, beginning 1992; freelance writer, 1992—. Presenter at schools.

AWARDS, HONORS: British Booktrust Teenage Prize shortlist, and Carnegie Medal shortlist, both 2008, both for *Apache;* Phoenix Book Award shortlist, 2009, for *Mondays Are Murder;* Carnegie Medal longlist, 2009, for *The Goldsmith's Daughter.*

WRITINGS:

PICTURE BOOKS

One Hundred Percent Pig, illustrated by Judy Brown, A. & C. Black (London, England), 2005.

The Little Egg, illustrated by Shoo Rayner, Collins (London, England), 2006.

The World's Bellybutton, illustrated by Ross Collins, Walker (London, England), 2007.

The Kranken Snores (sequel to *The World's Bellybutton*), illustrated by Ross Collins, Walker (London, England), 2008.

Mary's Penny, illustrated by Richard Holland, Candlewick Press (Somerville, MA), 2010.

Geronimo, Barrington Stoke (Edinburgh, Scotland), 2010.

"MERLIN" SERIES

Merlin's Apprentice, illustrated by Thomas Taylor, Walker (London, England), 2006.

Waking Merlin, illustrated by Thomas Taylor, Walker (London, England), 2006.

"FLOTSAM AND JETSAM" SERIES

Flotsam and Jetsam, illustrated by Ruth Rivers, Walker (London, England), 2006.

Flotsam and Jetsam and the Stormy Surprise, illustrated by Ruth Rivers, Walker (London, England), 2007.

Flotsam and Jetsam and the Grooof, illustrated by Ruth Rivers, Walker (London, England), 2008.

"POPPY FIELDS MYSTERIES" SERIES

Mondays Are Murder, Walker (London, England), 2009.

Dead Funny, Walker (London, England), 2009.

Dying to Be Famous, Walker (London, England), 2009.

The Head Is Dead, Walker (London, England), 2009.

The Scent of Blood, Walker (London, England), 2010.

Certain Death, Walker (London, England), 2010.

YOUNG-ADULT NOVELS

Useless, illustrated by Julia Page, Barrington Stoke (Edinburgh, Scotland), 2007.

Apache, Walker (London, England), 2007, published as *I Am Apache,* Candlewick Press (Cambridge, MA), 2008.

Two Words, illustrated by Julia Page, Barrington Stoke (Edinburgh, Scotland), 2008.

The Goldsmith's Daughter, Walker (London, England), 2008, Candlewick Press (Somerville, MA), 2009.

Contributor to anthologies, including *Winter Magic.*

SIDELIGHTS: Tanya Landman is a British writer whose books include the middle-grade novels *Waking Merlin* and *The World's Bellybutton* as well as beginning readers featuring the characters Flotsam and Jetsam. Turning to older readers, Landman has also produced several critically praised teen novels, both contemporary fiction such as *Useless* and *Two Words* and the historical novels *I Am Apache* and *The Goldsmith's Daughter.* In addition to her work as a writer, Landman helps run Storybox Theatre, a touring puppet theatre for children that was founded by her partner, Rod Burnett.

First published in England as *Apache, I Am Apache* draws readers into a family tragedy set in what is now Arizona: after a four-year-old boy is horribly killed when Mexican soldiers overrun his village, his fourteen-year-old sister, Siki, resolves to avenge his death. Orphaned, she has only vengeance to live for, and she now trains to master the skills that will make her a warrior. In her training, Siki is aided by Golahka, an elder of the (fictional) Black Mountain Apache tribe who is also suffering the loss of family. As Siki becomes skilled as a fighter, her once-proud people are slowly becoming dispirited at the increasing migration of white settlers into their tribal lands, and a truth about the girl's parentage ultimately affects both her path and that of her people. Noting that the scenes between Siki and Golahka are "riveting and unusual," *Kliatt* critic Claire Rosser praised *I Am Apache* as "a dramatic story" that is based on the true story of an Apache woman named Lozez, who fought with Geronimo. Although Riva Pollard maintained in *School Library Journal* that the story's "historical accuracy is questionable," she asserted that, as fiction, *I Am Apache* draws readers into "a complex adventure full of jealousy, romance, . . . bloody battles, [and] daring rescues." Landman's story "ring[s] with authenticity," Francisca Goldsmith stated in *Booklist,* the critic adding that the author's "artistic" prose benefits from "an eloquent voice and [a] dignified pace." In *Publishers Weekly* a contributor also cited Landman's "deliberately exotic" narrative voice, and added that Siki's "fiery spirit" will register with many teens.

Although Landman is British, her decision to focus on Native Americans in *I Am Apache* was sparked by the grave of Pocahontas, which is located in her home town of Gravesend, England. "There's this beautiful statue of her by the Thames silhouetted against this cold, grey expanse of the river," Landman explained to British Booktrust online interviewer Madelyn Travis. "I used to find it very moving, and when I learned more about the story of what had happened to her and how she'd died before she'd made it home I found it terribly sad. That image of her must have sunk somewhere into my subconscious." In 2008 *I Am Apache* was shortlisted for the prestigious Carnegie Medal.

BIOGRAPHICAL AND CRITICAL SOURCES:

PERIODICALS

Booklist, October 1, 2008, Francisca Goldsmith, review of *I Am Apache,* p. 38.

Kirkus Reviews, July 1, 2008, review of *I Am Apache.*

Kliatt, July, 2008, Claire Rosser, review of *I Am Apache,* p. 17.

Publishers Weekly, July 14, 2008, review of *I Am Apache,* p. 67.

School Library Journal, August, 2008, Riva Pollard, review of *I Am Apache,* p. 126.

ONLINE

British Book Trust Web site, http://www.booktrustchildrensbooks.org.uk/ (November 1, 2009), Madelyn Travis, interview with Landman.

Storybox Theater Web site, http://www.storyboxtheatre.co.uk/ (November 11, 2009).

Tanya Landman Home Page, http://www.tanyalandman.com (November 15, 2009).*

LEARNER, Tobsha 1959-

PERSONAL: Born 1959, in London, England. *Education:* Trained as a sculptor in London.

ADDRESSES: *Home*—Australia, England, and America.

CAREER: Novelist, short story writer, and playwright.

AWARDS, HONORS: Silver Medal for Best Drama Special, New York Festival Radio Awards, 1993, and Prix Italia commendation, Auteursbureau Almo bvba, Belgium, both for *Lionheart.*

WRITINGS:

Quiver: A Book of Erotic Tales, Viking (Ringwood, Victoria, Australia), 1996, Plume (New York, NY), 1998.

My Grandfathers Grave "Enough Already"—Anthology, Allen & Unwin (Australia), 1999.

Madonna Mars, Droemer-Knaur (Munich, Germany), 2001.

Tremble: Sensual Fables of the Mystical and Sinister, HarperCollins (Pymble, New South Wales, Australia), 2004.

The Witch of Cologne, Forge (New York, NY), 2005.

Some Girls Do . . . , Allen & Unwin (Australia), 2006.

Dying for It: Tales of Sex and Death, Thunder's Mouth Press/Avalon Publishing (New York, NY), 2006.

Soul, Forge (New York, NY), 2008.

In Bed with . . . , Penguin Books (Australia), 2008.

Meine Feuerroten Stilettos, Droemer-Knaur (Munich, Germany), 2008.

Sphinx, Harper Collins (New York, NY), 2009.

PLAYS

Wolf: A Dedication to Priapus, Currency Press/Playbox Theatre Co., Melbourne (Paddington, New South Wales, Australia), 1992.

The Glass Mermaid, Currency Press/Playbox Theatre Centre, Monash University Melbourne (Sydney, New South Wales, Australia), 1994.

Miracles, Currency Press/Playbox Theatre Centre, Monash University (Sydney, New South Wales, Australia), 1998.

Also author of radio plays and stage plays, including *Les enfants du paradis, Seven Acts of Love, Fidelity, Feast, The Gun in History, Witchplay, S.N.A.G (Sensitive New Age Guy), Homage, Volkov* (radio play), *Lionheart* (radio play), *Queen Song* (radio play), *Antonio's Angel,* and *Succubus.*

SIDELIGHTS: Tobsha Learner was born in London, England, in 1959 and grew up there, where she trained to be a sculptor. She believes that this training has helped to give her writing a keen feeling for eliciting the visual senses when she describes scenes and locations, and is one reason she is most interested in the relationships between characters, objects, and ideas. She has written many novels, but is best known, especially in Australia, for her stage plays and screenplays. In her plays and novels she likes to put ordinary people into extraordinary circumstances. Learner lives in the United Kingdom, the United States, and Australia in turn.

Learner's *Quiver: A Book of Erotic Tales* is a collection of stories, told from a variety of viewpoints, that use eroticism to examine issues such as power and domination, self esteem and body image, and personal relationships through characters that hunger for extreme experiences, lust for revenge, and express the doubts that creep into middle age. Although most stories are told from the point of view of a heterosexual woman, Leaner also writes from the perspective of men and bisexuals, and from multiple perspectives on a given situation, with an element of voyeurism that creates added interest. The reviewer for *Publishers Weekly* praised *Quiver* saying, "It's no mystery why this explicit debut has found an enthusiastic audience Down Under."

The Witch of Cologne is an historical novel set in medieval Germany. The protagonist is Ruth, a skilled and much sought after young Jewish midwife and the daughter of the chief rabbi of Deutz, the Jewish ghetto in the German city of Cologne. It is the time of the Inquisition, when agents of the Roman Catholic Church sought out and persecuted people considered to be "heretics," those who did not adhere to Roman Catholic doctrine and practices. Jews were special targets of prejudice, as were women who practiced traditional healing arts. Ruth has become the target of the Dominican inquisitor Archbishop Carlos Vicente Solitario because, when he was young, Ruth's mother refused his overtures, and he is now obsessed with destroying her daughter. His ammunition is Ruth's use of the Kabbalah—mystical teachings of the Jewish religion that are seen by the Inquisition as magical arts—as part of her spiritual practice. Ruth is arrested for sorcery and thrown into prison where she meets and falls in love with a churchman who is struggling with his faith, leading to an unusual and tenuous marriage. Learner describes Ruth's spirituality, the pain of her torture, and the passion of her love as she tells Ruth's story.

Reviewers praised *The Witch of Cologne.* In her review for *Booklist,* Ilene Cooper commented, "This is the kind of all-consuming novel that readers hate to see end." The reviewer for *Publishers Weekly* declared, "This steamy, riveting page-turner is also a paean to the triumph of a woman's spirit." Marika Zemka, in her review for *Library Journal,* called the book "bawdy, romantic, and filled with well-developed characters."

In *Soul,* Learner explores the theme of biology as destiny. Geneticist and researcher Julia Huntington has been looking into the question of whether or not there is a gene for violence—an inherited characteristic that allows a person to kill without regret or a backlash of emotional disorder. On her return from a difficult research trip to Afghanistan, she finds that her husband has run off with her best friend, leading her to wonder if there is an inherited characteristic in her own line. The story turns to Julia's ancestor Lavinia Huntington, who was convicted of murdering her husband, and recounts the events leading up to his death. Through the book, Learner parallels the lives of the two women, leading the reader to wonder if Julia will follow in Lavinia's footsteps and end up murdering her unfaithful husband in an uncontrolled rage.

Reviews were extremely mixed in their responses to *Soul.* The review in *Piaw's Blog* called it "awfully heavy-handed and obvious," but Jen Baker, in her review for *Booklist,* thought it was "a page-turner." The reviewer for *Publishers Weekly* commented, "Learner details the science behind the question [of how the two women deal with their husbands] nicely, but underpowers the story's emotion and drama."

Sphinx is about an unusual couple who are living in Egypt in 1977. Oliver is a geophysicist, a pragmatist, and able to instinctively know where there is oil beneath the surface of the ground. His wife, Isabella, is a marine archaeologist and mystic, as well as a member of an old Alexandrian family. She is searching for an ancient Egyptian astrolabe, and Oliver begins to realize that there are mysterious groups of people who are also looking for it and would do anything to get it. There ensues a story of spies, ghosts, mysterious deaths, and an international chase. In a review for *Straits Times,* Niki Bruce said that *Sphinx* was "a substantial novel with quality prose, interesting ideas and a relatively twisty plot."

BIOGRAPHICAL AND CRITICAL SOURCES:

PERIODICALS

Booklist, August 1, 2005, Ilene Cooper, review of *The Witch of Cologne,* p. 1993; April 1, 2008, Jen Baker, review of *Soul,* p. 27.

Bulletin with Newsweek, April 29, 2003, "Eau No, Cologne," p. 74.

Library Journal, July 1, 2005, Marika Zemke, review of *The Witch of Cologne,* p. 69.

Publishers Weekly, June 1, 1998, review of *Quiver: A Book of Erotic Tales,* p. 48; June 20, 2005, review of *The Witch of Cologne,* p. 56; March 3, 2008, review of *Soul,* p. 31.

ONLINE

Fantastic Fiction, http://www.fantasticfiction.co.uk/ (August 12, 2009), short author profile.

Macmillan Web site, http://us.macmillan.com/ (August 12, 2009), summary of *Soul* and short author profile.

Piaw's Blog, http://piaw.blogspot.com/ (August 12, 2009), review of *Soul.*

Straits Times, http://blogs.straitstimes.com/ (August 12, 2009), Niki Bruce, "A Relatively Twisty Read."

Tobsha Learner Home Page, http://www.tobshalearner.com (August 12, 2009), author profile.*

* * *

LEE, Janice Y.K.

PERSONAL: Born in Hong Kong; immigrated to the United States as a teenager; married; children: four. *Education:* Harvard University, B.A.; Hunter College, M.F.A.

ADDRESSES: Agent—Theresa Park, The Park Literary Group, 270 Lafayette St., Ste. 1504, New York, NY 10012. *E-mail*—janice@janiceyklee.com.

CAREER: Novelist.

WRITINGS:

The Piano Teacher, Viking Press (New York, NY), 2009.

Served as an editor for several women's magazines, including *Elle* and *Mirabella. The Piano Teacher* has been translated into numerous languages.

SIDELIGHTS: Born in Hong Kong to Korean parents, Janice Y.K. Lee came to the United States to attend boarding school at fifteen. She went on to study literature at Harvard, and then to serve in several editorial positions with the popular women's magazines *Elle* and *Mirabella.* She left publishing to attend the M.F.A. writing program at Hunter College, where she began the five-year process of writing her historical novel *The Piano Teacher.* During that period she married, had four children, and returned to Hong Kong with her family. Just two weeks after publication, *The Piano Teacher* shot up the *New York Times* best- seller list, earning critical accolades from all quarters, and has since been translated into twenty-one languages.

The Piano Teacher, Lee's first novel, takes place in mid-twentieth century Hong Kong, following the two ill-fated love affairs of British ex-patriot Will Truesdale: One with an exotic Hong Kong socialite during the height of the WWII Japanese Occupation of Hong Kong, and the second a decade later, with a young British wife recently arrived in Hong Kong (the piano teacher of the title). In an interview with a *Publishers Weekly* contributor, Lee explained, "I wrote a lot of fiction with twenty-something narrators in New York, so I'm surprised that this was my first book. The story kind of found me. It was something I kept coming back to, something that kept staying in my head." Despite the level of detail and research that a historical novel calls for, Lee told a reporter with the *Yonhap News Agency of Korea* that writing this novel was a "very unconscious, unplanned process. . . . The plot of the book came as I wrote. I just tried to write the best book I could and worry about other stuff later."

Reviewers were impressed by the book's exploration of the collision and collusion of cultures. A *Kirkus Reviews* contributor called the book "a lush examination of East-West relations." A reviewer for *Publishers Weekly* likewise noted that "Lee covers a little-known time in Chinese history without melodrama, and deconstructs without judgment the choices people make." Others saw the book as primarily an exploration of personal psychology. As Carolyn Kubisz wrote in *Booklist,* Lee's "interesting, complex characters . . . drive a rich and intimate look at what happens to people under extraordinary circumstances." In a review for the Minneapolis *Star Tribune,* Katherine Bailey suggested that "perhaps the book's strongest feature is its theme: moral choice during torturous times of war is not black and white, with the result that sometimes one must strike bargains in order to survive."

Few reviewers failed to mention the simple pleasure of reading this exquisitely crafted tale. According to Lisa Fugard, contributor for the *New York Times Book Review,* "Lee has made the bold (and successful) decision to write a novel in which none of her characters are particularly endearing. Will can be cruel and self-absorbed; Claire is often prejudiced. And the upper echelons of Hong Kong society, through which they both pass, are rife with pettiness and jealousy." In a review for the *Chicago Tribune,* Jessica Reaves concluded: "Evocative, poignant and skillfully crafted, 'The Piano Teacher' is more than an epic tale of war and a tangled, tortured love story. It is the kind of novel one consumes in great, greedy gulps, pausing (grudgingly) only when absolutely necessary." Reviewing *The Piano Teacher* for *Library Journal,* Beth E. Andersen concluded: "Her adept pacing slowly exposes the inevitability of tragedy that engulfs her characters. Highly recommended."

BIOGRAPHICAL AND CRITICAL SOURCES:

PERIODICALS

Booklist, December 1, 2008, Carolyn Kubisz, review of *The Piano Teacher,* p. 24.

Books & Media, January 3, 2009, "Powerful Love Stories Shape Exotic Tale," p. 1.

Chicago Tribune, January 3, 2009, "Powerful Love Stories Shape Exotic Tale: *The Piano Teacher* by Janice Y.K. Lee."

Kirkus Reviews, October 1, 2008, review of *The Piano Teacher.*

Library Journal, October 1, 2008, Beth E. Andersen, review of *The Piano Teacher,* p. 58.

Marie Claire, January 1, 2009, Lizzie Dunlap, review of *The Piano Teacher,* p. 43.

New York Times Book Review, January 18, 2009, "Colonial Rondo," p. 19.

Publishers Weekly, September 8, 2008, review of *The Piano Teacher,* p. 34 October 13, 2008, "PW Talks," p. 36.

Star Tribune (Minneapolis, MN), January 11, 2009, "A Song of Loves Affected by War; Fiction: An Englishwoman Blossoms in Tropical Hong Kong," p. 13.

Yonhap News Agency of Korea, February 11, 2009, "'Unconscious, Unplanned' Passion for Writing Leads to Delightful Debut Novel."

ONLINE

Fantastic Fiction, http://www.fantasticfiction.co.uk/ (July 25, 2009), profile of author.

Janice Y.K. Lee Home Page, http://www.janiceyklee.com (July 26, 2009).

Laura's Reviews, http://lauragerold.blogspot.com/ (April 20, 2009), review of *The Piano Teacher.*

* * *

LEWIS, Sarah Katherine 1972-

PERSONAL: Born 1972.

ADDRESSES: Home—Ann Arbor, MI. *E-mail*—Sarah@sarahkatherinelewis.com.

CAREER: Author. Former worker in the sex industry. Appeared on National Public Radio.

WRITINGS:

Indecent: How I Make It and Fake It as a Girl for Hire, Seal Press (Emeryville, CA), 2006.

Sex and Bacon: Why I Love Things That Are Very, Very Bad for Me, Seal Press (Berkeley, CA), 2008.

Also author of the *Sarah Katherine Lewis* Web log.

SIDELIGHTS: Writer Sarah Katherine Lewis began a ten-year career in the adult sex industry at the age of twenty-three when she applied for a job as a lingerie model. This first job opened her eyes to the world of adult entertainment and was the impetus for her later work. She explores her past and her experiences working several different jobs in which she used her body to pay her bills in the 2006 book *Indecent: How I Make It and Fake It as a Girl for Hire.* Nicole Solomon, who talked with Lewis in an interview on the *PopMatters* Web site, stated that her "wit and candor make for delightful reading, even when she's discussing unsavory aspects of the sex industry or her own struggle with depression," which she does so frequently in her first work. Lewis takes a lighthearted look at some important topics that have played a significant role in her life. She especially examines the plight of the other workers in the industry who struggle to try to make ends meet, as well as those individuals who utilize the services offered, sparing no feelings offering her thoughts on client habits. A reviewer in *Publishers Weekly* took issue with some of Lewis's comments in the book, however. The reviewer believed that the author is "slippery about her own background and motivation" for being a part of the sex trade. The reviewer wrote that although Lewis provides an "astute analysis" of the industry, the book ultimately "misses the mark."

The author's second book, *Sex and Bacon: Why I Love Things That Are Very, Very Bad for Me,* includes further discussion of the sex trade. Additionally, Lewis includes her thoughts on how sex is equated with food. In an interview in the *Seattle Times,* Lewis stated, "I want people to really celebrate their own appetite for whatever it is that they really want, whatever it is that's really savory to them or really sexy to them. And I want them to sort of feel a sense of permission, or at least a sense of kinship in the pursuit of satisfaction and appetite." Lewis's acceptance of sexual desire of all sorts leads to the same response as desire for food. The author advocates changing the way people eat. She believes that eating what one really wants will better satiate hunger than trying to fill the void with the diet version of whatever food one craves. Lewis supplements this belief by including several recipes in her book for sensual meals and food that elicits a visceral response. Joanne Wilkinson, reviewing the book in *Booklist,* called *Sex and Bacon* "provocative reading." The reviewer also stated that while some of the essays in the work "don't always mesh well," she offers "thought-provoking" tales about her life. *Sex and Ba-*

con is also "painfully candid" and "frank" according to Wilkinson. The author's opinionated style was explained by a critic reviewing the book in *Publishers Weekly,* who stated, "in the same way that she celebrates . . . politically incorrect food—Lewis is not interested in pleasing everyone." Lewis's style led the reviewer to conclude that some will not be entertained by the book, but much of it offers a "joyful sensuality" and comedy.

While Lewis hoped to provide an insider's view of the sex industry and explain her own experiences, she also offers a way to make the most out of life. Solomon on *PopMatters* praised both of Lewis's books, calling them "at the same time heavy, hilarious, and rejuvenating reads."

BIOGRAPHICAL AND CRITICAL SOURCES:

PERIODICALS

America's Intelligence Wire, April 9, 2007, "Cornell U.: Sex Worker Speaks to Cornell U. about Industry"; November 25, 2008, "Cornell U.: Sex Veteran Links Appetite for Food to Erotica."

Biography, fall, 2008, Lisa Crystal Carver, review of *Sex and Bacon: Why I Love Things That Are Very, Very Bad for Me,* p. 794.

Booklist, April 15, 2008, Joanne Wilkinson, review of *Sex and Bacon,* p. 10.

Curve, January-February, 2009, Colleen McCaffrey, review of *Sex and Bacon,* p. 56.

Publishers Weekly, August 21, 2006, "Indecent: How I Make It and Fake It as a Girl for Hire," p. 63; March 24, 2008, review of *Sex and Bacon,* p. 62.

ONLINE

PopMatters, http://www.popmatters.com/ (May 13, 2009), Nicole Solomon, "How It Could Be Different: An Interview with Sarah Katherine Lewis."

Sarah Katherine Lewis Home Page, http://www.sarahkatherinelewis.com (August 23, 2009).

Sarah Katherine Lewis MySpace Page, http://www.myspace.com/sarah_katherine_lewis (August 23, 2009).

Seal Press Web site, http://www.sealpress.com/ (August 23, 2009), author information.

Seattle Times Online, http://seattletimes.nwsource.com/ (June 2, 2008), Mark Rahner, "Rahner Q&A: Sarah Katherine Lewis, 'Sex & Bacon.'"

Sex and Bacon, http://www.sexandbacon.com (August 23, 2009).*

* * *

LEWIS, Simon 1971-

PERSONAL: Born 1971, in Wales.

ADDRESSES: *E-mail*—info@simonlewiswriter.com.

CAREER: Writer.

WRITINGS:

FICTION

Go, Pulp Books (New York, NY), 1999.

Bad Traffic: An Inspector Jian Novel, Scribner (New York, NY), 2008.

NONFICTION

China: The Rough Guide, Rough Guides (New York, NY), 2000.

The Rough Guide to Shanghai, Rough Guides (New York, NY), 2008.

The Rough Guide to Beijing 3, Rough Guides (New York, NY), 2008.

SIDELIGHTS: Welsh travel writer Simon Lewis is the author of *Go,* a novel detailing the exploits of a group of backpackers as they make their way across Europe and Asia. The text features exotic and foreign locales, such as Hong Kong and London, accompanied by a diverse cast of characters who all share a common willfulness to want to escape the realities of their lives.

Lewis released his second fiction publication, titled *Bad Traffic: An Inspector Jian Novel,* in 2008. The narrative centers on the efforts of Chinese Public Security

Bureau inspector Ma Jian who learns of his daughter's abandonment of her university studies and subsequent disappearance while living in the United Kingdom. Suspecting the involvement of illegal human trafficking organizations, Jian seeks out the help of an illegal immigrant who also serves as his translator. A *Reading Matters* Web site contributor found, "Ultimately, *Bad Traffic* is a brilliantly paced and well constructed story that speeds along at a terrific pace. It has plenty of thrills and spills throughout, but underpinning it all is a quietly disturbing and shocking expose on an issue I've not ever read about in contemporary fiction—that of human trafficking and the terrible fate so many desperate people find themselves in." Not only does the text address the real life dangers of kidnapping and human trafficking but also the plight of a foreigner who is handicapped by his linguistic limitations yet bolstered by his knowledge of the verisimilitudes of criminal operations.

Maxine Clarke, in an article for the *Euro Crime* Web site, reported that Lewis modeled the narrative after "real-life recent crimes in the UK: the death by suffocation of more than fifty illegal Chinese immigrants in a lorry container; and the drowning of cockle-pickers in Morecombe Bay, when they were caught out by the tides. His excursion into the sleazy and violent world of the gangs responsible for these crimes, as well as his extraordinary ability to see England with the fresh and uncomprehending eyes of a range of Chinese characters, is nothing short of superb." The realism that Lewis employs serves to provide the reader with an identifiable environment for the unfolding crime story. A *Necessary Acts of Devotion* Web site reviewer concluded, "Lewis has written a very accessible book. Short, declarative sentences make the writing clear and concise. Combined with scenes that average no more than five pages, the pace is swift. The lead characters can be thoughtful and reflective, yet they are always active, never captured in a dull moment. . . . The universal threats lend an immediacy to the story, and give the reader reason to cheer for the compromised protagonists."

In addition to fiction writing, Lewis has written several travel books detailing the Chinese cities of Shanghai and Beijing. In particular, *The Rough Guide to Shanghai* offers an introduction to the city that serves as a world financial center, indicator of progress, and a modern entertainment behemoth. After a comprehensive introduction, the text discusses the basic concerns regarding travel to Shanghai, including visitation times, holiday information, culture and etiquette, and tips regarding travel with children. Detailed maps of the city are provided and are divided into eight main sections, such as the Old City and Pudong. Moreover, the guidebook offers suggestions for overnight accommodations, dining, and nighttime entertainment options. The text concludes with a glossary of terms and a helpful language aid which details common words, phrases, and pronunciation options. Likewise, Lewis's *The Rough Guide to Beijing 3,* also released in 2008, includes much of the same information regarding the city and its elements as well as a brief history of Beijing and a list of publications which provide contextual materials.

BIOGRAPHICAL AND CRITICAL SOURCES:

PERIODICALS

Booklist, November 1, 2008, Jessica Moyer, review of *Bad Traffic: An Inspector Jian Novel,* p. 26.

Publishers Weekly, October 6, 2008, review of *Bad Traffic,* p. 35.

ONLINE

Euro Crime Web site, http://www.eurocrime.co.uk/ (October 1, 2008), Maxine Clarke, review of *Bad Traffic.*

Its a Crime! (Or a Mystery. . .)?, http://itsacrime.typepad.com/ (July 7, 2008), review of *Bad Traffic.*

Mostly Fiction, http://www.mostlyfiction.com/ (February 21, 2009), Poornima Apte, review of *Bad Traffic.*

Necessary Acts of Devotion, http://beggarsofazure.blogspot.com/ (February 1, 2009), review of *Bad Traffic.*

Reading Matters, http://kimbofo.typepad.com/readingmatters/ (February 1, 2009), review of *Bad Traffic.*

Simon & Schuster Web site, http://authors.simonandschuster.com/ (July 20, 2009), author interview.

Simon Lewis Home Page, http://www.simonlewiswriter.com (July 20, 2009).

Washington Post Online, http://www.washingtonpost.com/ (December 29, 2008), Patrick Anderson, review of *Bad Traffic.**

LIEBERT, Elizabeth 1944-

PERSONAL: Born July 28, 1944, in Seattle, WA. *Education:* Vanderbilt University, Ph.D., 1986.

ADDRESSES: Office—San Francisco Theological Seminary, 105 Seminary Rd., San Anselmo, CA 94960. *E-mail*—eliebert@sfts.edu.

CAREER: Writer and educator. San Francisco Theological Seminary, San Anselmo, CA, professor of spiritual life, 1987—.

WRITINGS:

NONFICTION

Changing Life Patterns: Adult Development in Spiritual Direction, Paulist Press (New York, NY), 1992, reprinted, Chalice Press (St. Louis, MO), 2000.

(With John C. Endres) *A Retreat with the Psalms: Resources for Personal and Communal Prayer,* Paulist Press (New York, NY), 2001.

(With Katherine Dyckman and Mary Garvin) *The Spiritual Exercises Reclaimed: Uncovering Liberating Possibilities for Women,* Paulist Press (New York, NY), 2001.

Exploring Christian Spirituality: Essays in Honor of Sandra M. Schneiders, Paulist Press (New York, NY), 2006.

The Way of Discernment: Spiritual Practices for Decision Making, Westminster John Knox Press (Louisville, KY), 2008.

Contributor of essays and articles to periodicals, including *Theological Studies.*

SIDELIGHTS: American nonfiction writer Elizabeth Liebert was born July 28, 1944, in Seattle, Washington. Liebert, a graduate of Vanderbilt University, has served as professor of spiritual studies at the San Francisco Theological Seminary in California since 1987. Additionally, Liebert has released several books detailing adult spiritual development, women's spirituality, and employing spirituality in one's decision making.

In 1992, Liebert released *Changing Life Patterns: Adult Development in Spiritual Direction,* which was reprinted in 2000. The text correlates age and experience with spiritual development and provides a series of indicators which help one gauge their own development. *Changing Life Patterns* also discusses using spirituality to mitigate conflict and applies the general tenets of Christianity as the framework for adult spiritual development. Liebert's subsequent release, *A Retreat with the Psalms: Resources for Personal and Communal Prayer,* employs a more formal method for achieving spiritual growth. The text, released in 2001 and written with John C. Endres, offers ten thematic options for employing psalms in one's prayer. Chapter one discusses the general structure of the book of Psalms, with a focus on structure and coherency, and chapter two offers an analysis of five various prayer styles to be implemented with the psalms. The following eight chapters group like Psalms into distinct subgenres, such as personal and communal lamentation, thanksgiving prayer, praise and devotions, penitential prayer, and euphemistic offerings. Stephen Brachlow, in a review for *Interpretation,* claimed that the text involves the reader "in creative and playful ways that press beyond an analytical approach to Bible study and plumb the depths of human experience through praying the psalms."

Unlike her previous publications, Liebert's 2001 release of *The Spiritual Exercises Reclaimed: Uncovering Liberating Possibilities for Women* specifically addresses a particular segment of the laity in order to offer a perspective through which women may fully connect with the material. The *Spiritual Exercises* were authored in the early sixteenth century by Ignatius Loyola in an attempt to provide the pious with a means through which they could discern God's personal influence in their lives. Liebert provides a discussion of these *Exercises* which is relevant to the modern woman's implementation of traditional, and somewhat exclusive, texts in order to gain divine insight. Furthermore, the *Exercises* stress the power of retreat and one's exclusion from the habitual, and Liebert does not omit this important textual component. In Liebert's *Theological Studies* review of Philip Sheldrake's *Spaces for the Sacred: Place, Memory, and Identity,* a theoretical analysis of the importance of a physical space on religious practice, she stated, "Place, however, is hardly a straightforward concept," it "is a cultural category, subject to multiple interpretations, and it includes the notion of person as embodied and therefore located." This statement coupled with her earlier works suggests a holistic view of spirituality wherein exterior as well as interior elements contribute to one's spiritual achievement.

Likewise, Liebert's *The Way of Discernment: Spiritual Practices for Decision Making* focuses on a particular dimension of spirituality in order to provide information regarding applied religious study. The text offers answers to questions regarding how one can parallel free will with God's will, employ spiritual practice in secular decision making, and draw upon spiritual wisdom in order to positively influence personal acts. *The Way of Discernment,* influenced by the works of fundamental Christian theologians, makes clear that the application of discernment is simultaneously a natural and practiced talent. In other words, the text suggests that, even though one is born with the ability to discern and employ divine will, without conscious effort to that effect even inherited ability cannot be fully realized.

BIOGRAPHICAL AND CRITICAL SOURCES:

PERIODICALS

Interpretation, April 1, 2002, Stephen Brachlow, review of *A Retreat with the Psalms: Resources for Personal and Communal Prayer,* p. 214.

Publishers Weekly, June 9, 2008, review of *The Way of Discernment: Spiritual Practices for Decision Making,* p. 47.

Theological Studies, June 1, 2004, Elizabeth Liebert, review of "Spaces for the Sacred: Place, Memory and Identity," p. 441; June 1, 2008, Elizabeth Liebert, review of "Spaces for the Sacred," p. 483.

ONLINE

San Francisco Theological Seminary Web site, http://www.sfts.edu/ (July 19, 2009), faculty profile.*

* * *

LITTLE, Terra 1973-

PERSONAL: Born March 5, 1973.

ADDRESSES: *E-mail*—writeterralittle@yahoo.com.

CAREER: Writer, corrections officer, and crisis counselor.

WRITINGS:

Running from Mercy, Q-Boro Books (Queens, NY), 2008.

Where There's Smoke, Q-Boro Books (Queens, NY), 2009.

Also author of the blog *Terra Little.*

SIDELIGHTS: Terra Little, a corrections officer and crisis counselor, is the author of *Running from Mercy* and *Where There's Smoke.* Released in 2008, *Running from Mercy* tells the story of Pamela Mayes, an African American woman, who leaves her hometown of Mercy, in Georgia, in order to free herself from the perceived judgmental mentality of her fellow townsfolk. Mayes develops a successful career in the music industry; however, when her sister, Paris, dies in an automobile accident, Mayes returns to Mercy. The narrative recounts Mayes difficult childhood as an orphan, her deep relationship with her twin sister, and her ambitions as a young woman. Anticipating remaining only long enough to attend her sister's funeral, Mayes has no intentions of remaining in Mercy any longer than necessary. Nevertheless, Mayes's stay lengthens as she discovers her sister's journal and some long forgotten, yet painful, memories. Other characters in the story include Miles Dixon, a hopeful biographer who seeks out Mayes for an article, and Nikki, Paris's only daughter. These secondary characters facilitate Mayes's interactions with her past and her self-development. The overarching theme of the story centers of the inability of a person to wholly avoid or escape their past despite the years of distance and effort. Additionally, the story addresses the subject of familial loss and serenity gained through self reflection.

In Little's subsequent release, *Where There's Smoke,* published in 2009, the subject of the inescapability of one's past returns in a new context. In the narrative, Alex Avery, as a successful African American, has overcome his underprivileged background in order to become an educator and a working professional. Nevertheless, elements of Avery's past resurface and cause him a significant amount of stress. Specifically,

Avery learns that he may have fathered a child, unbeknownst to him at the time of the boy's birth, who is now a wily teenager. Little introduces contemporary social problems into the narrative which are well documented in American society. Race and gender also fulfill large roles in the story, as Avery is presented as a well-meaning but absent father and the mother, Anne, is shown to have obscure intentions in revealing Avery's parental status after such a lengthy period of time. A *Kirkus Reviews* contributor concluded that Little presents "a solid, believable cautionary tale" that is "comfortable" written "in a range of registers, from N-word-laced ghetto slang to the more refined speech of the aspirational main characters."

BIOGRAPHICAL AND CRITICAL SOURCES:

PERIODICALS

Kirkus Reviews, November 15, 2008, review of *Where There's Smoke.*

ONLINE

Terra Little Home Page, http://www.terralittle.com (June 24, 2009).*

* * *

LORENZ, Ralph 1969-

PERSONAL: Born August 24, 1969, in Lanark, Scotland; married Elizabeth Turtle, June 3, 1996. *Education:* University of Southampton, England, B.E., 1990; University of Kent, Canterbury, England, Ph.D., 1994.

ADDRESSES: Office—Space Department, Planetary Exploration Group, Johns Hopkins University Applied Physics Lab, 11100 Johns Hopkins Rd., MP3-E104, Laurel, MD 20723-6099. *E-mail*—ralph.lorenz@jhuapl.edu.

CAREER: Astronomer and engineer, science writer, and instructor. University of Surrey, Guilford, England, UoSAT Spacecraft Engineering Research Unit, engineer; European Space Agency, Noordwijk, The Netherlands, Cassini-Huygens project, engineer; Jet Propulsion Laboratory, Pasadena, CA, engineer; University of Arizona, Lunar and Planetary Laboratory, Tucson, research associate; Johns Hopkins University, Applied Physics Laboratory, Laurel, MD, instructor.

MEMBER: Royal Astronomical Society, Division of Planetary Sciences of American Astronomical Society, Royal Aeronautical Society, American Geophysical Union.

AWARDS, HONORS: International Astronautical Federation Congress, Luigi Napolitano prize for most significant contribution by scientist under thirty, 1994.

WRITINGS:

(With Jacqueline Mitton) *Lifting Titan's Veil: Exploring the Giant Moon of Saturn,* Cambridge University Press (Cambridge, MA), 2002.

(Editor, with A. Kleidon) *Non-equilibrium Thermodynamics and the Production of Entropy: Life, Earth, and Beyond,* Springer (New York, NY), 2005.

(With David M. Harland) *Space Systems Failures: Disasters and Rescues of Satellites, Rockets and Space Probes,* Springer (New York, NY), 2005.

Spinning Flight: Dynamics of Frisbees, Boomerangs, Samaras, and Skipping Stones, Springer (New York, NY), 2006.

(With Andrew Ball, James Garry, Viktor Kerzhanovich) *Planetary Landers and Entry Probes,* Cambridge University Press (Cambridge, MA), 2007.

(With Jacqueline Mitton) *Titan Unveiled: Saturn's Mysterious Moon Explored,* Princeton University Press (Princeton, NJ), 2008.

SIDELIGHTS: Ralph Lorenz is an astronomer and engineer who was born August 24, 1969, in Lanark, Scotland. He earned a B.E. from the University of Southampton in England in 1990 and a Ph.D. from the University of Kent in Canterbury, England, in 1994.

Lorenz worked on a number of engineering projects at such notable scientific organizations as the European Space Agency, Jet Propulsion Laboratory, University of Arizona's Lunar and Planetary Laboratory, and the University of Surrey in England.

As part of the Johns Hopkins University's Applied Physics Laboratory, Lorenz worked as an engineer on the Cassini-Huygens spacecraft that explored Saturn's moon Titan. He left the project to earn his doctorate, then returned to it as a scientist. Lorenz helped build a probe on the spacecraft, was a primary interpreter of the data it sent back, and was a member of the craft's radar team that analyzed Titan's atmosphere and surface.

In 2002 Lorenz published *Lifting Titan's Veil: Exploring the Giant Moon of Saturn* with Jacqueline Mitton that describes the combined NASA and European Space Agency exploration of Saturn's largest moon through the Cassini-Huygens mission two years before the spacecraft's arrival.

The book starts with some history, such as the discovery of Titan in 1655 by Dutch scientist Christiaan Huygens, and the invaluable information the Voyager spacecraft beamed back of Saturn's system in 1980. The final section of the book centers on the Cassini-Huygens mission beginning with its inception and political considerations between the two continents' involvement, the craft's design and construction, operations, and launch.

Titan had been found to be submerged within 200 kilometers of smog composed of the same prebiotic chemicals, such as hydrocarbons, organic molecules, and nitriles, that Earth's atmosphere may have had billions of years ago. This composition is why Titan is so important. It gives scientists a window into examining the chemical evolution that may lead to formation of amino acids and nucleic-acid bases, which is what happened on Earth to create life. The book speculates what the Cassini-Huygens mission will find when it reaches Saturn.

Despite the book's couple of glaring errors, Darrell F. Strobel wrote in *Science,* "Lorenz's experiences, amplified in passages labeled 'Ralph's Log,' lend the book a personal flavor and give the reader insight into the inner workings of these complex missions." "Their prose is, accordingly, lively and captivating," said Strobel. "The authors present some material at the level of *Scientific American* or *Sky and Telescope,* but most of the text would be appropriate in an introduction to astronomy for nonscientists," commented Strobel. "I recommend *Lifting Titan's Veil* to anyone having an interest in planetary exploration."

Lorenz cowrote and coedited a number of other fun-fact science book, including *Space Systems Failures: Disasters and Rescues of Satellites, Rockets and Space Probes,* and *Non-equilibrium Thermodynamics and the Production of Entropy: Life, Earth, and Beyond,* both in 2005, the 2006 *Spinning Flight: Dynamics of Frisbees, Boomerangs, Samaras, and Skipping Stones,* and *Planetary Landers and Entry Probes* in 2007.

Following up the speculated results of the Cassini-Huygens mission in *Lifting Titan's Veil,* Lorenz and coauthor Mitton present actual results in their 2008 book, *Titan Unveiled: Saturn's Mysterious Moon Explored.* The book describes the mission of the Huygens probe, the first craft to land on the satellite of another planet. In 2005, the probe plunged into Titan's thick atmosphere, landed on the moon's surface, and sent back pictures and scientific analysis. Using near-infrared mapping and other instruments, the probe discovered frozen water in the moon's crust, an atmosphere of ammonia and methane, methane rain, and a landscape of river channels, volcanoes, lakebeds, and deserts. The data will provide scientists with much work in the years ahead. In an interview following the receipt of data from Titan, Lorenz famously described the surface of the moon as "crème brulee" because it has a hard crust covering a softer material underneath.

Reviewers were fascinated with the book's science and charmed by the firsthand account from Lorenz. Commenting in *Natural History,* Laurence A. Marschall wrote, "[Lorenz's] firsthand experience, expressed in a series of bloglike entries, makes one appreciate the compromises that have to be made to design instruments that are durable, lightweight, and effective . . . and the ingenious ways in which Earth-bound engineers turn technical problems into research opportunities." Michael Gross mentioned in *Chemistry and Industry,* that the book's timing is off, as it was published in 2008 but includes data only up to 2006. "Thus, at the time of reading it, as Cassini has started its extended mission and ethane lakes have finally been confirmed, it already looks dated."

Nevertheless, Fred Taylor wrote in *American Scientist,* "The book's prose is polished, making it an easy read. The result is an engrossing firsthand account of one of humankind's greatest adventures of recent years." He added, "*Titan Unveiled* provides the general reader with a lively narrative that combines a reliable, nontechnical account of the Cassini-Huygens mission with personal and often intimate insights into these efforts to explore a fascinating planetary analogue to the Earth."

BIOGRAPHICAL AND CRITICAL SOURCES:

PERIODICALS

American Scientist, July 1, 2008, Fred Taylor, "Saturn's Earthlike Moon," review of *Titan Unveiled: Saturn's Mysterious Moon Explored.*

Booklist, April 15, 2008, Gilbert Taylor, review of *Titan Unveiled,* p. 14.

Chemistry and Industry, March 23, 2009, Michael Gross, "Space Exploration," p. 30.

Choice: Current Reviews for Academic Libraries, September 1, 2008, M. Dickinson, review of *Titan Unveiled,* p. 122.

Journal for the History of Astronomy, February 1, 2004, review of *Lifting Titan's Veil: Exploring the Giant Moon of Saturn,* p. 121.

Natural History, September 1, 2008, Laurence A. Marschall, review of *Titan Unveiled,* p. 38.

Nature, May 22, 2008, Henry Roe, "A Rough Guide to Titan," review of *Titan Unveiled,* p. 453.

New Scientist, June 8, 2002, David W. Hughes, "World Apart," p. 49; May 3, 2008, Richard A. Lovett, "Mystery Moon," p. 47; April 30, 2008, review of *Titan Unveiled.*

Science, November 29, 2002, Darrell F. Strobel, "Photochemical Smog Hides an Icy World," p. 1721.

Science News, May 10, 2008, review of *Titan Unveiled,* p. 34.

Scientific American, July 1, 2008, Michelle Press, review of *Titan Unveiled,* p. 98.

Times Higher Education, June 12, 2008, Kevin Beurle, "Titanic Tales of Creme Brulee," review of *Titan Unveiled,* p. 50.

ONLINE

Astrobiology, http://library.thinkquest.org/ (August 1, 2009), "An Interview with Dr. Ralph Lorenz," author interview.

University of Arizona University Web site, http://www.lpl.arizona.edu/ (August 1, 2009), author profile.*

LOWE, Jaime 1976-

PERSONAL: Born November 20, 1976.

ADDRESSES: Home—Brooklyn, NY.

CAREER: Writer.

WRITINGS:

Digging for Dirt: The Life and Death of ODB, Faber & Faber (New York, NY), 2008.

Contributor of essays and articles to periodicals, including *Village Voice, Interview, Radar,* and *Sports Illustrated.*

SIDELIGHTS: Jaime Lowe, a Brooklyn, New York, resident, has contributed articles to periodicals such as *Interview, Radar, Sports Illustrated,* and the *Village Voice.* In 2008, Lowe released her debut biographical publication titled *Digging for Dirt: The Life and Death of ODB.* The text chronicles the life and career of hip hop innovator Russell Tyrone Jones, better known as Ol' Dirty Bastard (ODB), who died as the result of an accidental drug overdose while recording studio music in New York City on November 13, 2004.

In the narrative, Lowe tells of how ODB was one of the original members, along with RZA, GZA, Raekwon, U-God, Ghostface Killah, Inspectah Deck, Method Man, and Masta Killa, of the groundbreaking Wu-Tang Clan. The text informs that while ODB was with the group he participated as a lyricist on three albums with the Wu-tang Clan, including *Enter the Wu-Tang (36 Chambers), Wu-Tang Forever,* and *The W,* before embarking on his career as a solo artist. Furthermore, as a solo artist, ODB released four albums, including *Return to the 36 Chambers: The Dirty Version, Nigga Please, The Dirty Story: The Best of Ol' Dirty Bastard,* and *The Trials and Tribulations of Russell Jones.*

Lowe also discusses how ODB became more publicly unpredictable after the group found widespread popularity, most notably at the 1998 Grammy Awards where he appeared uninvited on the stage while another artist was giving a speech. Additionally, ODB was arrested numerous times for charges ranging from robbery to drug possession. A *Publishers Weekly* contributor acknowledged that Lowe exhibits "occasional flashes of insight, especially when she writes on the subject of ODB's probable mental illness." The text speculates that ODB's public antics and encounters with law enforcement were the result of a protracted mental health issue which was, to public knowledge, never treated. Mike Tribby, in a review for *Booklist,* also felt that ODB "devolved into a more and more disturbed state, and some of his entertaining traits came to suggest" a type of mental disability.

A *Kirkus Reviews* contributor concluded that "Lowe's strong and quite welcome vein of generosity toward her subject is winning in the end, particularly in describing the tragedy of a life that collapsed so spectacularly and so publicly." Lowe succeeds in telling a story of ODB's life which is not obscured by his many challenges. Joshua Finnell, in an article for the *Library Journal,* wrote that *Digging for Dirt* presents "ODB as a far more complex character than what the headlines would lead people to believe."

BIOGRAPHICAL AND CRITICAL SOURCES:

PERIODICALS

Booklist, November 1, 2008, Mike Tribby, review of *Digging for Dirt: The Life and Death of ODB,* p. 14.

Giant, October 1, 2008, Zakiya Walden, review of *Digging for Dirt.*

Kirkus Reviews, October 1, 2008, review of *Digging for Dirt.*

Library Journal, September 1, 2008, Joshua Finnell, review of *Digging for Dirt,* p. 128.

Publishers Weekly, August 25, 2008, review of *Digging for Dirt,* p. 59.

ONLINE

Macmillan Web site, http://us.macmillan.com/ (July 23, 2009).*

* * *

LOWNDES, Joseph E. 1966-

PERSONAL: Born April 12, 1966. *Education:* Antioch College, B.A., 1990; New School for Social Research, M.A., 1996, Ph.D., 2004.

ADDRESSES: Home—Eugene, OR. *E-mail*—jlowndes @uoregon.edu.

CAREER: Writer and educator. University of Oregon, Eugene, assistant professor of political science, 2003—.

WRITINGS:

(With Julie Novkov and Dorian Warren) *Race and American Political Development,* Routledge (New York, NY), 2008.

From the New Deal to the New Right: Race and the Southern Origins of Modern Conservatism, Yale University Press (New Haven, CT), 2008.

Contributor of essays and articles to periodicals, including the *International Journal of Politics, Culture and Society* and *International Labor and Working-Class History.*

SIDELIGHTS: Joseph E. Lowndes, an associate professor of political science at the University of Oregon, in Eugene, is the author of *Race and American Political Development* and *From the New Deal to the New Right: Race and the Southern Origins of Modern Conservatism. Race and American Political Development,* written with Julie Novkov and Dorian Warren, was released in 2008. The text chronicles the role of race and ethnicity in American politics. Lowndes presents over three hundred years of political history and highlights the significant benchmarks wherein race played a significant role. The text calls attention to the conservative and liberal shifts in politics and draws parallels between efforts towards racial equality and political change. The text, in a compilation of essays, analyzes how race has mitigated political and social action and served as a catalyst for change.

Lowndes's *From the New Deal to the New Right,* also released in 2008, refutes previous scholarship which suggests that the Southern constituency transitioned from a Democratic to a Republican platform due to a mere conflict in equal civil rights ideology. Instead, Lowndes asserts that the conservative Republican Party maintained a venerable effort at challenging the South's allegiance to the Democratic Party through a focus on segregationist goals, state authority, and middle-class values. A *Publishers Weekly* contributor claimed, "Lowndes breaks fresh ground in this history of contemporary conservatism, refuting the backlash thesis, which holds that" the South broke with the Democratic Party over the adoption of civil liberties as their primary platform. Lowndes discusses such party members as Charles Wallace Collins, George Wallace, Richard Nixon, and Asa Carter. These individuals, Lowndes asserts, helped to shape the modern conception of Democratic and Republican Party ideologies. Specifically, after the introduction detailing the inconsistencies of the "Backlash Thesis," *From the New Deal to the New Right* offers a discussion of Collins's involvement in the Dixiecrat Revolt of 1948. The revolt centered on the Democrats' party split and the subsequent Dixiecrat refusal to support to desegregation. The Dixiecrat platform was backed by the then popular Senator James Strom Thurman, one of the 1948 presidential candidates, who advocated not only segregation but also a general opposition to federal involvement in state governmental affairs. Moreover, Thurman's change from a Democratic to Republican Party member is deemed significant in the context of a developing and strong Southern conservative constituency. After establishing the role of the Dixiecrats in early Democratic infighting, Lowndes points out the effects of the *National Review,* a highly polemical publication founded by William F. Buckley, Jr., in 1955. The periodical rivaled the *Saturday Evening Post* and the *Readers' Digest* for popularity and publicized conservative values and the Republican political ideology. Lowndes uses these examples of early conservative activity to underpin the significance of Richard Nixon's creation of a "New Majority," which consisted of the underrepresented Americans who ascribed to the conservative dogma. After Nixon's acknowledgement of the conservatives, and his resulting successful presidential reelection, Lowndes asserts that the Republican Party continued to modernize itself in the wake of social change. In a review for the *Journal of American History,* Catherine Maddison wrote that the final chapter exposes "Lowndes's aptitude for forging unlikely but revealing connections, such as Carter's antistatist conservatism and the New Left's antiauthoritarianism." Lowndes employs Carter as an illustration of Party progression and as a distinct example of how Democratic Party objectives were both reactionary and evolutionary; consequently, Lowndes's index provides a reference to the many individuals mentioned in the course of his discussions. Maddison concluded, "While *From the New Deal to the New Right* contains much to interest specialists in the field, it is also clear and lively enough to engage undergraduates."

BIOGRAPHICAL AND CRITICAL SOURCES:

PERIODICALS

Choice: Current Reviews for Academic Libraries, November 1, 2008, J.P. Sanson, review of *From the New Deal to the New Right: Race and the Southern Origins of Modern Conservatism,* p. 586; March 1, 2009, S.E. Horn, review of *Race and American Political Development,* p. 1406.

Journal of American History, June 1, 2009, Catherine Maddison, review of *From the New Deal to the New Right,* p. 267.

Publishers Weekly, April 28, 2008, review of *From the New Deal to the New Right,* p. 126.

ONLINE

University of Oregon Web site, http://polisci.uoregon.edu/ (July 20, 2009), faculty profile.

Yale University Press Web site, http://yalepress.yale.edu/ (July 20, 2009), author profile.*

* * *

LUONGO, Julie

PERSONAL: Education: Temple University, M.A.

ADDRESSES: E-mail—julieluongo@gmail.com.

CAREER: Writer, instructor, journalist, business consultant, and researcher.

WRITINGS:

The Hard Way, Forge (New York, NY), 2008.

SIDELIGHTS: Julie Luongo is a writer from Stroudsburg, Pennsylvania. She was writing for a newspaper when the call to write fiction and short stories struck her. Pursuing that vocation she attended graduate school for creative writing where she learned about rigor and technique to perfect her craft. After graduation she taught writing and research at a college but was not happy with the life of a teacher. In addition to university instructor, she has been a researcher, editor, freelance writer, business consultant, and reporter. She has written about theater, fishing, and entertainment.

The call of fiction hit again and Luongo quit her job, moved into a cabin in the woods with no running water or electricity, and wrote her first novel in six weeks. She sent it to an agent, who shopped it around and sold it.

Luongo published her first novel, *The Hard Way,* in 2008. The wacky romantic comedy covers thirty years in the life of wayward Lucy Venier and follows her long search for self-awareness and personal fulfillment. Her strange, detached life begins in her childhood when the painter her parents are supporting uses her as his subject. While in college, Lucy travels with her mother, her mother's new boyfriend, and her shrill sister Nancy.

Grown and on her own, Lucy muddles through a variety of professions—journalist, advertising writer, crime reporter, Web writer, lawyer, artist. Her luck choosing and settling on a man in her life is equally misguided and tragic. Mourning the loss of her father, she hooks up with a self-possessed older man who uses her for sex and is unfaithful. Another man gambles away money from her credit card, a recovering alcoholic is abusive to her, and an ill-mannered store manager talks in outdated slang. Only charming, confident, and sweet Ben is a keeper. But when he proposes, Lucy begins to feel smothered.

Written as a collection of short stories, the episodes of Lucy's life reveal her heroic determination to adjust, grow, be happy, and simply survive. Through it all, she realizes that life is a work in progress.

Reviewers appreciated the humor in an otherwise dark series of tales. "Though it has the trappings of chick lit, this is much wiser and frequently funnier," said a writer in *Publishers Weekly.* "Teens will connect with Lucy's youthful mistakes and her teenage attraction to an older painter," commented a writer in *Booklist.*

BIOGRAPHICAL AND CRITICAL SOURCES:

PERIODICALS

Booklist, April 15, 2008, Kristine Huntley, review of *The Hard Way,* p. 25.

Publishers Weekly, February 25, 2008, review of *The Hard Way,* p. 46.

ONLINE

Julie Luongo Home page, http://julieluongo.wordpress.com (August 1, 2009), author profile.

My Book, The Movie, http://mybookthemovie.blogspot.com/ (May 27, 2008), Marshall Zeringue, review of *The Hard Way.*

Once Written, http://www.oncewritten.com/ (August 1, 2009), short author profile.

* * *

LYONS, Gabe 1975-

PERSONAL: Born 1975.

ADDRESSES: Home—Atlanta, GA. *E-mail*—glyons@fermiproject.com.

CAREER: Writer.

WRITINGS:

(With David Kinnaman) *Unchristian: What a New Generation Really Thinks about Christianity . . . and Why It Matters,* Baker Books (Grand Rapids, MI), 2007.

The Faith: What Christians Believe, Why They Believe, and Why It Matters (kit), Zondervan (Grand Rapids, MI), 2008.

SIDELIGHTS: Gabe Lyons, founder of the Fermi Project, is the author, with Dave Kinnaman, of *Unchristian: What a New Generation Really Thinks about Christianity . . . and Why It Matters. Unchristian* is the end result of several years of research conducted with the goal of discerning how American culture, particularly youth culture, receives and responds to Christianity. In nine chapters, the text analyzes the major elements which contribute to a negative perception of the Christian faith: hypocritical, salvation oriented, anti-homosexual, sheltered, political, and judgmental. Not only does the text discuss the six aforementioned facets of unchristian behavior but it also describes how these elements are individually and collectively projected. *Unchristian* asserts that Christian followers need to reexamine the fallibility of their lives and employ a more humble and understanding approach to ministry and missionary activities. Although the text itemizes the major faults facing the Church, the tone is nevertheless sanguine in that the language stresses possibility. A *Christianity Today* contributor noted that the text reminds Christians to treat others "the way a missionary approaches a host society—with eyes and ears open, expecting differences but seeking points of connection." In other words, one needs to employ respect and sympathy in order to make constructive progress.

BIOGRAPHICAL AND CRITICAL SOURCES:

PERIODICALS

Atlanta Journal-Constitution, October 6, 2007, "Faith & Values: Christians' 'Image Problem': Book Details Attitudes about Faithful," p. 6.

Booklist, October 1, 2007, June Sawyers, review of *Unchristian: What a New Generation Really Thinks about Christianity . . . and Why It Matters,* p. 28.

Christianity Today, December 1, 2007, "Who Do People Say We Are? It Doesn't Hurt to Listen to What Non-Christians Think of Us," p. 21.

Herald & Review, June 14, 2008, "Interest in Faith Is Growing among Teens."

Leadership, January 1, 2008, David Swanson, review of *Unchristian,* p. 65.

Library Journal, September 15, 2007, Steve Young, review of *Unchristian,* p. 65.

Publishers Weekly, August 13, 2007, review of *Unchristian,* p. 65.

ONLINE

Calvin College Web site, http://www.calvin.edu/ (July 22, 2009), author profile.

Common Grounds Online, http://commongrounds online.typepad.com/ (July 22, 2009), Les Newsome, review of *Unchristian.*

Crusader, http://media.www.crusaderonline.com/ (February 26, 2009), Corey Beebe, "Q&A with David Kinnaman."

FaithfulReader.com, http://www.faithfulreader.com/ (July 22, 2009), Marcia Ford, review of *Unchristian.*

Fermi Project Web site, http://www.fermiproject.com/ (July 22, 2009), author profile.

Forever Yours, http://brentbailey.blogspot.com/ (April 18, 2009), Brent Bailey, review of *Unchristian.*

New Wineskins, http://www.wineskins.org/ (June 13, 2008), Keith Brenton, author interview.

Relief, http://www.reliefjournal.com/ (May 16, 2008), Kimberley Culbertson, "Changing the Unchristian Perception with David Kinnaman."

SOMA, http://www.somareview.com/ (July 22, 2009), Robert Cornwall, review of *Unchristian.*

Unchristian Web site, http://www.unchristian.com (July 22, 2009).

Xposed2Jesus, http://brianford.wordpress.com/ (December 17, 2007), Brian Ford, review of *Unchristian.*

Zondervan Web site, http://www.zondervan.com/ (July 22, 2009), author profile.*

M

MacDONALD, Samuel A.
See MacDONALD, Sam

* * *

MacDONALD, Sam 1972-
(Samuel A. MacDonald)

PERSONAL: Born November 11, 1972.

ADDRESSES: Office—English Department, University of Pittsburgh, 526 Cathedral of Learning, 4200 5th Ave., Pittsburgh, PA 15260-0001.

CAREER: Writer and educator. University of Pittsburgh, Pittsburgh, PA, instructor in creative writing.

WRITINGS:

The Agony of an American Wilderness: Loggers, Environmentalists, and the Struggle for Control of a Forgotten Forest, Rowman & Littlefield (Lanham, MD), 2005.

The Urban Hermit: A Memoir, St. Martin's Press (New York, NY), 2008.

SIDELIGHTS: Sam MacDonald, a creative writing instructor at the University of Pittsburgh in Pennsylvania, released his debut nonfiction release, *The Agony of an American Wilderness: Loggers, Environmentalists, and the Struggle for Control of a Forgotten Forest,* in 2005. The text explores the environmental implications of long- term logging pursuits in America's wilderness. *The Agony of an American Wilderness* also discusses such questions as the right to ownership, commercialization, and commodification of American forests.

In 2008, MacDonald released *The Urban Hermit: A Memoir,* an autobiographical account of his experiences with alcohol and poverty. "MacDonald says that some advance readers (including some folks he describes in the book) found the story's tenor to be mean—say, in the way that a hectoring and righteous ex-smoker can come off as mean, full of indignation that it's not so hard after all to leave your evil ways behind. Reading the book and enjoying yourself despite constantly cringing might suggest watching the edgier, more cruel British version of *The Office,*" wrote Melissa Meinzer in an article for the *Pittsburgh City Paper.* Thus, the narrative's tone is one of wry humor and candid honesty. Meinzer also observed, "While prodigal sons returned from the brink make for popular fare these days, MacDonald denies that his book chronicles any kind of redemption. Yet *The Urban Hermit* hews close to addiction narratives, with control and lack thereof looming large."

Despite his recognition of poor choices and unrealized opportunities, MacDonald maintains an unapologetic attitude which allows him to relate events through the point of view of someone who has grown from experience. In the narrative, MacDonald admits that his downward spiral into obesity and alcoholism was not the result of his being an underprivileged youth. In a question-and-answer session with Deirdre Donahue for *USA Today,* MacDonald stated, "I had wonderful parents and a wonderful education." However, as the text reveals, the stress of mounting debt and his affinity for large quantities of food and drink compromised his health and ambitions. In a review for the *Los Angeles Times,* Erika Schickel pointed out, "Though MacDonald presents himself as a chucklehead, he's really quite savvy, setting his personal struggle against the rise and fall of our overindulgent consumer culture." MacDonald exposes the temptations surrounding the availability of credit, unhealthy food, and alcohol in excess. Schickel continued, "MacDonald's new life was fraught with temptation. Even a piece of cake at an office party threw him into moral disarray. Although he never uses the word "addiction," it's clear that excess is his drug."

The narrative makes clear that if someone with an athletic and Ivy League background can fall victim to the allures of excessive consumption, then virtually anyone is at risk for the type of dangerous self indulgences that MacDonald describes. A *Kirkus Reviews* contributor mentioned, "If MacDonald had presented himself as an exemplar of our fat, consumerist society, his book wouldn't work half as well as it does." However, MacDonald never claims to be the exception or the ideal. Living on a diet of lentils, cabbage, and tuna, MacDonald eventually achieved his goals of frugality and weight loss. A *Pittsburgh Tribune-Review* contributor concluded, "Stories like MacDonald's are not prone to fairy tale endings, but he certainly gained entrance to his own version of the Magic Kingdom. He met a woman—an attractive woman—who worked in the same building as the weekly newspaper. He had been there a year, but such was his weight loss that she thought he had just started working there. They fell in love, got married, had kids. A happy ending."

BIOGRAPHICAL AND CRITICAL SOURCES:

PERIODICALS

Booklist, November 1, 2008, Carol Haggas, review of *The Urban Hermit: A Memoir,* p. 13.

Kirkus Reviews, October 1, 2008, review of *The Urban Hermit.*

Library Journal, October 1, 2008, Dale Farris, review of *The Urban Hermit,* p. 77.

Pittsburgh Tribune-Review, December 28, 2008, "Memoir Traces Broke Barfly's Path to Solvent Sobriety."

ONLINE

Los Angeles Times Online, http://www.latimes.com/ (November 26, 2008), Erika Schickel, review of *The Urban Hermit.*

Macmillan Web site, http://us.macmillan.com/ (July 20, 2009), author profile.

Pittsburgh City Paper Online, http://www.pittsburghcitypaper.ws/ (December 18, 2008), Melissa Meinzer, "Sam McDonald's Journey from 'Fat Bastard' to Published Author Invites Questions about Whether Self-Control Can Be Its Own Kind of Addiction."

Reason Online, http://www.reason.com/ (July 20, 2009), author profile.

USA Today Online, http://www.usatoday.com/ (December 23, 2008), Deirdre Donahue, "5 Questions for *Urban Hermit* Author Sam MacDonald."*

* * *

MacKLAN, Anna
See DOUGLAS, Anne

* * *

MacMEANS, Donna

PERSONAL: Female.

ADDRESSES: *E-mail*—dmacmeans@aol.com.

CAREER: Writer and accountant.

WRITINGS:

FICTION

The Education of Mrs. Brimley, Berkley Sensation (New York, NY), 2007.

The Trouble with Moonlight, Berkley Sensation (New York, NY), 2008.

The Seduction of a Duke, Berkley Sensation (New York, NY), 2009.

(With others) *Tails of Love,* Berkeley Books (Berkeley, CA), 2009.

SIDELIGHTS: Donna MacMeans, a writer and practicing accountant, released her debut fiction publication, *The Education of Mrs. Brimley,* in 2007. The narrative centers on Emma Brimley, an inexperienced young schoolteacher who accepts a position as an instructor at the Pettibone School for Young Ladies. Upon her arrival, Brimley discovers that she is tasked with making the young women ready for their duties as a newly married wife and as an intimate partner. Brimley, who lied on her employment application, has no experience in intimate or sexual matters, and she seeks the cooperation of an infamous local noble so that she may gain the knowledge necessary to maintain her position and fulfill her teaching duties. MacMeans told Cathy Sova, in an interview for the *Romance Reader* Web site, that Brimley's "only hope of maintaining her place lies with the alluring Lord Nicholas Chambers, a neighboring artist whose behavior is scarcely consistent with that of a gentleman." However, in return for his knowledge on the subject of intimacy and marriage, Chambers cryptically requests that Brimley model for a classically themed portrait. Bordering on the inappropriate, Brimley nevertheless accepts Chambers's condition thus risking her reputation, her employment, and, most importantly, her affections. John Charles, in a review for *Booklist,* concluded that MacMeans's debut novel is sure "to dazzle readers with its irresistible combination of complex characters and very sexy romance."

MacMeans's subsequent release, *The Trouble with Moonlight,* was published in 2008. The narrative, also modeled in the romantic genre, follows James Locke, an agent in Her Majesty's Secret Service, as he meets a mysterious woman named Lusinda Havershaw, who has the unusual ability to achieve invisibility only in natural moonlight. The duo meets while Locke is investigating the contents of a safe in a suspected traitor's residence. Locke witnesses an invisible force in the process of absconding with a precious piece of jewelry, and he is immediately captivated by the woman responsible for the theft. Havershaw, forced to work with Locke under penalty of exposure, reluctantly accompanies the spy on a mission to recover information that has been taken by a Russian agent. A *Romance Novel* Web site contributor found, "Eventually, at the end of a journey that is suspenseful, humorous and poignant, James and Lusinda both discover that trust is essential to true love and true love is worth any risk."

The Seduction of a Duke, like *The Trouble with Moonlight,* features a seemingly incompatible pair of protagonists. Released in 2009, the narrative centers on the mismatched union of Francesca Winthrop, the product of an eagerly social mobile family, and Duke William Chambers, a romantically inclined bachelor who is in need of the wealth to support his title. The pair meets in ignorance of each other's identities at a costume party, and they find that they are somewhat attracted to each other. As Amy Wroblewsky reported in an article for the *Romance Reader* Web site, "Fran finds out that her beloved Randolph, who has been away for work, has married another woman, despite promising to wait for her. Franny is devastated but resigns herself to the marriage with the Duke, only hoping that she will become pregnant quickly so that she will be able to return to America as her father has put a clause in the marriage contract that his grandchildren should be educated there." After Winthrop employs the techniques she learned in a courtesans' memoir, the couple's passion for each other increases and a pregnancy appears quite possible albeit premature. "However, her past surfaces and threatens the marriage between the heiress and the duke," according to an article by Harriet Klausner for the *Genre Go Round Reviews*Web site.

BIOGRAPHICAL AND CRITICAL SOURCES:

PERIODICALS

Booklist, October 1, 2007, John Charles, review of *The Education of Mrs. Brimley,* p. 39.

ONLINE

Berkley Jove Web site, http://berkleyjoveauthors.com/ (July 21, 2009), author profile.

COFW, http://www.cofw.org/ (July 21, 2009), author profile.

Donna MacMeans Home Page, http://www.donnamacmeans.com (July 21, 2009).

Genre Go Round Reviews, http://genregoroundreviews.blogspot.com/ (February 28, 2009), Harriet Klausner, review of *The Seduction of a Duke.*

Romance Novel, http://www.romancenovel.tv/ (June 27, 2008), review of *The Trouble with Moonlight.*

Romance Reader, http://www.theromancereader.com/ (July 21, 2009), author interview with Cathy Sova; (July 21, 2009), Amy Wroblewsky, review of *The Seduction of a Duke.**

* * *

MALARKEY, Don 1921-

PERSONAL: Born 1921.

ADDRESSES: Home—OR.

CAREER: Writer. *Military service:* U.S. Army, 1942-46, served in the 101st Airborne, Easy Company; promoted to technical sergeant; received Bronze Star.

WRITINGS:

(With Bob Welch) *Easy Company Soldier: The Legendary Battles of a Sergeant from World War II's "Band of Brothers,"* St. Martin's Press (New York, NY), 2008.

SIDELIGHTS: Don Malarkey is a World War II veteran and a retired member of the 101st Airborne division, also known as the Screaming Eagles, of the U.S. Army. Malarkey was assigned to Easy Company, which stormed the beaches at Normandy, France, on D-Day. The company would later be paid homage to in a Home Box Office (HBO) series titled *Band of Brothers,* which chronicled the formation, deployment, and movement of Easy Company throughout their involvement in World War II's European campaign. Malarkey, one of the first trained paratroopers to engage in front-line combat, landed in Normandy on Tuesday, June 6, 1944. Malarkey's autobiographical text, *Easy Company Soldier: The Legendary Battles of a Sergeant from World War II's "Band of Brothers,"* details his experience as a soldier in the 101st Airborne in WWII. Released in 2008, the text details how, on the night before the official start of the invasion, Malarkey jumped from a C-47 transport airplane into Normandy under intense fire from enemy lines and thus began his experience in the Eastern campaign of the war. Gary Mortensen, in an article for the *Combat Report* Web site, described, "Once out, he fell for what felt like an eternity through the smoke and the lethal metal fragments on this fateful morning of June 6th, 1944. Finally, his chute snapped open and the ground came up hard to greet him. High above him in the night sky were burning C-47 carcasses as they plummeted towards the ground filled with desperate men who had lived their last day." However, according to Malarkey, this was only the beginning of his experience in combat. From there onward, Easy Company engaged in regular fights against Nazi occupation forces. The company was present at such monumental encounters as Brecourt Manor, the Battle of the Bulge, Operation Market Garden, and Bastogne. Regarding Easy Company's experience at Brecourt Manor, Mortensen wrote, "Three of the guns were destroyed that day in what has become a text book example of a frontal assault against a fixed position. In 1984 Don Malarkey went back to Brecourt Manor and met with its owner. He walked over and pointed out large shrapnel marks on the wall. "This is where your mortar round landed" the farmer said in his thick French accent. Malarkey walked over and touched the wall still damaged after all these years. His fingers traced the scars and he smiled."

In addition to the combat narrative, Malarkey details his thoughts on soldiering, and Easy Company's legacy. In an article for the *Associated Content* Web site, Greg Brian wrote, "Anybody seeing the beginnings of Malarkey's journey might not equate such a person with becoming one of the greatest soldiers of all time. When you see that Malarkey was born in Astoria, Oregon, one could easily think of a naïve soldier being thrown into the throes of battle that instantly brings on a breakdown of his mental and physical faculties. Instead, Malarkey's appreciation of nature in Oregon already set up a mental reserve he'd be able to tap into later when experiencing the worst hell on planet earth in the winter of Bastogne Forest." Thus, the text details how Malarkey maintained his sanity while serving in the most violent and protracted campaign of the war. *Easy Company Soldier,* which Malarkey wrote with Bob Welch, features an alphabetical index that provides access to persons and locations noted in the narrative as well as important events and terms of interest. Brian concluded, "Malarkey's story is arguably the greatest example of how one mentally prepares to be a soldier beforehand and during times of the most horrific wars."

BIOGRAPHICAL AND CRITICAL SOURCES:

PERIODICALS

Booklist, April 1, 2008, Roland Green, review of *Easy Company Soldier: The Legendary Battles of a Sergeant from World War II's "Band of Brothers,"* p. 20.

ONLINE

Associated Content, http://www.associatedcontent.com/ (April 15, 2009), Greg Brian, "Easy Company's Don Malarkey: 65 Years after D-Day and Changing History."

Combat Report, http://www.thecombatreport.com/ (December 16, 2006), Gary Mortensen, "One Day in War: Don Malarkey and the 101st Screaming Eagles."

Macmillan Web site, http://us.macmillan.com/ (July 23, 2009), author profile.*

* * *

MALONE, Jill
(Jill Amy Malone)

PERSONAL: Education: Holds an M.F.A.

ADDRESSES: E-mail—jillamymalone@gmail.com.

CAREER: Writer.

AWARDS, HONORS: Bywater Books Prize for Fiction, 2008, for *Red Audrey and the Roping.*

WRITINGS:

Red Audrey and the Roping, Bywater Books (Ann Arbor, MI), 2008.

A Field Guide to Deception, Bywater Books (Ann Arbor, MI), 2009.

SIDELIGHTS: Jill Malone is a writer living in Spokane, Washington. Growing up a military brat, she spent her school years in Germany, the American east coast, rural south, and Hawaii. She attended college in Hawaii and earned an M.F.A. in Washington state, where she settled, managed an independent bookstore, and lives with her partner, son, and dogs.

Expanding a short story she wrote in graduate school, Malone published her debut novel, *Red Audrey and the Roping,* in 2008. Amid the backdrop of beautiful Hawaii, Jane Elliott, a long-board surfer and Latin teacher, is distraught by her mother's suicide and finds comfort in the arms of her landlady, Emily. Jane suffers even more after a crushing accident that leaves her with survivor's guilt.

Told from her hospital bed, the story flashes forward and backward through time settling on Jane's friends, her sadistic male lover, her hesitation to get close to anyone else, her yearning for her mother, and her eventual willingness to live and be loved.

In an interview with Bett Norris in *Lambda Book Report,* Malone talked about the process of organizing the scenes in a nonlinear fashion. "The time hops create another layer of tension to the narrative, and they are textually representative of Jane's nonlinear thinking as a result of the accident."

Reviewers found the Hawaiian landscapes lush and inviting and the story far too short. "Finely tuned, daring, and perceptive, Malone's auspicious debut leaves us wanting more," said Whitney Scott in *Booklist.* A writer in *Lambda Book Report* noted, "Malone has accomplished an enormous feat with her wonderful writing and characterization in *Red Audrey.*" Bett Norris wrote in *Lambda Book Report* that, "Jill Malone has created characters that are fully wrought, layered, and complicated. No one is completely bad or completely good. Jane and her circle of friends, lovers and acquaintances are uncomfortably real. Jane's sexuality is as fluid as the rest of her identity and sense of self." A recipient of lesbian press Bywater Books' Prize for Fiction, *Red Audrey and the Roping* was lauded as literary fiction worthy of a crossover into mainstream interest.

In 2009 Malone released her second novel, *A Field Guide to Deception.* Upon the death of her aunt, Claire Bernard loses her livelihood, her best friend, and her son's co-parent. Now raising her son alone, Claire begins a journey to the discovery of parenthood, the nature of goodness and love, shifting alliances, and heroes found in unexpected places. Characters propel the story toward a climax of plot twists.

BIOGRAPHICAL AND CRITICAL SOURCES:

PERIODICALS

Booklist, May 1, 2008, Whitney Scott, review of *Red Audrey and the Roping,* p. 72.

Lambda Book Report, spring-summer, 2008, Bett Norris, "Jill Malone," review of *Red Audrey and the Roping;* fall, 2008, review of *Red Audrey and the Roping,* p. 27.

ONLINE

Bywater Books Web site, http://www.bywaterbooks.com/ (August 1, 2009), short author profile.

Jill Malone Home Page, http://www.jillmalone.com (August 1, 2009), short author profile.*

* * *

MALONE, Jill Amy
See MALONE, Jill

* * *

MARS, Julie 1951-

PERSONAL: Born 1951.

ADDRESSES: *E-mail*—julie@juliemars.com.

CAREER: Fiction writer.

AWARDS, HONORS: Recipient of grants from New York Fellowship for the Arts and from the New Jersey Arts Council for *The Secret Keepers.*

WRITINGS:

The Secret Keepers (novel), GreyCore Press (Pine Bush, NY), 2000.

A Month of Sundays: Searching for the Spirit and My Sister (memoir), GreyCore Press (Pine Bush, NY), 2005.

Anybody Any Minute (novel), St. Martin's Press (New York, NY), 2008.

SIDELIGHTS: Julie Mars is a fiction writer who lives in Albuquerque, New Mexico. She has written screenplays, fiction, nonfiction, and short stories, some through grants from the New York Fellowship for the Arts and the New Jersey Arts Council. Mars has also taught writing workshops in such diverse venues as the Taos Writers Conference and prison education programs.

In 2000 Mars published her debut novel, *The Secret Keepers,* a book that transcends the generic mystery genre. In the story, Steve Dant, a former junkie who functions well enough in society but has no friends, spots Christine Timberlake at the post office. When she forgets her keys, he has them duplicated so he can sneak into her apartment and admire her through the objects that make up her life. Christine is also being followed by a private investigator her sinister ex-husband hired to discover in which institution Christine has hidden their autistic child. Steve sets off to find the child, the PI in hot pursuit.

Reviewers praised *The Secret Keepers* for its cinematic voice, eloquent descriptions, and plot driven by characters. A writer in *Publishers Weekly* noted, "Mars's theme, that everybody harbors secrets . . . adds dimension to the characterization and also to the intrigue and suspense in this unusually smart debut." "What Mars has accomplished here is something akin to the creation of a new genre—one that is not easily categorized. As spellbinding and entertaining as it is [the book] is also a morality tale with its heart poignantly set on redemption," according to a writer in *Yomiuri Shimbun/Daily Yomiuri.*

Mars published a memoir, *A Month of Sundays: Searching for the Spirit and My Sister,* in 2005 that focuses on her sister. After spending seven months taking care of her dying older sister, Mars went searching for spiritual absolution and ways to cope with her grief. In thirty-one weeks she visited thirty-one houses of worship, including Christian churches, Jewish temples, Muslim mosques, and Buddhist temples. The book was a finalist for the Independent Press Book Award in 2005 and was selected by Barnes & Noble for its "Discover Great New Writers Series."

In 2008 Mars published another novel, *Anybody Any Minute,* a quirky story in which middle-aged, ex-hippie, and newly unemployed Ellen Kenny spontaneously buys a dilapidated country house in upstate New York on her way to visit her sister in Montreal. While Ellen deals with the strain the impromptu purchase puts on her marriage, she finds herself caring for her sister's young son who doesn't speak English. A redneck who nicknamed his ex-wife "Wide Load," exotic neighbors, and a depressed dog also test Ellen's free spirit. Through it all she rejects the hesitant and suspicious nature of native New York residents by bonding with her new friends, and she comes to learn what is important in life.

Reviewers were mixed on Mars's follow-up to her successful memoir. A writer in *Publishers Weekly* commented, "Though there's nothing that really sings, it's a passable story of self-discovery and self-improvement." "Mars leavens Ellen's potentially annoying idiosyncrasies with sly humor, and she revels in her heroine's '60s-cum-New Age mentality. . . . This '60s survivor is a hoot," noted a writer in *Kirkus Reviews.* Harriet Klausner wrote on the *Genre Go Round Reviews* Web site. "This is a fine look at a former hippie turned middle class trying to regain the idealism of her lost youth paradise." "For anyone who was young in the 1960s or for women over forty, *Anybody Any Minute* will have particular interest. The historical context is melded neatly with the psychological," remarked Maggie Ball on the *Blogcritics* Web site.

BIOGRAPHICAL AND CRITICAL SOURCES:

BOOKS

Mars, Julie, *A Month of Sundays: Searching for the Spirit and My Sister,* GreyCore Press (Pine Bush, NY), 2005.

PERIODICALS

Booklist, May 1, 2008, Katherine Boyle, review of *Anybody Any Minute,* p. 69.

Kirkus Reviews, May 15, 2008, review of *Anybody Any Minute.*

Publishers Weekly, May 29, 2000, review of *The Secret Keepers,* p. 52; March 17, 2008, review of *Anybody Any Minute,* p. 45.

Reviewer's Bookwatch, March 1, 2005, Christina Francine Whitcher, review of *A Month of Sundays.*

Virginia Quarterly Review, December 22, 2001, review of *The Secret Keepers,* p. 23.

Yomiuri Shimbun/Daily Yomiuri, June 11, 2000, "Mars' Debut Novel a Shot at Redemption," review of *The Secret Keepers.*

ONLINE

Blogcritics, http://www.blogcritics.org/ (May 2, 2008), Maggie Ball, review of *Anybody Any Minute.*

Genre Go Round Reviews, http://genregoroundreviews.blogspot.com/ (May 10, 2008), Harriet Klausner, review of *Anybody Any Minute.*

Julie Mars Home Page, http://www.juliemars.com (August 1, 2009), author profile.

Macmillan Web site, http://us.macmillan.com/ (August 1, 2009), author profile.

Mystery Reader, http://www.themysteryreader.com/ (August 1, 2009), Andy Plonka, review of *The Secret Keepers.*

Pif magazine, http://www.pifmagazine.com/ (June 1, 2000), Candace Moonshower, review of *The Secret Keepers.**

* * *

MARTIN, C.K. Kelly

PERSONAL: Born in Canada; married. *Education:* York University (Toronto, Ontario, Canada), B.A. (with honors).

ADDRESSES: Home—Toronto, Ontario, Canada. *E-mail*—ckkellymartin@hotmail.com.

CAREER: Writer.

WRITINGS:

FOR YOUNG ADULTS

I Know It's Over, Random House (New York, NY), 2008.

One Lonely Degree, Random House (New York, NY), 2009.

The Lighter Side of Life and Death, Random House (New York, NY), 2010.

Also author of the *C.K. Kelly Martin Web Log.*

SIDELIGHTS: After earning a university degree in Toronto, Canadian author C.K. Kelly Martin moved to Ireland, "spen[ding] the majority of the nineties there in forgettable jobs meeting unforgettable people," as she explained on her home page. During her stay in Ireland, Martin also began working seriously on her writing after discovering her interest in literature for teen readers. As she told *Cynsations* online interviewer Cynthia Leitich Smith, "It wasn't until 1999, after several years of living in Ireland, that I discovered I specifically wanted to write YA. I hadn't read any young adult literature in years." Once she became aware of her desire to write for the young-adult audience, she said, "I started snatching up all the teen books I could get my hands on. The process of becoming a writer was largely an unconscious one—just doing what felt right at the time, learning things by osmosis from reading."

Martin's work resulted in the publication of *I Know It's Over,* a novel about a teenaged couple facing an unplanned pregnancy. Told from the perspective of sixteen-year-old Nick, *I Know It's Over* traces the development of Nick's relationship with Sasha, from their initial infatuation with each other, to their first awkward attempts at intimacy, to their eventual break up. Martin earned much attention from reviewers for her ability to develop a convincing character in a book dealing with teen pregnancy. According to *School Library Journal* reviewer Lynn Rashid, *I Know It's Over* rises above other books about the same topic due to "the authentic voice and emotion of the protagonist." A *Kirkus Reviews* critic offered similar comments, writing that "rich characters and honest interactions set Martin's debut novel apart." Martin also earned favorable remarks from a *Publishers Weekly* contributor who suggested that the author "displays uncanny insight" in her first book, crafting "an emotionally complex and disarmingly frank coming-of-age tale."

BIOGRAPHICAL AND CRITICAL SOURCES:

PERIODICALS

Booklist, November 15, 2008, Ilene Cooper, review of *I Know It's Over,* p. 54.

Kirkus Reviews, August 1, 2008, review of *I Know It's Over;* April 1, 2009, review of *One Lonely Degree.*

Kliatt, September, 2008, Claire Rosser, review of *I Know It's Over,* p. 16.

Publishers Weekly, August 18, 2008, review of *I Know It's Over,* p. 63.

School Library Journal, November, 2008, Lynn Rashid, review of *I Know It's Over,* p. 130.

ONLINE

C.K. Kelly Martin Home Page, http://www.ckkellymartin.com (November 8, 2009).

Cynsations, http://cynthialeitichsmith.blogspot.com/ (December 4, 2008), Cynthia Leitich Smith, interview with Martin.

* * *

MARTIN, Deborah L. 1962-

PERSONAL: Born May 27, 1962.

ADDRESSES: *Home*—PA. *E-mail*—deb@compostgardening.com.

CAREER: Writer.

WRITINGS:

NONFICTION

(Editor, with Grace Gershuny) *The Rodale Book of Composting,* Rodale Press (Emmaus, PA), 1992.

(With Barbara W. Ellis and Joan Benjamin) *Rodale's Low-Maintenance Gardening Techniques: Shortcuts and Time-Saving Hints for Your Greatest Garden Ever,* Rodale Press (Emmaus, PA), 1995.

(Editor) *1,001 Ingenious Gardening Ideas: New, Fun, and Fabulous Tips That Will Change the Way You Garden—Forever!,* Rodale Press (Emmaus, PA), 1999.

(With Barbara W. Ellis and Joan Benjamin) *Rodale's Low-Maintenance Landscaping Techniques: Shortcuts and Timesaving Hints for Your Greatest Garden Ever,* Rodale Press (Emmaus, PA), 1999.

(Editor, with Joan Benjamin) *Great Garden Formulas: The Ultimate Book of Mix-It-Yourself Concoctions for Gardeners,* Rodale Press (Emmaus, PA), 2000.

(Editor, with Jill Jesiolowski Cebenko) *Insect, Disease & Weed I.D. Guide: Find-It-Fast Organic Solutions for Your Garden,* Rodale Press (Emmaus, PA), 2001.

Natural Stain Removal Secrets: Powerful, Safe Techniques for Removing Stubborn Stains from Anything, Fair Winds Press (Beverly, MA), 2007.

Best-Ever Backyard Birding Tips: Hundreds of Easy Ways to Attract the Birds You Love to Watch, Rodale Press (New York, NY), 2008.

(With Barbara Pleasant) *The Complete Compost Gardening Guide: Banner Batches, Grow Heaps, Comforter Compost, and Other Amazing Techniques for Saving Time and Money, and Producing the Most Flavorful, Nutritious Vegetables Ever,* Storey Press (North Adams, MA), 2008.

(With Barbara Pleasant) *Compost Gardening: A New Time-Saving System for More Flavorful Vegetables, Bountiful Blooms, and the Richest Soil You've Ever Seen,* Rodale Press (Emmaus, PA), 2008.

SIDELIGHTS: Deborah L. Martin is an avid gardener and the author of several nonfiction selections that detail topics regarding olericulture, horticulture, and botany.

Many gardeners experience trouble when attempting to compost, and Martin addresses these concerns as well as composting methodology in her fertilizer-related book releases. In both *The Rodale Book of Composting* and *The Complete Compost Gardening Guide: Banner Batches, Grow Heaps, Comforter Compost, and Other Amazing Techniques for Saving Time and Money, and Producing the Most Flavorful, Nutritious Vegetables Ever,* Martin addresses the history and culture of composting, including a list of benefits for the gardener, reasons to put one's effort into composting, and the contributions to plant health. Moreover, these texts detail the intricate anatomy of the compost heap which involves the symbiotic nature of rhizomes with decaying plant matter, the life cycle of nutrients, and the repurposing of materials for newly forming plant life. Specifically, Martin's *The Rodale Book of Composting* focuses on materials and methods for composting, such as manure and the use of shredders, while *The Complete Compost Gardening Guide* discusses the difference between slow and fast composting and the usefulness of banner batches. Regarding the former text, Karen Van Eppen, in a review for *Whole Earth,* found that Martin "answers almost every question you might have about the alchemy of transforming garbage into magical humus." Moreover, *The Complete Compost Gardening Guide,* which Martin wrote with Barbara Pleasant, offers customization tips and illustrations to further aid both well-practiced gardeners as well as the compost novice. Carol Haggas, in a review for *Booklist,* observed that the text is founded on the authors' personal "trial-and-error experiences" and that the instructional passages serve to "calm the fears that can wriggle through gardeners' psyches." Additionally, *Compost Gardening: A New Time-Saving System for More Flavorful Vegetables, Bountiful Blooms, and the Richest Soil You've Ever Seen,* also written with Barbara Pleasant, focuses on time-saving techniques and offers personal anecdotal journal sections from the authors.

However, Martin's work regarding gardening technique and method is not restricted to composting. In *Rodale's Low-Maintenance Gardening Techniques: Shortcuts and Time-Saving Hints for Your Greatest Garden Ever,* written with Barbara W. Ellis and Joan Benjamin, Martin attempts to demystify the complexities of gardening by explaining organic practices and the philosophy of health wherein a healthy garden is achieved through maintaining healthy soil. Likewise, *1,001 Ingenious Gardening Ideas: New, Fun, and Fabulous Tips That Will Change the Way You Garden—Forever!* not only expresses the potential ease with which one can achieve a beautiful garden but also creative solutions for common garden problems like the destruction of plants by animals, preservation of garden yields, and garden aesthetics. A *Publishers Weekly* contributor claimed that, due to the number of tips, "the only risk readers may run is wanting to rush out into the garden to try them all at once." *1,001 Ingenious Gardening Ideas* features twelve chapters organized according to subject. Select themes include: fruit-bearing plants, flower gardens, landscaping techniques, herb gardens, vegetable gardens, and seasonal selections. In his *Booklist* review, George Cohen noted that the text covers "using containers, hanging baskets, cold frames, and pit greenhouses; and starting seeds," and *Library Journal* contributor Dale

Luchsinger remarked that *1,001 Ingenious Gardening Ideas* is "a true idea book for organic gardeners." Similarly, Martin's *Great Garden Formulas: The Ultimate Book of Mix-It-Yourself Concoctions for Gardeners,* contains, according to Cohen, "hundreds of organic recipes and techniques."

Furthermore, Martin combines horticultural and entomological knowledge in her *Insect, Disease & Weed I.D. Guide: Find-It-Fast Organic Solutions for Your Garden.* Edited with Jill Jesiolowski Cebenko, the 2001 publication seeks to inform the reader that insects are a healthy part of the garden ecosystem. Using illustrative data, the text provides educational material regarding both beneficial and pestilent bugs. Species discussed in the text's entries include: ants, wasps, bees, weevils, flies, aphids, leafhoppers, mealybugs, scales, whiteflies, psyllids, cicadas, and crickets. Martin also includes a chapter detailing nonbug organisms, such as diseases and fungi, which may harm garden variety plants. A *Science News* contributor pointed out that the section regarding botanical disease features "photos of infected plants and information about how the disease is transmitted between plants." Aside from a description aimed at entomologic identification, the *Insect, Disease & Weed I.D. Guide* provides an alphabetical index of terms as well as an illustrated overview of the insect body.

BIOGRAPHICAL AND CRITICAL SOURCES:

PERIODICALS

American Gardener, September 1, 2008, Kirsten Winters, review of *The Complete Compost Gardening Guide: Banner Batches, Grow Heaps, Comforter Compost, and Other Amazing Techniques for Saving Time and Money, and Producing the Most Flavorful, Nutritious Vegetables Ever.*

Birder's World, October 1, 2008, review of *Best-Ever Backyard Birding Tips: Hundreds of Easy Ways to Attract the Birds You Love to Watch,* p. 54.

Booklist, June 1, 1998, George Cohen, review of *Great Garden Formulas: The Ultimate Book of Mix-It-Yourself Concoctions for Gardeners,* p. 1699; April 1, 1999, George Cohen, review of *1,001 Ingenious Gardening Ideas: New, Fun, and Fabulous Tips That Will Change the Way You Garden—Forever!,* p. 1375; April 1, 2008, Carol Haggas, review of *The Complete Compost Gardening Guide,* p. 14.

Library Journal, June 1, 1998, Molly Newling, review of *Great Garden Formulas,* p. 141; May 1, 1999, Dale Luchsinger, review of *1,001 Ingenious Gardening Ideas,* p. 101; March 15, 2008, Edward J. Valauskas, review of *The Complete Compost Gardening Guide,* p. 84.

Publishers Weekly, May 18, 1998, review of *Great Garden Formulas,* p. 75; April 5, 1999, review of *1,001 Ingenious Gardening Ideas,* p. 236.

Reference & Research Book News, October 1, 1992, review of *The Rodale Book of Composting,* p. 33.

Science News, April 27, 2002, review of *Insect, Disease & Weed I.D. Guide: Find-It-Fast Organic Solutions for Your Garden,* p. 271.

SciTech Book News, June 1, 2008, review of *The Complete Compost Gardening Guide.*

Whole Earth, March 22, 1999, Karen Van Epen, review of *The Rodale Book of Composting,* p. 30.

ONLINE

Compost Gardening Web site, http://www.compostgardening.com/ (July 22, 2009), author profile.

Workman Web site, http://www.workman.com/ (July 23, 2009), author profile.*

* * *

MASHIMA, Ted Y.

PERSONAL: Married; wife's name Julie. *Education:* University of Hawaii, Manoa, B.A.; Colorado State University, Fort Collins, D.V.M.

ADDRESSES: Office—Virginia-Maryland Regional College of Veterinary Medicine, 8075 Greenmead Dr., College Park, MD 20742. *E-mail*—tmashima@umd.edu.

CAREER: Veterinarian, instructor, and administrator. Virginia-Maryland Regional College of Veterinary Medicine, College Park, MD, instructor; Center for Public and Corporate Veterinary Medicine, Blacksburg, VA, associate director; Geraldine R. Dodge

Foundation, consultant; National Association of Physicians for the Environment, project director; Asian & Pacific Islander American Scholarship Fund, Washington, DC, president, CEO, and executive director; Mashima Communications, LLC, founder; Association of American Veterinary Medical Colleges, Washington, DC, director of academic affairs and research.

MEMBER: National Association of Physicians for the Environment, Association of American Veterinary Medical Colleges, American College of Zoological Medicine, Alliance of Veterinarians for the Environment.

WRITINGS:

(With James W. Carpenter and David J. Rupiper) *Exotic Animal Formulary,* W.B. Saunders (Philadelphia, PA), 2004.

(Editor, with Lucy H. Spelman) *The Rhino with Glue-On Shoes: And Other Surprising True Stories of Zoo Vets and Their Patients,* Delacorte Press (New York, NY), 2008.

SIDELIGHTS: Ted Y. Mashima is a veterinarian, college instructor, and executive of a nonprofit organization. He earned his B.A. in zoology from the University of Hawaii at Manoa and his D.V.M. from Colorado State University at Fort Collins. Mashima completed his internship in zoological medicine at Kansas State University and his residency in wildlife studies at North Carolina State University. He is board certified by the American College of Zoological Medicine and the American College of Veterinary Preventive Medicine.

Mashima is active in philanthropy, nonprofit organizations, and environmental conservation. He was a consultant to the Geraldine R. Dodge Foundation; project director for the National Association of Physicians for the Environment; secretary and administrative officer of the American College of Zoological Medicine; research associate with the Smithsonian Institute's Department of Animal Health; director of academic affairs and research at the Association of American Veterinary Medical Colleges, Washington, DC; and member of the board of directors for the Alliance of Veterinarians for the Environment.

Committed to teaching the next generation of veterinarians, he coordinates hands-on veterinary programs in the Washington, DC, area; coordinates clerkships for senior veterinary students at government agencies, corporations, zoos, aquariums, and other conservation outlets; and mentors hundreds of veterinary students and veterinarians. Mashima has been associate director of the Center for Public and Corporate Veterinary Medicine, part of the Virginia-Maryland Regional College of Veterinary Medicine at the University of Maryland. The innovative center trains veterinary students and veterinarians for nontraditional veterinary careers, such as zoological medicine.

After seven years at the Center, he left academia in 2007 for the Asian & Pacific Islander American Scholarship Fund, where he became its president, CEO, and executive director. The Fund assists Asian and Pacific Island American students in achieving higher education through scholarships to first-year undergraduate college, university, and vocational students. Mashima also founded Mashima Communications, LLC, a company that provides consultative services in communications, development, and strategic planning for nonprofit organizations. Commenting on his passion for treating animals and teaching others to care for them, Mashima said on the *Dr. Lucy Spelman* Web site, "I live vicariously through the people I mentor, helping them attain their dreams of making this world a better place for animals, people, and . . . ecosystems."

In 2004 Mashima wrote *Exotic Animal Formulary,* with James W. Carpenter and David J. Rupiper. The reference book for zoological medicine veterinarians presents recent data on veterinary drug therapy for exotic pets including antimicrobials, antiparasitics, anesthetics, vitamins, hormones, and chemotherapy protocols for many animal species. Bairbre O'Malley noted in the *Irish Veterinary Journal,* "This manual is an excellent user-friendly reference and is an essential requirement for any veterinary surgeon seeing exotic pets."

With coeditor Dr. Lucy Spelman, Mashima published *The Rhino with Glue-On Shoes: And Other Surprising True Stories of Zoo Vets and Their Patients* in 2008. The book collects twenty-eight stories about exotic pets and wild animals from zoos, aquariums, and wildlife sanctuaries around the world and the dedicated veterinarians who have to devise ways to treat them.

The book features touching and humorous stories about a 5,000-pound rhino with worn-through feet from walking on his cement enclosure, a baby giraffe with a broken hip, a polar bear with a hernia, a panda who needed a colonoscopy, a giant octopus that needed an MRI, and a moray eel who refused to eat.

Reviewers favored the short, readable stories and descriptions of exotic animals. According to Nancy Bent in *Booklist,* "The episodic nature of the individual stories makes it a perfect book for dipping into." Craig Wilson wrote in *USA Today,* "That's what makes these essays so readable. Mini life-and-death dramas told by vets who love their patients." Julie M. Mckinnon said in Toledo, Ohio's *Blade,* "Those true stories go far beyond what many animal lovers typically imagine, offering glimpses of what happens beyond a zoo's barricades. . . . Some stories take place in the wilds, not a zoo. Some prompt laughs, like one veterinarian's recollections of going into a drained pool with a fully awake crocodile or the thought of giving a hippo a root canal."

BIOGRAPHICAL AND CRITICAL SOURCES:

PERIODICALS

Blade (Toledo, OH), July 6, 2008, Julie M. Mckinnon, "Zoo Vets Talk about the Joys and Problems of Caring for Animals."

Booklist, May 15, 2008, Nancy Bent, review of *The Rhino with Glue-On Shoes: And Other Surprising True Stories of Zoo Vets and Their Patients,* p. 12.

DVM Newsmagazine, September 1, 2008, "Collection of Zoo Stories: Random House," review of *The Rhino with Glue-On Shoes,* p. 58.

Irish Veterinary Journal, February 1, 2007, Bairbre O'Malley, review of *Exotic Animal Formulary.*

Publishers Weekly, May 19, 2008, review of *The Rhino with Glue-On Shoes,* p. 48.

Science News, August 2, 2008, review of *The Rhino with Glue-On Shoes,* p. 30.

USA Today, July 10, 2008, Craig Wilson, "Why a Glued-Shoed Rhino? It's in the Book!," review of *The Rhino with Glue-On Shoes,* p. 4.

ONLINE

Dr. Lucy Spelman Home Page, http://www.drlucyspelman.com (August 1, 2009), author profile.

Environmental Medicine Consortium http://emc.ncsu.edu/ (August 1, 2009), author profile.

Random House Web site, http://www.randomhouse.com/ (August 1, 2009), short author profile.

University of Maryland Newsdesk http://www.newsdesk.umd.edu/ (August 1, 2009), author profile.*

* * *

MASTRAS, George 1966-

PERSONAL: Born April 10, 1966, in Boston, MA. *Education:* Graduate of Yale University and the University of California, Los Angeles.

ADDRESSES: Home—Los Angeles, CA. *E-mail*—george@fidalisway.com.

CAREER: Writer. Worked as a litigator for over ten years.

WRITINGS:

Fidali's Way (novel), Scribner (New York, NY), 2009.

Contributor to television series, including *The Evidence,* Warner Bros., 2006; *The Dresden Files,* Dresden File Productions, 2007; and *Breaking Bad,* Sony Pictures Television, 2008.

SIDELIGHTS: George Mastras, a graduate of Yale University and the University of California, Los Angeles, spent several years working in litigation and public service before he began writing for television series, including *The Evidence, The Dresden Files,* and *Breaking Bad.* In 2009, Mastras released his debut novel, *Fidali's Way.* The narrative tells the story of the protagonist, an American named Nick Sunder, as he is arrested and detained in Pakistan. What began as an exciting opportunity to see the Central Asian landscape quickly turns into a horrific experience, as Sunder is implicated in the death of one of his backpacking companions, a French woman who had become his girlfriend. While in captivity, Sunder is tortured and repeatedly urged to confess to the woman's murder. However, confident of his innocence, Sunder stubbornly refuses to comply, which further infuriates the policemen. In a moment of desperation, Sunder escapes the Pakistani prison by murdering a police officer and absconds to India. In poor health and with no resources, Sunder encounters two of his fellow escapees, Ghulam and Fidali, who take pity on him and guide him into Kashmir. Alternatively, the narrative also follows the story of an ambitious young woman named Aysha. Aysha falls in love with a young extremist named Kazim. While Aysha pursues a career as a physician, Kazim becomes an infamous fighter who seeks the conquest of Kashmir. Tragically, their divergent goals ultimately prevent the couple from fully realizing their love for each other.

These two seemingly disparate stories eventually converge in a climactic scene in which the characters meet at the height of military insurgency only to witness the cost of using violence to achieve moral imperatives. Mastras introduces many contemporary topics into the narrative, such as the true cost of religious conflict, the result of using violence as a means to an end, and whether or not love can compete with ingrained religious devotion. Moreover, the landscape and characters are indelibly linked through circumstances which cannot be controlled. In a review for the *Book Chase* Web site, Sam Sattler claimed that Mastras provides a "strong sense of place," and he concluded: "Mastras very successfully places a human face on those involved in a tragic struggle (on both sides) that is little more than headline news to most of the rest of the world." Similarly, a *Publishers Weekly* contributor noted that Mastras "delivers a winding, character-rich plot full of authentic detail and regional history."

BIOGRAPHICAL AND CRITICAL SOURCES:

PERIODICALS

Kirkus Reviews, November 15, 2008, review of *Fidali's Way.*

Publishers Weekly, October 13, 2008, review of *Fidali's Way,* p. 37.

ONLINE

Book Chase, http://bookchase.blogspot.com/ (April 17, 2009), Sam Sattler, review of *Fidali's Way.*

George Mastras Home Page, http://georgemastras.com (July 24, 2009).*

* * *

MATOUSEK, Mark 1957-

PERSONAL: Born February 5, 1957, in Los Angeles, CA. *Education:* University of California, Berkeley, B.A., 1979; University of California, Los Angeles, M.A., 1981.

ADDRESSES: Agent—Joy Harris, 156 5th Ave., Ste. 617, New York, NY 10010.

CAREER: Writer. V-Men, New York, NY, creative director, 2009—.

WRITINGS:

NONFICTION

A Day in the Life of Hollywood: As Seen by 75 of the World's Leading Photographers on One Day, May 20, 1992, HarperCollins (San Francisco, CA), 1992.

(Editor) *Dialogues with a Modern Mystic,* Theosophical Press (Wheaton, IL), 1994.

Sex, Death, Enlightenment: A True Story, Riverhead Books (New York, NY), 1996.

The Boy He Left Behind: A Man's Search for His Lost Father, Riverhead Books (New York, NY), 2000.

(Editor) *Still Here: Embracing Aging, Changing, and Dying,* Riverhead Books (New York, NY), 2000.

When You're Falling, Dive: Lessons in the Art of Living, Bloomsbury (New York, NY), 2008.

Ethical Wisdom: What Makes Us Good, Random House Inc. (New York, NY), 2010.

Contributor to books, including *The Tibetan Book of Living and Dying,* Harper (New York, NY), 1992. Contributor of essays and articles to periodicals, including *Newsweek, Common Boundary, New Yorker, Details, Harper's Bazaar,* and *Interview.*

SIDELIGHTS: American author Mark Matousek has worked as a magazine editor, journalist, and author of nonfiction and fiction. His publication credits consist of periodicals such as *Newsweek, Common Boundary, New Yorker, Details,* and *Harper's Bazaar* as well as contributions to texts, including *The Tibetan Book of Living and Dying* and *Dialogues with A Modern Mystic.* Moreover, Matousek has published several book-length works, including *The Boy He Left Behind: A Man's Search for His Lost Father.*

Despite these accomplishments, Matousek's experience has not always translated as an allegory of success. "Matousek was diagnosed as HIV-positive in 1989. In his case, terminal illness was more than a metaphor; it allowed him to feel human for the first time in his life. A senior editor at Andy Warhol's *Interview,* he had transcended the relative poverty of a dysfunctional single-parent home in California for bacchanalian promiscuity, drug and alcohol abuse, seventy-hour working weeks, and daily interaction with the international leaders of every field—financial, social, artistic, athletic, and intellectual," wrote *This is a War* Web site contributor Antonella Gambotto-Burke. In *Sex, Death, Enlightenment: A True Story,* he recounts the daily surrealism of working with Warhol and how his employment at *Interview* magazine led to a demystification of the celebrity culture. Gambotto-Burke observed, "Warhol embodied the spiritual vacuity of our civilisation to Matousek, who recalls the artist as emotionally frigid and exploitative, materialistic and pathologically detached. Their association began with a handshake . . . and ignominiously ended when Warhol ordered an assistant to escort Matousek from the premises to ensure that he didn't 'steal' anything." During his employment at *Interview,* Matousek grew increasingly more dissatisfied with the culture of publicity and consumption, although the experience was not without gains. Eventually, as *Sex, Death, Enlightenment* relates, Matousek achieved a measure of self realization and an understanding of his circumstances. Gambotto-Burke noted, "Matousek documents his paradigm shift with humorous severity: the celebrity which he had imagined to be his goal was, in fact, no more than the starting point of his quest for wisdom." Specifically, prior to his HIV diagnosis, Matousek found himself in need of spiritual fulfillment. With this realization also came the knowledge that he had been using other means to fulfill his need for transcendence, namely drugs and sex. In the text, Matousek traces the formation of his sexual identity to the behavior of his mother, a lascivious woman whose concept of womanhood was rooted in sexual experience. Gambotto-Burke found, "This philosophy—transhistorically that of the sexually abused—was, in turn, passed on to her son. It is in writing of his later pilgrimage to India and of his mother that Matousek displays his prose skills at their finest." Matousek informs that, neglected by his mother, he was drawn into the company of a pedophile who freely, albeit through dehumanization, bestowed attention upon alienated young boys.

Through his reflections on his youth, *Sex, Death, Enlightenment* articulates how the abuses Matousek endured as the result of a neglectful mother coupled with his early exposure to a sexual predator led to his self- destructive behaviors. However, as the text also reveals, Matousek does not realize the extent of his emotional malaise until he becomes disillusioned with the environment perpetuated by Warhol and the celebrity culture. In the narrative, it is while Matousek is attempting to discern the cause of his dissatisfaction with his situation that he meets the poet Alexander Maxwell. Matousek reveals that he and Maxwell developed an intimate relationship and that Maxwell facilitated his journey to India. This journey proves transformational for Matousek, and the narrative details his experiences with Mother Meera and India itself. Whether or not these experiences served as a type of preparation for his HIV diagnosis is speculative. Will Blythe, in a review for *Esquire,* felt that "Matousek's growing apprehension of the reality of spiritual life came just in time," as he was diagnosed with HIV shortly after his return to the United States. Regardless, Matousek describes how he dealt with his initial surprise, dismay, and anxiety when he learned of his illness. Blythe claimed that Matousek's illness "has lent an extra urgency to his attempts to come to grips with life, although, as his soulful, charming book makes clear, we are all—sick or not—under comparable death sentence."

In Matousek's subsequent publication, *When You're Falling, Dive: Lessons in the Art of Living,* he extrapolates wisdom gathered from his prior experiences while also relating the experiences of others. In an interview with Valerie Reiss for the *Beliefnet* Web site, Matousek related that he set about to answer such questions as: "How do you survive as a soul? How do you reinvent yourself after catastrophe? How do you handle the really extreme things that life deals you and come through intact—and with curiosity and interest and enthusiasm in your life?" In the wake of a tragic experience, Matousek explains how one can recover and not only live as a survivor but also become satisfied with life again. In the narrative, Matousek states that life's annoyances lead to one's greater understanding of the world and their place in it. Matousek told Reiss, "One of the prerequisites for change is the inability to escape. And one of the side effects of the inability to escape is irritation. And what is irritation? Irritation is going against the grain. We're just talking about working against the grain. And that's actually how evolution happens." In addition to the more abstract elements of self realization, the text presents specific examples of spiritual triumph. Reiss considered Matousek's description of "a mother who lost her child but remains open-hearted" and "a photographer who started creating his best work after going blind" as two instances of people who used their "pain to grow." Consequently, the premise of working through pain in order to overcome adversity is the major theme of the text. In response to a question posed by Reiss, Matousek maintained, "When you're in a situation you can't escape, how do you get through it? Raging against the dying of the light? No. You end up killing yourself that way. You get through it by cooperating with something."

BIOGRAPHICAL AND CRITICAL SOURCES:

PERIODICALS

Advocate, April 30, 1996, Peter Galvin, review of *Sex, Death, Enlightenment: A True Story,* p. 61; May 23, 2000, Alaric Blair, review of *The Boy He Left Behind: A Man's Search for His Lost Father,* p. 106.

Booklist, April 1, 1996, Whitney Scott, review of *Sex, Death, Enlightenment,* p. 1325; March 1, 2000, GraceAnne A. DeCandido, review of *The Boy He Left Behind,* p. 1193.

Bulletin with Newsweek, May 15, 2001, Kathy Hunt, review of *The Boy He Left Behind,* p. 78.

Entertainment Weekly, April 12, 1996, Lisa Schwarzbaum, review of *Sex, Death, Enlightenment,* p. 60.

Esquire, June 1, 1996, Will Blythe, review of *Sex, Death, Enlightenment,* p. 33.

Lambda Book Report, March 1, 2001, review of *The Boy He Left Behind,* p. 31.

Library Journal, February 15, 2000, Pam Kingsbury, review of *The Boy He Left Behind,* p. 174; June 15, 2008, Shawna Thorup, review of *When You're Falling, Dive: Lessons in the Art of Living,* p. 83.

New York Times Book Review, May 14, 2000, review of *The Boy He Left Behind,* p. 34.

O, the Oprah Magazine, July 1, 2008, "Worth a Read," p. 132.

People, May 27, 1996, Clare McHugh, review of *Sex, Death, Enlightenment,* p. 34.

Publishers Weekly, February 19, 1996, review of *Sex, Death, Enlightenment,* p. 197; February 14, 2000, review of *The Boy He Left Behind,* p. 182; May 5, 2008, review of *When You're Falling, Dive,* p. 55.

Saturday Night, June 1, 1996, review of *Sex, Death, Enlightenment,* p. 68.

Times Literary Supplement, January 3, 1997, review of *Sex, Death, Enlightenment,* p. 32.

Tribune Books, March 23, 1997, review of *Sex, Death, Enlightenment,* p. 6.

ONLINE

Beliefnet, http://www.beliefnet.com/ (September 1, 2008), Valerie Reiss, "The Alchemy of Crisis."

Mark Matousek Home Page, http://www.markmatousek.com (July 22, 2009).

This Is a War, http://www.thisisawar.com/ (July 22, 2009), author interview with Antonella Gambotto-Burke.

* * *

McCLOSKEY, Patrick J.

PERSONAL: Education: Attended Columbia School of Journalism.

ADDRESSES: E-mail—pjm@thestreetstopshere.com.

CAREER: Writer, journalist. *New York Times,* New York, NY, writer; contributor to various publications.

WRITINGS:

The Street Stops Here: A Year at a Catholic High School in Harlem, foreword by Samuel G. Freedman, University of California Press (Berkeley, CA), 2008.

Contributor to the *New York Times* and various other periodicals.

SIDELIGHTS: Writer and journalist Patrick J. McCloskey has contributed to a wide range of periodicals over the course of his career, most notably the *New York Times.* He is also the author of *The Street Stops Here: A Year at a Catholic High School in Harlem,* his debut effort. The book addresses the broader issue of education in the United States and the quality of learning that most high school students have available to them, and focuses in particular on a school that features the parochial standards within a Harlem neighborhood of New York City.

In order to write *The Street Stops Here,* McCloskey spent a year inside the walls of a Catholic high school with a high record of success among its students, particularly when measured against the fact that—as is true with many parochial schools—the staff struggles to do and to achieve more for their numbers with less funding and less resources than do most private schools and, in some instances, many public schools. Rice High School is a parochial institution for boys only, located in Harlem. The population of the school is made up primarily of African Americans, who comprise eighty-five percent of the student body, with Hispanic students making up the balance. Over the course of the year he spent in the school, McCloskey sat in on classes, school events, teacher meetings, and so on. He also interviewed students, teachers, and parents, and even spent time with some students away from school, allowing him to get a broader impression of the circumstances that served as a foundation for many of Rice's population. His book reflects this diverse approach, and allows readers to understand that the school is not an easy or luxurious atmosphere, but it is one that takes education seriously. While moral standards are upheld, there is no overt preaching of Catholicism, so non-Catholic students are able to attend with no pressure regarding their beliefs. Ultimately, McCloskey points out that while the school is far from perfect, their methods enable them to produce more graduates each year than the typical public school facing a similar population. A writer for *Kirkus Reviews* commented that "the unadorned narrative is convincing in its portrayal of Rice's mission to put an education, not a creed, into young men's heads." Joan Frawley Desmond, in a review for the *Weekly Standard,* remarked that McCloskey's book "calls on Roman Catholic leaders, education reform groups, and large philanthropic institutions such as the Bill and Melinda Gates Foundation to coordinate a systemwide rescue/reinvention that would protect the legacy of Rice High School, and similar institutions, for generations to come."

BIOGRAPHICAL AND CRITICAL SOURCES:

PERIODICALS

Kirkus Reviews, November 15, 2008, review of *The Street Stops Here: A Year at a Catholic High School in Harlem.*

National Catholic Reporter, April 3, 2009, "Rice Men: Lessons at a Harlem High School: Heroes Defy the Odds in Author's Portrait of a Catholic Educational Oasis," p. 1.

National Post, January 31, 2009, review of *The Street Stops Here,* p. 14.

Publishers Weekly, October 27, 2008, review of *The Street Stops Here,* p. 46.

Wall Street Journal, December 5, 2008, "Parochial-School Lessons: *The Street Stops Here,*" p. 19.

Weekly Standard, March 2, 2009, "Motivation High: Schools That Work Need a System That Sustains Them."

ONLINE

Street Stops Here Web site, http://www.thestreetstopshere.com (August 17, 2009).

University of California Press Web site, http://www.ucpress.edu/ (August 17, 2009), author profile.*

* * *

McCORMACK, Win

PERSONAL: Education: Attended Harvard University and the University of Oregon.

ADDRESSES: Home—Portland, OR. *E-mail*—info@winmccormack.com.

CAREER: Writer. *Oregon,* publisher, 1976-88; *Tin House,* publisher.

WRITINGS:

You Don't Know Me: A Citizen's Guide to Republican Family Values, Tin House Books (Portland, OR), 2008.

Contributor of essays and articles to periodicals, including *Oregon, Tin House, Oregonian, Military History Quarterly,* and *Oregon Humanities.*

SIDELIGHTS: Win McCormack has worked in the publishing industry for over twenty-five years, first as the publisher of *Oregon* magazine and then as the publisher of *Tin House.* Consequently, Eric Bryant, in an article for *Library Journal,* commented on *Tin House*'s "impressive editorial board" which includes "Dorothy Allison, Rick Moody, and Irvine Welsh." In addition to acting as a publisher, McCormack has contributed numerous articles and essays to periodicals, including the *Oregonian, Military History Quarterly,* and *Oregon Humanities.*

In 2008, McCormack released his debut book *You Don't Know Me: A Citizen's Guide to Republican Family Values.* The text chronicles the hypocrisy of politicians, specifically those persons who espouse family values and religious morals. According to a *Publishers Weekly* contributor, "McCormack catalogues over one hundred cases of sexual misconduct and criminality committed by Republican officials and supporters." The duplicity of these individuals is presented in detail and coupled with illustrations as well as primary source materials which lend credibility to the narrative.

Among the charges included are the representations of the sexual escapades of highly public political figures, such as Newt Gingrich and Bill O'Reilly, as well as their seeming lack of judgment. These compromising selections serve as evidence of a moral void in American politics. These selections also imply that wrongdoing by politicians is conveniently and quickly disregarded, for many of the persons discussed have been active in twenty-first-century politics despite their transgressions. McCormack details how prominent politicians have ascribed to normative family values while simultaneously engaging in sexual misconduct, child pornography, adultery, drug abuse, and prostitution. These umbrages range from mildly to blatantly offensive in nature, as the content often recounts explicit acts. Using these lurid details from the lives of civic representative figures, the text primarily endeavors to illustrate the discord between the public and private spheres of political lives. Twenty-six sections, each one corresponding with a letter of the alphabet, represent the range of depravity and misconduct that can be attributed to well-known leaders in state and federal government institutions. Moreover, McCormack includes an appendix that provides selections from documents supporting various charges and an alphabetical index which serves to orient the reader with persons of interest. Most recent scandals include the Clinton impeachment proceedings, Rudy Giuliani's marital history, Stephen R. Johnson's affair with a staff member, Clarence Thomas's sexual harassment of Anita Hill, and Eliot Spitzer's alleged engagement with a prostitute.

BIOGRAPHICAL AND CRITICAL SOURCES:

PERIODICALS

Library Journal, July 1, 1999, "Tin House," p. 146.

Publishers Weekly, June 30, 2008, review of *You Don't Know Me: A Citizen's Guide to Republican Family Values,* p. 176.

ONLINE

Huffington Post Online, http://www.huffingtonpost.com/ (July 23, 2009), author profile.

Red Room, http://www.redroom.com/ (July 23, 2009), author profile.

Tin House Web site, http://www.tinhouse.com/ (July 23, 2009), author profile.

Win McCormack Home Page, http://www.winmccormack.com (July 23, 2009).*

* * *

McCULLOUGH, Kelly 1967-
(Kelly David McCullough, Kelly Sorsoleil)

PERSONAL: Born 1967. *Education:* Attended Hamline University and the University of Minnesota.

ADDRESSES: Home—WI.

CAREER: Writer.

WRITINGS:

Chronicles of the Wandering Star: Interactions in Physical Science (novel), It's About Time (New York, NY), 2006.

"RAVIRN" SCIENCE FICTION SERIES

WebMage, Berkley Press (New York, NY), 2006.
Cybermancy, Ace Books (New York, NY), 2007.
CodeSpell, Ace Books (New York, NY), 2008.
MythOS, Ace Books (New York, NY), 2009.

SIDELIGHTS: Kelly McCullough is a science fiction and fantasy writer. McCullough's "Ravirn" series is set in a futuristic high tech universe where characters from Greek legends make regular appearances and magic has the ability to conjoin with technology. In an extension of Greek mythology, McCullough's characters have both ordinary and extraordinary talents. In *WebMage,* for example, the reader is introduced to the series protagonist, Ravirn, who is a digital code breaker with paranormal ability, a divine lineage, and a familiar named Melchior. In an interview with a *Penguin* Web site contributor, McCullough stated, "I decided to go for a fantasy world rather science fiction because I hadn't seen anyone doing anything with magic and computers or magic and crosstime stories and I really wanted to try something new. Once I had that, the character of Ravirn was a natural."

What differentiates McCullough's work from the science fiction genre and aligns it more with fantasy is the influential deific pantheon that he employs to construct his characters and the mechanics of the universe. The Greek Fate Lachesis and Thalia are Ravirn's progenitures. This is significant, for Greek legend holds that Lachesis, the second of the Moirae, has the responsibility to judge the lifespan of mortals, and Thalia is a muse that inspires poetry and comedy. So, Ravirn has the ability to test fateful situations with comedic relief during his exploits. McCullough told the *Penguin* Web site contributor, "The Greek mythos architecture was added when I started trying to figure out what sort of entity would have built a huge interworld web. I tend to think along classical lines and the idea of the Fates upgrading their operation to make use of modern technology struck me as a great framework."

In *WebMage,* according to an *Apex Book Company* Web site contributor, "The Fates have upgraded their magic—they have blended magic with computer programming, creating their own 'mweb' which runs on the Fate Core, the server that governs Destiny. To the consternation of the Fates, this programming contains a major bug." This situation facilitates Ravirn's reluctant interaction with the cosmic powers, and he quickly enters the fray. However, Ravirn is not a willing participant in the Fates' manipulations, and he undermines their efforts by refusing to become the architect for a program intended to remove human volition. "Thus the adventure begins and we are led on a fast-paced adventure through familiar and sometimes new territory," wrote a *Blogcritics* Web site contributor. Atropos, the Fate that attempted to gain Ravirn's assistance, retaliates by afflicting Ravirn with Cassandra's curse which causes those he speaks with to immediately disbelieve him. The curse acts as a protracted obstacle throughout the story. Mel Odom, in a review for the *Blogcritics* Web site, claimed, "Gripping and imaginative, rooted carefully in the real world, *WebMage* is an exciting chase novel filled with techno jargon the cyber-crowd will enjoy as well as Greek mythology for the fantasy enthusiasts. The first-person narrative rings especially true and drives the tale. Dialogue between Ravirn and Melchior is sharp and cutting, and sounds like two old friends who constantly pick at each other." Moreover, in a review for *Kliatt,* Sherry Hoy remarked that *WebMage* is "a unique first novel" with "a charming, fresh combination of mythological, magical, and computer elements."

McCullough's second installment in the series, *Cybermancy,* was released in 2007. The narrative follows Ravirn as he attempts to rescue his girlfriend Cerice's familiar, Shara, from Hades. Cerice's devotion to Shara is both emotional and practical, for she uses the familiar as an external memory device. When Shara is transported to Hades, Cerice's doctoral research goes with her. Therefore, the impetus is established for Ravirn's involvement. Likewise, in *CodeSpell,* Ravirn is tasked with the rescue of an important figure. The universe's computer, called Necessity, has been infected with a virus, and Ravirn must find a solution and restore the system's health or risk the destruction of reality. Unfortunately, not only are Ravirn's enemies conspiring against him, his former girlfriend is also seeking his failure. Adding to his difficulties, "Ravirn finds his affections torn between Eris (a Discord) and Tisiphone (a Fury)," as a *Publishers Weekly* contributor observed.

In McCullough's fourth novel, *MythOS,* the pantheon is expanded to include Norse myths as well as the familiar Greek characters. In *MythOS,* a 2009 release, Ravirn is conveyed to an alternative universe and he is subjected to a steep learning curve when he discovers that the Fates do not control every plane in the multiverse. While he is endeavoring to decipher the new programming system, he is also preoccupied by his romantic involvement with Tisiphone. Furthermore, in another layer of complication, Ravirn learns of a conflict between Odin and his son Loki which he is anxious to avoid but also compelled to participate in.

BIOGRAPHICAL AND CRITICAL SOURCES:

PERIODICALS

Booklist, August 1, 2006, Frieda Murray, review of *WebMage,* p. 57; October 1, 2007, Frieda Murray, review of *Cybermancy,* p. 41; May 15, 2008, Frieda Murray, review of *CodeSpell,* p. 36.

Kliatt, November 1, 2006, Sherry Hoy, review of *WebMage,* p. 29.

Publishers Weekly, June 26, 2006, review of *WebMage,* p. 38; May 5, 2008, review of *CodeSpell,* p. 51.

Voice of Youth Advocates, October 1, 2007, Michael Levy, review of *Cybermancy,* p. 354.

ONLINE

Apex Book Company Web site, http://apexdigest.livejournal.com/ (September 28, 2006), review of *WebMage.*

Blogcritics, http://blogcritics.org/books/ (August 11, 2006), Mel Odom, review of *WebMage;* (October 23, 2006), review of *WebMage.*

Bookhound, http://bookhound.wordpress.com/ (November 20, 2007), review of *Cybermancy.*

Fresh Fiction, http://freshfiction.com/ (July 23, 2009), author profile.

Kelly McCullough Home Page, http://www.kellymccullough.com (July 23, 2009).

Penguin Web site, http://us.penguingroup.com/ (July 23, 2009), author profile.

Red Room, http://www.redroom.com/ (July 23, 2009), author profile.

Science Fiction and Fantasy Novelists, http://www.sfnovelists.com/ (May 26, 2009), author interview.*

* * *

McCULLOUGH, Kelly David
See McCULLOUGH, Kelly

* * *

McKERRIGAN, Sarah
[A pseudonym]
(Glynnis Talken Campbell)

PERSONAL: Female.

ADDRESSES: *Home*—Arleta, CA.

CAREER: Writer and voice-over artist. Voice-over artist for television series, including *The Maxx,* Rough Draft, 1995; *Fables of Regis,* Castle Builders. Voice-over artist for audiobooks, including *Star Wars: Dark Empire,* Dark Horse, 1997; *Star Wars: Dark Empire II,* Dark Horse, 2006; *Star Wars: Dark Lords,* Art Insana, 2008; and *Dragon Lover's Treasury,* Art Insana, 2008. Voice-over artist for video games, including *Starcraft,* Blizzard Entertainment, 1998; *Savage,* S2 Games, 1998; *Diablo,* Blizzard Entertainment, 1998; *Diablo II,* Blizzard Entertainment, 2000.

WRITINGS:

ROMANCE NOVELS

My Champion, Jove Books (New York, NY), 2000.

My Warrior, Jove Books (New York, NY), 2001.

A Knight's Vow, Jove Books (New York, NY), 2001.

My Hero, Berkley Press Group (New York, NY), 2002.

Captive Heart, Warner Forever (New York, NY), 2006.

Lady Danger, Warner Books (New York, NY), 2006.

Knight's Prize, Warner Books (New York, NY), 2007.

Danger's Kiss, Forever Books (New York, NY), 2008.

SIDELIGHTS: Sarah McKerrigan, a pseudonym of Glyniss Talken Campbell, is a romance writer and voice-over artist. McKerrigan has provided the vocals for fictional characters in television and audiobook projects, including *The Maxx, Fables of Regis, Star Wars: Dark Empire, Star Wars: Dark Lords,* and *Dragon Lover's Treasury.* In an interview with an *Insomniac Mania* Web site contributor, McKerrigan revealed, "I did my very first voice-over when I was about ten years old. I had a small reel-to-reel deck, and I roped my little brother into doing an audio skit with me. It was a play I'd written about Amenhotep the Egyptian [pharaoh], and we recorded it complete with satirical commercials. Little did I know what it would lead to." Since then, McKerrigan has worked in many media genres, including video games, and provided the vocalizations for leading characters in such popular games as *Starcraft, Savage,* and the *Diablo* series. McKerrigan told the *Insomniac Mania* Web site contributor, "Probably my favorite thing about voice-over is completely immersing myself into a character to the extent that people don't know it's the same person. I've done voices for old men, little girls, rubber duckies, tavern wenches, pterodactyls, even Yoda's sister."

In addition to her diversity in working with audiovisual media, McKerrigan has authored numerous romantic novels. In the *Insomniac Mania* interview, McKerrigan told the contributor, "I've been fascinated with the written word from the time I won a limerick contest at the age of eleven. And I've had a lifelong love of towering castles, trusty swords, and knights in shining armor. These passions came together when I started writing historical romance a few years ago." *My Champion,* released in 2000, serves as the introduction to McKerrigan's romantic fourteenth-century trilogy. In *My Champion,* Linet de Montfort is placed in a dangerous situation when she requests, with the permission of King Edward, that a pirate known as El Gallo relinquish his property to her. Duncan de Ware, in the disguise of a lowly gypsy, resolves to watch over de Montfort so that no harm befalls her. De Ware not only has noble intentions, he is the son of Lord James de Ware. However, he keeps his true identity a secret from the woman he has taken a keen interest in. Thus, the romantic adventure ensues wherein de Montfort is abducted by the pirate and de Ware acts as her defender and savior. Nancy J. Silberstein, in a *Romantic Reader* Web site review described de Montfort as "a sharp little businesswoman who appraises every situation as though it were a variation on her business of weaving, dying, and selling cloth." However, despite her business acumen, de Montfort is not easily swayed by de Ware because she is reluctant to give her affections to someone she perceives as a commoner. Silberstein felt that McKerrigan "writes a competent prose, with tantalizing glints of humor," and, "if she can build on her strengths while improving her plots and characterization, the result should be worth checking out."

My Warrior, the second installment in the "Knights of de Ware" trilogy, was released in 2001. The narrative continues the de Ware saga with the story of Holden de Ware and, under the command of King Edward, his attempted subjugation of Scottish lands owned by Laird Gavin. De Ware is forced to use aggressive tactics to claim the lands, and he acquires the enmity of Cambria Gavin in the process of his hostile conquest. When de Ware apprehends the Lady Gavin for suspicion of murder, the duo develops a dynamic relationship. Kathe Robin, in the *Romantic Times Online,* claimed *My Warrior* "is filled with dangerous battles and good historical backdrop" as well as "great characters" and an abundance of romantic drama.

The series' conclusion, *My Hero,* features Garth de Ware who is the third son of Lord de Ware. As the youngest de Ware progeny, and as was common in the fourteenth century, "there are few opportunities open to him, so he chooses the church," noted *Romantic Times Online* contributor Kathe Robin. De Ware takes a vow of silence, which proves to be problematic when Lady Cynthia le Wyte attempts to garner his attentions. Soon thereafter, de Ware, according to Robin, "finds himself torn between piety and passion."

Like her preceding works, McKerrigan's *Lady Danger* features a trio of medieval relations who are distinguished by their overt personalities. However, in this narrative, the story presents three sisters, Dierdre, Helena, and Muriel of the Clan Rivenloch, and the family drama heightens when the sisters are divided over the opportunity to marry an accomplished knight and facilitate the preservation of their lands. Shirley Lyons, in an article for the *Romance Reader* Web site, concluded, "The story moves along nicely and anon, there is adventure, friction, seduction, loving and even some laughing." After the knight weds one of the Rivenloch sisters, the family sets about to do battle with their English aggressors.

BIOGRAPHICAL AND CRITICAL SOURCES:

PERIODICALS

Booklist, April 1, 2008, Diana Tixier Herald, review of *Danger's Kiss,* p. 34.

ONLINE

Berkeley Jove Authors Web site, http://berkleyjove authors.com/ (July 21, 2009), author profile.

Glynnis Talken Campbell Home Page, http://www.glynnis.net (July 21, 2009).

Insomniac Mania, http://insomniacmania.com/ (July 21, 2009), author interview.

Internet Movie Database, http://www.imdb.com/ (July 21, 2009), "Glynnis Talken."

Jandy's Reading Room, http://www.jandysbooks.com/ (April 20, 2008), review of *Danger's Kiss.*

Romance Reader, http://www.theromancereader.com/ (July 21, 2009), Nancy J. Silberstein, review of *My Champion;* (July 21, 2009), Shirley Lyons, review of *Lady Danger.*

Romantic Times Online, http://www.romantictimes.com/ (July 21, 2009), Kathe Robin, review of *My Warrior;* (July 21, 2009), Kathe Robin, review of *My Hero;* (July 21, 2009), Kathe Robin, review of *Lady Danger;* (July 21, 2009), Kathe Robin, review of *Lady Danger;* (July 21, 2009), Kathe Robin, review of *Knight's Prize;* (July 21, 2009), Kathe Robin, review of *Danger's Kiss;* (July 21, 2009), Kathe Robin, review of *Captive Heart.*

Sarah McKerrigan Home Page, http://www.sarah mckerrigan.com (July 21, 2009).*

* * *

McMANUS, Erwin Raphael 1958-

PERSONAL: Born August 28, 1958. *Education:* Attended University of North Carolina and Southwestern Theological Seminary.

ADDRESSES: Home—Los Angeles, CA.

CAREER: Writer, artist, speaker, filmmaker, and innovator in creative development.

WRITINGS:

NONFICTION

An Unstoppable Force: Daring to Become the Church God Had in Mind, Group (Loveland, CO), 2001.

Seizing Your Divine Moment: Dare to Live a Life of Adventure, Thomas Nelson Press (Nashville, TN), 2002, reprinted as *Chasing Daylight: Seize the Power of Every Moment,* Thomas Nelson Press (Nashville, TN), 2006.

Uprising: A Revolution of the Soul, Thomas Nelson Press (Nashville, TN), 2003.

The Barbarian Way: Unleash the Untamed Faith Within, Thomas Nelson Press (Nashville, TN), 2005.

Soul Cravings: An Exploration of the Human Spirit, Thomas Nelson Press (Nashville, TN), 2006.

Stand against the Wind: Awaken the Hero Within, J. Countryman (Nashville, TN), 2006.

Wide Awake: For Those Who Would Live Their Dreams, Thomas Nelson Press (Nashville, TN), 2008.

SIDELIGHTS: Writer and motivational speaker Erwin Raphael McManus was born August 28, 1958. He has appeared at public speaking events for various organizations, including the National Football League, Lionsgate Films, New Line Cinema, and ILOG. McManus also is credited with engaging his congregation in multimedia experiences which facilitate religious discussions. In an article for the *Los Angeles Business Journal,* RiShawn Biddle noted, "Whether or not 'Framing Reality' actually gets McManus' message across, the viewings do allow him to indulge his love of cinema." Additionally, McManus has released several texts detailing topics in spirituality and personal development.

The Barbarian Way: Unleash the Untamed Faith Within, published in 2005, explains how one can serve God without the rigor of a traditional model of prayer, churchgoing, and Christian behavior. In other words, McManus suggests that when one is devoted to Jesus they forsake the confines of civilization and live like a barbarian. McManus, however, does not imply a negative connotation to the "barbarian way," rather he elevates this form of spiritual living to the ideal. "McManus opens up to readers by sharing many of his own life experiences and allows readers to come along with him on his journey to discovering what it really means to live as a barbarian for Christ," according to Sara Christine in a review for the *Blogcritics* Web site.

McManus seeks to remove the perceptual barriers to becoming a practicing Christian so that those outside of the Church can find a way to participate that is unobstructed by tradition, membership, or even language. The text underscores the importance of open and unpretentious communication within a congregation so that it remains welcoming and hospitable to outsiders. McManus also contextualizes biblical stories so that a more contemporary audience can easily identify with the characters and messages. Christine pointed out that "the book shares how to let go of this life" so that one can live devoted to Christ. In an essay for the *FaithfulReader* Web site, Lisa Ann Cockrel explained, "McManus advocates a more romantic, adventurous, and arguably reckless paradigm for Christian living. He defines the "barbarian way" as being about love, intimacy, passion and sacrifice." Furthermore, Cockrel noted that by framing the barbarism of living devoted to Christ as courageous, "McManus effectively argues that the Christian life is about a lot of things, but it's never about being safe—emotionally or physically. It's about becoming strong via bold vulnerability, the call of Christ to engage with a dangerous world. It's not an insurance plan." Alternatively, McManus reveals the risk and reward of barbarian living.

Soul Cravings: An Exploration of the Human Spirit, McManus's 2006 release, seeks to expose those outside of the Church to the philosophy of Christianity while also presenting the image of hope. As a *Joanna Muses* Web site contributor observed, "McManus attempts to communicate how our desire for intimacy, meaning and destiny point to the existence of God and our need for him." In four primary sections, the text offers selections which discuss themes of searching for spirituality, divining meaning, and destiny. An *Internet Bookwatch* contributor found that McManus maintains that the soul's spiritual longings "suggest a human connection with God." Moreover, *Christianity Today* contributor Elisa Weeks commented on the text's "stylish red, white, and black cover" and suggested that the cover is an indication of *Soul Cravings*'s aesthetic contents.

McManus told *CA:* "I've loved writing for as long as I can remember. I love not only the satisfaction of a finished product, but the wonder of the process. In the end though I became a writer as the result of so may people asking for help and it was the only way I could answer with a yes."

In describing his influences, McManus said, "Life influences my work. All the people who matter to me and everyone who touches my life—they all influence my work."

"I have said many times I don't write books, they write me. The book consumes me over time then it demands its release. I write fast and frenzied. I finished one of my books in ten hours from beginning to end. Others have taken up to sixty hours. I speak and Holly (my assistant) types up to 150 words a minute." McManus then said that the most surprising thing he has learned as a writer is "that you know more than you know and that you know less than you know."

When asked what his favorite book he's written is, McManus commented: "The one I haven't written yet. It is definitely my best work. It is the one that still holds me captive and inspires me to imagine and dream."

BIOGRAPHICAL AND CRITICAL SOURCES:

PERIODICALS

Christianity Today, October 1, 2005, "The Christian Visigoth," p. 94; June 1, 2007, Elisa Weeks, review of *Soul Cravings: An Exploration of the Human Spirit,* p. 72.

Internet Bookwatch, June 1, 2007, review of *Soul Cravings.*

Leadership, June 22, 2005, "Q: Does Church Membership Really Matter? 4 Pastors Debate and Define the Value of Formal Commitment," p. 105.

Los Angeles Business Journal, September 1, 2003, "God Is His Co-Star," p. 4.

Publishers Weekly, May 12, 2008, review of *Wide Awake: For Those Who Would Live Their Dreams,* p. 51.

ONLINE

Blogcritics, http://blogcritics.org/ (October 20, 2008), Sara Christine, review of *The Barbarian Way.*

Erwin McManus Home Page, http://erwinmcmanus.com (July 23, 2009).

FaithfulReader, http://www.faithfulreader.com/ (July 23, 2009), Lisa Ann Cockrel, review of *The Barbarian Way: Unleash the Untamed Faith Within.*

Joanna Muses, http://www.joannamuses.com/ (May 17, 2009), review of *Soul Cravings.*

Thomas Nelson Web site, http://www.thomasnelson.com/ (July 23, 2009), author profile.

* * *

MENZEL, Peter 1948-

PERSONAL: Born 1948, in Farmington, CT; married Faith D'Aluisio (a writer); children: Josh, Jack, Adam, Evan. *Education:* Boston University, B.S.

ADDRESSES: *Office*—Material World Books, 199 Kreuzer Ln., Napa, CA 94559. *E-mail*—peter@menzelphoto.com.

CAREER: Photojournalist. *Exhibitions:* Work exhibited at United Nations, New York, NY; Museum of Science and Industry, Chicago, IL; National Museum of Natural History, Washington, DC; and other venues in the United States and Europe.

AWARDS, HONORS: Harry Chapin Media Award, 1994, for *Material World* by Charles C. Mann; Books for the Teen Age selection, New York Public Library, 1996, for *Women in the Material World;* James Beard Foundation Award, 1999, for *Man Eating Bugs;* Best Science Portfolio Award, World Press Photo, and Independent Publisher Book Award in Science Category, both 2000, both for *Robo Sapiens;* Book of the Year selection, Harry Chapin World Hunger Media Foundation, 2005, and James Beard Foundation Award, 2006, both for *Hungry Planet;* has also received World Press Awards for photography.

WRITINGS:

AND PHOTOGRAPHER

(With wife, Faith D'Aluisio) *Women in the Material World,* Sierra Club Books (San Francisco, CA), 1996.

(With Faith D'Aluisio) *Man Eating Bugs: The Art and Science of Eating Insects,* Ten Speed Press (Berkeley, CA), 1998.

(With Faith D'Aluisio) *Robo Sapiens: Evolution of a New Species,* MIT Press (Cambridge, MA), 2000.

(With Faith D'Aluisio) *Hungry Planet: What the World Eats,* Ten Speed Press (Berkeley, CA), 2005, children's edition, Tricycle Press (Berkeley, CA), 2008.

(With Faith D'Aluisio) *What the World Eats: Around the World in Eighty Diets,* Random House (New York, NY), 2010.

PHOTOGRAPHER

David Weber, *Oakland, Hub of the West,* Continental Heritage Press (Tulsa, OK), 1981.

Charles C. Mann, *Material World: A Global Family Portrait,* introduction by Paul Kennedy, Sierra Club Books (San Francisco, CA), 1994.

Julieta Ramos-Elorduy, *Creepy Crawly Cuisine: The Gourmet Guide to Edible Insects,* translated by Nancy Esteban, Park Street Press (Rochester, VT), 1998.

Contributor to periodicals, including *GEO, Stern, Figaro, Der Spiegel, Paris Match, Focus, Muy Interesante, El País, Life, National Geographic, Smithsonian, New York Times Magazine, Newsweek,* and *Time.*

ADAPTATIONS: *Women in the Material World* was adapted as an audiobook, Sierra Club Audio Library, 1998.

SIDELIGHTS: Photojournalist Peter Menzel and his wife, Faith D'Aluisio, have collaborated on nonfiction books that include *Hungry Planet: What the World Eats,* winner of the James Beard Foundation Award. The duo has traveled the globe in search of interesting stories; their works have introduced readers to a restaurant that serves live scorpions, the development of anthropomorphic robots, and the daily activities of a Mongolian family. Menzel told *Photo.net* interviewer Philip Greenspun that "having a partner who is your wife traveling with you can be great. We each have our roles in the work and then can help each other out on the emotional front when things get stressful, which they are. Most of the time when you try to get a lot done in an efficient and timely manner it's stressful. I would recommend trying it for other husband-wife teams. If you don't get divorced or kill each other after the first few months, you might learn to like it."

Menzel and D'Aluisio's first book, *Women in the Material World,* offers portraits of twenty women, their homes ranging from China, Mali, and Jordan to Italy and Haiti. The work, which is illustrated with full-color photographs taken by a host of female photojournalists, includes interviews with these women, who discuss their day-to-day lives and reflect on social, cultural, and political issues in their native lands. A contributor in *Publishers Weekly* called the work a "beautiful and moving photo-essay," and Leon Wagner, writing in *Booklist,* described *Women in the Material World* as a "great book for a wide range of readers and thinkers."

In *Man Eating Bugs: The Art and Science of Eating Insects,* Menzel and D'Aluisio present a global study of entomophagy: the practice of devouring bugs. While entomophagy is common in many parts of the world, including Asia and Africa, many Westerners frown upon it, Menzel notes. As he told Jonathan Dyson in the London *Independent,* "I remember . . . thinking it was just inconceivable that people could eat something so lowly and disgusting. But then I came across this piece in the *Wall Street Journal* about the *Food Insect Newsletter,* and it had some recipes and talked about the strange people who subscribed to the newsletter, and I just became fascinated with it. I made a point of looking for insect-eating whenever I went abroad on assignment." A reviewer in *Whole Earth* called *Man Eating Bugs* "by far the most informative, fun, and mind/stomach-bending book ever on insect eating." The critic added that D'Aluisio and Menzel's narrative "chronicles their journeys with lovely anecdotes of each day's new events."

Menzel and D'Aluisio profile the creation of synthetic beings in *Robo Sapiens: Evolution of a New Species.* The volume includes interviews with scientists who research and design robots, and it examines the different types of machines they construct, such as those with industrial and military applications and others that mimic human skills. Reviewing *Robo Sapiens* in *Publishers Weekly,* a critic deemed the work "an informative—and handsome—view of some current work in robotics, from out-there A[rtificial] I[ntelligence] research to practical (and profitable) surgical technology."

In *Hungry Planet* the husband-and-wife team describes the food consumption of families from more than twenty nations. Each entry opens with a photograph of family members standing with a week's worth of food purchases, along with a list of the items and their prices in both local and U.S. currency. The work also includes narratives about the family members' lifestyles and the food traditions of their native lands. "We found it shocking that a lot of people don't know what they're eating," Menzel remarked to *USA Today* interviewer Shawn Sell, "and by that I mean not just what's in food, in terms of preservatives and additives, but many people don't know where their food comes from or how it's processed."

Hungry Planet, which was released in two versions—one for adults and another for younger readers—earned strong reviews. Gillian Engberg, writing in *Booklist,* called the book "a fascinating, sobering, and instructive look at daily life around the world," while a *Publishers Weekly* critic described it as a "beautiful, quietly provocative volume." In the words of *Geographical* critic Jo Sargent, by examining "how our spending patterns reflect cultural traditions and how globalisation is affecting our diet, *Hungry Planet* offers plenty of food for thought."

BIOGRAPHICAL AND CRITICAL SOURCES:

PERIODICALS

Booklist, September 15, 1996, Leon Wagner, review of *Women in the Material World,* p. 186; March 15, 2000, review of *Man Eating Bugs: The Art and Science of Eating Insects,* p. 1360; July 1, 2008, Gillian Engberg, review of *Hungry Planet: What the World Eats,* p. 65.

Environment, October, 2006, Robert W. Kates, review of *Hungry Planet,* p. 40.

Geographical, February, 2006, Jo Sargent, review of *Hungry Planet,* p. 90.

Independent (London, England), February 13, 1999, Jonathan Dyson, "Eating Insects," p. 28.

New York Times Book Review, November 9, 2008, Regina Marler, review of *Hungry Planet,* p. 42.

PhotoMedia, August 1, 2007, Eric Rudolph, "Peter Menzel: Food for Thought," pp. 34-40.

Publishers Weekly, Jly 29, 1996, review of *Women in the Material World,* p. 77; July 3, 2000, review of *Robo Sapiens: Evolution of a New Species,* p. 55; August 22, 2005, review of *Hungry Planet,* p. 47; September 1, 2008, review of *Hungry Planet,* p. 55.

School Library Journal, April, 2006, Eva Elisabeth VonAncken, review of *Hungry Planet,* p. 68; July, 2008, Joyce Adams Burner, review of *Hungry Planet,* p. 111.

Technology Review, September, 2000, Wade Roush, review of *Robo Sapiens,* p. 127.

UN Chronicle, June, 1995, Elsa B. Endrst, review of *Material World: A Global Family Portrait,* p. 64.

USA Today, December 15, 2005, Shawn Sell, interview with D'Aluisio and Menzel.

U.S. News & World Report, December 26, 2005, Diane Cole, review of *Hungry Planet,* p. 87.

Whole Earth, spring, 1999, review of *Man Eating Bugs,* p. 73.

ONLINE

Light Connection Web site, http://www.lightconnection.us/ (November, 2008), Jennifer Joe, interview with D'Aluisio and Menzel.

Peter Menzel and Faith D'Aluisio Home Page, http://www.menzelphoto.com (September 1, 2009).

Photo.net, http://photo.net/ (April, 2007), Philip Greenspun, interview with D'Aluisio and Menzel.

* * *

MEYER, Philipp 1974-

PERSONAL: Born May 1, 1974; son of an artist and an electrician turned college science instructor. *Education:* Attended colleges in Baltimore, MD; Cornell University, B.A.; Michener Center for Writers, Austin, TX, M.F.A.

ADDRESSES: Home—TX; NY. *Agent*—Esther Newberg, International Creative Management, 825 8th Ave., New York, NY 10019. *E-mail*—reader@philippmeyer.net.

CAREER: Writer. Worked as bicycle mechanic, investment banker with Swiss investment bank UBS, construction worker, and emergency medical technician.

AWARDS, HONORS: Fellowship at the Michener Center for Writers, 2005-08; also fellowships or residencies from Yaddo, Ucross, Blue Mountain Center, and the Anderson Center for the Arts.

WRITINGS:

American Rust, Spiegel & Grau (New York, NY), 2009.

Contributor to periodicals and Web sites, including *McSweeney's, Iowa Review, New Stories from the South,* and *Salon.com.*

SIDELIGHTS: After graduating from Cornell University, Philipp Meyer worked with a Swiss investment bank to pay back his student loans. Once he paid off his debt, he quit the bank to pursue his dream of becoming a writer. In the process, he earned his M.F.A. from the Michener Center for Writers. Meyer's first novel, *American Rust,* about failed dreams in a Pennsylvania town resulting from the collapse of the steel industry, has received widespread, favorable reviews.

"*American Rust* is a bold, absorbing novel with a keen interest in how communities falter," wrote Lewis Robinson for the *New York Times Book Review,* adding: "Meyer knows that reductive explanations aren't sufficient, and he moves deftly from the panoramic to the microscopic—from sweeping views of a dying valley to the quiet ruminations of a mind behind bars." A *Publishers Weekly* contributor wrote that the author "has a thrilling eye for failed dreams and writes uncommonly tense scenes of violence."

Buell, Pennsylvania, is a steel town devastated by the faltering of the American steel industry. The extremely bright Isaac English is looking to get out of Buell and find a better life. However, his mother has committed suicide and his sister left for Yale University and now has a new life. As a result, Isaac has been caring for his elderly father, a distant and bitter man. Isaac's best friend is Billy Poe, a high school football star who turned down a scholarship to college and has become a heavy drinker. Billy decides to join Isaac as he begins hitchhiking to California along with 4,000 dollars he has taken from his father. The two twenty-year-olds do not get far, however, when they become accidentally involved in a murder. Isaac and Billy come across vagrants staying at a shutdown steel mill not far out of town, and a confrontation evolves between the vagrants and the volatile Billy. Isaac steps in to protect Billy and ends up killing one of the men.

"Through this act the author lays bare the minds of Isaac, Billy and the members of their respective families," wrote Roger Perkins in a review for the *Telegraph Online.*

The novel also features Poe's mother, who has a troubled relationship both with Poe's alcoholic father and with Bud Harris, chief of police. Harris has often treated Poe like his own son by getting him out of trouble on numerous occasions. Now he finds himself torn between his allegiance to Billy's mother and his role as a policeman whose job it is to see justice done. "Meyer's debut novel is peopled with characters both complex and deeply in tune with who they are, their flaws and capabilities, and their place in their world, even as they struggle against their circumstances and question the inevitability of their situations," noted a contributor to the *Linus's Blanket* Web site. *Mostly Fiction* Web site contributor Poornima Apte pointed out: "While allowing us glimpses into these characters' lives (or perhaps even through these glimpses), Meyer also chronicles the crippling effect of massive job losses in a town like Buell."

As the novel continues, Billy has remained in Buell and becomes the prime suspect in the murder. He is arrested and sent off to a high-security prison to await trial. Isaac, meanwhile, has gone on the run and ends up in Michigan, another place where people are suffering from the end of American industry. Readers witness Isaac's fall into the dark side of American life until he finally decides to return home. The author also reveals Billy's experiences in the American prison system, and the pains and fears of both young men's families. The author tells the tale in alternating chapters narrated by six different characters. "By cutting from one character's point of view to another, Mr. Meyer is not only able to create a richly layered narrative with multiple perspectives, but he's also able to climb inside his people's heads and channel their thoughts and feelings," noted *New York Times* contributor Michiko Kakutani.

In an interview for the *Popcorn Youth* Web site, the author commented on his presentation of the story from the perspective of several characters. Meyer noted: "I spent a lot of time studying the way people's thoughts and speech patterns interact, and a lot of time studying the mechanics of my own thoughts—how quickly the mind moves from one topic to another, circles around and examines things from different angles. As for the writing style I think it's just me, writing in the most honest and accurate way I can."

Several reviewers lauded Miller's debut novel. "Mr Meyer's voice is assured, and the story crackles with narrative tension," remarked a contributor to the *Economist,* adding: "He develops his characters with impressive psychological and sociological insight." Calling the novel "part earnest Dreiserian tragedy, part Cormac McCarthy," a *Kirkus Reviews* contributor went on in the same review to note: "Meyer does a terrific job capturing the tone and ethos of his setting, half postindustrial wasteland and half prelapsarian Eden."

BIOGRAPHICAL AND CRITICAL SOURCES:

PERIODICALS

Economist, April 25, 2009, "Nailing It; New Fiction," review of *American Rust,* p. 84.

Kirkus Reviews, November 1, 2008, review of *American Rust.*

Library Journal, October 15, 2008, Leigh Anne Vrabel, review of *American Rust,* p. 58.

Marie Claire, February, 2009, Lauren Iannotti, review of *American Rust,* p. 55.

National Post, March 14, 2009, review of *American Rust,* p. 13.

New Yorker, March 30, 2009, review of *American Rust,* p. 71.

New York Times, February 27, 2009, Michiko Kakutani, "Steel Town Roots, Huck Finn Dreams," review of *American Rust,* p. 23.

New York Times Book Review, March 22, 2009, Lewis Robinson, "In the Noir Belt," review of *American Rust.*

Observer (London, England), May 24, 2009, Mary Fitzgerald, "Voices form America's Underbelly," review of *American Rust.*

Publishers Weekly, April 28, 2008, "Spiegel Takes Debut," p. 6; September 15, 2008, review of *American Rust,* p. 40.

USA Today, March 5, 2009, Bob Minzesheimer, "Corrosive Realities Underpin Remarkable *American Rust,*" review of *American Rust,* p. 05.

ONLINE

Linus's Blanket, http://www.linussblanket.com/ (March 9, 2009), review of *American Rust.*

Mostly Fiction, http://www.mostlyfiction.com/ (March 24, 2009), Poornima Apte, review of *American Rust.*

Philipp Meyer Home Page, http://www.philippmeyer.net (July 22, 2009).

Popcorn Youth, http://www.ithacatimesartsblog.com/ (July 22, 2009), "An interview with *American Rust* Author Philipp Meyer."

Random House Web site, http://www.randomhouse.com/ (July 22, 2009), brief profile of author.

Red Room, http://www.redroom.com/ (July 22, 2009), brief profile of author.

Rumpus, http://therumpus.net/ (July 10, 2009), Stacy Muszynski, "Don't Be a Coward: The Rumpus Interview with Philipp Meyer."

Telegraph Online, http://www.telegraph.co.uk/ (May 24, 2009), Roger Perkins, review of *American Rust.**

* * *

MILLER, Keith 1966-

PERSONAL: Born May 25, 1966.

ADDRESSES: *Home*—London, England.

CAREER: Journalist, writer, and lecturer.

WRITINGS:

St. Peter's ("Wonders of the World" series), Harvard University Press (Cambridge, MA), 2007.

SIDELIGHTS: In his first book, *St. Peter's,* author Keith Miller provides a cultural history of St. Peter's Basilica in Rome, the largest and perhaps the most important Christian church in the world. "It is huge: not only in space but in time and structure; and in the nonmaterial sphere of the complex interplay of meanings, symbols and significances," wrote Magda Healey in a review for the *Bookbag* Web site. "Miller's book, intentionally combining cultural and political history, art criticism and travel writing, manages to reflect that hugeness without weighting the reader down with too much austere detail."

Miller's architectural history closely examines one of the most ambitious architectural undertakings in history and analyzes the project's results. "It will examine the ways in which St. Peter's has been used to express the special relationship between imperial and papal authority, and how it has actually worked as a place of worship, pilgrimage, assembly and tourism at various points in its history," the author writes in the book's prologue, adding that he will also examine "the complex spatial and temporal dialogues entered into by the building, its many conversations with and appeals to other structures of every date and type across the uniquely elegant Roman cityscape." The author goes on to write in the prologue that the book reveals the many "layers" of the building, going back to the "telling remains of the old fourth-century basilica." Miller adds that he also discusses "the enigma of the tombs beneath it."

In his history of the building of St. Peter's, Miller writes of the various people and factors that played a role in St. Peter's construction, from the decree by Constantine to begin the construction project to rebuilding efforts by some of Italy's most distinguished architects. He also examines how the architecture of St. Peter's has influenced subsequent building projects, including the building of various other Catholic churches and the architectural plans of Hitler's Third Reich for the Great Hall of Germania. The author reveals much about the artwork within St. Peter's, including mosaics, tombs, and Michelagelo's *Pieta.* He examines the "street of tombs" deep within the basilica and discusses the efforts to identify bones recovered from beneath the church's altar as those of St. Peter, coming to the conclusion that this ultimately must be accepted on faith since documented history has been lost. Miller includes tips for further reading and a chapter that is essentially a guidebook for visiting St. Peter's.

"Keith Miller's *St. Peter's* joins other outstanding titles in Profile's "Wonders of the World" series . . . with its elegant design, its scholarly enthusiasm, and its respect for the general reader," wrote Mark Bostridge in a review for the *Telegraph Online.* "Like the best guides, it makes one long to visit the place in question, armed with book in hand." Donna Seaman, writing for *Booklist,* remarked that the author "weaves a sharply patterned brocade of facts and informed opinion."

BIOGRAPHICAL AND CRITICAL SOURCES:

BOOKS

Miller, Keith, *St. Peter's,* Harvard University Press (Cambridge, MA), 2007.

PERIODICALS

Booklist, October 1, 2007, Donna Seaman, review of *St. Peter's,* p. 28.
Contemporary Review, winter, 2007, review of *St. Peter's,* p. 533.
Times Literary Supplement, November 23, 2007, Lucy Beckett, "The Rock and the Baroque," review of *St. Peter's,* p. 25.

ONLINE

Bookbag, http://www.thebookbag.co.uk/ (July 24, 2009), Magda Healey, review of *St. Peter's.*
Independent Online, http://www.independent.co.uk/ (April 27, 2007), Mark Bostridge,"Michelangelo's Monster," review of *St. Peter's.**

* * *

MILLER, Laura 1960-

PERSONAL: Born February 12, 1960.

ADDRESSES: Home—NY. *E-mail*—magiciansbook@yahoo.com.

CAREER: Journalist, critic, writer. Cofounded *Salon.com* and staff writer, 1995—.

WRITINGS:

(Editor, with Adam Begley) *The Salon.com Reader's Guide to Contemporary Authors,* Penguin Books (New York, NY), 2000.
The Magician's Book: A Skeptic's Adventures in Narnia, Little, Brown (New York, NY), 2008.

Contributor to periodicals, including the *New York Times Book Review, New Yorker, Los Angeles Times,* and *Wall Street Journal.* Wrote "Last Word" column for *New York Times Book Review.*

SIDELIGHTS: Cofounder of *Salon.com,* Laura Miller was a child when she became fascinated with C.S. Lewis's "The Chronicles of Narnia" fantasy series for children after being introduced to the books by a teacher. Miller would often reread the series, which begins with *The Lion, the Witch and the Wardrobe.* She continued to be intrigued by the books until, as a teenager, she learned of its Christian themes. Miller no longer wanted to find her own Narnia as she became skeptical and then estranged from the story. Nevertheless, years later Miller found herself still thinking of the series and how "the first book we fall in love with shapes us every bit as much as the first person we fall in love with," as Miller writes in *The Magician's Book: A Skeptic's Adventures in Narnia.*

The Magician's Book grew out of Miller's decision to revisit Lewis's series and see what she thought and felt about the book as an adult. "I guess you would have to put *The Magician's Book* into the category of creative nonfiction," wrote Kevin Holtsberry in a review for the *Collected Miscellany* Web site. "Good thing too, because otherwise it would be hard to categorize. Part memoir, literary criticism, biography, and current events reporting it frequently slides between childhood memories, academic criticism, Freudian analysis, personal opinion, and interviews with other authors."

Miller focuses much of her attention on Lewis and discovers that the man was nothing like her ideal conception of him. As she researches Lewis's life, an effort that took her to his Irish hometown to visit the landscape that influenced Narnia, the author discovers a man whose faith, politics, and education played a large role in his biases and his prejudices. In her analysis of Lewis's religious beliefs and his insertion of these beliefs into his "Narnia" series, the author reflects on her rejection of much of Lewis's philosophy. As noted by *Collected Miscellany* contributor Holtsberry, the author "evidences little sympathy for Lewis's faith or political worldview." Although Holtsberry disagreed with Miller's inability to see others' points of view, he praised the book's chapters concerning the author's reflections on her love of the series as a child and her "insights into what Lewis was attempting to accomplish in his literary efforts."

Miller explores Lewis's friendship with J.R.R. Tolkien, author of the "The Lord of the Rings" fantasy series. The author points out that Tolkien felt that the religious subtext of Lewis's fantasy series undermined one of the basic goals of fantasy writers, which is to build a unified world. Miller examines many critical aspects of the series, noting that people such as John Goldthwaite held a contrary viewpoint to Tolkien. Goldthwaite found the "Narnia" series lacking, and, according to Miller, Goldthwaite believed that the fantasy elements of the book took away from its "religious integrity." "Although faith is an issue in *The Magician's Book,* it's readerly faith rather than religious faith that really interests me," the author noted in an interview with Rose Fox for *Publishers Weekly.*

The author still has much praise for the series as she examines the many creative accomplishments by Lewis, noting the pure exuberance of the storytelling and Lewis's obvious pleasure in writing the series. Miller explores how the series reflects both Lewis's own childhood reading habits and his later adult literary pursuits, including influences from the novels of Jane Austen and references to the works of classic writers such as Dante, Edmund Spenser, and Sir Thomas Malory.

Writing for *Horn Book,* Deirdre F. Baker commented that "through the sheer range of her [Miller's] allusions and commentary, she's likely to make most Narnia buffs say, 'Aha! Interesting . . . ' more than once." A *Kirkus Reviews* contributor called *The Magician's Book* "a rewarding study by a first-rate arts writer."

BIOGRAPHICAL AND CRITICAL SOURCES:

BOOKS

Miller, Laura, *The Magician's Book: A Skeptic's Adventures in Narnia,* Little, Brown (New York, NY), 2008.

PERIODICALS

Booklist, August, 2000, review of *The Salon.com Reader's Guide to Contemporary Authors,* p. 2100; November 1, 2008, Michael Cart, review of *The Magician's Book,* p. 12.

Book World, December 14, 2008, Elizabeth Ward, "Saving C.S. Lewis," review of *The Magician's Book,* p. 7.

Horn Book, May-June, 2009, Deirdre F. Baker, review of *The Magician's Book.*

Kirkus Reviews, October 1, 2008, review of *The Magician's Book.*

Library Journal, July, 2000, Shana C. Fair, review of *The Salon.com Reader's Guide to Contemporary Authors,* p. 80.

Publishers Weekly, July 3, 2000, review of *The Salon.com Reader's Guide to Contemporary Authors,* p. 65; September 15, 2008, review of *The Magician's Book,* p. 53; September 29, 2008, Rose Fox, "PW Talks with Laura Miller: To Narnia and Back," p. 68.

Reference & Research Book News, May, 2009, review of *The Magician's Book.*

Vanity Fair, December, 2008, Elissa Schappell, "The Chronicles of Lewis," review of *The Magician's Book,* p. 158.

Virginia Quarterly Review, winter, 2009, Britt Petersen, review of *The Magician's Book,* p. 242.

ONLINE

Collected Miscellany, http://collectedmiscellany.com/ (June 5, 2009), Kevin Holtsberry, review of *The Magician's Book.*

Laura Miller Home Page, http://lauramiller.typepad.com (July 24, 2009).*

* * *

MILLS, Linda G. 1951-
(Linda Gayle Mills)

PERSONAL: Born October 21, 1951. *Education:* Holds Ph.D., L.C.S.W., J.D.

ADDRESSES: Office—New York University, Silver School of Social Work, Office of Admissions, Ehrenkranz Center, 1 Washington Sq. N., New York, NY 10003-6654. *E-mail*—linda.mills@nyu.edu.

CAREER: Lawyer, sociologist, social worker, educator, and writer. New York University, Silver School of Social Work, New York, NY, professor of social work, public policy, and law, and senior vice provost for undergraduate education and university life; previously on the faculty at the University of California, Los Angeles. Founder of the Hawkins Center of Law and Services for People with Disabilities, 1984, and the Center on Violence and Recovery.

AWARDS, HONORS: Recipient of research grants, including grants from the Department of Homeland Security and the U.S. Department of Health and Human Services.

WRITINGS:

The Heart of Intimate Abuse: New Interventions in Child Welfare, Criminal Justice, and Health Settings, Springer Publishing (New York, NY), 1998.

A Penchant for Prejudice: Unraveling Bias in Judicial Decision Making, University of Michigan Press (Ann Arbor, MI), 1999.

Insult to Injury: Rethinking Our Responses to Intimate Abuse, Princeton University Press (Princeton, NJ), 2003.

Violent Partners: A Breakthrough Plan for Ending the Cycle of Abuse, Basic Books (New York, NY), 2008.

Contributor to professional journals, including *Harvard Law Review, Cornell Law Review, Social Work, Children and Youth Services Review,* and *Criminal Justice and Behavior.* Contributor of editorials to *USA Today,* the *Los Angeles Times,* and *Newsday.*

SIDELIGHTS: Linda G. Mills combines her expertise in law and social work to examine issues such as intimate abuse, law and emotion, and alternative responses to traumatic events. She is one of the leading advocates in the United States for legal training and interventions that takes into consideration race, gender, and emotional states in an effort to address the entire person.

In her 1999 book *A Penchant for Prejudice: Unraveling Bias in Judicial Decision Making,* Mills examines the meaning of impartiality in the legal justice system and discusses modern myths about judging. In the process, the author challenges the idea that judicial impartiality is readily maintained in the U.S. courts of law. In fact, according to Mills, bias is an inherent part of the judicial process and argues that how the legal system now defines impartial decision making is itself a type of bias. Instead, writes Mills, the dualistic idea of impartiality as maintained in the legal system should be replaced by a more sensitive definition of bias based on history and context. This approach, writes the author, should take into consideration important aspects of various cultures and communities as their members face judgment in the legal system.

Writing in the introduction, Mills notes that *A Penchant for Prejudice* "provides the material and impetus for exploring a new definition of judicial impartiality and for formulation of an innovative method for adjudicating claims. This method realistically incorporates the negative and positive features of stereotyping that inevitably affects the process of decision making when resolving the claims of disaffected applicants who are easily stereotyped. The cornerstone of such an approach, I argue, is a self-reflective method in which judges would have the tools not only to resolve the facts in any given dispute and to apply the law but also to be conscious of their propensity to stereotype negatively and positively."

The author's next book, *Insult to Injury: Rethinking Our Responses to Intimate Abuse,* presents Mills's case for a restorative justice approach to domestic violence. The author writes that the modern criminal justice system may negatively impact domestic violence cases in several ways. For example, the author believes that mandatory imprisonment does not help bring about reform efforts in domestic violence. Mills writes in the book's prologue that many studies have shown that "arrest, prosecution, and incarceration do not necessarily reduce the problem of domestic violence and may even be making the problem worse." The author goes on to note that only "people who have something to lose" are deterred by the prospect of arrest and facing the legal justice system. The author writes: "On the other hand, the men most likely to be arrested because of the criminal justice system's inherent class and race bias can become more violent in response to arrest." The author also comments in the prologue: "At worst, the criminal justice system increases violence against women. At best, it has little or no effect."

Mills calls her alternative approach to dealing with domestic violence "Intimate Abuse Circles." This approach involves abusers, abusees, and various family and friends meeting to discuss issues surrounding abuse. The author writes that this approach seeks to transform those involved instead of focusing on mandatory punishments. "Going where few have gone before, and many dare not go in today's current political environment, Linda Mills bravely challenges the current ideology surrounding domestic violence and its etiology, dynamics, and the manner in which the criminal justice system currently addresses this social problem," wrote a contributor to *Criminal Justice Policy Review.*

In her 2008 book *Violent Partners: A Breakthrough Plan for Ending the Cycle of Abuse,* the author continues her examination of intimate abuse and presents her case that the American culture does not understand the basic causes and effects of abuse. Mills argues that some widespread changes have to be made in how society approaches intimate abuse. In the process, she outlines several programs that show promise for providing new and effective ways to address intimate abuse. Among these programs are Peacemaking Circles and Healing Circles, both of which focuses on couple and group encounters designed to deemphasize people's sense of guilt and shame. Peacemaking Circles is a program designed especially for the criminal justice system and has been adopted by a court in Nogales, Arizona. The author writes about several success stories associated with this program. Healing Circles is a community-based program focusing on intervention prior to arrest for intimate violence. The idea of Healing Circles is to have a circle keeper who keeps the discussion moving among participants, who may include the perpetrator, the victim, family members, and others important to the couple. The circle can also expand as the people involved progress and want to widen their circle of discussion.

The author also points out in her book that intimate abuse is not always solely the fault of men and that both partners often play a role in the dynamics of a situation. "The ideas are highly controversial, yet this book is authoritative, reasonable, and easy to grasp," wrote Antoinette Brinkman for *Library Journal.* The book, which features numerous case studies, also includes a discussion of the overall patterns of violence dynamics and tips for men who have been abused by women.

"It is an excellent read and features . . . stories that lead the reader on a journey from ignoring DV [dometic violence] issues to where we are today—to an alternative way of attempting to end the cycle of abuse," wrote Matthew A. Sciarrino, Jr., in a review for the *New York Law Journal.* Calling *Violent Partners* "scrupulously researched," a *Publishers Weekly* contributor also wrote in the same review that the author's exploration of "new treatments" may be "the book's most valuable part."

BIOGRAPHICAL AND CRITICAL SOURCES:

BOOKS

Mills, Linda G., *A Penchant for Prejudice: Unraveling Bias in Judicial Decision Making,* University of Michigan Press (Ann Arbor, MI), 1999.

Mills, Linda G., *Insult to Injury: Rethinking Our Responses to Intimate Abuse,* Princeton University Press (Princeton, NJ), 2003.

PERIODICALS

Affilia Journal of Women and Social Work, winter, 1999, Diana M. Filliano, review of *The Heart of Intimate Abuse: New Interventions in Child Welfare, Criminal Justice, and Health Settings,* p. 503.

California Bookwatch, August, 2008, review of *Violent Partners: A Breakthrough Plan for Ending the Cycle of Abuse.*

Children and Youth Services Review, August, 1999, Mieko Yoshihama, review of *The Heart of Intimate Abuse,* p. 696.

Choice, April, 2004, R.T. Sigler, review of *Insult to Injury,* p. 1515.

Criminal Justice Policy Review, March 1, 2005, review of *Insult to Injury,* pp. 115-117.

Harvard Law Review, June, 2000, review of *A Penchant for Prejudice,* p. 2146.

JAMA: The Journal of the American Medical Association, October 22, 2008, Carl C. Bell, review of *Violent Partners,* p. 1949.

Justice System Journal, spring, 2000, Robert M. Howard, review of *A Penchant for Prejudice,* p. 349.

Law and Social Inquiry, spring, 2004, review of *Insult to Injury,* p. 500.

Library Journal, June 1, 2008, Antoinette Brinkman, review of *Violent Partners,* p. 112.

National Review, March 8, 2004, C. Douglas Kern, "Sparing the Abusers," review of *Insult to Injury,* p. 53.

New York Law Journal, March 3, 2006, Thomas Adcock, "Professor Targets Roots of Violence"; October 3, 2008, Matthew A. Sciarrino, Jr., "Lawyer's Bookshelf"; October 8, 2008, Matthew A. Sciarrino, Jr., "Lawyer's Bookshelf," review of *Violent Partners.*

Ottawa Law Review, spring, 2004, Diana Majury, review of *Insult to Injury,* p. 313.

Publishers Weekly, April 28, 2008, review of *Violent Partners,* p. 127.

Social Service Review, December 1, 2000, review of *A Penchant for Prejudice,* p. 685.

ONLINE

New York University Silver School of Social Work Web site, http://www.nyu.edu/socialwork/ (July 25, 2009), faculty profile of author.

Violent Partners Web site, http://www.violentpartners.com (July 25, 2009).*

* * *

MILLS, Linda Gayle
See MILLS, Linda G.

* * *

MONTANDON, Mac 1971-

PERSONAL: Born March 10, 1971; married; children: two daughters.

ADDRESSES: Home—Brooklyn, NY. *E-mail*—macmontandon@gmail.com.

CAREER: Journalist and writer.

WRITINGS:

(Editor) *Innocent When You Dream: The Tom Waits Reader,* foreword by Frank Black, Thunder's Mouth Press (New York, NY), 2005.

Jetpack Dreams: One Man's Up and Down (but Mostly Down) Search for the Greatest Invention That Never Was, Da Capo Press (New York, NY), 2008.

Contributor to periodicals, including *New York Times, New York, Details, Radar* and *Spin;* founding editor of the *Silence of the City* Web site.

SIDELIGHTS: Mac Montandon is a journalist whose book *Jetpack Dreams: One Man's Up and Down (but Mostly Down) Search for the Greatest Invention That Never Was* chronicles the author's fascination with the iconic jetpack. The book examines the jetpack's history and the science that makes it work. The author also delves into why people have had a long collective fascination with flight.

Montandon writes in his book that the idea of the jetpack dates back to an *Amazing Stories* magazine feature in 1928 in which Buck Rogers was introduced to readers in a story that also featured Buck using a jetpack to fly around. Montandon writes that ever since then people have envisioned this amazing form of travel as one day coming to fruition. He notes that real efforts to develop jetpacks occurred in the 1950s and 1960s when Bell Aerosystems produced a jetpack that enabled someone to fly for approximately twenty seconds. Montandon comments that he and many others have believed that jetpacks would one day be a common form of transportation only to be disappointed that the development of jetpacks has faltered.

"Whatever happened to what must surely be the greatest promise never kept?," the author writes in *Jetpack Dreams.* He goes on to note: "Soon an idea began to take shape. I could go out into the world, wherever it made sense to go, and some places that perhaps it did not, and find out what happened to our jetpacks. I mean, is this the future or is it not? And as a serious bonus, perhaps my quest would lead me to someone who could still make the dream come true."

In addition to delving into the history of government efforts to develop a viable jetpack, the author examines Hollywood's fascination with jetpacks, from the *King of the Rocket Men* serial of 1949 to James Bond movies to the film *The Rocketeer.* However, much of the book focuses on the author's efforts to meet several individuals who continue to work on the technology. The author's other goal is to take a ride with a jetpack if he gets the chance.

In one profile, the author writes of "The Mexican Rocket Man," whom Montandon visits only to find him hampered by injuries he obtained in a serious accident with a jetpack. In another story, the author recounts the strange tale of the American Rocketbelt Corporation. With three owners, the corporation actually developed a jetpack that worked, proven by a demonstration at a National Basketball Association championship game in 1995. However, the three owners soon had a falling out. One owner ended up dead. Another owner found himself in jail following his kidnapping and torturing of a partner to learn the whereabouts of the jetpack, which is still missing.

"Montandon's entertaining adventures highlight a strange footnote of the space age," wrote Gilbert Taylor in a review of the book in *Booklist.* A *Publishers Weekly* contributor remarked: "This snappily written, often funny book should attract dreamers of both sexes and all ages."

Montandon is also the editor of *Innocent When You Dream: The Tom Waits Reader.* The book features interviews with and stories about the songwriter and musician dating back to the 1970s. The book also includes album reviews and a conversation with Elvis Costello, another noted singer and songwriter.

Noting that Waits "delivers the best quotes of any composer on the planet," *New Statesman* contributor Mark Ellen went on to write in his review of *Innocent When You Dream:* "In this splendid compilation, you see the ruffled old rascal dancing lightly around his less gifted examiners, locking horns with others, and launching himself into dazzling, spontaneous trajectories of thought and conjecture when he occasionally meets an inquisitor he considers a kindred spirit." Bill Walker, writing for *Library Journal,* remarked: "This first anthology on Waits is essential reading for his myriad fans."

BIOGRAPHICAL AND CRITICAL SOURCES:

BOOKS

Montandon, Mac, *Jetpack Dreams: One Man's Up and Down (but Mostly Down) Search for the Greatest Invention That Never Was,* Da Capo Press (New York, NY), 2008.

PERIODICALS

Booklist, May 15, 2005, June Sawyers, review of *Innocent When You Dream: The Tom Waits Reader,* p. 1626; October 15, 2008, Gilbert Taylor, review of *Jetpack Dreams,* p. 9.

Kirkus Reviews, September 15, 2008, review of *Jetpack Dreams.*

Library Journal, May 1, 2005, Bill Walker, review of *Innocent When You Dream,* p. 86.

New Statesman, January 30, 2006, Mark Ellen, "Dream Ticket," review of *Innocent When You Dream,* p. 53.

Publishers Weekly, September 15, 2008, review of *Jetpack Dreams,* p. 57.

Science Books & Films, January-February, 2009, Wilton T. Adams, review of *Jetpack Dreams.*

Wall Street Journal, October 27, 2008, Steve Kemper, "Great Idea, Limited Uplift: *Jetpack Dreams,* by Mac Montandon," p. 17.

ONLINE

Huffington Post, http://www.huffingtonpost.com/ (July 25, 2009), brief profile of author.

Jetpack Dreams Web site, http://www.jetpackdreams.com (July 25, 2009).

SF Signal, http://www.sfsignal.com/ (July 25, 2009), review of *Jetpack Dreams.**

*   *   *

MOROWITZ, Laura

PERSONAL: Married; children: two daughters. *Education:* Brooklyn College, B.A.; Institute of Fine Arts, New York University, M.A., Ph.D.

ADDRESSES: Home—NJ. *Office*—Art Department, Wagner College, 1 Campus Rd., Staten Island, New York 10301.

CAREER: Art historian, educator, and writer. Wagner College, Staten Island, NY, faculty member, 1996—, appointed professor of art history. Previously taught at other colleges, including Hunter College, New York,

NY; the Cooper Union for the Advancement of Art and Science, New York, NY; Yale University, New Haven, CT; and Pratt University, Brooklyn, NY.

WRITINGS:

(Editor, with William Vaughan) *Artistic Brotherhoods in the Nineteenth Century,* Ashgate (Burlington, VT), 2000.
(With Elizabeth Emery) *Consuming the Past: The Medieval Revival in Fin-de-Siècle France,* Ashgate (Burlington, VT), 2003.
(With Laurie Albanese) *The Miracles of Prato,* William Morrow (New York, NY), 2009.

SIDELIGHTS: Laura Morowitz is an art historian whose scholarship covers various artistic issues and periods. Her first two books focus on medievalism in the nineteenth-century Europe. In *Artistic Brotherhoods in the Nineteenth Century,* Morowitz and coeditor William Vaughan feature essays exploring the emergence of numerous artistic brotherhoods in the nineteenth century. These brotherhoods were organized into communal groups that shared both aesthetic and spiritual goals. Contributors to the book situate the brotherhoods within an historical context that includes the social, economic, political, and cultural milieu of the times. Among the groups discussed are the Nazarenes, the Russian Abramatsova, the Primitifs, the Nabis, and the Pre-Raphaelites.

"A particularly compelling component of the book is its engaging exploration of the homosocial nature of the brotherhoods," wrote Debra L. Cumberland in a review for *Nineteenth-Century French Studies,* adding later in the same review: "With its careful attention to economic, historical, cultural and social movements, this far-reaching, innovative collection of essays should appeal to a broad audience, ranging from those interested in art and art history to gender studies."

Morowitz is also the author, with Elizabeth Emery, of *Consuming the Past: The Medieval Revival in Fin-de-Siècle France.* The book examines the fin-de-si-ècle (end of the century) French fascination with the Middle Ages. Writing in the book's introduction, the authors note that an "important shift had taken place in the last three quarters of the nineteenth century as scholars and archaeologists began to share their knowledge of he period [the Middle Ages] with the wide public: with artists, scientists, students, the cultural elite and even the working classes." The authors go on to note that "at this time everything associated with the medieval world—from works of art to religious belief—caught the attention of the intelligentsia and society at large. At the end of the nineteenth century, people from all over the political and social spectrum praised the Middle Ages and avidly consumed 'medieval' products."

The authors follow the cultural history of the era beginning with the end of the Franco-Prussian war. They write that the demand for medieval products and interest in medieval thought evolved from numerous developments, including an increased literacy among the general public and the growth of the popular press. Morowitz and Emery point out that various factions of French society, including writers, artists, and church people, also began to focus on the Middle Ages as a period that perhaps reflected France at the height of its greatness. "Herein lies one meaning of 'consuming the past': constructing a narrative of the medieval for contemporary political and artistic purposes," noted *Church History* contributor Anthony J. Steinhoff. Steinhoff went on to write that the authors are also referring to the actual consumption of medieval art, from decorating homes to using medieval themes in cabarets and elsewhere as attractions to pilgrims and others.

The authors point out that critics of that time saw the public's widespread attraction to this time period as vulgar because of such outcomes as mass-produced reproductions of art. The authors, however, argue that the general public's interest ultimately helped scholars not only research the country's medieval heritage but also to protect it. In addition, the authors explore how a broad interest in medieval art also impacted the growth of the artistic avant-garde movement. The book includes numerous illustrations.

In a review for *Nineteenth-Century French Studies,* Dominic Janes noted that the "authors examine the role of domestic decoration, cafes and cabarets, but are perhaps at their most vibrant when examining popular pilgrimages and, above, all, popular attendance at medieval exhibitions in Paris which recreated whole medieval streets." Janes went on to write later in the same review that the "popular sense of romantic longing for an authenticity can make the period an object of fascination and it also infuses, almost despite of the authors' best intentions, this fascinating study of reception."

The Miracles of Prato, written by Morowitz and Laurie Albanese, is an historical novel about the illicit love affair between Fra Filippo Lippi and Lucrezia Buti. In the story, Fra Fillipo is a Renaissance painter who creates masterpieces for the Catholic Church and Cosimo de' Medici. He is also a Carmelite monk who serves as a chaplain at the Convent Santa Margherita. Despite his religious affiliations, Filippo has a reputation as a rogue. At the convent, he comes across the young and beautiful nun Lucrezia and begins to use her as his inspiration and model. As time passes, however, their relationship develops into a passionate love affair that can destroy them both.

Karen Ballinger wrote in her review for the *Story Circle Book Reviews* Web site that the authors "do a great job of setting the mood of the time period with the dialogue between characters and the descriptions of their concerns and daily life." A *Publishers Weekly* contributor called the novel "a saccharine, tidy and satisfying romance."

BIOGRAPHICAL AND CRITICAL SOURCES:

BOOKS

Morowitz, Laura, and Elizabeth Emery, *Consuming the Past: The Medieval Revival in Fin-de-Siècle France,* Ashgate (Burlington, VT), 2003.

PERIODICALS

Art History, September, 2005, review of *Consuming the Past.*

Choice, September, 2004, E. Edson, review of *Consuming the Past,* p. 180.

Church History, March, 2005, Anthony J. Steinhoff, review of *Consuming the Past,* p. 173.

Journal of Pre-Raphaelite Studies, fall, 2002, Stephen Wildman, review of *Artistic Brotherhoods in the Nineteenth Century,* p. 126.

Library Journal, February 15, 2009, "Xpress Reviews: First Look at New Books," review of *The Miracles of Prato,* p. 5.

Medieval Review, January, 2005, Bonnie Effros, review of *Consuming the Past.*

Nineteenth-Century French Studies, spring-summer, 2003, Debra L. Cumberland, review of *Artistic Brotherhoods in the Nineteenth Century;* spring-summer, 2006, Dominic Janes, review of *Consuming the Past.*

Publishers Weekly, October 13, 2008, review of *The Miracles of Prato,* p. 34.

Reference & Research Book News, August, 2001, review of *Artistic Brotherhoods in the Nineteenth Century,* p. 197.

ONLINE

HarperCollins Web site, http://www.harpercollins.com/ (July 25, 2009), brief profile of author.

Story Circle Book Reviews, http://www.storycirclebook reviews.org/ (April 5, 2009), Karen Ballinger, review of *The Miracles of Prato.*

Wagner College Web site, http://www.wagner.edu/ (July 25, 2009), faculty profile of author.*

* * *

MORTENSEN, Kurt W.

PERSONAL: Married; wife's name Denita; children: Brooke, Mitchell, Bailey, and Madison. *Education:* Brigham Young University, bachelor's degree, 1992; University of Pittsburgh, M.B.A., 1993.

ADDRESSES: Home—Provo, UT.

CAREER: Educator, consultant, public speaker, and writer. Conducts motivational speaking, training, and consulting programs.

WRITINGS:

Magnetic Persuasion: How to Create Instant Influence: Get What You Want, When You Want & Win Friends for Life, 2M Publishing (Provo, UT), 2003.

Maximum Influence: The 12 Universal Laws of Power Persuasion, American Management Association (New York, NY), 2004.

Persuasion IQ: The 10 Skills You Need to Get Exactly What You Want, American Management Association (New York, NY), 2008.

ADAPTATIONS: Persuasion IQ has been adapted for audio, Brilliance Audio, c. 2009.

SIDELIGHTS: A leading authority on persuasion, motivation and influence, Kurt W. Mortensen conducts consulting, speaking, and training programs nationwide. Mortensen proposes that a person's life, from business success to personal relationships, depends on the individual's ability to influence, motivate, and persuade others. The author's approach to success is trademarked as Magnetic Persuasion, which focuses on how to attract people.

Mortensen is the author of several books on persuasion and attracting people into your life. In *Magnetic Persuasion: How to Create Instant Influence: Get What You Want, When You Want & Win Friends for Life,* Mortensen presents his Magnetic Persuasion philosophy and program. Basing his guide on both academic and scientific research focusing on areas such as persuasion psychology and motivation triggers, the author draws from numerous strategies, techniques, and principles to teach people, especially in business areas such as sales, how to incorporate good persuasion talents into their career goals. For example, the author points out that the sales field has greatly changed, largely due to more cynical and skeptical consumers. In his sales approach, Mortensen emphasizes attracting customers as a more successful modern-day sales approach as opposed to old sales approaches based on convincing people. One area that the author emphasizes is verbal skills, noting that a person with skilled language abilities can be more persuasive. "Successful people all share a common ability to use language in ways that evoke vivid thoughts, and actions in their audiences," the author writes in his book. The author also discusses ten obstacles that limit persuasion success.

Mortensen's next book, *Maximum Influence: The 12 Universal Laws of Power Persuasion,* presents the author's basic laws of persuasion. Mortensen writes that many techniques of persuasion are subtle and often work on the unconscious level. He points to basic persuasive traits such as offering compliments and dressing professionally as examples. The author instructs readers on how to bring the twelve laws from the realm of the unconscious to the conscious level where they can be employed daily. He reveals several "secrets" to becoming persuasive, such as the willingness to share secrets, which creates both an immediate bond and a sense of trust and responsibility. He also notes that humor is important in making the persuader appear more friendly. He points out, however, that bad humor is counterproductive to the goal of persuasion. Giving "sincere" praise is yet another tip for effective persuasion. The author also emphasizes the importance of language, listing sixteen words that, if not persuasive by themselves, do work as attention grabbers. For example, the author points out how the words "free" and "new" used in sales pitches have a much higher sales rate than pitches that do not use these words. "He backs up each of his principles with real-life examples and scientific studies of human nature," wrote Kelly Quigley in a review for *Realtor* magazine.

In *Persuasion IQ: The 10 Skills You Need to Get Exactly What You Want,* the author discusses his concept of "Persuasion IQ," which Mortensen bases on research concerning multiple forms of intelligence conduced by Howard Gardner and the Emotional Intelligence work of Daniel Goleman. Presenting his concept of Persuasion IQ in a step-by-step structure, the author includes ten essential skills and techniques for developing persuasion abilities. Emphasizing the need to understand how other people think and the ability to establish a rapport with them based on trust, Mortensen also outlines the primary obstacles to being persuasive. In addition to discussing nonverbal persuasion techniques such as mirroring, the author explores how to develop self-knowledge as a crucial component of persuasion. The book includes a persuasion IQ test, illustrations, and links to other related Web sites. A contributor to the *Reference & Research Book News* Web site commented that the author emphasizes that persuasion "skills can be learned in a scientifically exact way."

BIOGRAPHICAL AND CRITICAL SOURCES:

BOOKS

Mortensen, Kurt W. *Magnetic Persuasion: How to Create Instant Influence: Get What You Want, When You Want & Win Friends for Life,* 2M Publishing (Provo, UT), 2003.

PERIODICALS

AORN Journal, December, 2008, Stacy M. Joiner, review of *Persuasion IQ: The 10 Skills You Need to Get Exactly What You Want,* p. 1022.

Business Line, July 10, 2006, "'Leverage' Language," review of *Maximum Influence: The 12 Universal Laws of Power Persuasion.*

Lawyers Competitive Edge, January, 2005, John W. Olmstead, review of *Maximum Influence,* p. 14.

Realtor, October 1, 2004, Kelly Quigley, review of *Maximum Influence.*

Reference & Research Book News, February, 2009, review of *Persuasion IQ.*

ONLINE

EmpoweringMessages.com, http://www.empowering messages.com/ (July 25, 2009), profile of author.

Kurt W. Mortensen Home Page, http://www.kurt mortensen.com (July 25, 2009).*

* * *

MR. CUTLET
See OZERSKY, Josh

* * *

MUN, Nami 1968-

PERSONAL: Born 1968, in Seoul, South Korea; immigrated to the United States, c. 1976. *Education:* University of California, Berkeley, B.A., 1998; University of Michigan, M.F.A., 2007.

ADDRESSES: *Home*—Chicago, IL. *E-mail*—MilesfromNowheretheNovel@gmail.com.

CAREER: Writer and educator. Columbia College, Chicago, IL, assistant professor of creative writing, 2009—. Previously worked as an Avon Lady, a street vendor, a photojournalist, a waitress, an activities coordinator for a nursing home, and a criminal defense investigator.

AWARDS, HONORS: Hopwood Award for fiction, University of Michigan; Pushcart Prize; shortlisted for the Orange Prize for New Writers for *Miles from Nowhere;* scholarships from Yaddo, MacDowell, Eastern Frontier, Squaw Valley Writers' Conference, Tin House Writers' Conference, and Key West Literary Seminar.

WRITINGS:

Miles from Nowhere (novel), Riverhead Books (New York, NY), 2009.

Contributor of stories to the 2007 *Pushcart Prize Anthology* and to various periodicals, including the *Iowa Review, Evergreen Review, Tin House,* and *Witness.*

SIDELIGHTS: Nami Mun grew up in Seoul, South Korea, where she was born, and in the Bronx, New York. Mun's first novel, *Miles from Nowhere,* has received widespread acclaim from reviewers. In a review for *Library Journal,* Eveyln Beck called the novel "a haunting debut." Viviane Crystal, writing for the *Crystal Reviews* Web site, referred to *Miles from Nowhere* as "a wise, literate, fresh story from an author to closely follow in the days to come."

The novel revolves around a Korean American teenager named Joon. Living in the Bronx in the 1980s, Joon watches as her father's loss of Korean identity leads him to leave the family. Joon's mother also develops a severe mental illness that sends her into catatonic-like states. Joon decides to leave home at the age of thirteen, which leads her to a traumatic journey from homeless shelters to working in an escort club. Eventually, Joon falls into drug addiction and begins committing small crimes to pay for her habit. Sliding into the dark side of American life in the big city, Joon goes on to find the will to try and turn her life around.

Several reviewers and interviewers noted that the story of Joon has definite aspects that coincide with the author's own life story. Like Joon, Mun left home at age thirteen and lived on the streets of New York, staying in abandoned buildings and sleeping on park benches. Nevertheless, the author says that only part of the story reflects her own life, noting that her experiences were not as bad as Joon's experiences. "You squeeze from your own experience every drop, sweet or bitter, it can possibly give," the author told Alice O'Keeffe in a profile article for the *Bookseller.* The author also told O'Keeffe: "If I had to give a number I'd say it's about one percent based on real-life events that either I've experienced or I've witnessed . . . but it is ninety-nine percent fiction."

The author's decision to write about Joon began with a series of short stories. In an interview with Mark Pritchard for the *San Francisco Metblogs* Web site, the author noted that, while writing several short stories, she noticed that she was focusing more and more on the character of Joon. The author told Pritchard that she "realized that these stories, while self-contained, could also be cogs working toward a larger narrative arc." The author also remarked that she then made a "crucial decision . . . to keep the episodic structure, primarily because I felt it gave a truer, more visceral reflection of Joon's fractured mindset." Mun told Pritchard: "The initial surge to write *Miles from Nowhere* began with the voice of Joon, the narrator of my book. I found her voice to be both naïve and wise, as well as vulnerable and strong, and I suppose I liked the tension these dichotomies created on the page, especially when she tried to describe certain adult settings and situations." A *Publishers Weekly* contributor commented on Mun's use of Joon as the book's narrator. The reviewer remarked that "Joon's voice, purged of self-pity, sounds clear and strong on every page."

In several reviews of *Miles from Nowhere,* reviewers commented on the author's use of language. For example, *Sun Sentinel Online* contributor Chauncey Mabe commented that the author "writes with strong verbs," adding that, "given the overwrought, undercooked prose of the 'literary' novels [of today] . . . , a simple, inventive verb choice is a thing to be celebrated." Mabe went on to write in the same review: "Mun's use of firm, unshowy language is just one of the sinews in her first novel." Other reviewers commented on the bleakness of the novel and the author's ability to provide Joon with some prospect for a better future. "The book's depiction of the desperation brought on by homelessness is raw and jarring," remarked Julia Keller in a review for the *Chicago Tribune.* "But amid all the gloom, Mun also sneaks in hope, like somebody smuggling shiny contraband under a tattered jacket."

BIOGRAPHICAL AND CRITICAL SOURCES:

PERIODICALS

Booklist, November 15, 2008, Donna Seaman, review of *Miles from Nowhere,* p. 30.

Books & Media, January 3, 2009, Julia Keller, "Amid Urban Bleakness, a Fragile Beauty Blooms," review of *Miles from Nowhere,* p. 1.

Bookseller, October 24, 2008, Alice O'Keeffe, "Runaway Success: Nami Mun's Remarkable Debut Is the Tale of a Teenager's Life on the Streets of New York. Alice O'Keeffe Met Her," p. 17.

Chicago, February, 2009, Joe Meno, review of *Miles from Nowhere,* p. 23.

Chicago Tribune, January 3, 2009, Julia Keller, review of *Miles from Nowhere.*

Kirkus Reviews, October 1, 2008, review of *Miles from Nowhere.*

Library Journal, October 1, 2008, Evelyn Beck, review of *Miles from Nowhere,* p. 61.

Publishers Weekly, September 1, 2008, review of *Miles from Nowhere,* p. 33.

ONLINE

Creative Loafing, http://blogs.creativeloafing.com/ (January 12, 2009), Wyatt Williams, "Speakeasy with . . . Author Nami Mun."

Crystal Reviews, http://www.crystalreviews.com/ (November 3, 2008), Viviane Crystal, review of *Miles from Nowhere.*

Fantastic Fiction, http://www.fantasticfiction.co.uk/ (July 26, 2009), profile of author.

Miles from Nowhere Web site, http://milesfromnowherethenovel.wordpress.com (July 26, 2009).

Nami Mun Home Page, http://www.namimun.com (July 26, 2009).

Penguin Speaker Web site, http://penguinspeakersbureau.com/ (July 26, 2009), profile of author.

San Francisco Metblogs, http://sf.metblogs.com/ (January 4, 2009), Mark Pritchard, "Interview: Novelist Nami Mun."

Sun Sentinel Online, http://www.sun-sentinel.com/ (January 4, 2009), Chauncey Mabe, review of *Miles from Nowhere.**

MUSGROVE, Marianne

PERSONAL: Born in Sydney, New South Wales, Australia. *Education:* University of Adelaide, B.A.; Flinders University, B.S.W. *Hobbies and other interests:* Reading, visiting the beach, spending time with friends and family.

ADDRESSES: *Home*—South Australia, Australia. *E-mail*—marianne@mariannemusgrove.com.au.

CAREER: Author. Former social worker; worked as a museum guide and for Australian *Daily Mirror.*

MEMBER: Society of Children's Book Writers and Illustrators (Australian chapter), Australian Society of Authors.

AWARDS, HONORS: National Children's Peace Literature Award shortlist, 2007, and Queensland Premier's Literary Award shortlist, and South Australia Festival Award for Children's Literature shortlist, both 2008, and Australian Family Therapists' Award for Children' Literature, 2008, all for *The Worry Tree;* Speech Pathology Australia Children's Book of the Year shortlist, and Victorian Premier's Reading Challenge selection, both 2009, both for *Lucy the Good.*

WRITINGS:

The Worry Tree, Random House Australia (Sydney, New South Wales, Australia), 2007, Henry Holt (New York, NY), 2008.

Lucy the Good, illustrated by Cheryl Orsini, Random House Australia (Sydney, New South Wales, Australia), 2009.

Don't Breathe a Word, Random House Australia (Sydney, New South Wales, Australia), 2009.

Lucy the Lie Detector, Random House Australia (Sydney, New South Wales, Australia), 2010.

Author's work has been published in Germany and Indonesia.

ADAPTATIONS: Musgrove's books have been adapted for audiobook by Bolinda Books Audio.

SIDELIGHTS: Australian author Marianne Musgrove always enjoyed writing, which is not surprising given that she is a descendent of England's King Henry VIII's librarian. It was a lucky brush with her past that prompted her to begin what became her first published novel. "I come from a family of storytellers," Musgrove explained on her home page. "My grandma used to give dramatic public poetry recitals and make the audience cry. I also had a string of excellent teachers who inspired me to write and write and write. In my late twenties, I spent an afternoon reading back over my old diaries. I came across an entry I'd written when I was sixteen: 'I think I'd like to write a book,' it said. Not long after I read this, the opening chapter of *The Worry Tree* came to me."

In *The Worry Tree,* readers meet a preteen who worries way too much. In her busy family, Juliet Jennifer Jones finds a lot to worry about, from her annoying little sister to her beloved Nana's health to her friendships with Gemma and Lindsay. After a move to a new bedroom—more worries!—Juliet discovers a painting of a tree hidden under layers of wallpaper. Nana explains that the room was once hers and that the painting can help take care of her worries. Juliet's challenge comes when a family tumult puts Nana's claim to the test in a chapter book that a *Kirkus Reviews* writer cited for portraying a "delightfully normal and realistically flawed family."

Other books by Musgrove include the middle-grade novel *Don't Breathe a Word,* as well as two humorous books for younger readers that focus on a girl named Lucy van Loon. In *Lucy the Good,* a feisty young girl spends a great portion of her day sitting in the Time Out chair until an unusual present from a traveling relative threatens even worse reprisals.

BIOGRAPHICAL AND CRITICAL SOURCES:

PERIODICALS

Booklist, May 1, 2009, Connie Rockman, review of *The Worry Tree,* p. 94.

Kirkus Reviews, July 15, 2008, review of *The Worry Tree.*

School Library Journal, March, 2009. Elaine Morgan, review of *The Worry Tree,* p. 124.

ONLINE

Marianne Musgrove Home Page, http://www.mariannemusgrove.com.au (November 10, 2009).

* * *

MUSSO, Guillaume 1974-

PERSONAL: Born 1974, in Antibes, France. *Education:* College graduate.

CAREER: Writer and educator. Teaches at an international school. Once worked as an ice cream vendor in the United States.

WRITINGS:

Skidamarink, Éditions Anne Carrière (Paris, France), 2001.
Et Après, XO Editions (Paris, France), 2004.
Sauve-moi, XO Editions (Paris, France), 2005.
Seras-tu là?, XO Editions (Paris, France), 2006, translation by George Holoch published as *Will You Be There?,* Hodder & Stoughton (London, England), 2008.
Parce que je t'aime, XO Editions (Paris, France), 2007.
Je reviens te chercher, XO Editions (Paris, France), 2008.
Que serais-je sans toi?, XO Editions (Paris, France), 2009.

Author's novels have been translated into thirteen languages.

ADAPTATIONS: Et Après was adapted for film by Gilles Bourdos, 2008; film rights to *Seras-tu là* have been purchased by Les Films Christian Fechner; film rights for *Parce que je t'aime* have been purchased by UGC.

SIDELIGHTS: French novelist Guillaume Musso, who was in love with reading by the age of ten, has stated that he often went on reading marathons, including one that consisted of *War and Peace, Sentimental Education,* and *The Stranger* in quick succession. The author has said that it was his interest in reading that led to his desire to write fiction.

Musso has written several novels well-accepted in France. Commenting on his novels in a "reader interview" section for his Home Page, Musso noted that he sees the thriller, supernatural, and mystery genres as giving the author the opportunity to write about important subjects in a more lighthearted manner. He went on to note the various themes of his novels, such as *Et Après,* which the author noted is about people's trials and ordeals and their ability to get through them. The author also commented that other themes include destiny and coincidence, aging and regrets, and resilience.

Musso's 2006 French novel *Seras-tu là?* appeared in English in a 2008 translation by George Holoch titled *Will You Be There?* Noting that the author provides "a refreshing take on the notion of time travel," *M/C Reviews* Web site contributor Mary-Anne Mangano added: "*Will You Be There?* is a beautiful, heart-warming, and often . . . [humorous] story of the strength of love, hope, and friendship even in the midst of death, and what can happen when destiny, regret, and time travel are thrown into the mix."

Will You Be There? revolves around Elliott Cooper, who is dying from cancer. The sixty-year-old surgeon practices in San Francisco but is in Cambodia as a volunteer working for the Red Cross. Following an operation on a child, Elliott is given a peculiar bottle of pills from a relative of the child. The relative tells Elliott he can have his dearest wish fulfilled by taking a pill. Elliott is longing to see Ilena, a beautiful young woman who died thirty years earlier, just one more time before he dies. The secret of the pills is that they allow the user to go back in time, and they allow Elliott to fulfill his wish. Nevertheless, Elliott is never sure "if they're just inducing dreams, however vivid," as noted by a contributor to *Kirkus Reviews.*

The author commented on his Home Page that he began thinking of the story after a car accident and the impact of realizing death can come at any time. Musso also remarked that the novel was inspired by several movies containing similar themes, including the American film *It's a Wonderful Life* by director Frank Capra, *Wings of Desire* by director Wim Wenders, and Jacques Tournier's *La Féline.*

In *Will You Be There?,* Elliott takes the pills and revisits San Francisco in 1976, a pivotal time in the then thirty-year-old doctor's life. The novel follows Elliott as he goes back and forth in time, slowly beginning to perceive that his choice to seek out Ilena and his decision to try to change the past could have disastrous repercussions. "Each chapter begins with a poignant quote, which complements the themes of time travel and fate," noted Mary-Anne Mangano in her article for the *M/C Reviews* Web site. At odds with his past self, Elliott begins to realize with each trip that the future is changing little by little. When he discovers that his efforts to change the past could have life-changing consequences for many people, including his best friend Matt and Matt's daughter, Angie, Elliott must work feverishly to protect the future before he dies from cancer.

In a review for the *Bookbag* Web site, Paul Harrop wrote that "the scenes are vividly drawn, and the central character sufficiently-developed to enable a willing suspension of disbelief." Harrop added: "Despite a shaky start, the book is an accessible, undemanding read."

BIOGRAPHICAL AND CRITICAL SOURCES:

PERIODICALS

Bookseller, July 7, 2006, Nicholas Clee, "Hodder Wins French Bestseller," p. 13; November 9, 2007, James Smith, review of *Will You Be There?,* p. 11; May 30, 2008, Caroline Allen, review of *Will You Be There?,* p. 11.

Kirkus Reviews, October 1, 2008, review of *Will You Be There?*

Swiss News, February, 2009, review of *Will You Be There?,* p. 64.

ONLINE

Bookbag, http://www.thebookbag.co.uk/ (July 26, 2009), Paul Harrop, review of *Will You Be There?*

Guillaume Musso Home Page, http://www.guillaumemusso.com/?lang=en (July 26, 2009).

M/C Reviews, http://reviews.media-culture.org.au/ (April 6, 2009), Mary-Anne Mangano, review of *Will You Be There?**

N

NESS, Patrick 1971-

PERSONAL: Born 1971, in Alexandria, VA. *Education:* University of Southern California, B.A.

ADDRESSES: *Home*—London, England.

CAREER: Writer. Former corporate writer in CA; freelance writer, beginning c. 1997. Oxford University, Oxford, England, instructor in creative writing.

AWARDS, HONORS: London *Guardian* Children's Fiction Prize and Booktrust Teenage Prize, both 2008, both for *The Knife of Never Letting Go.*

WRITINGS:

"CHAOS WALKING" TRILOGY; FOR YOUNG ADULTS

The Knife of Never Letting Go, Walker Books (London, England), 2008, Candlewick Press (Cambridge, MA), 2009.

The Ask and the Answer, Candlewick Press (Somerville, MA), 2009.

Monsters of Men, Candlewick Press (Somerville, MA), 2010.

OTHER

The Crash of Hennington (adult novel), Flamingo (London, England), 2003.

Topics about Which I Know Nothing (short fiction), Flamingo (London, England), 2004.

Contributor to periodicals, including *Genre.*

SIDELIGHTS: Patrick Ness combines fantasy with science fiction in his award-winning novel *The Knife of Never Letting Go.* Born in the United States but living in London, England, Ness began working as a fiction writer in the late 1990s and produced his first novel, *The Crash of Hennington,* in 2003. *Topics about Which I Know Nothing,* a book of short fiction, followed before Ness turned his attention to teen readers.

The first book in Ness's "Chaos Walking" trilogy, *The Knife of Never Letting Go* takes readers to Prentisstown, a rural community on a newly colonized planet in which no women can be found. Prentisstown has another odd characteristic: every thought of every resident—human and animal—can be heard by all, resulting in the total lack of privacy and the unceasing, overbearing mental cacophony called Noise. At twelve years of age, Todd Hewitt is the youngest resident of Prentisstown. It is almost time for Todd to undergo initiation when he discovers a place where he is immune from the Noise. This discovery prompts Todd's adoptive parents to help him escape from town. Pursued by the army of Mayor Prentiss, the preteen discovers the wreckage of a space ship in a local swamp and finds a young girl named Viola hiding in the woods nearby. Todd had assumed all the women had been killed by the Noise; however, he now realizes, the actual history of Prentisstown is far more horrific and far more deadly.

In *Kliatt,* Paula Rohrlick called *The Knife of Never Letting Go* a "haunting page-turner" featuring "edge-of-your-seat chase scenes" and "moments of both anguish and triumph." Although a *Kirkus Reviews* critic found the novel's pacing to be "uneven" and the premise "unbelievable," its "emotional, physical, and intellectual drama is well-crafted and relentless," wrote *School Library Journal* contributor Megan Honig. In *Horn Book,* Claire E. Gross cited Ness's "subtle world-building" and his ability to create relationships between characters that are "nuanced" and feature "considerable emotional depth." Calling *The Knife of Never Letting Go* a "troubling, unforgettable [series] opener," *Booklist* critic Ian Chipman concluded of the novel that Ness's "cliffhanger ending is as effective as a shot to the gut."

Ness's "Chaos Walking" trilogy continues with *The Ask and the Answer* and *Monsters of Men.* Pursued by the army of Prentisstown in *The Ask and the Answer,* Todd and Viola arrive at the city of Haven only to become separated when they are captured by the maniacal Mayor Prentiss. With his freedom gone, Todd must now cooperate with Prentiss's scheme for creating the perfect society, even as that plan begins to drive him mad. Meanwhile, Viola is sent to a female compound where she joins a loosely formed resistance group that selectively bombs area targets. In *Publishers Weekly,* a contributor praised *The Ask and the Answer* as a "grim and beautifully written sequel" that prompts readers to question "the nature of evil and humanity." The "Chaos Walking" trilogy "continues to develop a fascinating world," wrote *Horn Book* critic Claire E. Gross, "and its fully formed characters and conflicts draw attention to difficult issues with a rare, unblinking candor." In *The Ask and the Answer,* "Ness delivers a leaner, meaner narrative," concluded a *Kirkus Reviews* writer, and in *Booklist,* Chipman wrote that, while the novel is slightly "less exhilarating" than *The Knife of Never Letting Go,* it is "far weightier and no less stunning to read."

BIOGRAPHICAL AND CRITICAL SOURCES:

PERIODICALS

Booklist, September 1, 2008, Ian Chipman, review of *The Knife of Never Letting Go,* p. 97; August 1, 2009, Ian Chipman, review of *The Ask and the Answer,* p. 66.

Financial Times, April 26, 2008, James Lovegrove, review of *The Knife of Never Letting Go,* p. 19.

Horn Book, November-December, 2008, Claire E. Gross, review of *The Knife of Never Letting Go,* p. 712; September-October, 2998, Claire E. Gross, review of *The Ask and the Answer,* p. 570.

Kirkus Reviews, August 15, 2008, review of *The Knife of Never Letting Go;* August 15, 2009, review of *The Ask and the Answer.*

Kliatt, September, 2008, Paula Rohrlick, review of *The Knife of Never Letting Go,* p. 18.

Publishers Weekly, August 31, 2009, review of *The Ask and the Answer,* p. 59.

School Library Journal, November, 2008, Megan Honig, review of *The Knife of Never Letting Go,* p. 133.

ONLINE

Patrick Ness Home Page, http://www.patrickness.com (November 10, 2009).

* * *

NEVINS, Thomas

PERSONAL: Born in Brooklyn, NY; married; wife's name Debbie; children: three daughters. *Education:* Attended New York University School of Continuing Education and the College of Staten Island.

ADDRESSES: *Home*—Brooklyn, NY. *E-mail*—tomnevs@aol.com.

CAREER: Salesperson and writer. Random House, New York, NY, sales representative. Previously worked for Doubleday Bookshops, New York, NY, began as sales clerk, became assistant manager, manager, buyer, sales representative, and national account manager.

WRITINGS:

The Age of the Conglomerates: A Novel of the Future, Ballantine Books (New York, NY), 2008.

SIDELIGHTS: Thomas Nevins is a longtime sales representative and manager in the book business who has worked for the Doubleday Bookshops and Random House. The author's first book, *The Age of the Conglomerates: A Novel of the Future,* tells the story of the rise of a powerful political party called the Conglomerate, which takes Draconian control of the government and people's lives in the name of preventing an economic collapse. For example, the Family Relief Act passed by the Conglomerate states that all people over eight years old, referred to as "coots," are to be sent to a community in Arizona called "Cootsville" run by the government. The act also states that the former property and assets of the elderly revert automatically to their children. Genetics research also plays a role in government's plans to form a more stable society. Any family who has a child that they don't want for some reason—whether it be a medical or some other problem—can turn the child, termed a "dyscard," over to the government. Then they can have a specially bred child designed to be a good member of society. Furthermore, the Conglomerate has placed cameras everywhere and any laws concerning the elderly, children, or any other aspect of society and family life are enforceable at gunpoint.

As director of genetic development at the New York Medical Center, Christine Salter has helped create the perfect child for families via genetic manipulation. Christine is also working on a way to use genetic engineering to make the Conglomerate chair more youthful. Christine, however, begins to develop questions about the Conglomerate and the nature of her work. Her suspicions are heightened when one of her top coworkers, for whom Christine was developing a personal interest, disappears. Christine becomes further disllusioned when her own parents are sent to the elderly camp in Arizona and her sister becomes a dyscard living with other dyscards in the subway system. Eventually, Christine uncovers a nefarious plan and places her own life on the line to save the very people that the Conglomerate and most of society have deemed to be undesirables.

"As a vision of the future; Nevins' *The Age of the Conglomerates* is backed up by enough things (happening right now) to make it plausible enough to give the reader more than a slight chill," noted Flory Graeme, writing for the *Graeme's Fantasy Book Review* Web site. A *Publishers Weekly* contributor commented: "Readers willing to pardon the oversimplification of good versus evil may enjoy the slick presentation and Hollywood-like setup."

BIOGRAPHICAL AND CRITICAL SOURCES:

PERIODICALS

Publishers Weekly, June 2, 2008, review of *The Age of the Conglomerates: A Novel of the Future,* p. 30.

ONLINE

Graeme's Fantasy Book Review, http://www.graemesfantasybookreview.com/ (July 14, 2008), Flory Graeme, review of *The Age of the Conglomerates.*

Random House Web site, http://www.randomhouse.com/ (July 27, 2009), brief profile of author.

Thomas Nevins Home Page, http://www.ageoftheconglomerates.com (July 27, 2009).*

* * *

NIMOY, Adam 1956-

PERSONAL: Born August 9, 1956, in Los Angeles, CA; son of Leonard Nimoy (an actor and director) and Sandra Zober; divorced; children: Maddy and Jonah.

ADDRESSES: *Agent*—The Gersh Agency, 232 N. Canon Dr., Beverly Hills, CA 90210.

CAREER: Television director and writer. Worked as an entertainment attorney before beginning career as television director; teaches writing, directing, and acting at the New York Film Academy, Los Angeles, CA. Director of numerous television show episodes, including "Rascals," 1992, and "Timescape," 1993, both for *Star Trek: The Next Generation;* "Cold Heaters," *NYPD Blue,* ABC, 1995; "I, Robot," *The Outer Limits,* Showtime and syndicated, 1995; "Passing through Gethsemane," *Babylon 5,* syndicated, 1995; "The Practical Joker," *Deadly Games,* UPN, 1995; "Chapter Seven, Year Two," *Murder One,* ABC, 1996; "The Guardian," and "Post Traumatic Slide Syndrome," both for *Sliders,* Fox, both 1996; "Lost and Found," *Nash Bridges,* CBS, 1997; "Tom and Geri,"

NYPD Blue, ABC, 1997; "Checkmate," and "State of Mind," *The Practice,* ABC, 1998; "Kill the Buddha," *The Net,* USA Network, 1998; "Scents and Sensibility," V.I.P., syndicated, 1998; "You Never Can Tell," *Ally McBeal,* Fox, 1998; "Bye, Bye, Love," *Party of Five,* Fox, 1999; "Decisions," *Family Law,* CBS, 1999; "Funny Valentine," *Early Edition,* CBS, 1999; "A Wicked Good Time," *Hercules: The Legendary Journeys,* syndicated, 1999; "Kill Me Now," *Gilmore Girls,* The WB, 2000; "Ralph," *The Invisible Man,* Sci-Fi Channel, 2000; "The Long Con," *Thieves,* ABC, 2001; "The Time/Sex Continuum," *Jack and Jill,* The WB, 2001; and "Skulls," *Veritas: The Quest,* ABC, 2003.

WRITINGS:

My Incredibly Wonderful, Miserable Life: An Anti-Memoir, Pocket Books (New York, NY), 2008.

SIDELIGHTS: Adam Nimoy is the son of actor and director Leonard Nimoy, most famous for his role as Mr. Spock on the *Star Trek* television series and several features films based on the series. A successful television director, Adam Nimoy is also the author of *My Incredibly Wonderful, Miserable Life: An Anti-Memoir.* The memoir examines Nimoy's life from his time as a child, who had to deal with a famous father who was often away working, to the author's own adulthood trials and tribulations, including a failed marriage and a long addiction to alcohol and marijuana.

In an article for *LJWorld.com,* Susan Salter Reynolds noted that Nimoy worked hard to get an agent to represent him and to allow him to write the memoir that he wanted to write. "Agents wanted the dirt on growing up with [the] *Star Trek* television actor," wrote Reynolds, noting that the author wanted to focus on many other aspects of his life. Reynolds noted: "Writing the book was a way to pull himself out of the depressing hole his life had become. Not necessarily finding himself—that obnoxious baby-boomer phrase—but asserting his identity, separate from his father, from the marriage, from drugs."

In his memoir, Nimoy writes about his life as a child and how his father, prior to the success he achieved in *Star Trek,* was a rugged kid who had to hustle for work as an actor and rarely had time for the family. However, the author is more concerned with his own adult life, how he handled adversity, and how he nearly lost everything. He begins his book writing: "Today is Tuesday and I'm waking up in my sleeping bag on my air mattress in my new two-bedroom apartment off Venice Boulevard where the only furniture is my fold-out camping chair. Just last Sunday, I was sleeping in my bed in my big beautiful house in Cheviot Hills in West L.A. Now I'm staring at the ceiling, the white stucco ceiling of my apartment, trying to remember how the hell I got here."

The author goes on to relate that his career as a director appeared to be over when no one wanted to hire him. The problem wasn't that the product he produced was bad but rather that his antagonistic personality was more than what people wanted to deal with on the sets. Nimoy traces much of his problem to his thirty years of smoking marijuana almost daily. When he decides to quit smoking pot, the author also undergoes the realization that he is in an unhappy marriage and has to change his life. Nimoy goes on to write about his relationship with his two children, as he tries to stay connected while being a single dad in Los Angeles. Writing for *Booklist,* Allison Block commended the author for the sections of his book focusing on his children, noting that "his discussions with teenage daughter Maddy are especially poignant."

Although much of the book deals with how Nimoy handles his children, who are devastated by their parents' divorce, the author also details his adjustment to living a life without marijuana or alcohol. For example, he writes of attending Alcoholics Anonymous (AA) meetings, where he found himself chasing beautiful blondes. The author also examines the new direction his life took as he joined a writer's workshop, began teaching film production, and started to write his memoir.

A *Publishers Weekly* contributor wrote that Nimoy is able "to tell an instantly recognizable story of heartache and recovery with deceivingly simple honesty." A *Kirkus Reviews* contributor remarked that "the narrative brilliantly mirrors the author's progression toward awareness," adding: "Initially riddled with unrelieved tension and unexpressed feelings, the prose becomes more expansive and reflective as Nimoy's self-realization unfolds."

BIOGRAPHICAL AND CRITICAL SOURCES:

BOOKS

Contemporary Theatre, Film, and Television, Volume 52, Gale (Detroit, MI), 2009.

Nimoy, Adam, *My Incredibly Wonderful, Miserable Life: An Anti-Memoir,* Pocket Books (New York, NY), 2008.

PERIODICALS

Booklist, July 1, 2008, Allison Block, review of *My Incredibly Wonderful, Miserable Life,* p. 25.

Entertainment Weekly, July 25, 2008, Adam B. Vary, review of *My Incredibly Wonderful, Miserable Life,* p. 75.

Kirkus Reviews, May 15, 2008, review of *My Incredibly Wonderful, Miserable Life.*

Los Angeles Magazine, August 1, 2008, "This Gift Is Most Illogical," includes review of *My Incredibly Wonderful, Miserable Life,* p. 98.

Publishers Weekly, May 26, 2008, review of *My Incredibly Wonderful, Miserable Life,* p. 55.

ONLINE

Adam Nimoy MySpace.com Web site, http://www.myspace.com/adamnimoy (July 27, 2009).

LJWorld.com, http://www2.ljworld.com/ (August 10, 2008), Susan Salter Reynolds, "Identity Crisis: Adam Nimoy Writes Anti-Memoir about 'Wonderful, Miserable Life' as Son of Spock."*

* * *

NUNN, Malla

PERSONAL: Born in Swaziland, South Africa; immigrated to Australia, 1970s; married; children: two. *Education:* University of Western Australia, B.A.

ADDRESSES: Home—Sydney, New South Wales, Australia.

CAREER: Writer, novelist, scriptwriter, and filmmaker. Producer and writer of documentaries, corporate videos, and short films. Producer of films *Fade to White, Sweetbreeze,* and *Servant of the Ancestors.*

AWARDS, HONORS: Winner of awards for films *Fade to White, Sweetbreeze,* and *Servant of the Ancestors.*

WRITINGS:

A Beautiful Place to Die (novel), Atria Books (New York, NY), 2009.

SIDELIGHTS: Malla Nunn is a novelist and filmmaker based in Sydney, New South Wales, Australia. Born in Swaziland, South Africa, Nunn and her family immigrated to Western Australia in the 1970s. She attended the University of Western Australia, where she earned a B.A. degree in English and history, according to a biographer on the *Mostly Fiction* Web site. Nunn lived for a while in the United States, where she met her husband. Afterward, she and her family moved back to Australia where Nunn became an award-winning producer of short films, documentaries, and corporate videos. Her films, including *Sweetbreeze, Servant of the Ancestors,* and *Fade to White,* have been shown at festivals both in the United States and abroad.

A Beautiful Place to Die is Nunn's debut novel, a story set in the violent, racially explosive environment of 1950s South Africa, when the restrictive policies of apartheid have excavated a vast social and cultural gulf between blacks and whites. In the small town of Jacob's Rest, near the border of South Africa and Mozambique, the local police captain, Willem Pretorius, has been murdered. Pretorius, an Afrikaner white man, was well known and well liked, and suspicion immediately falls upon the black population. When Detective Emmanuel Cooper arrives to begin his investigation, however, he refuses to conduct his grim business along racial lines, and considers suspects of all races. Soon, Cooper has aroused the ire of Pretorius's family and brutish sons, and must contend with thuggish investigators from the Security Branch. Elsewhere, Cooper explores the possibility of a suspect from the town's black community, so oppressed that they are banned from even traveling the streets and are restricted to walking along Kaffir footpaths crisscrossing the hidden sections of town. Cooper discovers a link between the murder and a Peeping Tom case that Pretorius had been investigating, and uncovers dark secrets about the dead policeman that many people in Jacob's Rest would rather keep hidden. With no shortage of suspects, Cooper struggles against ingrained racism, threatening authorities, and personal demons to find justice where little hope exists.

In writing her novel, the first in a proposed series, Nunn remarked to a reviewer on the Simon & Schuster Web site, she wanted to "explore, through crime fiction, the crippling racial segregation laws that forced my parents out of Southern Africa. Any society that elevates a 'pure' minority to the pinnacle has a dark underbelly. My book explores the unlit spaces in 1950's South African society."

"One thing that will strike readers of *A Beautiful Place to Die* firmly between the eyes is how an apartheid society is so incredibly foreign from the ways in which others of us live," observed a reviewer on the *Austcrime* Web site. The reviewer continued, "The way that people's lives were so fundamentally affected by something as minor as the color of their skin is really very sobering indeed."

Reviewer Mary Mann, writing on the *Lit Mob* Web site, stated that "Nunn nicely shines a light on a complex society where whites are divided from each other (Dutch Boers and Englishmen), and black and mixed race are two entirely different entities." The *Austcrime* Web site reviewer called Mann's novel "an extremely good thriller, with lots of twists and turns in the story," while Mary Whipple, writing on the *Mostly Fiction* Web site, found it to be "extremely cinematic." Throughout the novel, Nunn "gets the politics exactly right: the farce, cruelty, sorrow, and rebellion in daily life," commented Hazel Rochman in *Booklist.* "Smooth prose and a deft plot make this novel a welcome addition to crime fiction" with a South African setting, remarked a *Publishers Weekly* contributor. *Entertainment Weekly* writer Chris Nashawaty commented, "This first installment in a proposed series has all the right smells and dialects."

BIOGRAPHICAL AND CRITICAL SOURCES:

PERIODICALS

Booklist, December 1, 2008, Hazel Rochman, review of *A Beautiful Place to Die,* p. 27.

Entertainment Weekly, January 9, 2009, Chris Nashawaty, review of *A Beautiful Place to Die,* p. 65.

Kirkus Reviews, October 15, 2008, review of *A Beautiful Place to Die.*

Library Journal, January 1, 2009, "Xpress Reviews: First Look at New Books," review of *A Beautiful Place to Die,* p. 5.

Publishers Weekly, October 27, 2008, review of *A Beautiful Place to Die,* p. 32.

ONLINE

Austcrime, http://www.austcrimefiction.org/ (July 26, 2009), review of *A Beautiful Place to Die.*

BookBrowse, http://www.bookbrowse.com/ (December 29, 2008), biography of Malla Nunn.

Innocent Bystander Web log, http://innocentbystander.typepad.com/ (March 22, 2009), review of *A Beautiful Place to Die.*

Lit Mob, http://litmob.com/ (November 16, 2008), Mary Mann, review of *A Beautiful Place to Die.*

Mostly Fiction, http://www.mostlyfiction.com/ (January 22, 2009), Mary Whipple, review of *A Beautiful Place to Die;* (July 26, 2009), biography of Malla Nunn.

Simon & Schuster Web site, http://www.simonandschuster.com/ (July 26, 2009), interview with Malla Nunn.*

O

OLMSTED, Kathryn S.

PERSONAL: Education: Stanford University, B.A.; University of California, Davis, M.A., Ph.D.

ADDRESSES: Office—History Department, University of California, 2216 Social Sciences and Humanities, 1 Shields Ave., Davis, CA 95616. *E-mail*—ksolmsted@ ucdavis.edu.

CAREER: University of California, Davis, professor of history.

WRITINGS:

Challenging the Secret Government: The Post-Watergate Investigations of the CIA and FBI, University of North Carolina Press (Chapel Hill, NC), 1996.

Red Spy Queen: A Biography of Elizabeth Bentley, University of North Carolina Press (Chapel Hill, NC), 2002.

Real Enemies: Conspiracy Theories and American Democracy, World War I to 9/11, Oxford University Press (New York, NY), 2009.

Contributor of articles to books, including "Lapdog or Rogue Elephant? CIA Controversies from 1947 to 2004," in *The Central Intelligence Agency: Security under Scrutiny,* Athan Theoharis, editor, Greenwood Press (Westport, CT), 2006; and "Linus Pauling: A Case Study in Counterintelligence Run Amok," for *Handbook on Intelligence Studies,* Loch Johnson, editor, Routledge (London, England), 2007. Contributor to journals, including *Intelligence and National Security.*

SIDELIGHTS: Writer and educator Kathryn S. Olmsted serves on the faculty at the University of California at Davis, where she is a professor in the Department of History. Early in her career, she intended to be a journalist, but a brief stint on a newspaper and a love of history shifted her goal and she ultimately studied the history of journalism. Her primary academic and research interests revolve around the twentieth century and the cultural and political history of the United States at that time, which dovetails well with her earlier interest in journalism. Olmsted is a frequent contributor to various journals, including *Intelligence and National Security,* and has provided articles to numerous books. Her own book-length publications include *Challenging the Secret Government: The Post-Watergate Investigations of the CIA and FBI,* which stems from her doctoral dissertation, *Red Spy Queen: A Biography of Elizabeth Bentley,* and *Real Enemies: Conspiracy Theories and American Democracy, World War I to 9/11.*

In *Challenging the Secret Government,* Olmsted focuses on the changes in the attitude between journalists and government that took place starting in 1974 as a result of the Watergate scandal and the national discontent regarding the country's role in the Vietnam War. She was particularly interested in how reporters became investigators, as evidenced specifically by the work of Bob Woodward and Carl Bernstein in uncovering the culpability of various individuals within the government, with the trail leading all the way to the presidency. It was later revealed that the CIA was investigating dissidents within the country in relationship to the Vietnam War. Over the course of her book, Olmsted ties together the various threads of the covert government agency actions that were revealed after Watergate, providing readers with a thorough understanding of the underhanded behavior that was taking place. Through detailed research and a number of interviews, she pieces together both the motivations behind much of the activities and the reactions of both the public and the government in the aftermath. She also addresses the line drawn by the media in general when it comes to government and what appeared to motivate various publications from backing down rather than pursuing certain lines of questioning or reportage of events. Stanley I. Kutler, writing for the *Nation,* remarked that Olmsted offers readers "a useful summary of the Frank Church and Otis Pike investigations. She has mastered the voluminous reports of the C.I.A.'s sensational domestic and foreign transgressions, including planned assassinations of foreign leaders. In addition, she addresses the question of how Congress, the executive branch, the American people and, most of all, the media responded to the investigations. Her conclusions are devastating." Kutler went on to conclude that "Olmsted successfully confronts and refutes the heroic myths surrounding post-Watergate journalism." A reviewer for *Publishers Weekly* found the book to be "a fascinating study of how, just months after Watergate, both press and Congress quietly retreated to the same silk-gloved handling of the CIA and FBI."

Olmsted's *Red Spy Queen* chronicles the life and activities of Connecticut resident Elizabeth Bentley who, in 1945, turned herself in to the FBI in New Haven as a spy for the Soviet Union. Bentley's information was devastating to the Soviets and their ongoing espionage efforts in the United States, as she revealed the identities of various other operatives, including Julius and Ethel Rosenberg, and provided the United States with a stronger footing in the ongoing cold war. Olmsted provides readers with Bentley's early life as well as depicting her years as a spy, discussing her youth and her years at Vassar, when all indications pointed to her future as a party girl rather than as a spy. Bentley initially showed more interest in social activities than in politics, but eventually began providing the Soviets with information before graduating to courier and working her way up to a far more involved role. Olmsted's effort shows Bentley in part to have been somewhat naïve and unprepared for the tangled web in which she found herself trapped. David Pitt, reviewing the volume for *Booklist,* declared that "this is a revealing and compassionate biography."

With *Real Enemies,* Olmsted delves into the world of conspiracy theories and how they have affected the United States over the course of the twentieth century and into the twenty-first. She begins by analyzing the aftermath of World War One, when the nation found itself doing well financially and able to expend resources to follow the efforts of more dubious individuals, particularly dissidents and anyone prone to speaking out against the country. War was blamed on evil-minded individuals behind the government and some of the earliest conspiracies began to surface. From there Olmsted tracks the history of conspiracy theories and their validity, or lack of, through the events of September 11, 2001. A contributor for *Kirkus Reviews* found the book to be a "convincing study of how alternative histories develop."

BIOGRAPHICAL AND CRITICAL SOURCES:

PERIODICALS

American Historical Review, October 1, 1998, John Robert Greene, review of *Challenging the Secret Government: The Post-Watergate Investigations of the CIA and FBI,* p. 1354.

Biography, June 22, 2003, "Bentley, Elizabeth," p. 515.

Booklist, September 1, 2002, David Pitt, review of *Red Spy Queen: A Biography of Elizabeth Bentley,* p. 29.

Choice: Current Reviews for Academic Libraries, May 1, 1996, review of *Challenging the Secret Government,* p. 1557; May 1, 2003, A. Yarnell, review of *Red Spy Queen,* p. 1610.

Chronicle of Higher Education, October 11, 2002, review of *Red Spy Queen,* p. 22.

Diplomatic History, November 1, 2003, "The 'Red Spy Queen' in a Male World," p. 741.

Historian, June 22, 1998, Leo P. Ribuffo, review of *Challenging the Secret Government,* p. 868.

History Today, November 1, 2002, review of *Red Spy Queen,* p. 82.

Journal of American History, March 1, 1997, Jonathan Marshall, review of *Challenging the Secret Government,* p. 1500; December 1, 2003, Rhodri Jeffreys-Jones, review of *Red Spy Queen,* p. 1079.

Journal of American Studies, August 1, 2003, Christine K. Erickson, review of *Red Spy Queen,* p. 351.

Kirkus Reviews, July 1, 2002, review of *Red Spy Queen,* p. 938; November 15, 2008, review of *Real Enemies: Conspiracy Theories and American Democracy, World War I to 9/11.*

Library Journal, July 1, 2002, "Women Who Spy," p. 97.

Nation, March 18, 1996, Stanley I. Kutler, review of *Challenging the Secret Government,* p. 29.

National Review, February 24, 2003, "The Truth-Spiller," p. 52.

New England Quarterly, September 1, 2004, Alan Wald, review of *Red Spy Queen,* p. 505.

New York Times Book Review, November 3, 2002, Dorothy Gallagher, "The Witness," review of *Red Spy Queen.*

Publishers Weekly, February 26, 1996, review of *Challenging the Secret Government,* p. 99; August 5, 2002, review of *Red Spy Queen,* p. 61.

ONLINE

Printed Matter, http://dcn.davis.ca.us/ (April 21, 1996), Elizabeth Sherwin, "Olmsted's Book Challenges US Secret Government."

University of California at David Web site, http://history.ucdavis.edu/ (August 17, 2009), faculty profile.*

* * *

ONUF, Peter S. 1946-

PERSONAL: Born October 6, 1946. *Education:* Johns Hopkins University, B.A., 1967, Ph.D., 1973.

ADDRESSES: Office—Corcoran Department of History, University of Virginia, P.O. Box 400180, Randall Hall, Charlottesville, VA 22904. *E-mail*—pso2k@virginia.edu.

CAREER: Writer, historian, educator. Worcester Polytechnic Institute, Worcester, MA, former assistant professor; University of Virginia, Charlottesville, Thomas Jefferson Memorial Foundation professor, 1989—.

MEMBER: American Antiquarian Society

WRITINGS:

The Origins of the Federal Republic: Jurisdictional Controversies in the United States, 1775-1787, University of Pennsylvania Press (Philadelphia, PA), 1983.

Statehood and Union: A History of the Northwest Ordinance, Indiana University Press (Bloomington, IN), 1987.

(With Andrew R.L. Cayton) *The Midwest and the Nation: Rethinking the History of an American Region,* Indiana University Press (Bloomington, IN), 1990.

(With Cathy D. Matson) *A Union of Interests: Political and Economic Thought in Revolutionary America,* University Press of Kansas (Lawrence, KS), 1990.

(Editor and author of introduction) *Establishing the New Regime: The Washington Administration,* Garland Publishing (New York, NY), 1991.

(Editor and author of introduction) *The Federal Constitution,* Garland Publishing (New York, NY), 1991.

(Editor and author of introduction) *New American Nation, 1775-1820,* Garland Publishing (New York, NY), 1991.

(Editor and author of introduction) *Patriots, Redcoats, and Loyalists,* Garland Publishing (New York, NY), 1991.

(Editor and author of introduction) *Ratifying, Amending, and Interpreting the Constitution,* Garland Publishing (New York, NY), 1991.

(Editor and author of introduction) *Federalists and Republicans,* Garland Publishing (New York, NY), 1991.

(Editor and author of introduction) *The Revolution in the States,* Garland Publishing (New York, NY), 1991.

(Editor and author of introduction) *America and the World: Diplomacy, Politics, and War,* Garland Publishing (New York, NY), 1991.

(Editor and author of introduction) *American Culture, 1776-1815,* Garland Publishing (New York, NY), 1991.

(Editor and author of introduction) *American Society, 1776-1815,* Garland Publishing (New York, NY), 1991.

(Editor and author of introduction) *Congress and the Confederation,* Garland Publishing (New York, NY), 1991.

(Editor and author of introduction) *The Revolution in American Thought,* Garland Publishing (New York, NY), 1991.

(Editor and author of introduction) *State and Local Politics in the New Nation,* Garland Publishing (New York, NY), 1991.

(With Nicholas Onuf) *Federal Union, Modern World: The Law of Nations in an Age of Revolutions, 1776-1814,* Madison House (Madison, WI), 1993.

(Editor) *Jeffersonian Legacies,* foreword by Daniel P. Jordan and afterword by Merrill D. Peterson, University Press of Virginia (Charlottesville, VA), 1993.

(Author of introduction) Mason Locke Weems, *The Life of Washington,* M.E. Sharpe (Armonk, NY), 1996.

(With Edward L. Ayers, Patricia N. Limerick, and Stephen Nissenbaum) *All Over the Map: Rethinking Region and Nation in the United States,* Johns Hopkins University Press (Baltimore, MD), 1996.

(Editor, with Jan Ellen Lewis) *Sally Hemings & Thomas Jefferson: History, Memory, and Civic Culture,* University Press of Virginia (Charlottesville, VA), 1999.

Jefferson's Empire: The Language of American Nationhood, University Press of Virginia (Charlottesville, VA), 2000.

(With Leonard J. Sadosky) *Jeffersonian America,* Blackwell Publishers (Malden, MA), 2002.

(Editor, with James Horn and Jan Ellen Lewis) *The Revolution of 1800: Democracy, Race, and the New Republic,* University of Virginia Press (Charlottesville, VA), 2002.

(Editor, with Eliga H. Gould) *Empire and Nation: The American Revolution in the Atlantic World,* Johns Hopkins University Press (Baltimore, MD), 2005.

(Editor, with Douglas Seefeldt and Jeffrey L. Hantman) *Across the Continent: Jefferson, Lewis and Clark, and the Making of America,* University of Virginia Press (Charlottesville, VA), 2005.

(With Nicholas Onuf) *Nations, Markets, and War: Modern History and the American Civil War,* University of Virginia Press (Charlottesville, VA), 2006.

The Mind of Thomas Jefferson, University of Virginia Press (Charlottesville, VA), 2007.

(Editor, with Christian Y. Dupont) *Declaring Independence: The Origin and Influence of America's Founding Document: Featuring the Albert H. Small Declaration of Independence Collection,* University of Virginia Library (Charlottesville, VA), 2008.

Contributor of scholarly articles to journals.

SIDELIGHTS: American historian and author Peter S. Onuf is a distinguished authority on early American history. Onuf focuses particularly on the life and times of Thomas Jefferson, and has edited or written numerous books dealing with federalism, sectionalism, and American democracy.

Working with Jan Ellen Lewis, Onuf served as editor for the 1999 collection of essays *Sally Hemings & Thomas Jefferson: History, Memory, and Civic Culture.* Written following the 1998 DNA results that proved Jefferson was the father of at least one of his slave's children, this volume examines the formerly private world of the third president. The eleven essays gathered in the book deal with topics including Jefferson and his opinions on race, the efforts of Jefferson's white family to ignore and avoid the issue of Hemings and her children, and the history of the Hemings clan. Douglas R. Egerton, writing in the *Journal of Southern History,* termed this book a "splendid anthology," and further remarked that it "goes a long way" to making sense of the then recent DNA findings regarding Jefferson's children. Stuart Leibiger, reviewing the same title in the *Historian,* felt that the essays in the collection "seek to understand how [Jefferson] reconciled slavery with the Declaration of Independence and racism with miscegenation." Leibiger also wrote, "This book makes it abundantly clear that with so much hitherto uncertain information now confirmed, historians need completely to reinterpret Jefferson's life." Further praise for *Sally Hemings & Thomas Jefferson* came from *Mississippi Quarterly* reviewer Stephanie M.H. Camp, who commented, "By contextualizing the Hemings-Jefferson liaison, Lewis and Onuf's consistently excellent anthology does much to bring the story down to size."

Onuf continues to focus on Jefferson in several other volumes. *Jefferson's Empire: The Language of American Nationhood* is a book, according to *Journal of Southern History* reviewer Eliga H. Gould, that explores "the invention of the American nation and the principle of national self-determination." Gould found the work "marvelous," as well as "splendid" in its analysis of Jefferson's role in establishing the new nation along federalist lines. Onuf is frank in his evaluation of Jefferson's rather hypocritical stance regarding the status of African Americans and Native Americans in this new democracy of free men. While the Native Americans needed to assimilate into the dominant society of the whites, the slaves were, in Jefferson's mind, only fit to be colonized and held in slavery. "Not everyone will take comfort from this rendering of Jefferson's politics," Gould remarked. *History: Review of New Books* contributor Gene A. Smith concluded of the same book, "Professional historians and graduate students alike will appreciate this study because it offers a new, nonbiographical view of Jefferson." Joseph C. Morton, writing for the *Historian,* remarked, "This well-researched, fresh look at Jefferson's political vision is a happy reminder that there is much more to the Thomas Jefferson legacy than the recent controversy over the nature and extent of his relationship with Sally Hemings." Similarly, *Philadelphia Inquirer* reviewer Carlin Romano noted, "Onuf's tightly argued book offers one vehicle by which we can . . . honor the Founders by comprehending a little better what they thought."

Onuf collaborated with Leonard J. Sadosky for the 2002 work *Jeffersonian America,* a "marvelous recreation" of the epoch, according to Daniel Sisson, writing in the *Journal of Southern History.* Sisson observed that the authors "link the early years of the new nation to the aspirations of the Founders and demonstrate how the then-revolutionary principles of republicanism were intentionally infused into every institution in society—family, county, state, and nation—each of which had a purpose related to the whole." *Canadian Journal of History* reviewer Reginald C. Stuart noted, "Peter Onuf and Leonard Sadosky argue that the ramifications of Thomas Jefferson's republican world view offer a panoramic picture-window on the first half-century's career of the United States." Stuart also felt that the authors' "synthesis is greater than the sum of its parts and will introduce students at undergraduate and graduate levels, as well as lay readers, to Jefferson, his times, and the richness of this era's scholarship." *Institute of Historical Research* Web site contributor Michael A. McDonnell also commended the work, terming it "a rich book that moves well beyond summarising principal lines of Jeffersonian scholarship and provides much food for thought for those who might tackle Jefferson yet." However, McDonnell also had reservations about how well the authors achieved their goal of saving Jefferson from the "rising tide of confusing interpretive currents." McDonnell concluded: "This is certainly a convincing book about Jefferson's America. Yet because we never see the view from the cleaner's floor, the authors do not quite succeed in convincing this reader that all America during this period was definitively Jeffersonian."

Working with Eliga H. Gould, Onuf edited the 2005 collection *Empire and Nation: The American Revolution in the Atlantic World.* Writing for *History: Review of New Books,* Timothy Roberts explained that this work attempts to "refute scholarship of the new social history and the neo-Whig school, which, the editors argue, have interpreted the American Revolution as too parochial and predetermined." Essays in the volume range from a discussion of the role of American farmers in the Revolution to the impact of Irish immigrants on the rise of evangelical Christianity in the formation of the United States. Reviewing this book in the *Journal of Southern History,* Michael A. McDonnell noted that Onuf and Gould set out "to explore the influence of events and ideas from elsewhere in the British Empire on political developments in the thirteen mainland colonies and to trace the effect of the American Revolution on the wider Atlantic world." McDonnell felt that "the essays in this collection are in turns stimulating, provocative, and enlightening," and added, "They represent some of the best new work on the political history of the American Revolution and highlight some promising new directions in Atlantic history."

Writing on his own, Onuf returned to Jeffersonian themes with the 2007 work *The Mind of Thomas Jefferson,* a collection of previously published essays that focuses on two aspects: they explore Jefferson's import in his era and also examine the man's private life. Steven Sarson, writing in the *Journal of Southern History,* noted, "Both recontextualizations, especially the former, offer striking insights." Sarson also noted that the volume is "full of novel findings." Onuf writes widely in this collection, looking at Jefferson's contradictions and moralizing tendencies, his firm belief in federal unity as the surest way to make the new country successful, and his views on religion and race, among other topics. "Onuf makes Jefferson's sense of historical place and its implications for our understanding of him clearer than any historian has before," stated Sarson. *Historian* reviewer Thomas S. Engeman also had praise for the collection, noting that the author "addresses many of the contested aspects of Jefferson's thought" in these thirteen essays. Engeman added, "Onuf offers a savory intellectual feast for scholar and neophyte alike."

BIOGRAPHICAL AND CRITICAL SOURCES:

PERIODICALS

American Historical Review, December, 2001, James Roger Sharp, review of *Jefferson's Empire: The*

Language of American Nationhood, p. 1793; April, 2006, H.T. Dickinson, review of *Empire and Nation: The American Revolution in the Atlantic World,* p. 435.

Canadian Journal of History, April, 2004, Reginald C. Stuart, review of *Jeffersonian America,* p. 184.

Choice, September, 2000, H.M. Ward, review of *Jefferson's Empire,* p. 204; April, 2002, G.A. Smith, review of *Jeffersonian America,* p. 1484; January, 2006, L.T. Cummins, review of *Empire and Nation,* p. 916.

Early American Literature, winter, 2001, Robert S. Levine, review of *Sally Hemings & Thomas Jefferson: History, Memory, and Civic Culture,* p. 89.

English Historical Review, June, 2006, P.J. Marshall, review of *Empire and Nation,* p. 861.

Historian, summer, 2001, Stuart Leibiger, review of *Sally Hemings & Thomas Jefferson,* p. 839; winter, 2002, Joseph C. Morton, review of *Jefferson's Empire,* p. 423; summer, 2009, Thomas S. Engeman, review of *The Mind of Thomas Jefferson,* p. 377.

History: Review of New Books, spring, 2000, Gene A. Smith, review of *Jefferson's Empire,* p. 107; fall, 2005, Timothy Roberts, review of *Empire and Nation,* p. 5.

Journal of American History, March, 2001, Sharon Block, review of *Sally Hemings & Thomas Jefferson,* p. 1476; September, 2001, Emory G. Evans, review of *Jefferson's Empire,* p. 629; March, 2006, Colin Bonwick, review of *Empire and Nation,* p. 1416; June, 2006, William E. Foley, review of *Across the Continent: Jefferson, Lewis and Clark, and the Making of America,* p. 199.

Journal of American Studies, December, 2001, Sharon Monteith, review of *Sally Hemings & Thomas Jefferson,* p. 530; December, 2006, Paul Giles, review of *Empire and Nation,* p. 664; August, 2008, Frank Cogliano, review of *The Mind of Thomas Jefferson,* p. 376.

Journal of British Studies, April, 2006, Erik R. Seeman, review of *Empire and Nation,* p. 413.

Journal of Cultural Geography, spring, 2006, Ralph K. Allen, review of *Across the Continent.*

Journal of Historical Geography, July, 1997, Stanley D. Brunn, review of *All Over the Map: Rethinking Region and Nation in the United States,* p. 373.

Journal of Southern History, August, 2001, Douglas R. Egerton, review of *Sally Hemings & Thomas Jefferson,* p. 640; November, 2001, Eliga H. Gould, review of *Jefferson's Empire,* p. 833; May, 2003, Daniel Sisson, review of *Jeffersonian America,* p. 407; February, 2007, Brian Steele, review of *Across the Continent,* p. 168; August, 2007, Michael A. McDonnell, review of *Empire and Nation,* p. 683; May, 2008, Steven Sarson, review of *The Mind of Thomas Jefferson,* p. 431.

Journal of the Early Republic, winter, 2000, Ronald L. Hatzenbuehler, review of *Jefferson's Empire,* p. 725; fall, 2000, Barbara Oberg, review of *Sally Hemings & Thomas Jefferson,* p. 566; winter, 2006, Edward Countryman, review of *Empire and Nation,* p. 668.

Mississippi Quarterly, spring, 2000, Stephanie M.H. Camp, review of *Sally Hemings & Thomas Jefferson,* p. 275.

New York Review of Books, May 13, 1993, Gordon S. Wood, review of *Jeffersonian Legacies,* p. 6.

Pacific Historical Review, November, 2002, Stephen Aron, review of *Across the Continent,* p. 494.

Pacific Northwest Quarterly, summer, 2001, Michael A. Morrison, review of *Jefferson's Empire,* p. 160.

Philadelphia Inquirer, July 3, 2000, Carlin Romano, review of *Jefferson's Empire.*

Reference & Research Book News, August, 2000, review of *Jefferson's Empire,* p. 49; August, 2005, review of *Empire and Nation,* p. 65; May, 2007, review of *The Mind of Thomas Jefferson,* February, 2009, review of *Declaring Independence: The Origin and Influence of America's Founding Document: Featuring the Albert H. Small Declaration of Independence Collection.*

Sixteenth Century Journal, winter, 2008, Wayne F. Anderson, review of *Empire and Nation,* p. 1177.

Times Literary Supplement, November 24, 2000, Gary McDowell, review of *Jefferson's Empire,* p. 30.

Virginia Magazine of History and Biography, summer, 2000, William C. DiGiacomantonio, review of *Jefferson's Empire,* p. 313; fall, 2005, Ian K. Steele, review of *Empire and Nation,* p. 416; winter, 2008, Richard B. Bernstein, review of *The Mind of Thomas Jefferson,* p. 79.

Virginia Quarterly Review, fall, 2000, review of *Jefferson's Empire,* p. 121.

William and Mary Quarterly, fall, 2000, Martha Hodes, review of *Sally Hemings & Thomas Jefferson,* p. 883; winter, 2001, James T. Kloppenberg, review of *Jefferson's Empire,* p. 291.

ONLINE

Institute of Historical Research, http://www.history.ac.uk/ (January 1, 2003), Michael A. McDonnell, review of *Jeffersonian America.*

Organization of American Historians, http://www.oah.org/ (August 3, 2009), "Peter S. Onuf."

University of Virginia Web site, http://www.virginia.edu/ (August 3, 2009), "Peter S. Onuf."*

* * *

OPPEGAARD, David 1979-

PERSONAL: Born 1979, in St. Paul, MN. *Education:* St. Olaf College, B.A., 2002; Hamline University, M.F.A.

ADDRESSES: Agent—Jonathan Lyons, Lyons Literary LLC, 27 W. 20th St., Ste. 1003, New York, NY 10011. *E-mail*—oppegaard@gmail.com.

CAREER: Writer. Has worked as an optician, receptionist at the University of Minnesota, standardized test scorer, farmhand, editorial assistant, trash picker for St. Paul public housing, library circulation assistant, and child minder on a British cruise ship.

WRITINGS:

The Suicide Collectors (novel), St. Martin's Press (New York, NY), 2008.

Wormwood, Nevada (novel), St. Martin's Press (New York, NY), 2009.

SIDELIGHTS: Writer David Oppegaard was born in 1979 in St. Paul, Minnesota. He earned his undergraduate degree at St. Olaf College in 2002, then went on to earn a master of fine arts degree from Hamline University. Over the course of his career, Oppegaard has held a wide range of jobs. He has worked as an optician, a receptionist at the University of Minnesota, a standardized test scorer, a farmhand, an editorial assistant, a trash picker for St. Paul public housing, a library circulation assistant, and a child minder on a British cruise ship. His debut novel, *The Suicide Collectors,* was published by St. Martin's Press in 2008, with his second novel, *Wormwood, Nevada,* released the following year.

In *The Suicide Collectors,* Oppegaard offers readers a twist on the post-apocalyptic novel, setting his work in the near future with the action revolving around a new type of global epidemic. While the spread of disease or the aftermath of war are common themes for this type of story, Oppegaard sought a fresh approach. Though he had never intended to write a horror novel, his fascination with the various types of epidemics that might result in the decimation of the planet ultimately inspired his story. Having shied away from killer viruses, zombies, and other types of plagues, he finally settled on the idea of a global suicide epidemic. He had read of a number of such epidemics that had taken place throughout history, and so decided on mass suicide as his central plot point, with the self-inflicted deaths resulting from an epidemic known as the "Despair." Though *The Suicide Collectors* is Oppegaard's first published work, it was actually the fifth book he completed. It was nominated for a Bram Stoker award.

The novel's hero is Norman, a man whose wife has recently succumbed to the suicide epidemic. Without his wife, Norman begins to drift, feeling as though he has nothing to live for and so must find a purpose. He finds that purpose in the plague that surrounds him, and sets out on a journey in search of a cure. With two companions, he travels from Florida across the country to Kansas, Seattle, and further, hoping to find some indication that the sadness leading to the epidemic of suicides can somehow be stopped. The country no longer resembles its previous state; it has become dangerous and, in some areas, sparsely populated. During his journey, Norman encounters a group known as the Collectors, individuals that show up at the scene of death whenever another person has killed himself, in order to remove the body. Ultimately, Norman discovers what is causing this terrible global situation, though the journey is difficult and long.

The heavy subject matter of the book wore on Oppegaard as he wrote. There was always a sense of possibility—a feeling that this type of epidemic could strike at any moment—a tone he deliberately cultivated by setting the story just a small step into the future. But the themes of death and hopelessness were the most difficult to deal with. John Joseph Adams reported for the *Sci-fi* Web site that "Oppegaard said it was a difficult book to write, since he had to dwell in a world devastated by suicide for several years. 'The author commented that "I basically 'lived' suicide as I wrote this book."'"

Oppegaard's debut garnered a nomination for the Bram Stoker award, as well as many positive comments and reviews. Rick R. Reed, in a review for the *Dark Scribe* Web site, declared that "this is one of those books that succeed on more than one level: it's a contemplation of death, a treatise on the bleakness that lives in all of our hearts, an homage to hope and human perseverance, and simply a damn good, page-turning read." Johnny Butane, reviewing for the *Dread Central* Web site, found some faults with the book, but praised it as a whole, stating that it "showcases an author with a lot of promise, despite some of the book's character drawbacks. That is the most common stumbling block of a first novel anyway, and believe me it's far better and more skillfully written than most debuts I've read." A contributor for *Kirkus Reviews* dubbed Oppegaard's effort "an inventive but erratic meditation on waiting for the end of the world." A reviewer for *Publishers Weekly* opined that "eloquent prose and haunting characters lift Oppegaard's astonishing debut." Writing for the *Book Reporter* Web site, Joe Hartlaub concluded: "At heart a metaphoric work, it is a book with which almost everyone can identify. Who among us hasn't heard the hum of the Despair at one point or another?"

Oppegaard told *CA:* "I can't recall any one thing that got me interested in writing, really, but it was probably television and movies like *Star Wars.* I wrote my first novel when I was fifteen. The novel began as a short story and just kept growing. From there I was hooked."

When asked about his influences, Oppegaard explained: "It's a huge mishmash of all the pop culture junk I've consumed over the years, the solid advice I've received from several teachers, and the books I've read and loved. In particular, I try to keep in mind the plotting and characterizing skills of someone like Charles Dickens, with an ear toward snappy dialogue *à la* Ray Carver, while sneaking in as much philosophy as I can, like Dostoevsky.

"I try to always create a world that really interests me, keeping in mind that as a novelist I will be living with this world for a long time and through many drafts. I start with one or two characters and build the world from there.

"A good day of writing maxes out at about 1,200 words, or five pages. I try to write five days a week when I'm working on a first draft. I consider a full second draft, and all subsequent drafts, a two-part process in which I edit the manuscript on the computer all the way through and then print it out and edit it again with a pen. Each novel averages at least ten drafts, with later drafts aided along by comments from my agent or comments from one or two other readers. Sometimes the story wants to end its own way, in defiance of the reader's wishes or the author's best interest. I love all of my books. I love *The Suicide Collectors* because it's my first published novel, and I love *Wormwood, Nevada* because it's what comes next."

When asked what kind of effect he hopes his books will have, Oppegaard said, "A good one."

BIOGRAPHICAL AND CRITICAL SOURCES:

PERIODICALS

Booklist, December 1, 2008, Keir Graff, review of *The Suicide Collectors,* p. 26.

Kirkus Reviews, October 1, 2008, review of *The Suicide Collectors.*

National Post, January 31, 2009, review of *The Suicide Collectors,* p. 13.

Publishers Weekly, October 27, 2008, review of *The Suicide Collectors,* p. 34.

ONLINE

Book Reporter, http://www.bookreporter.com/ (July 19, 2009), Joe Hartlaub, review of *The Suicide Collectors.*

Dark Scribe, http://www.darkscribemagazine.com/ (April 11, 2009), Rick R. Reed, review of *The Suicide Collectors.*

David Oppegaard Home Page, http://www.davidoppegaard.com (July 19, 2009).

Decider Twin Cities, http://twincities.decider.com/ (January 21, 2009), Stephanie Ash, "Dead-on Writing."

Dread Central, http://www.dreadcentral.com/ (July 19, 2009), Johnny Butane, review of *The Suicide Collectors.*

Fantasy Book Critic Blog, http://fantasybookcritic.blogspot.com/ (December 5, 2008), Robert Thompson, review of *The Suicide Collectors.*

IO9, http://io9.com/ (December 28, 2008), Charlie Jane Anders, "What If *The Happening* Was a Novel?"

Minnesota Post, http://www.minnpost.com/ (March 25, 2009), Amy Goetzman, "St. Paul Novelist Is a Finalist for Bram Stoker Award."

Quiet Earth, http://www.quietearth.us/ (December 30, 2008), "New Post Apocalyptic Novel *The Suicide Collectors.*

Robots and Vamps, http://robotsandvamps.com/ (February 23, 2009), review of *The Suicide Collectors.*

St. Olaf College Web site, http://fusion.stolaf.edu/ (April 9, 2009), Kari VanDerVeen, "David Oppegaard, '02, Talks about *Suicide Collectors.*"

Sci-fi, http://www.scifi.com/ (July 19, 2009), John Joseph Adams, "In Collectors, Suicide Isn't Painless."

Soulless Machine Review, http://www.soullessmachine.com/ (October 13, 2008), author interview.

Suicide Collectors MySpace Page, http://www.myspace.com/thesuicidecollectors (July 19, 2009).

Worlds of Wonder Blog, http://worldsofwonder.blogspot.com/ (January 1, 2009), Harriet Klausner, review of *The Suicide Collectors.*

* * *

OZERSKY, Josh 1967-
(Mr. Cutlet)

PERSONAL: Born August 22, 1967. *Education:* Notre Dame University, M.A., 1996.

ADDRESSES: Home—New York, NY. *E-mail*—editor@the-feedbag.com.

CAREER: Writer, journalist, editor. *Feedbag* Web site, editor; *Citysearch* local guide Web site, restaurant editor, 2008—; *New York* magazine Web site, food editor.

AWARDS, HONORS: James Beard Award for Food Writing/Multimedia, 2008.

WRITINGS:

(Compiler, with William Vesterman) *Readings for the 21st Century: Tomorrow's Issues for Today's Students,* 2nd edition, Allyn & Bacon (Boston, MA), 1994, 4th edition, 2000.

Archie Bunker's America: TV in an Era of Change, 1968-1978, foreword by Mark Crispin Miller, Southern Illinois University Press (Carbondale, IL), 2003.

The Hamburger: A History, Yale University Press (New Haven, CT), 2008.

Also author, as Mr. Cutlet, of *Meat Me in Manhattan: A Carnivore's Guide to New York,* 2003, *Meat-Men I Have Known, Tasty Talons of Belgium, The Cutlets Way in Business, At Table, Stampede,* and *Henry Porter and the Magic Wurst.* Contributor to periodicals, including the *New York Times, New York Post,* and *Saveur.* Contributor, *Oxford Dictionary of American Biography.*

SIDELIGHTS: A cultural historian, American writer Josh Ozersky also writes on food for numerous online publications and in that capacity is a one-man cheering section for meat. He has published books in both areas of expertise, including *Readings for the 21st Century: Tomorrow's Issues for Today's Students* and *Archie Bunker's America: TV in an Era of Change, 1968-1978,* and *Meat Me In Manhattan: A Carnivore's Guide to New York* and the 2008 title *The Hamburger: A History.*

Ozersky's work in cultural history deals with futurology and television. In *Readings for the 21st Century,* compiled with William Vesterman, Ozersky provides a selection of writing dealing with the single theme of the future. These writings vary in length, points of view, and style. Each section begins with a well-known essay by a prominent writer that gives some historical perspective on the theme at hand. This theme is then further explored by a myriad of contributions from contemporary writers, such as Amy Tan or Tom Wolfe, or from celebrities or business people like Bill Gates or former vice president Al Gore. The writings are designed to supply students with talking points about how the world is changing in their lifetime and what challenges might face their generation.

In *Archie Bunker's America,* on the other hand, Ozersky looks at television programming as an index to society and cultural changes from the era of the Vietnam War to the late 1970s. Here Ozersky looks at such shows as the contentious *All in the Family* whose protagonist appears in the title, to utterly non- or apolitical programs such as *Happy Days.* By doing so

Ozersky demonstrates in his study how television mirrors or echoes cultural and societal trends in American society as a whole. As *History: Review of New Books* contributor Amy Henderson remarked, Ozersky's study attempts to demonstrate how television "manifested and reflected the platetechtonic changes that knocked America off its middle-aged pins between 1968 and 1978." Ozersky does not simply use his own firsthand research of watching and reporting on the programs analyzed but further employs interviews with cast members of the shows in question, as well as producers and other industry insiders, including journalists for publications such as *Variety.* Ozersky also shows in his study that television, because of its ceaseless search for ratings, tends to be behind the culture in its content. Television is devoted to the status quo, and thus there is always a certain lag time between the creation of social movements and change and their portrayal on television. As a result of the tumultuous decade of the 1960s, television finally found a theme in relevancy and dealing with topical issues in the late 1960s. Similarly, after the Watergate years, there came some lighter and more family-friendly entertainment on television as a palliative. Henderson found Ozersky's work a "a well-reasoned book aimed at a general, television-viewing public."

Ozersky has also written under the pseudonym Mr. Cutlet, penning guides to eating out, such as *Meat Me in Manhattan,* a tribute to the carnivore life style in the Big Apple. Additionally, Ozersky plays the role of cultural historian in some of his food writing, as well, putting the lowly hamburger into historical as well as culinary context. *The Hamburger* is an attempt to make that supremely American food icon a cultural and business artifact of the twentieth century. It is, as John Gapper noted in the *Financial Times,* an "ode to the beef patty on a bun." Ozersky provides a history of the hamburger, tracing it back to nineteenth-century roots, and goes on to explain how, through shrewd marketing stratagems, it became the food of everyman, enjoyed not only in the United States, but also all around the world. The hamburger descended, as Ozersky shows, from the Hamburg sausage, which even then was recognized as the steak for poor people. Ozersky demonstrates how hamburger marketing strategies helped to give rise to modern marketing. The author looks at some of the most popular and successful hamburger chains, beginning with White Castle, founded by Billy Ingram in Kansas in 1916. White Castle actually pioneered many of the services, such as standardized production and the drive-in, which later Ray Kroc put to such powerful use in McDonald's, founded in 1955. What made the difference between the two chains, the author explains, was Ingram's inherent conservative view of business and Kroc's more freewheeling capitalism of property ownership and franchising. The difference between the two is now easily discernible; while McDonald's has a worldwide presence and a market capitalization of 67.2 billion dollars, White Castle is still primarily a much more modest and regional player. Ozersky looks at other chains, such as Wendy's and Burger King, examining their unique marketing systems, and concludes that, though nutritionists might bemoan the food value of hamburgers, they are certainly here to stay as a symbol of America.

Writing for the *Weekly Standard,* Victorino Matus observed, "How did a sandwich once reviled as something unsanitary and purchased outside factories and at carnivals come so far?" Matus's response to his own question: "The answer can be found in this little book, *The Hamburger.*" A contributor for the *Economist* also had praise for *The Hamburger,* terming it an "entertaining and informative book, which traces the burger's evolution from working man's snack during the Depression to symbol of American corporatism." As such, the same reviewer further commented, it "is nothing less than a brief history of America in the 20th century." Similarly, *Chicago Tribune* contributor Ted Anthony thought that "Ozersky's unusual blend of passion and common sense sets his book apart from others of its kind," while *Guardian* reviewer P.D. Smith called the same work "a sizzling homage to the hamburger, from working-class trash food to pop-art pin-up."

In an interview with Eric Butterman for the *Notre Dame Magazine Online,* Ozersky explained the origins of his food passion: "I always had an analytic bent on what I was eating. . . . I think it started when I was a kid with the Big Plain, a plain Whopper from Burger King. I started putting fries on the sandwich because it was too unadorned. Most kids don't think like that."

BIOGRAPHICAL AND CRITICAL SOURCES:

PERIODICALS

American Historical Review, April, 2004, Aniko Bodroghkozy, review of *Archie Bunker's America: TV in an Era of Change, 1968-1978,* p. 562.

Booklist, April 15, 2008, Mark Knoblaunch, review of *The Hamburger: A History,* p. 15.

Chicago Tribune, July 5, 2008, Ted Anthony, review of *The Hamburger.*

Choice, October, 2008, S. Hammer, review of *The Hamburger,* p. 323.

Economist, April 26, 2008, review of *The Hamburger,* p. 107.

Financial Times, May 17, 2008, John Gapper, review of *The Hamburger,* p. 16.

Guardian (London, England), June 6, 2009, P.D. Smith, review of *The Hamburger.*

History: Review of New Books, September 22, 2003, Amy Henderson, review of *Archie Bunker's America,* p. 5.

Independent (London, England), July 5, 2009, Lesley McDowell, review of *The Hamburger.*

Journal of American History, June, 2004, Michael Curin, review of *Archie Bunker's America,* p. 334.

Library Journal, June 1, 2008, Courtney Greene, review of *The Hamburger,* p. 120.

PR Newswire, August 18, 2008, "Award-Winning Writer Josh Ozersky Joins Citysearch to Dish about Food and New York's Dynamic Restaurant Scene."

Weekly Standard, September 29, 2008, Victorino Matus, review of *The Hamburger.*

ONLINE

Feedbag, http://www.the-feedbag.com/ (August 3, 2009), "Josh Ozersky."

Hamburger Today, http://aht.seriouseats.com/ (January 9, 2009), Adam Kuban, "Josh Ozersky and Hamburgers on 'Nightline.'"

Notre Dame Magazine Online, http://magazine.nd.edu/ (August 7, 2009), Eric Butterman, "Josh Ozersky, New York's Well-Seasoned Writer."

Yale University Press Web site, http://yalepress.yale.edu/ (August 3, 2009), "Josh Ozersky."*

P

PAGE, Tyler 1976-

PERSONAL: Born December 7, 1976; married Cori Doerrfeld (an illustrator); children: Charlotte. *Education:* St. Olaf College, B.A.; Minneapolis College of Art and Design, M.F.A.

ADDRESSES: *Home*—Minneapolis, MN. *E-mail*—mail@stylishvittles.com.

CAREER: Writer, artist, comics author. Minneapolis College of Art and Design, Minneapolis, MN, director of print technology; *Stylish Vittles* comics, Demention Comics, creator; *Nothing Better* comics, Webcomics Nation, creator; freelance illustrator.

AWARDS, HONORS: Eisner Award for Talent Deserving of Wider Recognition nomination, 2003.

WRITINGS:

"STYLISH VITTLES" SERIES; GRAPHIC NOVELS

Stylish Vittles: I Met a Girl, Demention Comics (Minneapolis, MN), 2002.

Stylish Vittles: All the Way, Demention Comics (Minneapolis, MN), 2003.

Stylish Vittles: Fare Thee Well, Demention Comics (Minneapolis, MN), 2005.

OTHER

(Illustrator) Bill Zimmerman, *100 Things Guys Need to Know,* Free Spirit Publishing (Minneapolis, MN), 2005.

Creator and author of *Nothing Better* comics for Webcomics Nation; maintains a blog at http://thetylerpage.blogspot.com.

SIDELIGHTS: Writer, artist, and comics author Tyler Page was born December 7, 1976. He attended St. Olaf College, where he earned his undergraduate degree in studio art, then continued his education at the Minneapolis College of Art and Design, where he earned his master of fine arts degree. He began drawing when he was just a small child, inspired partly by the comics that he loved to read and then emulate, such as *Transformers, GI Joe,* and the *Smurfs.* Later he moved on to more classic comics, focusing primarily on the strip comic variety that appeared daily in the newspaper over the standard comic books that required both an outlay of money and a trip to purchase them. He also had little patience when he was anxious to read the next installment. In addition, he had already started to create his own comics, and was ultimately far more interested in working on the books of his own devising than he was in reading existing stories, even in famous series such as *Superman* or *Batman.* His goal was to use his own drawings to tell a story, and by the time he started junior high school, he was serious about making comics of his very own, from design to art to text. Regarding the process of becoming a comics writer/artist, Page is adamant that the only way to improve is to practice and to absorb the details of everything one reads, until it becomes clear just what makes good work versus promising or simply amateur work. In an interview with Rachel Dukes for the *Poseur Ink* Web site, Page commented about the importance of reading in the medium: "Don't just read 'em and put them down. Read them, yes, but go back and look at the art, look at the arrangement of panels, etc., and figure out what about it works for you—what the successes are and what doesn't work. It will help in your own work." Page has applied this advice to his own work, and the results include his first comics series, "Stylish Vittles," which he publishes under his own label, Demention Comics, and his follow-up effort, *Nothing Better,* for Webcomics Nation. He has also provided the illustrations for Bill Zimmerman's *100 Things Guys Need to Know.*

The "Stylish Vittles" series of graphic novels, which received an Eisner Award nomination in 2003 for Talent Deserving of Wider Recognition, includes a number of issues originally published separately. The first of these is *Stylish Vittles: I Met a Girl.* This particular issue covers very personal material, as it delves into a relationship with a girl named Nanette, whom Page had dated while he was still in college. The comic grew out of an exercise that Page attempted, where he worked on short, one-page vignettes based on things and situations he experienced when he was in college. They all had an autobiographical bent to them, but Nanette soon became the focus. Page had yet to get over her, so it felt natural to write about her in order to exorcise the ghosts of their relationship. The story grew into the comic series from there, tracking their romance step by step. Page tries to maintain a very clear, honest attitude when depicting himself through his work, though he makes sure that the people from his life whom he includes in his comics are fine with his using their stories as an adjunct to his own impressions of the events. A reviewer for *Comic Books Resource* Web site commented of the series that "it's all the small quiet moments that bring a smile to your face as you realize these two people are destined for each other. They are two likable characters who you can't help but root for as they circle each other."

In *Nothing Better,* Page once again looks at college life, this time addressing larger questions of religion and belief and whether or not God exists and thereby giving the series a fresh voice and a new twist. The characters are rich and complicated, and Page's art has matured to match the more adult themes. A number of reviewers noted that Page has grown artistically since his earlier work. Randy Lander, writing for the *Fourth Rail* Web site, declared that "Page creates a variety of interesting characters, all representing very different points of view, and manages to make them all sympathetic or at least understandable, and the resulting mix will resonate with anyone who remembers their college days, fondly or otherwise." Alan David Doan, in a review for the *Comic Book Galaxy* Web site, stated that "Page's exploration of early college life is flawlessly convincing. . . . A moment when a character returns home and is shocked to learn her parents expect her to follow her high school curfew feels expertly observed, as do many other moments."

BIOGRAPHICAL AND CRITICAL SOURCES:

PERIODICALS

Publishers Weekly, August 18, 2003, review of *Stylish Vittles: All the Way,* p. 60; April 18, 2005, review of *Stylish Vittles: Fare Thee Well,* p. 46.

School Library Journal, May 1, 2006, Joyce Adams Burner, review of *100 Things Guys Need to Know,* p. 158.

ONLINE

Comic Book Galaxy Web site, http://www.comicbookgalaxy.com/ (August 7, 2009), Alan David Doan, review of *Nothing Better,* issue 1.

Comic Book Resources Web site, http://www.comicbookresources.com/ (August 7, 2009), review of *Nothing Better,* issues 1-3; review of *Stylish Vittles: I Met a Girl* and *Stylish Vittles: Fare Thee Well.*

Comic World News Web site, http://www.comicworldnews.com/ (August 7, 2009), "Young Artists in Love: A Conversation with Tyler Page and Cori Doerrfeld."

Fourth Rail Web site, http://thefourthrail.com/ (August 7, 2009), Randy Lander, review of *Nothing Better,* issues 1-3.

Poseur Ink Web site, http://poseurink.com/ (August 7, 2009), Rachel Dukes, author interview.

Precocious Curmudgeon Web site, http://precur.wordpress.com/ (August 7, 2009), review of *Nothing Better,* issue 1.

Simply Comics Blog, http://www.simpleweblog.com/ (August 7, 2009), Alan David Doan, review of *Stylish Vittles.*

Stylish Vittles Web site, http://www.stylishvittles.com (August 7, 2009), author profile.*

PAREKH, Hema 1964(?)-

PERSONAL: Born c. 1964, in Bombay (now Mumbai), India; immigrated to Japan, c. 1983; married; husband's name Atul (a businessman); children: two. *Education:* College graduate; headmaster's license in ikebana; studied bonseki. *Religion:* Jain.

ADDRESSES: *Home*—Tokyo, Japan.

CAREER: Teacher of vegetarian cooking.

WRITINGS:

The Asian Vegan Kitchen: Authentic and Appetizing Dishes from a Continent of Rich Flavors, Kodansha International (New York NY), 2007.

SIDELIGHTS: Born in Bombay, India, around 1964, Hema Parekh was raised in the Jain religion, which, as part of its philosophy of nonviolence, teaches vegetarianism. She attended university where she studied commerce and economics, but was married when she was nineteen and before graduation immigrated to Japan where her husband held a business partnership. She returned to India to complete her examinations and graduation, but has made Tokyo her home ever since. Parekh threw herself into learning about the new culture, taking an intensive course in the Japanese language; receiving a headmaster's license in *ikebana,* the meticulous art of Japanese flower-arranging, and studying *bonseki,* in which miniature landscapes are created with sand and pebbles on black lacquer trays.

Surprised by how many of her new friends were unfamiliar with vegetarian cooking, Parekh soon began teaching cooking classes featuring vegetarian recipes that had no meat and vegan recipes that contained no animal products, such as milk or eggs, at all. The people she met in Japan from all over the world, combined with her interest in vegetarian dishes, has culminated in her teaching vegetarian cuisine in the styles of many different countries. Initially invited to teach vegetarian cooking to classes at the Tokyo American Club, Parekh soon found herself on a new career path to teach others how tasty and nutritious a vegetarian diet can be. She lives in Tokyo, Japan, with her husband, Atul. They have two children.

In *The Asian Vegan Kitchen: Authentic and Appetizing Dishes from a Continent of Rich Flavors,* Parekh brings together recipes from nine Asian countries—India, Japan, China, Thailand, Vietnam, Burma, Indonesia, Malaysia and Korea. All the dishes are vegan, containing no animals products, and encompass a range of ideas that includes salads, soups, rice and noodle-based dishes, breads, desserts, and drinks. Being careful to suggest ingredients that are readily available in the United States and Great Britain, Parekh provides detailed instructions on how to use combinations of vegetables, herbs, and spices to prepare flavorful and healthy food, accompanying the recipes with colorful illustrations.

Reviewers enjoyed *The Asian Vegan Kitchen.* In her review for *BookLoons Reviews,* Mary Ann Smyth wrote, "*The Asian Vegan Kitchen* cookbook should satisfy the person already dedicated to vegan living as well as that soul who is contemplating going vegan," and the Eccentric Vegan said in *Vegan Soapbox,* "I think the cookbook is fantastic. It's a great addition to my kitchen and I'm sure it will improve my cooking."

BIOGRAPHICAL AND CRITICAL SOURCES:

PERIODICALS

Booklist, May 1, 2008, Barbara Jacobs, review of *The Asian Vegan Kitchen: Authentic and Appetizing Dishes from a Continent of Rich Flavors,* p. 62.

Christian Science Monitor, May 28, 2008, "Dressed-Up Veggies," p. 17.

Vegetarian Journal, July 1, 2008, Debra Wasserman, review of *The Asian Vegan Kitchen.*

ONLINE

BookLoons Reviews, http://www.bookloons.com/ (September 2, 2009), Mary Ann Smyth, review of *The Asian Vegan Kitchen.*

Japan Times, http://search.japantimes.co.jp/ (September 2, 2009), Vivienne Kenrick, "Hema Parekh."

Kodansha International, http://www.kodansha-intl.com/books/ (September 2, 2009), short author profile and summary of *The Asian Vegan Kitchen.*

Porter Square Books, http://www.portersquarebooks.com/ (September 2, 2009), author profile and summary of *The Asian Vegan Kitchen.*

Vegan Soapbox, http://www.vegansoapbox.com/ (September 2, 2009), Eccentric Vegan, review of *The Asian Vegan Kitchen.**

* * *

PARKER, Alan Michael 1961-

PERSONAL: Born January 11, 1961; partner of Felicia van Bork (an artist); children: Eli. *Education:* Washington University, B.A.; Columbia University School of the Arts, M.F.A.

ADDRESSES: Home—P.O. Box 7010, Davidson, NC 28035-7010. *E-mail*—amparker@davidson.edu.

CAREER: Poet, writer, educator. Davidson College, Davidson, NC, faculty member, 1998—, professor of English, director of creative writing; Queens University, Low-Residency MFA program, Core Faculty Member; previously on the faculty at Rutgers University, NJ, and Penn State Erie University, Behrend College, PA.

AWARDS, HONORS: Pushcart Prize for poetry, 1999; Lucille Medwick Memorial Award, Poetry Society of America, 2003; Editor's Choice Award, *Marlboro Review,* 2003; awarded fellowships from the New Jersey and Pennsylvania Councils on the Arts, and the Arts and Sciences Council; awarded residencies at the Seaside Institute, the MacDowell colony, and the Virginia Center for the Creative Arts.

WRITINGS:

(Editor, with Mark Willhardt) *The Routledge Anthology of Cross-Gendered Verse,* Routledge (New York, NY), 1996.

Days Like Prose (poems), Alef Books (New York, NY), 1997.

The Vandals: Poems, BOA Editions (Rochester, NY), 1999.

(Editor, with Mark Willhardt) *Who's Who in Twentieth-Century World Poetry,* foreword by Andrew Motion, Routledge (New York, NY), 2000, 2nd edition, 2002.

Love Song with Motor Vehicles: Poems, BOA Editions (Rochester, NY), 2003.

(Editor) *The Imaginary Poets,* Tupelo Press (Dorset, VT), 2005.

Cry Uncle (novel), University Press of Mississippi (Jackson, MS), 2005.

Elephants & Butterflies: Poems, BOA Editions (Rochester, NY), 2008.

Contributor of poetry to journals, including *American Poetry Review, Gettysburg Review, Kenyon Review, New Republic, New Yorker, Paris Review, Pleiades,* and the *Yale Review;* contributor of prose to various periodicals, including the *Believer, New York Times Book Review, New Yorker,* and the *San Francisco Chronicle.*

SIDELIGHTS: Poet, writer, and educator Alan Michael Parker was born January 11, 1961. He attended Washington University, where he earned his undergraduate degree, then went on to the Columbia University School of the Arts, where he earned a master of fine arts degree. He has served on the faculty of several universities, including Rutgers University in New Jersey, and Penn State Erie in Pennsylvania. As a faculty member for Davidson College in North Carolina, he serves as a professor of English and director of creative writing. He is also a core faculty member for the low-residency M.F.A. program at Queens University. Parker's poetry has appeared in numerous journals and other periodicals, including *American Poetry Review, Gettysburg Review, Kenyon Review, New Republic, New Yorker, Paris Review, Pleiades,* and the *Yale Review.* He has also contributed prose to various periodicals, including the *Believer, New York Times Book Review, New Yorker,* and the *San Francisco Chronicle.* Parker has published five books of poetry, as well as the novel *Cry Uncle,* and has served as editor or coeditor on several other volumes. He has been honored with several awards, including the Pushcart Prize, the Lucille Medwick Memorial Award from Poetry Society of America, and an Editor's Choice Award from *Marlboro Review.*

In *Days Like Prose,* Parker's first collection of poems, he addresses different ways of being alone, touching on everything from widowhood to the way one can feel solitary even within the confines of a relationship. A reviewer for *Publishers Weekly* praised the book for "the deft, formal quality of these poems coupled with Parker's eye for the telling detail."

The Vandals: Poems is a collection of humorous poems in which Parker, acting as narrator, pokes fun at his own medium and provides the reader with a light-hearted experience. He addresses the connection between reality and the words on the page, using heroism as a theme through many of his poems, linking the poems to the reality of history and also the myths that so often grow up out of heroic events. John Taylor, in a contribution for *Antioch Review,* declared of Parker's book that "it is a complex, hilarious, but also at times unexpectedly moving collection in which fragmentary, haunting, melancholic melodies alternate eerily with the brassy, percussive music of the vandals."

In *Elephants & Butterflies: Poems,* the title signifies the opposing sides of the poems that Parker has included in the volume. On the one hand, they are equal to the massive beast that is the elephant, and yet they range to the frail delicacy of the butterfly as well, coexisting within one book. Many of the poems deal with the commonplace, images as simple as a dog drinking water or someone commuting to work, but at the same time Parker is capable of taking the sublime and making it accessible, as he does in "Jelly Jar Ode," where heaven features a God who tidies up his office. A reviewer for *Publishers Weekly* described Parker's approach to the poems in this collection as "stumbling sometimes or telling too much, and sometimes anchoring his poems with poignant ironies and vivid images."

Parker's debut novel, *Cry Uncle,* tells the story of Ray Stanton, who has just undergone something terrible, even though he cannot quite remember what it was. He has obviously been tortured, and on a spring night finds himself thrown from the back of a truck, naked and confused, onto the side of a road in Ohio. Aside from the obvious problems, he understands that he cannot account for all of his time, that he has lost his memory of or blocked out a chunk of the evening. He has plenty of enemies as a result of his job, firing people from the local textile mill in the small town of Brighton, so it takes time and his slowly returning memory to piece together what truly happened. Parker uses his poetic talents in choosing words for his novel, making for a precise and powerful narrative. Mindy Friddle, in a review for her *Mindy Friddle* Web site, remarked: "Part mystery, part love story, *Cry Uncle* is steadily entertaining and a memorable debut."

BIOGRAPHICAL AND CRITICAL SOURCES:

PERIODICALS

American Book Review, September 1, 2006, "Climbing Sylvester's Ladder."

Antioch Review, March 22, 2000, John Taylor, review of *The Vandals: Poems,* p. 247.

Harvard Review, December 1, 2006, Molly McQuade, review of *The Imaginary Poets,* p. 203.

New Statesman & Society, January 12, 1996, Boyd Tonkin, review of *The Routledge Anthology of Cross-Gendered Verse,* p. 40.

New Yorker, July 14, 1997, review of *Days Like Prose,* p. 80; September 13, 1999, review of *The Vandals,* p. 106.

Prairie Schooner, June 22, 1999, Constance Merritt, review of *Days Like Prose,* p. 205.

Publishers Weekly, April 28, 1997, review of *Days Like Prose,* p. 71; May 19, 2008, review of *Elephants & Butterflies: Poems,* p. 36.

Times Literary Supplement, May 30, 1997, review of *The Routledge Anthology of Cross-Gendered Verse,* p. 25.

ONLINE

Alan Michael Parker Home Page, http://www.amparker.com (August 7, 2009), author profile.

Davidson College Web site, http://www3.davidson.edu/ (August 7, 2009), faculty profile.

Marlboro Review, http://www.marlbororeview.com/ (August 7, 2009), author profile.

Mindy Friddle Web site, http://www.mindyfriddle.com/ (August 7, 2009), Mindy Friddle, review of *Cry Uncle.*

North Carolina Arts Council Web site, http://www.ncarts.org/ (August 7, 2009), Aliki Barnstone, author critique.

Scene Missing, http://www.scenemissingmagazine.com/ (August 7, 2009), author interview.

* * *

PAULEY, Garth E. 1971-

PERSONAL: Born April 29, 1971. *Education:* Pennsylvania State University, Ph.D.

ADDRESSES: Office—CAS-DeVos, Communication Center, 1810 E. Beltline S.E., Grand Rapids, MI 49546. *E-mail*—gpauley@calvin.edu.

CAREER: Calvin College, Grand Rapids, MI, assistant professor of communication arts and sciences.

WRITINGS:

The Modern Presidency and Civil Rights: Rhetoric on Race from Roosevelt to Nixon, Texas A&M University Press (College Station, TX), 2001.

LBJ's American Promise: The 1965 Voting Rights Address, Texas A&M University Press (College Station, TX), 2007.

SIDELIGHTS: Garth E. Pauley was born on April 29, 1971. He received his Ph.D. from Pennsylvania State University in State College, Pennsylvania, and is an assistant professor of communication arts and sciences at Calvin College in Grand Rapids, Michigan.

Pauley's *The Modern Presidency and Civil Rights: Rhetoric on Race from Roosevelt to Nixon* is his examination of the rhetoric used by Presidents Truman, Eisenhower, Kennedy, and Johnson when addressing the issue of race and race relations in the United States. Pauley uses as examples an important speech that each of these presidents made about civil rights. In each, the speaker makes promises, which he cannot necessarily keep because of the limitations imposed on the president, but Pauley contends that the rhetoric used did, in fact, make a social and political difference, even if that president could not hold to his pledge. Pauley's intent is to show that the rhetoric used by a president can actually bring about change by encouraging discourse on a subject—in this case the issues of race and civil rights. He looks in depth at each speech, including the events and issues leading up to it, the personal opinion of the president who made it, how the speech was written, and how the audience reacted to it. Pauley believes that the presidents who made these speeches were courageous to take the stands that they did, but also believes that they could have said more.

Reviewers' responses were generally positive. The reviewer for the *Journal of Negro History* called the book "an intriguing look at how the modern presidency views race," and Mary E. Stuckey, in her review for the *Presidential Studies Quarterly,* commented, "This book offers a solid example of how political realities are reflected in presidential rhetoric." In his review of the book for the *Journal of Southern History,* Paul Frymer declared, "The strength of Pauley's book lies in its analysis of the particular speeches. Those interested in presidential rhetoric and communication will find this a valuable resource." David Zarefsky, reviewing *The Modern Presidency and Civil Rights* for *Argumentation and Advocacy,* stated: "Pauley's book can be read with profit by specialists and laypeople alike. Specialists will appreciate the fresh insight, carefully grounded appraisals, and seamlessness of text and context. Laypeople will benefit from the clear exposition of what a rhetorical perspective involves and how rhetoric contributes to Presidential leadership. And both groups should find value in Pauley's judicious judgments, including his admirable practice of not condemning a President's choices without offering an alternative that is realistic, feasible, and available."

LBJ's American Promise: The 1965 Voting Rights Address is another examination of a presidential speech. This speech, given on March 15, 1965, is considered by historians to be the best speech Lyndon Johnson ever gave. It was given to Congress to announce that Johnson and his administration were in favor of legislation to support African Americans' civil right to vote. In the address, Johnson managed to smooth over the subject of blame for the violence that recently had occurred in Selma, Alabama, thereby refraining from upsetting Southerners, while at the same time evoking "the American promise" and the mythic American dream of equality and justice for all. According to Pauley, the text of the speech was just as important as the historical moment at which it was given, and he carefully analyzes both the words Johnson used and how he used them. Pauley includes who the speechwriters were and how their input was used, basing some of his research on President Johnson's personal correspondence. Pauley also devotes a chapter to the reactions the speech received from the public.

In her review of *LBJ's American Promise* for the *Journal of Southern History,* Jill Ogline wrote, "The author's shrewd commentary highlights the speech's deft manipulation of the tropes of national mythology."

BIOGRAPHICAL AND CRITICAL SOURCES:

PERIODICALS

Argumentation and Advocacy, January 1, 2002, David Zarefsky, review of *The Modern Presidency and*

Civil Rights: Rhetoric on Race from Roosevelt to Nixon, p. 179.

Choice: Current Reviews for Academic Libraries, July 1, 2001, S.E. Schier, review of *The Modern Presidency and Civil Rights*; August 1, 2007, P.E. Kane, review of *LBJ's American Promise: The 1965 Voting Rights Address,* p. 2099.

Journal of American Ethnic History, September 22, 2002, James N. Giglio, review of *The Modern Presidency and Civil Rights,* p. 108.

Journal of Negro History, January 1, 2001, review of *The Modern Presidency and Civil Rights,* p. 83.

Journal of Southern History, August 1, 2003, Paul Frymer, review of *The Modern Presidency and Civil Rights,* p. 731; May 1, 2008, Jill Ogline, review of *LBJ's American Promise,* p. 518.

Presidential Studies Quarterly, September 1, 2001, Mary E. Stuckey, review of *The Modern Presidency and Civil Rights,* p. 550.

Southwestern Historical Quarterly, April 1, 2008, Jesus F. De La Teja, review of *LBJ's American Promise,* p. 465.

Western Legal History, June 22, 2002, Kenneth O'Reilly, review of *The Modern Presidency and Civil Rights.*

ONLINE

Calvin College, https://www.calvin.edu/ (September 2, 2009), author profile.

Texas A&M University Press, http://www.tamu.edu/ (September 2, 2009), review of *The Modern Presidency and Civil Rights* and short author profile.*

* * *

PAUVERT, Olivier 1973(?)-

PERSONAL: Born c. 1973, in France.

ADDRESSES: Home—France.

CAREER: Writer, pharmacist.

AWARDS, HONORS: Prix Carrefour for Best First Novel for *Noir.*

WRITINGS:

Noir, translated by Adriana Hunter, Counterpoint (Berkeley, CA), 2007.

SIDELIGHTS: Olivier Pauvert was born circa 1973 in France. A pharmacist by trade, he wrote his first novel, *Noir,* which won the Prix Carrefour for Best First Novel, released in the United States in 2007 and translated from the original French by Adriana Hunter. Set in the not-too-distant future in France, Pauvert's novel is a dystopian thriller that features a fascist government that has been democratically elected. France has become a very different type of country, where an atmosphere of fear is all-pervasive and a daylight curfew is under enforcement, limiting travel severely and forcing large portions of the nonwhite population to live in very isolated, rural areas. The protagonist, a white man whom Pauvert never names, discovers a woman who has been murdered—her harshly mutilated body strung up in a tree for anyone to stumble upon. Inexplicably, the man is arrested under suspicion of having killed the woman himself. He never reaches jail, however, as the van in which he is being transported is in a crash, and only the protagonist survives. At loose ends in Paris, he wanders around attempting to discover what precisely is going on, only to realize that he has somehow found himself twelve years in the future. From that point on, the book reveals one strange occurrence after another. First, the man discovers he has no reflection when he looks in a mirror or in shop windows; then he appears to be someone else entirely, his face and body having transformed while his consciousness remains his own. Finally, the man discovers he has the power to kill someone just by staring at them. Turned fugitive, the narrator travels the width of France, seeking answers to the state of the country. He himself has taken on ghostlike characteristics, while the people he encounters appear to have become zombies.

Ultimately, Pauvert has created a thriller that serves to criticize the French government as structured by President Sarkozy, as well as those French citizens who voted him into office. The themes of *Noir* reflect a near-future where the leadership's extreme adherence to more traditional policy and political thought results in restricted freedom, racial profiling, and extreme discrimination and control of the population. While reviewers had mixed opinions regarding the novel as a thriller, several noted that what makes it stand apart is its timely look at the culture and politics of France, and the applicability of its themes to many other nations as well. Lee Rourke, reviewing for *Book Forum* Web site, declared that "*Noir* is guilty of moments of clunky, plot-driven excess. It is shocking and occasionally brilliant but would have benefited from a steadier pace." However, Rourke also found Pauvert's work to be "a cheerless vision, explored with great vim, that grows brutal at an alarming rate." Jonathan Gibbs, in a review for the *Telegraph* online, remarked that "if you do want to find a political message in the book, beyond 'Fascism is Bad,' it is actually a rather conservative one. *Noir* is marked by a deep appreciation of la France Profonde, the alpine landscapes, sea ports and small towns through which its undead murderer hurtles." Keir Graff, in a review for *Booklist,* described the novel as "a powerful and promising debut, marred only by Pauvert's tendency to explain what he's quite capably shown." A reviewer for *Publishers Weekly* noted that "those expecting a traditional thriller with narrative drive will be disappointed," but praised the book as a different sort of achievement, dubbing it an "episodic, poetic book." Harriet Klausner, writing for the *Genre Go Round Reviews Blog,* opined that "readers who appreciate a forbidding gloomy suspense saga will appreciate the cat and mouse French morality tale in which fascism rules."

BIOGRAPHICAL AND CRITICAL SOURCES:

PERIODICALS

Booklist, October 15, 2008, Keir Graff, review of *Noir,* p. 26.

Books & Media, February 7, 2009, Paul Goat Allen, "Thriller *Noir* Blends Chills, Mystery, Sci-fi," p. 3.

Financial Times, June 2, 2007, "French Dread a Psychological Thriller Examines a Fascistic, Dystopian Future," p. 38.

Kirkus Reviews, October 1, 2008, review of *Noir.*

Library Journal, October 1, 2008, Jim Coan, review of *Noir,* p. 62.

Publishers Weekly, October 6, 2008, review of *Noir,* p. 36.

ONLINE

Book Forum, http://www.bookforum.com/ (August 7, 2009), Lee Rourke, review of *Noir.*

French Publisher's Agency Web site, http://frenchpubagency.com/ (August 7, 2009), author profile.

Genre Go Round Reviews Blog, http://genregoroundreviews.blogspot.com/ (August 7, 2009), Harriet Klausner, review of *Noir.*

No BS Book Reviews, http://nobsbookreviews.today.com/ (August 7, 2009), review of *Noir.*

Raymond Chandler Drank Here Blog, http://rcdhbookclub.blogspot.com/ (August 7, 2009), David Worsley, review of *Noir.*

Reviewing the Evidence Blog, http://www.reviewingtheevidence.com/ (August 7, 2009), Sarah Dudley, review of *Noir.*

Salonica Blog, http://blog.salonicaworldlit.com/ (August 7, 2009), "Babies, JFK, and *Noir.*"

San Francisco Chronicle Online, http://www.sfgate.com/ (August 7, 2009), Alan Cheuse, review of *Noir.*

Telegraph Online, http://www.telegraph.co.uk/ (August 7, 2009), Jonathan Gibbs, "Life on Mars in La France Profonde."*

* * *

PEARSE, Meic 1955-

PERSONAL: Born December 29, 1955; married; wife's name Anne (a nurse); children: Ieuan (son), Bethan and Rhian (daughters). *Education:* University of Wales, B.A.; Polytechnic of Wales, D.M.S.; Oxford University, M.Phil., D.Phil.

ADDRESSES: Home—Croatia and the United States. *E-mail*—Meic.Pearse@houghton.edu.

CAREER: London School of Theology, London, England, faculty member, head of theology program, ten years; Evangelical Theological Seminary, Osijek, Croatia, visiting professor of Church History, 1995—; Houghton College, Houghton, NY, professor. Has also taught at Oxford University; University of Newcastle; SS. Cyril and Methodius University, Skopje, Macedonia; Osijek University, Croatia; Timisoara University, Romania; and St. Bonaventure University, New York. Has worked with student ministries and churches and spent ten years aiding in the establishment of a new church in Swansea, Wales. Has additionally worked as a pipe valve maker in Germany and as a tax collector.

WRITINGS:

Why the Rest Hates the West: Understanding the Roots of Global Rage, InterVarsity Press (Downers Grove, IL), 2004.

The Gods of War: Is Religion the Primary Cause of Violent Conflict?, IVP Books (Downers Grove, IL), 2007.

SIDELIGHTS: Meic Pearse's first book, *Why the Rest Hates the West: Understanding the Roots of Global Rage,* was published in 2004. Given the volume's relevance to conflicts between Islamic fundamentalist groups and the United States, the book was widely reviewed and received a great deal of media coverage. Indeed, in an interview posted on the *Christian Book Previews* Web site, Pearse noted that "most Westerners have completely lost touch with the fundamental realities that underpin human social existence in the areas of morality, political order and social organization." Thus, Pearse finds more fault with Westerners than he does with fundamentalist ideologies. This interesting and controversial take was often commented on by reviewers. Yet, as Pearse explained in his *Christian Book Previews* interview, his intent was to do far more than provoke controversy. He stated: "Any writer of a serious book wants to change the world. . . . I would hope at least to introduce the terms anticulture and antivalues (as descriptors of how our outlook is perceived by non-Westerners) into public discourse. If so, we will have an ongoing reminder of what we need to move away from, of what we need to move back toward and of what is causing the real trouble that we have got ourselves into."

According to a *PR Newswire* reviewer, Pearse's first book "unpacks the deep divides" that exist between North America and parts of Europe and many countries in the rest of the world. The reviewer also noted that the author's "analysis offers insight into perspectives not often understood in the West, and provides a starting point for intercultural dialogue and rapprochement." Yet more praise was proffered by *Christianity Today* writer J. Dudley Woodberry, who found that "attempts to explain anti-Western feelings among Muslims have centered on weaknesses in Islamic societies and opposition to U.S. foreign policy. Church historian Meic Pearse bucks the trend by focusing on cultural differences—and along the way makes some prickly points about Western ways." Indeed, Woodberry went on to note that "Islam itself contributes to the rage against the onslaught of Western culture. These factors too—foreign policy and Islam—must be added to Pearse's insightful analysis to understand more fully why the rest hates the West." In a glowing *Booklist* review of *Why the Rest Hates the West,* Ray Olson commented that it is "possibly the best, most intelligent, most humane brief argument that the West, rather than the Rest, needs reform."

Pearse's second book, *The Gods of War: Is Religion the Primary Cause of Violent Conflict?,* was published in 2007. Like its predecessor, the volume was widely reviewed. Bill Meuhlenberg, writing in the online *Culture Watch,* found that "Pearse is no hawk, and he certainly does not let Christianity off easily in this volume. It has made plenty of mistakes, and has too readily been a cause of, or a contributing factor to, war and bloodshed. Yet when this complex and multifaceted issue is examined in close historical detail, the reckless charges of the secularists quickly unravel. Warfare is a multi-causal phenomenon, and religion is only one component of it at times, and certainly not the most important factor." This, then, is the main theme of the book; one that results, according to *Booklist* writer Olson, in "essential reading for those caught up in the new war about, not of, religion." Gary W. Jenkins, writing in the *Journal of Church and State,* applauded the book as well, finding that "Pearse's final section, the last three chapters, . . . contains by far the best and most engaging aspects of this work." Jenkins also stated that the volume is "a thought-provoking read, good perhaps for introductory college classes in which such issues arise, or among adult reading groups."

BIOGRAPHICAL AND CRITICAL SOURCES:

PERIODICALS

Booklist, June 1, 2004, Ray Olson, review of *Why the Rest Hates the West: Understanding the Roots of Global Rage,* p. 1678; October 1, 2007, Ray Olson, review of *The Gods of War: Is Religion the Primary Cause of Violent Conflict?,* p. 24.

Choice, May, 2008, J.W. Frost, review of *The Gods of War,* p. 1594.

Christianity Today, March, 2005, J. Dudley Woodberry, "Islam's Culture War: Author Says Muslims Are Troubled by Our Morals More Than Our Politics," p. 83.

Journal of Church and State, autumn, 2008, Gary W. Jenkins, review of *The Gods of War,* p. 717.

PR Newswire, February 8, 2005, "Houghton Professor Speaks to Senators and President Bush."

ONLINE

Christian Book Previews, http://www.christianbookpreviews.com/ (August 2, 2009), author interview.

Culture Watch, http://www.billmuehlenberg.com/ (February 15, 2008), Bill Meuhlenberg, review of *The Gods of War.*

Houghton College Web site, http://campus.houghton.edu/ (August 2, 2009), author profile.

Intervarsity Press Web site, http://www.ivpress.com/ (August 2, 2009), author profile.*

* * *

POMFRET, Scott
(Scott D. Pomfret)

PERSONAL: Partner of Scott Whittier. *Religion:* Catholic.

ADDRESSES: Home—Boston, MA. *E-mail*—scott@scottpomfret.com.

CAREER: Ropes & Gray LP, litigation associate; Gay & Lesbian Advocates & Defenders, cooperating attorney; United States Securities and Exchange Commission, Boston District Office, Boston, MA, enforcement attorney.

WRITINGS:

"ROMENTICS" NOVELS; WITH PARTNER, SCOTT WHITTIER

Razor Burn, BookSurge (Charleston, SC), 2003.
Spare Parts, BookSurge (Charleston, SC), 2004.
Nick of Time, BookSurge (Charleston, SC), 2004.
Hot Sauce, Warner Books (New York, NY), 2005.
E-Male, Palari (Richmond, VA), 2009.

OTHER

(With Scott Whittier) *The Q Guide to Wine and Cocktails: Stuff You Didn't Even Know You Wanted to Know . . . about Spirits, Stemware, and the Ultimate Way to Pop Your Cork,* Alyson Books (London, England), 2007.

Since My Last Confession: A Gay Catholic Memoir, Arcade (New York, NY), 2008.

Contributor of short stories to periodicals and anthologies, including *Fourteen Hills, Fugue, Ecotone, Post Road, New Delta Review, Genre Magazine, Fresh Men: Best New Gay Voices, Best Gay Love Stories 2005,* and *Best Gay Love Stories 2006.*

SIDELIGHTS: Scott Pomfret is a lawyer and author. He has worked as a litigation associate at Ropes & Gray LP, as a cooperating attorney for the Gay & Lesbian Advocates & Defenders, and as an enforcement attorney for the U.S. Securities and Exchange Commission, Boston District Office. Pomfret is also a Catholic who is openly gay. In fact, the seeming contradictions of Pomfret's faith and his lifestyle have been discussed in his writing, particularly in his 2008 memoir *Since My Last Confession: A Gay Catholic Memoir.* Notably, before publishing his memoir, Pomfret teamed with his partner, Scott Whittier, to write "Romentics," a series of romantic novels for gay men. The series was a homegrown success; the first few books were published via *Amazon.com*'s on-demand publishing service, BookSurge. As the books grew in popularity, however, Warner Books purchased the series.

Pomfret and Whittier's novels contain sexually explicit scenes, but they also include romantic plotlines and thus span both the romance and erotica genres. Indeed, as Pomfret told *Advocate* interviewer Michael Glitz, when Whittier and I have "just had sex, both erotica and romance are impossible to write because there's no motivation to get worked up again. But I think tenderness is a little harder to write. You've got to stay focused on your characters, so one sex scene can't be so different from another that it seems like different people." Discussing the series yet again in a joint interview with *Lambda Book Report* writer Chelsea Jennings, Pomfret and Whittier explained that "we draw from all kinds of stories and novels, ranging from Jhumpa Lahiri's work to Edmund White's novels to David Sedaris' wry observations on life. Also, Michael Bronski's *Pulp Friction* was invaluable to us in understanding the historical and social impact and the evolution of gay literature." The authors added that "for romantic inspiration, specifically, we draw on *Bridget Jones's Diary* and pop classic movies such as *Pretty Woman* and *Dirty Dancing.* All of these provide improbable but plausible tales of true love, with an infusion of comedy, drama and tenderness." Praising the 2005 "Romentics" novel, *Hot Sauce,* a *Publishers Weekly* contributor noted that "this is fun, fast-moving, fairy tale fluff custom-built for the softhearted gay beach set."

In addition to their "Romentics" novels, Pomfret and Whittier authored *The Q Guide to Wine and Cocktails: Stuff You Didn't Even Know You Wanted to Know . . . about Spirits, Stemware, and the Ultimate Way to Pop Your Cork* in 2007. The following year, Pomfret wrote his first solo full-length effort, the memoir *Since My Last Confession.* In an online *Denver Westword* interview with Amber Taufen, Pomfret stated that he wrote the book out of "sheer anger." He then went on to explain that "in Boston in the early part of this decade, it became increasingly hard to be both gay and Catholic, first with the pedophile priest scandal, which the Vatican tried to pin on gay priests, followed by Catholic Charities . . . ending its adoption program rather than comply with state law that requires them, if they do any adoptions, to work with gay parents as well as straight parents. Then the Vatican ban on gay men entering seminaries and the opposition . . . to same-sex marriage. My anger about that kind of robs the Mass, my worship experience, of a spiritual element."

Thus, Pomfret was inspired to write about his own experiences as a gay man in the Catholic Church. He even interviewed the friars in his archdiocese as part of the research efforts for his book. Yet, while the memoir itself was critically acclaimed, Pomfret was removed from his leadership position at St. Anthony's Shrine following its publication. Indeed, as Pomfret said to a contributor to the online *Lead Us Not into Temptation* Web site: "I anticipated in my book that perhaps the archdiocese might boot me out, but it never occurred to me that it would be the friars. . . . I am still kind of speechless." Indeed, given that the friars participated in Pomfret's research process, their reaction was a surprise. Regardless of the friars' reaction, online *Rainbow Reviews* critic Alan Chin said of the memoir: "I especially liked the helpful, tongue-in-cheek sidebars that enlightened me on such topics as how to detect a gay Catholic, three easy steps to being excommunicated, and the ten commandments of reading gay porn." Chin added: "I also was impressed Pomfret's interpretations of church doctrines." A *Publishers Weekly* reviewer, however, was far less impressed, finding that "although unfailingly lively, the book suffers from a lack of focus and a dizzying dependence on 'fun facts.'" Nevertheless, a *Lambda Book Report* writer observed that "Pomfret, a Boston trial attorney and a lay minister, is a committed gay Catholic. He writes of his experiences as an involved parishioner with the satirical sagacity of a latter-day Art Buchwald. This highly enjoyable memoir touches on every aspect of parish life, from eccentric fellow parishioners to the anti-gay edicts of the Cardinal-Archbishop of Boston, Cardinal Sean O'Malley."

BIOGRAPHICAL AND CRITICAL SOURCES:

BOOKS

Pomfret, Scott, *Since My Last Confession: A Gay Catholic Memoir,* Arcade (New York, NY), 2008.

PERIODICALS

Advocate, August 16, 2005, Michael Glitz, "Scott Pomfret & Scott Whittier," p. 8; September 11, 2007, review of *The Q Guide to Wine and Cocktails: Stuff You Didn't Even Know You Wanted to Know . . . about Spirits, Stemware, and the Ultimate Way to Pop Your Cork,* p. 60.

Lambda Book Report, June-July, 2004, Jameson Currier, "The Battle for Romance," p. 50; January-March, 2005, Chelsea Jennings, "Two for Romance"; fall, 2007, review of *The Q Guide to Wine & Cocktails,* p. 37; spring, 2009, review of *Since My Last Confession,* p. 21.

National Catholic Reporter, October 17, 2008, "Scott Pomfret," p. 4.

Publishers Weekly, August 30, 2004, "They'll Take Romance," p. 23; April 4, 2005, review of *Hot Sauce,* p. 40; May 5, 2008, review of *Since My Last Confession,* p. 58.

Reviewer's Bookwatch, March, 2005, Lori L. Lake, review of *Nick of Time.*

UPI NewsTrack, September 24, 2008, "Gay Memoir Too Racy for Catholic Shrine."

ONLINE

Boston Bibliophile, http://www.bostonbibliophile.com/ (August 2, 2009), review of *Since My Last Confession.*

Denver Westword, http://blogs.westword.com/ (October 8, 2008), Amber Taufen, "Q&A with Scott Pomfret, author of *Since My Last Confession.*"

Lead Us Not into Temptation, http://votingcatholic in2008.blogspot.com/ (September 24, 2008), "Erotic Male Fiction Writer Scott Pomfret Removed from Leadership at St. Anthony's Shrine."

Rainbow Reviews, http://rainbow-reviews.com/ (October 8, 2008), Alan Chin, review of *Since My Last Confession.*

Scott Pomfret Home Page, http://www.scottpomfret.com (August 2, 2009).

Since My Last Confession Web site, http://www.since mylastconfession.com (August 2, 2009).*

* * *

POMFRET, Scott D.
See POMFRET, Scott

* * *

POON, Janice

PERSONAL: Born in Alberta, Canada. *Education:* Holds an art degree.

ADDRESSES: *Home*—Toronto, Ontario, Canada.

CAREER: Graphic designer and writer. Has designed movie sets, created storyboards for animation, and worked as a fashion designer. Also a painter and sculptor.

AWARDS, HONORS: Merit Award, Annual International Cook Books and Culinary Arts, 2007, for *The Cocktail Chef Entertaining in Style.*

WRITINGS:

(With Dinah Koo) *The Dinah's Cupboard Cookbook: Recipes and Menus for Elegant Home Entertaining,* Totem Books (Toronto, Ontario, Canada), 1986.

(With Dinah Koo) *The Cocktail Chef: Entertaining in Style,* Douglas & McIntyre, 2007.

Claire and the Bakery Thief (children's graphic novel), Kids Can Press (Tonawanda, NY), 2008.

Claire and the Water Wish (children's graphic novel), Kids Can Press (Tonawanda,NY), 2009.

SIDELIGHTS: Janice Poon was born in Alberta, Canada, and attended an art college in Washington. Then after graduating, she began a career as a writer and graphic designer. She has also designed movie sets, created storyboards for animation, and worked as a fashion designer. Poon has also been a painter and sculptor, and her work has been purchased and displayed in the United States and Canada. Her work in graphic design has led her to live in such Canadian locales as Vancouver, British Columbia; Calgary, Alberta; and Toronto, Ontario. Her fashion design work led her to London and Paris. Later, after returning to Toronto, Poon began coauthoring cookbooks, ultimately becoming the sole author of two children's graphic novels as well. Poon's first book, written with Dinah Koo, was released in 1986. The volume, *The Dinah's Cupboard Cookbook: Recipes and Menus for Elegant Home Entertaining,* was well received by critics. Indeed, Leslie McGrath, writing for the *Manitoba Library Association Bulletin,* noted that "ambitious beginners and expert cooks alike will enjoy the *Dinah's Cupboard Cookbook.*" Twenty-one years after the release of *Dinah's Cupboard Cookbook,* Poon and Koo teamed up again to write *The Cocktail Chef: Entertaining in Style.* Like its predecessor, the volume was a success, winning the 2007 Merit Award from Annual International Cook Books and Culinary Arts.

A year after the release of *The Cocktail Chef,* Poon published her first solely authored project, a children's graphic novel titled *Claire and the Bakery Thief.* The story features Claire, who is sad about having to move with her family from the city to Bellevale, a rural town that is the direct opposite of everything Claire has known and loved all her life. Her parents have initiated the move to open an organic bakery, but the stress is causing them to bicker, upsetting Claire further. Applauding the book in a *Kirkus Reviews* article, a critic noted that the story "starts out as a perfectly nice bit of realistic fiction." Online *Quill & Quire* contributor Jean Mills was also impressed. She found that "while the story wavers, the illustrations never falter, depicting the action with clarity and style." Mills also went on to note that the book's protagonist "certainly has the potential to be an engaging heroine." In the 2009 *Claire and the Water Wish,* Poon presents a sequel to *Claire and the Bakery Thief.* Applauding the book in *Booklist,* Kat Kan praised the volume's "simple and clear black-and-white art, with expressive faces."

BIOGRAPHICAL AND CRITICAL SOURCES:

PERIODICALS

Booklist, April 15, 2009, Kat Kan, review of *Claire and the Water Wish,* p. 44.

Canadian Book Review Annual, January 1, 2006, John R. Abbott, review of *The Cocktail Chef: Entertaining in Style,* p. 131.

Kirkus Reviews, March 1, 2008, review of *Claire and the Bakery Thief;* March 1, 2009, review of *Claire and the Water Wish.*

Manitoba Library Association Bulletin, May, 1987, Leslie McGrath, review of *The Dinah's Cupboard Cookbook: Recipes and Menus for Elegant Home Entertaining.*

ONLINE

Cocktail Chef Web site, http://www.cocktailchef.com (August 2, 2009).

Cordon d'Or Cuisine Web site, http://www.cordondorcuisine.com/ (August 2, 2009), profile of author.

Douglas & McIntyre Web site, http://www.dmpibooks.com/ (August 2, 2009), author profile.

Kids Can Press Web site, http://www.kidscanpress.com/ (August 2, 2009), author profile.

Quill & Quire, http://www.quillandquire.com/ (March, 2008), Jean Mills, review of *Claire and the Bakery Thief.**

* * *

PORTER, Linda 1947-

PERSONAL: Born 1947; married; children: one daughter. *Education:* University of York, B.A., D. Phil.

ADDRESSES: *Home*—England. *Agent*—Andrew Lownie Literary Agency, Ltd., 36 Great Smith St., London SW1P 3BU, England. *E-mail*—mailmaster@lindaporter.net.

CAREER: Historian and academic. Lectured for ten years at Fordham University and City University of New York; British Telecommunications, international public relations senior advisor.

AWARDS, HONORS: Biographers' Club prize, 2004-05.

WRITINGS:

Mary Tudor: The First Queen, Portrait (London, England), 2007, also published as *The First Queen of England: The Myth of "Bloody Mary,"* St. Martin's Press (New York, NY), 2008.

Katherine the Queen: The Remarkable Life of Katherine Parr, Macmillan (London, England), 2010.

Contributor to *History Today* and *BBC History* magazine.

SIDELIGHTS: Linda Porter is a historian and academic. Born in 1947, she completed a bachelor of arts and a doctor of philosophy degree from the University of York before entering academia as a career. She lectured for ten years at universities in the United States, including Fordham University and the City University of New York. At that point, then married with a daughter, she returned to England and began working with British Telecommunications as an international public relations senior advisor. In 2004 she won the Biographers' Club prize, which reportedly gave her a nudge to become a writer.

Porter published her first book, *Mary Tudor: The First Queen,* in 2007. The following year, the book was released in the United States as *The First Queen of England: The Myth of "Bloody Mary."*

Steve Donoghue, reviewing the book in *Open Letters,* observed that when Porter discusses the relationship between Mary and Elizabeth, she follows the pattern laid down by previous chroniclers. Both women wanted desperately to be queen, but "English historians have always been reluctant to attribute the animosity between the two women to" this obvious fact. Donoghue further explained that "her subject was a prickly, willful individual, and Porter is to be given credit for not overlooking that fact. Readers . . . will not encounter hagiography. . . . Something like a three-dimensional portrait emerges." Donoghue pointed out that Porter cleverly evokes "the emotional subtleties that must have riddled relations between the two most problematic Tudors."

Donoghue continued, remarking that all of the historians who have written about Mary agree on one point, that she was every inch a Tudor. In fact, of all the Tudors, only she and her grandfather, Henry VII, had to fight for their right to the monarchy. Like all of the other members of this dynasty, Mary I was amply endowed with "raw physical courage." In the end, Donoghue concluded that "Porter has done a superb and richly rewarding job illuminating it for a new generation. Difficult woman though she might have been, Mary Tudor is at last lucky in her biographer." Frances Wilson, reviewing the book in the London *Telegraph,* recalled of Mary that "hers is a story we already know, but no amount of retelling can erase its grimness." Wilson concluded that "this is a richly researched, marvelously realised historical biography, which might not establish its subject as a humanitarian but shows that Mary certainly was contrary."

A contributor reviewing the book in *WalesOnline.co.uk* thought that the author "possibly takes too dismissive a view of the barbaric treatment of the religious dissenters," adding that "even in those brutal times, the burnings at the stake shocked Roman Catholic observers from abroad." A contributor writing in *Kirkus Reviews* remarked that the book "properly accentuates this much-maligned queen's achievements, but [is] not always convincing when trying to explain away her failures." Tonya Briggs, writing in *Library Journal,* claimed that the account would teach readers "something about the events of Mary's time and the people she knew." However, Briggs felt that insight into Mary's "personality and thinking" were absent. A contributor reviewing the book in *Publishers Weekly* commented that "this intelligent, engrossing biography succeeds somewhat in restoring Mary's reputation as trailblazer and crucial link in the" dynasty of Tudor kings and queens. Claire Ridgway, writing in *AnneBoleynFiles.com,* found the book to be an "incredibly well researched" account of Mary's life, adding that the section on her childhood "gives readers a good understanding of this misunderstood, and much maligned, monarch of England."

A person representing Porter told *CA:* "Linda became interested in writing at a very early age. Her love of history was kindled at the age of seven, when her grandfather picked a book off the shelf in a house her parents were renting, to show her the illustrations. The book was H.E. Marshall's *Our Island Story,* a child's history of England written in the early twentieth century and still in print today. Linda was unimpressed by the pictures, but she could not stop reading the words. Only recently did she learn that the author, Henrietta Marshall, was a woman. Linda was taught how to do historical research, and how to refine her writing, by two brilliant historians, Gwyn Williams and Gerald Aylmer, when she studied at the University of York. Her writing process is straightforward: begin researching the topic through secondary sources, to get the broader context and also an understanding of the latest scholarship, then move back into primary sources, both printed and manuscript. Visits to places associated with her subjects also form part of the research. She finds writing isolating and demanding but enjoys the process. Some authors claim that writing is an affliction. She has always considered it a great gift."

BIOGRAPHICAL AND CRITICAL SOURCES:

PERIODICALS

Kirkus Reviews, May 15, 2008, review of *The First Queen of England: The Myth of "Bloody Mary."*

Library Journal, June 1, 2008, Tonya Briggs, review of *The First Queen of England,* p. 104.

Publishers Weekly, May 26, 2008, review of *The First Queen of England,* p. 51.

Telegraph (London, England), November 8, 2007, Frances Wilson, review of *The First Queen of England.*

ONLINE

AnneBoleynFiles.com, http://reviews.theanneboleynfiles.com/ (July 7, 2009), Claire Ridgway, review of *Mary Tudor.*

Linda Porter Home Page, http://www.lindaporter.net (August 6, 2009), author biography.

Macmillan Books, http://us.macmillan.com/ (August 6, 2009), profile of author.

Open Letters, http://openlettersmonthly.com/ (July 30, 2008), author interview; (September 30, 2008), Steve Donoghue, review of *The First Queen of England.*

WalesOnline.co.uk, http://www.walesonline.co.uk/ (November 3, 2007), review of *Mary Tudor.*

*   *   *

POWELL, Diane Hennacy

PERSONAL: Married; has children. *Education:* Johns Hopkins University, M.D.; studied at Queen Square and the Institute of Psychiatry.

ADDRESSES: Home—Medford, OR. *E-mail*—info@dianehennacypowell.com.

CAREER: Psychiatrist and academic. Harvard Medical School, Cambridge, MA, former faculty member; Cambridge Hospital, Cambridge, former consultation-liaison service assistant clinical director; Brockton Multi-Service Center, Cambridge, former chief psychiatrist of the emergency room; McCandliss Center for Women, Chula Vista, CA, former clinical director; John E. Mack Institute, Boulder, CO, former director of research; in private practice, San Diego, CA, and Medford, OR. Survivors of Torture, International, San Diego, former branch founder of the psychiatry program; former Salk Institute member; Jean Houston Foundation board of directors.

WRITINGS:

The ESP Enigma: The Scientific Case for Psychic Phenomena, Walker (New York, NY), 2009.

SIDELIGHTS: Diane Hennacy Powell is a psychiatrist and academic. After completing her undergraduate studies in neuroscience, she finished an M.D. at Johns Hopkins University. Powell supplemented her education with further studies in London at Queen Square and the Institute of Psychiatry. She has held a number of positions, including being a faculty member at the Harvard Medical School, the consultation-liaison service assistant clinical director at Cambridge Hospital, and as the chief psychiatrist of the emergency room at the Brockton Multi-Service Center. She eventually opened her own private practice in Medford, Oregon.

Powell published her first book, *The ESP Enigma: The Scientific Case for Psychic Phenomena,* in 2009. The book opens new insight into the nature of consciousness by presenting a theory that can account for the positive results of experiments done on phenomena such as clairvoyance and telepathic interconnection.

In an interview in *Time* magazine with M.J. Stephey, Powell claimed that everybody is capable of having psychic visions and abilities, or extrasensory perception (ESP), but she admitted that certain people are more in tune with it than others, explaining that "genetics are likely behind it. . . . We know that it runs in families." In the same article, Powell discussed the stigma scientists face when dealing with the study of psychic phenomena. Powell explained that "there are theories about how the brain works, and what people do is design experiments to generate data that fits with that theory. If they run into data that doesn't fit into their theory, they just ignore it." Therefore, she concluded that "a true scientist will throw out the existing theory if they have a lot of data that cannot be explained."

In an interview in the *Parapsychology Informational Portal* with Maria Grazia, Powell continued her thoughts about the discrimination faced by scientists working with psychic phenomena. She revealed that "science will not accept anecdotal evidence," adding that "within science a single study is not considered sufficient proof because the data needs to be repeatable. So the greatest evidence is actually what is called a meta-analysis of the studies that have been done on ESP." Powell admitted that "there hasn't been a comprehensive and persuasive model to explain consciousness and psychic abilities." In addition to this, Powell asserted that "there is more evidence for ESP than there is for the use of aspirin to prevent strokes or heart attacks. The lack of a viable theory for the mechanism behind ESP has contributed to the skepticism."

Penny Cockerell, reviewing the book in *News OK,* agreed with Powell in finding that the scientific community "has thought too narrowly for too long"; she summarized by writing that the author "uses intriguing anecdotes and scientific findings to address the curious world of psychic phenomena. Much is unknown about why some people seemingly can predict future happenings or connect with the thoughts of others. Powell asks what is consciousness anyway? Does the brain actually create consciousness or merely process it?" Peter Rogerson, reviewing the book in *John Rimmer's Magonia Blog,* criticized that "as with many such writers, Powell really does not do justice to the many complexities and disputes within this field, and barely touches upon the skeptical critiques of many of the topics and personalities covered. The approach to parapsychology is not really scientific, and I doubt that this book will convince many agnostics let alone skeptics."

A contributor writing in *Kirkus Reviews* remarked that Powell "makes a persuasive argument that with the spectacular advances in particle physics will come a scientific revolution" leading to a new understanding of the human brain. The same contributor said that *The ESP Enigma* constituted "a cogent argument offering many striking examples of the power and potential of the unconscious." A contributor writing in the *California Bookwatch* suggested that new age and general readers alike "will find it involving." *Booklist* contributor Gilbert Taylor pointed out that "incorporating Powell's knowledge of neuroscience, this work should appeal to those open to the idea that" parapsychology and ESP are real phenomena. A contributor reviewing *The ESP Enigma* in *Publishers Weekly* stated: "Undaunted by the weak evidence, Powell asserts that she is on the forefront of a" neuroscientific breakthrough.

BIOGRAPHICAL AND CRITICAL SOURCES:

PERIODICALS

Booklist, December 1, 2008, Gilbert Taylor, review of *The ESP Enigma: The Scientific Case for Psychic Phenomena,* p. 17.

California Bookwatch, April, 2009, review of *The ESP Enigma.*

Kirkus Reviews, October 1, 2008, review of *The ESP Enigma.*

Publishers Weekly, October 6, 2008, review of *The ESP Enigma,* p. 45.

Time, December 24, 2008, M.J. Stephey, "The Science behind Psychic Phenomena."

ONLINE

Diane Hennacy Powell Home Page, http://dianehennacypowell.com (August 4, 2009), author biography.

John Rimmer's Magonia Blog, http://pelicanist.blogspot.com/ (February 12, 2009), Peter Rogerson, review of *The ESP Enigma.*

News OK, http://newsok.com/ (March 27, 2009), Penny Cockerell, review of *The ESP Enigma.*

Parapsychology Informational Portal, http://parapsych.info/ (January 30, 2009), Maria Grazia, author interview.

Walker Books Web site, http://www.walkerbooks.com/ (August 4, 2009), profile of author.

* * *

PRIESTLY, A.M.
See DOUGLAS, Anne

* * *

PROPHET, Erin L.

PERSONAL: Married; daughter of Mark and Elizabeth Clare Prophet.

ADDRESSES: *Home*—Boston, MA. *Agent*—Justin Loeber, Mouth Public Relations, LLC, 915 Broadway, Ste. 1009, New York, NY 10010.

CAREER: Church spokesperson. Church Universal and Triumphant, MT, former minister, messenger, and media spokesperson.

WRITINGS:

(With Elizabeth Clare Prophet) *Reincarnation: The Missing Link in Christianity,* Summit University Press (Corwin Springs, MT), 1997.

Prophet's Daughter: My Life with Elizabeth Clare Prophet inside the Church Universal and Triumphant, Lyons Press (Guilford, CT), 2009.

SIDELIGHTS: Erin L. Prophet is the daughter of Montana-based cult leaders. Raised within the Church Universal and Triumphant, or CUT, that her father founded and her mother popularized, she was nurtured to be a messenger of the church. Part of the way through her studies, she decided that her role of messenger carried too much sway over people and could easily be abused. After one of the church's failed predictions of Armageddon, Prophet left the group and began writing about her experiences. The result is her memoir, *Prophet's Daughter: My Life with Elizabeth Clare Prophet inside the Church Universal and Triumphant,* which was finally published in 2009.

Joe Szimhart, reviewing the book in his cult research information portal, the *Joe Szimhart Web site,* noted that much of the narrative that Erin has to tell was omitted from the book. However, what is left is more than sufficient to develop her thesis, which is partly that her mother had a definite gift for leadership but that what she taught was not a result of divine communication but simply a figment of her own imagination. The world of the Church Universal and Trimphant "was primarily dependent on one woman's stability in reason, ethics, and health." Szimhart continued, noting that the leaders of the church "depended on her parents the Prophets for their very existence." Not one of the children in the family was willing to continue the legacy begun by their parents. Szimhart concluded that "overall, I think this is a well-written book that serves a niche purpose beyond the author's personal story. For those thousands whose lives were personally impacted for better or for worse by Elizabeth Prophet's movement, Erin provides a valuable testament. I was among those thousands when I participated in CUT conferences from 1979 to 1980 before rejecting the 'Teachings.' However, when Erin departs from her family and personal story, her commentary is much less compelling."

A contributor writing in *Nonfiction Book Reviews* said: "I have mixed feelings about the book. I am glad to have learned more about cult culture, especially its history here in the US, but on the other hand, I think this is a book that I'll easily forget about. There are some books that stay with you long after you turn the last page, . . . but for me, this just won't be one of them." A contributor writing in the *California Bookwatch* remarked that this book "is an essential acquisition for any . . . new age library." *Booklist* contributor Mike Tribby remarked that the book is "good stuff about a powerful religious entrepreneur and her flock." A contributor writing in *Kirkus Reviews* concluded that *Prophet's Daughter* is "a must-read for anyone seeking to understand how cults operate and view themselves in relation to the world."

BIOGRAPHICAL AND CRITICAL SOURCES:

BOOKS

Prophet, Erin L., *Prophet's Daughter: My Life with Elizabeth Clare Prophet inside the Church Universal and Triumphant,* Lyons Press (Guilford, CT), 2009.

PERIODICALS

Booklist, October 1, 2008, Mike Tribby, review of *Prophet's Daughter,* p. 16.

California Bookwatch, January, 2009, review of *Prophet's Daughter.*

Kirkus Reviews, September 15, 2008, review of *Prophet's Daughter.*

ONLINE

Bozeman Chronicle, http://www.rickross.com/ (March 16, 1998), Scott McMillion, "Prophet's Daughter Is Writing a Book about CUT."

Joe Szimhart Web site, http://home.dejazzd.com/jszimhart/ (October 31, 2008), Joe Szimhart, review of *Prophet's Daughter.*

Lively Times (Charlo, MT), http://www.livelytimes.com/ May 4, 2009, Kristi Niemeyer, "Prophet's Daughter."

Nonfiction Book Reviews, http://nonfictionlover.today.com/ (January 13, 2009), review of *Prophet's Daughter.*

Prophet's Daughter Web site, http://www.prophetsdaughter.com (August 4, 2009), author profile.

Write Question, http://thewritequestion.blogspot.com/ (February 19 2009), Chérie Newman, author interview.*

R

RADOSH, Daniel 1969-
(Daniel Lord Radosh)

PERSONAL: Born March 12, 1969, in New York, NY; son of Ronald (a researcher) and Alice (an academic administrator) Radosh; married Gina Martinez Duclayan (a science writer); children: two. *Education:* Oberlin College, B.A., 1991.

ADDRESSES: *Home*—New York, NY. *E-mail*—radosh@gmail.com.

CAREER: Writer and editor. Freelance writer, 1992—; *Transom,* senior producer, 1995-97; *Mode* magazine, executive editor, 2003—.

WRITINGS:

Rapture Ready! Adventures in the Parallel Universe of Christian Pop Culture, Scribner (New York, NY), 2008.

Contributor to periodicals, including *GQ, New York Times, Playboy, Esquire, Entertainment Weekly, New York, Salon.com, Slate, McSweeney's, Spin, Details, Might, Forward, Mademoiselle, Talk,* and the *New Yorker;* entertainment editor for *New Youth Connections,* 1984-85; monthly columnist for *Scholastic Choices,* 1985-87; editor in chief with *Below the Belt,* 1988-91; staff writer and editor with *Spy* magazine, 1991-94; weekly columnist with the *New York Press,* 1993-96; senior editor with *Modern Humorist,* 2000-01; contributing editor to the *Week,* 2002—; contributing editor to *Radar,* 2003—; author of the *Radosh.net* Web log; contributor to anthologies; writer for television programs for VH1 and United Paramount Network (UPN).

SIDELIGHTS: Daniel Radosh is an American writer and editor. Born in New York on March 12, 1969, he graduated from Oberlin College with a bachelor of arts degree in 1991. Radosh began working as a freelance writer that following year and has contributed to a range of periodicals, including *GQ, New York Times, Playboy, Esquire, Entertainment Weekly, New York, Salon.com, Slate, McSweeney's, Spin, Details, Might, Forward, Mademoiselle, Talk,* and the *New Yorker.* He is a contributing editor to *Week* and *Radar* and is the author of the *Radosh.net* Web log.

Radosh published his first book, *Rapture Ready! Adventures in the Parallel Universe of Christian Pop Culture,* in 2008. The account examines the world of Christian pop culture by giving insight into Christian rock concerts, Christian retail shows, biblically based theme parks, Christian book publishers, Kentucky's Creation Museum, and Christian comedy clubs.

Ben Myers, reviewing the book in *Faith and Theology,* found that "although Radosh rightly critiques (and occasionally ridicules) these diverse aspects of Christian pop culture, his overall impressions remain hopeful and positive." In fact, Myers continued, Radosh is mostly "surprised by what he encounters." Myers concluded that "Radosh provides valuable insight into the workings of American evangelical pop culture. The book is . . . littered with surprising discoveries, zany characters, humorous observations and wise insights." Myers suggested that "in the end, though, I just can't share Radosh's optimism about the future of Christian pop culture. Instead, my hope would be for the demise of this pop culture, and for the appearance instead of a church that knows its own identity."

Hanna Rosin, reviewing the book in *Slate,* remarked that "reading Radosh's book is like coming across another planet hidden somewhere on Earth where everything is just exactly like it is here except blue or made out of plastic. Every American pop phenomenon has its Christian equivalent, no matter how improbable. And Radosh seems to have experienced them all." A contributor writing in *Flight into Fantasy* claimed that "the heart and soul of this book, actually, is Radosh himself. His style is chatty and confiding, and yet incredibly honest. There were times I was laughing with him, and times I wanted to cry for him. When he gets angry, as he sometimes does, he explains why, and I never felt that he was actually attacking anyone." The same contributor concluded that "if you're a fan of *This American Life* style journalism" and you appreciate or wonder about subcultures like the one described here, "I highly recommend this book."

Reviewing the book in *Forward,* Marjorie Ingall summarized that "Radosh presents a delightfully varied compendium of Christian items known among many actual Christians as 'Jesus junk.'" Ingall appended that "Daniel's a terrific reporter and a funny writer, but I think the book's strongest, most heartfelt moments come when he loses his poise." Peter Suderman, writing in the *American Conservative,* revealed that "Radosh approaches his project much as the Christians he meets approach theirs. . . . Being Jewish, he is naturally sensitive about anti-Semitic slights, and, being liberal, he is resistant to religious notions about abortion, homosexuality, and evolution. He hopes his words will prove meaningful to Christians, yet it is clear he is writing primarily for his own culture and class." Suderman claimed that "for all the respect he shows, his evenhandedness only goes so far. . . . Secular elite or not, Radosh has issued a brief for conversion—an altar call of his own."

Alexander Zaitchik, writing in *Alter.Net,* pointed out that while Radosh may not have begun his book expecting to respect some of the people he met during his research, he actually "ends by arguing for . . . openness on the part of secular culture when it comes to its Christian counterpart." Zaitchik countered that Radosh's plea for understanding runs almost immediately into a barrier: "many evangelicals do not want accommodation or cooperation with secular culture for the simple reason that they think this culture is evil." Once evil and Satan enter the dialogue, conversations become so polarized that they generally cease altogether. Zaitchik contended, nevertheless, that "the parallel world Radosh explores in his entertaining book will [not] remain frozen where it is in relation to the dominant secular culture. . . . Both Christian culture and its secular counterpart are fluid and overlapping; they are constantly interacting, with leading figures in each groping toward some kind of understanding (and higher sales)."

Kristen Scharold, writing in *First Things,* found that having researched the world of Christian pop culture, Radosh better understands it than many other outsiders do. However, because he is "operating from a completely different worldview," he cannot possibly grasp that Christianity will always exist as "a sort of parallel universe." Scharold proposed that "the greatest lesson in the book is not in what Radosh says with words but what he teaches by way of his tremendous example. If Christians treated American pop culture with the same respectful criticism and discerning openness that Radosh employed when examining the evangelical universe—neither rejecting nor accepting everything—these two cultures could have a productive encounter. . . . And rather than an apocalyptic collision, these two worlds could exist like neighbors, perhaps even offering to do the laundry every once in a while." *Boston Globe* writer Robin Abrahams, reviewing the work in *Miss Conduct's Web log,* mentioned that "it's a serious book. It's also a really funny book, because Mr. Radosh is one funny guy, and because he's got a rich, rich lode of material to work with."

A contributor reviewing the book in the *Atlantic* commented that "Radosh's exploration of Christian pop culture brings him in contact with some serious hot button issues—abstinence only education, creationism—and he offers some sharp observations on them. But I found the book most interesting when Radosh gets away from the political to engage with individual Christians about their lives as believers." *Booklist* contributor June Sawyers observed that Radosh "isn't afraid to use his well-honed wit to good advantage."

BIOGRAPHICAL AND CRITICAL SOURCES:

PERIODICALS

Atlantic, March 10, 2008, review of *Rapture Ready! Adventures in the Parallel Universe of Christian Pop Culture.*

Booklist, April 1, 2008, June Sawyers, review of *Rapture Ready!,* p. 11.

Dallas Morning News, August 16, 2008, Brad A. Greenberg, review of *Rapture Ready!*

Jerusalem Post, July 24, 2008, David Brinn, review of *Rapture Ready!*

New York Times, July 13, 1997, "Gina Duclayan, Daniel Radosh."

Reason, July, 2008, David Weigel, "Pop Christianity," p. 13.

ONLINE

Alter Net, http://www.alternet.org/ (April 22, 2008), Alexander Zaitchik, review of *Rapture Ready!*

American Conservative, http://www.amconmag.com/ (June 16, 2008), Peter Suderman, review of *Rapture Ready!*

BeliefNet, http://www.beliefnet.com/ (May 14, 2008), review of *Rapture Ready!*

Ebony Jet, http://www.ebonyjet.com/ (September 4, 2008), Patrice Evans, author interview.

Faith and Theology, http://faith-theology.blogspot.com/ (May 14, 2008), Ben Myers, review of *Rapture Ready!*

First Things, http://www.firstthings.com/ (August 14, 2008), Kristen Scharold, review of *Rapture Ready!*

Flight into Fantasy, http://www.flightintofantasy.com/ (March 15, 2009), review of *Rapture Ready!*

Forward, http://www.forward.com/ (May 16, 2008), Marjorie Ingall, "Stranger in a Strange Land," review of *Rapture Ready!*

Gelf, http://www.gelfmagazine.com/ (August 4, 2009), Adam Rosen, "Enlightened Consumerism."

Gothamist, http://gothamist.com/ (May 28, 2004), author interview.

Millions, http://www.themillions.com/ (May 11, 2008), C. Max Magee, author interview.

Miss Conduct's Web log, http://www.boston.com/ (June 9, 2008), Robin Abrahams, review of *Rapture Ready!*

Radosh.net, http://www.radosh.net (August 4, 2009), author Web log.

Rapture Ready! Web site, http://getraptureready.com (August 3, 2009), author profile.

Slate, http://www.slate.com/ (May 5, 2008), Hanna Rosin, review of *Rapture Ready!*

Soma Review, http://www.somareview.com/(August 4, 2009), Timothy Beal, review of *Rapture Ready!**

* * *

RADOSH, Daniel Lord
See RADOSH, Daniel

* * *

RAMSLAND, Morten 1971-

PERSONAL: Born 1971; married; children: three. *Education:* Earned degree.

ADDRESSES: Home—Aarhus, Denmark.

CAREER: Writer.

AWARDS, HONORS: Danish Book Award, Golden Laurel Prize, Author of the Year, Book of the Year, Reader's Prize, and Premio Berto, all for *Doghead.*

WRITINGS:

Hundehoved, Rosinante (Copenhagen, Denmark), 2005, translation by Tiina Nunnally published as *Doghead,* Thomas Dunne Books/St. Martin's Press (New York, NY), 2009.

SIDELIGHTS: Morten Ramsland is a Danish writer. He earned a degree in Danish and art history. Ramsland began writing poetry in 1993 and published his first novel, *Hundehoved,* in 2005. The novel was translated into English in 2009 by Tiina Nunnally and published as *Doghead.* The novel won a range of awards, including the Danish Book Award, Golden Laurel Prize, Author of the Year, Book of the Year, Reader's Prize, and the Premio Berto. The story spans three generations of the narrator's family, highlighting humorous moments dotted around the family tree, ranging from infidelity to financial problems.

In an article in *EdinburghGuide.com,* Ramsland confessed that the novel does not represent "the story of my own family," explaining: "I drew inspiration from my own family. There is a treasure of good stories in my own family, and I took the best stories from it." Ramsland also commented that "if you are using humour, it's often the right way you can come closer to serious subject matter. It's a better path to the truth."

Annette Hougaard, reviewing the book on the *Nordic Literature 2006 Web site,* said that "the tone in which the book is written, together with the way in which, whatever happens to the characters, they carry on their unhappy lives notwithstanding—and become whole human beings in the few brighter moments which, after all, do occur—ensures that one isn't just left with a bad taste in one's mouth, but on the contrary feels challenged to look at one's own life in a different light." Hougaard concluded that "with its blend of social, psychological, and grotesque realism, *Hundehoved* (*Doghead*) has added a new dimension to Danish family sagas." A contributor writing in *World of Books* noted that "the stories are even wilder than the characters." The same contributor concluded that "*Doghead* is a strange book. A dark book. I am not sure I liked it. But I will remember it. And I do think it is well worth reading."

A contributor reviewing the book in *Lanew-Yorkaise.com* commented that the narrator "illuminates how pain, loss, and laughter are carried through generations to manifest themselves in the most unexpected of places." The same contributor concluded that "*Doghead* is an unapologetic exploration of the ugly sides of marriage and the legacy that parents can leave to children, but there is hope in the humor and, Ramsland seems to say, the creation of art to tell stories." *Booklist* contributor Thomas Gaughan said that the novel "is brilliant, exhilarating, and haunting. The characters and their stories will stay with thoughtful readers."

A contributor reviewing the book in *Publishers Weekly* claimed that the author "masterfully captures a zigzagging litany of recollections across generations and the cold North Sea." Kate Ward, reviewing the book in *Entertainment Weekly,* commented that the novel, "which has plenty of bite—is definitely worth the effort." A contributor writing in *Kirkus Reviews* called the book "an earthy, funny, unflinching family history." On the other hand, Clare Clark, writing in the *New York Times Book Review,* found that "despite its earthy comedy," the novel "is ultimately a bleak book. The thread that binds the stories is a belief in endurance, in the ability of ordinary people to survive no matter the horrors they suffer and the cruelties they effect. In the characters' rare moments of reflection there is self-pity in abundance but precious little tenderness or compassion." Reviewing the novel in *Library Journal,* K.H. Cumiskey "enthusiastically recommended" *Doghead,* appending that it "is so entertaining readers will want to devour it in a sitting or two."

BIOGRAPHICAL AND CRITICAL SOURCES:

PERIODICALS

Booklist, December 1, 2008, Thomas Gaughan, review of *Doghead,* p. 21.

Entertainment Weekly, March 6, 2009, Kate Ward, review of *Doghead,* p. 77.

Kirkus Reviews, November 15, 2008, review of *Doghead.*

Library Journal, February 15, 2009, K.H. Cumiskey, review of *Doghead,* p. 97.

New York Times Book Review, March 1, 2009, Clare Clark, review of *Doghead,* p. 17.

Publishers Weekly, October 6, 2008, review of *Doghead,* p. 33.

ONLINE

Booklounge.ca, http://www.booklounge.ca/ (August 5, 2009), author profile.

EdinburghGuide.com, http://www.edinburghguide.com/ (August 20, 2007), Per Fischer, "Talk by Authors Rodge Glass and Morten Ramsland."

Lanew-Yorkaise.com, http://lanew-yorkaise.com/ (August 5, 2009), review of *Doghead.*

Macmillan Web site, http://us.macmillan.com/ (August 5, 2009), profile of author.

Nordic Literature 2006 Web site, http://www.nordic-literature.org/ (August 5, 2009), Annette Hougaard, review of *Doghead.*

PEN American Center Web site, http://www.pen.org/ (August 5, 2009), author profile.

World of Books, http://www.leserglede.com/engblogg/ (June 8, 2009), review of *Doghead.**

* * *

READ, Frank T. 1938-

PERSONAL: Born July 16, 1938, in Ogden, UT. *Education:* Brigham Young University, B.A., 1960; Duke University, J.D., 1963.

CAREER: Writer and educator. University of Florida, College of Law, professor and dean, 1981-88; University of California, Hastings College of Law, San Francisco, dean and chief executive officer, 1988-93; South Texas College of Law, dean and president, 1995—.

WRITINGS:

NONFICTION

Let Them Be Judged: The Judicial Integration of the Deep South, Scarecrow Press (Metuchen, NJ), 1978.

Oklahoma Evidence Handbook: A Practitioner's Guide to the Oklahoma Evidence Code and to the Federal Rules of Evidence, Oklahoma Bar Review (Norman, OK), 1979.

Read's Florida Evidence, Callaghan (Wilmette, IL), 1987.

(With Rennard Strickland) *The Lawyer Myth: A Defense of the American Legal Profession,* Ohio University Press (Athens, OH), 2008.

SIDELIGHTS: Frank T. Read was born on July 16, 1938, in Ogden, Utah. Educated at Brigham Young University and Duke University, Read later served as a professor of law at the University of Florida and as a dean for the University of California Hastings College of Law and the South Texas College of Law.

Released in 1978, Read's *Let Them Be Judged: The Judicial Integration of the Deep South* chronicles the evolution in judicial policy from the passage of *Brown v. Board of Education.* Covering approximately twenty years of legal history, Read presents the cause-and-effect relationship between historical events and legal policy which have shaped the modern judicial system. Read also details the landmark issues the justice system encountered during the Civil Rights movement. Exposing the weakness of the southern legal system with regard to segregation and other racist policy, the text exposes how federal courts dealt with changing legal precedent involving racism, ethnicity, and class division. Read's subsequent release also explores judicial history and offers a comprehensive overview of Oklahoma legal standards and codes. In the *Oklahoma Evidence Handbook: A Practitioner's Guide to the Oklahoma Evidence Code and to the Federal Rules of Evidence,* Read presents information regarding professional codes, rules for state and district courts, as well as appellate, criminal, and bankruptcy procedures wherein evidentiary requirements are practiced. Additionally, within the text's 326 pages, Read details evidentiary precedent and the case law pertaining to the inclusion of evidence in case proceedings.

Widening his scope from judicial practice to perceptions of the legal system, Read chronicles the evolution of negativity regarding the practice of law in *The Lawyer Myth: A Defense of the American Legal Profession,* written with Rennard Strickland. The text seeks to explain why lawyers have acquired such a negative reputation during the profession's very recent history. *The Lawyer Myth* explains why society needs lawyers and how the degradation of the profession does not benefit those people who rely on the law to preserve and protect their freedoms. A *Reference & Research Book News* contributor claimed that the authors "make a good case for the accused and end with a rousing exhortation." Moreover, Vernon Ford, in an article for *Booklist,* concluded that although the text "is not likely to stop lawyer jokes," it does offer "an insightful look at a much-maligned profession."

BIOGRAPHICAL AND CRITICAL SOURCES:

PERIODICALS

ABA Journal, January 1, 1980, Patrick E. Higginbotham, review of *Let Them Be Judged: The Judicial Integration of the Deep South,* p. 82.

Bench & Bar of Minnesota, April 1, 2008, review of *The Lawyer Myth: A Defense of the American Legal Profession,* p. 35.

Booklist, May 1, 2008, Vernon Ford, review of *The Lawyer Myth,* p. 59.

Howard Law Journal, June 22, 1980, Caliph Johnson, review of *Let Them Be Judged,* p. 599.

Reference & Research Book News, August 1, 2008, review of *The Lawyer Myth.*

Vanderbilt Law Review, March 1, 1980, Steven F. Lawson, review of *Let Them Be Judged,* p. 517.

ONLINE

Chapman University School of Law Web site, http://www.chapman.edu/ (August 14, 2009), faculty profile.

University of Florida Levin College of Law Web site, http://www.law.ufl.edu/ (August 14, 2009), faculty profile.*

* * *

REID, Verna 1928-

PERSONAL: Born 1928. *Education:* University of Calgary, Ph.D., 2003.

CAREER: Writer and educator. Alberta College of Art and Design, Calgary, Alberta, Canada, lecturer emerita, 1971—.

WRITINGS:

Women Between: Construction of Self in the Work of Sharon Butala, Aganetha Dyck, Mary Meigs and Mary Pratt, University of Calgary Press (Calgary, NY), 2008.

SIDELIGHTS: Verna Reid, born in 1928, has served as a lecturer at the Alberta College of Art and Design since 1971. In 2003, she received her Ph.D. from the University of Calvary. Using materials she had acquired during her doctoral research, Reid released *Women Between: Construction of Self in the Work of Sharon Butala, Aganetha Dyck, Mary Meigs and Mary Pratt.* "*Women Between* explores the practice of autobiographically based art, literary or visual or both, of a group of senior Canadian women," according to an article by Linda Quirk for *Canadian Literature.* The text, released in 2008, covers works of self reflective literature, painting, and mixed media compositions by women who created original works during their senior years. Reid explains that Sharon Butala, a Canadian novelist, produced much of her acclaimed work while in her fifties and sixties. Likewise, visual artist Aganetha Dyck, born in 1937, attended college in her forties and has produced a series of exhibitions for the Burnaby Art Gallery, including *Collaborating in the Darkness of the Bee Hive,* which she created while in her sixties. The late Mary Meigs, Reid explains, not only lived openly as a lesbian during the conservative 1950s but also published a memoiresque novel titled *In the Company of Strangers* in 1991 at the age of seventy-four. And, Mary Frances Pratt, perhaps the youngest of Reid subjects, won the Canadian Molson Prize in 1997 at the age of sixty-two.

Quirk explained, "Frequently reading against the texts and reading life writing as well as fictional and visual forms as autobiographical, Reid supplements such readings with extensive interviews and relies on a range of theorists (from sociologists to theologians to literary critics) to develop a highly structured portrait of shifting personal identities." Reid attempts to unify these identities with shared elements, such as age, generational background, professional experience, and domestic attachments. Reid's conclusion suggests that these artists provide a canon of work defined by a particular attitude, spirit, and ambition. From comparative theory to close readings, Reid examines these women's works within the context of exceptionalism. Moreover the text has an increasingly positive and hopeful tone underpinned by the examples of mature creativity and talent. Quirk claimed the narrative presents "a highly unified portrait" of mature artists who redefine the meaning of aging and thwart stereotypes of senior practices. Reid's "sense of sisterhood with her subjects enriches this inspiring work," concluded a *Reference & Research Book News* contributor.

BIOGRAPHICAL AND CRITICAL SOURCES:

PERIODICALS

Reference & Research Book News, November 1, 2008, review of *Women Between: Construction of Self in the Work of Sharon Butala, Aganetha Dyck, Mary Meigs, and Mary Pratt.*

ONLINE

Calgary Herald Online, http://www2.canada.com/ (February 1, 2009), Eric Volmers, "A New Golden Age."

Canadian Literature Online, http://www.canlit.ca/ (August 17, 2009), Linda Quirk, "Love and Liminality."

Michigan State University Press Web site, http://msupress.msu.edu/ (August 17, 2009), author profile.

University of Calgary Web site, http://www.ucalgary.ca/ (August 17, 2009), author profile.*

* * *

RESNICK, Rachel 1964(?)-

PERSONAL: Born c. 1964. *Education:* Yale University, B.A.; Vermont College, M.F.A.

ADDRESSES: *Home*—Topanga, CA. *Agent*—Pilar Queen, McCormick & Williams, 37 W. 20th St., New York, NY 10011. *E-mail*—info@rachelresnick.com.

CAREER: Creative writing instructor and writer. University of California, Los Angeles, writing instructor; Writers on Fire, founder and chief executive officer. Has also lectured at University of Southern California, Loyola Marymount University, CalArts, Los Angeles Community College, Whittier College, Emerson College, and Antioch College.

WRITINGS:

*Go West Young F*cked-up Chick: A Novel of Separation,* St. Martin's Press (New York, NY), 1999.

Love Junkie: A Memoir, Bloomsbury USA (New York, NY), 2008.

Contributor to periodicals, including *Los Angeles Times, Marie Claire, Women's Health,* and *BlackBook;* contributor to anthologies; contributing editor to *Tin House* magazine.

SIDELIGHTS: Rachel Resnick is a writer and creative writing instructor. A graduate of Yale University and Vermont College's M.F.A program, she went on to teach creative writing at a number of colleges and universities in the Los Angeles area. She also heads the Writers on Fire writer's retreat.

Resnick published her first novel, *Go West Young F*cked-up Chick: A Novel of Separation,* in 1999. Somewhat autobiographical, the novel follows Rebecca Roth on her cross-country trip to get away from a dark past and the suicidal death of her troubled mother.

Whitney Scott, reviewing the novel in *Booklist,* said that it is a "darkly comic vision of wanna-be redemption in a modern hell Dante could appreciate." Scott found it "oddly compelling." A contributor writing in *Publishers Weekly* criticized all the jumping around in the nonchronological telling of the story, adding that "the distanced reader gains only a fractured portrait of Rebecca, the city and the time period." The same contributor observed that "the prose is outweighed by the pose."

In 2008 Resnick published *Love Junkie: A Memoir.* The memoir tells of the author's troubled childhood, dangerous relationships, and her path to recovery. Kelly Hartog, writing in the *California Literary Review,* observed that "reconciling her life and her relationships . . . is a slow, painful process that is not tied up in neat little bows at the end of the memoir. This is real life. It's Resnick's life to be sure, but there are elements of despair, hope and the need for love, recognition and acceptance that are part of all of our lives." Hartog added: "That Resnick has managed to lead a successful life as a writer . . . is a testament to her facing her demons head on and undertaking a 12-step program for those addicted to love, sex, romance, and fantasy." Writing in the *Chronicle of Higher Education,* Carlin Romano discussed the topic of writers who pen memoirs using their own unique styles, adding that Resnick is "full frontal in that genre."

Martha Frankel, writing in the *New York Post,* revealed that "Resnick writes about her Dickensonian past with no plea for sympathy; she lets the sex stories turn you on, and then riddle you with revulsion." Frankel pointed out that one flaw in the book, however, is "Resnick's not-so-cute idea of addressing the reader directly every now and then. It's jolting, but not as much as the high octane stories Resnick chooses to tell." Sara Vilkomerson, reviewing the memoir in the *New York Observer,* noted that the memoir had the potential to be "seriously annoying—whiny, victimy, self-indulgent. Except that Ms. Resnick is so brutally honest about her own complicit behavior—to the point where you just can't believe anyone would be willing to admit such embarrassing—and (unfortunately for some of us) occasionally familiar—behavior."

Writing in the *San Francisco Chronicle,* Christina Eng stated: "That Resnick gets the professional help she needs to finally save herself is admirable. . . . We trust that she is better now than she was then." Eng remarked, however, that "the reassurance does not make her narrative any more pleasant to read. It does not negate the humiliation and degradation to which she repeatedly subjects herself over the years." William Leith, reviewing the book in London's *Evening Standard,* called the account "gripping." Kate Whiting, reviewing the book in *IOMToday.co.im,* pointed out that "there is real emotion in the tender passages about her parents." Hephzibah Anderson, writing in the London *Observer,* claimed: "To describe this book as soul-baring is to undersell its bloodied candour. Its revelations are gynaecological, its prose thrumming with overwrought images." Anderson added: "Yet this cocktail of obsession, scattershot humour and self-excoriating insights is also readable enough that you don't realise how jading it is until you put it down."

Elizabeth Bachner, writing in *Bookslut,* observed that Resnick tells her story "with raw honesty, although, since names and details are changed to protect everyone's privacy, only the particulars of the abuse are true. It's hard to read, and hard to put down. There may be a dark value to this literary nakedness, but it's not actually healing, at all. In fact, for people working through abuse . . . this genre is probably more triggering than anything else." *Booklist* contributor Allison Block noticed that the memoir's prose is "as direct and uninhibited as her subject matter," adding that it "may be a bit too racy for some." Vanessa Juarez, writing in *Entertainment Weekly,* also found it "difficult to slog through more than 200 pages of gory self-destruction." A contributor writing in *Kirkus Reviews* nevertheless stated that *Love Junkie* is "an important memoir about romantic/sexual addiction and the potential cures . . . if it's accurate."

BIOGRAPHICAL AND CRITICAL SOURCES:

BOOKS

Resnick, Rachel, *Love Junkie: A Memoir,* Bloomsbury USA (New York, NY), 2008.

PERIODICALS

Booklist, March 1, 1999, Whitney Scott, review of *Go West Young F*cked-up Chick: A Novel of Separation,* p. 1156; December 1, 2008, Allison Block, review of *Love Junkie,* p. 13.

Chronicle of Higher Education, November 28, 2008, Carlin Romano, review of *Love Junkie,* p. B5.

Entertainment Weekly, November 28, 2008, Vanessa Juarez, review of *Love Junkie,* p. 79.

Evening Standard (London, England), January 23, 2009, William Leith, review of *Love Junkie.*

Kirkus Reviews, October 1, 2008, review of *Love Junkie.*

New York Observer, November 28, 2008, Sara Vilkomerson, review of *Love Junkie.*

New York Post, November 23, 2008, Martha Frankel, review of *Love Junkie.*

Observer (London, England), January 11, 2009, Hephzibah Anderson, review of *Love Junkie.*

Publishers Weekly, February 1, 1999, review of *Go West Young F*cked up Chick,* p. 73; September 22, 2008, review of *Love Junkie,* p. 47.

San Francisco Chronicle, December 12, 2008, Christina Eng, review of *Love Junkie,* p. E2.

ONLINE

Austinist, http://austinist.com/ (August 5, 2009), author interview.

Bookslut, http://www.bookslut.com/ (October 31, 2008), Elizabeth Bachner, review of *Love Junkie.*

California Literary Review, http://calitreview.com/ (November 12, 2008), Kelly Hartog, review of *Love Junkie.*

IOMToday.co.im, http://www.iomtoday.co.im/ (January 22, 2009), Kate Whiting, review of *Love Junkie.*

Loose Girls and Love Junkies, http://loosegirlsandlovejunkies.com/ (August 5, 2009), author profile.

Rachel Resnick Home Page, http://www.rachelresnick.com (August 5, 2009), author biography and interview.

Rachel Resnick MySpace Profile, http://www.myspace.com/rachelresnick (August 5, 2009), author profile.

University of California, Los Angeles, Extension Writers' Program Web site, http://www2/uclaextension.edu/writers/ (August 5, 2009), author profile.

Writers on Fire Web site, http://www.writersonfire.com/ (August 5, 2009), author profile.*

* * *

RETTSTATT, Chris
See ASHLAND, Monk

* * *

REYNOLDS, Richard

PERSONAL: Male.

ADDRESSES: *E-mail*—richard@guerrillagardening.org.

CAREER: Writer.

WRITINGS:

On Guerrilla Gardening: A Handbook for Gardening without Boundaries, Bloomsbury (New York, NY), 2008.

SIDELIGHTS: Richard Reynolds is the author of *On Guerrilla Gardening: A Handbook for Gardening without Boundaries,* released in 2008. The book advocates a new philosophy regarding gardening. Instead of merely maintaining a garden within the boundaries of one's personal space, Reynolds suggests taking the pastime outside of one's own walls and engaging in civic beautification. Using a term known as "guerilla gardening," Reynolds suggests that gardeners should use common public space for the continuation of their skills. The text offers numerous reasons why one should partake in guerilla gardening, namely the opportunity to engage in civic progress and environmental cleanup. Alice O'Keeffe, in a review for the *New Statesman,* claimed, "This is gardening repackaged for the 21st century: forget Arthur Fowler sipping tea in his potting shed, think instead a dashing Comandante Marcos figure, sowing maize and beans while holding forth on the flaws of global capitalism."

Reynolds explains that he began his foray with guerilla gardening while he lived in a monolithic high-rise in the city of London, England. While living in the city was necessary, Reynolds found he missed gardening. So, he embarked upon a nightly adventure wherein he gardened other people's property. Starting with the empty or ill-kempt planters outside of his building, Reynolds expanded his operation to plots of empty land or spaces within the city in need of beautification, such as roadside or roundabout green areas. Reynolds chronicled his experiences in his blog, which attracted an increasing amount of attention from a diverse readership. As Reynolds relates in the text, he found that he is part of an international movement for beautification and environmentally aimed civic responsibility. In other words, his activity with gardening in civic spaces is mirrored by gardeners the world over. O'Keeffe remarked, "Soon Reynolds found himself tapping in to an international movement of activist gardeners from Montreal to Brisbane—who take on unused public land and transform it into lush, cultivated flower displays and allotments." Moreover, Emily-Jane Dawson, in an essay for *Library Journal,* noted that Reynolds "peppers the text with stories from clandestine gardeners around the world." *On Guerrilla Gardening* also relates how others came to join Reynolds in his outings. Reynolds uses military-themed language to explain the concept of guerilla gardening, including references to his materials as forms of weaponry and other participants as troops. Additionally, an *Internet Bookwatch* contributor concluded, "A scattering of color photography enhances this eyebrow-raising gardening guide."

BIOGRAPHICAL AND CRITICAL SOURCES:

PERIODICALS

Booklist, May 15, 2008, Alice Joyce, review of *On Guerrilla Gardening: A Handbook for Gardening without Boundaries,* p. 14.

Internet Bookwatch, June 1, 2008, review of *On Guerrilla Gardening.*

In the Black, March 1, 2009, "The Guerilla Gardener," p. 67.

Library Journal, May 1, 2008, Emily-Jane Dawson, review of *On Guerrilla Gardening,* p. 89.

New Statesman, June 23, 2008, "How Green Was My Alley," p. 56.

ONLINE

Bloomsbury Press Web site, http://www.bloomsbury.com/ (August 15, 2009), author profile.*

RHODES, Tricia McCary 1952-

PERSONAL: Born July 23, 1952; married; husband's name Joe (a pastor); children: two sons. *Education:* Earned B.A. and M.S.

ADDRESSES: Home—San Diego, CA. *Office*—The Soul at Rest, 10330 Carmel Mountain Rd., San Diego, CA 92129. *E-mail*—soulatrest.rhodes@yahoo.com; contact@soulatrest.com.

CAREER: Christian minister and writer. New Hope Church, San Diego, CA, cofounder, 1981—. Has worked as a missionary in rural Alaska, India, and Bangladesh.

WRITINGS:

The Soul at Rest, Bethany House (Minneapolis, MN), 1996.

Contemplating the Cross, Bethany House (Minneapolis, MN), 1998, also published as *Contemplating the Cross: A 40-day Pilgrimage of Prayer,* Thomas Nelson (Nashville, TN), 2004.

Taking Up Your Cross: The Incredible Gain of the Crucified Life, Bethany House (Minneapolis, MN), 2000.

At the Name of Jesus: Meditations on the Exalted Christ, Bethany House (Minneapolis, MN), 2003.

Intimate Intercession: The Sacred Joy of Praying for Others, Thomas Nelson (Nashville, TN), 2005.

Sacred Chaos: Spiritual Disciplines for the Life You Have, IVP Books (Downers Grove, IL), 2008.

Author of the *Sacred Chaos* blog; contributor to periodicals, including *Pray!, Discipleship Journal, Guideposts, Decision,* and *Moody Monthly.*

SIDELIGHTS: Tricia McCary Rhodes is a Christian minister and writer. Born on July 23, 1952, she has dedicated most of her life to spreading her religious beliefs around the world. With her pastor husband, Joe, she founded the New Hope Church in San Diego, California, and has also served as a missionary in rural Alaska, India, and Bangladesh.

Rhodes published her second book, *Contemplating the Cross,* in 1998. The account was also published as *Contemplating the Cross: A 40-day Pilgrimage of Prayer* in 2004. The book looks at the final days of the life of Jesus Christ from a number of perspectives and incorporates meditative exercises at the start of each section. Bernadette McGrath, writing in *Library Journal,* remarked that the writing in the book "stirs the soul." McGrath found it to be "neither too maudlin nor detached."

Rhodes published *Taking Up Your Cross: The Incredible Gain of the Crucified Life* in 2000. The account mixes evangelical and classical Christian theology to highlight the connections one should feel with God and also encourages private time to reflect in peace on this relationship. Jana Riess, reviewing the book in *Publishers Weekly,* noted that "Rhodes is long on God's grace," appending that the author "writes well."

In 2003 Rhodes published *At the Name of Jesus: Meditations on the Exalted Christ.* The book looks at the many names and roles of Jesus and shows readers how to experience the meaning of these roles in their lives. A contributor writing in *Publishers Weekly* criticized the writing as occasionally "overdone." Nevertheless, the same contributor concluded that *At the Name of Jesus* "speaks ardently about the love and power of the risen Christ."

The following year Rhodes published *Intimate Intercession: The Sacred Joy of Praying for Others.* The book defines the concept of intercession and shows how significant it can be in life to experience this moment. Rhodes guides readers to move closer to God and share a closer intimacy. Michele Howe, reviewing the book in *FaithfulReader.com,* suggested that "readers will learn more about the holy calling as apprentices to the school of prayer." Howe concluded that "Rhodes's entire primer on intercession is lovely, inspiringly presented, and all the more palatable because of its plucky honesty," adding that "intercession is not for the weak-kneed—but then again, maybe it is." Joyce Handzo, reviewing the account in *In the Library Reviews,* found the book to be "reader-friendly and Spirit-inspired." Handzo assured that "although the idea of intercession may seem intimidating, the author makes this concept completely understandable through her sensitive and discerning writing."

In 2008 Rhodes published *Sacred Chaos: Spiritual Disciplines for the Life You Have.* The book directs readers to achieve a spiritual life with what they already have, as opposed to how they would like to make their lives in order to meet this goal. Again, Rhodes emphasizes the importance of quiet time and prayer, even if for just a minute. A contributor writing in the *Link Between* Web log concluded: "While I've read some books in the spiritual disciplines genre that [are] either too ethereal or too common-sense-y . . . *Sacred Chaos* is simple yet profound, practical yet deeply spiritual. Don't let one more 'Sacred ___' title scare you away. This one's a keeper." A contributor reviewing the book in *Today's Christian Woman* found the chapters of *Sacred Chaos* to be both "brief" and "evocative," offering practical advice for busy mothers. A contributor writing in *Publishers Weekly* observed that in addition to her own personal experiences, "Rhodes capably draws on" a range of Christian "traditions to advocate small, realistic steps on the path to holiness." Carol B. Boren, writing in the *Baptist Standard,* realized that "the tone of Rhodes' writing is never academic or removed, but always encouraging," adding that the author's "words resonate with the heart of our Father."

BIOGRAPHICAL AND CRITICAL SOURCES:

PERIODICALS

Library Journal, March 1, 1998, Bernadette McGrath, review of *Contemplating the Cross,* p. 94.

Publishers Weekly, February 21, 2000, Jana Riess, review of *Taking Up Your Cross: The Incredible Gain of the Crucified Life,* p. 52; February 24, 2003, review of *At the Name of Jesus: Meditations on the Exalted Christ,* p. 28; April 21, 2008, review of *Sacred Chaos: Spiritual Disciplines for the Life You Have,* p. 55.

Today's Christian Woman, July-August, 2008, review of *Sacred Chaos,* p. 10.

ONLINE

Baptist Standard, http://www.baptiststandard.com/ (March 6, 2009), Carol B. Boren, review of *Sacred Chaos.*

FaithfulReader.com, http://www.faithfulreader.com/ (August 5, 2009), Michele Howe, review of *Intimate Intercession: The Sacred Joy of Praying for Others.*

Intervarsity Press Web site, http://www.ivpress.com/ (August 5, 2009), author profile.

In the Library Reviews, http://www.inthelibrary reviews.net/ (September 26, 2005), Joyce Handzo, review of *Intimate Intercession.*

Link Between, http://thelinkbetween.wordpress.com/ (July 12, 2008), review of *Sacred Chaos.*

Soul at Rest Web site, http://www.soulatrest.com/ (August 5, 2009), author profile.

Thomas Nelson Web site, http://www.thomasnelson.com/ (August 5, 2009), author profile.*

* * *

ROBBINS, Jann
(Jann Stapp)

PERSONAL: Born in Oklahoma City, OK; married Harold Robbins (an author), 1992 (deceased, 1997). *Education:* Attended University of Oklahoma.

ADDRESSES: *Home*—Valencia, CA. *E-mail*—Jann@haroldrobbinsnovels.com.

CAREER: Editor and writer. Executive assistant, Los Angeles, CA, beginning 1982; worked previously as a commercial writer for print, radio, and television, book writer and editor, and ad executive.

AWARDS, HONORS: Colby Award, 2005, for *Hope and Honor.*

WRITINGS:

(With Sidney Shachnow) *Hope and Honor,* Forge (New York, NY), 2004.

Harold and Me: My Life, Love, and Hard Times with Harold Robbins, Forge (New York, NY), 2008.

SIDELIGHTS: Born in Oklahoma City, Oklahoma, Jann Robbins attended the University of Oklahoma and later opened her own advertising agency. However, it was in 1982, when renowned and polarizing author Harold Robbins hired her as his personal assistant, that she made the move to Los Angeles, California. Their working relationship soon became a romantic one, with the pair marrying in 1992. The two worked on Harold Robbins's works together until his death in 1997. His wife continues to edit the writings he left behind. Jann Robbins also boasts of her own writing career, authoring and cowriting several works.

In 2004, Robbins wrote, with Holocaust survivor and United States Army Major General Sidney Shachnow, *Hope and Honor.* The book details the youth of the man once known as Schaja and his experience as a Jew in Lithuania. As a young boy Shachnow and his family were transported to a concentration camp where his mother was able to beguile her way into helping her family survive. After continuing to struggle after the war, the family eventually was able to immigrate to the United States. It was there that Shachnow gained a new name and a new life in the United States Army. A reviewer in *Library Journal* called the work "interesting," while also noting that the book "is almost entirely anecdotal." However, the reviewer also commented that grammatical errors took away from the book as a whole. A reviewer in *Publishers Weekly* made mention of a similar issue, wording it that the author's "telling . . . is not always graceful." Despite this, the reviewer complimented that the "story comes through clearly and with conviction." J.H. Crerar in *Special Warfare* offered a different critique for the book stating that it is more of a book categorized as a family story and biography, rather than military. However, Crerar mentioned that *Hope and Honor* offers an important glimpse into human nature and the ability to survive despite difficult circumstances. The reviewer also noted, "One could wish for more," as an important part of the story "cries for expansion beyond the . . . lines allocated." Crerar concluded however, "Readers will find this a highly readable account of courage and character."

Robbins used her relationship with her husband as inspiration for the 2008 book *Harold and Me: My Life, Love, and Hard Times with Harold Robbins.* A reviewer on *Midwest Book Review Online* called the book a "deep perspective" as Robbins explores not only her husband's writing and raucous life, but also their relationship. A reviewer in *Publishers Weekly* commented that the author offers "a fair amount of schmaltz and low-level gossip," but concluded that the book is "an intimate look" at their life together. Likewise, the reviewer on the *Midwest Book Review Online* called the book "an intriguing insight."

BIOGRAPHICAL AND CRITICAL SOURCES:

PERIODICALS

Kirkus Reviews, October 1, 2008, review of *Harold and Me: My Life, Love, and Hard Times with Harold Robbins.*

Library Journal, September 15, 2004, Edward Metz, review of *Hope and Honor,* p. 65.

Publishers Weekly, June 21, 2004, review of *Hope and Honor,* p. 49.

Special Warfare, November 1, 2005, J.H. Crerar, review of *Hope and Honor.*

Vietnam, February 1, 2007, James H. Willbanks, review of *Hope and Honor,* p. 62.

ONLINE

Harold Robbins Web site, http://haroldrobbinsnovels.com/ (July 13, 2009), author information.

Macmillan Web site, http://us.macmillan.com/ (July 13, 2009), author information.

Midwest Book Review Online, http://www.midwestreview.com/ (August 7, 2009), review of *Harold and Me.**

* * *

ROSENBERG, Saralee 1955-

PERSONAL: Born January 13, 1955; married Lee Rosenberg (a financial planner); children: three.

ADDRESSES: Home—Long Island, NY. *Agent*—Cornerstone Literary, 4525 Wilshire Blvd., Ste. 208, Los Angeles, CA 90010. *E-mail*—Saralee@saraleerosenberg.com.

CAREER: Writer.

WRITINGS:

Destination Florida: The Guide to a Successful Relocation, Rex (Clearwater, FL), 1989.

(With husband, Lee Rosenberg) *50 Fabulous Places to Retire in America,* Career Press (Hawthorne, NJ), 1991.

(With Lee Rosenberg) *50 Fabulous Places to Raise Your Family,* Career Press (Hawthorne, NJ), 1993.

(With Lee Rosenberg) *Lee and Saralee Rosenberg's 50 Fabulous Places to Raise Your Family,* Career Press (Franklin Lakes, NJ), 1996.

A Little Help from Above, Avon Books (New York, NY), 2003.

Claire Voyant, Avon Trade (New York, NY), 2004.

Fate and Ms. Fortune, Avon Trade (New York, NY), 2006.

Dear Neighbor, Drop Dead, Avon (New York, NY), 2008.

Also author of the *Saralee Rosenberg* blog. Contributor to the *New York Times* and *ORT* newsletter.

SIDELIGHTS: Author Saralee Rosenberg had her first work published in the *New York Times* and it was the mere beginning of the publishing of several informational books. A chance acquaintance of her husband's led to her writing a book about Florida relocation called *Destination Florida: The Guide to a Successful Relocation,* published in 1989. The book includes helpful hints and tips to make moving south as simple as possible. This first book opened up an opportunity for both Rosenberg and her husband, and they began to write books together. They began their series in 1991 with *50 Fabulous Places to Retire in America.* After investigating and researching cities around the country, they put together a list of the best places for retirees, focusing on topics, including activities and medical facilities. They continued with *50 Fabulous Places to Raise Your Family,* published in 1993. Again, the couple created a comprehensive list of cities after researching what cities around the country have to offer. Jan Lewis reviewing the book in *Booklist* stated that the authors "try to give the reader a realistic view of" the cities they rank. It was this book that caught the attention of Oprah Winfrey, who invited the couple to be on her show to discuss their book.

After several years, publishing attempts, and man hours, Rosenberg published her first novel in 2003, and *A Little Help from Above* was called a "busy debut novel" by Kathleen Highes when she reviewed the book in *Booklist.* When a reporter receives word that her father and stepmother have been critically injured, she is forced to return home, begrudgingly doing so. During her trip she also must come face-to-face with the pain from losing her mother years ago, as well as her sister's pleas to be her surrogate. Harriet Klausner, reviewing the work on the *Best Reviews* Web site, considered the work "whimsical," but believed that "too many different crises" keep the characters from retaining "audience empathy." However, the reviewer ultimately complimented the author's talent and plot. Samantha J. Gust applauded Rosenberg's "snappy writing style on the *Romantic Times Online.* She ultimately called *A Little Help from Above* "a promising debut."

Rosenberg's next book, published in 2004, was *Claire Voyant.* In a fit of guilt after bearing witness to the death of the elderly man sitting next to her on an airplane, an out-of-work actress seeks out his family and past with surprising results. The discoveries she makes about the old man also lead to her own self-discovery. Donna Carter, on the *Romantic Times Online,* raved that the book is "witty and romantic, with sparkling dialogue and lifelike characters." Meanwhile, Lisa Davis-Craig critiqued in *Library Journal* that a portion of the work "drags," however she also believed the main character has "a sense of humor and plenty of attitude" to add to the tone of the book.

Rosenberg's next novel, *Fate and Ms. Fortune,* published in 2006, deals with the personal life of a down-and-out makeup artist for the local news station, who also happens to be a struggling stand-up comedian. While she tries to navigate through a constant stream of set-ups, the main character must deal with her mother's decision to leave her father and move in, as well as the constant work struggles that seem to always be around. Nasha Kanai reviewing the book on the *Romantic Times Online,* called it "charming," and stated that the main character's "efforts to be optimistic and true to herself make for some funny moments."

Rosenberg's book *Dear Neighbor, Drop Dead,* published in 2008, came out of a previously unpublished novel as well as the author's own life. A woman who feels constant inadequacy and irritation at the existence of her "perfect" neighbor finds her life revolving around their dealings. However, she learns there is more to the story when her neighbor's personal information ends up public. In *Booklist,* reviewer Carol Haggas believed Rosenberg's book is a successful "blend of hip and humble humor" and found that the author "simultaneously skewers and celebrates the institution of suburban sisterhood." Rosenberg explores being a neighbor in the modern world of technology and distractions, along with the time old familial relationships. A reviewer in *Publishers Weekly* believed Rosenberg acknowledges this in her novel enough to resonate with suburban moms. The reviewer also felt that the number of plot twists and disruptions could cause a distraction to the book, except the main character's personality and tone keep the reader involved. Ultimately, the reviewer applauded the work by stating that for those who are looking for "giddy diversions" this story "can be surprisingly sweet and . . . well worth the trip." As with many of Rosenberg's previous works, reviewers found her main characters and their dialogue the highlights of the book as a whole.

BIOGRAPHICAL AND CRITICAL SOURCES:

PERIODICALS

Booklist, March 1, 1993, Denise Perry Donavin, review of *50 Fabulous Places to Retire in America,* p. 1141; April 15, 1993, review of *50 Fabulous Places to Raise Your Family,* p. 1534; January 1, 1996, Jan Lewis, review of *50 Fabulous Places to Raise Your Family,* p. 874; January 1, 2003, Kathleen Hughes, review of *A Little Help from Above,* p. 851; July 1, 2008, Carol Haggas, review of *Dear Neighbor, Drop Dead,* p. 34.

Library Journal, March 1, 1992, Karen McNally Bensing, review of *50 Fabulous Places to Retire in America,* p. 80; October 1, 2004, Lisa Davis-Craig, review of *Claire Voyant,* p. 73.

Money, September 22, 1991, "Finding Where You Should Retire to Today," p. 26.

Publishers Weekly, June 2, 2008, review of *Dear Neighbor, Drop Dead,* p. 30.

Tribune Books, February 2, 2003, review of *A Little Help from Above,* p. 6.

ONLINE

Ask Wendy—The Query Queen, http://askwendy.wordpress.com/ (June 24, 2009), author interview.

Best Reviews, http://thebestreviews.com/ (December 5, 2002), Harriet Klausner, review of *A Little Help from Above.*

BookDivas blog, http://www.bookdivas.com/ (October 23, 2007), review of *Claire Voyant.*

Bookstove, http://bookstove.com/ (June 2, 2009), Mary Patricia Bird, review of *Dear Neighbor, Drop Dead.*

HarperCollins Web site, http://www.harpercollins.com/ (July 14, 2009), author information.

Jenny Gardiner Web site, http://jennygardiner.net/ (December 7, 2008), author interview.

Joanne Rendell Web site, http://www.joannerendell.com/ (November 18, 2008), author interview.

Reader's Place Web site, http://www.hcplonline.info/ (August 1, 2008), author information.

Romantic Times Online, http://www.romantictimes.com/ (July 19, 2009), Samantha J. Gust, review of *A Little Help from Above;* Donna Carter, review of *Claire Voyant;* Nasha Kanai, review of *Fate and Ms. Fortune.*

Saralee Rosenberg Home Page, http://www.saraleerosenberg.com (July 14, 2009).

Side Dish, http://ellenmeister.blogspot.com/ (November 24, 2008), author interview.

Wendy Nelson Tokunaga Blog, http://blog.wendytokunaga.com/ (November 18, 2008), author interview.*

* * *

RUSS, Daniel 1949-

PERSONAL: Born 1949; married; wife's name Kathy; children: four. *Education:* University of Evansville, B.A.; Dallas Theological Seminary, M.A. (biblical studies); University of Dallas, M.A. (English), Ph.D. *Religion:* Christian.

ADDRESSES: *Home*—Danvers, MA. *E-mail*—dan.russ@gordon.edu.

CAREER: Author, scholar, and educator. Trinity Christian Academy, Dallas, TX, headmaster, 1994-2002; Dallas Institute of Humanities and Culture, Dallas, managing director; Studies in Leadership program, founder; Gordon College, Wenham, MA, Christians in the Visual Arts, executive director, 2002-03, Center for Christian Studies, director; Trinity Forum, Children of Prometheus: Technology and the Good Life curriculum, project director, *Provocations* journal, editor.

AWARDS, HONORS: Trinity Forum, senior fellow.

WRITINGS:

Flesh-and-Blood Jesus: Learning to Be Fully Human from the Son of Man, Baker Books (Grand Rapids, MI), 2008.

Contributor to various books, including *The Terrain of Comedy, The Epic Cosmos, Classic Texts and the Nature of Authority, Invitation to the Classics,* and *The Tragic Abyss.*

SIDELIGHTS: Author and scholar Daniel Russ is a senior fellow with the Trinity Forum, an organization founded in 1991. A contributor to the Trinity Forum Web site stated that the Trinity Forum is a leadership academy that engages leaders "with the great ideas in the context of faith for personal and societal renewal." Russ, who holds an M.A. and Ph.D. from the University of Dallas, also serves as a director of the Center for Christian Studies at Gordon College in Wenham, Massachusetts. In this position, Russ strives to bring Christian scholarship to higher-education institutions and the public at large. He has written extensively on theology, ethics, and biblical and classical texts. His work experience includes a position as headmaster of Trinity Christian Academy in Dallas, Texas, and managing director of the Dallas Institute of Humanities and Culture. He has edited *Provocations,* served as a project director and resource scholar for Trinity's various curriculum projects, and contributed to numerous books examining Christian theology and doctrine, including *The Terrain of Comedy, The Epic Cosmos, Classic Texts and the Nature of Authority, Invitation to the Classics,* and *The Tragic Abyss.* Russ also helped create Studies in Leadership, a program training civic and business leaders through the use of classical and biblical texts.

Russ further developed his research of Christianity and its modern applications in his first book, *Flesh-and-Blood Jesus: Learning to Be Fully Human from the Son of Man,* published by Baker Books in 2008. The author describes the human failings and struggles of Jesus Christ, even touching on the somewhat controversial subject of Jesus' family life and sexuality. A contributor to *Campus Life's Ignite Your Faith* noted that the author remarks that "Life is pain; life is joy" and Jesus Christ emphasized the brilliance of "being human." The author applies his findings to similar emotional issues—anger, failure, doubt, and the problems of authority and friendship—faced by people of the modern world. The founder of Christianity dealt with frequent failure and disappointment, both in himself and in others, as Russ explains, yet learned to "fail gracefully," a talent that in the author's view can well serve anyone in the twenty-first century.

A *Publishers Weekly* review praised *Flesh-and-Blood Jesus* as "revealing, disturbing yet ultimately freeing," emphasizing the notion that "Jesus failed many times and disappointed others, yet remained sinless." A contributor to *Campus Life's Ignite Your Faith* called the book "refreshing" and noted that it explains to readers that "Jesus can understand your failures, questions, and struggles."

BIOGRAPHICAL AND CRITICAL SOURCES:

PERIODICALS

Campus Life's Ignite Your Faith, March 22, 2009, "Faith and Belief," review of *Flesh-and-Blood Jesus: Learning to Be Fully Human from the Son of Man,* p. 23.

Publishers Weekly, April 28, 2008, review of *Flesh-and-Blood Jesus,* p. 132.

ONLINE

Trinity Forum Web site, http://www.ttf.org/ (July 24, 2009), author biography.*

*   *   *

RYAN, Amy Kathleen

PERSONAL: Born in Jackson, WY; married. *Education:* Attended college in Omaha, NE, and Madrid, Spain; graduated from the University of Wyoming; University of Vermont, M.A.; The New School, M.F.A.

ADDRESSES: *Home*—CO. *E-mail*—amy@amykathleenryan.com.

CAREER: Writer. Worked various jobs over the course of her career.

WRITINGS:

YOUNG ADULT NOVELS

Shadow Falls, Delacorte Press (New York, NY), 2005.
Vibes, Houghton Mifflin (New York, NY), 2008.

SIDELIGHTS: Writer Amy Kathleen Ryan was born and raised in Jackson, Wyoming, where she grew up loving outdoor adventures such as climbing trees and writing stories. The books of Madeleine L'Engle made her a devoted reader as well, introducing her to a world of fantasy and literary adventures that led her to the works of Susan Cooper, Isaac Asimov, and Jack London. Early on, Ryan set her sights on being a writer, starting her first novel when she was in fifth grade. Though other interests took precedence over the intervening years, writing always remained a major interest. She attended various colleges in Omaha, Nebraska, and Madrid, Spain, before finally returning home to graduate from the University of Wyoming. It was during her final semester that she took a creative writing class that got her back into serious thoughts of a career as a writer. She ultimately continued to write while working various jobs to pay the rent, working on her fiction at night. Ryan continued her education at the University of Vermont, where she earned a master 's degree in English, and then went on for a master of fine arts degree at the New School in New York City, where she honed her craft. Now a full-time writer, Ryan is the author of *Shadow Falls* and *Vibes,* both novels aimed at a young adult audience.

Shadow Falls tells the story of fifteen-year-old Annie, whose brother Cody has been killed in a climbing accident in the Andes. It has been six months since his death and Annie is still haunted by the incident, feelings made worse when she goes to visit her grandfather's cabin in the Tetons of Wyoming, where she and Cody used to summer when they were younger. Annie also blames her grandfather for initially teaching Cody how to climb during those summer vacations, rationalizing that had her brother never learned, he never would have had his accident. Ryan shows how Annie slowly works through her grief over the course of the summer, facing dangers like a near-tragic run-in with a grizzly bear, and everyday tasks such as babysitting for a local boy with issues of his own. Cindy Dobrez, writing for *Booklist,* opined that "teens will enjoy Annie's honest emotions and her wilderness adventures." *Kliatt* reviewer Myrna Marler wrote that "a varied cast of memorable characters . . . along with lyrical descriptions of nature, reinforces the themes of grief, love, loss, and healing."

In *Vibes,* Ryan introduces readers to Kristi, a girl with the ability to read minds. Kristi is not a likeable character at first. An outcast at her school, she insists on making her own clothes and refers to herself in highly negative terms, calling herself a bitch and describing herself as ugly. While much of this negativity is her own, she also feeds off negative feelings she perceives in others due to her abilities, and her inability to trust anyone since her father abandoned her family two years earlier makes it all the more difficult to feel anything positive to counteract her misery. However, when Mallory, a young man with similar feelings of negativity, starts at Kristi's school, she is suddenly able to see her own downward spiral in his behavior and attitude. This vision brings with it a better understanding of her own dilemma and she sets out to turn her life around, deciding she does not want to live her life from such an angry perspective. Stephanie L. Petruso, writing for *School Library Journal,* commented of Kristi that "many teens will relate to her feelings of isolation and the defensiveness it causes." A reviewer for *Publishers Weekly* called the book "an exceptional second novel."

BIOGRAPHICAL AND CRITICAL SOURCES:

PERIODICALS

Booklist, June 1, 2005, Cindy Dobrez, review of *Shadow Falls,* p. 1789.

Kirkus Reviews, June 1, 2005, review of *Shadow Falls,* p. 643; September 1, 2008, review of *Vibes.*

Kliatt, May, 2005, Myrna Marler, review of *Shadow Falls,* p. 17; November, 2008, Aimee Cole, review of *Vibes,* p. 18.

Publishers Weekly, October 13, 2008, review of *Vibes,* p. 55.

School Library Journal, November, 2005, Morgan Johnson-Doyle, review of *Shadow Falls,* p. 147; December, 2008, Stephanie L. Petruso, review of *Vibes,* p. 136.

ONLINE

Amy Kathleen Ryan Home Page, http://www.amykathleenryan.com (August 12, 2009), author profile.

Bookshelves of Doom Blog, http://bookshelvesofdoom.blogspot.com/ (August 12, 2009), review of *Vibes.*

Curled Up with a Good Kid's Book, http://www.curledupkids.com/ (August 12, 2009), Douglas R. Cobb, review of *Vibes.*

Teen Reads, http://www.teenreads.com/ (August 12, 2009), review of *Vibes.*

YA Books and More Blog, http://naomibates.blogspot.com/ (August 12, 2009), review of *Vibes.**

S

SALVATORE, Chris

ADDRESSES: Home—Brooklyn, NY.

CAREER: Tor Books, publicist of science fiction, fantasy, and horror.

WRITINGS:

Necking, Pocket Books (New York, NY), 2008.

SIDELIGHTS: An English major and former publicist for Tor Books specializing in science fiction, fantasy, and horror, Chris Salvatore applies her eleven years in the publishing business and her love of the horror genre to her debut work, *Necking,* published in 2008 by Pocket Books. Gia Felice, the hero of *Necking,* works as an "underworld publicist," promoting the works of vampires, witches, werewolves, and deep-space alien travelers. "Once upon a time I was a book publicist too," commented Salvatore in an interview for the *Chris Salvatore Home Page.* "You know what they say: write what you know." Salvatore points out several autobiographical features of her central character, including blonde hair, modesty, a love for high heels, a preference for scrawny men, and a poor ability to sleep. Gia has some unique fictional problems, however, in her complicated relations with a cast of otherworldly, sometimes horrifying, clients. In an interview for the *Number One Novels* Web log, Salvatore told Rebecca Chastain, "Gia's Rolodex full of supernatural contacts has become the obsession of a centuries-old vampire . . . [and] Gia can't fight her attraction to the beautiful, charismatic, and funny Jonathan. Well, who could blame her? He's had hundreds of years to perfect that smile." Gia faces a series of dangerous occurrences, highlighted by the author's dryly humorous view of her romantic adventures.

Inspired by her idea of a publicist whose nightmarish clients are the "real deal," Salvatore imagined a host of unique problems and plot twists. Her main client, who goes by the name of Belladonna Nightshade, sets Gia an important task: find the vampire that "turned" her and who was responsible for the death of her formerly "undead" lover. In the meantime, Belladonna's vampirish manager, Johnny, is having a strange and not-unpleasant effect on Gia, who must decide whether to fall head over heels and eventually join the world of the living dead, or remain among the single, normal, and mortal. Salvatore completed her book in just six weeks and promptly brought it to an agent, who rejected the manuscript and advised on an extensive rewrite. After a revision that took longer than the creation of the original story, the author turned to a different agent and soon landed her publication with Pocket Books, a division of Simon & Schuster. Knowing the book world's publicity ropes as she did, Salvatore brought the book to the attention of various radio and television outlets, appeared on a local television comedy show, and landed her name and title on "Page Six," a popular gossip feature column of the *New York Post.*

Reviewers had mixed opinions on *Necking,* giving the author high marks for her new take on the very familiar vampire genre. A contributor to the Web site

Dear Author graded the book a "C+" and offered some constructive criticism: "While this was a nice change of pace from the darker urban fantasies I usually read, I think it ultimately wasn't the book for me. I like my books with more externally driven plot and fewer unconnected slice of life scenes." In a review of *Necking* for the *Romantic Times Online,* Whitney Kate Sullivan called the book a "thoroughly engaging tale about the humanity of the inhuman." "The story line is fast-paced, filled with action and stars a full blooded heroine," commented Harriet Klausner in a review for the *Genre Go Round Reviews* Web log, adding, "Fans will enjoy this lighthearted satirizing of the latest publishing rage." A reviewer for *Publishers Weekly* wrote that Salvatore's work exhibits strength in "blend[ing] paranormal romance and chick lit" and called *Necking* "a fun, fast-paced read."

BIOGRAPHICAL AND CRITICAL SOURCES:

PERIODICALS

Publishers Weekly, June 2, 2008, review of *Necking,* p. 33.

ONLINE

Beth's Hobbies Web log, http://bethshobbies.blogspot.com/ (July 4, 2009), review of *Necking.*

Chris Salvatore Home Page, http://www.chrissalvatore.com (July 24, 2009).

Dear Author, http://dearauthor.com/ (August 20, 2008), review of *Necking.*

Genre Go Round Reviews, http://genregoroundreviews.blogspot.com/ (June 19, 2008), Harriet Klausner, review of *Necking.*

Number One Novels Web log, http://numberonenovels.blogspot.com/ (March 23, 2009), Rebecca Chastain, author interview.

Romantic Times Online, http://www.romantictimes.com/ (July 24, 2009), Whitney Kate Sullivan, review of *Necking.*

Scooper Speaks Web log, http://scooper.wordpress.com/ (June 28, 2009), review of *Necking.**

* * *

SCHANZER, Jonathan

PERSONAL: Education: Emory University, B.A., 1994; Hebrew University of Jerusalem, M.A., 2000.

ADDRESSES: Home—Washington, DC. *E-mail*—jschanzer@jewishpolicycenter.org.

CAREER: Author, research fellow, commentator, and specialist on Middle East topics. Middle East Forum, research fellow, 2000-02; Washington Institute for Near East Policy, Soref fellow, 2002-04; U.S. Department of the Treasury, Office of Intelligence and Analysis, counterterrorism analyst, 2004-07; Jewish Policy Center, deputy executive director, 2007—. Has appeared as a guest on U.S. television networks, including Cable News Network and Fox News, and on the Arabic-language network Al-Jazeera.

WRITINGS:

Al-Qaeda's Armies: Middle East Affiliate Groups & the Next Generation of Terror, Specialist Press International (New York, NY), 2005.

Hamas vs. Fatah: The Struggle for Palestine, Palgrave Macmillan (New York, NY), 2008.

SIDELIGHTS: Jonathan Schanzer is a scholar of Middle East affairs with long experience as a researcher and commentator on the region's complex politics, cultural affairs, and religious and socioeconomic turmoil. He has been associated with the Washington Institute for Near East Policy and the Middle East Forum as a researcher, and currently holds the position of director of policy at the Jewish Policy Center. He holds a bachelor's degree from Emory University and a master's from the Hebrew University of Jerusalem. He has traveled widely in the Middle East, studied Arabic at Cairo University, and authored numerous journal articles and editorials on the subject of Middle East politics and terrorism. Schanzen is the author of two titles on international terrorism and the Israeli-Palestinian conflict: *Al-Qaeda's Armies: Middle East Affiliate Groups & the Next Generation of Terror,* published in 2005, and *Hamas vs. Fatah: The Struggle for Palestine,* published in 2008.

Al-Qaeda's Armies examines the various nationalist Islamic groups that have affiliated with al-Qaeda in many countries of the Middle East. After the terrorist attacks of September 11, 2001, al-Qaeda decentralized itself, changing into a loosely organized structure which gave direction, but not direct orders, to smaller organizations throughout the region. In Schanzer's view, this change has brought about the next generation of terrorism, with affiliate groups in Lebanon, Yemen, Algeria, Iraq, and Egypt posing a challenge to U.S. allies and interests. In a televised interview with Jim Angle for the Fox News Channel, Schanzer commented on the advantages of modern electronic media and its instantaneous, worldwide transmission of events, to these al-Qaeda affiliates: "What they're seeing is the effect that is having on U.S. population here. We watch it, you know, from our televisions at home and see how this is affecting us. It clearly shakes the administration. It shakes the average citizen here in the United States. And they know by reading our media and by looking at our reactions that this is a tactic that works." To combat them, in Schanzer's view, the U.S. government should undertake small-scale operations with the assistance of Muslim governments. "Convincing these," as noted by Avi Jorisch in a review of the book for *Middle East Quarterly,* "[is] an unlikely prospect under the best of circumstances [that] would demonstrate to Al-Qaeda and other jihadis that the West and the Muslim world alike consider them pariahs.

Hamas vs. Fatah is a scholarly study of the recent struggle between these two factions for political dominance over territories governed by the Palestinian Authority. The book explores the partition of Palestine in the early twentieth century, the rise of Islamic fundamentalism with the founding of the Muslim Brotherhood in the 1920s, and the conflicts that endure in the region despite the separation of Arab Palestinian and Jewish Israeli populations behind political and physical boundaries.

The author provides links between the Israeli-Palestinian conflict, the civil war in Lebanon, and the rise of al-Qaeda and other groups seeking to return the Arab states of the Middle East to the social and legal strictures of fundamentalist Islam. Schanzer concludes that the endless struggle between Hamas and Fatah has frustrated the aspirations of the Palestinians to achieve social stability and economic progress. The conflicts of the Middle East give rise to sharply conflicting opinions, and in the reviews of Schanzer's books the result has been no different. A *Kirkus Reviews* contributor commented that "this well-argued account helps sort out the two groups' tangled history of nationalism and terrorism, the latter of which Hamas refuses to give up." The same contributor stated that the book is "recommended for students of current events in the Middle East." A *Publishers Weekly* reviewer praised the book as a "serious, no-frills account," and a "concise historical survey."

BIOGRAPHICAL AND CRITICAL SOURCES:

PERIODICALS

America's Intelligence Wire, May 15, 2004, "Interview with Jonathan Schanzer"; June 18, 2004, "Analysis with Jonathan Schanzer"; September 18, 2004, "Interview with Harlan Ullman, Jonathan Schanzer."

Kirkus Reviews, September 15, 2008, review of *Hamas vs. Fatah: The Struggle for Palestine.*

Middle East Quarterly, September 22, 2005, Avi Jorisch, review of *Al-Qaeda's Armies: Middle East Affiliate Groups & the Next Generation of Terror,* p. 82.

Publishers Weekly, September 1, 2008, review of *Hamas vs. Fatah,* p. 47.

ONLINE

Atlantic Free Press Web site, http://www.atlanticfreepress.com/ (December 2, 2008), Jim Miles, review of *Hamas vs. Fatah.*

David Project Web site, http://www.davidproject.org/ (July 24, 2009), author biography.

FrontPage, http://www.frontpagemag.com/ (July 24, 2009), author biography.

Jewish Policy Center Web site, http://www.jewishpolicycenter.org/ (July 24, 2009), author biography.

Macmillan Web site, http://us.macmillan.com/ (July 24, 2009), author biography.

* * *

SCHAUBERT, Steve

PERSONAL: Education: Yale University, B.S. (summa cum laude); Harvard Business School, M.B.A. (with high distinction); Northeastern University, M.S.

ADDRESSES: Home—Boston, MA. *Office*—Bain & Co., Inc., 131 Dartmouth St., Boston, MA 02116.

CAREER: Bain & Co., Inc., Boston, MA, 1979—, partner, 1980—, CIO; previously worked for several health-care industry firms in general management.

MEMBER: Phi Beta Kappa.

AWARDS, HONORS: Named a George F. Baker scholar, Harvard Graduate School of Business.

WRITINGS:

(With Mark Gottfredson and others) *The Breakthrough Imperative: How the Best Managers Get Outstanding Results,* Collins (New York, NY), 2008.

SIDELIGHTS: A graduate of Yale University and the Harvard Graduate School of Business, Steve Schaubert has served for more than two decades with the Boston-based office of Bain and Company Incorporated, rising from consultant to partner. He is also the author of *The Breakthrough Imperative: How the Best Managers Get Outstanding Results,* written with Mark Gottfredson and with additional assistance from John Case and Kath Tsakalakis. *The Breakthrough Imperative* addresses the ever-changing global marketplace and the speed at which those changes are occurring, noting that as a result, it is more important than ever for managers to hit the ground running when they take on a new position so that they can prove their worth and achieve their goals as rapidly as possible. As speed and a competitive edge become more and more important to maintaining a foothold in the marketplace, managers will have even less time than they have traditionally had to show that they are capable of handling the high demands of their job. According to the book, three years is the most time that a manager has to make some sort of an impression through their efforts. Through a series of real-life examples gleaned from interviews with more than forty leaders across a wide spectrum of industries, Gottfredson and Schaubert illustrate how that impact can be made, and offer readers a number of steps or "laws" they have developed to achieve similar results. Kim Lumpkin, in a review for the *Cultural Cartel* Web site, concluded: "This is not a book for a casual entrepreneur; to successfully apply the four laws outlined within requires insight, discipline, and leadership skills. But for a serious new (or not so new) CEO, Gottfredson and Schaubert's advice could well make the difference between success and failure."

BIOGRAPHICAL AND CRITICAL SOURCES:

PERIODICALS

Booklist, April 15, 2008, Barbara Jacobs, review of *The Breakthrough Imperative: How the Best Managers Get Outstanding Results,* p. 12.

New Zealand Management, May 1, 2008, Reg Birchfield, review of *The Breakthrough Imperative,* p. 24.

ONLINE

Culture Cartel, http://www.culturecartel.com/ (July 1, 2008), Kim Lumpkin, review of *The Breakthrough Imperative.*

Garamond Agency Web site, http://www.garamond-agency.com/ (August 12, 2009), author profile.

HarperCollins Web site, http://www.harpercollins.com/ (August 12, 2009), author profile.

Zubon Book Reviews Blog, http://zbooks.blogspot.com/ (January 25, 2008), review of *The Breakthrough Imperative.**

* * *

SCHÖNBORN, Christoph
See SCHÖNBORN, Cardinal Christoph

* * *

SCHÖNBORN, Cardinal Christoph 1945-
(Christoph Schönborn)

PERSONAL: Born January 22, 1945, in Skalsko, Czechoslovakia. *Education:* Attended Le Saulchoir; University of Vienna; Catholic Institute of Paris; University of Paris, Sorbonne; and University of Regensburg. *Religion:* Roman Catholic.

CAREER: University of Graz, Graz, Austria, student pastor, 1973-75; University of Fribourg, Fribourg, Switzerland, associate professor of dogmatics, professor of dogmatic theology, 1975-91. Auxiliary bishop of Vienna, Vienna, Austria, 1991-95; coadjutor bishop of Vienna, 1995-98; archbishop of Vienna, 1995—; cardinal of the Catholic church, 1998—.

Served on several religious commissions, including Swiss Commission for Dialogue between Roman Catholics and Christians, 1980-84; Orthodox-Roman Catholic Dialogue Commission of Switzerland, 1980-87; Theological Commission of the Swiss Bishop's Conference, 1980-91; Foundation Pro Oriente, 1984—; International Commission of Theologians, 1980—; editorial secretary for the commission drafting the catechism of the Roman Catholic church, 1987-92.

MEMBER: Congregations for the Doctrine of the Faith, Oriental Churches, and Catholic Education; Commission on the Cultural Heritage of the Church; Special Council for Europe of the General Secretariat of the Synod of Bishops; Austrian Bishop's Conference, president, 1998—.

WRITINGS:

The Mystery of the Incarnation, Ignatius Press (San Francisco, CA), 1992.
God's Human Face: The Christ Icon, translated by Lothar Kraugh, Ignatius Press (San Francisco, CA), 1994.
From Death to Life: The Christian Journey, Ignatius Press (San Francisco, CA), 1995.
(With David Kipp) *Living the Catechism of the Catholic Church: The Creed,* Ignatius Press (San Francisco, CA), 1995.
Loving the Church: Spiritual Exercises Preached in the Presence of Pope John Paul II, Ignatius Press (San Francisco, CA), 1998.
Living the Catechism of the Catholic Church: The Sacraments, translated by John Saward, Ignatius Press (San Francisco, CA), 2000.
Living the Catechism of the Catholic Church, Volume III: Life in Christ, Ignatius Press (San Francisco, CA), 2001.
Living the Catechism of the Catholic Church: Paths of Prayer, translated by Michael J. Miller, Ignatius Press (San Francisco, CA), 2003.
My Jesus: Encountering Christ in the Gospel!, translated by Robert J. Shea, Ignatius Press (San Francisco, CA), 2005.
Chance or Purpose? Creation, Evolution, and a Rational Faith, translated by Henry Taylor, Ignatius Press (San Francisco, CA), 2007.
Who Needs God?, Ignatius Press (San Francisco, CA), 2009.

SIDELIGHTS: A staunch defender of religious tradition in modern and largely secular Europe, Cardinal Christoph Schönborn is the archbishop of Vienna, a member of the Roman Catholic college of cardinals and one of the most prominent voices in the contemporary Catholic Church. Born in Skalsko, Czechoslovakia (now the Czech Republic), he moved to Austria at a young age and joined the Dominican order at the age of eighteen. He studied at several Catholic institutions, and with Professor Joseph Ratzinger at the University of Regensburg in Germany, before receiving his doctorate in theology in 1974. In 1992, a commission on which he served as secretary completed the modern catechism of the Catholic Church. He was appointed as the archbishop of Vienna in 1995 and in 1996 received the pallium, the archbishop's symbol of authority, from Pope John Paul II, and in 1998 received the cardinal's red beretta from the same pope. Schönborn was one of the youngest members of the conclave that took place in 2005 and elected Cardinal Joseph Ratzinger as Pope Benedict XVI. He has allied closely with Pope Benedict on theological issues but has also criticized the Vatican publicly for not properly vetting its appointments to important positions. He has taken noted positions on other controversial church issues, including the church's stand on the Holocaust, the debate over evolution, and cooperation with leaders of the Islamic faith. He has been a frequent traveler in Europe, Africa, North America, and Asia, where he visited Indonesia in the wake of the devastating tsunami of late 2004. Schönborn serves on several high church commissions and has been active in liaisons with Jewish, Orthodox, and Islamic organizations; he has also been active in cooperating with new Christian organizations such as the Charismatic Renewal.

Schönborn has been outspoken in his warnings of the increasing secularization of Europe. He has also raised controversy over his defense of the teaching of "intelligent design" in school science classes. In doing so, Schönborn has emphasized the consequences of a stridently materialistic view of life, intelligence, and the origins of the universe. This dogma of "evolutionism," as he explained in an interview for *Beliefnet.com,* "is an ideological view that says evolution can explain everything in the whole development of the cosmos, from the Big Bang to Beethoven's Ninth

Symphony. I consider that an ideology. It's not good for science if it becomes ideological, because it leaves its own field and enters the area of philosophy, of world views, maybe of religion. . . . What I would like to see in schools is a critical, open, and positive spirit so that we don't make a dogma of evolution theory."

On July 7, 2005, Schönborn placed his stand plainly before the reading public with "Finding Design in Nature," an opinion piece solicited by the Discovery Institute, a Seattle-based advocacy group favoring the teaching of intelligent design, and published in the *New York Times.* A contributor to the *National Review* stated that the editorial explained, "Evolution in the sense of common ancestry might be true, but evolution in the neo-Darwinian sense . . . is not." The article touched off a minor storm in the ongoing, often-acrimonious campaign between supporters of evolution and creationists. Soon afterward, three U.S. scientists—all churchgoers—published an open letter to the pope, requesting that he state his views on the debate and reaffirm that evolution is compatible with modern church teaching. Schönborn was also challenged in the pages of *Commonweal* by reviewer John F. Haught, who pointed out the contradiction in Schönborn's stand to the endorsement of evolution research by the late Pope John Paul II, and who commented, "The cardinal is intent on making science itself a defender of the notion of divine design, an old mistake still repeated today. To claim that a divine mind or designer lurks behind natural phenomena is not a conclusion that science as such is ever permitted to make."

Schönborn elaborated on his views in his book *Chance or Purpose? Creation, Evolution, and a Rational Faith,* published in 2007. The book made the point, consistent with Schönborn's opinion piece, that excluding the notion of design or purpose from scientific discussions of the origins of life is irrational. Simple common sense, in the author's view, would lead a rational thinker to conclude that chance, random events cannot bring about the elaborately ordered world surrounding us. The book again stirred the evolution versus creationism debate, inspiring reviewer John F. McCarthy to a lengthy analysis and refutation of the cardinal's points in the *Roman Theological Forum.* McCarthy began by stating: "Common sense and reason tell the Cardinal that there is, indeed, order and planning in the universe, even though it may stand outside of the approach of the natural sciences . . . the Cardinal sees no difficulty in combining faith in the Creator with the theory of evolution." McCarthy opposed the cardinal's view that the Christian doctrine can be ultimately reconciled with Darwinian evolution: "The Cardinal clearly presents the viewpoint of a theistic evolutionist, but it is odd that he accepts so confidently Darwin's claim of the descent of man from lower animals while, at the same time, admitting that, concerning the validity of the theory of evolution, 'so many questions still remain open.'" Ray Olson, in a review for *Booklist,* gave the book a brief and positive review, characterizing it as "beautiful and rational theology, elegantly expressed."

BIOGRAPHICAL AND CRITICAL SOURCES:

PERIODICALS

America, February 20, 2006, Robert John Russell, "Evolution and Christian Faith: A Response to Cardinal Christoph Schönborn: Intelligent Design Is an Ideology, Not a Science," p. 12.

Booklist, October 1, 2007, Ray Olson, review of *Chance or Purpose? Creation, Evolution, and a Rational Faith,* p. 20.

Commonweal, August 12, 2005, John F. Haught, "Darwin & the Cardinal," p. 39.

Contra Costa Times, February 8, 2002, "Catholic Theologian: Westerners Need to Reach Out to Islamic Faithful."

First Things: A Monthly Journal of Religion and Public Life, May 1, 2008, review of *Chance or Purpose?,* p. 63.

Houston Chronicle, February 10, 2007, "Cardinal Says Barring the Teaching of 'Intelligent Design' Is Censorship," p. 2.

National Catholic Reporter, May 28, 1999, "European Papers Say Schönborn May Be Vatican Education Chief," p. 9; July 29, 2005, "Questions of Faith and Science," p. 2; July 29, 2005, "Catholic Experts Urge Caution in Evolution Debate; Scientists, Theologians Take Issue with Schönborn's Op-Ed Article," p. 5.

National Review, August 8, 2005, "Christoph Cardinal Schönborn, the Catholic Archbishop of Vienna, Wrote an Op-Ed for the *New York Times* Arguing that While the Church Has No Objection to 'Evolution,' That Does Not Mean It Accepts Everything that Travels under That Name," p. 12.

Theological Studies, September 1, 2006, "Evolution, Randomness, and Divine Purpose: A Reply to Cardinal Schönborn," p. 653.

U.S. Newswire, April 6, 2008, "World Congress Controversy: Cardinal Schönborn Defuses Concern over Orthodox Bishop's Remarks."

ONLINE

Austrian Times, http://www.austriantimes.at/ (April 13, 2009), Thomas Hochwarter, "The End Is Nigh, Warns Schönborn."

Beliefnet.com, http://www.beliefnet.com/ (July 25, 2009), Tom Heneghen, "Catholics and Evolution: Interview with Cardinal Christoph Schönborn."

Cardinal Christoph Schönborn Home Page, http://www.cardinalschonborn.com (July 25, 2009), author Web site.

Evolution News and Views, http://www.evolutionnews.org/ (June 6, 2008), Logan Gage, "O'Leary Reviews Cardinal Schönborn's *Chance or Purpose?*"

Ignatius Insight, http://www.ignatiusinsight.com/ (July 25, 2009), author biography.

Roman Theological Forum, http://www.rtforum.org/ (May 1, 2008), John F. McCarthy, "Reviewing Cardinal Schönborn's Stand on Evolution by Chance or by Purpose."

Telegraph Online, http://www.telegraph.co.uk/ (January 30, 2009), Damian Thompson, "Cardinal Schönborn: Someone at the Vatican Screwed Up over Williamson."

Whispers in Loggia, http://whispersintheloggia.blogspot.com/ (March 2, 2009), Rocco Palmo, "As the Protege Turns."

Zenit, http://www.zenit.org/ (May 2, 2003), "Cardinal Ratzinger on the Abridged Version of Catechism."*

* * *

SCHWARTZ, Sunny 1954-

PERSONAL: Born June 13, 1954.

ADDRESSES: Agent—Priscilla Gilman, Janklow and Nesbit, 445 Park Ave., New York, NY 10022. *E-mail*—sunny@sunnyschwartz.com.

CAREER: Writer and criminal justice reform activist. San Francisco Sheriff's Department, San Francisco, CA, program administrator, 1990—.

WRITINGS:

(With David Boodell) *Dreams from the Monster Factory: A Tale of Prison, Redemption and One Woman's Fight to Restore Justice to All,* Scribner (New York, NY), 2009.

SIDELIGHTS: Sunny Schwartz is a social justice and prison reform pioneer. In 1990, Schwartz was appointed as the San Francisco Sheriff's Department's program administrator. While serving in that capacity, Schwartz implemented several large-scale prison reforms that provided access to educational and rehabilitation programs for inmates and established a program for victims and victims' families in the San Francisco area. Schwartz has lectured across the United States regarding the future of law enforcement and the prison system. In an interview with Heidi Benson for the *San Francisco Chronicle,* Schwartz discussed the concept of restorative justice and stated, "Restorative justice recognizes that crime hurts everyone—victim, offender and community. And it creates an obligation to make it right. It really differs from what we have, which is retributive justice, punishment. Restorative justice is an effort to put the humanity back into the system. Authentic accountability is the backbone of restorative justice." Schwartz also told Benson her hopes for the prison system and stated, "My dream is that every jail and prison will be a place of no-nonsense change and responsibility."

In 2009, Schwartz released *Dreams from the Monster Factory: A Tale of Prison, Redemption and One Woman's Fight to Restore Justice to All.* Written with David Boodel, the text details the ideas underlying the practice of restorative justice. In a question-and-answer selection for the Simon & Schuster Web site, Schwartz stated, "I wanted to write a book to reveal a more civilized society that is based on restoration rather than retribution." In other words, Schwartz believes there is a better way to conduct the business of inmate incarceration and rehabilitation in America's prison systems. Schwartz chronicles the issues plaguing the prison system, such as repeat offenders, underpaid guards, and understaffed correctional institutions. The overcrowded conditions of many of America's prisons, the text reveals, lends a tension to an already volatile housing situation wherein violent criminals are lodged in close quarters with little to no reprieve in the form of exercise or activity. Furthermore, with no training and no rehabilitation, upon release these ex-convicts return to the practices that they know. Thus, Schwartz lends the moniker the "monster factory" to the jails that house these cyclical offenders. A *Tenured Radical* Web site contributor summarized the life cycle of the average repeat offender and reported, "After their trial, if they're convicted, many don't change their mind-set. Why should they? To truly confront what they've done requires confronting the shame and fear and reality of their situation. Few people choose to do this, because it's difficult. . . . So criminals blame someone or something else—the cop who caught them or their lousy upbringing—for their circumstances and spend their time growing angrier and angrier about being treated like an animal. They are usually full of rage when they are released, and less prepared to function as citizens; the predictable products of the monster factory."

In order to change the repetitious cycle of violence and incarceration, the text offers a model solution in the form of Schwartz's Resolve to Stop the Violence Project (RSVP). The program, according to a *Kirkus Reviews* contributor, worked to reduce "violent recidivism by eighty percent and won an Innovations in Government Award." As the text explains, the program advocates developing the criminals' perception of personal responsibility and atonement for their ills against society. Moreover, the program allows the inmates to become involved in a community process wherein they can relearn how one functions within the boundaries of society. "Lucid, gritty and penetrating, this book is perhaps one of the most effective testaments available," concluded a contributor for *Publishers Weekly.*

BIOGRAPHICAL AND CRITICAL SOURCES:

PERIODICALS

Kirkus Reviews, December 1, 2008, review of *Dreams from the Monster Factory: A Tale of Prison, Redemption and One Woman's Fight to Restore Justice to All.*

Library Journal, November 1, 2008, Frances Sandiford, review of *Dreams from the Monster Factory,* p. 89.

Publishers Weekly, October 20, 2008, review of *Dreams from the Monster Factory,* p. 44.

ONLINE

San Francisco Chronicle Online, http://www.sfgate.com/ (February 1, 2009), Heidi Benson, author interview.

Simon & Schuster Web site, http://authors.simonandschuster.com/ (August 16, 2009), author profile.

Sunny Schwartz Home Page, http://sunnyschwartz.com (August 16, 2009).

Tenured Radical, http://tenured-radical.blogspot.com/ (August 2, 2009), review of *Dreams from the Monster Factory.**

* * *

SEMPLE, Maria 1964-

PERSONAL: Born May 21, 1964, in Los Angeles, CA; daughter of Lorenzo Semple, Jr. (a television writer and producer); partner of George Meyer; children: one daughter. *Education:* Graduated from Barnard College.

ADDRESSES: Home—Seattle, WA. *E-mail*—maria@mariasemple.com.

CAREER: Writer, television screenwriter, movie screenwriter, and novelist.

WRITINGS:

This One Is Mine (novel), Little, Brown (New York, NY), 2008.

Screenwriter for television series, including *Beverly Hills 90210, Ellen, Saturday Night Live, Mad about You,* and *Arrested Development.*

SIDELIGHTS: Maria Semple is a novelist, screenwriter, and television scriptwriter. She was born May 21, 1964, in Los Angeles, California, but spent her first two years in Spain with her family, where her father had gone to write a play, noted a contributor to the *Maria Semple Home Page.* Instead, the elder Semple wrote the screenplay for a television phenomenon—Maria Semple is the daughter of screenwriter Lorenzo Semple, Jr., perhaps best known as a writer for the extremely popular mid-sixties television series *Batman* and the screenwriter of notable films such as *Three Days of the Condor* and *Papillion.* She attended Barnard College with dreams of becoming a novelist or English teacher, the same contributor stated. After graduation, however, she sold a movie script to Twentieth Century-Fox. "I could have happily spent my life as an English major—reading books, writing papers, maybe teaching, eventually writing a novel—but I wrote a screenplay and that sold to Fox," she told Jason Rice in an interview for the *Red Room* Web site. After her movie-writing success, she followed a professional course (and her father's footsteps) into the entertainment industry and television screenwriting. For more than fifteen years, Semple wrote scripts and material for a wide variety of programs such as *Saturday Night Live, Ellen, Mad about You,* and *Arrested Development.* After her daughter was born, Semple left television, but "when it was time to get back to work, she resisted Hollywood and gave novel-writing a try," noted a contributor to the *Maria Semple Home Page.*

In Semple's debut novel, *This One Is Mine,* "Semple takes Hollywood stereotypes—a wealthy music producer who is by all accounts a jerk, and his languishing wife—and makes you care about them. She's unflinching, but compassion isn't sacrificed," commented *Seattle Post-Intelligencer* contributor Lisa Albers. "It doesn't sound like this kind of character turnaround could work in print, but Semple's prose pins his psyche to a board as if it were a butterfly." *Los Angeles Times* reviewer Mary McNamara remarked, "Indeed, Semple's greatest strength is the courage to stock her book with characters who are, upon first glance, largely unsympathetic and then gently peel them until they become, if not entirely likable, then at least recognizably and even endearingly human."

The story line explores the complicated relationships of a trio of interconnected family members in high-stakes Hollywood. Violet Parry is a former television writer caught up in the apparent contradiction of being thoroughly trapped by her freedom; now the wife of music industry mogul David Parry, she is wealthy, unfettered by the need to work, and tied only to her luxurious home and child. Despite her advantageous economic status, Violet feels frustrated, neglected, unappreciated, and depressed as she sees herself as little more than David's servant. When she meets musician Terry Reyes, an unlikely and potentially devastating affair is sparked. Reyes is, in most ways, her opposite: he is unhygienic, crass, rude, and impoverished. Though Reyes is a drug addict with Hepatitis C, Violet soon becomes deeply involved with him. Elsewhere in the story, David's unmarried sister Sally is envious of Violet's apparently carefree lifestyle. In an attempt to seize her own share of what Violet owns, Sally schemes to find a wealthy husband, finally settling on Jeremy, a sports statistician on the cusp of a lucrative television career. Even the fact that Jeremy has Asperger's Syndrome cannot derail Sally's determined attempts to wed him, and soon their relationship is consummated and complicated. When David discovers his wife's infidelity, he is devastated, but he experiences a life-altering transformation at a yoga retreat that sets him on the path of repairing his damaged marriage relationship. "Almost everyone gets what's coming to them, including a shot at redemption—which is unsurprising," commented *New York Observer* writer Meredith Bryan. "What is surprising is that the reader cares at all for these hapless creatures, and that, in our era of schadenfreude as public sport, the novel's mostly happy ending is . . . deeply satisfying," Bryan concluded.

McNamara called *This One Is Mine* a "keenly observed, well-written book," while *Booklist* contributor Katherine Boyle found it to be "fun and engrossing light reading." A *Publishers Weekly* reviewer noted that Semple's observations and portrayals are "tack sharp as her delightful cast is driven comically and tragically ever deeper into a culture of artifice."

BIOGRAPHICAL AND CRITICAL SOURCES:

PERIODICALS

Booklist, November 1, 2008, Katherine Boyle, review of *This One Is Mine,* p. 26.

Kirkus Reviews, October 1, 2008, review of *This One Is Mine.*

Library Journal, November 1, 2008, Karen Core, review of *This One Is Mine,* p. 59.

Los Angeles Times, January 1, 2009, Mary McNamara, "A Hollywood-ish Novel Takes on the Complications of Modern Marriage and Parenthood," review of *This One Is Mine.*

New York Observer, December 11, 2008, Meredith Bryan, "Postcards from the Past," review of *This One Is Mine.*

Publishers Weekly, September 15, 2008, review of *This One Is Mine,* p. 41.

Seattle Post-Intelligencer, January 15, 2009, Lisa Albers, "Maria Semple Takes Hollywood Stereotypes and Makes Readers Care about Them," profile of Maria Semple.

USA Today, December 16, 2008, Patty Rhule, "*This One Is Mine:* Hey, You Can Have It," review of *This One Is Mine,* p. 06.

ONLINE

A 'n' E Vibe, http://www.anevibe.com/ (July 26, 2009), Nickky Renault, review of *This One Is Mine.*

Arrested Development Web log, http://arresteddevelopmentblog.com/ (July 26, 2009), author interview.

Author Interviews Web log, http://writerinterviews.blogspot.com/ (February 3, 2009), Marshal Zeringue, author interview.

BookPage, http://www.bookpage.com/ (July 26, 2009), Amy Scribner, "Motherhood on the Edge," review of *This One Is Mine.*

Bookreporter.com, http://www.bookreporter.com/ (July 26, 2009), Donna Volkenannt, review of *This One Is Mine.*

Book Zombie, http://www.thebookzombie.com/ (January 28, 2009), review of *This One Is Mine.*

Fantastic Fiction, http://www.fantasticfiction.co.uk/ (July 26, 2009), author profile.

Huffington Post, http://www.huffingtonpost.com/ (July 26, 2009), "A Touch of Reality in Print and on Screen," author profile.

January, http://januarymagazine.com/ (January 30, 2009), Linda L. Richards, "Author Snapshot: Maria Semple," author interview.

Maria Semple Home Page, http://www.mariasemple.com (August 3, 2009).

Red Room, http://www.redroom.com/ (July 26, 2009), Jason Rice, author interview.

SEUFERT, Lisa Genova
See GENOVA, Lisa

* * *

SHABI, Rachel

PERSONAL: Born in Israel; immigrated with family to Great Britain.

ADDRESSES: *Home*—Tel Aviv, Israel.

CAREER: Journalist and writer.

WRITINGS:

We Look Like the Enemy: The Hidden Story of Israel's Jews from Arab Lands, Walker Books (New York, NY), 2008.

Contributor to periodicals, including the London *Guardian, Sunday Times,* and the *Sunday Express.*

SIDELIGHTS: Rachel Shabi was born in Israel and immigrated to Great Britain with her family, where she grew up in England. A journalist who contributes to periodicals in Great Britain, Shabi is also the author of *We Look Like the Enemy: The Hidden Story of Israel's Jews from Arab Lands.* Published in 2008, the book focuses on the tense relationship between Mizrahi and Ashkenazi Jews in Israel. Ashkenazi Jews are of European descent and have historically belittled and scorned the Middle Eastern Jews, or Mizrahi, who have immigrated to Israel. Shabi, who returned to Israel for a year to conduct research for her book, examines the history and ongoing struggle of the Ashkenazi and Mizrahi Jews. "Virtually all of those with broad Israeli contacts, and many others, are well acquainted with the prejudices of Ashkenazim, Jews whose traditions have been shaped by centuries of exile in Europe and America, toward Mizrahim, whose traditions evolved during their long dispersion in Arab lands," noted Charles A. Radin in a review for the *Boston Globe Online.*

Shabi provides a history of the tensions between the Mizrahi and Ashkenazi, tracing it back centuries earlier to the Jewish Diaspora. She relates the role that the

Mizrahi played in establishing the Jewish state of Israel and documents their ongoing problems, including the first major confrontations between Jewish groups in Israel when the Mizrahi Black Panther Party staged protests in 1971. According to the author, many Ashkenazi Jews have long-held stereotypes concerning the Mizrahi, which have led to discrimination within the Israeli society. For example, Shabi writes of the Yemenis who came to Palestine in the early twentieth century and picked up many of the cultural aspects of the Middle Eastern society around them. As a result, they were looked upon as Arabs by the Ashkenazi, who came to establish Israel following World War II. The author notes that the Mizrahi traditionally were relegated to the role of Hebrew labor and employed in low-paying jobs. Another example is the many peripheral towns created between 1952 and 1964. These towns, which primarily house Mizrahi immigrants, are among the poorest sections of Israel.

The author writes that many Mizrahi have tried to pass for Ashkenazi to avoid prejudice and discrimination. She also points out that the life of the Mizrahi in Israel has improved but also documents that they still face many types of subtle discrimination. In the process of telling the story of the rift between these two Jewish groups, the author also includes her own story of being born in Israel to a Baghdadi Jewish family, which subsequently moved to England. The author also draws from numerous interviews and cultural and academic analyzes. Jay Freeman, writing for *Booklist,* commented that the author "hits hard and effectively in pointing out the fissures in contemporary Israeli society." A *Kirkus Reviews* contributor called *We Look Like the Enemy* "a finely calibrated, intimate portrait of a diverse people, imbued with . . . sympathy."

BIOGRAPHICAL AND CRITICAL SOURCES:

PERIODICALS

Booklist, January 1, 2009, Jay Freeman, review of *We Look Like the Enemy: The Hidden Story of Israel's Jews from Arab Lands,* p. 30.

Kirkus Reviews, December 1, 2008, review of *We Look Like the Enemy.*

Middle East Journal, spring, 2009, Jacob Passel, review of *We Look Like the Enemy,* p. 347.

ONLINE

Boston Globe Online, http://www.boston.com/ (March 26, 2009), Charles A. Radin "A 'Hidden Story' with Preconceived Notions," review of *We Look Like the Enemy.*

Guardian Online, http://www.guardian.co.uk/ (August 13, 2009), brief author profile.

Walker Books Web site, http://www.walkerbooks.com/ (August 13, 2009), brief author profile.*

* * *

SHAH-KAZEMI, Reza 1960-

PERSONAL: Born June 1, 1960. *Education:* Graduated from Sussex University and Exeter University; University of Kent, Ph.D., 1994.

CAREER: Writer, editor, researcher, consultant, and translator. Institute of Ismaili Studies, London, England, research fellow. Institute for Policy Research, Kuala Lumpur, Malaysia, consultant.

WRITINGS:

(Editor) *Algeria: Revolution Revisited,* Islamic World Report (London, England), 1997.

(Translator and editor) Ja'far Sobhani, *Doctrines of Shi'i Islam: A Compendium of Imami Beliefs and Practices,* Imam Sadeq Institute (Qom, Iran), 2003.

Paths to Transcendence: According to Shankara, Ibn Arabi, and Meister Eckhart, World Wisdom (Bloomington, IN), 2006.

(With M. Ali Lakhani and Leonard Lewisohn) *The Sacred Foundations of Justice in Islam: The Teachings of Ali; Ibn Abi Talib,* edited by M. Ali Lakhani, introduction by Seyyed Hossein Nasr, World Wisdom (Bloomington, IN), 2006.

Justice and Remembrance: Introducing the Spirituality of Imam Ali, I.B. Tauris/Institute of Ismaili Studies (New York, NY), 2006.

My Mercy Encompasses All: The Koran's Teachings on Compassion, Peace, & Love, Shoemaker & Hoard (Emeryville, CA), 2007.

Also author of *Crisis in Chechnya,* Islamic World Report, 1995; and *Avicenna: Prince of Physicians,* Hood Hood, 1997. Contributor to periodicals and academic journals. *Islamic World Report,* founding editor.

SIDELIGHTS: Reza Shah-Kazemi is a writer, translator, and researcher who specializes in subjects related to spirituality, metaphysics, Islam, and religious doctrine. He is a research fellow at the Institute for Ismaili Studies in London, England, in the institute's department of academic research and publications. There, he studies and translates important religious texts, such as *Nahj al-Balagha,* a work by the noted Imam Ali and other books in Arabic, Persian, and other Middle Eastern languages. Shah-Kazemi holds degrees in international relations and politics from Sussex University and Exeter University, and a Ph.D. in comparative religion from the University of Kent. He is the founding editor of the *Islamic World Report,* and has been a consultant with the Institute for Policy Research in Kuala Lumpur, Malaysia.

In *My Mercy Encompasses All: The Koran's Teachings on Compassion, Peace, & Love,* Shah-Kazemi presents translations of several "key verses from the Koran that illustrate the important role of compassion, love, and peace in Islam," remarked Frederic Brussat and Mary Ann Brussat in a contribution to the Web site *Spirituality & Practice.* These verses from the Muslim holy book demonstrate that these emotions form the core of Islam, in contrast to well-publicized episodes of Islamic violence and terrorist activities that have occurred throughout the world. Shah-Kazemi points out that there is a wrathful side to Islam, but that it is not the fundamental tenet of the religion. He states that those who use the Koran to justify violence and hatred on religious grounds display a "blatantly unIslamic political ideology."

Shah-Kazemi notes that while the Christian God embodies love, the Muslim God represents mercy, and this theme and associated ideas of forgiveness, love, and peacefulness best represent the true nature of Islam. For example, the Brussats stated, he presents a translated verse in English as, "Whoever saves the life of one human being, it shall be as if he had saved the whole of humankind. (5:32)." He points out that in Islam, God's love and mercy are the dominant forces of creation, and that they are supreme over all else, even God's wrath and anger. Hatred, Shah-Kazemi relates, is not an emotion consistent with Islam, according to this verse from the Koran: "O you who believe, be steadfast and upright for God, bearing witness with justice, and never let hatred of a people cause you to deal unjustly with them. Be just—that is closest to piety. (5:8)." *Booklist* contributor Ray Olson remarked that the author's "introduction and notes learnedly and companionably complete the lovely and enlightening little volume."

BIOGRAPHICAL AND CRITICAL SOURCES:

BOOKS

My Mercy Encompasses All: The Koran's Teachings on Compassion, Peace, & Love, Shoemaker & Hoard (Emeryville, CA), 2007.

PERIODICALS

African Studies Review, December, 1999, Maati Monjib, review of *Algeria: Revolution Revisited,* p. 251.

Booklist, October 1, 2007, Ray Olson, review of *My Mercy Encompasses All,* p. 27.

Choice: Current Reivews for Academic Libraries, June, 1999, L.J. Cantori, review of *Algeria,* p. 1860.

International Journal of African Historical Studies, spring-summer, 1999, John P. Entelis, review of *Algeria,* p. 610.

Middle East Journal, summer, 1999, review of *Algeria,* p. 503; winter, 2000, review of *Algeria,* p. 155.

Parabola, fall, 2007, Barry McDonald, review of *Justice and Remembrance: Introducing the Spirituality of Imam Ali,* p. 115.

ONLINE

Institute of Ismaili Studies Web site, http://www.iis.ac.uk/ (July 26, 2009), author biography.

Macmillan Web site, http://us.macmillan.com/ (July 26, 2009), author biography.

Spirituality & Practice Web site, http://www.spiritualityandpractice.com/ (July 26, 2009), Frederic Brussat and Mary Ann Brussat, review of *My Mercy Encompasses All.*

World Wisdom Web site, http://www.worldwisdom.com/ (July 26, 2009), author biography.*

* * *

SHARPE, Isabel 1962(?)-
[A pseudonym]
(Muna Shehadi Sill)

PERSONAL: Born c. 1962; divorced; children: two sons. *Education:* Yale University, B.A.; Boston University, M.A.

ADDRESSES: Home—Wauwatosa, WI. *E-mail*—isabel@isabelsharpe.com.

CAREER: Writer. Worked in fundraising and as a professional opera singer.

MEMBER: Romance Writers of America.

WRITINGS:

ROMANCE NOVELS

The Wild Side, Harlequin (New York, NY), 2001.
Hot on His Heels, Harlequin (New York, NY), 2002.
A Taste of Fantasy, Harlequin (New York, NY), 2003.
Take Me Twice, Harlequin (New York, NY), 2004.
Before I Melt Away, Harlequin (New York, NY), 2004.
Thrill Me, Harlequin (New York, NY), 2005.
All I Want—, Harlequin (New York, NY), 2005.
What Have I Done for Me Lately?, Harlequin (New York, NY), 2006.
Women on the Edge of a Nervous Breakthrough, Avon Books (New York, NY), 2007.
Indulge Me, Harlequin (New York, NY), 2008.
My Wildest Ride, Harlequin (New York, NY), 2008.
As Good as It Got, Avon (New York, NY), 2008.
No Holding Back, Harlequin (New York, NY), 2009.
(With Sharon Sala and Linda Cardillo) *A Mother's Heart,* Harlequin (New York, NY), 2009.

OMNIBUS NOVELS

(With Cathie Linz) *The Cowboy Finds a Bride; The Way We Weren't,* Harlequin (New York, NY), 2000.
(With Cathie Linz) *The Lawman Gets Lucky/Beauty and the Bet,* Harlequin (New York, NY), 2000.
(With Carrie Alexander) *Tryst of Fate/Counterfeit Cowboy,* Harlequin (New York, NY), 2000.
(With Jacqueline Diamond) *Excuse Me?, Whose Baby?,* Harlequin (New York, NY), 2001.
One Fine Prey/Two Catch a Fox, Harlequin (New York, NY), 2002.

ANTHOLOGIES

Windfall, Harlequin (New York, NY), 2003.
(With Jane Sullivan, Julie Kistler) *Always a Bridesmaid,* Harlequin (New York, NY), 2004.
(With Janelle Denison and Jennifer LaBrecque) *Secret Santa: A Naughty but Nice Christmas Collection,* Harlequin (New York, NY), 2006, also published as *Secret Santa: He'd Better Watch Out!/The Nights before Christmas/Mistletoe Madness,* 2006.

SIDELIGHTS: Isabel Sharpe is the pseudonym of prolific romance novelist Muna Shehadi Sill. Sharpe grew up in New England and attended Yale University, where she earned her bachelor of arts degree in music. She then attended Boston University, where she received her master of arts degree in vocal performance. After completing her academic career, Sharpe worked in fundraising and as a professional opera singer. Sharpe, however, found that she was not cut out for a job in fundraising. Later, after marrying and moving to Wisconsin with her husband and newborn son, Sharpe found herself bored as a stay-at-home mother in a new town. So, she tried writing. Although her first manuscript was rejected by the Harlequin Press, Sharpe's subsequent work was accepted. As Sharpe related in a *Milwaukee Journal Sentinel* interview, "I honestly can't remember what made me think I could write a novel." However, she added, "If I see two people on a sidewalk, I start making up a story subconsciously." The author also noted: "I don't try to do it. I think I've always been a writer. I just didn't know it."

Sharpe's first book, *The Wild Side,* was published in 2001. It was followed a year later by *Hot on His Heels.* In 2003, Sharpe authored *A Taste of Fantasy.* Applauding the novel in the online *Best Reviews,* Janice Bennett stated, "I found the plot . . . to be interestingly unique with an amusing narrative and snappy dialogue to move things along." Sharpe next wrote *Take Me Twice* in 2004, as well as *Before I Melt Away.* Praising the latter novel in a contribution to *BookReview.com,* Harriet Klausner called it "a delightful contemporary romance starring two wonderful hard working and hard loving individuals who bring to life Milwaukee." Yet more applause was given by Page Traynor in a review for the *Romantic Times Online.* Traynor found that the "heartwarming story shines with finely drawn characters that touch your heart."

In 2005, Sharpe wrote *Thrill Me* and *All I Want—.* Traynor, again writing for the *Romantic Times Online,* noted that the latter story "has strong, well-drawn characters." The following year, Sharpe continued her publishing successes with *What Have I Done for Me Lately?* She then wrote *Women on the Edge of a Nervous Breakthrough* in 2007. The book is one of her more widely reviewed to date. The novel is set in Kettle, Wisconsin, and features Vivian Harcourt. Vivian is returning to Kettle after living in New York. There, her lover, Ed, was murdered. After arriving in Kettle, Vivian meets Erin Hall, a woman who has just left her abusive husband. Sarah, a wife and mother in the midst of a midlife crisis also befriends Vivian. Together, the three women recover from their respective pasts. Like Sharpe's previous works, *Women on the Edge of a Nervous Breakthrough* was praised by reviewers. Sheri Melnick, in a contribution to the *Romantic Times Online,* said the novel is "filled with laughter and dark humor." A *Publishers Weekly* contributor was also impressed, declaring that "this feel-good story won't disappoint women readers looking for a light read."

In 2008, Sharpe published *Indulge Me,* a novel that *Romantic Times Online* contributor Traynor called "a fast, sexy read." She also went on to praise the "heartwarming characters" in the book. Also in 2008, Sharpe wrote *My Wildest Ride,* which Traynor called "moving and heartwarming" in a review for the *Romantic Times Online.* Another of Sharpe's more popular romance novels is *As Good as It Got.* The story again features three women in emotional crisis. This time, they are all at the tail end of bad relationships. Although Cindy Matterson has overlooked her husband's affairs for years, he is the one leaving her. Anne Redding is recently widowed by her husband's suicide; she is overwhelmed by the debt he has left behind. Martha Danvers is unable to maintain a relationship, so she imagines that she is the mistress of a politician who is in a coma. Critics found the book to be an inspiring tale of women who finally learn the value of their own self-worth. Praising the volume in the *Romantic Times Online,* Leslie L. McKee stated that "all of Sharpe's strong female characters become empowered to make changes in their lives after dealing with a loss." Klausner, again writing for *BookReview.com,* stated that *As Good as It Got* is "a strong sharp tale that focuses on females recovering from dead relationships in which they were the losing party." A *Publishers Weekly* writer also found much of value in the novel, stating that "Sharpe delivers a cheeky overcoming-adversity narrative that's laced with wisdom and humor."

BIOGRAPHICAL AND CRITICAL SOURCES:

PERIODICALS

MBR Bookwatch, January 1, 2005, Harriet Klausner, review of *Before I Melt Away.*

Milwaukee Journal Sentinel, January 15, 2006, "Wauwatosa Mom Churns Out Red-Hot Romance Novels," author interview.

Publishers Weekly, December 11, 2006, review of *Women on the Edge of a Nervous Breakthrough,* p. 48; May 19, 2008, review of *As Good as It Got,* p. 33.

ONLINE

Best Reviews, http://thebestreviews.com/ (January 31, 2003), Janice Bennett, review of *As Good as It Got.*

BookReview.com, http://www.bookreview.com/ (July 27, 2009), Harriet Klausner, review of *Before I Melt Away;* (July 27, 2009), Harriet Klausner, review of *As Good as It Got.*

Isabel Sharpe Home Page, http://www.isabelsharpe.com (July 27, 2009).

Romantic Times Online, http://www.romantictimes.com/ (July 27, 2009), Page Traynor, reviews of *Windfall, All I Want, Indulge Me, My Wildest Ride,* and *Before I Melt Away;* (July 27, 2009), Leslie L. McKee, review of *As Good as It Got;* (July 27, 2009), Sheri Melnick, review of *Women on the Edge of a Nervous Breakthrough.**

* * *

SHAWL, Nisi 1955(?)-

PERSONAL: Born c. 1955; divorced. *Education:* Attended the University of Michigan.

ADDRESSES: *Home*—Seattle, WA. *E-mail*—nisis@aol.com.

CAREER: Writer. Has worked as a janitor, dorm cook, artists' model, and au pair. Worked at a natural foods warehouse and as salesperson of structural steel, aluminum, and used books. Clarion West Writers Workshop, board of directors.

MEMBER: Carl Brandon Society (founding member).

AWARDS, HONORS: James Tiptree, Jr., Award, 2008, for *Filter House: Short Fiction.*

WRITINGS:

(With Cynthia Ward) *Writing the Other,* Aqueduct Press (Seattle, WA), 2005.

Filter House: Short Fiction, Aqueduct Press (Seattle, WA), 2008.

Author maintains a blog at http://nisi-la.livejournal.com. Contributor of short stories to *Semiotext(e).* Contributor to periodicals, including the *Seattle Times, Ms.,* and *Shawl.*

SIDELIGHTS: Nisi Shawl is the author of the award-winning short story collection *Filter House: Short Fiction.* Shawl began writing at an early age, and she told an interviewer for the online *Enter the Octopus*: "When I was about 20, I dropped out of college, because that place wasn't teaching me a thing I needed to know about writing. That's when I started sending stories out to editors." She also said in the same interview, "My favorite piece is always the most recent. . . . But I love all my writing. I know there are people who can't stand their own work. Not me. I love rereading what I've written. It's like sleep, or chocolate mousse; I sink right down into it and smile." Discussing the odd title of her collection in an online *Ambling along the Aqueduct* interview with Jesse Vernon, Shawl explained that *Filter House* "is sort of like an underwater, 3-D spiderweb that [appendicularia] use to trap food. They are filter feeders but they build these filters outside their body that last for about two or three hours, until the appendicularia outgrows it or they become clogged, useless. Then they release them and they drift down to the lower levels of the ocean. If you've read about anything in marine ecology, you've heard about 'marine snow'—all the lower levels of life subsist on [it]; that's the basic element of their ecology. So [discarded filter houses are] a large component of marine snow. [I liked] the idea that it was something so basic, too." Thus, Shawl went on to tell Vernon: "I wanted to have the title of the collection not be a story and I wanted it to be the sort of combination of words that would make people think, 'Well, what is that?' I also was drawn by this idea that the structure of the short story collection is ephemeral, that it's made up of other elements that are brought together in this moment—because they are so short, short stories are sort of ephemeral too." Furthermore, Shawl admitted: "I was just really attracted to the idea of something that was so ephemeral and beautiful."

In yet another interview, this time with Eileen Gunn in the online *Fantasy* magazine, Shawl explained how *Filter House* came to be published. "Timmi Duchamp, who is the editor at Aqueduct, approached me about doing a collection of my short stories. It was her idea. I mean—of course I had wanted to put a book together for a long time. I had a whole list I wrote down of titles for this imaginary collection. But the book wouldn't exist without her impetus." Indeed, Shawl noted that her editor "asked me to send her all my stories, and I took her at her word. I sent the first story I'd ever sold, 'I Was a Teen Age Genetic Engineer,' and several others simply not suitable for publication. She picked fourteen of the twenty-eight I offered her. When people ask me if there's an underlying theme to *Filter House,* I want to tell them: 'Stuff Timmi liked.' Of course there's more to it than that. When I told her about the Tiptree she said, 'I knew the stories needed to be in a book for people to see what you were doing with them. And I was right.'" Later in the same interview, Shawl stated: "It's true I had some things in mind when I was writing various of the collection's stories. Usually more than one thing. But they're not just about what I think," adding: "Is a story something I create to communicate ideas, or something I participate in with my readers? I'm always thrilled when someone gets out of a story what I was trying to put into it. And I'm also often thrilled when someone gets out of a story a totally other thing I didn't even know was up in there."

Shawl's collection, regardless of its intended or perceived meaning, was well received by critics. Matthew Cheney, in the online *Strange Horizons,* stated that "the primary virtue of Shawl's stories is their wide range in influence, genre, and setting. There are stories set in the past, present, and future; there are stories of fantasy, science fiction, and horror; there are stories whose inspiration comes from folktales and fairy tales; and all of the stories include characters who are not white, middle-class men (still the most common protagonists in fiction). More writers should strive for such range." Brian Charles Clark, writing in the online

Curled up with a Good Book, declared: "Call Nisi Shawl's first collection of stories slipstream, call it speculative, call it curvy fiction for the straight-ahead twists—they're all grounded in experience." Clark added: "In Shawl's realities, imagination is a force to be reckoned with, and the universe teems with life and spirit and desire."

BIOGRAPHICAL AND CRITICAL SOURCES:

PERIODICALS

Booklist, July 1, 2008, Regina Schroeder, review of *Filter House: Short Fiction,* p. 48.

Publishers Weekly, June 9, 2008, review of *Filter House,* p. 35.

ONLINE

Ambling along the Aqueduct, http://aqueductpress.blogspot.com/ (April 8, 2008), Jesse Vernon, author interview.

Curled Up with a Good Book, http://www.curledup.com/ (July 27, 2009), Brian Charles Clark, review of *Filter House.*

Enter the Octopus, http://entertheoctopus.wordpress.com/ (July 27, 2009), author interview.

Fantasy, http://www.darkfantasy.org/ (July 27, 2009), Eileen Gunn, author interview.

Nisi Shawl Home Page, http://www.sfwa.org/members/shawl (July 27, 2009).

Strange Horizons, http://www.strangehorizons.com/ (October 22, 2008), Matthew Cheney, review of *Filter House.*

* * *

SHORT, Brendan 1969-

PERSONAL: Born May 10, 1969; married; children: daughter. *Education:* University of Notre Dame, B.A.; University of Texas James A. Michener Center for Writers, M.F.A.; attended graduate school in Maryland.

ADDRESSES: Home—Chicago, IL. *Agent*—InkWell Management, 521 5th Ave., 26th Fl., New York, NY 10175. *E-mail*—brenshort@hotmail.com.

CAREER: Novelist, poet, and short story writer. Writer-in-residence fellow, St. Albans School, Washington, DC, 2000-01. Formerly an AmeriCorps VISTA volunteer; works as a fund-raiser for nonprofit agencies. Also wrote captions for photographs for an online database.

AWARDS, HONORS: Artist fellowship, DC Commission on the Arts and Humanities; Larry Neal Writer's Award for Fiction (twice); received Pushcart Prize nomination.

WRITINGS:

Dream City (novel), MacAdam/Cage Publishing (San Francisco, CA), 2008.

Contributor of fiction and poetry to periodicals, including *Literary Review* and *River Styx.*

SIDELIGHTS: Novelist and short story writer Brendan Short is the author of *Dream City,* which "is partially a social history of Chicagoland from the 1930s to the present," wrote *San Francisco Chronicle* reviewer Marcus Banks, "but it's principally about the life of a fractured man named Michael Halligan. Short successfully weaves together many people's lives, all the while with a keen understanding of how people interact with each other." This understanding, the author suggested, came to him only slowly; his original impulses were in other directions (although he did spend several years working in fundraising, writing proposals for antipoverty organizations in Washington, DC), and he recognizes that the process of composition is one that takes a toll on a writer's creativity. "In grade school and high school, I was always better at math than English," Short told an interviewer for the blog *Oh, the Writing You Can Do.* "Once I started enjoying and working at reading and writing and gave up on math, I realized that all writing relies on some sort of structure and logic, just like with equations and formulas." "I assume," he said in an interview for the online *Writers Read,* "that many first-time novelists hit a period shortly after publication when they feel disoriented. . . . The artistic impulse, after a scramble through the publishing world, emerges weary and timid. At least that is where I find myself."

Describing the character of Michael Halligan, wrote a contributor to the *Rick Librarian* blog, "the author pulls off a really difficult feat—creating an antisocial character with various vices who is still strangely likable." From the age of six, Michael Halligan is caught up in the breaking of his family during the Great Depression. He first begins to understand that his family is not having the idyllic existence he had come to expect from the comics pages his mother pasted on the walls of his bedroom when the family visits the great Chicago World's Fair in 1933. Michael's father, Paddy Halligan, had been a small-time boxer who turned to the mob for employment after his career faltered. His mother, Elizabeth, accidentally died as the result of a home abortion. As a result, Michael turns to what will become the great obsession of his lifetime: the collection of Big Little Books, a kind of precursor to modern graphic novels, but which were designed as ephemera and never meant to last. For Michael, however, the Big Little Books represent a kind of stability, an evocation of the time when his family was still a unit and his mother was still alive. "What starts out as an idle pastime becomes an obsession as Michael chases down every title at the cost of all relationships and a life of any consequence," Poornima Apte explained in a *Mostly Fiction* review. "The novel shows us snapshots of Michael's life—as he makes a break from his abusive father, his awkward and ultimately sad relationship with his aunt, a failed attempt at marriage."

"Michael ends up spending much of his life trying to recapture the innocence and purity that he had with Elizabeth even as he becomes ever more aware that his youth is fading," Michael Leonard declared in a review for the Web site *Curled Up with a Good Book.* "Ironically, those childhood dreams and their made-up stories of heroes and villains give him the strength to continue and imbue him with a sense of courage to follow his heart no matter the cost." "Short doesn't bring much new to the family saga potluck," declared a *Publishers Weekly* critic, yet "a bevy of eccentric characters and some tense moments" help maintain readers' interest. "The moral dilemmas that can complicate family commitment," said Kevin Greczek, writing for *Library Journal,* "are presented very clearly here."

BIOGRAPHICAL AND CRITICAL SOURCES:

PERIODICALS

Austin American-Statesman, November 23, 2008, Jeff Salamon, review of *Dream City.*

Library Journal, August 1, 2008, Kevin Greczek, review of *Dream City,* p. 72.

Publishers Weekly, June 30, 2008, review of *Dream City,* p. 159.

San Francisco Chronicle, November 11, 2009, Marcus Banks, review of *Dream City.*

ONLINE

Brendan Short Home Page, http://www.brendanshort.net (July 29, 2009).

Curled Up with a Good Book, http://www.curledup.com/ (July 29, 2009), Michael Leonard, review of *Dream City.*

Mostly Fiction, http://mostlyfiction.com/ (July 29, 2009), Poornima Apte, review of *Dream City.*

Oh, the Writing You Can Do, http://ohwriteucando.blogspot.com/ (July 29, 2009), author interview.

Rick Librarian, http://ricklibrarian.blogspot.com/ (July 29, 2009), review of *Dream City.*

Time Out Chicago, http://chicago.timeout.com/ (July 29, 2009), Jonathan Messinger, review of *Dream City.*

Writers Read, http://whatarewritersreading.blogspot.com/ (July 29, 2009), Vivian Darkbloom, author information.

* * *

SIGER, Jeffrey M.

PERSONAL: Born in Pittsburgh, PA. *Education:* Washington and Jefferson College, degrees in political science and biology; Boston College Law School, law degree.

ADDRESSES: Home—Mykonos, Greece. *Agent*—Shannon Vander Hook, Linden Alschuler & Kaplan, 1251 Ave. of the Americas, New York, NY 10020. *E-mail*—jeffsiger@mac.com.

CAREER: Novelist. Formerly worked as a lawyer in New York, NY.

WRITINGS:

Murder in Mykonos (novel), Poisoned Pen Press (Scottsdale, AZ), 2009.

Assassins of Athens (novel), Poisoned Pen Press (Scottsdale, AZ), 2009.

SIDELIGHTS: Former Wall Street lawyer Jeffrey M. Siger is the author of the mystery novels *Murder in Mykonos* and *Assassins of Athens.* After a legal career in which he helped change prison conditions in New York, New York, he created an organization to bring lawyers working in private practice and volunteer opportunities together, and helped found his own private practice that dealt with national and international litigation. Then Siger retired to Mykonos, Greece, and began a new career as a mystery writer. "I wanted to write about Greek culture," Siger explained in an interview with Ken Coffman for the Web site *Gather.* The stories he composes, he also told Coffman, "can be read in three or four different levels. If you read it at one level it talks about the culture of Greece. Another level is the mystery. You want to make sure the level the reader chooses works for them, don't bounce back and forth. Make sure what you're trying to get across runs smoothly. Otherwise, you're putting in things meaningful to you, but you're not the person who counts."

Murder in Mykonos, explained a reviewer for the Web site *Reading Is Vital to My Sanity,* "starts with a beautiful young woman arriving on the island to enjoy the island and revel in the all night partying that Mykonos is known for. She is only able to enjoy the nightlife for a few days before she disappears." Investigating the girl's disappearance is Andreas Kaldis, the new chief of police for the island of Mykonos. Kaldis is a transfer from Athens, Greece, where he had been a homicide detective. Like many of the visitors to Mykonos, Kaldis is undergoing culture shock; because he is not a native of the island, many of the local residents withhold information from him and refuse to cooperate with his inquiry. The matter becomes even more complicated when a girl's corpse is discovered buried beneath the floor of an abandoned church. "As more bodies turn up in churches around the island," wrote Ginger K.W. Stratton in *Reviewing the Evidence,* "Andreas seeks the help of Tassos Stamatos, chief homicide investigator for the Cyclades. Were they dealing with a serial killer or merely coincidence?" Soon the two are involved in a breakneck chase to discover the identity of the murderer before he can claim another victim. "In the end, Andreas finds more than he bargained for," stated *Booklist* reviewer Stephanie Zvirin, "and readers will be well pleased."

Critics celebrated Siger's evocation of the place and spirit of the Greek islands in his novels. "I thought my weakness was the description of a scene, but reviewers say that's my strongest skill," the author told Coffman. "I should have known the easy things are sweet spots, everybody has some and if you think they're no good, you'll wreck them. The thing I thought was my weakness—people are lauding. I'm more comfortable now and I just write descriptions the way I write them." "Siger sprinkles the novel with information on Greek history, customs and legend, which show he has done his research and add authenticity to the story," declared Katherine Petersen in a *Mysterious Reviews* contribution. "Readers who enjoy gaining knowledge through their fiction will learn of the panegyria, celebrations of saints on their name days," and many other aspects of local Aegean culture. Harriet Klausner, writing for the *Mystery Gazette,* stated that *Murder in Mykonos* is "an engaging Greek police procedural due to the locale and the lead detective," adding that "the rounding up of the usual suspects is fun to follow." "Kaldis's feisty personality and complex backstory are appealing," wrote a *Publishers Weekly* reviewer, and the novel provides "solid foundations for a projected series." The author's close "knowledge of Mykonos adds color and interest to his serviceable prose and his simple premise," concluded a *Kirkus Reviews* contributor. "The result is a surprisingly effective debut novel."

BIOGRAPHICAL AND CRITICAL SOURCES:

PERIODICALS

Booklist, November 15, 2008, Stephanie Zvirin, review of *Murder in Mykonos,* p. 21.

Kirkus Reviews, October 1, 2008, review of *Murder in Mykonos.*

Publishers Weekly, September 29, 2008, review of *Murder in Mykonos,* p. 62.

Science Letter, February 10, 2009, "A Mama Mia Sort of Setting for a No Country for Old Men Style Story," p. 217.

ONLINE

Gather, http://www.gather.com/ (July 29, 2009), Ken Coffman, "Writin' Wombat Interview—Jeffrey Siger."

Jeffrey Siger Home Page, http://www.jeffreysiger.com (July 29, 2009), author profile.

Mysterious Reviews, http://www.mysteriousreviews.com/ (July 29, 2009), Katherine Petersen, review of *Murder in Mykonos.*

Mystery Gazette, http://themysterygazette.blogspot.com/ (July 29, 2009), Harriet Klausner, review of *Murder in Mykonos.*

Reading Is Vital to My Sanity, http://www.cadycorner.com/ (July 29, 2009), review of *Murder in Mykonos.*

Reviewing the Evidence, http://www.reviewingthe evidence.com/ (July 29, 2009), Ginger K.W. Stratton, review of *Murder in Mykonos.**

* * *

SILL, Muna Shehadi
See SHARPE, Isabel

* * *

SIMONSON, Walter 1946-

PERSONAL: Born September 2, 1946; married Louise Jones (a writer). *Education:* Graduate of Rhode Island School of Design, 1972.

CAREER: Comic-book writer and illustrator. Worked for DC Comics and Marvel Comics.

AWARDS, HONORS: Shazam Award for best individual short story (dramatic) for *The Himalayan Incident,* 1973, for *Gotterdammerung,* 1974, and (with Archie Goodwin) for *Cathedral Perilous,* 1974; Haxtur Prize for best writer for *Mighty Thor.*

WRITINGS:

(With others) *Havok & Wolverine: Meltdown,* Epic Comics (New York, NY), 1990.

X-Men: Days of Future Present, Marvel Comics (New York, NY), 1991.

Stan Lee Presents the New Fantastic Four: Monsters Unleashed, Marvel Comics (New York, NY), 1992.

(With Bob Wiacek and William Rosado) *Iron Man 2020,* Marvel Comics (New York, NY), 1994.

Legends of the World's Finest, DC Comics (New York, NY), 1995.

Edgar Rice Burrough's Tarzan versus Predator: At the Earth's Core, Dark Horse Comics (Milwaukie, OR), 1997.

(And illustrator) *Orion: The Gates of the Apokolips,* DC Comics (New York, NY), 2001.

World of Warcraft, Book 1, WildStorm Productions (La Jolla, CA), 2008.

ILLUSTRATOR:

(With Bob Wiacek) Michael Moorcock, *Blitz Kid,* 1991.

(With Mark Reeve and John Ridgway) Michael Moorcock, *Michael Moorcock's Multiverse,* DC Comics (New York, NY), 1999.

Contributor, as author and/or illustrator, to comic book series including *Star Slammers, Battlestar Galactica, Raiders of the Lost Ark, Manhunter, X-Factor, Mighty Thor, Cyberforce, GEN-13, Avengers, Fantastic Four, Orion, Hawkgirl, Multiverse,* and *Wonder Woman.*

SIDELIGHTS: Walter Simonson is a renowned, award-winning comic-book writer and illustrator who has made important contributions to popular series at both DC Comics and Marvel, the two major comics publishing houses. He broke into the business in the early 1970s. Originally an undergraduate student of geology who was planning a career in paleontology, Simonson abandoned science and in 1969 transferred to the Rhode Island School of Design, where he graduated in 1972. As a thesis project, he created *Star Slammers,* a graphic science-fiction story that was used as a promotional item for the 1974 World Science Fiction Convention. He was hired out of art school by editor-in-chief Carmine Infantino of DC Comics, and in a short time had contributed illustrations to several award-winning numbers of the *Manhunter* series written by Archie Goodwin. In the meantime he also illustrated books, including an edition of J.R.R. Tolkien's *The Hobbit,* produced by New York art-house publisher Harry N. Abrams. In 1978 Simonson cofounded Upstart Associates, a comics studio he owned and operated with several colleagues in the Garment District of New York City. After

Upstart folded in 1987, Simonson took advantage of the new working arrangements made possible by the Internet and left the city for a new home in upstate New York.

In the meantime, Marvel Comics had hired him away from DC Comics. Collaborating with his wife, Louise, Simonson wrote *X-Factor,* starring the five original X-men. In 1983 Simonson began working on *The Mighty Thor,* a series originated by comic-book legends Stan Lee and Jack Kirby and over which Simonson took nearly complete creative control for forty-five issues. During the 1990s Simonson also contributed to *Avengers, Fantastic Four, Cyberforce,* and *GEN-13* series. In 2000, he began working on the monthly *Orion* series for DC Comics, and for the same company he wrote *Hawkgirl,* beginning in 2006. Simonson has also contributed covers and "backup features" to several Marvel series, including *Fourth World* and *Kanto the Assassin.* As of 2009, he was contributing stories to the *Multiverse* series written by Michael Moorcock and contributing story and dialogue to a series of graphic novels based on the massively popular World of Warcraft online game.

Like many of his colleagues at Marvel and DC, Simonson began creating comics at an early age. First inspired by dinosaurs and early earth history, he used crayons, colored pencils, and a typewriter to complete his first book at the age of ten, calling it "The Origin of Life." He discovered Marvel Comics while in college. At first he tried to imitate the commercial superheroes; later he started doing continuous stories with characters and settings of his own invention. His first paid published work appeared in DC Comics' *Weird War* in 1972. Simonson penciled, inked, and lettered the short story. After starting his professional career, he gradually developed a regular routine for his original books: developing a short story, creating a version of the story across a series of thumbnail pages on typing paper, tracing the thumbnails onto the comic-artist's medium known as Bristol board (indicating titles, word balloons, and sound effects), then sending out the boards to the letterer. After the lettered boards came back, he completed and inked the drawings. The entire process still demands great attention to detail and the collaboration of several people—all with their own ideas and talents—as the work goes through a process of constant review, criticism, revision, and improvement.

In interviews, Simonson claims to take a story-oriented approach. "You should never forget," he is quoted by *Mahalo.com,* "that the entire purpose of comics as a medium is to tell a story." A post on the blog *That Chip Guy* commented on Simonson's talent for storytelling. "Simonson's Thor stories are heavily plot-driven, but he finds a way to use the limited space of 22-page comics to develop the supporting cast to an extent never before accomplished in the title, creating a true ensemble piece. . . . His art is still distinctive even eighteen years later. He uses graphic ornamentation to strong effect within and outside panel borders, draws with angular and dynamic lines, and mixes ancient, modern, and futuristic environments almost seamlessly." In a *Booklist* review of *Michael Moorcock's Elric: The Making of a Sorcerer,* Tina Coleman wrote, "Simonson's fluid artwork [presents] a stunning view of Melnibone and give new texture to Moorcock's universe." Writing in *School Library Journal,* reviewer Benjamin Russell commented on the *World of Warcraft, Book 1,* which Simonson wrote, "The dialogue and narration both gamely try to provide detail and expression that the art cannot." Jesse Karp noted in *Booklist* that *World of Warcraft* "will appeal to even those few boys who are not familiar with the game."

BIOGRAPHICAL AND CRITICAL SOURCES:

PERIODICALS

Booklist, October 1, 2006, Gordon Flagg, "Walter Simonson: Modern Masters," p. 17; October 1, 2007, Tina Coleman, review of *Michael Moorcock's Elric: The Making of a Sorcerer,* p. 42; October 15, 2008, Jesse Karp, review of *World of Warcraft, Book 1,* p. 38.

School Library Journal, January, 2009, Benjamin Russell, review of *World of Warcraft, Book 1,* p. 134.

ONLINE

Comic Book DB.com, http://www.comicbookdb.com/ (July 29, 2009), author profile.

Comicvine, http://www.comicvine.com/ (July 29, 2009), author profile.

Lambiek.net, http://lambiek.net/ (July 29, 2009), author profile.

Mahalo, http://www.mahalo.com/ (July 29, 2009), author profile.

Man-Size Live Journal, http://man-size.livejournal.com/ (July 29, 2009), author interview.

Meanwhile . . . Interviews, http://www.mikejozic.com/ (July 29, 2009), Mike Jozic, "Walt Simonson: All Across the Multiverse."

NYC Graphic, http://graphicnyc.blogspot.com/ (April 13, 2009), Christopher Irving, author interview.

Sequential Tart, http://www.sequentialtart.com/ (July 29, 2009), Jennifer M. Contino, "Gods and Dinosaurs," author interview.

SF Site, http://www.sfsite.com/ (July 29, 2009), Steven H. Silver, review of *Multiverse.*

That Chip Guy, http://blog.tp.org/ (August 24, 2003), "Thor Visionaries: Walt Simonson, Vol. 1."*

* * *

SINGER, Margot

PERSONAL: Married; children: two. *Education:* Harvard University, B.A., 1984; Oxford University, M.Phil., 1986, University of Utah, Ph.D., 2005.

ADDRESSES: *Home*—Granville, OH. *E-mail*—singerm@denison.edu.

CAREER: McKinsey & Company, New York, NY, principal, 1986-87; faculty member at Denison University, Granville, OH, and Queens University, Charlotte, NC.

AWARDS, HONORS: Bosler Endowed Faculty fellowship, Denison University; Flannery O'Connor Award for Short Fiction, Shenandoah/Glasgow Prize for Emerging Writers, 2008, and Reform Judaism Prize for Jewish Fiction, all for *The Pale of Settlement;* National Endowment for the Arts fellowship; Carter Prize for the Essay; honorable mention, PEN/Hemingway Award.

WRITINGS:

The Pale of Settlement: Stories, University of Georgia Press (Athens, GA), 2007.

Contributor to literary journals, including *Agni, Prairie Schooner, Gettysburg Review, Shenandoah, Western Humanities Review, North American Review,* and *Sun.*

SIDELIGHTS: Margot Singer's first book, the short story collection *The Pale of Settlement: Stories,* has been hailed as an exceptional literary debut, winning not only the prestigious Flannery O'Connor Award but also the Shenandoah/Glasgow Prize for Emerging Writers and the Reform Judaism Prize for Jewish Fiction. The book contains nine linked stories centering on Susan, an Israeli American journalist who, despite having spent most of her life in New York City, remains haunted by her ties to her ethnic homeland. Singer connects her material to political events of the 1980s and 1990s, showing how the Israeli invasion of Lebanon and the ensuing Intifadas, suicide bombings, and facts of the Occupation affect the lives of Jews and Palestinians. The opening story, "Helicopter Days," begins in Israel in the first days of the 1982 war with Lebanon and ends with the death of Susan's grandfather shortly after Saddam Hussein's invasion of Kuwait in 1990. In "Lila's Story," Susan returns to Haifa for the first time since her grandmother's death in 1997. This event evokes memories of Lila and the stories she would tell her granddaughter about her earlier life, when she was forced to leave Germany for Palestine in the 1930s. Susan recalls Lila describing her first meeting with a man she calls Lev, shortly after the end of World War II; though she is already married, Lila is drawn to this man and Susan wonders what may have actually happened between them: "Maybe nothing happens" that first day, Susan thinks, "but I want to believe it does. I want to believe that desire rises out of smoke and ruin, out of loneliness and loss. I want to believe that there are infinite cultivars of love."

As a journalist, Susan is adept at telling other people's stories; in addition to her grandmother's, she tells her mother's story and those of other extended family and former lovers. Even during a trip to Nepal, Susan's thoughts are expressed through the narratives of others, as she muses on the possible story of another journey of obvious Israeli origin. Reviewer Gili Warsett, writing on the *Venus Zine* Web site, felt that Susan's distanced perspective undermines the coherence of the collection's various narrative threads and makes the character disappointingly unknowable. But in the end, wrote Warsett, Singer's approach succeeds "for the specific reason that these issues of identity and how politics figure into our personal stories is not a linear or simple story line. We are composed of our family's choices and our own, and this is true on a micro and macro level. Singer gets that her subject must match her tone."

Speaking about the political content in her stories in an interview with *Table* Web site contributor Stacy Perman, Singer said that the complexity of Israeli-Palestinian relations, "so politically and socially complex and contradictory," was a major inspiration in her writing. "Only in fiction or in literary nonfiction," she said, "can you work with complex issues in a way that honors the competing narratives." And doing so can lead to ambiguous results, because in fiction as well as real life, things are not always satisfactorily resolved. "Fragmentation is an important theme in the book," explained Singer. "Identity is incomplete. We try to piece together pieces of memory and history and create a narrative of who we are and that isn't easy. . . . Jews and Arabs tell stories about the causes of their historical situation that cannot be reconciled. The stories don't add up and I think there is truth in that."

Praise for *The Pale of Settlement* has been copious, with the Reform Judaism Prize judges, quoted on the Union for Reform Judaism Web site, calling the book "the most impressive literary representation to date of the complex relationship between contemporary American Jews and the State of Israel." Leah Strauss, writing in *Booklist,* observed that the stories create "a fascinating, many-hued narrative fabric," and *World Literature Today* reviewer Alan Cheuse wrote that "the triumph of this collection is that we enjoy [its] questions as much as any answers that might appear."

BIOGRAPHICAL AND CRITICAL SOURCES:

PERIODICALS

Booklist, October 1, 2007, Leah Strauss, review of *The Pale of Settlement: Stories,* p. 31.

Books, October 27, 2007, "Common Threads: Recurring Characters and Places Provide Link in 2 New Short-Story Collections," p. 12.

Choice, March 1, 2008, C.E. O'Neill, review of *The Pale of Settlement,* p. 1162.

Columbus Dispatch (Columbus, OH), Margaret Quamme, review of *The Pale of Settlement.*

Publishers Weekly, August 20, 2007, review of *The Pale of Settlement,* p. 45.

World Literature Today, March 1, 2008, Alan Cheuse, review of *The Pale of Settlement.*

ONLINE

Binghamton University Web site, http://www.2binghamton.edu/ (July 24, 2009), "Gardner Award Finalist for 2008."

JBooks.com, http://www.jbooks.com/ (July 24, 2009), Bezalel Stern, review of *The Pale of Settlement.*

Jew Wishes, http://jewwishes.wordpress/com/ (July 24, 2009), "Margot Singer Wins 2008 Reform Judaism Prize for Fiction."

Kenyon Review Online, http://www.kenyonreview.org/ (July 24, 2009), Erika Dreifus, review of *The Pale of Settlement.*

Margot Singer Home Page, http://www.margot-singer.com (July 24, 2009).

Shenandoah, http://shenandoah.wlu/edu/ (July 24, 2009), "The Shenandoah/Glasgow Prize for Emerging Writers."

Short Review, http://theshortreview.blogspot.com/ (July 24, 2009), "Margot Singer Wins 2008 Glasgow-Shenandoah Prize for Emerging Writers."

Tablet, http://tabletmag.com/ (July 24, 2009), Stacy Perman, interview with Singer.

Union for Reform Judaism Web site, http://urj.org/ (July 24, 2009), "Margo Singer Wins Reform Judaism Prize for Jewish Fiction."

Venus Zine, http://www.venuszine.com/ (July 24, 2009), GiliWarsett, review of *The Pale of Settlement.**

* * *

SIV, Sichan 1948-

PERSONAL: Born March 1, 1948, in Phochentong, Cambodia; immigrated to the United States, 1976, became naturalized citizen, 1982; son of Siv Chham and Chea Aun; married Martha Lee Pattillo (a staff worker), 1983. *Education:* Royal University of Phnom Penh, bachelor's degree; Columbia University, M.A., 1981.

ADDRESSES: *Home*—San Antonio, TX.

CAREER: High school English teacher, Cambodia; CARE relief worker, Cambodia, 1970s; Cambodian refugee resettlement worker, U.S., 1977-89; White House deputy assistant for public liaison, and State Department deputy assistant secretary of South Asian Affairs, Washington, DC, 1989-93; financial consultant and director, 1993-2001; U.S. ambassador to United Nations, 2001-06. Also worked as flight attendant, cab driver, apple picker, ice cream server, and short order cook.

WRITINGS:

Golden Bones: An Extraordinary Journey from Hell in Cambodia to a New Life in America, Harper (New York, NY), 2008.

SIDELIGHTS: Sichan Siv was a young relief agency worker in Cambodia when Pol Pot's Khmer Rouge army overtook the country and set about eradicating any vestige of western influence. Millions of people, particularly those with formal education, were sentenced to reeducation programs, slave labor, or summary execution. Some two million Cambodians were either killed outright or died of exhaustion or starvation. Siv was one of the few to escape, eventually immigrating to the United States as a refugee. His memoir, *Golden Bones: An Extraordinary Journey from Hell in Cambodia to a New Life in America,* chronicles his ordeal and expresses his gratitude for his new life as an American citizen.

Siv describes the horrors of life under Pol Pot: being forced to work long hours on starvation rations; seeing decomposing bodies, their hands still bound behind their backs, showing evidence of torture; risking torture or death for speaking. After serving one year of hard labor under the Khmer Rouge, Siv determined to risk an escape attempt, knowing that he would be killed if caught. He jumped off a logging truck in February 1976, and walked three days through the forest before making it over the border into Thailand. When a Connecticut couple agreed to sponsor him, he was able to immigrate to the United States, arriving with only two dollars in his pocket. He insisted on pulling his own weight as soon as possible. He drove a cab in New York City and also picked apples, scooped ice cream, and flipped burgers, working to perfect his English and to further his education. He earned a master's degree from Columbia University, and became a naturalized citizen in 1982. Siv became interested in the democratic political process after watching televised coverage of the national conventions in 1976, and in 1988 he volunteered for George H.W. Bush's campaign. To his surprise and delight, Bush appointed him White House deputy assistant for public liaison, and State Department deputy assistant secretary of South Asian Affairs. In 2001, President George W. Bush appointed Siv U.S. Ambassador to the United Nations.

But Siv's new life was haunted by sorrow as well. He learned that his entire family, including his mother and all of his siblings, their spouses, and children, had perished at the hands of the Khmer Rouge. In 1992 Siv returned to Cambodia, where, he told *Bangkok Post* Web site contributor Pichaya Svasti, he "played a key role in the peace process."

As his memoir makes clear, Siv has profound respect for democratic government. "I came out of a Communist dictatorship," he explained in an interview with *Asian American Policy Review* contributor Christina Hu. "There was nothing in correction of law except the death penalty. I mean, you made a mistake, you die." Observing American elections, he said, was an exciting and revelatory experience. "I said, 'People have the right to say what they have in mind. People are choosing those who are going to govern them. This is fantastic! This is great!'" Siv also spoke about the importance of hard work and education. "My favorite letter in the English alphabet is A," he said. "The first letter. A stands for adaptation and adoption. A stands for altruism. You can adapt yourself to a new circumstance, you will be adopted, and you will be successful."

Reviewers noted this positive message in *Golden Bones,* as well as the book's harrowing account of Siv's suffering, escape, and early struggles to make a new life in the United States. *Houston Chronicle* reviewer Steve Weinberg observed that the memoir "sheds no special insight on the disturbing phenomenon" of Pol Pot's genocidal policies and "relies heavily on cliché, name dropping and oversimplified scenarios," but found that Siv's "heart-rending account bears witness to the inhumanity of men and women when various factors coalesce."

BIOGRAPHICAL AND CRITICAL SOURCES:

BOOKS

Siv, Sichan, *Golden Bones: An Extraordinary Journey from Hell in Cambodia to a New Life in America,* Harper (New York, NY), 2008.

PERIODICALS

American Spectator, October 1, 2008, "An American from Cambodia," p. 75.

Asian American Policy Review, January 1, 2008, Christina Hu, "On Political Empowerment: From the Refugee Camp to the White House, an Interview with Former UN Ambassador Sichan Siv," p. 17.

Houston Chronicle, August 17, 2008, Steve Weinberg, review of *Golden Bones,* p. 14.

Kirkus Reviews, May 15, 2008, review of *Golden Bones.*

New York Times, June 16, 2005, "Bush Sends Regrets on U.N. Celebration," p. 18.

Publishers Weekly, May 5, 2008, review of *Golden Bones,* p. 53.

Texas Monthly, July 1, 2008, Mike Shea, interview with Siv.

Washington Post, March 31, 1989, Bill McAllister, "A Cambodian Emigre's Route from Killing Fields to White House," p. 23; March 6, 1992, Bill McAllister, "A Return to Cambodia," p. 21.

ONLINE

Andy's Cambodia, http://andybrouwer.blogspot.com/ (July 27, 2009), interview with Siv.

Bangkok Post Online, http://www.bangkokpost.com/ (July 27, 2009), Pichaya Svasti, "'Never Give Up Hope.'"

Sichan Siv Home Page, http://www.sichansiv.com (July 27, 2009).

Vietnam Center & Archive Web site, http://vietnam archive.blogspot.com/ (July 27, 2009), interview with Siv.

* * *

SLOVIC, Scott 1960-
(Scott H. Slovic)

PERSONAL: Born June 20, 1960. *Education:* Stanford University, B.A.; Brown University, M.A., Ph.D.

ADDRESSES: *Office*—University of Nevada, Reno, 1664 N. Virginia St., Reno, NV 89557-0208. *E-mail*—slovic@unr.edu.

CAREER: Southwest Texas State University, San Marcos, faculty member, 1991-95; University of Nevada, Reno, professor, 1995—, director, Center for Environmental Arts and Humanities, 1995-2002.

AWARDS, HONORS: Fulbright scholar, University of Bonn, 1986-87, and University of Tokyo, Sophia University, and Rikkyo University, Japan, 1993-94.

WRITINGS:

Seeking Awareness in American Nature Writing: Henry Thoreau, Annie Dillard, Edward Abbey, Wendell Berry, Barry Lopez, University of Utah Press (Salt Lake City, UT), 1992.

(Editor, with Terrell F. Dixon) *Being in the World: An Environmental Reader for Writers,* Macmillan (New York, NY), 1993.

(Compiler, with Lorraine Anderson and John P. O'Grady) *Literature and the Environment: A Reader on Nature and Culture,* Longman (New York, NY), 1999.

(Editor) *Getting Over the Color Green: Contemporary Environmental Literature of the Southwest,* University of Arizona Press (Tucson, AZ), 2001.

(Editor, with Michael P. Branch) *The ISLE Reader: Ecocriticism, 1993-2003,* University of Georgia Press (Athens, GA), 2003.

(Editor, with George Hart) *Literature and the Environment,* Greenwood Press (Westport, CT), 2004.

(Editor, with Terre Satterfield) *What's Nature Worth? Narrative Expressions of Environmental Values,* University of Utah Press (Salt Lake City, UT), 2004.

(Editor, with Roberta Moore) *Wild Nevada: Testimonies on Behalf of the Desert,* University of Nevada Press (Reno, NV), 2005.

Going Away to Think: Engagement, Retreat, and Ecocritical Responsibility, University of Nevada Press (Reno, NV), 2008.

Editor, "Credo Series," "Milkweed Editions," and "Environmental Arts and Humanities Series," University of Nevada Press. Editor, *American Nature Writing Newsletter,* 1992-95; editor, *ISLE: Interdisciplinary Studies in Literature and Environment,* 1995—.

SIDELIGHTS: Scott Slovic spent his childhood in Oregon, where he developed a love of the outdoors. His academic training and his teaching career has focused on environmental literature. His first book, *Seeking Awareness in American Nature Writing: Henry Thoreau, Annie Dillard, Edward Abbey, Wendell Berry, Barry Lopez,* examines the psychological and philosophical aspects of works by these writers, as well as the significance of their rhetorical strategies. Slovic has also edited numerous anthologies and collections, including *Being in the World: An Environmental Reader for Writers,* edited with Terrell F. Dixon, and *Literature and the Environment: A Reader on Nature and Culture,* which he compiled with Lorraine Anderson and John P. O'Grady.

Getting Over the Color Green: Contemporary Environmental Literature of the Southwest is a collection of fiction, nonfiction, and poetry on environmental subjects. The book's title comes from Wallace Stegner's remark that one must stop thinking in terms of green grass and lush gardens in order to appreciate the beauty of the dry landscape of the American west. His intent in the book, said Slovic, is to "suggest the exceptional diversity of contemporary southwestern culture—this is, indeed, one of the defining features of the 'human landscape' of the region." The collection focuses on established and emerging writers associated with the southwest, including Edward Abbey, Charles Bowden, Ann Zwinger, Rick Bass, Rudolfo Anaya, Terry Tempest Williams, John Daniel, Joy Harjo, Gloria Bird, Linda Hogan, Luci Tapahonso, and Simon J. Ortiz, as well as Ray Gonzalez, Ofelia Zepeda, Benjamin Alire Sánz, and Jimmy Santiago Baca. Their works, writes Slovic in the book's introduction, will sensitize readers to "issues of 'environmental justice,' to the ways that technology and economics impact the lives of particular groups of people living in the region." Many of the texts included in the collection, Slovic goes on to say, "aim to demonstrate that there is grace and beauty in this long-disparaged, long-neglected part of the world—beauty in the human traditions that have developed in the desert and in the natural features of the desert itself." Reviewing the book in *Environment,* William Rossi called *Getting Over the Color Green* a "rich collection" that "shows how environmental literature . . . can complement policy and science approaches."

With Terre Satterfield, Slovic edited *What's Nature Worth? Narrative Expressions of Environmental Values,* a collection of twelve interviews in which nature writers discuss the benefits and difficulties of narrative strategy as a means to communicate environmental values. Praising the book's attention to a topic of great relevance, *Environment* reviewer Glen A. Love called *What's Nature Worth?* a "necessary and important work."

Going Away to Think: Engagement, Retreat, and Ecocritical Responsibility is a collection of Slovic's own personal essays on environmental themes. In the title essay he considers the environmental costs of travel; in "Be Prepared for the Worst," the author writes about how a personal devastation—in his case, the death of his child—presents more "emotional sharpness" than the more vast, but emotionally distanced, devastation of ecological harm. Other topics include changes in the approaches of ecocriticism after 9/11; the environmental ethics of xenotransplantation; and the challenges of presenting scientific information to readers in a manner consistent with environmental sensitivity. *Going Away to Think* also includes essays on writers Rick Bass, Randy Malamud, and Robinson Jeffers. A reviewer for *Publishers Weekly* found that the collection "veers between the pedantic and profound," praising Slovic's attempt at emotional engagement despite the book's academic tone. Similarly, a writer for *Internet Bookwatch* described Slovic's writing as "insightful" and "informative."

Slovic has been awarded two Fulbright awards, the first for study at the University of Bonn and the second for study in Japan at the University of Tokyo, Sophia University, and Rikkyo University. Since 1995 he has been professor of literature and environment at the University of Nevada, Reno, where he prefers to conduct meetings with students and colleagues on the hiking trail rather than his office.

BIOGRAPHICAL AND CRITICAL SOURCES:

BOOKS

Slovic, Scott, *Going Away to Think: Engagement, Retreat, and Ecocritical Responsibility,* University of Nevada Press (Reno, NV), 2008.

Slovic, Scott, editor, *Getting Over the Color Green: Contemporary Environmental Literature of the Southwest,* University of Arizona Press (Tucson, AZ), 2001.

PERIODICALS

American Literature, March 1, 1993, John A. Kinch, review of *Seeking Awareness in American Nature Writing: Henry Thoreau, Annie Dillard, Edward Abbey, Wendell Berry, Barry Lopez,* p. 193.

Choice: Current Reviews for Academic Libraries, September 1, 2004, M.W. Cox, review of *What's Nature Worth? Narrative Expressions of Environmental Values,* p. 104.

Environment, June 1, 1993, review of *Being in the World: An Environmental Reader for Writers,* p. 30; September 1, 2002, William Rossi, review of *Getting Over the Color Green,* p. 44; January 1, 2005, Glen A. Love, review of *What's Nature Worth?*

Georgia Review, December 22, 2004, Douglas Carlson, review of *What's Nature Worth?,* p. 973.

Green Teacher, March 22, 2000, review of *Literature and the Environment: A Reader on Nature and Culture,* p. 42.

Internet Bookwatch, November 1, 2008, review of *Going Away to Think.*

Journal of American Culture, March 1, 2005, Ray B. Browne, review of *Literature and the Environment,* p. 143.

Nineteenth-Century Literature, September 1, 1992, review of *Seeking Awareness in American Nature Writing,* p. 269.

Publishers Weekly, June 30, 2008, review of *Going Away to Think,* p. 174.

Reference & Research Book News, November 1, 2001, review of *Getting Over the Color Green,* p. 234; February 1, 2004, review of *The ISLE Reader: Ecocriticsm, 1993-2003,* p. 220; November 1, 2004, review of *Literature and the Environment,* p. 240; November 1, 2008, review of *Going Away to Think.*

Sewanee Review, October 1, 1995, review of *Being in the World,* p. 621; October 1, 1995, review of *Seeking Awareness in American Nature Writing,* p. 613.

ONLINE

University of Nevada, Reno Web site, http://www.unr.edu/ (July 27, 2009), Slovic faculty profile.*

*   *   *

SLOVIC, Scott H.
See SLOVIC, Scott

SMART, Bradford D. 1944-

PERSONAL: Born July 3, 1944. *Education:* Purdue University, Ph.D.

ADDRESSES: Office—37202 N. Black Velvet Ln., Wadsworth, IL 60083.

CAREER: Psychologist, consultant, and writer. Smart & Associates, Chicago, IL, president.

WRITINGS:

Selection Interviewing: A Management Psychologist's Recommended Approach, Wiley (New York, NY), 1983.

The Smart Interviewer, Wiley (New York, NY), 1989.

Topgrading: How Leading Companies Win by Hiring, Coaching, and Keeping the Best People, Prentice Hall Press (Paramus, NJ), 1999, revised edition, Portfolio (New York, NY), 2005.

(With Kathryn Smart Mursau) *Resourcefulness Parenting: How to Raise Happy, Successful Kids,* Perigee Book (New York, NY), 2003.

(With Greg Alexander) *Topgrading for Sales: World-Class Methods to Interview, Hire, and Coach Top Sales Representatives,* Portfolio (New York, NY), 2008.

SIDELIGHTS: Bradford D. Smart is an industrial psychologist and business consultant who is recognized throughout the world for his expertise on hiring. In his 1989 book *The Smart Interviewer,* the author discusses the employee selection interviewing process and provides a step-by-step approach to planning and conducting the interview. Smart delves into the psychology upon which interview questions are based and instructs interviewers on how to interpret answers to various questions. The book includes both an examination of interviewing's legal aspects as pertaining to employment and information on writing job descriptions and personal specifications needed to fulfill a position. A contributor to the *Dallas Business Journal* commented that the author provides "a simple, elegant technique."

Smart's next book, *Topgrading: How Leading Companies Win by Hiring, Coaching, and Keeping the Best People,* was published in 1999 with a revised edition published in 2005. The book introduces the author's "Topgrading" concept, pointing out that it is the people that a company employs that have the greatest influence on a company's ultimate success or failure. "The basic theory is that one can transform hiring from an art guided by intuition and chemistry into a science," noted *Inc.* contributor Leigh Buchanan.

Smart explains that Topgrading is a system developed to enable companies to not only fill their staff with "A" players but also to turn "B" players into "A" players. The system also provides information on how to rid the company of those only playing on the "C" level, including a discussion of the ethics of firing people. Smart includes case studies and real-life examples from companies that have employed his technique. The book features both guidelines and checklists that emphasize objectivity in staffing, assessing, and developing employees. Since the development of the program, the author and his team have conducted more than 6,500 interviews and case studies to validate the process. "The book is written in a concise and easy-to-understand format," wrote *HR* magazine contributor Jeanine Brannon in a review of the book's first edition. Also reviewing the first edition, *Booklist* contributor Mary Whaley noted that "useful lessons can be learned from this approach to developing corporate talent."

Smart and Greg Alexander wrote *Topgrading for Sales: World-Class Methods to Interview, Hire, and Coach Top Sales Representatives.* This book extends the Topgrading concept to a focus on sales and sales managers. The principles are refined to apply to the special needs of sales managers and sales directors. Noting that successful sales depend on hiring the best possible sales reps, the authors point out that surveys have revealed that approximately one-half of all those hired for sales positions or promoted are actually not qualified and end up in the wrong job. To support this observation, the authors note that statistics show that a forty percent of all sales reps fail each year and that sales managers' tenure is typically about nineteen months.

In *Topgrading for Sales,* Smart and Alexander focus on teaching sales managers how to conduct systematic interviews to get the best people for their sales teams. They also discuss how to improve employees capabilities and weed out employees who do not make the "A" grade or have the potential to make the grade. The book includes forms, worksheets, and guidelines that point to thirty-six areas of competency in sales that include assertiveness, resourcefulness, and self-awareness. The authors also feature one hundred "smart" questions. "Readers may never again have to have an original thought about sales hiring," wrote Leigh Buchanan for *Inc.* In a review for *Booklist,* Barbara Jacobs remarked that the approach is "based on sound human-resources practices and policies" that have received outside validation.

BIOGRAPHICAL AND CRITICAL SOURCES:

PERIODICALS

Booklist, February 15, 1999, Mary Whaley, review of *Topgrading: How Leading Companies Win by Hiring, Coaching, and Keeping the Best People,* p. 1017; May 15, 2008, Barbara Jacobs, review of *Topgrading for Sales: World-Class Methods to Interview, Hire, and Coach Top Sales Representatives,* p. 11.

Dallas Business Journal, July 7, 2000, review of *The Smart Interviewer,* p. 42.

HR, May, 1990, Lloyd N. Dosier, review of *The Smart Interviewer,* p. 12; July, 1999, Jeanine Brannon, review of *Topgrading,* p. 146.

Inc., June, 2008, Leigh Buchanan, "A Skimmer's Guide to the Latest Business Books," review of *Topgrading for Sales,* p. 26.

Journal of Property Management, March-April, 2008, "High Grade Hiring," review of *Topgrading.*

Personnel Psychology, winter, 1990, review of *The Smart Interviewer,* p. 906.

Philadelphia Business Journal, August 11, 2000, review of *The Smart Interviewer,* p. 27.

Planet IT, May 6, 2000, review of *Topgrading.*

ONLINE

Penguin Web site, http://us.penguingroup.com/ (August 15, 2009), brief author profile.

Topgrading Web site, http://www.topgrading.com (August 15, 2009).*

* * *

SMITH, Anthony Neil

PERSONAL: Born in MS.

ADDRESSES: *E-mail*—a.neil.smith@gmail.com.

CAREER: Writer; coeditor, *Plots with Guns* (online noir journal); associate editor, *Mississippi Review.*

WRITINGS:

(Editor) *Plots with Guns: A Noir Anthology,* Dennis McMillan Publications (Tucson, AZ), 2005.

NOVELS

Psychosomatic, Point Blank/Wildside Press (Rockville, MD), 2006.
The Drummer, Two Dollar Radio (San Diego, CA), 2006.
Yellow Medicine, Bleak House Books (Neenah, WI), 2008.
Hogdoggin', Bleak House Books (Neenah, WI), 2009.

Author of *Anthony Neil Smith* blog.

SIDELIGHTS: Anthony Neil Smith is a writer of crime fiction and an associate editor at the *Mississippi Review.* He also coedited the online noir journal *Plots with Guns.* The anthology *Plots with Guns: A Noir Anthology,* which Smith edited, includes twenty-four stories culled primarily from that publication, and most of them, according to a *Publishers Weekly* reviewer, "hit their targets as bulls-eyes." As its title indicates, the book's material features significant firearms action and plenty of blood. Authors include Eddie Muller, Jim Nisbet, Kevin James Miller, Robert Skinner, and Sean Doolittle. *Booklist* contributor Keir Graff considered the collection uneven, but the *Publishers Weekly* reviewer concluded that the best pieces in the book show "the breadth and creative reach of the modern hard-boiled tale.

Smith's first novel, *Psychosomatic,* is set along the coast of the author's native Mississippi and tells the story of a vengeance plot that goes very wrong. In a review of the book quoted on the *Point Blank* Web site, Sean Doolittle observed that the author "takes hard-boiled, crunches it, peels back the shell, and finishes it off with a flamethrower."

The protagonist of *The Drummer* is a former rock star whose tax evasion problems had sent him underground years earlier. He ends up in New Orleans, where he is content to live anonymously until his former band mate tracks him down with the idea of launching a comeback tour. Merle, as the drummer sometimes calls himself, is not interested—but his adrenaline shoots up when his band mate is killed and he realizes he may be next in the crosshairs.

Yellow Medicine introduces Deputy Billy Lafitte, Gulf Coast law enforcement officer who is transferred to Minnesota after Hurricane Katrina. Before long, the divorced Billy becomes involved with Drew, a sexy chanteuse who prefers her other boyfriend's company to Billy's. When the boyfriend is murdered and decapitated, Billy becomes the prime suspect. The effort to clear his name draws Billy into the nasty doings of a drug gang as well as a group of terrorists. *Booklist* contributor Steve Glassman found some plot elements less than plausible, but nevertheless hailed *Yellow Medicine* as "quite a romp."

In the sequel, *Hogdoggin',* Billy has moved to South Dakota, where he serves an enforcer for the ailing ruler of a motorcycle gang whose control over his bikers is wavering as his health deteriorates. Called home on an emergency, Billy encounters Franklin Rome, the FBI agent whom Billy had once assaulted and who has vowed to get some payback. A writer for *Publishers Weekly* noted the novel's "brutality": its title refers to a sport that pits fighting dogs against pigs. *Booklist* reviewer Elliott Swanson, however, found the book fresh and engaging, and hailed Smith as a "very fine [writer] indeed."

BIOGRAPHICAL AND CRITICAL SOURCES:

PERIODICALS

Booklist, October 15, 2005, Keir Graff, review of *Plots with Guns: A Noir Anthology,* p. 33; April 1, 2008, Steve Glassman, review of *Yellow Medicine,* p. 34; May 1, 2009, Elliott Swanson, review of *Hogdoggin',* p. 25.
Books, June 11, 2006, Dick Adler, review of *The Drummer,* p. 8; June 21, 2008, Paul Goat Allen, review of *Yellow Medicine,* p. 8.
Publishers Weekly, September 19, 2005, review of *Plots with Guns,* p. 47; April 13, 2009, review of *Hogdoggin',* p. 32.

ONLINE

Bill Crider's Pop Culture Magazine, http://billcrider.blogspot.com/ (July 28, 2009), Bill Crider, review of *Hogdoggin'* and *The Drummer.*

BSC Review, http://www.bscreview.com/ (July 28, 2009), review of *Hogdoggin'.*

Fantastic Fiction, http://www.fantasticfiction.co.uk/ (July 28, 2009), Smith profile.

Tim Maleeny Web site, http://www.timmaleeny.com/ (July 28, 2009), Tim Maleeny, review of *Yellow Medicine.**

* * *

SMITH, Gwen 1970-

PERSONAL: Born September 4, 1970; married; husband's name Brad; children: Preston, Hunter, Kennedy. *Hobbies and other interests:* "Loves to cheer loudly at her kids' ballgames, play guitar, relax at the piano, and chat with her girlfriends."

ADDRESSES: *Office*—Audio 31 Music, P.O. Box 1311, Huntersville, NC 28070. *E-mail*—Audio31@aol.com.

CAREER: Writer, public speaker, worship leader, and song writer. Girlfriends in God (conference and devotional ministry), Huntersville, NC, cofounder and worship leader; Great Worship Songs Christian record label, Nashville, TN, recording artist, 2008—; Brentwood and Benson Publishing Group, Nashville, staff songwriter; Audio 31, Huntersville, founder.

WRITINGS:

Broken into Beautiful: How God Restores the Wounded Heart, Harvest House Publishers (Eugene, OR), 2008.

Maintains a blog at http://gwensmithsblog.blogspot.com.

SIDELIGHTS: Writer, worship leader, and public speaker Gwen Smith was born September 4, 1970. The founder of Girlfriends in God, a devotional ministry and conference based in Huntersville, North Carolina, Smith is motivated not only by her own Christian beliefs but by a strong conviction that there is a need for women to have an outlet and an organization geared toward their specific spiritual needs. This idea led her to take her place as a spiritual advocate for women, traveling around the country to minister them in particular, as well as to the creation of her daily devotions that are sent to subscribers by e-mail in an effort to provide ongoing support and spiritual encouragement. Smith preaches the unconditional love of Jesus Christ, and stresses the importance of allowing oneself to trust in the healing power of religion. A singer and songwriter, Smith also performs as a recording artist for Great Worship Songs, a Christian record label owned by Brentwood-Benson Music Publishing in Nashville, Tennessee. In addition, Smith is the author of *Broken into Beautiful: How God Restores the Wounded Heart,* which offers readers insight into the ways in which religion and spiritual belief can provide one with the strength to overcome heartbreaking events and to continue on through tragedies that might seem too difficult to bear.

In *Broken into Beautiful,* Smith provides readers with an open and loving view of religion and the power of spirituality to both heal wounds and forgive earlier missteps along the journey of one's life. She shares her own painful story of becoming pregnant while in college and choosing to have an abortion, a decision that she always looked back at with pain, sorrow, and regret, though imagining giving birth and caring for a child at that point in her life seemed impossible. Later in life, Smith believes that God encouraged her to use that experience and her memories of it to help reach out to other individuals who believed that similar choices in their own lives cut them off from leading a spiritual life in the present. By sharing her story, Smith hopes to show that religion can provide support and understanding to anyone in need, acknowledging that spirituality does not mean perfection or lack of doubts about one's personal struggles and demons. She addresses issues ranging from surviving abuse to the pain of losing a loved one, and how spirituality can help one through any struggle. A reviewer for *Publishers Weekly* remarked that "Smith exhorts Christians to stop hiding behind their smiles and be brave enough to get real."

BIOGRAPHICAL AND CRITICAL SOURCES:

BOOKS

Smith, Gwen, *Broken into Beautiful: How God Restores the Wounded Heart,* Harvest House Publishers (Eugene, OR), 2008.

PERIODICALS

Publishers Weekly, May 12, 2008, review of *Broken into Beautiful,* p. 51.

ONLINE

Gwen Smith Home Page, http://www.gwensmith.net (August 12, 2009), author profile.*

* * *

SMITH, Nigel 1958-

PERSONAL: Born November 29, 1958. *Education:* Oxford University, D.Phil.

ADDRESSES: *Office*—Princeton University, Center for the Study of Religion, 5 Ivy Ln., Princeton, NJ 08540; fax: 609-258-6940. *E-mail*—nsmith@princeton.edu.

CAREER: Scholar, educator, writer, and editor. Princeton University, Princeton, NJ, professor of English, chair of the Renaissance Studies Committee, and Senior Behrman fellow. Previously reader in English at Oxford University and tutor in English and fellow of Keble College, Oxford. Also active in radio and television broadcasting in the United Kingdom and United States, 1989—.

AWARDS, HONORS: Recipient of fellowships from the British Academy, National Endowment for the Humanities, John Simon Guggenheim Memorial Foundation, and the National Humanities Center.

WRITINGS:

Perfection Proclaimed: Language and Literature in English Radical Religion, 1640-1660, Clarendon Press (Oxford, England), 1989.

Literature and Revolution in England, 1640-1660, Yale University Press (New Haven, CT), 1994.

Is Milton Better Than Shakespeare?, Harvard University Press (Cambridge, MA), 2008.

EDITOR

A Collection of Ranter Writings from the 17th Century, foreword by John Carey, Junction Books (London, England), 1983.

Literature and Censorship, D.S. Brewer (Cambridge, England), 1993.

(And author of introduction and notes) George Fox, *The Journal,* Penguin Books (New York, NY), 1998.

(With Timothy Morton) *Radicalism in British Literary Culture, 1650-1830: From Revolution to Revolution,* Cambridge University Press (New York, NY), 2002.

The Poems of Andrew Marvell, Pearson/Longman (New York, NY), 2003, revised edition, 2006.

SIDELIGHTS: Nigel Smith is an English professor whose work has focused primarily on early modern literature, especially pertaining to the seventeenth century. In this area his interests include poetry and poetic theory; the social role of literature, including its relation to politics and religion; literature and the visual arts; heresy and heterodoxy; radical and women's literature; and the history of linguistic ideas. As editor of *Literature and Censorship,* published in 1993, Smith presents a series of essays that "explore ways in which literary texts negotiate the tacit or implicit constraints of their culture," as noted by Janet Clare in the *Review of English Studies.* Some contributors examine how writers challenge censorship that can either be real or a cultural perception. They also discuss views of authors and their works in terms of censorship and perceptions in their own times and in modern society. Contributors write about authors and works from William Shakespeare to Virginia Woolf. Clare called the essays "eclectic in both subject and in methodological approach."

In his 1994 book *Literature and Revolution in England, 1640-1660,* the author examines the effects of the British Civil War on literature, from poetry and literary writings to pamphlets and other printed public discourse. "Smith's spotlight is turned less on the inky fabrications of the pen than on those of the printing press; consequently, our sense of what counts in the history of literature expands healthily—out of the coterie and into the public," noted Sharon Achinstein in a review for *Criticism.*

The author begins by examining the conditions under which the writings were completed and within the context of the growing amount of printed publications and news that were becoming available. He explores how news writing changed dramatically with the lessening of censorship while writing for the theater became inhibited by theater closings. Smith goes on to examine the works of apologists within the parliamentary debate and various political theorists with distinct partisan affiliations. In the final third of the book, Smith explores how political, ideological, and religious debates significantly impacted nearly every genre of poetry and prose, and he examines a wide range of authors in various genres.

"Smith brings a wealth of knowledge of texts, both traditional classics and the more obscure items like newsbooks and commonplace books, combined with a subtle understanding of the nuances of literary form and genre (matters often neglected by historians and until recently out of favour in some literary circles as well) to his study, and the result is a valuable study," wrote D.R. Woolf in a review for the *Canadian Journal of History.* Noting that the author's "work can be usefully placed alongside the best recent literary studies of the civil war period," Laura Lunger Knoppers, writing for the *Journal of English and Germanic Philology,* remarked, "Smith . . . provides an important new paradigm for civil war historiography, shifting ground to look at the causes and effects of print culture and the rapid transformation of both rhetoric and literary genres."

Smith is the editor, with Timothy Morton, of *Radicalism in British Literary Culture, 1650-1830: From Revolution to Revolution.* Published in 2002, the book features scholarly essays that examine Great Britain's radical literary culture from the time of the English Revolution on through to the French Revolution. The various essays reveal that radical writing in Great Britain during the 1640s remained important on through to the 1770s, during which time it helped to incite the American and French Revolutions. In the process, contributors set about to disprove the belief held by many historians that this period lacked significant radical thought in terms of politics. The author also contributes an essay. Writing for *Albion,* Chris Mounsey commented that the book "follows in a tradition of historical writing that attempts to discover sources of political radicalism and its transmission from one period of revolution to another."

In his 2008 book *Is Milton Better Than Shakespeare?* Smith presents his case that John Milton is better than William Shakespeare in terms of being more pertinent to modern times by addressing eternal issues that remain important concerns. Writing for *Time International,* Gary Taylor remarked: "Smith dares to confront two big questions that most scholars nowadays scrupulously avoid: Does poetry matter? And, if it does, which poets matter most?"

In advocating Milton as the more pertinent poet, the author points to Milton's emphasis on liberty while also stressing the poet's dedication "to positive transformation in all spheres of human activity." Writing in the book's preface, the author notes: "Milton's presence may be discerned in the formation of much of the English-speaking world's understanding of how the individual belongs to the world and how a just society should be ordered. He considers the nature or even the necessity of rebellion, the need to overcome the deadening hold of custom, and the belief that liberty comes through the confrontation of contrary experiences and contrariness itself." Smith goes on to write that Milton's willingness "to address these vital public and personal themes . . . and to make them part of an astonishingly exciting, innovative visionary literary practice . . . is what seems to me to put Milton in front."

The author examines how the seventeenth-century poet, most noted for *Paradise Lost,* theorized about issues such as political, civil, and religious liberty. He points out that Milton's thoughts not only influenced America's Founding Fathers and their conception of individuality and independence but his thoughts also pertain to our modern society as well. He examines Milton's life within the literary and political scenes of his day and explores some of Milton's key themes, including free will, freedom, slavery, love, and sexual liberty. In his analysis, the author, who draws on Milton's poetry and prose, shows that the poet was not necessarily consistent in his philosophies except as they pertained to "inviting difference and dissent."

Some reviewers pointed out that the title is misleading in that the book does not really compare Milton and Shakespeare but rather focuses primarily on Milton and his works. Nevertheless, the book received favorable reviews. Ray Olson, writing for *Booklist,* called *Is Milton Better Than Shakespeare?* "an inquiry as fascinating as it is demanding."

Smith is also the editor of *The Poems of Andrew Marvell.* Writing for the *Modern Language Review,* Warren Chernaik remarked that the collection of Marvell's works "is far superior to all previous editions of Marvell in several respects: its annotation of linguistic detail, the puns and verbal ambiguities so abundant in Marvell; its notes identifying possible sources and analogues, classical and biblical; its citation of parallel passages from the poet's contemporaries; and its consistent attempts to situate Marvell's writings in their historical context."

BIOGRAPHICAL AND CRITICAL SOURCES:

BOOKS

Smith, Nigel, *Is Milton Better Than Shakespeare?,* Harvard University Press (Cambridge, MA), 2008.

PERIODICALS

Albion, summer, 2003, Chris Mounsey, review of *Radicalism in British Literary Culture, 1650-1830: From Revolution to Revolution,* p. 296.

Booklist, May 1, 2008, Ray Olson, review of *Is Milton Better Than Shakespeare?,* p. 65.

Canadian Journal of History, April, 1995, D.R. Woolf, review of *Literature and Revolution in England, 1640-1660,* p. 115.

Choice: Current Reviews for Academic Libraries, March, 1995, review of *Literature and Revolution in England, 1640-1660,* p. 1121; November, 2008, E.D. Hill, review of *Is Milton Better Than Shakespeare?,* p. 514.

Contemporary Review, July, 2004, review of *The Poems of Andrew Marvell,* p. 64.

Criticism, summer, 1995, Sharon Achinstein, review of *Literature and Revolution in England, 1640-1660,* p. 493.

English Historical Review, July, 1992, J.F. McGregor, review of *Perfection Proclaimed: Language and Literature in English Radical Religion, 1640-1660,* p. 721; November, 1996, Derek Hirst, review of *Literature and Revolution in England, 1640-1660,* p. 1285; September, 2004, Mark Philip, review of *Radicalism in British Literary Culture, 1650-1830,* p. 1062.

Essays in Criticism, January, 1996, Alastair Fowler, review of *Literature and Revolution in England, 1640-1660,* p. 52.

Historical Journal, September, 1990, J.C. Davis, review of *Perfection Proclaimed,* p. 693; June, 1991, J.C. Davis, review of *Perfection Proclaimed,* p. 479.

History, June, 1990, Austin Woolrych, review of *Perfection Proclaimed,* p. 323.

Journal of English and Germanic Philology, July, 1996, Laura Lunger Knoppers, review of *Literature and Revolution in England, 1640-1660,* p. 425.

Journal of Religion, October, 1990, W. Clark Gilpin, review of *Perfection Proclaimed,* p. 633.

Journal of the History of Ideas, January, 1995, review of *Literature and Revolution in England, 1640-1660,* p. 174.

Journal of Theological Studies, April, 1991, B.R. White, review of *Perfection Proclaimed,* p. 396.

Keats-Shelley Journal, annual, 2006, Andrew McCann, review of *Radicalism in British Literary Culture, 1650-1830,* p. 261.

Modern Language Review, April, 1996, David Norbrook, review of *Literature and Revolution in England, 1640-1660,* p. 453; July, 2005, Warren Chernaik, review of *The Poems of Andrew Marvell,* p. 782.

New Statesman, October 7, 1983, Christopher Hill, review of *A Collection of Ranter Writings from the 17th Century,* p. 24.

Notes and Queries, March, 1990, George Parfitt, review of *Perfection Proclaimed,* p. 90; December, 2003, Nicholas McDowell, review of *Radicalism in British Literary Culture, 1650-1830,* p. 4742.

Renaissance Quarterly, winter, 1996, Maija Jansson, review of *Literature and Revolution in England, 1640-1660,* p. 886.

Review of English Studies, November, 1990, John Morrill, review of *Perfection Proclaimed,* p. 563; February, 1996, Janet Clare, review of *Literature and Censorship,* p. 120; August, 1996, Graham Parry, review of *Literature and Revolution in England, 1640-1660,* p. 415.

Shakespeare Survey, annual, 1994, Martin Wiggins, review of *Literature and Censorship,* p. 221.

Sixteenth Century Journal, fall, 1995, Rudolph P. Almasy, review of *Literature and Revolution in England, 1640-1660,* p. 682.

Southern Humanities Review, winter, 1997, review of *Literature and Revolution in England, 1640-1660,* p. 80.

Time International, May 26, 2008, Gary Taylor, "Battle of the Bards," review of *Is Milton Better Than Shakespeare?,* p. 60.

Times Higher Education (London, England), June 23, 1995, Nick Moschovakis, review of *Literature and Revolution in England, 1640-1660,* p. 33; February 26, 2009, Frank Kermode, review of *Is Milton Better Than Shakespeare?,* p. 45.

Times Literary Supplement (London, England), June 30, 1995, David Loewenstein, review of *Literature and Revolution in England, 1640-1660,* p. 31; December 12, 2003, Alastair Fowler, "Garden Gates," review of *The Poems of Andrew Marvell,* p. 7.

Virginia Quarterly Review, autumn, 1989, review of *Perfection Proclaimed,* p. 122; spring, 1995, review of *Literature and Revolution in England, 1640-1660,* p. 48.

ONLINE

Harvard University Press Web site, http://www.hup.harvard.edu/ (August 15, 2009), brief author profile.

Oxford University Press Web site, http://www.oupcanada.com/ (August 15, 2009), brief author profile.

Princeton University Center for the Study of Religion Web site, http://www.princeton.edu/csr/ (August 15, 2009), author faculty profile.*

* * *

SOBEY, Ted Woodall
See SOBEY, Woody

* * *

SOBEY, Woody
(Ted Woodall Sobey)

PERSONAL: Son of Edwin J.C. Sobey.

ADDRESSES: *Office*—Discovery Center of Idaho, 131 Myrtle St., Boise, ID 83702.

CAREER: Discovery Center of Idaho, Boise, director of education; Invent Idaho invention competition, state coordinator.

WRITINGS:

(With father, Edwin J.C. Sobey) *The Way Toys Work: The Science behind the Magic 8 Ball, Etch a Sketch, Boomerang, and More,* Chicago Review Press (Chicago, IL), 2008.

SIDELIGHTS: Woody Sobey, whose full name is Ted Woodhall Sobey, serves as the director of education for the Discovery Center of Idaho. In addition, he works as state coordinator for Invent Idaho, a competition held on a state-wide level among grade-school students, with participants offering up their various inventions for scrutiny. He is the son of Edwin J.C. Sobey, the founder of the National Toy Hall of Fame, as well as the founding director of the National Inventors Hall of Fame. Along with his father, Sobey is the author of *The Way Toys Work: The Science behind the Magic 8 Ball, Etch a Sketch, Boomerang, and More,* which was published by the Chicago Review Press in 2008.

The Way Toys Work is a book that appeals to the inner child in everyone, particularly those who have fond memories of taking apart their toys as children in order to see what made them tick. As preparation for writing this volume, Sobey and his father did just that, taking popular toys and deconstructing them in order to determine how they had been assembled in the first place, and them putting them back together again in order to examine the results once they understood their inner workings. In most cases, science is the key to the secrets held by most favored childhood pastimes, and by examining the parts and principles of assembly behind the various toys, Sobey and his father were able to see just which scientific concepts provided the behind-the-scenes magic. One example of such a toy is the whiffle ball. Originally designed by David N. Mullany, the toy includes slots that send air currents through the ball in a specific way that makes it curve when thrown, thereby providing Mullany's son with a curve ball that he could achieve without hurting his arm. Not only do the Sobeys explain the science behind the various toys included in the book, but they include tips for making toys on your own, the history of various favorite toys, and a list of scientific experiments that help to demonstrate the principles behind the items. David Pitt, in a review for *Booklist,* declared the volume "perfect for collectors, for anyone daring enough to build homemade versions of these classic toys." A reviewer for the *ARS Geek* Web site commented that "children can benefit from the brief explanations of how their favorite toys work, and adults can benefit from the interesting backgrounds and inner workings of their childhood playthings."

BIOGRAPHICAL AND CRITICAL SOURCES:

PERIODICALS

Booklist, April 1, 2008, David Pitt, review of *The Way Toys Work: The Science behind the Magic 8 Ball, Etch a Sketch, Boomerang, and More,* p. 14.

Boys' Life, May 1, 2009, "Read All about It," p. 12.

School Library Journal, June 1, 2008, Robert Saunderson, review of *The Way Toys Work,* p. 175.

ONLINE

ARS Geek, http://www.arsgeek.com/ (August 12, 2009), review of *The Way Toys Work.*

Chicago Review Press Web site, http://www.chicagoreviewpress.com/ (August 12, 2009), author profile.

Ingram Library Web site, http://www.theingramlibrary.com/ (August 12, 2009), review of *The Way Toys Work.**

* * *

SORSOLEIL, Kelly
See McCULLOUGH, Kelly

* * *

SOUSSAN, Michael

PERSONAL: Born in Denmark. *Education:* Brown University, B.A.; Science-Po, Paris, M.A.; earned a certificate in film from New York University.

ADDRESSES: Home—New York, NY. *Agent*—Jennifer Gates, Zachary Shuster Harmsworth, 1776 Broadway, Ste. 1405, New York, NY 10019. *E-mail*—michaelsoussan@yahoo.com.

CAREER: Writer, educator. New York University, New York, NY, Center for Global Affairs, faculty member; previously worked for Cable News Network (CNN), and for the United Nations, New York, NY, as program director for the Iraq program, 1997-2000. Frequent guest lecturer at organizations and universities, such as United States Central Command, the Ditchley House in Oxford, the Harvard Club of New York, the London School of Economics, Johns Hopkins, the MIT book club, and the World Affairs Council.

WRITINGS:

Backstabbing for Beginners: My Crash Course in International Diplomacy, Nation Books (New York, NY), 2008.

Contributor to various periodicals, including the *International Herald Tribune, New Republic, Prospect Magazine, Salon.com, Irish Times, New York Post, Commentary,* and the *Wall Street Journal.*

SIDELIGHTS: Writer and educator Michael Soussan was born in Denmark. He attended Brown University, where he earned his undergraduate degree, then continued his education with a master's degree from Science-Po in Paris, France, and a certificate in film from New York University. He serves on the faculty of New York University in the Center for Global Affairs, and previously worked for the Cable News Network (CNN). Soussan is best known, however, for his work on the United Nations' Iraq program from 1997-2000, where he served as program director of the oil-for-food plan. The premise behind the plan was that, in the wake of the first Gulf War, money from Iraqi oil was supposed to be filtered back into support for the country, specifically making sure that the citizens of Iraq had sufficient food, medicine, and other consumer goods, rather than that money getting funneled directly back to Saddam Hussein. The United Nations had taken on the goal of making sure this strategy was followed. The reality of the situation was far different, however. Very little of the funding in question actually reached the people of Iraq, either in the form of cash or goods. Instead, there was a steady stream of money into the hands of the Iraqi government, with considerable kickbacks going to the various members of the security program designed to prevent such corruption, including participants from France, Russia, and the United States. Disgusted with the situation, Soussan eventually exposed the scandal, a revelation that led to an investigation in the form of the Volker Commission. However, even this form of checks and balances proved ineffective, as far too many high-ranking members of the United Nations Security Council were actually part of the scandal itself, and the Volker Commission was relegated to a superficial investigation rather that risking the complete undermining of the United Nations as a whole. Soussan chronicles his experiences with the United Nations and his thoughts about the outcome of the situation in his book *Backstabbing for Beginners: My Crash Course in International Diplomacy,* which was published by Nation Books in 2008.

Backstabbing for Beginners delves into the scandal at the United Nations from an insider's perspective, and as a result Soussan reveals many of his own personal experiences as he participated in the Iraq program, including how the United Nations conducted business with Saddam Hussein during the last years of the twentieth century. He explains how he gradually came to realize that the program was not working in the ways prescribed, and discusses his own struggles to continue at his job despite his growing awareness of the situation. The book received mix reactions from reviewers, though all agree that the information contained in the volume is important and revelatory. John Green, writing for the *Morning Star* Web site, found Soussan's writing style a distraction from the meat of his argument, remarking that "Soussan loves over-personalizing things and his anecdotal reminiscences of drinking sessions in Kurdistan bars or verbatim conversations with his . . . intern, . . . only distract from what is at its core—an important revelatory work." A reviewer for *Publishers Weekly* praised Soussan both for coming forth with the information that launched the investigation into the oil-for-food program, and with his story of the scandal, declaring that "Soussan brings provocative wit, a keen eye for detail and a knack for revealing anecdotes to this important account." A contributor for *Kirkus Reviews* stated that "United Nations whistleblower Soussan jauntily recounts his tenure coordinating the Iraq Oil-For-Food program, revealing why bribery and kickbacks were tolerated," and went on to conclude that Soussan's revelatory book is "an insightful expose, spiked with outraged wit."

BIOGRAPHICAL AND CRITICAL SOURCES:

BOOKS

Soussan, Michael, *Backstabbing for Beginners: My Crash Course in International Diplomacy,* Nation Books (New York, NY), 2008.

PERIODICALS

Kirkus Reviews, October 1, 2008, review of *Backstabbing for Beginners.*

Library Journal, October 15, 2008, Marcia L. Sprules, review of *Backstabbing for Beginners,* p. 84.

Middle East, November 1, 2008, Fred Rhodes, review of *Backstabbing for Beginners,* p. 65.

Publishers Weekly, September 8, 2008, review of *Backstabbing for Beginners,* p. 46.

Wall Street Journal, November 14, 2008, John R. Bolton, review of *Backstabbing for Beginners,* p. 15.

ONLINE

Michael Soussan Home Page, http://www.michaelsoussan.com (August 12, 2009), author profile.

Morning Star Online, http://www.morningstaronline.co.uk/ (August 12, 2009), John Green, review of *Backstabbing for Beginners.*

Times Online, http://entertainment.timesonline.co.uk/ (August 12, 2009), Dominic Lawson, review of *Backstabbing for Beginners.**

* * *

SPENSER, Jay 1952-
(Jay P. Spenser)

PERSONAL: Born July 5, 1952; married; wife's name Deborah; children: two. *Education:* Graduated from Middlebury College.

ADDRESSES: Home—Seattle, WA. *E-mail*—jay@jayspenser.com.

CAREER: Historian, writer; Smithsonian Institution, Washington, DC, National Air and Space Museum, positions up through assistant curator, 1975-86; freelance writer, 1986-87; Museum of Flight, Seattle, WA, 1987-89; freelance writer, 1989—; Boeing, Seattle, WA, technical writer, 1990—.

WRITINGS:

Aeronca C-2: The Story of the Flying Bathtub, National Air and Space Museum/Smithsonian Institution Press (Washington, DC), 1978.

Bellanca C.F.: The Emergence of the Cabin Monoplane in the United States, National Air and Space Museum/Smithsonian Institution Press (Washington, DC), 1982.

Moskito, Monogram Aviation Publications (Boylston, MA), 1983.

Focke-Wulf FW 190, Workhorse of the Luftwaffe, National Air and Space Museum/Smithsonian Institution Press (Washington, DC), 1987.

Vertical Challenge: The Hiller Aircraft Story, University of Washington Press (Seattle, WA), 1992.

Whirlybirds: A History of the U.S. Helicopter Pioneers, University of Washington Press/Museum of Flight (Seattle, WA), 1998.

(With Joe Sutter) *747: Creating the World's First Jumbo Jet and Other Adventures from a Life in Aviation,* Smithsonian (New York, NY), 2006.

The Airplane: How Ideas Gave Us Wings, Smithsonian Books (Washington, DC), 2008.

Maintains a blog at http://jayspenser.blogspot.com.

SIDELIGHTS: Born July 5, 1952, Jay Spenser has led a colorful life, with a multi-tiered career revolving around his love of airplanes and the history of flight. A historian and writer, Spenser was privileged to be in charge of the Boeing team that designed and engineered the famed 747 airplane during the 1960s. Later, having graduated from Middlebury College, he moved to Washington, DC, where he joined the staff of the National Air and Space Museum at the Smithsonian Institution, arriving in time to help celebrate the museum's official opening on July 1, 1976, marked by the landing of the Viking Lander on Mars. As of the early 1980s, Spenser had climbed to the position of assistant curator for the museum, a job that not only included overseeing new exhibits, but gave him ample opportunity to write articles and books and to learn a myriad of details about the history of aviation. Although he enjoyed the position, which allowed him to conduct research and work with the public, as well as to meet various heads of state, aviators, astronauts, and politicians, the writing side of the job only served to further convince him that he wished to continue his career as a writer. In 1986, Spenser left his position at the National Air and Space Museum to write as a full-time freelancer. Although he was lured back into a formal job by the chance to work at the Museum of Flight in Seattle, he left that position after two years in order to resume his writing once more. Over the course of his career, Spenser has written a number of books, including *Aeronca C-2: The Story of the Flying Bathtub; Bellanca C.F.: The Emergence of the Cabin Monoplane in the United States; Moskito; Focke-Wulf FW 190, Workhorse of the Luftwaffe; Vertical Challenge: The Hiller Aircraft Story; Whirlybirds: A History of the U.S. Helicopter Pioneers;* and *The Airplane: How Ideas Gave Us Wings,* as well as *747: Creating the World's First Jumbo Jet and Other Adventures from a Life in Aviation,* which he wrote with Joe Sutter.

The Airplane offers readers an in-depth look into the history of flight, chronicling the many dreamers responsible for eventually putting man into the air. Spenser looks back at the various inventors who worked toward the creation of the airplane. He also delves into the numerous ways in which those inventors sought inspiration from creatures that possessed the ability they longed to have themselves, such as birds and insects, as well as other creatures that might also give clues as to how to achieve a streamlined physique, such as fish and mammals that spend the bulk of their time in the water. He then goes on to discuss man's various improvements on the airplane over the course of its history, and includes thoughts of where the future of flying might lead. A reviewer for *Bookmarks* Web site dubbed the book an "entertaining history of the jetliner." A contributor for *Kirkus Reviews* found the book to be "a satisfying journey guided by an able pilot."

In *747,* Spenser explains the development of the first wide-bodied jet that included two aisles with three sections of seating. During the 1960s, the Boeing

Corporation was working on numerous projects, and due to the attention paid to the 2707 supersonic plane, there was little manpower or time to devote to the brand new jetliner. Spenser was ultimately recruited to work on the project, and as a result is able to discuss both the progress of the plane itself and the corporate politics that sprang up between various parties within the company, each of whom has their own agendas to meet through the construction of the plane. A writer for *Kirkus Reviews* declared the book "well-written and intelligent: a must for aviation buffs, and convincing backup for Charles Lindbergh's appreciative comment that the 747 was 'one of the great ones.'"

Spenser told *CA:* "I have always loved writing and anything that flies, including birds and airplanes. It was only natural that these interests be combined, I suppose. My professional life has been dedicated to learning more about human achievement in the arena of flight, first at the Smithsonian and the Museum of Flight (my aviation history phase) and then for the past nineteen years at Boeing, where I have learned about current progress and activities (I work closely with engineering teams across the enterprise). I had the best possible education during my ten years at the National Air and Space Museum/Smithsonian Institution. I also have a passion for writing and believe that 'doing good history' is not enough; one must also be able to communicate it broadly and effectively.

"The favorite of my books is *The Airplane.* As to why, here's something from an e-mail I sent recently to a friend who enjoyed it and asked me what led me to write it: The challenge wasn't so much in the content (although a lot of that is new and revisionist) but rather in finding a new way of presenting a familiar story. I call the result 'the antidote of the usual flight history' because previous works invariably overwhelm us with names, dates, record flights, horsepowers, wingspans, etc.—tough going even for those of us who like flying machines. Aviation is too wondrous and inspiring a subject to bore people or ask them to remember vast amounts of information, yet it's hard to avoid doing just that because the history of flight itself is so complex. I knew I needed and wanted to push all that information aside and instead offer insight—i.e., what it all means, why it's important, what truths it reveals about ourselves, where it fits in the greater scheme of things, and so on. But how does one do this in a mass-market book that must hook, entertain, and broadly inform rather than just cater to buffs? My solution was to come up with a highly unconventional structure that looks at the airplane's conception, its birth, and then the different aspects of this key invention each in turn. This approach let me unweave the overly complex tapestry of flight to trace its individual strands in linear fashion. This in turn allowed me to explain the technology, evoke key people and places, and make lateral leaps through time and space to put readers at the elbows of pioneers during their epiphanies. The result was rich, fun, and ultimately very human storytelling infused with more than a bit of the thrill of the hunt. My top theme is that flying is humankind's oldest dream. Exploring this idea, I also posit that we as a species draw our inspiration from nature, can accomplish a great deal when working toward a shared vision, and are adept at applying what we've learned to do in one field of endeavor to meet the needs of another.

"I suspect people find this book is so different and appealing because it masquerades as a history of flight but is in fact a history of technology told in simple, human terms. This alternative approach allowed me to follow the flow of simple yet powerful ideas to show in a memorable way how aviation came about."

BIOGRAPHICAL AND CRITICAL SOURCES:

PERIODICALS

Booklist, November 1, 2008, Gilbert Taylor, review of *The Airplane: How Ideas Gave Us Wings,* p. 10.

Business History Review, December 22, 1993, William F. Trimble, review of *Vertical Challenge: The Hiller Aircraft Story,* p. 666.

Choice: Current Reviews for Academic Libraries, March 1, 1999, W.M. Leary, review of *Whirlybirds: A History of the U.S. Helicopter Pioneers,* p. 1286.

Kirkus Reviews, April 15, 2006, review of *747: Creating the World's First Jumbo Jet and Other Adventures from a Life in Aviation,* p. 399; September 15, 2008, review of *The Airplane.*

Library Journal, June 15, 2006, Sara Tompson, review of *747,* p. 101; October 15, 2008, Sara R. Tompson, review of *The Airplane,* p. 91.

Public Historian, September 22, 1999, review of *Whirlybirds,* p. 83.

Publishers Weekly, March 27, 2006, review of *747,* p. 67; September 22, 2008, review of *The Airplane,* p. 54.

Reference & Research Book News, February 1, 1999, review of *Whirlybirds,* p. 187.

Science Books & Films, May 1, 1983, review of *Bellanca C.F.: The Emergence of the Cabin Monoplane in the United States,* p. 267; March 1, 2009, Eugene E. Nalence, review of *The Airplane.*

SciTech Book News, March 1, 2009, review of *The Airplane.*

ONLINE

Bookmarks Web site, http://www.bookmarksmagazine.com/ (August 12, 2009), review of *The Airplane.*

Jay Spenser Home Page, http://www.jayspenser.com (August 12, 2009), author profile.

* * *

SPENSER, Jay P.
See SPENSER, Jay

* * *

SPILLER, Nancy

PERSONAL: Born in San Francisco, CA; married. *Education:* San Francisco State University, B.A.

ADDRESSES: *Home*—Los Angeles, CA. *E-mail*—nancy@nancyspiller.org.

CAREER: Journalist, artist, writer, novelist, and cook. Previously worked as a staff feature writer at the *San Jose Mercury News,* San Jose, CA, and the *Los Angeles Herald-Examiner,* Los Angeles, CA; as an editor at the *Los Angeles Times* syndicate, Los Angeles; and as a freelance food writer in Glendale, CA. Also instructor in the University of California, Los Angeles Extension Writers Program.

WRITINGS:

Entertaining Disasters: A Novel (with Recipes), Counterpoint (Berkeley, CA), 2009.

Contributor of articles to periodicals, including the *Los Angeles Times, Mother Jones, New West, Travel & Leisure, Coagula Art Journal,* and *New York* magazine. Contributor of fiction to *Rain City Review.*

SIDELIGHTS: Nancy Spiller is a former journalist and food writer whose first novel, *Entertaining Disasters: A Novel (with Recipes),* features an unnamed food writer whose articles about her dinner parties attended by exclusive Hollywood guests turn out to be lies. The truth is that the food writer suffers from a form of social paralysis when it comes to inviting people to her older hillside home. When Richard Cronenberg, the editor of a prestigious food magazine, arrives in town and requests an invitation to one of her bashes, the writer panics as she finally has to stage a real-life dinner.

In a contribution to the *Nancy Spiller Home Page,* Spiller noted that the novel is autobiographical in nature, pointing out she was once a freelance food writer living in an old house just as the character in the book. She also commented that her mother, like the food writer's mother, experienced mental illness. However, Spiller also stresses that she never faked any of her articles. She went on to note that she did not write a memoir because she did not want to disturb living friends, relatives, and colleagues. The novel form, remarked the author, also allowed her more freedom to delve into the lives of various characters, including the protagonist's mother's life before the food writer's birth.

Narrated by the food author, the novel follows not only the writer's dilemma concerning her upcoming gathering but also her dealings with her family, including her husband as their marriage has disintegrated into a loveless union. As for Lenore, the narrator's mother, the reader learns about her life in a series of flashbacks that reveal a single mom who led a life of isolation and sadness. Lenore eventually is institutionalized and undergoes electroshock treatments, leading to family ridicule. As for her dinner party, the food writer encounters numerous problems with the guests she invites, from making up excuses not to come to agreeing to attend only if the writer makes certain foods and promises not to serve other foods. Spiller includes a recipe with each chapter.

Calling some of the recipes "utterly hilarious and undoable," *Booklist* contributor Mark Knoblauch referred to a "simple coleslaw [recipe that] carries ill-written, self-defeating instructions" and another recipe that ends by recommending the reader forgo the cooking and go to a bakery to buy one instead. Another reviewer writing for *Publishers Weekly* noted "Spiller's clever way with words."

BIOGRAPHICAL AND CRITICAL SOURCES:

PERIODICALS

Booklist, November 15, 2008, Mark Knoblauch, review of *Entertaining Disasters: A Novel (with Recipes),* p. 27.

Kirkus Reviews, December 1, 2008, review of *Entertaining Disasters.*

Publishers Weekly, November 17, 2008, review of *Entertaining Disasters,* p. 42.

ONLINE

Nancy Spiller Home Page, http://www.nancyspiller.org (August 16, 2009).

UCLA Extension Writers Program Web site, http://www.uclaextension.edu/writers/ (August 16, 2009), author biography.*

* * *

STANGER-ROSS, Ilana

PERSONAL: Born in Brooklyn, NY; married Jordan Stanger-Ross (a historian); children: Eva, Tillie. *Education:* Barnard College, B.A.; Temple University, M.A., 2003; University of British Columbia, courses in midwifery. *Religion:* Jewish.

ADDRESSES: Home—Victoria, British Columbia, Canada. *E-mail*—ilana@ilanastangerross.com.

CAREER: Writer.

AWARDS, HONORS: Awarded a number of grants from the Leeway Foundation, the Toronto Arts Council, the Ontario Arts Council, the Barbara Deming Memorial/Money for Women Fund, and the Humber College Summer Writer's Workshop; awarded a residency at the Ragdale Foundation.

WRITINGS:

Sima's Undergarments for Women, Wheeler Publishing (Waterville, ME), 2009.

Contributor of short fiction to periodicals including the *Bellevue Review, Lilith Magazine,* and *KillingtheBuddha.com;* contributor of nonfiction to the *Globe and Mail, Walrus Magazine,* and the *Literary Review of Canada;* contributor to the anthology *My Wedding Dress: True-Life Tales of Lace, Laughter, Tears and Tulle.*

SIDELIGHTS: Writer Ilana Stanger-Ross was born in Brooklyn, New York, and received her undergraduate degree from Barnard College. She then went on to earn a master's degree with an emphasis on fiction from Temple University in Philadelphia, then later settled in Victoria, British Columbia, Canada, where she studies midwifery at the University of British Columbia. Stanger-Ross has been awarded a number of grants to support her writing endeavors, including from the Leeway Foundation, the Toronto Arts Council, the Ontario Arts Council, the Barbara Deming Memorial/Money for Women Fund, and the Humber College Summer Writer's Workshop. In addition, she was awarded a residency at the prestigious Ragdale Foundation. Stanger-Ross has contributed short fiction to a number of periodicals and Web sites, including the *Bellevue Review, Lilith Magazine,* and *KillingtheBuddha.com.* She has also written nonfiction for publications including the *Globe and Mail, Walrus Magazine,* and the *Literary Review of Canada.* Her work also appears in the anthology *My Wedding Dress: True-Life Tales of Lace, Laughter, Tears and Tulle.* Stanger-Ross's debut novel, *Sima's Undergarments for Women,* was published in 2009.

Sima's Undergarments for Women has gone through several incarnations over the course of Stanger-Ross's career. Originally a short story, the concept grew and eventually served as the author's dissertation for her master's degree. Later she continued to expand the work until it became the novel that was eventually published. Set in the Boro Park neighborhood of

Brooklyn, an area with a large population of Orthodox Jews, the book features Sima Goldner, a woman who runs a small, dingy underwear shop from her basement that has been catering to various ethnic women of all ages for more than three decades. In a Q&A on her home page, Stanger-Ross notes the idea for the shop springs from an experience out of her own childhood. When it was time to go shopping for her first bra, Stanger-Ross assumed her mother would take her to a bright, clean department store. However, instead they went to a tiny specialty shop on Coney Island Avenue run by a woman known as Miss Pauline, who saw to her fitting. Though Stanger-Ross began shopping at chain lingerie shops when she was old enough to go on her own, she later found herself returning to Miss Pauline's, having gained a greater appreciation for the wonders of personalized attention, a proper fit, and quality merchandise. Sima has no children, and her relationship with her husband is tense and lacking true communication, leaving her to focus on her shop and its routine. However, when Sima hires on a bright Israeli girl named Timna to work as a seamstress, she finds that the vibrant woman brings out many of her own fears and issues that have gone unexamined and unresolved for years, including her infertility and her crumbling marriage. A reviewer for *Publishers Weekly* found the book revealed great depth and multiple layers, declaring it "a subtly powerful treatise on friendship, trust and love, written with plenty of verve." In a review for *Book Reporter* Web site, Sarah Rachel Engelman declared that "this is a quiet novel. The drama is subtle yet emotional, and Stanger-Ross is never heavy-handed. It lags a bit towards the middle, but the descriptions and characterizations are usually spot-on and nicely rendered. There are some very well-written passages here, and the story feels real." Geraldine Sherman, reviewing for the *National Post* Web site, opined: "Stanger-Ross's great talent, at least on this occasion, lies in her understanding of the shadings of female friendship. She never pretends that all of it is benign. There are moments of revenge, of schadenfreude, of jealousy, but she wraps all of it within a richly authentic-sounding language and compassionate grace."

BIOGRAPHICAL AND CRITICAL SOURCES:

PERIODICALS

Booklist, December 1, 2008, Leah Strauss, review of *Sima's Undergarments for Women,* p. 24.

Entertainment Weekly, February 13, 2009, Kate Ward, review of *Sima's Undergarments for Women,* p. 61.

Kirkus Reviews, November 1, 2008, review of *Sima's Undergarments for Women.*

Library Journal, October 15, 2008, Marika Zemke, review of *Sima's Undergarments for Women,* p. 59.

National Post, March 14, 2009, Geraldine Sherman, review of *Sima's Undergarments for Women,* p. 14.

Publishers Weekly, September 29, 2008, review of *Sima's Undergarments for Women,* p. 57.

ONLINE

Book Reporter, http://www.bookreporter.com/ (April 3, 2009), author Q&A; Sarah Rachel Egelman, review of *Sima's Undergarments for Women.*

Boston Bibliophile, http://www.bostonbibliophile.com/ (February 12, 2009), review of *Sima's Undergarments for Women.*

Ilana Stanger-Ross Home Page, http://www.ilanastangerross.com (July 26, 2009).

Jenny's Books, http://jennysbooks.wordpress.com/ (May 4, 2009), review of *Sima's Undergarments for Women.*

National Post Web site, http://network.nationalpost.com/ (March 14, 2009), Geraldine Sherman, review of *Sima's Undergarments for Women.*

Sarah Weinman Web site, http://www.sarahweinman.com/ (January 7, 2009), Sarah Weinman, review of *Sima's Undergarments for Women.*

Temple University Web site, http://www.temple.edu/ (July 26, 2009), alumnus profile.*

* * *

STANLEY, Kelli 1964-

PERSONAL: Born June 11, 1964, in Tacoma, WA. *Education:* Holds a B.A. and M.A.

ADDRESSES: Home—San Francisco, CA. *Agent*—Kimberley Cameron, Reece Halsey North Literary Agency, 98 Main St., Ste. 704, Tiburon, CA 94920. *E-mail*—kelli@kellistanley.com; kstanley@sfsu.edu.

CAREER: Former co-owner of Funny Papers (a comic book store).

AWARDS, HONORS: Writer's Digest Notable Debut, 2008, and Bruce Alexander Memorial Historical Mystery Award, Left Coast Crime, 2009, both for *Nox Dormienda (A Long Night for Sleeping): An Arcturus Mystery.*

WRITINGS:

Nox Dormienda (A Long Night for Sleeping): An Arcturus Mystery, Five Star (Detroit, MI), 2008.

Author maintains a blog at http://kellistanley.blogspot.com.

SIDELIGHTS: Kelli Stanley is a classics scholar and author of the novel *Nox Dormienda (A Long Night for Sleeping): An Arcturus Mystery.* Discussing her writing career in the online *January* magazine, Stanley told Linda L. Richards: "Writing is something I've always done. Because of that, I think, as a child I never had the goal of becoming a writer. Writing was always there, and I suppose I sort of took it for granted. I planned to become an actress when I graduated from high school, and I wanted to direct films. But by the time I was an adult, I realized that I actually needed to write (and in a more disciplined way than scratching out poetry or essays). So I started with screenplays initially, and turned to novels when I was back in college, finishing up my master's degree. [*Nox Dormienda (A Long Night for Sleeping)*] was my first attempt at writing one. And now, of course, I wouldn't trade being a writer for anything."

Stanley's first novel is the beginning of a proposed series. It is a classic noir thriller and mystery, yet it is unique in that it is set in ancient Rome. Discussing the book's distinctive style and content in an interview with Bethany Hensel for the *Bethany Hensel Official Site,* Stanley explained: "I like cities with a lot of history, a lot of character, so to speak . . . one reason I resonate with the noir style, in literature and film. And you're so right about noir being atmospheric . . . born out of the hardboiled '20s and '30s prose of Dashiell Hammett and Raymond Chandler, it became ever darker in the late '40s, with the work of writers like Jim Thompson and films like *Out of the Past.*" Furthermore, she noted that "'Roman Noir' is a play on words, because that's what French critics call the hardboiled/noir prose of the '30s—'black novel,' adding that "Chandler and Hammett were the primary influences for [*Nox Dormienda (A Long Night for Sleeping)*] and the novel is set in the first century AD, in the Roman province of Britannia. So Roman history plus noir style equals 'Roman Noir' . . . and it marks a hybrid genre of historical mystery and classic hardboiled/noir storytelling."

Given her master's degree in classics, Stanley is well qualified to write of ancient Rome. As she told Hensel, "Thanks to my education, I really know this culture, the time and place. The noir part I was born with, I think . . . to me, it's an ideal way to make the history come alive for the reader. And that's what I want to do with my books . . . make you forget that you're reading history." Stanley is also fascinated by the noir genre, and she told Stefan Halley in the online *Pop Syndicate* that "noir is really so much a part of me that it's difficult to analyze why . . . I wrote my first noir play when I was in the third grade! As a writer, I like layers and complexity—what we experience in real life, as opposed to a streamlined simplicity of stereotypes. Human beings are full of surprises. Noir lets me upend expectations and explore characters struggling through life and death and guilt and innocence—epic themes, without the pretensions of 'The Great American Novel.'" Speaking of her decision to combine both of her passions, Stanley told Halley that "I started *NO* in grad school—I spent a long time in academia, between a B.A. and a M.A. in Classics. I did not want to pursue a terminal degree, feeling that it would live up to its name in terms of my creativity. So I thought, why not use the knowledge I've gained in a different, really fulfilling way?" She then stated that, "at the time, there was no other series featuring a Roman doctor—and I thought a medicus would make a perfect protagonist, a logical person to be involved in ancient forensics and investigation. After I received my publishing news, Ruth Downie's book *MEDICUS*—which I'd never heard about—debuted. But even though Arcturus is a doctor in Roman Britain—as is her protagonist—my series has a completely different feel, because of the noir style and pace."

Critics found Stanley's novel to be both compelling and distinctive. Harriet Klausner stated in the online *Mystery Gazette,* "Fans of ancient historical mysteries will enjoy" the book. Klausner also called it an "entertaining Britannia Noir as Arcturus escorts the audience to places not normally found in Roman Empire whodunits." However, in a rare dissenting opinion, a *Publishers Weekly* writer remarked that "readers should be prepared for a routine plot and prose." Even so, a *Kirkus Reviews* contributor was far more impressed, commenting that "first-timer Stanley is sure-footed and enthusiastic about history . . . and crafts a satisfyingly intricate puzzle."

BIOGRAPHICAL AND CRITICAL SOURCES:

PERIODICALS

Kirkus Reviews, May 15, 2008, review of *Nox Dormienda (A Long Night for Sleeping): An Arcturus Mystery.*

Library Journal, April 15, 2009, Wilda W. Williams, "The Great Escape: In Tough Times, Readers Turn to Mysteries," review of *Nox Dormienda (A Long Night for Sleeping),* p. 22.

Publishers Weekly, May 26, 2008, review of *Nox Dormienda (A Long Night for Sleeping),* p. 42.

San Francisco Business Times, August 16, 1991, Lisa Greim, "Funny Papers ZAPS! Teen Fantasies," author information, p. 1.

ONLINE

Bethany Hensel Official Site, http://bethanyhensel.blogspot.com/ (July 7, 2008), Bethany Hensel, author interview.

January, http://januarymagazine.com/ (August 1, 2008), Linda L. Richards, author interview.

Kelli Stanley Home Page, http://www.kellistanley.com (July 28, 2009).

Mystery Gazette, http://themysterygazette.blogspot.com/ (July 4 2008), Harriet Klausner, review of *Nox Dormienda (A Long Night for Sleeping).*

Pop Syndicate, http://www.popsyndicate.com/ (February 25, 2009), Stefan Halley, author interview.*

* * *

STAPP, Jann
See ROBBINS, Jann

STENNETT, Rob 1977-

PERSONAL: Born July 10, 1977; married; wife's name Sarah; children: Julianna. *Education:* Attended the University of Colorado, Colorado Springs, and the University of California, Los Angeles.

ADDRESSES: E-mail—robstennett3@yahoo.com.

CAREER: Novelist and screenwriter. New Life Church, creative director, 1998—.

WRITINGS:

The Almost True Story of Ryan Fisher, Zondervan (Grand Rapids, MI), 2008.

The End Is Now, Zondervan (Grand Rapids, MI), 2009.

Author maintains a blog dedicated to *The Almost True Story of Ryan Fisher* at http://www.almosttruestory.com/blog and a personal blog at http://robstennett.blogspot.com.

SIDELIGHTS: Rob Stennett attended the University of Colorado, Colorado Springs, and the University of California, Los Angeles. He then went on to work as a screenwriter. In 1998, he joined the New Life Church as a creative director. Stennett also maintains a personal blog and lives with his wife, Sarah, and their daughter, Julianna. His first novel, *The Almost True Story of Ryan Fisher,* was published in 2008. Stennett hosts a blog dedicated to the novel as well. In the book, the protagonist, Ryan Fisher, is attempting to found a megachurch. However, Ryan is not a religious person, and he is not aligned with any one faith. Ryan's aspirations began accidentally as a marketing ploy. As a realtor looking to build a larger customer base, Ryan put an advertisement in a Christian periodical. The ad led to a great deal of new business, but Ryan found himself faced with customers who would casually inquire as to his faith and the church he belonged to. Thus, rather than just attend a neighborhood church, Ryan decides to start his own. Strangely, Ryan's wife is so inspired by the idea that she sincerely finds her faith. In the meantime, Ryan hires a cowboy worship leader to be pastor of the new church. As it turns out, the pastor's faith is also somewhat elastic. Later, when a miracle healing is performed at the church, enrollment grows exponentially, even garnering national attention. Ryan's megachurch becomes so significant that he is an invited guest on the *Oprah Winfrey Show.*

Although there were some dissenting opinions, reviewers largely applauded *The Almost True Story of Ryan Fisher* as an entertaining and humorous satire. Several also noted the distinctive writing style, featuring experimental line breaks and innovative paragraph and sentence structure. Praising the story in a review for the online *Signs of Life,* a reviewer noted that "Stennett writes with great wit and satire, but also great warmth," stating that "all of the major characters are developed well," and added that "hopefully we'll be reading much more from him in the future." Timothy Fish, writing in the online *Timothy's Thoughts,* was also impressed with the work. He remarked that "if we look at just the story, *The Almost True Story of Ryan Fisher* is one of the best written Christian novels that I have read in quite a while." Offering additional praise, Fish commented that "the simple fact is that [Stennett] has managed to put together a strong story." A contributor to the online *YS Marko,* noted that the novel is quite accurate in its critiques. The same contributor found that the book is "painful to read at times, since the book is full of the kind of insider stuff that should make us wince." The contributor also felt that "it's also loaded with implications about church, power, worship styles."

Mike Moran, writing in the online *Christianity Today,* was also positive in his assessment of *The Almost True Story of Ryan Fisher.* He observed that "for me, reading Fisher was like literary déjà-vu—the distinct impression that I was reading a story from great literature. That's because in some twisted way, I was. There's an uncanny resemblance, whether intentional or not, between Fisher's plot and characters and those of Fyodor Dostoyevsky's *Crime and Punishment.*" In fact, Moran explained: "Both main characters, Ryan Fisher and Rodion Raskolnikov, concoct a plan to commit a 'crime' based on an irrational, unhealthy view of themselves as extraordinary men." Brittian Bullock, writing in the online *Sensual Jesus,* commented, "I wish I could say that the book was just a bit of silliness . . . but something in me says that this book is all true."

Stennett's second novel, *The End Is Now,* was published in 2009. The story is set in Goodland, Kansas, and the townspeople believe that they will disappear during the rapture first as a sign to the rest of the world that the apocalypse is coming. When one of the residents receives a prophecy indicating that the end is near, the town is divided into two groups; those who do believe and those who do not. Applauding the novel in the online *Scandalous Sanity,* a reviewer noted that "Goodland, Kansas is not only the scene of the 'test market' for the rapture, it is where Christian beliefs and human nature are exposed at their best and worst, stretched to their limits for the world to see." Dale Lewis, in a review of *The End Is Now* for *TitleTrack.com,* stated that the book is "more than a thrilling story based around the apocalypse." Lewis also called the novel "an unorthodox exploration of the two thousand-year-old Christian tradition of looking to the sky and longing for the eternal home promised so long ago." While the story itself is humorous, a *Publishers Weekly* reviewer declared that "examining the nature of belief whatever its content is not at all goofy."

BIOGRAPHICAL AND CRITICAL SOURCES:

PERIODICALS

Publishers Weekly, April 28, 2008, review of *The Almost True Story of Ryan Fisher,* p. 114; May 25, 2009, review of *The End Is Now,* p. 39.

ONLINE

Almost True Story of Ryan Fisher Web site, http://www.almosttruestory.com (July 28, 2009).

Christianity Today, http://www.christianitytoday.com/ (January 30, 2009), Mike Moran, review of *The Almost True Story of Ryan Fisher.*

Scandalous Sanity, http://scandaloussanity.blogspot.com/ (June 16, 2009), review of *The End Is Now.*

Sensual Jesus, http://sensualjesus.wordpress.com/ (July 10, 2008), Brittian Bullock, review of *The Almost True Story of Ryan Fisher.*

Signs of Life, http://signsoflifebooks.com/ (July 30, 2008), review of *The Almost True Story of Ryan Fisher.*

Timothy's Thoughts, http://timothyfish.blogspot.com/ (May 31, 2009), Timothy Fish, review of *The Almost True Story of Ryan Fisher.*

TitleTrack.com, http://www.titletrakk.com/book-reviews/ (July 28, 2009), Dale Lewis, review of *The End Is Now.*

YS Marko, http://ysmarko.com/ (July 28, 2009), review of *The Almost True Story of Ryan Fisher.**

* * *

STEVENS, Karl 1978-

PERSONAL: Born November 21, 1978, in Concord, MA. *Education:* Attended Montserrat College of Art and the Art Institute of Boston.

ADDRESSES: Home—Allston, MA. *E-mail*—stevens_karl@hotmail.com.

CAREER: Illustrator, artist, and writer. Works as a security guard at the Fogg Art Museum, Cambridge, MA.

WRITINGS:

(And illustrator) *Guilty* (graphic novel), Alternative Comics (Gainesville, FL), 2005.
(Illustrator) Anthony Apesos, *Anatomy for Artists: A New Approach to Discovering, Learning and Remembering the Body,* North Light Books (Cincinnati, OH), 2007.
(And illustrator) *Whatever* (graphic short stories), Alternative Comics (Gainesville, FL), 2008.

Illustrations have appeared in periodicals, including the *Boston Phoenix* and *Legal Action Comics.*

SIDELIGHTS: In his first graphic novel, *Guilty,* writer and illustrator Karl Stevens writes about "20-something angst in the familiar settings around Cambridge and Boston," as noted by Alvin Powell in an article for the *Harvard Gazette Online.* The sixty-four-page comic first came to life as a twenty-four-page short story, the author told Mike Miliard in an article for the *Boston Phoenix.* However, Stevens received a grant from the Xeric Foundation to work further on the story. "Once I got the grant, I decided that it was better to do a book," he told Miliard. "I wanted to expand on these characters."

The story features former lovers Ingrid and Mark accidentally meeting when they both get jobs at Harvard University's Fogg Art Museum, where Ingrid works the admissions desk and Mark toils as a security guard. (The author also works as a security guard at the actual museum and inserts himself in the story in a cameo role.) Mark asks Ingrid to have drinks one evening at a local bar called the Cellar, along with a friend that Mark brings along for support. The rest of the story is told primarily from the inside the minds of Ingrid and Mark as their insecurities and fears are revealed, as well as their struggle with whether or not they should begin dating again. Ingrid has had a series of bad relationships while Mark has not been able to get over Ingrid and has immersed himself in video games. The author also features the characters remembering their past together with various panels depicting their memories in a somewhat incoherent and scattered fashion.

Writing for the *Comics Reporter* Web site, a contributor noted that the author provides his characters with "clear motivations . . . that drive their actions." The contributor also remarked that both of them cheated on each other when they were dating and that they are not fully honest with each other as they make contact once again. Noting that the author also depicts numerous lesser emotions exhibited by the couple other than just Ingrid's guilt and Mark's loneliness, the reviewer wrote that, as a result, Stevens avoids the pitfall that many other younger writers succumb to when they "give their characters ambiguous feelings in an attempt to make them 'complex,' making their participation in the storyline feel like an arbitrary set of marching instructions."

Several reviewers commented on the author's use of staged photographs of his friends on which to base his drawings. Noting this approach and the author's "uncanny artwork," Suzette Chan, in a review for the *Sequential Tart* Web site, commented that "Stevens . . . underlines the characters static emotional states with deliberate drawings and tableau compositions," adding, "Stevens certainly captures a feeling—each ex-lover's quiet desperation." Steven N. Jacobs, writing for the *Harvard Crimson,* commented that the "artwork and the narrative it embodies hold the kind of profound and simple truth that could one day make for something great."

In his next graphic novel, *Whatever,* Stevens presents a series of short stories that first appeared as comic strips in the *Boston Phoenix.* The book also includes two full-color inserts of images. The stories revolve around the hero, Karl, and his friends as they go about their daily lives, from such mundane endeavors as drinking and smoking and waiting for a bus to going to parties and the beach. The stories feature the characters thinking and talking about life. Ray Olson, writing for *Booklist,* called Stevens "a much more thorough realistic artist than the label cartoonist suggests."

BIOGRAPHICAL AND CRITICAL SOURCES:

PERIODICALS

Booklist, May 15, 2008, Ray Olson, review of *Whatever,* p. 28.

Boston Phoenix, May 27, 2005, Mike Miliard, "Karl Stevens's Guilty Pleasure," review of *Guilty.*

Harvard Crimson, May 5, 2005, "'Guilty' Pleasures from Fogg to Cellar."

ONLINE

Comics Reporter, http://www.comicsreporter.com/ (March 14, 2005), review of *Guilty.*

Harvard University Gazette Online, http://www.news.harvard.edu/gazette/ (August 16, 2009), Alvin Powell, "The Big Picture," author profile.

Sequential Tart, http://sequentialtart.com/ (June 1, 2005), Suzette Chan, review of *Guilty.**

* * *

STOLL, Ira 1972-

PERSONAL: Born 1972, in Massachusetts. *Education:* Attended Harvard University. *Politics:* Conservative.

CAREER: Journalist and managing editor. *Jerusalem Post,* editor; *Wall Street Journal,* editorial page consultant; *Forward,* managing editor and Washington correspondent; *Los Angeles Times,* reporter; *Smarter times.com,* editor; *New York Sun,* cofounder, managing editor and vice president, 2002-08.

WRITINGS:

Samuel Adams: A Life, Free Press (New York, NY), 2008.

SIDELIGHTS: Former managing editor and a cofounder of the *New York Sun,* Ira Stoll has long experience in journalism, including a stint as editor of the *Jerusalem Post,* as a consultant to the *Wall Street Journal,* and as a reporter for the *Los Angeles Times.* He was born in Massachusetts, attended Harvard University, and resides in New York City. In partnership with editor-in-chief Seth Lipsky, Stoll gave the *New York Sun*a libertarian and conservative political stance, publishing the writings of many prominent conservative authors, including William F. Buckley, Daniel Pipes, and Mark Steyn. The paper staunchly supported the U.S. invasion and occupation of Iraq, and was outspoken in defense of the United States' military and political cooperation with Israel. The *New York Sun* was backed by investors who sought to create an alternative to what they viewed as the liberal bias of the *New York Times,* but its emphasis on local and state issues limited its appeal to a national audience. Its circulation numbers plunged during the economic problems that began to plague New York City in late 2007. The last edition of the paper was published on September 30, 2008, although Stoll and other contributors still post opinion and information on the paper's Web site.

In the same year the newspaper folded, Stoll published *Samuel Adams: A Life.* The book is a biography of the Massachusetts firebrand who, when George Washington and others were still seeking reconciliation with the British, called for armed resistance against the colonial government. One of Adams's many notable contributions to independence was to help to stiffen the spines of twenty frightened rebel leaders—all that remained of the Continental Congress—after Washington's defeat at the Battle of Brandywine. He continued to play a key role in the events that led to and followed the colonies' declaration of independence. In the years after the defeat of the British, Adams helped to write the Massachusetts constitution and served as governor of the state from 1793 until 1797.

In his book, Stoll argues that Adams has been unjustly neglected as one of the most important revolutionary leaders, and that many key events of the period, including the Boston Tea Party, the battles of Lexington and Concord, the Continental Congress, and the writing of the Declaration of Independence can be traced directly to his ideas and influence. Although Adams is honored by a prominent statue standing before Boston's Faneuil Hall, he has drawn the interest of only a handful of biographers since the early nineteenth century. One reason is the scant record he left behind for historians. He did not hold public office either before or during the revolution, did not keep an archive of his own papers, and out of fear of British reprisals instructed friends to burn any of his correspondence they possessed. Equally daunting for modern historians is Adams's strong religious convictions. Adams, for example, frequently compared the colonists to the ancient Israelites struggling to free themselves from bondage in Egypt. "Our secular times show little patience for anyone who was a self-righteous religious zealot," commented Edward Achorn in his review of Stoll's book for the *Weekly Standard,* "and who saw America as a 'Christian Sparta.'" Achorn concluded, "Sam's contemporaries seemed to share our revulsion, and as the years went by he faded into provincial politics rather than becoming a major figure in the new country's government." Adams was committed to the Puritan ideal that inspired the founding of Massachusetts; he sought to banish horse racing, gambling, and idle diversions or all kinds, and favored a law requiring public officeholders to denounce any non-Protestant faith. In the years following the revolution, he often expressed contempt for the vulgarization and commercialization of the young United States. For these and other reasons, Adams has never achieved the prominence of Benjamin Franklin, Thomas Jefferson, or his second cousin John Adams, and never attracted nearly as much interest among scholars as these more familiar founding fathers.

Reviewers of the book commented on the author's enthusiasm for his subject as well as his lack of scholarly expertise on the revolutionary period. Alan Pell Crawford wrote in the *National Review,* "Ira Stoll, in his well-researched biography . . . does an admirable job reminding us just who this indispensable man was, what contribution he made to this country, and why the British wanted him dead." In *Library Journal,* Michael O. Eshleman commented that "Stoll has mined primary sources, but his excessive fondness for quoting makes the narrative sag in places." Jay Freeman noted in *Booklist* that the author "effectively conveys both the virtues and defects of a somewhat neglected but very essential figure in our Revolutionary struggle." A review in *Publishers Weekly* pointed out: "This account might sustain a renewed interest in Adams as the founder of a distinctly American spirit." On the Web site *Bookpage.com,* Howard Shirley said, "Stoll goes a long way toward finding the man. . . . What results is the tale of a passionate, practical philosopher, a fiery provocateur, a dedicated public servant and a devoutly religious man."

BIOGRAPHICAL AND CRITICAL SOURCES:

PERIODICALS

America's Intelligence Wire, August 11, 2005, John Gibson, "Interview with Ira Stoll."

Booklist, October 15, 2008, Jay Freeman, review of *Samuel Adams: A Life,* p. 16.

Commentary, December, 2008, Philip Terzian, "The Revolutionist," p. 66.

Internet Bookwatch, December, 2008, review of *Samuel Adams.*

Kirkus Reviews, October 1, 2008, review of *Samuel Adams.*

Library Journal, September 1, 2008, Michael O. Eshleman, review of *Samuel Adams,* p. 137.

National Review, February 9, 2009, Alan Pell Crawford, "Righteous Rebel," p. 44.

Publishers Weekly, September 8, 2008, review of *Samuel Adams,* p. 44.

Wall Street Journal, November 3, 2008, Jonathan Karl, "Revolution Is No Tea Party," p. A17.

Weekly Standard, January 19, 2009, Edward Achorn, "Adams the Less: Making the Case for Samuel."

ONLINE

American Spectator, http://spectator.org/ (July 24, 2009), author articles and blog posts.

Bookpage, http://www.bookpage.com/ (July 24, 2009), Howard Shirley, "Raise a Glass to Sam Adams."

New York Sun Web site, http://www.nysun.com/ (July 24, 2009), articles by the author.

Simon and Schuster Web site, http://www.simonandschuster.net/ (July 24, 2009), author profile.*

* * *

STROUSE, Charles 1928-

PERSONAL: Born June 7, 1928, in New York, NY; son of Ira and Ethel Strouse; married Barbara Siman (a dancer, choreographer, and director); children: four. *Education:* Graduated from Eastman School of Music,

1947; further study with Aaron Copland at Tanglewood Music Center and privately with Copland, Nadia Boulanger, and David Diamond.

ADDRESSES: Office—Strouse IP, 350 W. 57th St., Ste. 19C, New York, NY 10019.

CAREER: Composer. Has written music for Broadway shows, including *Bye Bye Birdie,* 1960; *All American,* 1962; *Golden Boy,* 1964; *It's a Bird . . . It's a Plane . . . It's Superman,* 1966; *Applause,* 1970; *Annie,* 1977; *A Broadway Musical,* 1978; *Charlie and Algernon,* 1980; *Bring Back Birdie,* 1981; *Dance a Little Closer,* 1983; *Rags,* 1986; *Nick and Nora,* 1991; and *Annie Warbucks,* 1993. Composer of scores for films, including *Bonnie and Clyde,* 1967; *The Night They Raided Minsky's,* 1968; *There Was a Crooked Man,* 1970; *Just Tell Me What You Want,* 1980; and *All Dogs Go to Heaven,* 1989. Composer of music for television specials, including *Alice in Wonderland,* 1966; *Annie—A Royal Adventure,* 1982; *Lyle, Lyle Crocodile,* 1987; and *Alexander and the Terrible, Horrible No Good, Very Bad Day,* 1990. Composer of theme song, "Those Were the Days," with lyrics by Lee Adams, for television series *All in the Family.* Author of music, lyrics, and libretto for opera *Nightingale,* based on a story by Hans Christian Andersen. Composer of concert works, including *Concerto America,* 2002, and *On This Day,* 2003. Composer of popular songs, including "Born Too Late" and "We Love You Beatles" (based on "We Love You Conrad" from *Bye Bye Birdie*).

Bye Bye Birdie was adapted for film in 1963 and for television in 1995; *It's a Bird . . . It's a Plane . . . It's Superman* was adapted for television in 1975; *Applause* was adapted for television in 1973; *Annie* was adapted for film in 1982 and for television in 1999.

AWARDS, HONORS: Tony Award for best musical, American Theatre Wing, 1961, with librettist Michael Stewart, lyricist Lee Adams, and producer Edward Padula, for *Bye Bye Birdie,* 1970, with librettist Betty Comden, lyricist Lee Adams, and producers Joseph Kipness and Lawrence Kasha, for *Applause;* Tony Award for best score of a musical, 1977, with lyricist Martin Charnin, for *Annie;* Emmy Award for outstanding individual achievement in music and lyrics, Academy of Television Arts and Sciences, 1996, with Lee Adams, for song "Let's Settle Down," written for television adaptation of *Bye Bye Birdie;* Richard Rodgers Award for lifetime achievement in the American musical, American Society of Composers, Authors & Publishers (ASCAP) Foundation, 1999; named to Songwriters' Hall of Fame, 1985, and Theater Hall of Fame, 2002.

WRITINGS:

Put on a Happy Face: A Broadway Memoir, Union Square Press (New York, NY), 2008.

SIDELIGHTS: Charles Strouse has had a long and successful career as a composer of musical theater scores. He has also written music for film, television, and other media, but he is best known for his Broadway shows. He has more than thirty to his credit, including such hits as *Bye Bye Birdie, Applause,* and *Annie,* all of which earned Strouse Tony Awards. His wide-ranging body of work encompasses pop songs, including "Born Too Late," which reached number one on the *Billboard* charts in 1958; the music for the iconoclastic 1967 movie *Bonnie and Clyde,* which brought him a Grammy nomination for best film score; and the theme song "Those Were the Days" for the groundbreaking 1970s television series *All in the Family.* His most popular show tunes include "A Lot of Livin' to Do" from *Bye Bye Birdie,* "Once upon a Time" from *All American,* and "Tomorrow" from *Annie.* Another song from *Annie,* "It's the Hard Knock Life," was reworked by rap artist Jay-Z into a hip-hop hit, "Hard Knock Life (Ghetto Anthem)" in 1999.

Strouse used the title of another well-known tune from *Bye Bye Birdie* for his book *Put on a Happy Face: A Broadway Memoir.* Strouse writes not only about his successes but also his failures and the difficult periods in his life. He grew up in New York, New York, during the Great Depression, and his parents were both troubled people. His mother was melancholy, suicidal, and addicted to prescription drugs, and his father had numerous physical ailments. Amid all this, Strouse began his musical education early on; he started piano lessons at age ten and entered the Eastman School of Music at fifteen. After his graduation from Eastman in 1947, he studied with Aaron Copland, Nadia Boulanger, and David Diamond. Even with this background, he at first struggled to make a living. He played piano in such varied venues as strip clubs and acting classes, and he also wrote and performed music for film and television.

In 1949 he met lyricist Lee Adams, and they began a long collaboration. Initially they wrote musical revues performed at a summer resort in the Adirondack Mountains. Their Broadway break came when producer Edward Padula chose them to write the songs for a show about an Elvis Presley-like rock-and-roll star and his devoted teenage fans. That show, *Bye Bye Birdie,* opened on Broadway in 1960 and made Strouse's name famous. Strouse and Adams also collaborated on *Applause,* turning the 1950 Oscar-winning film *All about Eve* into a musical, while Martin Charnin was Strouse's lyricist on the composer's biggest success, *Annie,* based on the *Little Orphan Annie* comic strip. Other lyricists with whom Strouse has worked include Alan Jay Lerner, Stephen Schwartz, and Richard Maltby, Jr.

Strouse has had flops as well as hits, and his book examines both. Among the flops was *Nick and Nora,* during which Strouse had serious differences with writer-director Arthur Laurents. Sequels to *Bye Bye Birdie* and *Annie* failed to replicate the success of the originals. There were sometimes complications in creating the hits, too. When *Golden Boy,* starring African American entertainer Sammy Davis, Jr., was in a pre-Broadway run in Philadelphia in 1964, there were racist threats against Strouse and others involved with the show. (Strouse also recounts the racism he witnessed while touring the Deep South as accompanist to black singer-actress Butterfly McQueen of *Gone with the Wind* fame, and the prejudice he encountered in some quarters as a Jew.) Another problem on *Golden Boy* came from Davis's frequent demands for changes in the production; Strouse, frustrated, responded by writing a song called "No More," which found a fan in civil rights leader Martin Luther King, Jr.

Strouse relates disputes he had with some other stars, such as *Bonnie and Clyde*'s Warren Beatty, but critics noted that he had mostly positive things to say about his show-business colleagues, who have included such luminaries as Dick Van Dyke, Lauren Bacall, Chita Rivera, and Mike Nichols. Strouse also explores the self-doubt that has often haunted him. This combination of kindliness and self-effacement won him praise from several reviewers, who also found his backstage tales captivating. "His memoir is bouncy, candid, tragicomic and only occasionally horrifying," related David Patrick Stearns in the *Philadelphia Inquirer.* Jack Helbig, writing in *Booklist,* commented that the book is "free of ego and bitterness," while Stearns remarked that Laurents is the only figure "who receives a thorough trashing." A *Publishers Weekly* critic called the volume "superb," observing that Strouse "regales with fascinating, sometimes surprising, anecdotes." *Library Journal* reviewer Katherine Litwin characterized Strouse's memoir as "an entertaining story of genuine warmth," and Helbig was "utterly charmed by the man and his wit." Michael Elkin, who profiled Strouse for the Philadelphia *Jewish Exponent,* described *Put on a Happy Face* as Strouse's "happily engaging turn as author" and advised readers: "Let him entertain you."

BIOGRAPHICAL AND CRITICAL SOURCES:

BOOKS

Strouse, Charles, *Put on a Happy Face: A Broadway Memoir,* Union Square Press (New York, NY), 2008.

PERIODICALS

Back Stage, December 17, 1999, Robert Windeler, "Strouse: 'At Height of My Powers,'" p. 4.

Back Stage East, June 26, 2008, Erik Haagensen, review of *Put on a Happy Face,* p. 21.

Booklist, June 1, 2008, Jack Helbig, review of *Put on a Happy Face,* p. 35.

Financial Times, May 14, 2004, Hilary Ostlere, "Encores!/Bye Bye Birdie City Center, New York," p. 10.

Jewish Exponent (Philadelphia, PA), June 5, 2008, Michael Elkin, "Strouse Waltz," review of *Put on a Happy Face.*

Library Journal, June 15, 2008, Katherine Litwin, review of *Put on a Happy Face,* p. 70.

New York Times, June 2, 2008, "For Annie's Composer," p. 2; September 21, 2008, Joanne Kaufman, "A Theater Couple's Off Broadway Oasis," p. 4.

Philadelphia Inquirer, July 8, 2008, David Patrick Stearns, "In New Memoir, Broadway Composer Charles Strouse, 80, Looks Back on Success, Failure and Tumult," review of *Put on a Happy Face.*

Publishers Weekly, April 28, 2008, review of *Put on a Happy Face,* p. 120.

Record (Bergen County, NJ), March 21, 2004, Jim Beckerman, "Master of the Pick-Me-Up; Composer Charles Strouse Marvels at the Weight His 'Simple' Songs Can Carry," p. 1.

Sarasota Herald Tribune, October 23, 2008, Jay Handelman, "'Bye Bye Birdie' Puts on Happy Face," review of *Put on a Happy Face.*

ONLINE

Charles Strouse Home Page, http://www.charlesstrouse.com (July 28, 2009).

Internet Broadway Database, http://www.ibdb.com/ (July 28, 2009), list of author Broadway credits.

Internet Movie Database, http://www.imdb.com/ (July 28, 2009), list of author film and television credits.

Public Broadcasting Service Web site, http://www.pbs.org/ (July 28, 2009), brief author biography.

Scoffery.com, http://scoffery.com/ (August 24, 2008), review of *Put on a Happy Face.*

What's on Stage, http://www.whatsonstage.com/ (September 12, 2008), Terri Paddock, "Annie Composer Charles Strouse Marks 80th in UK," author biography.*

* * *

SUAREZ, Daniel 1964-
(Leinad Zeraus)

PERSONAL: Born December 21, 1964; married.

ADDRESSES: *Home*—CA. *E-mail*—dasuarez@thedaemon.com.

CAREER: Computer systems consultant and writer.

WRITINGS:

Daemon (novel), Dutton (New York, NY), 2009.

Daemon was originally self-published through Lightning Source (LaVergne, TN), 2006, under the pseudonym Leinad Zeraus.

Blogger at *Daniel Suarez.*

ADAPTATIONS: Screenwriters Walter Parkes and David DiGilio are adapting *Daemon* for a film to be produced by Parkes and Laurie MacDonald for Paramount Pictures.

SIDELIGHTS: Daniel Suarez's experience with his first novel, *Daemon,* is one of many authors' dreams. Initially unable to find a publisher, he self-published the novel through the print-on-demand firm Lightning Source in 2006 under the pseudonym Leinad Zeraus, "Daniel Suarez" spelled backward, as he found several other Daniel Suarezes on the Internet and wanted to avoid confusion. Suarez launched an Internet marketing campaign to attract readers, and word of mouth spread about the book, leading *Wired* magazine to do an article on it and major publishing houses to became interested. *Daemon* came out under Penguin Group's Dutton imprint in 2009. Paramount Pictures bought the movie rights, and Dutton contracted with Suarez for a sequel. The novel deals with the havoc wrought by a computer program called Daemon. Its creator, Matthew Sobol, was a successful game designer who set up the program to activate as soon as his obituary was published online. When Daemon goes live on the Internet after Sobol's death from cancer, it sets into motion Sobol's plans for identity and technology theft, corporate upheavals, multiple murders, and general chaos.

Suarez has said he came up with the idea for the book after he developed meteorological software that he sold online. Payments went in automatically, and he could go without checking the Web site for months at a time. "I realised—if I kicked the bucket, this thing would keep going, all automated," he told Claudine Beaumont in an interview for the London *Daily Telegraph Online,* adding: "It really played on my mind and I started to consider the outcomes." In an interview with *Entertainment Weekly* contributor Kate Ward, he further explained: "If you don't have to be a human being to do most of the things human beings do, that changes society. . . . It seems to me a scary prospect, having these not-self-aware bots running everything." He bases the novel's systems on existing technology, as he thought that would enhance his plot's believability. "I was really keen on using real technology," Suarez told Carol Memmott in *USA Today.* "To me, that was the whole point."

Numerous reviewers did find such a scenario within the realm of possibility and all the more horrifying because of that. "Suarez envisions a plausible apocalypse, and it is of course its conceivability which makes it so terrifying," commented Jessica Xanthe Cran in the online *Uinterview.* Cran also noted: "The themes explored are chillingly pertinent to our time. . . . This novel demonstrates that our technological interconnectedness can and will create as many problems as it solves." Beaumont observed that the book "provides a revealing and at times frightening insight into our impotence in the face of technology we can neither control nor understand," while Nathan Brazil, writing for the *SF Site,* said *Daemon* "lays bare the fragility of modern society." A critic for the online *Great Geek Manual* remarked that Suarez "takes what might have been the action novel of the year and uses [it] as a stage for an examination of some of the weightiest philosophic debates currently being waged by technologists."

Daemon is not lacking in action. The same *Great Geek Manual* critic put Suarez on a par with such thriller writers as Dan Brown, Michael Crichton, and Tom Clancy. Joe Hartlaub, reviewing the work for *BookReporter.com,* reported that the novel has "enough explosions and destruction to satisfy even the most jaded action junkie." In *Booklist,* Michael Gannon characterized *Daemon* as a "thrill-a-nanosecond novel," while a *Kirkus Reviews* contributor called it "a stunner." In a review for *Bookseller,* Kim Kovacs said the novel offers "breathtaking action" plus "a complex plot and plenty of surprises." *Blogcritics.org* commentator Ted Gioia maintained: "Suarez thinks cinematically, with car chases, explosions, and enough over-the-top gadgets to put agent Q to shame."

While many reviewers thought Suarez's concept believable, others questioned it. Robert Conroy, writing in *Library Journal,* thought the novel started well, but in its second half, "credulity is strained beyond the breaking point." Conroy wondered if one person could so stealthily cause all the damage Sobol produces. J.P. Frantz, a reviewer for the online *SF Signal,* reported: "I found some of the extrapolations to be far-flung at best, bordering on unbelievable. Technology doesn't always work right at the best of times." Frantz also doubted anyone could create a computer code both as complicated and as reliable as the one in book. Even so, Frantz added that he would "highly recommend" *Daemon,* citing its "breakneck pace" and "interesting uses of technology." The *Great Geek Manual* critic deemed the story "far-fetched" only in its totality, saying all the elements are "not only viable, but frighteningly plausible."

Jeff Craig, writing for the blog *Mad, Beautiful Ideas,* said his only quibble with this "great book" is that "it's clearly a setup to future novels." The conclusion, Craig explained, "sort of leaves you hanging." Craig welcomed the prospect of a sequel but wished for a "more complete and satisfying" finish to *Daemon.* Cran similarly described the ending as "fragmentary and slightly dissatisfying." Some other reviewers had no problem with the book's finale, although they predicted readers would be eager for the sequel. Suarez's "final twist . . . runs counter to expectations," related a *Publishers Weekly* contributor, noting that fans will be "anxiously awaiting" the next volume. Gioia saw the conclusion as one of several ways Suarez had revived and refined cyberpunk fiction, calling it "an eerily under-stated ending that violates every rule of the genre."

Further praise came from Harriet Klausner in a review for the Web site *Genre Go Round Reviews;* she dubbed *Daemon* a "superb science fiction book with a great finish." Hartlaub concluded: "My gut feeling is that the new world that Suarez is creating is too vast, too broad, to be contained on the canvas of two or even three books. Jump on now while you can still catch up." Brazil concluded: "As novels go, this is about as good as it gets."

BIOGRAPHICAL AND CRITICAL SOURCES:

PERIODICALS

Booklist, December 1, 2008, Michael Gannon, review of *Daemon,* p. 21.

Bookseller, March 20, 2009, Kim Kovacs, "A *Bookbrowse.com* Reviewer Takes to a Quercus Techno-thriller," p. 24.

California Bookwatch, March, 2009, review of *Daemon.*

Daily Variety, May 20, 2009, Tatiana Siegel, "Parkes Plants *Daemon* Seed," p. 1.

Entertainment Weekly, January 16, 2009, Kate Ward, "A Murderous Ghost in the Machine," author interview, p. 70.

Hollywood Reporter, January 14, 2009, Steven Zeitchik, "Polishing *Daemon:* Par, Tackle Technothriller," p. 1.

Kirkus Reviews, November 15, 2008, review of *Daemon.*

Library Journal, January 1, 2009, Robert Conroy, review of *Daemon,* p. 83.

Publishers Weekly, October 6, 2008, review of *Daemon,* p. 34; October 27, 2008, Allen Appel, "The Power of the Web: A Computer Game Developer Wreaks Havoc after His Death via the Interact in Daniel Suarez's Debut, Daemon," p. 31.

USA Today, January 6, 2009, Carol Memmott, "Tech Thriller *Daemon* Rises from Underground," p. 1D.

ONLINE

Blogcritics.org, http://blogcritics.org/ (January 23, 2009), Ted Gioia, review of *Daemon.*

BookReporter.com, http://www.bookreporter.com/ (July 28, 2009), Joe Hartlaub, review of *Daemon.*

Daemon Web site, http://www.thedaemon.com (July 28, 2009).

Daily Telegraph Online, http://www.telegraph.co.uk/ (April 20, 2009), Claudine Beaumont, author interview.

Gax Online, http://www.gaxonline.com/ (April 26, 2009), review of *Daemon.*

Genre Go Round Reviews, http://genregoroundreviews.blogspot.com/ (October 30, 2008), Harriet Klausner, review of *Daemon.*

Great Geek Manual, http://thegreatgeekmanual.com/ (March 18, 2009), review of *Daemon.*

Mad, Beautiful Ideas, http://blog.foxxtrot.net/ (April 3, 2009), Jeff Craig, review of *Daemon.*

Nicolai Wadstrom on Entrepreneurship, http://www.wadstrom.net/ (January 5, 2009), review of *Daemon.*

Ninja Monkeys, http://ninjamonkeys.co.za/ (July 8, 2009), review of *Daemon.*

SF Signal, http://www.sfsignal.com/ (February 10, 2009), J.P. Frantz, review of *Daemon.*

SF Site, http://www.sfsite.com/ (July 28, 2009), Nathan Brazil, review of *Daemon.*

Uinterview, http://www.uinterview.com/ (July 28, 2009), Jessica Xanthe Cran, review of *Daemon.**

* * *

SUDETIC, Chuck

PERSONAL: Male.

ADDRESSES: *Home*—Paris, France.

CAREER: Writer, journalist. *New York Times,* New York, NY, Eastern Europe correspondent, 1990-95; International Criminal Tribunal, The Hague, The Netherlands, analyst, 2001-05; Open Society Institute, Soros Foundation, Paris, France, senior writer. Previously served as a contributing editor to *Rolling Stone* magazine; contributor to periodicals including the *Atlantic Monthly* and *Mother Jones.*

WRITINGS:

Blood and Vengeance: One Family's Story of the War in Bosnia, W.W. Norton (New York, NY), 1998.

(With Carla Del Ponte) *Madame Prosecutor: Confrontations with Humanity's Worst Criminals and the Culture of Impunity,* Other Press (New York, NY), 2009.

Contributor to periodicals including the *Atlantic Monthly* and *Mother Jones.*

SIDELIGHTS: Paris-based writer and journalist Chuck Sudetic is a well-known expert on international politics, with a particular focus on the Balkan states, especially the former Yugoslavia. He spent the early 1990s serving as a foreign correspondent for the *New York Times,* covering the turmoil in the Balkans, including the fall of Yugoslavia and the subsequent war in Bosnia. He later served as an analyst during the Yugoslavia Tribunal at The Hague between 2001 and 2005. A senior writer for the Open Society Institute in France, which is part of the Soros Foundation, he has also contributed writings to an array of publications, including the *Atlantic Monthly, Rolling Stone,* and

Mother Jones, and in 1996, he was named a finalist for the National Magazine Award for his *Rolling Stone* article on the Srebrenica massacre. Sudetic is the author of *Blood and Vengeance: One Family's Story of the War in Bosnia,* and the author of *Madame Prosecutor: Confrontations with Humanity's Worst Criminals and the Culture of Impunity,* with Carla Del Ponte.

In *Blood and Vengeance,* Sudetic mines both his time spent covering the war in Bosnia and his own Croatian roots to provide readers with a thorough analysis of the racial and religious foundations for the long and bloody upheaval in that part of Eastern Europe. Although a long history of hatred exists between the various factions that made up the Bosnian war, few Americans are familiar with those tensions or have a sufficient knowledge of the region's political climate to understand how the war could become so violent so rapidly. In part due to a family link to one of the major parties involved—the Muslim Celik family—Sudetic relates the story of the massacre in Srebrenica, a mining town that was considered a safe location until the brutal reality proved it otherwise. Sudetic's account is detailed and personal, giving a face to the violence and death and making it much more poignant as a result. The book allows readers to see past the shallow reportage often provided by the media, where the reasons for the war alternated between a national tendency toward violence and the whims of power-mad government leaders. A reviewer for *Publishers Weekly* dubbed Sudetic's book "at once a stunning piece of war reporting and a heartbreaking, deeply personal story." A reviewer for the *Economist* noted that "what makes Mr Sudetic's book compelling is that he has no axe to grind. Unlike so many others he tells the whole story, not the bits that support one side or the other."

Madame Prosecutor focuses on the war- crime tribunals run by the United Nations in the aftermath of the fall of Yugoslavia and the Bosnian war and regarding the war in Rwanda, tribunals headed up by Carla Del Ponte, the attorney general of Switzerland, and for which Sudetic served as an analyst. The book offers readers an inside look at the tribunals themselves and at the determination of those in charge to see that justice was ultimately served. Del Ponte was a controversial figure over the course of the events, and this book helps shine a light on the intentions and motivation behind her decisions. Deirdre Bray Root, in a review for *Library Journal,* commented that the book offers readers "an important story."

BIOGRAPHICAL AND CRITICAL SOURCES:

PERIODICALS

Booklist, June 1, 1998, Jay Freeman, review of *Blood and Vengeance: One Family's Story of the War in Bosnia,* p. 1719.

Choice: Current Reviews for Academic Libraries, November 1, 1998, S.G. Mestrovic, review of *Blood and Vengeance,* p. 580.

Christian Century, November 18, 1998, Janet Varner Gunn, review of *Blood and Vengeance,* p. 1099.

Contemporary Review, January 1, 1999, review of *Blood and Vengeance,* p. 54.

East European Politics and Societies, September 22, 1999, Nick Miller, review of *Blood and Vengeance,* p. 606.

Economist, July 11, 1998, review of *Blood and Vengeance,* p. 9; July 11, 1998, review of *Blood and Vengeance,* p. 9; December 12, 1998, review of *Blood and Vengeance,* p. 3; December 12, 1998, review of *Blood and Vengeance,* p. 3.

Human Rights Quarterly, May 1, 1999, Laurel Fletcher, review of *Blood and Vengeance,* p. 545.

International Affairs, April 1, 1999, review of *Blood and Vengeance,* p. 377.

Journal of Modern History, March 1, 2001, review of *Blood and Vengeance,* p. 87.

Library Journal, January 1, 1999, Eric Bryant, review of *Blood and Vengeance,* p. 56; December 1, 2008, Deirdre Bray Root, review of *Madame Prosecutor: Confrontations with Humanity's Worst Criminals and the Culture of Impunity,* p. 143.

New York Review of Books, December 18, 1997, review of *Blood and Vengeance,* p. 65; February 19, 1998, review of *Blood and Vengeance,* p. 41; September 24, 1998, review of *Blood and Vengeance,* p. 63.

New York Times Book Review, March 29, 2009, "Justice of the Peace," p. 22.

Nieman Reports, March 22, 1999, Murray Seeger, review of *Blood and Vengeance,* p. 62.

Publishers Weekly, May 4, 1998, review of *Blood and Vengeance,* p. 193; November 2, 1998, review of *Blood and Vengeance,* p. 47; November 3, 2008, review of *Madame Prosecutor,* p. 49.

Times Literary Supplement, October 2, 1998, Charles King, review of *Blood and Vengeance,* p. 34.

ONLINE

Oberlin College Web site, http://www.oberlin.edu/ (July 26, 2009), author profile.

Other Press Web site, http://www.otherpress.com/ (July 26, 2009), author profile.*

* * *

SWIFT, Tom

PERSONAL: Married; wife's name Carrie. *Education:* Graduated from St. Olaf College.

ADDRESSES: *Home*—Northfield, MN. *E-mail*—tom@tom-swift.com.

CAREER: Writer, freelance journalist.

MEMBER: Society for American Baseball Research.

AWARDS, HONORS: Seymour Medal, Society for American Baseball Research, for *Chief Bender's Burden: The Silent Struggle of a Baseball Star,* 2009.

WRITINGS:

Chief Bender's Burden: The Silent Struggle of a Baseball Star, University of Nebraska Press (Lincoln, NE), 2008.

Maintains a blog at his home page.

SIDELIGHTS: Journalist and freelance writer Tom Swift graduated from St. Olaf College, and is now based in Northfield, Minnesota. Over the course of his career, Swift has had numerous intriguing encounters and experiences, primarily in the line of his work, including such varied events as covering a parade consisting entirely of white supremacists and having the chance to ride as part of a presidential motorcade. He has interviewed subjects ranging from the then-sitting majority leader of the United States Senate to the then-naked members of a major league baseball team. His debut book, *Chief Bender's Burden: The Silent Struggle of a Baseball Star,* was released in 2008, and garnered him the Seymour Medal from the Society for American Baseball Research the following year. The award is intended to honor the author of the best work of baseball history published in the prior year.

In *Chief Bender's Burden,* Swift recounts the story of Charles Albert Bender, who was considered to be the greatest American Indian baseball player in the history of the game. An Ojibwe from Harrisburg, Pennsylvania, Bender began playing professional baseball when he was just nineteen years old in 1903, as an anchor pitcher for the Philadelphia Athletics. He played with the team until 1914, and was immediately dubbed "Chief," which was the name accorded to every Native American athlete during that time. During his tenure with Philadelphia, Bender served as pitcher for a total of five World Series, three of which the team won. Only in the final series did he perform in a less than stellar manner, after which the team let him go and he eventually turned to managing players in the minor league. Swift follows Bender through not just his career, but from his childhood until his death. Originally from Minnesota, Bender was sent east to attend the Carlisle Indian Industrial School in Pennsylvania at the age of seven, where the intention was to both educate and encourage the assimilation of young Native Americans. Bender's mixed background—his father was of German heritage—helped him to fit in and to thrive despite the harsh atmosphere. Despite this, however, he was never treated as anything but a Native American baseball player, with the media reporting his game action using colorful and racially distinctive phrasing, including references to him as a "redskin" and to his "scalping of opponents." Prejudice did not keep Bender from having a successful career, however, and he was inducted into the Hall of Fame the year before his death.

Swift was inspired to write about Bender when he learned Bender was the first man born in Minnesota to end up in the Hall of Fame, something that Swift, as a native Minnesotan, had not known. In an interview for *Salon.com* with King Kaufman, Swift explained: "I was a baseball fan, but I didn't know anything about him. I started reading a little bit and the more I learned the more I wanted to learn. He had a rare ability to throw a baseball, but what grabbed me was just all the ways in which his success was so improbable. The human interest story was more of what I was after than the baseball games." The result is a book that offers readers an insight into American social history as well as the history of its national pastime. Wes Lukowsky, in a review for *Booklist,* found the book to be "carefully researched—and documented—as well as stylishly written (uncommon in the genre)." A writer for the *Philadelphia Athletics Historical Society* Web site opined that "the book will be a delightful read for A's fans"

Swift told *CA* how he first became interested in the story of Charles Albert "Chief Bender": "For almost fifty years Charles Bender was the only man from my home state—Minnesota—enshrined in the National Baseball Hall of Fame. When the next two guys (Dave Winfield, Paul Molitor) joined that club, newspaper articles often mentioned this name, 'Chief Bender,' almost as a footnote. I thought I should know more about Bender than I did—which is to say, not much—and so I started digging around. I did some research, wound up writing a magazine article about him, and the more I learned the more I wanted to learn.

"What I discovered was a man who, yes, had a rare ability to throw a baseball. But what fascinated me, what made me want to write this book, is what I consider an amazing human-interest story. Bender's success was improbable for so many reason, he had a fantastic run as one of the game's foremost clutch pitchers, and he was, without question, an interesting human being.

"No doubt, the rivers of intolerance ran through the City of Brotherly Love; Bender endured prejudice and racism from fans, fellow players, and newspapermen. In fact, there was scarcely a time when Bender was talked or written about when his race was not prominently mentioned—and usually in derogatory terms. No, it wasn't always easy. Nearly everywhere Bender went, on or off the field, he was reminded that people, most people, believed, and told him in so many words, that he was inferior. His very nickname is an example of that.

"Bender is the earliest-known pitcher to have, unquestionably, thrown the slider (though the pitch wasn't called a slider when he threw it). But few things in baseball history—like the origin of the game itself—can be correctly attributed to one clear and recognized inventor. Being historically accurate, we don't know for certain and almost certainly never will.

"Speaking subjectively, Bender was the kind of guy who was always thinking of new ways to get hitters out. Whether that meant changing speeds, developing excellent control, or using different deliveries—he was one of the first to be known for a big kick—and he was exceptionally bright. In other words, if you created a profile of the kind of guy who might have invented the slider, you would very likely sketch a guy like him."

Swift then explained how he came to writing: "Like an advertisement for produce, I came by way of the newspaper. There aren't many jobs recent college graduates with unremarkable transcripts can land that will allow them to both support themselves and write (actually, if you know much about small-time newspapers, you know the word 'support' is a relative term) and so that's what I did. I received my first assignment with the student newspaper during my freshman year in college. I didn't know what I was doing—as I recall, I wrote a piece about the baseball team that had something like eight introductory paragraphs and included sprinkles of fiction—but I knew I enjoyed putting words together and over time I took additional assignments, acquired a semblance of a clue, and by my senior year I had worked my way to the top of the masthead. Along the way I had completed summer internships with some papers in the Twin Cities metro area and so after graduation I took the first newspaper job I could find. This was the start of a glamorous career as a writer and editor; I have worked for numerous newspapers and magazines and almost certainly you haven't read any of them. No, I didn't find fame and for many years I didn't know what it was like to have a savings account. But the upside is that I was constantly learning, meeting different people, writing every day, and always writing about new things. I covered everything from a kiddie parade to a parade of racial supremacists, interviewed everyone from a state champion pickle grower to the sitting U.S. Senate majority leader, wrote about an American League batting champion and rode in a presidential motorcade. In a way, it was a continuation of my liberal arts education—with almost as much debt."

BIOGRAPHICAL AND CRITICAL SOURCES:

PERIODICALS

Booklist, April 1, 2008, Wes Lukowsky, review of *Chief Bender's Burden: The Silent Struggle of a Baseball Star,* p. 17.

Choice: Current Reviews for Academic Libraries, September 1, 2008, F.G. Polite, review of *Chief Bender's Burden,* p. 145.

ONLINE

Isportacus Web site, http://isportacus.com/ (June 29, 2009), Johnny Goodtimes, "Interview with *Chief Bender's Burden* Author Tom Swift."

Northfield Web site, http://northfield.org/ (May 3, 2009), Rob Hardy, "Northfield Writer: An Interview with Tom Swift."

Philadelphia Athletics Historical Society, http://www.philadelphiaathletics.org/ (July 26, 2009), Max Silberman, review of *Chief Bender's Burden.*

Red Room Web site, http://www.redroom.com/ (July 26, 2009), review of *Chief Bender's Burden.*

Salon.com, http://www.salon.com/ (May 23, 2008), King Kaufman, review of *Chief Bender's Burden.*

Society for American Baseball Research, http://www.sabr.org/ (March 31, 2009), "Swift's Biography of Chief Bender Wins Seymour Medal."

Tom Swift Home Page, http://tom-swift.com (July 26, 2009).

Twins Geek Blog, http://twinsgeek.blogspot.com/ (April 3, 2008), review of *Chief Bender's Burden.*

* * *

SYDOR, Colleen 1960-

PERSONAL: Born 1960, in Winnipeg, Manitoba, Canada. *Education:* University of Manitoba, B.A.

ADDRESSES: Home—Winnipeg, Manitoba, Canada. *E-mail*—sydor123@mts.net.

CAREER: Author and floral designer.

WRITINGS:

Ooo-cha!, illustrated by Ruth Ohi, Annick Press (New York, NY), 1999.

Smarty Pants, illustrated by Suzane Langlois, Lobster Press (Montreal, Quebec, Canada), 1999.

Fashion Fandango, illustrated by Lenka Vernex, Lobster Press (Montreal, Quebec, Canada), 2000.

Maxwell's Metamorphosis, illustrated by Lenka Vernex, Lobster Press (Montreal, Quebec, Canada), 2000.

Camilla Chameleon, illustrated by Pascale Constantin, Kids Can Press (Toronto, Ontario, Canada), 2005.

Raising a Little Stink, Kids Can Press (Toronto, Ontario, Canada), 2006.

My Mother Is a French Fry and Further Proof of My Fuzzed-up Life, Kids Can Press (Toronto, Ontario, Canada), 2008.

Timmerman Was Here, illustrated by Nicolas Debron, Tundra Books (Toronto, Ontario, Canada), 2009.

SIDELIGHTS: A native of Manitoba, Canadian author Colleen Sydor has written a variety of works for children, ranging from picture books to elementary-school chapter books to young-adult novels. After the appearance of *Ooo-cha!* in 1999, Sydor penned three books featuring a preteen girl named Norah. In the first installment, *Smarty Pants,* Norah stays with her namesake great aunt. While the two enjoy their time together, the younger Norah does not always believe all of her great aunt's superstitious stories, particularly the one which warns bad things will happen if she does not shake out her clothes in the evening. Disaster hits later when a forgotten pair of the previous day's underwear slips out from her pant leg while she is at school. While embarrassed by her exposed undergarment, Norah decides to take a lighthearted approach to the situation and turn her misfortune into a funny scene by claiming she had invented a new hat, with built-in holes for pig tails. The girl's unusual antics continue in *Fashion Fandango,* in which Norah hopes to be selected as a peer mediator at school, and *Maxwell's Metamorphosis,* which follows Norah as she must handle a classroom bully. Reviewing *Smarty Pants* in *Resource Links,* a reviewer applauded the "well-developed but not stereotypical characters," while another critic in the same periodical called *Fashion Fandango* an "engaging story . . . sure to be a hit."

Animal characters figure in several of Sydor's picture books, such as *Camilla Chameleon* and *Raising a Little Stink.* Illustrated by Pascale Constantin, *Camilla Chameleon* begins with a mother-to-be who has a craving for cream of chameleon soup. The daughter she bears consequently ends up with an unusual talent for camouflaging herself, particularly when it comes to activities she dislikes. A teacher, however, turns Camilla's disappearing act to good use when she recruits the girl to help actors remember their lines for the school play. A stinkbug also puts his unique skill to action in *Raising a Little Stink.* The insect, a mouse, a lion, and his tamer all leave the circus and settle in a small, abandoned home. Unfortunately, the other three leave all of the work to the stinkbug, forcing him to take care of the cooking and cleaning. Tiring of being taken advantage of, the insect resorts to releasing a powerful odor to drive out his freeloading friends. In her *School Library Journal* review, JoAnn Jonas described *Camilla Chameleon* as "a fresh story about an unusual child who gets into some bizarre situations." Discussing the same work in *Quill & Quire,* Carol L. MacKay commented favorably on the author's narrative, finding it full of "plenty of playful word choices and a penchant for descriptive silliness." *Raising a Little Stink* also found a favorable audience with *Resource Links* reviewer Linda Ludke who predicted "this funny fable will be a story-time hit."

In her first young-adult work, *My Mother Is a French Fry and Further Proof of My Fuzzed-up Life,* Sydor follows the coming-of-age angst of a teenager who is embarrassed by her over-friendly mother. The woman loves her job at a fast-food restaurant, part of which involves dressing in a French fry costume. Mortified by her mother's behavior, fifteen-year-old Eli believes that Mom behaves this way only to torment her, particularly when the woman announces that she is going to have another baby. This unexpected event proves to be a turning point in the relationship between mother and daughter, however, when it is revealed that much of Eli's resentment about her mom stems from the guilt she feels over the sudden death of a sibling years earlier. Several reviewers thought that Sydor captures the character of a self-centered adolescent exceptionally well, *Canadian Review of Materials* contributor Gregory Bryan writing that "the 15-year-old protagonist's irreverent, sarcastic, goo-eyed and love-struck voice is perfect." *School Library Journal* reviewer Lindsay Cesari also concluded of *My Mother Is a French Fry and Further Proof of My Fuzzed-up Life* that "readers will relate to Eli's conflicted feelings about her mother." Describing the characters as "wonderfully original," a *Publishers Weekly* critic praised Sydor's novel as "a funny and tender story," and Eli a "touching heroine."

BIOGRAPHICAL AND CRITICAL SOURCES:

PERIODICALS

Canadian Review of Materials, November 21, 2008, Gregory Bryan, review of *My Mother Is a French Fry and Further Proof of My Fuzzed-up Life.*

Kirkus Reviews, September 15, 2005, review of *Camilla Chameleon,* p. 1035; August 1, 2008, review of *My Mother Is a French Fry and Further Proof of My Fuzzed-up Life.*

Kliatt, September, 2008, Myrna Marler, review of *My Mother Is a French Fry and Further Proof of My Fuzzed-up Life,* p. 22.

Publishers Weekly, July 14, 2008, review of *My Mother Is a French Fry and Further Proof of My Fuzzed-up Life,* p. 67.

Quill & Quire, August, 2005, Carol L. MacKay, review of *Camilla Chameleon;* March, 2006, Gwyneth Evans, review of *Raising a Little Stink.*

Resource Links, February, 2000, review of *Ooo-cha!,* pp. 5-6, and review of *Smarty Pants,* p. 6; December, 2000, review of *Fashion Fandango,* p. 12; February, 2001, review of *Maxwell's Metamorphosis,* p. 20; February, 2006, Zoe Johnstone, review of *Camilla Chameleon,* p. 13; April, 2006, Linda Ludke, review of *Raising a Little Stink,* p. 12.

School Library Journal, March, 2000, Amy Lilien-Harper, review of *Ooo-cha!,* p. 214; June, 2006, JoAnn Jonas, review of *Camilla Chameleon,* p. 128; November, 2008, Lindsay Cesari, review of *My Mother Is a French Fry and Further Proof of My Fuzzed-up Life,* p. 138.*

U-V

UNSWORTH, Lilian
See HYLTON, Sara

* * *

UVILLER, Daphne 1972(?)-

PERSONAL: Born c. 1972, in New York, NY; married; children: two.

ADDRESSES: *Home*—New York, NY. *E-mail*—daphneuviller@gmail.com.

CAREER: Writer. Previously served as books/poetry editor for *Time Out New York;* former "Ethics" columnist, *Self* magazine. Also worked for a law enforcement agency in charge of investigating crime and corruption in the New York City public school system; served as a building superintendent in New York, NY, for ten years; currently co-owner and landlord.

WRITINGS:

(Editor, with Deborah Siegel) *Only Child: Writers on the Singular Joys and Solitary Sorrows of Growing Up Solo,* Harmony Books (New York, NY), 2006.

Super in the City (novel), Bantam Books (New York, NY), 2009.

Contributor to periodicals including the *Washington Post, New York Times, Newsday, Forward, New York, Oxygen, Allure,* and *Self.*

SIDELIGHTS: New York-based writer Daphne Uviller has had a diverse career, working for a number of years as the books and poetry editor for *Time Out New York* magazine, and also serving as the writer of the "Ethics" column for *Self.* In recent years she has focused more on writing as a freelancer, contributing to periodicals including the *Washington Post, New York Times, Newsday, Forward, New York, Oxygen, Allure,* and *Self.* She also edited the book *Only Child: Writers on the Singular Joys and Solitary Sorrows of Growing Up Solo,* with Debora Siegel, and is the author of *Super in the City* which is her debut novel.

Only Child takes a look at both the pluses and the minuses in growing up an only child. Uviller and Siegel look at the lives of a number of single children, all writers, and how they coped with their solitary experiences in the absence of siblings. The editors were inspired by their own different reactions to growing up single children. Uviller had loved being an only child, while Siegel felt oppressed by being the sole focus of her mother's attention. The reactions of these authors range from sadness at having no one with whom to share their daily adventures and a pervasive loneliness that extended into adulthood, to joy at having their parents' undivided attention as well as a complete share of all gifts and treats. In some cases, the status of being the only child is one that is reflected in writing, where only children form the foundation for a story—or are instead burdened with numerous fictional siblings. The editors included essays by writers who were also the children of writers themselves, such as Molly Jong-Fast, daughter of Erica Jong, and writer Alice Walker's daughter Rebecca. The book includes twenty-one essays, including offerings by both Uviller and Siegel, with a wide variety of theories about the joys and pain of growing up alone. Liesl Schillinger, in a review for the *New York Times,* remarked of the collection that "taken together, the reflections show what a crap shoot it can be for parents to stake all their chips on just one number. The luck is concentrated—when it's good it's magnificent; when it's bad, there's no fallback position."

In *Super in the City,* Uviller mines her own personal experiences working as the superintendent for a New York apartment building that her family co-owned. During her early twenties, Uviller was allowed to live in an apartment in the building at a greatly reduced rate—basically making the maintenance payment alone—in return for her services. Her novel features quirky heroine Zephyr Zuckerman and her group of fun-loving friends, who live and work in New York. Zephyr has dropped out of school and has no idea what to do with her life, particularly since she has recently broken up with her boyfriend. So when the super in her building gets arrested, Zephyr somehow ends up taking over the job. What seems like a natural move blows way out of control, however, when she discovers all her neighbors have crises and strange lives of their own. The result is a humorous, fun romp that defies the genre. A writer for *Publishers Weekly* declared that "the novel gallops at full speed," and concluded that "this is undoubtedly smarter and funnier than most other girls-in-the-city novels." A contributor for *Kirkus Reviews* found the plot a bit overcrowded, but praised the book for "a polished lead character, an ear for snappy dialogue and a propulsive storytelling style." The reviewer concluded the book is a "funny, enjoyable caper about a dirty job and the unlikely young woman who takes it on."

BIOGRAPHICAL AND CRITICAL SOURCES:

PERIODICALS

Booklist, January 1, 2009, Aleksandra Walker, review of *Super in the City,* p. 56.

Kirkus Reviews, December 1, 2008, review of *Super in the City.*

News & Observer, January 9, 2007, "When You're the One: New Book Explores the Pros and Cons of Growing Up as an Only Child."

New York Times, February 11, 2007, "And Baby Makes Three," p. 13.

Publishers Weekly, November 17, 2008, review of *Super in the City,* p. 41.

ONLINE

Best Reviews, http://thebestreviews.com/ (April 9, 2009), Bob Walch, "A New 'Take' on the Big Apple."

Curled Up with a Good Book, http://www.curledup.com/ (August 18, 2009), Jilian Vallade, review of *Super in the City.*

Daphne Uviller Home Page, http://www.daphneuviller.com (August 18, 2009).

Dear Author, http://dearauthor.com/ (January 29, 2009), review of *Super in the City.*

Genre Go Round Reviews Blog, http://genregoroundreviews.blogspot.com/ (December 1, 2008), Harriet Klausner, review of *Super in the City.*

Mother Talk, http://mother-talk.com/ (August 18, 2009), review of *Only Child: Writers on the Singular Joys and Solitary Sorrows of Growing Up Solo.*

Pop Culture Junkie Blog, http://aleapopculture.blogspot.com/ (March 29, 2009), review of *Super in the City.*

Random House Web site, http://www.randomhouse.com/ (August 18, 2009), author profile.*

* * *

VALELLY, Richard M. 1953(?)-

PERSONAL: Born c. 1953. *Education:* Attended University of Chicago, 1971-74; Swarthmore College, B.A. (with high honors), 1975; Harvard University, Ph.D., 1984.

ADDRESSES: Office—Department of Political Science, Swarthmore College, Swarthmore, PA 19081. *E-mail*—rvalell1@swarthmore.edu.

CAREER: Writer and educator. College of the Holy Cross, Worcester, MA, Department of Political Science, lecturer and assistant professor, 1983-85; Massachusetts Institute of Technology, Cambridge, MA, Department of Political Science, assistant professor and associate professor, 1985-93; Swarthmore College, Swarthmore, PA, Department of Political Science, associate professor, 1992-2000, professor, 2000-07, Claude C. Smith '14 Professor, 2008—. Also served as a visiting professor at Harvard University, 1993, and at the University of Pennsylvania, Philadelphia, PA, 2003, 2004, and 2007; frequent presenter of workshops and papers at various academic conferences.

MEMBER: American Political Science Association, Phi Beta Kappa.

AWARDS, HONORS: DeLancey K. Jay Prize, Harvard University, Graduate School of Arts and Sciences, 1985; Mary Parker Follett Award for Best Journal Article, 1992-93, Politics and History Organized Section, American Political Science Association, 1994; Ralph J. Bunche Book Award, American Political Science Association, 2005; J. David Greenstone Book Award, Politics and History Organized Section, American Political Science Association, 2005; V.O. Key, Jr., Book Award, Southern Political Science Association, for Best Book on Southern Politics published in 2004, 2006; awarded numerous research and travel grants.

WRITINGS:

Radicalism in the States: The Minnesota Farmer-Labor Party and the American Political Economy, foreword by Martin Shefter, University of Chicago Press (Chicago, IL), 1989.

The Two Reconstructions: The Struggle for Black Enfranchisement, University of Chicago Press (Chicago, IL), 2004.

(Editor) *The Voting Rights Act: Securing the Ballot,* CQ Press (Washington, DC), 2006.

(Editor) *Princeton Readings in American Politics,* Princeton University Press (Princeton, NJ), 2009.

Contributor to various compilations, and to journals, including the *Chronicle of Higher Education, New Republic, American Society and Politics, Political Science Quarterly,* and *American Prospect.* Also coeditor of the "American Governance: Politics, Policy, and Public Law" series, University of Pennsylvania Press. University of Pennsylvania Press, member of faculty editorial board.

SIDELIGHTS: Richard M. Valelly is a writer and educator who serves as the Claude C. Smith '14 Professor of Political Science at Swarthmore College in Pennsylvania. Over the course of his career, Valelly has been part of the faculty at several institutions of higher learning, including the College of Holy Cross in Worcester, Massachusetts, and the Massachusetts Institute of Technology in Cambridge, finally joining the Swarthmore faculty in 1992. He has also spent time at both the University of Pennsylvania and at Harvard University as a visiting professor. His primary academic and research interests include American politics and the American presidency and Congress in particular. Valelly is a regular contributor to various academic journals, including the *Chronicle of Higher Education, New Republic, American Society and Politics, Political Science Quarterly,* and *American Prospect.* In addition, he is the author of *Radicalism in the States: The Minnesota Farmer-Labor Party and the American Political Economy* and *The Two Reconstructions: The Struggle for Black Enfranchisement,* and served as editor for *The Voting Rights Act: Securing the Ballot* and for *Princeton Readings in American Politics.*

In *The Two Reconstructions,* Valelly takes a look at the two major periods of national reconstruction in the United States, the first directly following the Civil War and the second following World War Two, and discusses the ways in which these attempts to strengthen the country differed, including noting their failures and successes. Taken on the whole, it must be considered that the reconstruction of the nineteenth century in the wake of the Civil War was a failure, while the second reconstruction period during the mid-twentieth century was a far more successful endeavor. Valelly poses the question of why this was, and how the second reconstruction managed to make such great improvements where its predecessor failed. He looks at each attempt in broad context, considering the state of the world at large at the time and how differently people approached these two periods. The treatment of former slaves contributed in large part to the results of the post-Civil War reconstruction, as an entire portion of the population had been reclassified with very little support to ensure a smooth transition, not to mention the pervasive attitudes toward the former slaves by those who felt they should not be allowed any rights. The reconstruction period following World War Two ultimately served as a lead up to the civil rights movement, and therefore proved to provide a foundation of more inclusive behavior and policies.

Over the course of his book, Valelly offers readers a thorough recap of both the social and civil history of these two periods in the nation's history, and tracks the changes in public policy as they proceeded to give rights, remove rights, and the give them back once more. While there is a certain amount of back and forth, there is also a forward progression in these policy changes when one addresses the big picture. He looks at the role of political parties and how different factions were separated out as biracial or not. The advancement of the political system as a whole illustrates why the second reconstruction period different from the first. After the Civil War, there was no existing Republican coalition, the party that eventually stood most strongly in favor of rights for the former slaves. As a result, that party had to be built from the ground up, working for both membership and influence. Whereas in the wake of World War Two, the equivalent political party was the Democratic Party, and during that period the black membership swelled to the point where it became the majority, outnumbering white Southerners who had previously been the bulk of the party's weight. Valelly also addresses the question of voting rights, and how this differed from the actual ability to go to a polling location and successfully have one's vote included in the pool, a situation that has gradually improved through the years.

Valelly's book received warm reactions from a number of reviewers. Robert J. Norrell, reviewing for *Political Science Quarterly,* concluded that "there is probably little in this book that will be new to the close student of this nation's long struggle with political equality. What is original is the framework for a structural explanation about what kind of action succeeds in achieving fuller democracy and what does not. As that framework, this is a highly valuable work." Steven F. Lawson, in a review for the *Journal of Southern History,* noted that "chiefly a work of interpretive synthesis, this book borrows heavily from historians who have written about each of the two reconstructions. Because the author relies on history and generally offers light doses of political science theory and jargon, most historians will find this a readable and accessible work." He went on to conclude that "Valelly has made ample and judicious use of history. It is a timely and instructive book to read."

When asked what first got him interested in writing, Valelly told *CA:* "Admiring the writing of the *New Yorker.*" He then listed his main influences: Ben Yagoda, Hendrik Hertzberg, and Robert Kuttner. When asked to describe his writing process, he said, "Writing at least an hour every day, no matter what teaching obligations I have." He explained that the most surprising thing that he has learned as a writer is "that academics sometimes resent clear writing." Valelly said of his books, his favorite was *The Two Reconstructions* and he hopes they have will show "just how fascinating American political history and development have been."

BIOGRAPHICAL AND CRITICAL SOURCES:

PERIODICALS

American Historical Review, February 1, 1991, Lowell Dyson, review of *Radicalism in the States: The Minnesota Farmer-Labor Party and the American Political Economy,* p. 281; February 1, 2006, William E. Montgomery, review of *The Two Reconstructions: The Struggle for Black Enfranchisement,* p. 186.

American Journal of Sociology, January 1, 2006, Martin Ruef, review of *The Two Reconstructions,* p. 1243.

Black Issues in Higher Education, December 16, 2004, review of *The Two Reconstructions,* p. 36.

Choice: Current Reviews for Academic Libraries, September 1, 2005, J.P. Sanson, review of *The Two Reconstructions,* p. 174.

Dissent, January 1, 1992, James Green, review of *Radicalism in the States,* p. 102.

Election Law Journal, June 22, 2005, Chandler Davidson, review of *The Two Reconstructions,* p. 212.

Journal of American History, December 1, 1990, Stanley Shapiro, review of *Radicalism in the States,* p. 1075.

Journal of Economic History, March 1, 1992, W. Elliott Brownlee, review of *Radicalism in the States,* p. 242.

Journal of Interdisciplinary History, March 22, 2007, Michael Perman, review of *The Two Reconstructions,* p. 650.

Journal of Southern History, May 1, 2008, Steven F. Lawson, review of *The Two Reconstructions,* p. 516.

Labor Studies Journal, September 22, 1991, Sara B. Rasch, review of *Radicalism in the States,* p. 79.

Labour/Le Travail, September 22, 1991, review of *Radicalism in the States,* p. 360.

Law and History Review, June 22, 2007, J. Morgan Kousser, review of *The Two Reconstructions,* p. 430.

Law and Politics Book Review, March 1, 2005, Emery G. Lee, review of *The Two Reconstructions,* p. 221; July 1, 2006, Joseph N. Patten, review of *The Voting Rights Act: Securing the Ballot,* p. 550.

Political Science Quarterly, September 22, 2005, Robert J. Norrell, review of *The Two Reconstructions,* p. 520.

Reference Reviews, October 1, 2006, John Lawrence, review of *The Voting Rights Act.*

Social Forces, March 1, 2006, Jeff Manza, review of *The Two Reconstructions,* p. 1847.

Western Historical Quarterly, February 1, 1991, James N. Gregory, review of *Radicalism in the States,* p. 73.

ONLINE

Law and Politics Book Review Web site, http://www.bsos.umd.edu/ (March 1, 2005), review of *The Two Reconstructions.*

Swarthmore College Web site, http://www.swarthmore.edu/ (August 18, 2009), faculty profile.

University of Pennsylvania Fox Leadership Web site, http://www.sas.upenn.edu/ (August 18, 2009), award announcement and profile.

* * *

VAN METER, William 1975(?)-

PERSONAL: Born c. 1975, in Bowling Green, KY.

CAREER: Journalist.

WRITINGS:

Bluegrass: A True Story of Murder in Kentucky, Free Press (New York, NY), 2009.

SIDELIGHTS: Journalist William Van Meter was born in Bowling Green, Kentucky, and though he eventually moved on from his home town, his upbringing made him the logical choice to write *Bluegrass: A True Story of Murder in Kentucky,* a book that recounts the story of an eighteen-year-old college co-ed who was murdered in her dorm room on campus at Western Kentucky University in May 2003. The circumstances of the murder itself, which was followed by an inconclusive and poorly handled trial, resulted in vicious media coverage and harsh headlines. Van Meter was appalled that Bowling Green could be the setting for such a terrible event, and his curiosity was also piqued by the situation as a whole. Unsure what he would find, he determined that he would return to Kentucky and delve into the details of the case himself with an eye toward writing about it. He attended the trial and continued to work on the book, though a number of years had passed since the murder itself. In an interview with Deidre Wengen for the *Philly Burbs* Web site, he explained his motivation: "The Bowling Green of today is so different then what it was in the 80s and 90s. It really didn't compute that something like this could happen there to me. This incredulity was compounded with a kind of journalistic wanderlust that I was going through at the time. I really wanted to do something new and I just had a passion for this."

Bluegrass tells a sad story of a young girl, Katie Autry, who was a student by day and by night worked as a topless dancer. One night, after a frat party, she was raped, beaten, strangled, and ultimately set on fire in her dorm room. Two local men were charged for the crime, and eventually one pled guilty in exchange for testifying against the other, who was also a small-time drug dealer. Aside from the horror of the circumstances themselves, there is an aura of depression and economic hardship that surrounds the story. Katie and her younger sister were raised by foster parents, having been taken from their biological mother with her agreement, and Katie had a reputation on campus for being promiscuous and not particularly discriminating when it came to her partners. Stephen Soules, the first of the defendants, was a high school dropout. Luke Goodrum, the drug dealer and the second defendant in the case, was twenty-one, divorced, and had a baby he rarely visited, but had the best legal counsel available due to his stepfather's considerable wealth compared to the rest of the parties involved. A contributor for

Kirkus Reviews pointed out that "it's difficult to find any redeeming qualities in either of the suspects, their families or, for that matter, the victim's family."

Reviews were mixed for Van Meter's effort, though in part the fault was often placed on the material. Though the events of the murder case and trial were horrific, some reviewers noted that the people involved failed to garner sufficient sympathy to allow readers to truly become invested in the book. However, writing for the *Winston-Salem Journal,* Beth Woodard commented that in most true-crime books, "it's easy to feel sorry for the victim. With simple, compelling reporting, Van Meter persuades the reader to feel sorry for the perpetrator or perpetrators. At least temporarily." A reviewer for *Publishers Weekly* criticized the book for a lack of emphasis on the signs that the trial itself was mishandled, commenting that "Van Meter instead cobbles together a melodramatic narrative that doesn't do Autry's tragic death justice." Mike Tribby, writing for *Booklist,* opined that the book "should still satisfy dyed-in-the-wool true-crime fans."

BIOGRAPHICAL AND CRITICAL SOURCES:

PERIODICALS

Booklist, December 15, 2008, Mike Tribby, review of *Bluegrass: A True Story of Murder in Kentucky,* p. 6.

Interview, February 1, 2009, "William Van Meter's True-Crime Story," p. 52.

Kirkus Reviews, November 15, 2008, review of *Bluegrass.*

Lexington Herald-Leader, February 11, 2009, review of *Bluegrass.*

Publishers Weekly, October 13, 2008, review of *Bluegrass,* p. 47.

Winston-Salem Journal, March 29, 2009, Beth Woodard, "Dysfunctional Lives and Their Outcome," p. 18.

ONLINE

Fader Web site, http://www.thefader.com/ (January 9, 2009), "Book Release Party for William Van Meter's *Blue Grass.*"

Philly Burbs, http://www.phillyburbs.com/ (May 4, 2003), Deidre Wengen, "An Interview with Author William Van Meter."

Sang Bleu, http://sangbleu.com/ (May 3, 2009), "William Van Meter's Tattoos."

Style File Blog, http://www.style.com/ (January 8, 2009), "William Van Meter Digs Deep in the Bluegrass."*

* * *

VAN WINKLE, Clint

PERSONAL: Married; wife's name Sara (a kindergarten teacher) *Education:* Arizona State University, B.A., 2005; University of Wales-Swansea, M.A.

ADDRESSES: *Home*—Chesapeake, VA.

CAREER: Writer. *Military service:* United States Marine Corps, eight years, attaining rank of sergeant; served in Iraq as Amphibious Assault Vehicle section leader, attached to Lima Company 3rd BN 1st Marines.

WRITINGS:

Soft Spots: A Marine's Memoir of Combat and Post-Traumatic Stress Disorder, St. Martin's Press (New York, NY), 2009.

Contributor to various literary journals.

SIDELIGHTS: Writer Clint Van Winkle started his career in the military, serving for eight years in the United States Marine Corps, during which time he attained the rank of sergeant. While serving in the Iraq War, Van Winkle was a section leader for an Amphibious Assault Vehicle, attached to Lima Company 3rd BN 1st Marines. Once he was discharged from the service, he returned to the United States to complete his education, earning first an undergraduate degree in English from Arizona State University in 2005, and then moving on to earn a master's degree in creative writing and media from the University of Wales-

Swansea. His debut work, *Soft Spots: A Marine's Memoir of Combat and Post-Traumatic Stress Disorder,* is a memoir published by St. Martin's Press. Parts of the book were published earlier in various literary magazines.

In *Soft Spots,* Van Winkle shares with readers his own experiences in wartime, and the suffering that resulted when he finally returned home, only to face a battle against post-traumatic stress disorder. Memories of the devastation and the death that he faced on a daily basis in Iraq continued to haunt Van Winkle long after he left the country. While some memories were of combat or violence, other were more gruesome and disturbing, such as images of burned bodies or dead children. Although he and his compatriots were generally fighting the enemy, there were also times when they ceased fire only to realize that civilians had been in the path of their bullets. Once home, it took time, the care of his wife, and sessions with a number of therapists before Van Winkle was able to move past his memories and the horror of his experiences in Iraq and continue on with his life.

Over the course of his book, Van Winkle traces the evolution of his experiences as a Marine from his earliest days through his ongoing fight to maintain his sanity in the aftermath of the war. When he first shipped out to Iraq, Van Winkle had an image of what a Marine would be like in the face of war and danger, and that image included a certain amount of swagger and bravery that he was comfortable exuding himself. The reality of the situation, however, soon made him understand that war was far less about making the world safe for democracy or the spread of freedom and human rights, and much more about surviving until it was time to go home again. He learned that crude jokes and a brave front were simply a way of dealing the horrors that surrounded you in war, and that was a difficult attitude to turn off again once he returned to civilian life.

Van Winkle's book received mixed reactions from reviewers, who praised the substance but often found his style difficult to follow and a distraction from the material. A contributor for *Kirkus Reviews* found an arty approach to the writing that was not appropriate, and noted that the book was most successful "when he focuses on his emotions, confronting his doubts about the war and his guilt for doubting it while Marines are still fighting and dying in it." A reviewer for *Publishers Weekly* had a similar reaction to Van Winkle's approach, and suggested readers overlook "this exercise in creative writing techniques because it presents a vivid picture of what many vets endure." Writing for the *Washington City Paper* Web site, Eve Ottenberg commented that "Van Winkle's detailed account of how combat shattered his mind is as disturbing as his war imagery. Phantoms of Marine buddies he hasn't seen in months are as real as his wife or the useless psychiatrists he encounters at the VA hospital, where he is treated like a cipher—one more vet whose soul was mutilated in Iraq."

BIOGRAPHICAL AND CRITICAL SOURCES:

BOOKS

Van Winkle, Clint, *Soft Spots: A Marine's Memoir of Combat and Post-Traumatic Stress Disorder,* St. Martin's Press (New York, NY), 2009.

PERIODICALS

Book World, February 22, 2009, Juliet Wittman, review of *Soft Spots,* p. 6.

Kirkus Reviews, December 1, 2008, review of *Soft Spots.*

Publishers Weekly, December 15, 2008, review of *Soft Spots,* p. 43.

ONLINE

Arizona State University Web site, http://asunews.asu.edu/ (June 1, 2009), "ASU Alum, Iraq War Vet Finds Healing in His Book, *Soft Spots.*"

Macmillan Web site, http://us.macmillan.com/ (August 18, 2009), author profile.

Washington City Paper Web site, http://www.washingtoncitypaper.com/ (March 11, 2009), Eve Ottenberg, "Battle at Home."*

* * *

VROMEN, Suzanne

PERSONAL: Emigrated from Belgium to the Belgium Congo, 1941, and later settled in the United States; married; husband's name Ben; children: two. *Education:* University of Brussels, Licence ès Sciences Sociales and Première Licence ès Sciences Economiques; Columbia University, M.Sc.; New York University, M.A., Ph.D. *Religion:* Jewish.

ADDRESSES: Home—NY. *E-mail*—vromen@bard.edu.

CAREER: Writer, educator. Bard College, Annandale-on-Hudson, NY, Women's Studies Program, professor of sociology, 1978-2000, cofounder, 1979, coordinator, 1982-90, professor of sociology emeritus.

AWARDS, HONORS: National Endowment for the Humanities summer stipend, 1988; awarded two Senior Specialist Fulbright grants.

WRITINGS:

Hidden Children of the Holocaust: Belgian Nuns and Their Daring Rescue of Young Jews from the Nazis, Oxford University Press (New York, NY), 2008.

Contributor to journals, including *History of European Ideas, Jewish Women in America, Comparative Social Research, Focaal* (Dutch), *Journal of Arts Management, YIVO Annual, Knowledge and Society, American Behavioral Scientist, Contemporary Sociology,* and the *American Journal of Sociology.*

SIDELIGHTS: Writer and educator Suzanne Vromen earned her undergraduate degree at the University of Brussels in Belgium, then continued her studies at Columbia University, where she earned a master's degree in urban planning, and at New York University, where she earned both a master's degree and a doctorate in sociology. She is a professor emeritus at Bard College in Annandale-on-Hudson, New York, where she served as the cofounder and coordinator for the Women's Studies program. She is also a regular contributor to various academic journals, including *History of European Ideas, Jewish Women in America, Comparative Social Research, Focaal* (Dutch), *Journal of Arts Management, YIVO Annual, Knowledge and Society, American Behavioral Scientist, Contemporary Sociology,* and the *American Journal of Sociology.* Vromen is the author of *Hidden Children of the Holocaust: Belgian Nuns and Their Daring Rescue of Young Jews from the Nazis,* a book for which she mines her own childhood experiences fleeing the Nazi regime in Belgium.

In 1941, Vromen left Belgium with her family, settling in the Belgian Congo in order to escape the horrors of World War Two. Eventually moving to the United States, she raised a family with her husband and focused on her career. It was not until the 1970s, when her own daughter joined a protest at her college pressing for more courses covering the Holocaust, that Vromen felt able to talk about her own wartime experiences. She began by lecturing and offering workshops, and eventually moved on to write *Hidden Children of the Holocaust,* which focuses on the children who were sent to live as Catholics in order to protect them from anti-Semitism and from the concentration camps. Vromen herself went to a Catholic convent at the age of sixteen, though they had already fled Belgium. Belgian convents, too, however, served as sanctuaries for young Jewish students. Vromen discusses both her own experiences and the broader movement, as well as her own feelings once the war had ended and she was free to return home. She interviewed a number of children who experienced this adoption into a Christian atmosphere, as well as nuns and a priest who have survived from that time. A reviewer for the *Monsters and Critics* Web site called the book "a fascinating story which has been hidden for too long." Writing for *Booklist,* Donna Seaman declared that "Vromen's exacting and corrective work of history and remembrance is uniquely sensitive and illuminating." A writer for *Contemporary Review* remarked of Vromen that "she shows how complex were the relationships established in what was a 'story of cooperation and rescue.'"

BIOGRAPHICAL AND CRITICAL SOURCES:

BOOKS

Vromen, Suzanne, *Hidden Children of the Holocaust: Belgian Nuns and Their Daring Rescue of Young Jews from the Nazis,* Oxford University Press (New York, NY), 2008.

PERIODICALS

Booklist, May 15, 2008, Donna Seaman, review of *Hidden Children of the Holocaust,* p. 18.

Contemporary Review, December 22, 2008, review of *Hidden Children of the Holocaust,* p. 529.

ONLINE

Bard College Web site, http://www.bard.edu/ (August 18, 2009), faculty profile.

Jewish Women's Archive Web site, http://jwa.org/ (August 18, 2009), author profile.

Monsters and Critics Web site, http://www.monstersandcritics.com/ (August 18, 2009), review of *Hidden Children of the Holocaust.*

New Jersey Jewish News Web site, http://www.njjewishnews.com/ (March 19, 2009), Elaine Durbach, "Child of the Holocaust Tells of Rescue by Nuns."

Oxford University Press Web site, http://www.oup.com/ (August 18, 2009), author profile.*

W-Z

WAITE, Elizabeth

PERSONAL: Born in London, England; married.

ADDRESSES: *Home*—Pevensey Bay, Sussex, England.

CAREER: Writer. Worked as a bus conductress at Merton Garage, London, England, during World War Two; ran a guest house in Devon, England with her husband, beginning 1956.

WRITINGS:

NOVELS

Skinny Lizzie, Time Warner (London, England), 1993.
Cockney Waif, Sphere (London, England), 1993.
Cockney Family, Time Warner (London, England), 1994.
Second Chance, Time Warner (London, England), 1995.
Third Time Lucky, Time Warner (London, England), 1996.
Trouble and Strife, Little, Brown (New York, NY), 1997.
Nippy, Little, Brown (New York, NY), 1997.
Kingston Kate, Little, Brown (New York, NY), 1998.
Cockney Courage, Little, Brown (New York, NY), 1999.
Elizabeth Waite Omnibus, Little, Brown (New York, NY), 2000.
Time Will Tell, Little, Brown (New York, NY), 2000.
A London Lass, Little, Brown (New York, NY), 2001.
Skinny Lizzie [and] Nippy (omnibus edition), Time Warner (London, England), 2002.
Kingston Kate [and] Cockney Courage (omnibus edition), Time Warner (London, England), 2003.
Cockney Diamond, Time Warner, 2003.
Life's for Living, Little, Brown (New York, NY), 2005.
Wheeling and Dealing, Time Warner (New York, NY), 2006.
Never Say Never, Severn House (London, England), 2007.
A London Lass [and] Time Will Tell (omnibus edition), Sphere (London, England), 2007.
Safe Return Home, Severn House (London, England), 2007.
Wheeling and Dealing [and] Life's for Living (omnibus edition), Sphere (London, England), 2008.
Total Commitment, Severn House (London, England), 2008.

SIDELIGHTS: British writer Elizabeth Waite was born in the south of London, England, where she lived until her mid-thirties. During World War Two, she worked as a bus conductress, but then in 1956, she and her husband settled in Devon, where they opened a guest house. It was only after she retired that Waite began to write and publish novels. All set in England, both in London and in the countryside, Waite's books feature families struggling to survive the dangers of World War Two, poverty, family strife and abuse, and the hand of fate. Her titles include *Skinny Lizzie,* the story of ten-year-old Lizzie Collins, and how she and her family—mother, sisters, aunt, and grandmother—

survive the lean days of the early 1930s; *Cockney Waif,* the story of newly orphaned Patsy Kent who, though just thirteen, struggles to avoid life in an orphanage with the help of the Londoners who love her; and *Kingston Kate,* about a girl who is left on her own after her mother is hanged for the murder of her abusive father, as well as numerous others.

Never Say Never begins in 1930, during the heart of the Great Depression, and takes place in a small, quiet English village called North Waltham, which is located in Hampshire. Emma Pearson, who lives in the village with her family, is offering to take in orphaned children who live in London in order that they might have the chance to take a holiday outside the city. As a result, she finds herself caring for two young boys, John and Tommy, both of whom become as beloved to Emma as her own daughters. However, there is a price to pay for her attachment as, years later, when World War Two is underway, Emma has two more people to love and worry about as the world crumbles around them. Maria Hatton, in a review for *Booklist,* found the book to be a "sweetly told tale and poignant slice of life."

In *Safe Return Home,* Waite offers readers a follow up to *Never Say Never.* John, the near-son of the Pearson family, has been killed in the battle of Dunkirk, but Tom, as well as the Pearson's daughters Emily and Bella, are all well, with Bella working as a land girl locally to her parents, and the other two both working in London. The book describes the difficulties in London during the war, particularly as a result of frequent bombings, as Emma and her husband Sam attempt to bring as many of their friends as possible out of the city to the relative peace and safety of their village life. Again reviewing for *Booklist,* Maria Hatton dubbed the story a "detailed, heartwarming tale."

Waite's next novel, *Total Commitment,* tells the story of nineteen-year-old Paula O'Brien, a young girl in 1930 London who is desperate to start a new life. However, her father has been abusive to her as long as she can remember, and she fears she will never be able to escape from him or her difficult past. Particularly difficult for Paula are her memories of becoming pregnant at just thirteen, and of her parents' solution to her dilemma, which was to send her off to a nearby asylum that housed prostitutes, unwed mothers, and those with mental problems. However, Paula manages to find herself a job working for a family with twin babies, serving as nursemaid to the children. It is a live-in position and takes her away from her family and the constant reminders of her past. However, Paula finds forgetting is not as easy as she hoped, and it is only with the help of new friends that she finally begins to take control of both her life and her past. Once more reviewing for *Booklist,* Maria Hatton declared *Total Commitment* to be a "moving saga of overcoming the past so one can look forward."

BIOGRAPHICAL AND CRITICAL SOURCES:

PERIODICALS

Booklist, June 1, 2007, Maria Hatton, review of *Never Say Never,* p. 40; October 1, 2007, Maria Hatton, review of *Safe Return Home,* p. 32; January 1, 2009, Maria Hatton, review of *Total Commitment,* p. 50.

ONLINE

Fantastic Fiction Web site, http://www.fantasticfiction.co.uk/ (July 27, 2009), author profile.*

* * *

WANGERIN, Dave

See WANGERIN, David

* * *

WANGERIN, David
(Dave Wangerin)

PERSONAL: Born in Chicago, IL; immigrated to the United Kingdom, 1987.

ADDRESSES: *Home*—Kinross-shire, Scotland. *E-mail*—davidwangerin@onetel.com.

CAREER: Writer, sports historian, and coach.

WRITINGS:

Soccer in a Football World: The Story of America's Forgotten Game, Temple University Press (Philadelphia, PA), 2008.

Contributor to books, including *The Half-Decent Football Book,* WSC Books (London, England); *Always Next Year,* WSC Books (London, England); and *Power, Corruption, and Pies,* WSC Books (London, England). Contributor to magazines and periodicals, including *When Saturday Comes, Elfmeter,* and *The Absolute Game.*

SIDELIGHTS: David Wangerin is an American sportswriter, sports historian, and soccer coach living in Kinross-shire, Scotland. Born in Chicago and raised in Wisconsin, he moved to the United Kingdom in 1987. He is a frequent contributor to books and magazines on soccer, a sport better known as football in Europe.

With *Soccer in a Football World: The Story of America's Forgotten Game,* Wangerin "has taken on the daunting task of writing a comprehensive history of soccer in the United States," commented a reviewer on the *EPL Talk* Web site. "Telling the history of American soccer is no simple task," observed a writer on the *Culture of Soccer* Web site. Historians' efforts are complicated by the fact that record-keeping was inconsistent (or nonexistent) throughout much of the American leagues' history. Even many of the American leagues that sprang up and faded away in the twentieth century are not recorded. However, "The light Wangerin sheds on these leagues is the highlight of his book," the *Culture of Soccer* Web site reviewer remarked.

The author also covers a number of fundamental questions about American soccer, including the reason why Americans call the game soccer when players and fans elsewhere in the world refer to it as football. He assesses the rules of the game and how American rules differ from those affecting players in other countries. He also recounts numerous World Cup games and attendant victories and defeats.

Wangerin presents detailed information on long-forgotten leagues and franchises, such as the American Soccer League (ASL) that flourished in the early part of the twentieth century. He recounts the evolution of the game and the many governing bodies that affected soccer, up to and including today's Major League Soccer (MLS) organization. He profiles many of the sport's best-known stars, including Pele, David Beckham, and numerous others. The considerable media attention surrounding Beckham's arrival in America and commitment to MLS "shows how important David Wangerin's book is," remarked the *Culture of Soccer* Web site reviewer. "At a time when platitudes are spoken about the importance of Beckham's arrival, it is worth remembering that American soccer itself has a long and proud history."

In assessing Wangerin's work, the *EPL Talk* Web site reviewer stated, "Taken as a whole, the book was well researched and quite enjoyable to read," calling it a history that "can best be viewed as a cautionary tale of failed franchises, incompetent administrators and blindly idealist visionaries." *Booklist* reviewer Keir Graff suggested that libraries consider *Soccer in a Football World* a "good purchase where soccer-mad patrons—and there are more of them these days—provide demand."

BIOGRAPHICAL AND CRITICAL SOURCES:

PERIODICALS

Booklist, May 15, 2008, Keir Graff, review of *Soccer in a Football World: The Story of America's Forgotten Game,* p. 15.

Choice, February, 2009, J. Walker, review of *Soccer in a Football World,* p. 1143.

ONLINE

Culture of Soccer, http://cultureofsoccer.com/ (August 21, 2007), review of *Soccer in a Football World.*

David Wangerin Home Page, http://www.davidwangerin.net (August 18, 2009).

EPL Talk, http://eplleague.blogspot.com/ (February 12, 2007), review of *Soccer in a Football World.*

When Saturday Comes, http://www.wsc.co.uk/ (August 18, 2009).*

* * *

WARD, Jesmyn 1977(?)-

PERSONAL: Born c. 1977, in MS. *Education:* Stanford University; University of Michigan, M.F.A., 2005.

ADDRESSES: Home—DeLisle, MS. *E-mail*—ojaccc@gmail.com.

CAREER: University of New Orleans, New Orleans, LA, faculty member; previously worked for Random House, New York, NY.

AWARDS, HONORS: Wallace Stegner Fellowship, Stanford University.

WRITINGS:

Where the Line Bleeds, Bolden (Chicago, IL), 2008.

Maintains a blog at http://jesmimi.blogspot.com.

SIDELIGHTS: Mississippi native Jesmyn Ward is a graduate of Stanford University. After earning her undergraduate degree, she worked in publishing for a time, taking a job at Random House in New York City before she continued her education at the University of Michigan with a master of fine arts degree. Her writing later earned her a Wallace Stegner Fellowship from Stanford University. Ward serves on the faculty of the University of New Orleans. Her debut novel, *Where the Line Bleeds,* was released in 2008.

Ward began to write *Where the Line Bleeds* after the death of her brother. She had always intended to write a novel, but the story was still coalescing in her mind, and her brother's death somehow served as the impetus she needed to start. At the time she was working in New York in the publishing industry, but she ended up completing the novel while working toward her graduate degree in Michigan. Ward credits her relationship with her brother and with male friends growing up for her accurate portrayal of the twin boys who serve as the novel's focal point. A Southerner to the core, Ward also feels her writing is influenced by classic Southern writers. Brad Hooper, interviewing Ward for *Booklist,* remarked that "when asked whom she includes among her literary masters, Ward unhesitatingly answered, 'William Faulkner, particularly his novel *As I Lay Dying.*' She admits that 'it made my head explode' upon her first reading of it.' Ward cited Toni Morrison and poetry as a genre as additional influences on her style of writing.

Where the Line Bleeds takes place in the small rural town of Bois Sauvage, Mississippi, situated on the Gulf Coast. The residents are primarily black, and economically speaking, the town is at a stand still, with little to encourage young people to stay on and make their lives there after they have grown old enough to leave. The protagonists of the book are twins Christophe and Joshua. After graduating from high school, they set out to make their mark on the world, intent on leaving both their small town and parents of somewhat questionable morals far behind them. Unfortunately, neither twin gets very far. Joshua ends up working the docks, but when Christophe is unable to find a job, he begins to sell drugs with their cousin. There is little hope of them escaping the dead-end life ahead—no money for college, a father who is a junkie, and a mother who took off for Atlanta years earlier, leaving them behind. The boys strive to please their beloved grandmother, who virtually raised them and encouraged them to stay on the right path, but events conspire against all their efforts.

Critics praised Ward's debut effort as a strong and illuminating look at the rural South. A contributor for *Kirkus Reviews* remarked that Ward describes a place that has been little seen before in novels: "the rural African American South, a place of grinding poverty but enduring loyalties, tragic but somehow noble." Brad Hooper, in his *Booklist* review, declared that she "successfully escapes first-novel awkwardness, obviously knowledgeable of and comfortable with the milieu in which she sets her narrative." In a review for the *Dallas Morning News* Web site, William J. Cobb concluded of the boys' story that "the ending that eventually unfolds does not perhaps change their destiny as much as confirm it. This vision of the real America is not a pretty picture, but it's a powerful, realistic story." Elizabeth Jackson, writing for the *Austin Chronicle* online, commented that "Ward is an author to watch, to be sure, as one readily anticipates her sense of proportion and emphasis will gain subtlety."

BIOGRAPHICAL AND CRITICAL SOURCES:

PERIODICALS

Booklist, November 15, 2008, Brad Hooper, review of *Where the Line Bleeds,* p. 28.

Essence, November 1, 2008, "Boys to Men: Delve into Our Seventeenth Essence Book Club Pick, a Novel That Offers a Truthful View of Young Black Men in America Today," p. 79.

Kirkus Reviews, November 1, 2008, review of *Where the Line Bleeds.*

Publishers Weekly, September 22, 2008, review of *Where the Line Bleeds,* p. 39.

School Library Journal, December 1, 2008, Jamie Watson, review of *Where the Line Bleeds,* p. 157.

ONLINE

Apooo Book Club Web site, http://www.apooobooks.com/ (February 22, 2009), Darnetta Frazier, review of *Where the Line Bleeds.*

Austin Chronicle Online, http://www.austinchronicle.com/ (December 19, 2008), Elizabeth Jackson, review of *Where the Line Bleeds.*

Boston Globe Online, http://www.boston.com/ (December 28, 2008), Anna Mundow, "Tragedy, Loyalty on the Bayou."

Dallas Morning News Online, http://www.dallasnews.com/ (November 30, 2008), William J. Cobb, review of *Where the Line Bleeds.*

Literary Fiction Review Web site, http://www.litficreview.com/ (July 27, 2009), review of *Where the Line Bleeds.*

Warren County, Vicksburg Public Library Blog, http://wcvpl.blogspot.com/ (March 31, 2009), "Dive into Jesmyn Ward's World."*

* * *

WASSERMAN, Robin 1978-

PERSONAL: Born May 31, 1978, in Philadelphia, PA. *Education:* Harvard University, degree; University of California—Los Angeles, M.A. *Hobbies and other interests:* Watching television.

ADDRESSES: Home—Brooklyn, NY. *E-mail*—robin@robinwasserman.com.

CAREER: Novelist. Former associate editor at a New York, NY, publisher.

WRITINGS:

"SCOOBY-DOO&EXCL; PICTURE CLUE" SERIES

Search for Scooby Snacks, illustrated by Duendes del Sur, Scholastic (New York, NY), 2000.

Vanishing Valentines, illustrated by Duendes del Sur, Scholastic (New York, NY), 2001.

Snow Ghost, illustrated by Duendes del Sur, Scholastic (New York, NY), 2001.

Ghost School, illustrated by Duendes del Sur, Scholastic (New York, NY), 2002.

Stormy Night, illustrated by Duendes del Sur, Scholastic (New York, NY), 2002.

"FACE TO FACE" SERIES

Sharks, Scholastic (New York, NY), 2002.

Wolves, Scholastic (New York, NY), 2002.

Night Creatures, Scholastic (New York, NY), 2002.

Penguins, Scholastic (New York, NY), 2002.

Insects, Scholastic (New York, NY), 2002.

JUVENILE NOVELS

Oh, No! Why Me? II, Scholastic (New York, NY), 2002.

Grind (adapted from a screenplay by Ralph Sall), Scholastic (New York, NY), 2003.

Oops! I Did It (Again)!, illustrated by Angela Martini, Scholastic (New York, NY), 2003.

A Cinderella Story (novelization; based on a screenplay by Leigh Dunlap), Scholastic (New York, NY), 2004.

Raise Your Voice (novelization; based on a screenplay by Sam Schreiber), Scholastic (New York, NY), 2004.

Just My Luck! Embarrassing Moments and the Girls Who Survive Them ("Friends 4 Ever" series), Scholastic (New York, NY), 2006.

Callie for President ("Candy Apple" series), Scholastic (New York, NY), 2008.

Life, Starring Me! ("Candy Apple" series), Scholastic (New York, NY), 2009.

Wish You Were Here, Liza ("Candy Apple" series), Scholastic (New York, NY), 2010.

Bedtime Stories: School's Out?, Disney Press (New York, NY), 2011.

"UNFABULOUS" SERIES

Jinxed!, Scholastic (New York, NY), 2006.

Just Deal, Scholastic (New York, NY), 2006.

Meltdown, Scholastic (New York, NY), 2006.

So You Want to Be . . . , Scholastic (New York, NY), 2006.

Starstruck, Scholastic (New York, NY), 2006.

YOUNG-ADULT NOVELS

Hacking Harvard, Simon Pulse (New York, NY), 2007.

"SEVEN DEADLY SINS" SERIES; YOUNG-ADULT NOVELS

Lust, Simon Pulse (New York, NY), 2005.

Envy, Simon Pulse (New York, NY), 2006.

Pride, Simon Pulse (New York, NY), 2006.

Wrath, Simon Pulse (New York, NY), 2006.

Sloth, Simon Pulse (New York, NY), 2006.

Gluttony, Simon Pulse (New York, NY), 2007.

Greed, Simon Pulse (New York, NY), 2007.

"CHASING YESTERDAY" SERIES; YOUNG-ADULT NOVELS

Awakening, Scholastic (New York, NY), 2007.

Betrayal, Scholastic (New York, NY), 2007.

Truth, Scholastic (New York, NY), 2007.

"SKINNED" TRILOGY; YOUNG-ADULT NOVELS

Skinned, Simon Pulse (New York, NY), 2008.

Crashed, Simon Pulse (New York, NY), 2009.

OTHER

Extraordinary Dangerous Animals, Scholastic (New York, NY), 2003.

Extraordinary Sea Creatures, Scholastic (New York, NY), 2003.

Extraordinary Solar System, Scholastic (New York, NY), 2003.

Extraordinary Rain Forests, Scholastic (New York, NY), 2003.

Extraordinary Wild Weather, Scholastic (New York, NY), 2003.

Girl Talk: How to Deal with Friendship Conflicts, illustrated by Taia Marley, Scholastic (New York, NY), 2006.

Contributor to anthologies, including *First Kiss (Then Tell!): A Collection of True Lip-Locked Moments; 666: The Number of the Beast;* and *End Game,* Scholastic, 2005. Contributor to periodicals, including *Scholastic Choices.*

ADAPTATIONS: The "Seven Deadly Sins" novels were adapted for film by Lifetime.

SIDELIGHTS: Robin Wasserman got her start in children's publishing through her job as an assistant editor for a New York City publisher, and her experience there gave her a strong sense of what young readers want to read. Since making the break to author, she has produced books for both preteen and high-school readers, and is best known as the author of the "Chasing Yesterday" and "Seven Deadly Sins" novels. While many of her novels focus on problematic characters that socially savvy teens might enjoy vicariously but would studiously avoid, Wasserman's stand-alone novel, *Hacking Harvard,* was inspired by personal experience. Like the characters in her novel, Wasserman also had to face the daunting application process that culminated in her graduation from the prestigious Harvard University. In *Booklist,* Frances Bradburn dubbed *Hacking Harvard* a "harsh, funny, sophisticated, . . . and edgy" novel that treats teens to a "memorable reading experience," while Debra Mitts-Smith wrote in *Kliatt* that Wasserman's "tale of high achievers with high ambitions is anything but predictable."

Wasserman's "Chasing Yesterday" series begins with *Awakening,* as a young teen is injured and knocked unconscious during an explosion, and then awakens without any memories of who she is. "Addictive and fast-paced," according to *Kliatt* contributor Stephanie Squicciarini, *Awakening* follows the girl—nicknamed J.D. for Jane Doe—as she begins to sense that her physical strength and aggressive tendencies mark her as someone with a less-than-typical home life. When a woman claims J.D. as her own lost daughter, the teen worries that this may not be the case; although her doctors claim that she is skirting mental illness, J.D. knows that she must discover which of the vivid flashbacks she is experiencing are reality and which are something more sinister. The novels *Betrayal* and *Truth* round out Wasserman's "Chasing Yesterday" series.

Lust, Envy, Pride, Wrath, Sloth, Gluttony, and *Greed* chronicle the moral transgressions made by seven high-school seniors in Wasserman's popular "Seven

Deadly Sins" series. Beginning in *Lust,* the author takes readers to the small California town of Grace where Beth, Kane, Harper, Adam, Miranda, Kaia, and Reed discard professed loyalties, stated promises, and common compassion in favor of sexual conquest and popularity during their final year at Haven High. In *Booklist,* Bradburn characterized *Lust* as "a teen version of TV's 'Desperate Housewives,'" and *School Library Journal* critic Stephanie L. Petruso recommended the series to fans of YA writers Zoey Dean and Cecily von Ziegesar. Reviewing *Envy* in *School Library Journal,* Stephanie L. Petruso recommended the story as a "fast-paced," "compelling and frightening" view of contemporary adolescent culture, while *Pride* struck Rebecca M. Jones as an "addictive" chronicle of "cunning, lies, and emotional blackmail" in her review for the same periodical.

In *Skinned,* Wasserman salts her teen drama with elements of science fiction as seventeen-year-old Lia Kahn finds herself downloaded into a mechanical body following a terrible automobile accident. Formerly considered among the most popular, accomplished, and pretty girls in school, Lia is now shunned by both her superficial former friends and her own younger sister. As Lia attempts to craft a new life from the wreckage of the old, the harsh reality of her "mech head" status—she no longer eats, sleeps, aspirates, or ages—force her to accept her own failings and a less-than-promising future. Anticipating the "dystopian denouement" in *Skinned,* Francisca Goldsmith wrote in *Booklist* that Wasserman's story is "well composed and engaging," and *School Library Journal* critic Megan Honig stated that the fast-paced text contains "enough sarcasm, humor, and . . . momentum to engage reluctant readers." To a *Kirkus Reviews* writer, *Skinned* provides teens with more than a captivating story: it "intimately tackles tough ethical topics . . . through blunt dialogue and realistic characters."

BIOGRAPHICAL AND CRITICAL SOURCES:

PERIODICALS

Booklist, December 1, 2005, Frances Bradburn, review of *Lust,* p. 38; February 15, 2006, Gillian Engberg, review of *Pride,* p. 92; January 1, 2008, Frances Bradburn, review of *Hacking Harvard,* p. 58; October 15, 2008, Francisca Goldsmith, review of *Skinned,* p. 38.

Kirkus Reviews, August 1, 2008, review of *Skinned.*

Kliatt, September, 2007, Stephanie Squicciarini, review of *Awakening,* p. 26; January, 2008, Debra Mitts-Smith, review of *Hacking Harvard,* p. 17.

Publishers Weekly, December 5, 2005, review of *Lust,* p. 56; June 4, 2007, review of *Awakening,* p. 50.

School Library Journal, January, 2006, Stephanie L. Petruso, review of *Lust,* p. 145; February, 2006, Stephanie L. Petruso, review of *Envy,* p. 139; August, 2006, Rebecca M. Jones, review of *Pride,* p. 132; January, 2008, Vicki Reutter, review of *Hacking Harvard,* p. 128; January, 2009, Megan Honig, review of *Skinned,* p. 122.

ONLINE

Robin Wasserman Home Page, http://www.robinwasserman.com (November 10, 2009).*

* * *

WEITZ, Patricia 1973-

PERSONAL: Born April 30, 1973; married Paul Weitz (a filmmaker); children: two.

ADDRESSES: *Home*—Los Angeles, CA.

CAREER: Writer. Has worked variously for publications including the *Nation, New Yorker,* and the *Los Angeles Times.*

WRITINGS:

College Girl (novel), Riverhead Books (New York, NY), 2008.

SIDELIGHTS: Los Angeles-based writer Patricia Weitz was born April 30, 1973. Over the course of her career, she has worked for various periodicals, most notably the *Nation, New Yorker,* and the *Los Angeles Times.* Weitz has also tried her hand at writing fiction, and her debut novel, *College Girl,* was published by Riverhead Books in 2008. The book offers readers an inside look of the world of a young woman attending college, pulling no punches and, as a result of such an approach, garnering a number of comparisons to the novel *Prep,* by Curtis Sittenfeld, which served as a similar eye-opener in relation to the world of the American boarding school.

College Girl tells the story of Natalie Bloom, a twenty-year-old college student who, in appearances at least, has everything going for her. Natalie is bright, pretty, and has ambitions regarding her life. The one area in which she feels insecure is relationships, particularly those of a sexual nature. She is uncomfortable both thinking or discussing them and with the actual act of sex itself. As a result, despite what she considers to be an advanced age, she is still a virgin. While she finds it difficult to form lasting friendships with other girls, she is virtually paralyzed when facing boys, and has never even had a boyfriend. With no idea how to improve her ability to relate to others, Natalie simply hides out in the library on the weekends, intent on avoiding her fellow students in all but the most structured of settings. The situation is made worse by the fact that, halfway through her junior year, she has transferred to the University of Connecticut and is living in the dorms for the first time, having spent the early years of her college experience commuting back and forth from her parents' house. The school, despite being her dream, is unfamiliar, and she does not know anyone.

When Natalie meets Patrick one night in the library, however, everything begins to change. He flirts with her and eventually she succumbs to his charms, daydreaming about him and unable to concentrate on her school work. She begins going to parties with her older, rocker roommate, hoping to bump into Patrick, and at one such event agrees to smoke pot with him. Under the influence, she is easy to seduce. Natalie's grades fall steadily, and with them every last ounce of her self-esteem. She is chain smoking, miserable, and unsure of who she has become, and as her mood worsens, we learn that her older brother Jacob killed himself just a few years before—an added personal stress that acts like a ticking time bomb in Natalie's memories. Though Weitz takes the situation to extremes, she also effectively illustrates the way that a young woman's inexperience and vulnerability can lead her onto dangerous ground. A reviewer for *America's Intelligence Wire* found the extreme situation somewhat unbelievable, noting that "on the whole, it seems like Weitz tried to make *College Girl* realistic and all-encompassing, but instead came off as being unreal and depressing, offering the message that Natalie was almost better off not trying anything at all." A reviewer for *Publishers Weekly* observed that "the novel relies on its characters, but bland Natalie is surrounded by equally forgettable, interchangeable supporting personalities." Conversely, a reviewer for the *Eclectic Book Lover* Web site opined that Weitz's approach resulted in a realistic story, stating that "Natalie can be aggravating, endearing, sad and naïve—everything that a reader could hate in a more simple character in a more shallow story. But here, it works." Julie Kane, writing for *Library Journal,* remarked that the book "unwraps an intriguing downward spiral, deftly portraying social and psychological implications of college life."

BIOGRAPHICAL AND CRITICAL SOURCES:

PERIODICALS

America's Intelligence Wire, March 30, 2009, Alex Yuschik, "Carnegie Mellon U.: Book Review: *College Girl* Receives an 'R.'"

Booklist, December 1, 2008, Kristine Huntley, review of *College Girl,* p. 21.

Entertainment Weekly, January 9, 2009, Kate Ward, review of *College Girl,* p. 67.

Kirkus Reviews, October 1, 2008, review of *College Girl.*

Library Journal, September 15, 2008, Julie Kane, review of *College Girl,* p. 47.

Publishers Weekly, September 8, 2008, review of *College Girl,* p. 34.

USA Today, January 8, 2009, Korina Lopez, "Compelling *College Girl* Still Has a Lot to Learn, Plots to Develop," p. 5.

ONLINE

Blue Stocking Society, http://www.thebluestockings.com/ (December 1, 2008), review of *College Girl.*

Bookishly Reviews, http://www.bookishlyreviews.com/ (February 23, 2009), review of *College Girl.*

Book Reporter, http://www.bookreporter.com/ (July 27, 2009), Sarah Hannah Gomez, review of *College Girl.*

Book Zombie, http://www.thebookzombie.com/ (November 1, 2008), review of *College Girl.*

Confessions of a Bibliophile, http://www.bookconfessions.com/ (July 27, 2009), review of *College Girl.*

Eclectic Book Lover, http://www.eclecticbooklover.com/ (June 8, 2009), review of *College Girl.*

Muse Book Reviews Blog, http://musebookreviews.blogspot.com/ (February 26, 2009), review of *College Girl.*

New York Observer Online, http://www.observer.com/ (January 10, 2009), review of *College Girl.*

Penguin Group Web site, http://us.penguingroup.com/ (July 27, 2009), author profile.

Romantic Times Online, http://www.romantictimes.com/ (July 27, 2009), Lauren Spielberg, review of *College Girl.*

Under the Button, http://underthebutton.com/ (December 1, 2008), "*College Girl* Is So Your Life."*

* * *

WHEATLE, Alex 1963-

PERSONAL: Born January 3, 1963, in London, England; son of Jamaican immigrants; children: one son, one daughter.

ADDRESSES: Home—London, England. *Agent*—Susijn Agency, 3rd Fl., 64 Great Titchfield St., London W1W 7QH, England.

CAREER: Writer, DJ, and MC. Teaches creative writing in schools, colleges, and prisons.

AWARDS, HONORS: London New Writers Award, 2000, for *East of Acre Lane;* Order of the British Empire (MBE), 2008.

WRITINGS:

NOVELS

Brixton Rock, BlackAmber Books (London, England), 1999.

East of Acre Lane, Fourth Estate (London, England), 2001.

The Seven Sisters, Fourth Estate (London, England), 2002.

Island Songs (prequel to *East of Acre Lane*), Allison & Busby (London, England), 2002.

The Dirty South, Serpents Tail (London, England), 2002.

(With Mark Parham) *Checkers,* X Press (London, England), 2003.

ADAPTATIONS: Brixton Rock is being adapted for the stage by the Royal Stratford East theater; *East of Acre Lane* is being adapted as a feature film.

SIDELIGHTS: Alex Wheatle's novels about black families in London's gritty neighborhoods have earned him acclaim as the "Bard of Brixton," a term that refers to the West Indian section of London where he grew up. Born to parents who had immigrated to England from Jamaica, Wheatle spent his first five years with his father; his mother, who was married to another man when the boy was born, had returned to her husband and other children. By the time Wheatle reached school age, his father could not cope with him and placed the boy in government care. The young Wheatle did poorly in school and was expelled several times. In the 1980s he was arrested during the infamous Brixton riots, which erupted after the enforcement of drastic stop-and-search policies in the crime-infested neighborhood. When a black youth who had been stabbed received what residents felt was inappropriate treatment by the police, a riot ensued. Arson, looting, and other violence resulted in hundreds of police injuries, several dozen of civilian injuries, and damage to more than 150 buildings. Wheatle was among those arrested in the riot; he spent three months in prison. There, he began reading books—an experience that changed his life. "I began thinking that maybe I could achieve something, that I am worthwhile," he told *UKWatch.net* Web site writer Esme Choonara. "I see so many black youngsters today who feel that they are not worth anything. They need to be told by someone that they are. Instead they have a government that seems to despise them, calls them 'hoodies' and fears them."

Writing lyrics as a DJ and MC in Brixton, Wheatle began writing fiction in 1997. His first novel, *Brixton Rock,* is about a Brixton teen much like the author; it introduced Wheatle as a considerable new talent. Its sequel, *East of Acre Lane,* takes place during the Brixton riots as its young protagonists struggle to nurture dreams for the future amidst the relentless poverty and anger around them. The novel won a London New Writers Award.

The Seven Sisters is the story of four boys who grow up together in a rural governmen- care facility where they experience hardship and emotional cruelty. Desperate to get away from this loveless and confining place, they run away to the surrounding woods, where they at first revel in their newfound freedom. But before long, the friends begin to realize that they may have placed themselves in danger by failing to understand that the natural world is a force unto itself.

The inspiration for *Island Songs,* said Wheatle in an interview on the *African Survival and Creativity* Web site, came from his father's and grandfather's stories of their childhood. His grandfather was "a Maroon who came from the Akan district of Ghana," explained Wheatle, adding "That fired my imagination and I just had to write about it." The novel, which is a prequel to *East of Acre Lane,* follows the lives of two sisters who grow up in Jamaica in the 1940s and 1950s, later moving to England. But the novel also explores the wider historical context for this story, touching on seminal themes and events from the early history of Jamaica.

Wheatle returns to contemporary Brixton in *The Dirty South,* which is set some twenty years after the riots. The community has undergone considerable change, as newcomers have moved in and shifted the power relationships. The protagonist, Dennis, is the son of a schoolteacher and a library worker and does not suffer from poverty. But the excitement of street life proves too enticing for him to resist, and he ends up dealing drugs with his friend Noel. The novel begins with Dennis, age twenty-three, in Pentonville Prison, looking back over his life in flashbacks that reveal the several wrong turns he has made but that also illuminate his complex emotions and intelligence. The novel, observed a reviewer for the *Bookbag* Web site, "has many points to make about the black urban youth experience in Britain, but it makes them without bitter recrimination. Its told with wit, verve and style." American reviewers also praised *The Dirty South.* A writer for *Kirkus Reviews,* for example, commented that it is "often brutal but always compassionate," and is a "galvanizing" piece of writing.

Wheatle has been recognized for his literary achievements by being named a member of the Order of the British Empire in 2008. The recognition, he said in a *Deepest Red* Web site interview, is appreciated but overdue. "I write about black people. I write about working class people. The literary elite don't seem impressed with that at all. It wasn't always that way, though, years ago writing about the working class was celebrated—look at Charles Dickens and what he wrote about."

"We don't just need more Black writers," Wheatle told a writer for the *African Survival and Creativity* Web site. "We need more Black people going into publishing, going into marketing, sales, jacket design, all aspects of the book industry. And we need editors to trust Black writers more than they are doing so now. At the moment, editors are displaying maximum ignorance for us. That's why we are not represented in bookstores as much as I would like."

BIOGRAPHICAL AND CRITICAL SOURCES:

PERIODICALS

Booklist, November 1, 2008, Thomas Gaughan, review of *The Dirty South,* p. 26.

Europe Intelligence Wire, January 30, 2007, "Writer at Jail."

Guardian (London, England), May 3, 2008, Courttia Newland, review of *The Dirty South.*

Kirkus Reviews, October 1, 2008, review of *The Dirty South.*

Times Educational Supplement, July 12, 2002, "No Rest from the Wicked for Lost Boys of Summer."

World Literature Today, January 1, 2000, review of *Brixton Rock,* p. 162; June 22, 2001, Bruce King, review of *East of Acre Lane.*

ONLINE

African Survival and Creativity, http://www.kuumba-survivors.com/ (July 27, 2009), interview with Wheatle.

BookBag, http://www.thebookbag.co.uk/ (July 27, 2009), review of *The Dirty South.*

BookTin, http://www.booktin.com/ (July 27, 2009), Shira Bhamra, review of *The Dirty South.*

British Council Contemporary Writers Web site, http://www.contemporarywriters.com/ (July 27, 2009).

Catch a Vibe, http://www.catchavibe.co.uk/ (July 27, 2009), Elizabeth Salmon, interview with Wheatle.

Children's Discovery Centre Web site, http://www.childrensdiscoverey.org.uk/ (July 27, 2009), Wheatle profile.

Crime Scene NI, http://crimesceneni.blogspot.com/ (July 27, 2009), interview with Wheatle.

Deepest Red, http://aenisuoh.blogspot.com/ (July 27, 2009), "Alex Whatle—MBE."

Paste, http://www.pastemagazine.com/ (July 27, 2009), Ravi Howard, review of *The Dirty South.*

Reggaezine, http://www.reggaezine.co.uk/ (July 27, 2009), G. Parker, "Trodding out of Babylon: Alex Wheatle, South London Novelist."

Serpents Tail Web site, http://www.serpentstail.com/ (July 27, 2009), Wheatle profile.

Susijn Agency Ltd. Web site, http://www.thesusijnagency.com/ (July 27, 2009), Wheatle profile and bibliography.

UKWatch.net, http://www.ukwatch.net/ (July 27, 2009), Esme Choonara, interview with Wheatle.*

* * *

WINDSOR, Cooley

PERSONAL: Education: University of New Orleans, B.A.; Indiana University, M.F.A., 1985.

ADDRESSES: Office—California College of the Arts, 1111 8th St., San Francisco CA 94107-2247. *E-mail*—cwindsor@cca.edu.

CAREER: Writer, educator. California College of the Arts, San Francisco, senior adjunct professor of creative writing; Eureka Theater, San Francisco, annual Meant to Be Seen Festival, codirector. Headlands Center for the Arts in Sausalito, artist-in-residence, 2000. Bayview Hunters Point Community Advocates, founding board member.

AWARDS, HONORS: Ernest Hemingway fellowship; Wallace Stegner Fellowship, from Stanford University, 1986-87.

WRITINGS:

Visit Me in California: Stories, Northwestern University Press (Evanston, IL), 2008.

Contributor to journals including *Indiana Review, American Poetry Review, Ploughshares, Fourteen Hills,* and *Eleven Eleven.*

ADAPTATIONS: Windsor's monologue, "Sova, a Courtesan," was adapted as a ballet by Emily Keeler, and performed by the San Francisco State University dancers.

SIDELIGHTS: Writer and educator Cooley Windsor earned his undergraduate degree from the University of New Orleans, then continued his education at Indiana University, where he graduated with a master of fine arts degree. He serves on the faculty of the California College of the Arts in San Francisco, where he is a senior adjunct professor of creative writing, and also is the codirector of the annual Meant to Be Seen Festival run by the San Francisco Eureka Theater. In 2000, Windsor spent the year as the artist-in-residence for the Headlands Center for the Arts in Sausalito. He is a regular contributor to journals including *Indiana Review, American Poetry Review, Ploughshares, Fourteen Hills,* and *Eleven Eleven.* In addition, his monologue, "Sova, a Courtesan," was adapted by choreographer Emily Keeler as a ballet performed by the San Francisco State University dancers. Windsor's debut book, *Visit Me in California: Stories,* is a collection of short fiction that was published by Northwestern University Press in 2008.

Susan Larson, in a review for the *NOLA* blog, remarked that occasionally, "a writer comes along with an offbeat vision that gets the world just right, tilts it just enough so that you can laugh along at our common, bemused humanity, see it in a new, appreciative way," going on to note that Windsor meets these qualifications with his collection of short stories. The book is comprised of primarily works of flash fiction, each of which delves into literary tradition or classics and in some way turns them on end. He references everything from Homer and the Bible to the modern-day AIDS crisis, instilling pathos, wit, and understanding regardless of the scenario. In "The Last Israelite in the Red Sea," Windsor has his narrator joke about wearing improper shoes for the journey, while "The Omega Notebook" couches Judgment Day in the framework of an awards ceremony. Through that humor, Windsor is able to allow his characters to shine, and readers to connect with them on an emotional level. Heather Dewar, in a review for *Booklist,* declared of the collection that "these stories give new and devastating insight into what it means to yearn and what it means to falter." In a review for *Publishers Weekly,* one writer opined that "Windsor's stories possess the startling, memorable quality of the brightest fiction." Scott Bowen, writing for the *Prick of the Spindle* Web site, concluded of this collection that "Windsor helps us step outside the box of stereotypes and offers a generous helping of what it truly means to be human."

BIOGRAPHICAL AND CRITICAL SOURCES:

PERIODICALS

Booklist, July 1, 2008, Heather Dewar, review of *Visit Me in California: Stories,* p. 39.

Publishers Weekly, June 2, 2008, review of *Visit Me in California,* p. 30.

ONLINE

California College of the Arts Web site, http://www.cca.edu/ (July 27, 2009), faculty profile.

Cooley Windsor Home Page, http://www.cooleywindsor.com (July 27, 2009).

Headlands Center for the Arts Web site, http://www.headlands.org/ (July 27, 2009), author profile.

NOLA Blog, http://blog.nola.com/ (October 15, 2008), Susan Larson, review of *Visit Me in California.*

Prick of the Spindle, http://www.prickofthespindle.com/ (July 27, 2009), Scott Bowen, review of *Visit Me in California.**

* * *

WINTER, Clark

PERSONAL: Married.

ADDRESSES: E-mail—clark@clarkwinter.com.

CAREER: Investment strategist, writer. J.P. Morgan, New York, NY, managing director; Winter Enterprises and Winter Capital International (later acquired by Citigroup), New York, NY, founder; Citigroup Global Wealth Management, New York, NY, chief global investment strategist; Goldman Sachs & Co., New York, NY, president of global asset management, director of portfolio strategy, and managing director; SK Capital Partners, New York, NY, CIO; appears regularly on CNBC, and has been quoted in publications including the *Wall Street Journal, Financial Times,* and *Bloomberg.* Spanish Institute, chair emeritus; Mexican Cultural Institute, chair emeritus; Andrea Frank Foundation, board member; Committee on Photography at the Museum of Modern Art, board member; Belfer Center International Council at the Kennedy School of Government, Harvard University, member.

WRITINGS:

The Either/Or Investor: How to Succeed in Global Investing, One Decision at a Time, Random House (New York, NY), 2008.

SIDELIGHTS: Clark Winter is a writer and global investment strategist. Over the course of his career, Winter has held a number of prominent positions. He founded his own firm, Winter Enterprises and Winter Capital International, that specialized in bringing together independent investment managers from around the world in order to build portfolios with multiple managers, and then advising on the best means of maximizing and maintaining the integrity of those funds. Winter's firm was eventually acquired by Citigroup, and Winter himself became the chief global investment strategist there for the Citigroup Global Wealth Management, Citi Private Bank, and Smith Barney divisions. He has also worked at J.P. Morgan, serving as managing director, and where he was also instrumental in opening offices for that company in both Madrid and Mexico City; at Goldman Sachs & Co., as president of global asset management, director of portfolio strategy, and managing director; and as the chief investment officer for SK Capital Partners. Winters is frequently quoted in various financial publications, including the *Wall Street Journal, Financial Times,* and *Bloomberg,* and is a regular guest on CNBC. He is the author of *The Either/Or Investor: How to Succeed in Global Investing, One Decision at a Time,* which was published in 2008.

The Either/Or Investor suffers in some respect from a case of poor timing, in that the volume was released during a volatile time in the stock market and at a point where many industries that had previously been considered part of the fundamental bedrock of the American financial system began to falter, including the American automotive industry that Winter both praises and recommends in his book. However, beyond the fall in price and prestige for such companies as General Motors and Ford, there are other industries that Winter illuminates that might prove to be good investments in the near future. Over the course of the book, he examines different aspects of the global investment arena, addressing issues such as immigration and levels of global poverty. He includes anecdotes, both from the business world and his personal life, in an effort to make the book both entertaining and relevant. Matthew Rafat, in a review for the *Seeking Alpha* Web site, remarked that "Mr. Winter is obviously a man with both feet planted firmly on the ground. If you're skeptical of buy-and-hold investing, or if you just want to learn more about a different investment style, you may enjoy his book." A reviewer for *Publishers Weekly* declared that Winter's effort is "an admirably clear and encouraging guide to informed investing that is refreshingly free of jargon."

BIOGRAPHICAL AND CRITICAL SOURCES:

PERIODICALS

Booklist, June 1, 2007, Mary Whaley, review of *The Either/Or Investor: How to Succeed in Global Investing, One Decision at a Time,* p. 12.

Publishers Weekly, June 23, 2008, review of *The Either/Or Investor,* p. 52.

Wall Street Journal, August 27, 2008, Burton G. Malkiel, review of *The Either/Or Investor,* p. 13.

ONLINE

Clark Winter Home Page, http://www.clarkwinter.com (July 27, 2009).

Harvard Belfer Center Web site, http://belfercetner.kgs.harvard.edu/ (July 27, 2009), author profile.

Red Herring, http://www.redherring.com/ (July 20, 2005), author interview.

Seeking Alpha, http://seekingalpha.com/ (December 29, 2008), Matthew Rafat, review of *The Either/Or Investor.*

SK Capital Partners Web site, http://www.skcapitalpartners.com/ (July 27, 2009), author profile.

WOLFE, Inger Ash
[A pseudonym]

PERSONAL: Female.

ADDRESSES: Home—Canada.

CAREER: Writer.

WRITINGS:

The Calling, Harcourt (Orlando, FL), 2008.

SIDELIGHTS: Inger Ash Wolfe is the pseudonym of an unidentified North American writer living in Canada, whose debut novel under that name, *The Calling,* is a work of crime fiction. The advanced buzz for the novel focused far more on the mystery behind the author than on the book itself, with the media suggesting possible identities for Wolfe, including a number of female authors who share Wolfe's agent, Ellen Levine. However, all of the authors who were approached denied any connection to Wolfe or being the author behind *The Calling,* and Levine herself refused to provide any information about her elusive client. Suggested authors behind Wolfe's work include Michael Ondaatje, Russell Banks, Marilynne Robinson, and Jane Urquhart. Although Wolfe has not been identified, he or she (though speculation leans toward a female) has responded to interview requests, and through those provided some hint as to the motivation behind the pen name. In an interview for *January* magazine Web site, Wolfe explained her insistence on anonymity: "I wanted these novels to be read in their own context and to succeed or fail on their own terms. I can't do that under my own name. Also, the genre discussion—what does it mean to write genre, who is a genre writer, what does it mean to write more than one kind of fiction—is a heated one, and I didn't set out to write these books in order to take a side. I don't want to be co-opted into a debate I can't contribute to (or be directly accused of holding positions I don't hold)." Wolfe began using the shorter name of Inger Wolfe, but added the middle name of Ash to differentiate from Inger Wolfe the Danish writer.

Despite the distraction caused by the speculation regarding the author's identity, *The Calling* has made a fairly impressive debut based on quality alone. A mystery novel, it focuses on the exploits of a rather different serial killer, as this individual hunts victims who are already terminally ill across a range of small, rural towns in Canada. The police of Port Dundas, Ontario, find themselves chasing down the serial killer despite their limited manpower, led by Detective Inspector Hazel Micallef. Hazel is sixty-one years old, has an ailing mother and a bad back, and has recently gotten a divorce. Though her devotion to her job is most likely responsible for that divorce, it also enables her to escape her own reality, even if it is for a far more gruesome one. However, Hazel is somewhat handicapped by the slim resources of the police force, particularly given the fact that the serial killer appears to know his victims, the homes of the dead showing no sign of forced entry. Stubborn to the end, Hazel eventually manages to solve the mystery of the killer's identity, and in so doing garners the accolades she so richly deserves from her superiors.

The Calling has garnered its own share of praise since publication. Luan Gaines, in a review for the *Curled Up with a Good Book* Web site, commented of the book that "there are a number of interesting components: eccentric characters, a very human female protagonist and a serial killer not soon forgotten." Michele Leber, in a review for *Booklist,* declared that "this solid police procedural and its appealing cast make the pseudonymous Wolfe an author to watch." A reviewer for *Publishers Weekly* concluded that "Wolfe convincingly lays claim to a new mantle as a first-rate crime writer," dubbing the book a "bracingly original mystery." Caroline Mann, reviewing for *Library Journal,* wrote of the author that "whoever 'she' is, she has certainly written an excellent literary thriller, both riveting and precise."

BIOGRAPHICAL AND CRITICAL SOURCES:

PERIODICALS

Booklist, April 1, 2008, Michelle Leber, review of *The Calling,* p. 29.

Library Journal, March 15, 2008, Caroline Mann, review of *The Calling,* p. 62.

Maclean's, January 14, 2008, "Is Inger Wolfe Really Jane Urquhart? A Mysterious New Mystery Novelist Is Insisting on a Pseudonym, but There Are Clues," p. 81.

Publishers Weekly, March 24, 2008, review of *The Calling,* p. 55.

ONLINE

Confessions of an Idiosyncratic Mind, http://www.sarahweinman.com/ (February 6, 2008), "Inger Ash Wolfe Responds."

Curled Up with a Good Book, http://www.curledup.com/ (July 27, 2009), Luan Gaines, review of *The Calling.*

Galley Cat, http://www.mediabistro.com/ (July 27, 2009), Ron Hogan, "One Last Stab at the Inger Wolfe Mystery."

Harcourt Books Web site, http://www.harcourtbooks.com/ (July 27, 2009), author profile.

January, http://www.januarymagazine.com/ (December 1, 2008), author interview.

Ministry of Art Blog, http://ministryofart.blogspot.com/ (February 12, 2008), "Wolfe Eating Wolf."

Star, http://www.thestar.com/ (February 17, 2008), Vit Wagner, author interview.*

* * *

WOLVERTON, Mark 1960-

PERSONAL: Born 1960.

ADDRESSES: *Home*—P.O. Box 40322, Philadelphia, PA 19106. *E-mail*—mark@markwolverton.com.

CAREER: Writer, dramatist.

WRITINGS:

The Funnt File (sound recording), Tharsis Productions (Newtown, PA), 1998.

The Depths of Space: The Story of the Pioneer Planetary Probes, Joseph Henry Press (Washington, DC), 2004.

A Life in Twilight: The Final Years of J. Robert Oppenheimer, St. Martin's Press (New York, NY), 2008.

Also author of *The Science of Superman: The Official Guide to the Science of the Last Son of Krypton,* edited by Roger Stern, iBooks, 2004, and plays. Contributor of articles on science, technology, and history to various periodicals, including *Scientific American, American Heritage of Invention & Technology, Air & Space Smithsonian, Skeptical Inquirer, Quest,* and *American History.*

SIDELIGHTS: Writer and dramatist Mark Wolverton was born in 1960. He writes broadly about science, technology, and history and has contributed articles to a wide variety of periodicals, including *Scientific American, American Heritage of Invention & Technology, Air & Space Smithsonian, Skeptical Inquirer, Quest,* and *American History.* He is behind the creation of the sound recording *The Funnt File,* and also wrote *The Science of Superman: The Official Guide to the Science of the Last Son of Krypton,* which was edited by Roger Stern. Wolverton's more seriously toned works include *The Depths of Space: The Story of the Pioneer Planetary Probes* and *A Life in Twilight: The Final Years of J. Robert Oppenheimer.*

In *The Science of Superman,* Wolverton approaches the man of steel and his origins as based on the long-running comic book series and attempts to offer readers a scientific analysis of whether the superhero could really exist. Using his scientific background, Wolverton discusses whether or not Krypton, the world from which Superman supposedly hails, could have been real. He then goes on to look at potential ramifications from such a planet exploding, what sort of ship might have brought baby Kal-El—the infant Superman—to Earth, and how an alien of his biological makeup would have fared in our atmosphere. Wolverton breaks down each of Superman's abilities and both the biology and scientific principles behind them. David Maddox, in a review for the *SF Site,* noted that the book isn't "a hard-core science book, but it is entertaining in such a way that it could definitely be used to coerce stubborn school kids to enjoy science." Maddox went on to add that "Wolverton's research is thorough, his ideas sound and his asides quite humorous."

With *The Depths of Space,* Wolverton turns away from the more fanciful side of science and offers readers a history of Pioneer 10 and 11, as well as Pioneer Venus, the space probes sent out to explore the galaxy in the mid-1970s. The Pioneer 10 and 11 probes were notable for the gold notes on their sides that included the message "we are here" and a map of Earth, as well the image of a naked man and a naked woman, the latter of which caused something of a controversy at the time. But the technology of the day was limited and the circuitry used to run these probes was primitive in comparison to modern-day computers. Yet they accomplished far more than anticipated. Pioneer 10 traveled successfully through the asteroid belt after a thirty-year journey, ultimately heading for another solar system. Pioneer 11 was successful as well, reaching Saturn and traveling through the planet's rings, discovering a new moon on the way. Pioneer Venus, never intended to travel as far as the other two probes, delivered several smaller probes to the surface of Venus to gather further data. A reviewer for *Publishers Weekly* praised Wolverton's account of these intriguing participants in U.S. space exploration, remarking that "space buffs will revel in this well-told tale of the little space probes that could."

A Life in Twilight takes a look at the later years of Robert J. Oppenheimer, a man who in his heyday was in charge of the atom-bomb program for the United States, but by 1954 was deemed a security risk due to his obvious regrets regarding the way in which his technology was used to end the war with Japan. Wolverton looks at how Oppenheimer pulled his life back together in the wake of this verdict, and ultimately became a political entity. A reviewer for *Publishers Weekly* noted that Oppenheimer was a far less colorful character in his later life than during his years working on the Manhattan Project, but that Wolverton's book "opens a revealing window onto the intellectual climate of the cold war." *Booklist* contributor Bryce Christensen called the book a "nuanced and balanced portrait."

BIOGRAPHICAL AND CRITICAL SOURCES:

PERIODICALS

Booklist, October 15, 2008, Bryce Christensen, review of *A Life in Twilight: The Final Years of J. Robert Oppenheimer,* p. 8.

Bookwatch, September 1, 2004, review of *The Depths of Space: The Story of the Pioneer Planetary Probes,* p. 8.

Choice: Current Reviews for Academic Libraries, November 1, 2004, W.E. Howard, review of *The Depths of Space,* p. 506; April 1, 2009, A.M. Saperstein, review of *A Life in Twilight,* p. 1546.

Kirkus Reviews, September 15, 2008, review of *A Life in Twilight.*

Library Journal, October 1, 2008, Margaret F. Dominy, review of *A Life in Twilight,* p. 91.

Publishers Weekly, April 19, 2004, review of *The Depths of Space,* p. 47; September 1, 2008, review of *A Life in Twilight,* p. 46.

Science Books & Films, November 1, 2004, Roger D. Meicenheimer, review of *The Depths of Space.*

Science News, July 17, 2004, review of *The Depths of Space,* p. 47.

SciTech Book News, September 1, 2004, review of *The Depths of Space,* p. 44.

Sky & Telescope, September 1, 2004, Jeff Foust, review of *The Depths of Space,* p. 113.

ONLINE

Curled Up with a Good Book, http://www.curledup.com/ (July 27, 2009), Marie D. Jones, review of *The Depths of Space.*

Macmillan Books Web site, http://us.macmillan.com/ (July 27, 2009), author profile.

Mark Wolverton Home Page, http://www.markwolverton.com (July 27, 2009).

Scienticity, http://scienticity.net/ (July 27, 2009), review of *A Life in Twilight.*

SF Site, http://www.sfsite.com/ (July 27, 2009), David Maddox, review of *The Science of Superman.*

* * *

WOOD, Chris

PERSONAL: Born in Ontario, Canada; married; wife's name Beverley.

ADDRESSES: *Home*—Vancouver Island, British Columbia, Canada. *E-mail*—Info@bychriswood.com.

CAREER: Journalist.

WRITINGS:

Live to Air: The Craig Broadcast Story, Douglas & McIntyre (Vancouver, British Columbia, Canada), 2000.

(With wife, Beverley Wood) *Dogstar,* Raincoast Books (Vancouver, British Columbia, Canada), 2004.

(With Beverley Wood) *Jack's Knife,* Polestar (Vancouver, British Columbia, Canada), 2005.

(With Beverley Wood) *The Golden Boy,* Raincoast Books (Berkeley, CA), 2006.

Community Health, African Medical and Research Foundation (Nairobi, Kenya), 2008.

Dry Spring: When the Water Runs Out, Raincoast Books (Berkeley, CA), 2008.

Contributor to periodicals, including *Maclean's, Globe and Mail, Tyee, Walrus,* and *Reader's Digest Canada.*

SIDELIGHTS: Journalist Chris Wood was born in Ontario, Canada and has appeared in several periodicals, including the *Globe and Mail, Maclean's,* the *Tyee,* the *Walrus,* and *Reader's Digest Canada.* He has also published several books, including *The Golden Boy,* which he published in 2006 with his wife, Beverley. He has also published *Community Health* and *Dry Spring: When the Water Runs Out,* both in 2008.

In his mystery book *The Golden Boy,* a young boy finds himself in the middle of a new world in more than one sense after his family decides to leave on a trip around the world. Distraught at the idea, the boy runs away and ends up lost, but he soon realizes that not only is he in an unfamiliar place, but also an unfamiliar time. Susan Miller, reviewing the book in *Resource Links,* found the book "quite . . . complicated," but she also thought the work is "masterfully stitched together." The reviewer also complimented the authors for their ability to keep the plotline unpredictable, keeping it interesting for different types of readers. Miller also pointed out that the book contains "enough page to page action to keep most readers interested," while it also explores the rugged past of Alaska with plenty of historical information. The reviewer concluded that *The Golden Boy* is "well written and appealing."

Wood's book *Dry Spring* explores the idea of disappearing water in the United States and its possible effects on the Canadian water supply. The book details climbing temperatures, changes in weather patterns, and harmful water practices that put the supply in danger, while also denying that the United States will begin to drain Canadian water resources. Using previous reports, climatologists' interviews, and literature about the subject the author also examines how humans can attempt to avoid North American water shortage. Gilbert Taylor examining the book in his review appearing in *Booklist* stated that "American readers will be piqued" by the fear of some that the United States will attempt to commandeer some of the Canadian water supply in a waterless future. David Wellhauser reviewing the book in the *Alternatives Journal* raved that it is "politically astute and journalistically refined." The reviewer also calls the book a "must-read" because of the author's ability to provide suggestions to quelling the problem before it becomes too great that provide "ingenuity" and "diversity." The reviewer believed Wood offers an "insightful and well-informed perspective" on the water issue.

BIOGRAPHICAL AND CRITICAL SOURCES:

PERIODICALS

Alternatives Journal, January 1, 2009, "Water Woes."

Booklist, April 1, 2008, Gilbert Taylor, review of *Dry Spring: When the Water Runs Out,* p. 8.

Report on Business Magazine, April 1, 2008, "The True Price of Free Water," p. 52.

Resource Links, February 1, 2007, Susan Miller, review of *The Golden Boy,* p. 46.

SciTech Book News, December 1, 2008, review of *Dry Spring.*

Times Literary Supplement, May 30, 2008, Giles Slades, review of *Dry Spring,* p. 30.

ONLINE

Chris Wood Home Page, http://www.bychriswood.com (July 24, 2009).*

* * *

WYLY, Sam 1934-

PERSONAL: Born 1934, in Delhi, LA; married; wife's name Cheryl; children: six. *Education:* Louisiana Tech University, B.S.; University of Michigan Business School, M.B.A.

ADDRESSES: *Agent*—Travis J. Carter, Carter Public Relations, 5958 Sherry Lane, Ste. 1845, Dallas, TX 75225.

CAREER: Entrepreneur, philanthropist, and writer. Founder of University Computing, Sterling Software, Sterling Commerce, Earth Resources, Gulf Insurance, Bonanza Steakhouses, Michaels Stores, Maverick Capital, and Ranger Capital. Creator of Green Mountain Energy and Green Bull Fund.

WRITINGS:

1,000 Dollars and an Idea: Entrepreneur to Billionaire, Newmarket Press (New York, NY), 2008.

SIDELIGHTS: Entrepreneur and philanthropist Sam Wyly has cofounded and directed several leading companies, including University Computing, Michaels Stores, Maverick Capital, and Ranger Capital. More recently, he founded Green Mountain Energy Company, a joint venture with British Petroleum to provide electricity with a minimal carbon footprint. As of 2008, his net worth was estimated at more than one billion dollars. His memoir *1,000 Dollars and an Idea: Entrepreneur to Billionaire* is an account of his extraordinary business success.

As the book makes clear, Wyly was not born into wealth. He grew up in Louisiana in a family that farmed cotton and then published a local weekly newspaper. He earned a degree in journalism and accounting at Louisiana Tech University on a football scholarship before winning an academic scholarship to attend the University of Michigan Business School, where he earned a master's in business administration. He began his career in the computer industry, explaining in an interview with *Investor's Business Daily* contributor Curt Schleier: "In the beginning I thought of myself as a computer guy, but that kind of evolved. I came to think of myself as an entrepreneur and my job is to create companies and build them—and not just in the computer industry." Wyly joined IBM in 1958 at the beginning of the computer age, and two years later was recruited by Honeywell, a new competitor. As a sales executive, he quickly realized that many clients that needed computer services did not necessarily need to buy their own machines. He came up with the idea of leasing a computer to several different companies. He convinced officials at Southern Methodist University to provide space for the computer—which at that time was not only exorbitantly expensive but extremely large—if faculty and students could also be allowed to use it. Wyly eventually found a used computer for 600,000 dollars. But he had only a thousand dollars of his own to cover this initial expense. He got the money by getting clients to agree to pay for computer services in advance, and his first company, University Computing, was launched. The company went public in 1965.

Wyly's successful management style focuses on old-fashioned values such as hard work, loyalty, and respect. "I look to reward key contributors regardless of where they are in the hierarchy of the company," he told Schleier, explaining that these employees—and not just top management—receive stock options and other benefits. Another of Wyly's successful strategies is to hire skilled managers to supervise day-to-day operations at his companies. This gives him needed time to work on concepts and visualizations, which he considers his particular strengths. "The most important thing for a good manager," Wyly told *Forbes.com* Web site writer Andrew Farrell, "is that the people on his team feel like he or she has integrity." He takes inspiration from such business leaders as Tom Watson, Sr., Ross Perot, Michael Milken, T. Boone Pickens, and Sam Walton, as well as Christian Science Church founder Mary Baker Eddy. He believes that it is vital for companies to provide excellent service to customers, and that "you need happy employees to do this," as he emphasized in remarks quoted on the book's Web site. As for the ability to recognize and seize on business opportunities, Wyly wrote on the Web site: "It's real important to know who you are. If you don't, . . . then being an entrepreneur can be a very expensive way to find out. Doing what you love is more important than doing something you think is going to make you a lot of bucks. . . . The joy of the work to be done is more important than the dollars attached."

In 1997 Wyly founded Green Mountain Energy, which by 2009 had become the largest retail provider in the United States of cleaner energy and carbon offset solutions. In its first twelve years in operation, according to the company Web site, Green Mountain Energy provided more than six billion kilowatt hours of renewable electricity to consumers. This clean energy prevented as much carbon-based pollution as would be offset by the planting of 384 million trees. Indeed, as Wyly told Farrell, making businesses environmentally friendly is the most urgent issue facing the United States and the world. "Today it doesn't make a lot of difference if we cut electricity-making coal plants in Texas from ten down to three if China's building one a week." In his book Wyly proposes a "China tariff" which would impose a tariff and an internal tax on goods based on how much carbon they contained. Proceeds from the tax, which he argues should be gradually increased over a span of years, could be put toward reducing payroll taxes and to increase social security payments to retirees.

1,000 Dollars and an Idea received generally positive reviews. A writer for *Kirkus Reviews* described the book as "a business pep talk wrapped in a memoir," and admired Wyly's "folksy" philosophy. A contributor to *Publishers Weekly,* on the other hand, found the memoir's inspiring message obscured by its "meandering" style.

BIOGRAPHICAL AND CRITICAL SOURCES:

BOOKS

Wyly, Sam, *1,000 Dollars and an Idea: Entrepreneur to Billionaire,* Newmarket Press (New York, NY), 2008.

PERIODICALS

Business Week, September 3, 2001, "If at First You Don't Succeed," p. 39.

Corporate Board, November 1, 2008, "Sam Wyly: An Entrepreneur Looks at Boards."

Internet Bookwatch, October 1, 2008, review of *1,000 Dollars and an Idea.*

Investor's Business Daily, December 16, 2008, Curt Schleier, "Sam Wyly, One Shrewd Billionaire; Bulk Up: His Bonanza Steakhouse Boost Was Just One of His Choice Moves," p. 3.

Kirkus Reviews, May 15, 2008, review of *1,000 Dollars and an Idea.*

Library Journal, September 15, 2008, Richard Paustenbaugh, review of *1,000 Dollars and an Idea,* p. 67.

Long Island Business News, June 29, 2001, "Sam Wyly: The Wild Is Not Just in His Hair," p. 1.

Palm Beach Daily Business Review, January 3, 2008, Anthony Lin, "Court Rejects Billionaire's Bid to See Internal Documents."

Publishers Weekly, June 2, 2008, review of *1,000 Dollars and an Idea,* p. 36.
Reference & Research Book News, November 1, 2008, review of *1,000 Dollars and an Idea.*
Wall Street Journal, December 29, 2008, James Freeman, review of *1,000 Dollars and an Idea,* p. 11.

ONLINE

Bookreporter.com, http://www.bookreporter.com/ (July 27, 2009).
Forbes.com, http://www.forbes.com/ (July 27, 2009), Andrew Farrell, interview with Wyly.
Green Mountain Energy Web site, http://www.greenmountainenergy.com/ (July 27, 2009), company history and profile.
1,000 Dollars and an Idea Web site, http://www.1000dollarsandanidea.com (July 27 2009).
3R Blogging, http://3rliving.blogspot.com/ (July 27, 2009), interview with Wyly.
Trees Full of Money, http://www.treesfullofmoney.com/ (July 27, 2009), review of *1,000 Dollars and an Idea.*
Wyly Brothers Web site, http://www.charlesandsamwyly.com (July 27, 2009).*

* * *

ZERAUS, Leinad
See SUAREZ, Daniel

ISBN-13: 978-1-4144-3956-3
ISBN-10: 1-4144-3956-3

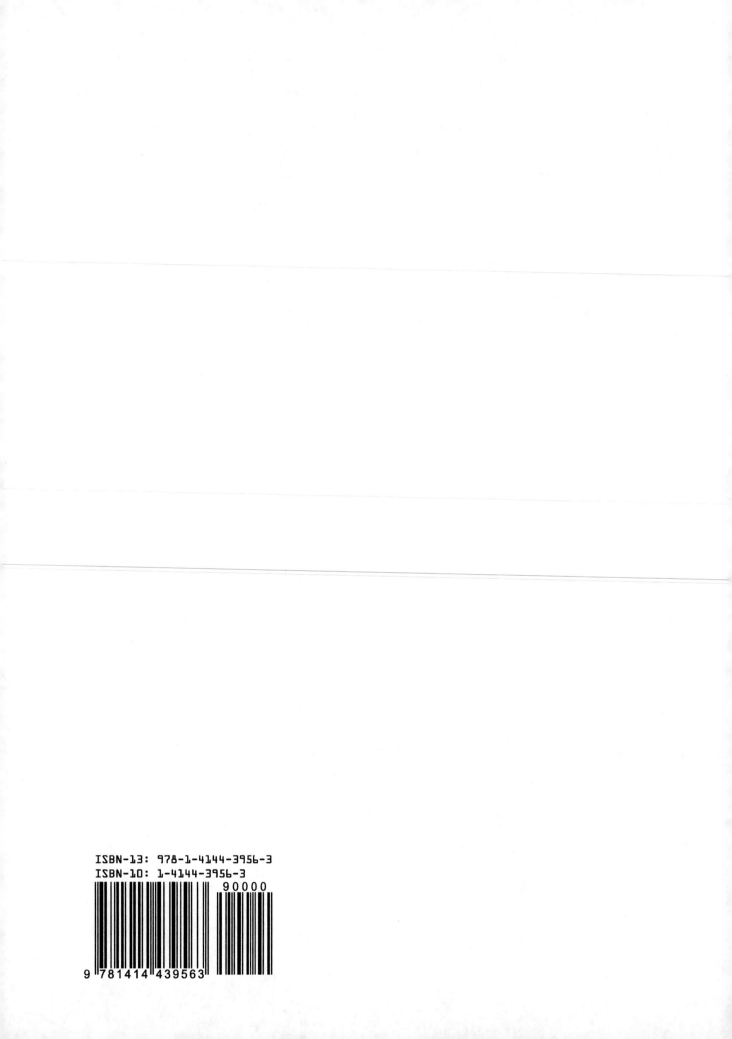